Spearhead

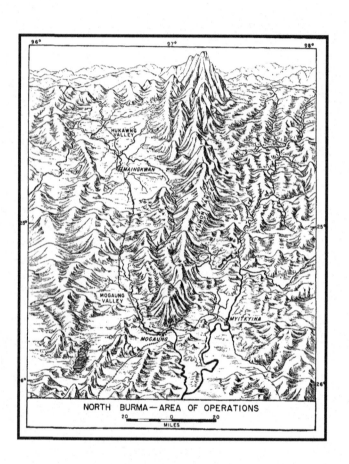

NORTH BURMA—AREA OF OPERATIONS

SPEARHEAD

A Complete History
of Merrill's Marauder Rangers

James E. T. Hopkins

in collaboration with
John M. Jones

MERRILL'S MARAUDERS ASSOCIATION, INC.

Ray Lyons, our long-term secretary and editor of the *Burman News*, has my thanks and that of all Marauders. Information from the *Burman News* has been used countless times throughout this book.

Published by
Merrill's Marauders Association, Inc.
111 Kramer Drive
Lindenhurst, NY 11757

Second Edition (Revised 2013)

Printed in the United States of America

ISBN 978-0-9898394-0-2
Library of Congress Control Number: 2013952656

Thanks to Sam B. Hopkins (oldest nephew of Dr. James E. T. Hopkins, Merrill's Marauder and author of *Spearhead*) and Matt Westbrook, editor of the original version, for making this updated edition of *Spearhead* available to a whole new generation of readers. Thanks also to Merrill's Marauders Historian Robert E. Passanisi for compiling the index for this Second Edition, and to Sheila Fredrickson (daughter-in-law of Merrill's Marauder Elmer G. "Buddy" Fredrickson) for revising the original layout of the book into this slightly larger format.

To the dead and living who served so courageously,

proudly, and effectively, in spite of almost insurmountable

odds, as infantry soldiers with Merrill's Marauders,

Burma, World War II

The patriot volunteer, fighting for his country and his rights,
makes the most reliable soldier on earth.

—General Thomas J. "Stonewall" Jackson

Foreword

Doctor James E. T. Hopkins tells it all, with no holds barred.

This is the true story of the most unique group of men in the annals of military history. No other American military unit, before or since, has fought behind enemy lines for so long, or has endured the hardships of arguably the worst jungle terrain in the world, with such determination and endurance.

Although no provision had been made for our return because we were not really expected to come back, our unit still beat all the odds, and managed to survive this secret suicide mission.

Spearhead paints a true understanding of what a human being can endure. Although the Marauders were all volunteers, they were ordinary men from all walks of life, from the New York City roughneck, and the Native American, to the Harvard graduate. As different as they were in civilian life, they were like one harmonious unit in combat.

This new edition of *Spearhead* has been resized to a slightly larger format, containing fewer pages than the original version; however, not one word has been left out.

With the addition of the needed index, *Spearhead* is better than ever. Searching for names, events and places is now much easier and faster.

— S/Sgt. Robert E. Passanisi, Chairman
Merrill's Marauders Association, Inc.

CONTENTS

Contents

CONTENTS

Illustrations

Photographs

ILLUSTRATIONS

ILLUSTRATIONS

Maps

MAPS

Preface

This account of the remarkable service of the 5307th Composite Unit (Provisional), the volunteer regiment that came to be known popularly as "Merrill's Marauders" or "Merrill's Marauder Rangers," is based on my records and recollections of service with the unit for the entire period of its existence. As a medical officer and field surgeon with the Orange Combat Team of the Third Battalion, I kept close day-to-day records of the casualties and the combat operations that produced them. Immediately after the Marauders' Burma campaign ended, I documented and submitted through military channels the medical history of the entire regiment. In combination, my field notes and those medical reports have been invaluable in telling this story fifty-three years after the events.

The role in this book of Major John M. Jones, who was an intelligence officer with the headquarters of both General Merrill and Colonel Charles N. Hunter, is that of indispensable collaborator. Shortly after the Marauders entered Burma in 1944, Jones suggested to General Merrill that an operations log be maintained and that the handwritten records be sent out when wounded soldiers were evacuated. Both suggestions were taken. Jones was not officially designated unit historian, but the comprehensive notes he wrote while the Burma action was under way, later organized as the "War Diary of the 5307th Composite Unit (Provisional)," made my task infinitely easier. Further, Jones has kindly read and commented on my manuscript at various stages and has made countless valuable suggestions. Sections from the War Diary appear throughout the book. I salute him as virtually my coauthor.

Anyone writing a history of the Marauders owes a debt to Colonel Charles N. Hunter for his book *Galahad* (1963). Hunter was a tower of strength and deserves much credit for the success of the Marauders.

Charlton Ogburn, Jr., who served as a communications officer with the First Battalion, was the first to bring the exploits and travail of the regiment to the attention of the public in his book *The Marauders*, published in 1956. His book has also been useful in the preparation of this one.

PREFACE

My records have been greatly augmented by a privately published manuscript, *The History of the Second Battalion,* written by the commanding officer, Colonel George A. McGee. He had the use of the daily log that was kept by the battalion's sergeant major, Master Sergeant William C. Collins, and the battalion clerk, Sergeant Joseph C. Magnetta. These accurate records have been of great help in checking battles, skirmishes, dates, place names, supply-flow data, and casualties.

I am grateful to David Quaid, who in the early phase of the campaign voluntarily joined the Third Battalion as a sergeant combat photographer. He has provided many of the U.S. Army Signal Corps photographs used in this book. He has also made available many video interviews with Marauder veterans, which I have freely used.

I am especially grateful to my wife, Mary Margaret Ayres Hopkins, and my nephew, Samuel Bloodgood Hopkins. She put up with the many hours devoted to the project, and he encouraged me to learn to type and master the mysteries of a computer. My editor, Matthew Westbrook, has corrected many deficiencies and given me invaluable advice and encouragement. Above all, I am thankful to the army for allowing me to join the American G.I.'s who accomplished what many believed were impossible missions in Burma.

Introduction

A complete history of Merrill's Marauder Rangers, the first American infantry regiment to fight on the Asiatic Continent since the Boxer Rebellion, has never been written. This document records the total history of the three loosely connected battalions that would become that proud and well-bonded regiment. They had been assembled to fight under British control in Burma but at the last minute were thrown into combat to spearhead two stalled Chinese divisions under the command of U.S. General Joseph W. Stilwell, the over-age and half-blind commander of the China-Burma-India theater. Stilwell had always dreamed of commanding American infantry troops in battle, and with the Marauders he got his chance (Stilwell 1948).

There is little doubt that few volunteers in the Marauders' unit had any significant idea of the political, personnel, governmental, and major military decisions that were responsible for the death, wounds, and illness in the precombat, combat, and immediate postcombat course of their lives. Approximately two-thirds of the Marauders had been overseas for eighteen months or more. The others had for the most part been in situations where they had little exposure to current events—an isolation that remained until well after the campaign was over. They had no means of knowing about decisions of the Combined Chiefs of Staff, the Joint Chiefs of Staff, the China-Burma-India directives and plans, or any information generated by the Southeast Asia Command.

In order to make this history of the Marauders' Burma campaign more interesting and informative, some important decisions must be discussed. Stilwell was taking his orders and cues from President Roosevelt, the Joint Chiefs of Staff, and the Southeast Asia Command, headed by Lord Louis Mountbatten. Stilwell also had to work with Chiang Kai-shek under an arrangement that was never satisfactory and eventually led to Stilwell's removal from his China-Burma-India duties.

Shortly after the sneak attack at Pearl Harbor and the declaration of war, Prime Minister Winston Churchill and President Roosevelt met at the Arcadia Conference in Washington (Romanus and Sunderland 1956, 3). It was essential that China be assisted because they, with massive manpower, had the potential to keep much of the Japanese army occupied. If airfields could be built and made available, U.S. bombers could reach Japan from China. The United States was already helping China with the American Flying Tigers. To give significant material help to China, our British Allies would either have to prevent the enemy from occupying Burma or—if prevention were impossible—would have to drive the invaders out.

After the Arcadia Conference, the Chinese leader Generalissimo Chiang Kai-shek was asked to be the supreme commander of a United Nations "China theater." After accepting that title, Chiang Kai-shek asked for a high-ranking U.S. Army officer to help him organize and command the China theater. General Marshall and President Roosevelt appointed General Joseph Stilwell to be that officer. He had extensive previous service in China and spoke the language. However, he was fifty-nine years old, had never commanded troops in battle, had poor vision in one eye, and was blind in the other.

Stilwell and his party left Miami on 11 February, 1942. At that time there was no Air Transport Command, and he and his party flew out on a Ferry Command, Pan American Airways flying boat. They had to turn back two times because of engine trouble, finally reaching India thirteen days later. He arrived only ten days before the Japanese took Rangoon (Stilwell 1948, 38).

The Chinese had sent seven divisions to the Burma border. One Chinese division was on a defensive line four hundred miles inside Burma (Stilwell 1948, 43). The British had two divisions, plus a brigade of tanks, on the defensive line. General Chennault's American Volunteer Group, the Flying Tigers, was ready to help with the defense of Burma (44). As soon as Stilwell visited the Generalissimo he was off to Burma, where the air and land battle had begun. He theoretically had command of the Chinese in Burma. The Japanese were rapidly pushing and crushing the disorganized Chinese, of which there were now four divisions: the 200th, 22nd, 96th, and 38th—plus two British divisions and an armored brigade (Dorn 1971, 41, 68). No record of the total lost by the Chinese and British is available, but all indications are that it was massive.

General Stilwell walked out, over the mountains between Burma and India, with about one hundred personnel, including General (then Major) Frank Merrill and the Burma surgeon Gordon Seagrave, with his Burmese nurses. During the retreat, Merrill had his first heart attack (Dorn 1971, 242). Numerous books dealing with the flight of civilians from Burma, retreating to the north with the remnants of the allied military forces before the advancing Japanese, have described the pitiful plight of these thirsty, sick, starving, and dying human beings. Various estimates have been given as to the number of survivors and dead. Brigadier General Frank Dorn, in his book *Walkout, with Stilwell in Burma,* estimated that only one-tenth of the nine hundred thousand who attempted to flee the country survived. Many have described the thousands of family groups, the bones of whom are in the mountains about the periphery of Burma (Dorn 1971, 148).

The 38th Chinese Division struggled through the Hukawng and Mogaung Valleys and then more than a hundred miles over the mountains into Assam, India. They arrived reasonably intact but with much illness and malnutrition. The 22nd Chinese Division soldiers, minus their equipment, made their way to Fort Hertz at the extreme northeast tip of Burma. Many had died from disease and starvation on the way. After months, the survivors hiked through the mountainous jungle two hundred miles to Ledo, Assam, India. It would appear that men from the other two Chinese divisions entered China by the Burma Road just before the Japanese destroyed the Salween River bridge.

General Stilwell, after difficult negotiations, was able to work out a plan to use Ramgarh Camp, which had been used to house Italian prisoners from the African campaign. The town of Ramgarh is located in Bihar Province about five hundred miles from Stilwell's New Delhi headquarters. The isolated desert camp of one-story buildings served as a training area for the Chinese troops in India until the war was over. The British provided food and pay, and the Americans supplied the equipment and training. Officers and enlisted men arrived from the States to run the training programs.

During January 1943 the Generalissimo provided twelve thousand replacements to the 22nd and 38th Divisions in training. These troops were flown from Kunming, China, to Dinjan, Assam, India, in the C-47's of the Ferrying Command, later to be called the Army Transport Service. At that time it was the greatest mass movement of troops by air in history. Over sixty thousand Chinese were eventually trained here, with American small arms and artillery, for Stilwell's 1943 and 1944 Burma operations (Dorn 1971, 244).

INTRODUCTION

During the retreat from Burma, Dr. Gordon Seagrave and his nurses were of great help to Stilwell and the retreating Chinese. As this group walked out with Stilwell's party, he became more and more grateful. He later took Seagrave and his nurses to Ramgarh and, after commissioning him a major in the U.S. Army, asked him to run a hospital at the training center with the aid of his Burmese nurses. He was soon able to keep his thousand-bed hospital full of grateful patients (Dorn 1971, 64).

Seagrave, with his mobile hospital and innovative surgical help, later gave brilliant and dedicated front-line service to the Chinese infantry until Burma was retaken. He and his assistants gave emergency care to many wounded Americans during the Battle of Myitkyina.

General Stilwell was ordered, in July 1942, to organize the U.S. air force and service troops in China, Burma, and India. Progress was rapid, and the American theater of operations and the U.S. Army in India was growing rapidly. Chennault's "Flying Tigers," the American volunteer group that had been operating, since Stilwell arrived, as the China-American Task Force, now came under the 10th Air Force as one division, the other being the India Task Force (Dorn 1971, 72). The Flying Tigers had a hundred old P-40's and about a hundred pilots of the American volunteer group (Stilwell 1948, 44).

The theater received little in the way of supplies in 1942 except transport aircraft in an effort to fly more tonnage over the "Hump" (the air-freight line from Assam, India, over the Himalayas to Kunming, China). Major General Claire L. Chennault was later the commander of the 14th U.S. Air Force in China when he convinced the Generalissimo and also President Roosevelt that if he had 105 fighters, 35 medium bombers, and 12 heavy bombers, he could open the way for the defeat of Japan. By March 1943 he had the president's firm support (Fischer 1991, 116).

By August 1942 the air force, the service of supply, and the China-Burma-India theater operations had eight thousand personnel. When the 5307th Composite Unit (Provisional) was ready to move toward Burma in January 1944, there were more than 105,000. None of these were combat troops, other than the men of the 5307th Composite Unit (Provisional) (Romanus and Sunderland 1956, 258). The India-based U.S. Army 10th Air Force grew slowly. At the end of December

INTRODUCTION

1943 the unit had a total of 285 planes, including 188 fighters, 23 medium bombers, 51 heavy bombers, and 23 others.

Some progress was made toward improving the Chinese Army in China. The Chinese agreed to put thirty divisions of infantry in west China at Yunnan and a similar number in east China, where they would be trained and equipped with the aid of the Americans. The Yunnan training operation started in March 1943. In spite of many requests by General Stilwell, these troops did not help with the battle for Burma until late 1945. The training center in east China began operations but was abandoned when the Japanese overran the area during 1944.

By December 1942 the Joint Chiefs of Staff had authorized the CBI theater to start construction of the road from Ledo, Assam, across the Patkai Mountain Range into the Hukawng Valley, North Burma. General Stilwell had not at first agreed to this approach to combat in North Burma. He called the Ledo-Shingbwiyang-Hukawng Valley-Myitkyina approach to combat "that rat hole." He had tried to convince the British and their commander General Wavell that the road should be built east from Imphal along the route he had used to escape from Burma in the spring of 1942. A paved road ran from the railhead at Manipur Junction to Imphal. The terrain from there to the old Burma Road was much more favorable than the approach from Ledo. The British would not listen to this brilliant plan, and the engineers had to start at Ledo (Romanus and Sunderland 1956, 11–15).

In late 1942 Stilwell was still planning to enter Burma in early 1943. The British had agreed to allow the necessary tonnage to pass over the Assam-Bengal Railway and the Brahmaputra Barge Line to support his Chinese divisions in North Burma. He planned to start them from Ledo on 15 February 1943. The British had agreed to have a diversionary operation using their 14th Division to advance on the Arakan, down the Mayu Peninsula, on Akyab in southwest Burma (Romanus and Sunderland 1956, 61).

In January 1943 the 38th Chinese Division was slowly moving down the ancient trails over the Patkai Mountains toward Burma. The British started out on schedule but, in February, were trapped and had to retreat. They did not put in any of the fifteen divisions they had in reserve on the India-Burma border. The Generalissimo wisely advised

General Stilwell to cancel his advance. His troops remained in the jungle, astride the slowly advancing Ledo Road, to protect the American engineers.

As part of this offensive, which seemed planned for failure, the British General Orde Wingate took his long-range penetration Chindits into north central Burma. His three thousand troops used pack animals and were supplied, in an irregular fashion, by air. They had no satisfactory way to care for their wounded or evacuate their sick and wounded. More than a third of the command was lost in a very tragic and unsuccessful campaign. In spite of lack of success, the fact that a small unit could continue to hit and run in the center of a Japanese-controlled country created a sensation back in England.

During January 1943 the Combined Chiefs of Staff met at Casablanca to discuss plans for further war effort in Southeast Asia. Here and at three other meetings the need to open communications from India to China by way of Burma was stressed. The British tried to get rid of Stilwell, but instead he got rid of Wavell. In spite of Lend-Lease, the British said it was impossible to start a major offensive in Burma because of lack of supplies. The British eventually agreed to conduct operations in the winter of 1943-44.

The Trident Conference took place at Washington in May 1943. The British said that training and supplies were inadequate to launch a Burma offensive. They favored an eventual amphibious operation in the south. They argued that construction of the Ledo Road was illogical and impossible. Stilwell argued that the road had to be built. It was the only way to get heavy equipment into China. North Burma had to be taken in order to keep China in the war. The British and Americans both agreed that any plans for extensive operations in Burma had to be scaled back because of the approaching invasion of Europe. Both sides agreed that any offensive would only involve northern Burma. If North Burma could be captured, the flight over the Hump could be eliminated, many pilots and planes could be saved, and much more freight could be delivered to increase China's war effort. Chennault wanted more planes because he was convinced he could defeat the Japanese in China by airpower. The Combined Chiefs of Staff argued that top priority had to be given to the Air Transport Command until it was capable of moving ten thousand tons per month over the Hump into China. Airfields were to be built in China. Air force commander General Bissell attempted to get rid of General Chennault—but with help from the Chinese, Bissell was recalled, and the China Air Force became the 14th Air Force with Chennault in command. General Howard C. Davidson assumed command of the 10th Air Force, based in India. President Roosevelt continued to stress that every effort had to be made to train and improve the Chinese army and air force (Romanus and Sunderland 1956, 5).

When Stilwell returned from Washington he found little progress on the construction of the Ledo Road. A new commander, Colonel Lewis A. Pick, was appointed to speed this massive engineering project. The two-lane dirt tract began to advance like magic, and jeeps were able to get through to Shingbwiyang by late December 1943 (Romanus and Sunderland 1956, 11–15). When the Marauders marched over the hilly, muddy, twisting and turning tract in February 1944, trucks were beginning to arrive at Shingbwiyang—the site of Stilwell's growing forward military base in North Burma.

With the aid of a directive from the Joint Chiefs of Staff, Stilwell got approval from the Generalissimo to launch an October 1943 offensive into Burma using the Chinese 38th and 22nd Divisions. In late 1943 Stilwell was able to move enough Chinese to Ramgarh to form and begin training another division, the 30th, minus one regiment. The 88th Regiment of this poorly equipped and trained division was later to be part of Galahad's K Force with the Marauder Third Battalion on the march to Myitkyina.

By the fall of 1943 Stilwell had four separate staffs, which in his case guaranteed inefficiency. He was known to hate paperwork and tended to delegate many important duties to subordinates. His Chungking office functioned largely as a liaison mission with the Chinese. The rear echelon staff in New Delhi was under the command of his Deputy Chief of Staff, Brigadier General B. G. Ferris. This officer was responsible for planning. The office was near the British general headquarters, where tonnage allocations on the Assam-Bengal Railway and the Brahmaputra Barge Line were set and authorized. Support for the Ledo Road, the Hump, and the North Burma operation had to be defined here. Reverse Lend-Lease requisitions had to be filed here. The third staff was run by Brigadier General Frank F. Dorn at the Yunnan Training School near Kunming, China. He had to run the school and watch over Chennault. The fourth staff was with the Chih Hui Pui (Chinese forces in India and Burma) near Ledo under General Boatner.

A big shake for the CBI took place at the Quadrant Conference of the Combined Chiefs of Staff at the Citadel in Quebec during the month of August 1943. The Southeast Asia Command was created and made responsible for ground, air, and sea operations. Admiral Lord Louis Mountbatten was named Supreme Allied Commander. The China-Burma-India theater was integrated into the Southeast Asia Command, with Stilwell named Deputy Supreme Commander in addition to his other duties. These duties still gave him four additional major titles:

1. Commanding General, United States Forces, China-Burma-India
2. Chief of Staff to Generalissimo Chiang Kai-shek.
3. Commanding General, Chinese Expeditionary Force (called Chinese Army in India)
4. Lend-Lease Administrator (Romanus and Sunderland 1956, 53).

For the most part, Mountbatten chose a British staff with American liaison officers attached.

To ensure the success of Stilwell's planned 1943 Burma operations, President Roosevelt and General Marshall promised to recruit a provisional regiment of American infantrymen from the Southwest Pacific, the Caribbean, and the continental United States. They were to be organized and sent immediately to train under the command and with the methods of General Orde Wingate. They were then to fight in Central Burma under his command in cooperation with and as part of his long-range penetration unit. The secret name of this proposed unit of approximately three thousand volunteers was to be Galahad. The War Department decided that the unlikelihood of their being restored to duty after the proposed guerilla operation did not warrant replacements. The War Department told the theater headquarters that the unit was provided for one major mission of three months' duration, whose closure might find the unit so exhausted and depleted that its survivors would require three months of hospitalization and rest. They expected eighty percent casualties. How right they were (Romanus and Sunderland 1956).

INTRODUCTION

The War Department sent a letter to Stilwell dated 7 September 1943:

> It is visualized that three battalions will be employed separately—probably two in Assam and one from Yunnan (China)—and that they will operate in front of the main effort. They will have pack transport and will be resupplied by air. Although operating separately, the three efforts should be coordinated by "Group" Headquarters composed of personnel who will train with the battalions and thus become familiar with their capabilities, personalities, communications and supply problems, and other vital factors, as well as maintain liaison and coordinate with other friendly troops in the area (Stuart 1984, 3).

General Stilwell had already received information, on 1 September 1943, that the American troops were to operate under Wingate (Stuart 1984, 4). To this day there is controversy about how Stilwell was able to have Galahad removed from General Wingate's command to his. A reference in *Stilwell's Command Problems* (Romanus and Sunderland 1956) is taken from the Stilwell Diary, 3 January 1944. On that date Stilwell asked General Wingate to move the U.S. long-range penetration group (Galahad) up to the Hukawng Valley. Wingate agreed.

Another theory is that the men of Galahad were so rough, undisciplined, and unruly that the British were glad to get rid of them. It is well known that Stilwell had used every move he knew to get the three battalions under his command in order to spearhead the Chinese advance into Burma. Stilwell is supposed to have said, "I don't know how I got them. I didn't have a leg to stand on."

General Wingate had arrived in England shortly before Churchill was to depart for Quebec. Churchill was fascinated by the action of Wingate's long-range penetration group, which had had such a tragic end due to enemy action, starvation, and disease. The unit was said to have accomplished nothing of military value. Yet Churchill took him to Quebec as an example of a man who knew how to fight. Churchill planned a new long-range penetration for Wingate as the commander of a six- (later changed to five-) brigade command of eighteen thousand men. They were to be part of the 1944 Burma campaign. Their zone would be Central Burma, where strongholds would be set about 150 miles south of the Japanese strongholds at Kamaing and

Mogaung. Here they would be able to block the main railway to Mogaung and Myitkyina. Most of the men would be flown in. Pack animals would also be transported by air. All supplies would be delivered on call by plane or parachute. The campaign also required American planes and gliders (Romanus and Sunderland 1956, 58).

General Arnold promised to send a complete air force to support Wingate's new operation. This pocket-size air force was designated as No. 1 Air Commando, AAF, and included fighter bombers, medium bombers, transports, gliders, and liaison craft. This was the origin of Colonel Philip Cochran's famous American Air Commandos. Among other items, General Arnold offered to send one hundred small liaison planes to aid in the evacuation of the sick and wounded. The Marauders were to unexpectedly discover the presence of these planes during the Battle of Walawbum. Their unplanned presence in our area of operations saved many American lives (Romanus and Sunderland 1956, 53).

At Quebec the British continued to agree that China should get as much help as possible, but they wanted to put the Hump under Mountbatten's control. This suggestion was turned down. Tonnage had to be increased to get essential supplies to the Chinese but most importantly to General Chennault's 14th Air Force. The Hump had begun a month after Burma fell. The India-China wing of the United States Air Transport Command was organized to carry personnel and freight at altitudes often over twenty thousand feet between Assam, India, and Kunming, China. After about one year, the C-47's were delivering six thousand tons per month. This small percentage of the desired tonnage was used as an argument that creating a land route to China—as soon as possible—was essential. The young pilots who were flying the C-46's and C47's were doing an increasingly dangerous job under extremely difficult conditions. The route over the Hump presented variable and at times extremely dangerous weather conditions. The planes tended to develop problems and were called "flying coffins" by the pilots. Living conditions for the pilots were primitive. They also had to contend with Japanese fighter planes. These young and largely inexperienced pilots were truly offering their lives for their country. Many died delivering an ever-increasing flow of goods to China. The Marauders were not aware that so much was being asked of other members of the armed forces in the CBI. Little was known about the operation. The Marauders would have had an additional reason to drive the Japanese out of North Burma if they had known their victory would allow these flyers to take a more reasonable and much safer flight by way of Myitkyina. This is only one of the many aspects of activity in the North Burma campaign that, if known and understood by our men, would have given them more understanding and appreciation of why they were risking life and limb for their country (Romanus and Sunderland 1956, 9).

The Quebec Conference had stressed the need to get supplies into China. Few of the Marauders knew that a road was under construction until we actually marched on it. There was no way for us to know that we were to be the spearhead that would allow the road to connect with the Old Burma Road. We were not made aware of the great need to get trucks rolling into China to take the strain off the fliers. In addition, we had no way of knowing that pipelines were following our advance in order to further speed the war effort (Romanus and Sunderland 1956, 9).

Stilwell first heard about the American volunteers on 2 September. He records in his diary, "Victory again. Radio from George Marshall on U.S. (combat) units for Stepchild. Only 3,000, but the entering wedge. Can we use them! And how!" (Stilwell 1948, 219). We, the American volunteers, were still listed as shipments 1688 A, B, and C. The name 5307th Combat Regiment (Provisional) was not assigned until 1 January 1944. We heard nothing of General Stilwell's activities and interest in the unit until General Merrill arrived as our commanding officer on 4 January 1945.

General Stilwell's American-trained Chinese 38th Division had remained in the jungle south of Ledo since the spring of 1943. In preparation for the proposed 1944 Burma campaign, which was being planned for March, General Stilwell had moved their forward elements to Shingbwiyang, a small, primitive village located at the northern tip of the Hukawng Valley.

American shipments A, B, and C were debarking from the *Lurline* in Bombay Harbor when the lead element of the 38th Division unexpectedly contacted outposts of Japanese General Tanaka's crack 18th Division. Two battalions from the 112th Regiment of the 38th Division were advancing to set up control of fords across the Tanai Hka and the Tarung Hka ("hka" means river). It was October 1943, and the 1944 Burma Campaign had begun prematurely without final decision as to whether or not it should even take place (Romanus and Sunderland 1956, 32–34).

Stilwell's Command Problems states, "Normally, planning precedes logistical preparation, and logistical preparation, fighting. One of the noteworthy aspects of the North Burma Campaign of 1943-44 is that the logistical preparations, the planning, and the fighting proceeded simultaneously. The troops moved forward before the commanders agreed on the plans, and the logistical preparations were months in being completed" (Romanus and Sunderland 1956, 10, 131). The Chinese battalions were soon surrounded and unable to break out. Fortunately they were able to survive because food and ammunition were dropped by air. The rest of the division was unable to get them out, and the situation was not much better when Stilwell went to Cairo for a meeting to begin in late November with the Combined Chiefs of Staff and the Joint Chiefs of Staff. He next traveled to Teheran, where Roosevelt and Churchill consulted with Stalin (Romanus and Sunderland 1956, 31).

At Cairo the Chinese, British, and Americans agreed that a major offensive in Burma should be set in motion immediately. The British were to mount a major landing from the sea into Southwest Burma. Stilwell's North Burma assignment was known as the Capital Plan. His forces were to continue their initial penetration from Ledo to Shingbwiyang and then fight through the Hukawng and Mogaung Valleys to Mogaung as the primary objective, with Myitkyina the ultimate and final objective. The Chinese Yoke Force was to attack on east Burma from Yunnan. Wingate's eighteen thousand long-range troops were to be flown in and deposited to set up bases as planned across the rail lines in North Central Burma, about 250 miles from Stilwell's entry point (Stilwell 1948, 242).

During the third week in November, General Stilwell was at the Teheran Conference. There was soon a drastic change in plans brought about by Roosevelt and Stalin's agreement that there had to be a massive cross-channel invasion in 1944. The sea invasion of Burma had to be called off because of the lack of landing craft.

INTRODUCTION

Roosevelt and Churchill returned to Cairo for further talks. The British refused to go forward with a strong invasion of Burma. When Chiang Kai-shek was told the British had pulled out, he refused to let his Yunnan troops get involved. He tried to hold Roosevelt up for a billion-dollar loan, demanding also that he double the size of the air force and establish a ferry route (Stilwell 1948, 250).

In spite of the critical situation on the northern Burma front, Stilwell had taken time off to see Jerusalem and parts of Egypt. He later spent a week at his Chungking Headquarters. Here on 18 December 1943 the Generalissimo gave him full command of the Chinese troops in North Burma (Fischer 1991, 120).

Stilwell arrived on the Burma front on 21 December and immediately took over duty as commanding general of the Chinese Army in India. During the next week the Chinese had limited success and by the first of the year were ready to advance further into Burma. The 38th Division had lost 17 officers and 298 enlisted men, with 20 officers and 409 enlisted men wounded (Romanus and Sunderland 1956, 28–29).

By this time Stilwell had accomplished his desire to acquire Galahad to spearhead the Chinese. All agreed that the immediate future of the North Burma campaign hung on the arrival of the approximately twenty-six hundred American infantrymen about 20 February. The men had heard rumors that they were to be removed from British control. On 4 January—before the 5307th's pack animals, communication equipment, and technicians had arrived and before all training, supply, and organization efforts were complete—they were under new command. They—we—were no longer a regiment but now a unit. (General Frank Merrill had arrived on this date to take command, and a general does not command a regiment.) We were now available for combat alongside General Stilwell's two Chinese divisions in North Burma. The men got no explanation as to when or why the change had taken place (Romanus and Sunderland 1956, 34–36).

Wingate's invasion was scheduled to start in early March 1944. Fortunately, Galahad's combat supplies were still in freight cars ready for shipment. Details were sent to Assam and warehouses requisitioned. The freight was soon on the way. All problems were solved except the lack of training, the chronic illness of many of the men, and the inability of General Merrill to give the medical sections a reasonable plan for the evacuation of the wounded. The outfit was declared ready for combat and was on its way to Assam, India.

Due to the great work of the men in the service of supply, the air force, and those in the NCAC and the Marauders' rear echelon, we were to be served as well as possible during most of our combat period in Burma. We were not given any hint that at times food and ammunition would not be available. Unfortunately the courage and dedication of the Marauders in spearheading the courageous but hesitant Chinese was constantly taken advantage of, serving as an excuse for the command to ask the impossible.

As the men advanced behind enemy lines deep into Burma, they were not informed of the critical situation. No one explained that the Chinese were stalled in their advance. Nor were the men told that, beyond the Japanese 18th Division, six other Japanese divisions waited and could easily move to the north at any time. The command also avoided telling us that General Wingate's long-range penetration troops would not start to fly into their assigned area, far to the south, for another week or more. We had understood, by rumor, that a massive British invasion was to take place from the west and several Chinese divisions were to be entering from the east. The rumors, of course, were not true. Without knowing it, we were alone and entering the territory of veteran Japanese troops who greatly outnumbered our small force. We would be surprised when we learned that we would be facing heavy Japanese artillery when we had no artillery and only limited and largely ineffective fighter-bomber support. Before the campaign and during the early part of the campaign, no one considered the possibility of an advance on Myitkyina (Romanus and Sunderland 1956, 136, 290).

The men of the Marauders never suspected that the so-called kindly General Stilwell, who was said to beloved by his service troops, would, unlike his British and Chinese allies, tend to drive his troops to accomplish the seemingly impossible even though it might have limited military value and could have waited for more suitable time and circumstances. The life, limb, and health of the men under his command seemed to be secondary in his drive to embarrass or outperform the leaders of his allies.

INTRODUCTION

The Marauders found Stilwell's tactics were superior when the plans were made by others and carried out by those who understood their duty to their country and army and did the best they could. No hint was ever given that, if the Chinese were not able to accomplish what they had been assigned to do, poorly trained and organized engineers and infantrymen would be sent into battle, where many would become unnecessarily sick, wounded, and killed.

Midway through the Battle of Burma, our men and officers were still unaware that Wingate's operation was not going well and three Japanese divisions were fighting a great battle on the India-Burma border. If the Japanese had been successful, the entire North Burma forces of General Stilwell would have been trapped in Assam and Burma. As the Marauders drove and gradually defeated the Japanese in Burma they never doubted that Stilwell's North Burma campaign would be declared one of the most brilliant and successful in World War II. They would never have guessed that near the end of the last battle, when Stilwell was given a fourth star, he would leave on vacation and never assemble them for congratulations and thanks as their unit was disbanded. The general's North Burma campaign was to result in a great victory—but it was pyrrhic. The cost would far exceed the results obtained.

Chronology

1941

7 December: Japanese make sneak attack on Pearl Harbor.

8 December: Japanese invade Malaya, Thailand, and the Philippines.

9 December: Japanese occupy Bangkok (Thailand) and invade the Gilbert Islands.

10 December: The small U.S. garrison at Guam surrenders.

11 December: Japanese invade Burma.

13 December: Japanese invade Borneo in the East Indies.

22 December–3 January: Arcadia Conference. At this British and American conference, military cooperation between the two nations is formulated; the Combined Chiefs of Staff, Washington, is created; an allied commander is named for each theater of operation; and General George Marshall is appointed Chief of Staff.

23 December: Wake Island falls.

25 December: Hong Kong falls, with the loss of a twelve-thousand-man garrison.

1942

January: Plans for allied landings and cooperation discussed. The Generalissmo (Chiang Kai-shek) accepts the title of supreme commander of a United Nations "China theater." He asks for a high-ranking American officer to help organize the China theater. General Joseph Stilwell is appointed allied (joint) chief of staff for the China theater.

January: Japanese capture Rabaul in New Britain.

27 January: Battle of Java Sea. Japanese crush a combined Dutch, U.S., and British fleet.

March: Stilwell directs the retreat of two Chinese divisions in Burma.

February and March: Singapore falls, with the loss of 138,000 British and Empire troops. Bali, Timor, and Java soon fall, as do the Dutch East Indies.

1 April: Dolittle raid on Tokyo.

May: The British and Chinese are driven out of Burma and the Japanese occupy territory in New Guinea and the Admiralty Islands.

6 May: The Philippines fall.

7–8 May: Battle of Coral Sea. The carrier *Lexington* is sunk and the carrier *Yorktown* damaged. The Japanese invasion force destined for Port Moresby, New Guinea, is turned back and two carriers are so badly damaged that they are not available for the Battle of Midway.

End of May: Burma falls to the Japanese.

3–6 June: The Battle of Midway. The Japanese attempt to occupy Midway, located one thousand miles west of Pearl Harbor, and destroy the Pacific Fleet. The Japanese lose four carriers and many experienced pilots.

7 August: The Japanese, who had begun to move into the Solomon Island group in May of 1942, set up a seaplane base on Tulagi, north of Guadalcanal. An airfield is soon under construction on Guadalcanal. The first landing of nineteen thousand of the U.S. Marine 1st Division is made on Guadalcanal, Tulagi, and Gavutu successfully. There are seven major land battles and six naval battles. The army and marines lose over one thousand dead, and the navy lose many ships and more than six thousand sailors and pilots. The Japanese lose several thousand sailors and pilots, and more than twenty thousand infantrymen.

1943

January: Casablanca Conference. After all matters dealing with Europe and Africa are settled, attention is turned to Asia and the Pacific. Aid is to be increased to China, and a tentative plan set up to retake Burma. Pacific operation is not to interfere with operations to defeat Germany.

March: Operation Cartwheel. Allied operation in the Pacific aimed at the Solomon Islands, New Guinea, and the eventual elimination of the great naval and air base at Rabaul. The defeat of the Japanese on New Georgia and Bougainville Islands, as well as numerous occupied areas on the north coast of New Guinea, opens the way to drive the enemy from the Philippines.

May: Trident Conference. A plan to advance on Japan through the Central Pacific is approved.

August: Quebec Conference. The commitment to the May 1944 invasion of France is confirmed. The Southeast Asia Command (SEAC) is created to direct and stimulate the conquest of Burma. Prime Minister Churchill brings along Brig. Gen. Orde Wingate. Churchill, Lord Louis Mountbatten, and Wingate request that the U.S. send troops to help with the conquest of Burma. George Marshall and President Roosevelt agree to immediately assemble three thousand volunteer infantry soldiers to fight under the command of Brig. Gen. Orde Wingate. The men are to be trained in jungle warfare and are to be in a state of rugged good health. Their campaign is to last no more than three months. Eighty-five percent casualties are assumed. This is the origin of Merrill's Marauders.

31 August: Assembly of Merrill's Marauders begins. On or about this date the War Department sends telegrams to the commanding generals in the South and Southwest Pacific asking for nine hundred volunteers battle-tested in jungle fighting. Eighteen hundred are requested from the Caribbean and the Continental United States. They are told that they face a "dangerous and hazardous mission."

29 October: The volunteers, after traveling by boat, arrive at Bombay, India.

29 October: Two Chinese divisions begin their advance against the Japanese 18th Division in North Burma.

November: Cairo and Tehran Conferences. Stalin gives his support to the invasion of France and agrees to declare war on Japan. Invasion of the Andaman Islands of the Burma coast cancelled.

1 November–21 January: Organization and training of Marauders in India.

1944

23 January–23 February: Movement of 1,200 miles by train and paddlewheel boat and 150 miles on foot to the battlefront.

24 February: D day for Merrill's Marauders. Battalions advance behind enemy lines into the Burmese jungle.

24 February–7 March: First Mission. Marauders ordered to spearhead the Chinese and to block the supply line (Ledo-Kamaing Road)

about twenty miles to the rear of the Japanese 18th Division. Three major battles and twelve skirmishes.

12 March–11 April: Second Mission. Marauders ordered to spearhead the Chinese and block the Japanese supply line in the Mogaung Valley at Shaduzup and Inkangahtawng. Two major battles and many skirmishes.

28 April–17 May: Third Mission. Marauders ordered to spearhead the Chinese across the Kumon Mountains and capture the Japanese airfield at Myitkyina. Two major battles and numerous skirmishes.

18 May–3 August: Fourth Mission—to assist in the destruction of approximately six thousand Japanese in the town of Myitkyina, to protect the airfield, and to train and assist two battalions of combat engineers and two thousand replacements. One major battle and numerous skirmishes. The engineers and infantry replacements are involved in a continuous offensive operation after 1 June in cooperation with the Chinese. The Marauders assist the American replacements and the Chinese in the capture of the town of Myitkyina, which falls on 3 August 1944.

10 August: Orders issued changing the designation of the Marauders and their New Galahad replacements to the 75th Infantry. The 75th Infantry is soon changed to the 475th Infantry Regiment. This regiment and the newly arrived 124th Cavalry Regiment are formed into a brigade. They train together and, in cooperation with the Chinese and British, open the Burma Road and defeat the Japanese army in Burma during 1945.

1969

1 January: In order to provide a regiment for the redesignated ranger companies of the active army, the 75th Infantry (Merrill's Marauders) is activated. The 75th Infantry, considered the most appropriate regiment with which to identify the ranger companies, traces its origins to the 5307th Composite Unit (Provisional).

CHAPTER ONE
THE BEGINNING

A Message from the President

On 6 September 1943, a dramatic message was read to the members of the medical detachment of the First Battalion, 148th Infantry Regiment, of the 37th Division (Ohio National Guard). The message explained that President Franklin D. Roosevelt was asking for volunteers to prepare for a "dangerous and hazardous" mission in another area of operation. Everyone was to be promoted one grade in rank. No mention was made about where the action would take place, when it would begin, how long it would last, or how many men would be needed. Of course, there was much discussion in our small unit. We soon learned that the offer was being made to other combat units on the Island of New Georgia. On 6 August, we had completed our part in the barbaric land, sea, and air battle of New Georgia Island and surrounding areas. The conflict had begun on 21 June and would continue—in all of its personal horror and military success—until 22 September 1943.

Why Volunteer?

My decision to volunteer was made quickly and for many reasons. Six medical technicians in the small medical detachment of about twenty men volunteered—but only one, Pvt. Dan Hardinger, was allowed to go. When the final list appeared on 12 September, it included one private first class and five privates as the only men taken from my battalion.

The special order from the 37th Infantry Division, dated 12 September 1943, listed 132 volunteers, including myself as the only medical officer, five first lieutenants, one second lieutenant, twelve sergeants, fifteen corporals, several technicians, and the rest privates first class and privates. Most of the men were from rifle companies, but some came from the pioneer, radio communications, and weapons platoons. First Lt. Vernon L. Beard from Ohio was a radio communications officer coming from the Second Battalion of the 148th Infantry Regiment. First Lt. Clarence C. Burch was also from Second Battalion. First Lt.'s Edward L. Sievers and Logan E. Weston each came from the Third Battalion. Lieutenants Sievers and Weston had been commissioned, after attending and graduating from Officer Candidate School, while with the 37th Division on Fiji Island. First Lt. Dominic A. Perrone, also a product of the Fiji Officer Candidate School, came from the 37th Division cavalry reconnaissance troop. Future events would show that the volunteers would serve their comrades and country well during the undefined mission ahead.

The men and officers of this group had their own reasons for volunteering. My belief was that we were all looking for a mission that was essential, well planned, and carried out under outstanding leadership. After the New Georgia operation and the many discouraging events that had occurred during our period of service, we were seeking to serve our country in a way that would make us proud of ourselves and our leaders.

As a student, I had followed the rise of Hitler and Mussolini and the march of the Japanese toward war. My knowledge of the uncivilized and barbaric actions of these countries was very limited. I had learned enough, however, to be firmly convinced of the aggressive and evil characteristics and actions of the leaders of the three aggressor nations, Germany, Italy, and Japan.

The events at Pearl Harbor soon showed how poorly prepared our country was for the necessary conduct of global war against the belligerent countries. Most Americans had no conception of the suffering, self-sacrifice, general misery, illness, battle wounds, and death that many of our men would encounter before the conflict would be over. The people were not given the full facts about the loss of life and property at Pearl Harbor. It was only after the war that I learned of the great loss. "In all, eighteen United States ships were either sunk or badly damaged, including four battleships destroyed and four crippled; 164 navy and army aircraft were destroyed and 124 damaged. For this the Japanese paid with twenty-nine planes destroyed with their crews and seventy-four damaged. The Americans reported 2,403 killed and 1,178 wounded, the vast majority from the navy" (van der Vat 1944, 21).

THE BEGINNING

Introduction to Military Duty

In April of 1942 I volunteered for military duty and was attached as a first lieutenant in the U.S. Army Medical Corps to go overseas with the 18th General Hospital, a five-hundred-bed hospital formed at Johns Hopkins Hospital. This unit of volunteer doctors, nurses, technicians, and all other necessary persons had a brief period for organization at Fort Jackson, South Carolina. We crossed the continent by train and sailed from San Francisco on 20 May 1942. Like most Americans, we citizens were doing our duty without hesitation, without considering the consequences to our own futures or to those of our loved ones. As far as I personally was concerned, I saw my duty to my country, responded as I felt appropriate, and did not look upon my action as any great sacrifice.

The passage from San Francisco to New Zealand took three weeks. The seven transports carried the 37th Infantry Division, our hospital, and many other smaller military units.

As we started across the vast Pacific Ocean we heard little about the great naval Battle of Coral Sea that had taken place on 7 and 8 May. This great effort by our navy stopped the attempt to capture Port Moresby on the southeastern coast of New Guinea. The Japanese had planned to eliminate the development of communication between Hawaii and Australia by capturing the French possession of New Caledonia, the Fiji Islands, and Samoa. On 4 and 5 June, when our convoy was two weeks in the Pacific, the Battle of Midway took place. This great victory for the U.S. Navy, with the destruction of four Japanese aircraft carriers, was the turning point in the Pacific War. During the passage we felt safe with the escort of the cruiser San Francisco and two destroyers. Our hospital soon moved to Fiji, where we began to get casualties from Guadalcanal, the island in the South Pacific that had been invaded by our marines on 7 August. It was from these men that we obtained information about the heroic actions of our marines, army infantry, air corps, and navy. It soon became apparent that many warships were being lost on each side. This meant loss of men. The ocean off northern Guadalcanal was controlled by the enemy. Supplies and replacements were arriving at Guadalcanal in very limited quantities, and the situation of the marines was critical.

Sick and wounded would continue to come from the land, sea, and air battles on and about Guadalcanal. We soon learned that the navy,

CHAPTER I

marine corps, and army air corps were barely hanging on. Due to the heroic action of all concerned, the situation turned for the better in October. Army infantry brought great help when elements of the American Division joined the ground forces. Later, parts of the 37th and 25th Divisions were used to help and replace marines.

The battle for Guadalcanal was not over until 7 February 1942, when the last Japanese were evacuated from the island. From time to time, those of us on Fiji Island discussed the probable number of casualties. It was thought that the Japanese land forces had left about twenty thousand dead. A conservative estimate of dead Japanese sailors and related persons was over five thousand. From various unofficial sources, some of us concluded that more than eight hundred Japanese planes and two thousand pilots and crewmen had been eliminated during the battle for control of "The Island of Death."

Our army, navy, and marine corps, including all air units of these services, controlled Guadalcanal, including the sea and air in the Eastern Solomons, during daylight hours after early December 1942. Because many ships had been sunk during the six-month conflict on and around Guadalcanal, the body of water directly to the north was called "Iron-Bottom Sound." Seven major naval battles had been fought, and approximately six thousand shipboard marines and American sailors had been drowned or killed. Many wounded in these battles were treated at the 18th General Hospital. An estimate of the loss of American warships came to twenty-five. Rumors suggested that we were losing more ships than the Japanese but were building replacement and additional vessels much faster than they were. From the little information available to those in the war zone and areas of major action, we concluded that Americans at home had little knowledge of the slaughter in the South Pacific.

While continuing to serve as a surgeon with the 18th General Hospital at Suva, Vita Levu—the largest of the Fiji Island group—I developed a profound interest in the welfare of the infantry soldier. I was very disturbed by the number of casualties that had been and were being produced by the Guadalcanal conflict. No official information was ever available until after the war, but the many wounded and sick who were patients in the hospital gave a disturbing picture of the number of dead and wounded. I estimated that over fifteen hundred marines and army infantrymen had been killed.

I and others began to have serious doubts about the ability of the admirals and generals responsible for planning and conducting the war in the Pacific—Guadalcanal in particular. Military operations had been initiated in spite of many deficiencies and unsolved problems that were apparent to the most casual observer. Many individuals, some of whom were in a position of command, often could not understand why certain missions were ordered when the odds were so heavily stacked against our forces. Training was frequently inadequate, the size of the force unnecessarily small, and military support and intelligence faulty or not available. Many men's lives and much equipment were lost unnecessarily. Heroic Americans and their Allies were doing their duty, no matter how illogical or seemingly impossible the mission, the burden thrust on them by senior officers who frequently were not in a position to have first-hand knowledge of the local situation.

Official casualty figures and data on loss of ships and planes by both sides eventually showed that Guadalcanal produced an important turning point in the war. The dead United States servicemen, including fewer than two hundred Australians and New Zealanders, totaled 7,100. One thousand seven hundred and sixty-nine ground troops died, while the sea claimed 4,911 and the air 420. The Japanese lost thirty thousand men. The loss in ships was far greater for the U.S. Navy: one heavy carrier, one light carrier, one battleship, four light cruisers, sixty-two destroyers, and eighteen submarines. The Japanese lost one light cruiser, seven destroyers, and fourteen submarines (Frank 1990, 615, 874).

A New Assignment

During late March 1943, Colonel George Finney, the commanding officer of the 18th General, explained to the four first lieutenants at the hospital that a surgeon was needed to join the 117th Combat Engineers. They were soon to depart for Guadalcanal with their parent outfit, the 37th Division. We had no knowledge of what plans were being prepared for this Ohio National Guard Division, which had been in training since 26 September 1940, when it had been

Federalized—three weeks before the draft of 16 October 1940. The colonel was looking for volunteers, and I saw this as an opportunity to help the infantry soldier. A decision was made to draw straws for the privilege of transferring to the combat unit.

I pulled the short straw and won the honor. My period with the 18th General had been very exciting and had done a lot to make me a better doctor. During my eleven months there, I had made many friends in this outstanding facility. My service as a surgeon had given me the opportunity to help the sick and wounded veterans of the South Pacific conflict. This had given me great satisfaction.

As I prepared to leave for this new assignment, I continued to be disturbed because of lack of information concerning past action and future plans in the South Pacific. No matter where we had been traveling or stationed, very little important information had been provided to the hospital personnel. We knew practically nothing of an official nature about the number of men available in the Pacific or elsewhere. Our knowledge of military leaders in our area was limited. Any official knowledge about troops, ships, planes, casualties, bases, military material, and plans for the future never reached us. There was little access to books, magazines, newspapers, or radio. The men realized that certain types of information could be of value to the enemy and were tolerant of many aspects of this censorship. Yet our lack of information was the chief cause of much speculation, and many looked at the policy of limiting our access to the facts as a convenient method of leading the lambs to slaughter.

Combat Engineers and Guadalcanal

During the last week in March 1943, I traveled by truck to the campsite of the 117th Engineer Battalion, located in a beautiful area surrounded by flourishing tropical vegetation. The camp was orderly, suggesting marvelous management. The men were living in spacious and neat tents. Kitchens and dining areas were screened and very satisfactory. Latrines and garbage facilities were exceptional. Their medical detachment had a well-appointed workplace. The battalion surgeon and his technicians seemed well trained and mentally and physically above average. The men of the battalion had been kept busy while on the island. They had been together as a unit for a long period and were well adjusted and ready for action.

On 1 April I had the frightening experience of climbing, with a full pack, up the side and onto the deck of the USS *Hunter Liggett*. The one-thousand-mile sea passage to Guadalcanal was enjoyable. At that time the Japanese Navy was not anxious to operate in this part of the South Pacific.

Due to the location of Guadalcanal near the equator, dawn and dusk always came very rapidly. Morning arrived at 0600 and evening at 1800 hours. Our convoy arrived 6 April 1943 off the northern coast of the island, just as the sun was appearing. At fifteen hundred yards off Lunga Point, the view was spectacular. There was this great, green, glorious land mass. The centrally located mountain ridges extended as far as we could see to the east and the west. Dense green, jungle-covered ridges sloped to the coast. Great groves of palm trees came down to the sea. We guessed that the island was about 30 miles wide and 150 miles in length. Maps would never be available to any men or junior officers. We could only hope that our leaders had and would continue to have them readily available. With great effort, we climbed down cargo nets—hung over the side of the ship—to the waiting boats that were to deposit men and material on the beach at Lunga Point.

Guadalcanal, the Island of Death

As the small Higgins boats rode the waves toward the beach, my thoughts turned to 7 August 1942 and the young marines who had landed and fought so gallantly to control this island and win the honor of their country. To those of us who had, during and after this historic battle, acquired bits of information, their action was considered a military miracle.

The First Marine Division and other marine units faced many obstacles immediately after Pearl Harbor. One of the biggest problems was the need to remove many men and officers from well-established and fully-trained units to help in developing new units. All available units had been rushed to the Pacific. Brig. Gen. Alexander Arthur Vandergrift had arrived in New Zealand with his First Marine Division in late June 1942. This was shortly after the 18th General Hospital had

CHAPTER I

departed for the Fiji Islands. He had counted on further training, planning, intelligence gathering, equipment, evaluation, and combat loading before embarking on a combat mission. He had a right to expect that the commander of the South Pacific force would have total belief in the operation and would give his full support. Conversation with marine casualties at our hospital led me to believe that the marines had been given a raw deal before and after the invasion. There was no time to carry out the general's plans, and Vice Admiral Robert L. Ghormley was not able to give the required support to the operation. Some of our group had heard accounts of the 7 August landings, including those of the marines on Tulagi, Gavutu, and Tanambogo. These Islands are located in the Florida group ten miles north of Guadalcanal. They were heavily defended by the Japanese. We had been told that the marines had taken heavy casualties during this brief period of brutal offensive action. One of my friends, Samuel Miles—a young doctor from Baltimore—was killed there by a Japanese sniper as he went to help two wounded marines.

The policy of speedy capture of Pacific islands was to cost many young Americans their lives. The men who had been in combat dreaded offensive action, especially when the operation was under supervision of the navy. Shelling from the sea usually did little to destroy enemy troops or fortifications. The unprotected infantrymen were left to confront machine-gun, artillery, mortar, and rifle fire.

After being an observer in many fire fights and battles, I came to understand that the marines who had occupied Tulagi and the smaller islands had been in an offensive action fighting against fixed defenses. Because of this they would be expected to take heavy casualties, even under ordinary circumstances. The marines on Guadalcanal were, for the most part, engaging in defensive combat. Units on the defensive could usually expect far fewer casualties—unless they were overrun, in which case they would be annihilated. During December, January, and February, the bulk of the fighting was offensive against fixed emplacements. This mostly took place on and about Mount Austen, a peak of over fifteen hundred feet. The Americal Division was committed here. This offensive operation was prolonged, difficult, and very brutal—resulting in very heavy casualties in this division and the 25th and 37th Divisions.

Guadalcanal

Our first night was spent in a coconut grove on Lunga Point where, during the early months of the battle, the enemy had dropped many bombs and done much shelling from the sea. The first night initiated me to sleeping in the open on the ground. About midnight our rest was disturbed when a Japanese bomber hit a nearby ammunition dump that exploded with a tremendous roar. Forty enemy fighters and fifty-eight bombers came over the next day. A spectacular air battle destroyed thirty-four Japanese planes, while seven of ours went down. During our stay on the island we were on the receiving end of approximately 130 alerts warning of enemy air action. The 117th Engineer Battalion soon set up a tent camp in a jungle area overlooking the Matanikau River. History would eventually document the many engagements that had taken place at this location, but at the time, few of our units were aware of the significance of this area. From my tent location I could look out and see the narrow grassy knolls, leading from the north side of the central mountain down to Henderson Airfield, that had been so gallantly and brilliantly defended by our ground and air forces. Bloody Ridge, where one battle that saved Guadalcanal took place, could be clearly seen.

The surviving heroes of these and other Guadalcanal battles were no longer on the island. It was impossible to find anyone who had any significant information about the heroic action of our men who had turned back the best that Japan could offer.

Assistant Battalion Surgeon, First Battalion, 148th Infantry, 37th Division (Ohio National Guard)

After a few days with the 117th Combat Engineer Battalion, I was transferred to the First Battalion of the 148th Infantry Regiment of the 37th Division. My post was about ten miles to the west on the northern coast of Guadalcanal. At this location I found the units, A and B companies, of my new battalion. They were isolated and knew little of future plans.

On 31 May we moved to the Russell Islands, sixty miles northwest of Guadalcanal, where we joined our battalion. I do not recall anyone explaining why we were there. We soon learned that the 43rd Division had occupied the area with little opposition a few weeks before.

In early July information was leaked that elements of the 43rd Division had invaded the Island of Rendova and several other islands off the southwest corner of New Georgia Island. Ground activity had been limited, but several major air battles had taken place between Rendova and Russell Island. The Navy had fought several destroyer battles with the Japanese in this area. Our troops soon set up artillery that could reach Munda Airfield.

Despite Japanese air attacks, Rendova was soon an important base—given its location five miles by sea from Munda Airfield, located on the southwest corner of New Georgia Island. Division artillery was placed on Kokorana, a smaller island about four miles from the airfield.

Battle of New Georgia

Over a period of several months, rumors suggested that small units of our forces had done patrol activity on New Georgia and surrounding islands. The actual invasion began, again according to rumors, on 22 June, when two companies of the First Battalion of the 103rd Infantry Regiment and two companies of the First Marine Raider Battalion landed on the northwest coast of New Georgia at Seigi Point. They then traveled seven miles by canoe and eight miles through jungle and swamp to capture a small Japanese base at Viru Harbor. It was rumored that they had to change their plans frequently. In spite of great hardship, they had fewer casualties than the enemy.

From 2 through 6 July, the 172nd and the 169th Combat Teams landed at Zanana Beach, nine thousand yards east of the airfield, without ground opposition. The command of these two regiments of the 43rd Division, as we were later to find out, soon realized that much swamp, jungle, and opportunity for enemy defense separated them from the Munda Airfield. The advance of these two regiments (less than six thousand infantry troops) started on 9 July. The infantry was supported by 105 howitzers on Kokorona Island, thirteen thousand yards away. They threw over five thousand rounds toward the enemy.

Four destroyers were said to have fired over two thousand five-inch shells. Eighty-eight bombers were also active. Little advance was made, however, and casualties were heavy. Many infantry soldiers were taken from the front to evacuate wounded and bring in food, water, and ammunition. Nervous exhaustion was rampant, and it was necessary to replan the attack. At this late date it was decided to establish a new base at Laiana Beach, five thousand yards closer to the main Japanese defense line.

Impossible terrain, inadequate food, water, and ammunition, and disabling weather conditions were worse than American infantry soldiers should have been asked to endure. The command was very disturbed because of the slow advance. Their plans and methods presented no means to improve supply, evacuate the sick and wounded, or obtain better support from artillery, air, or sea power. Their battle plans did not prevent small units of the enemy from attacking and terrorizing headquarters sections, blocking communications, and killing unprotected sick and wounded. The men on the front were dying for their country without adequate support and leadership from military superiors. The evacuation trails to and from the front were constantly harassed and broken by marauding groups of the enemy, infiltrating between the 169th and 172nd Infantries.

By 11 July it was obvious to all concerned, including the commanding general of the New Georgia Invasion Force, that more troops were needed.

On 12 July 1943, the 103rd Regiment of the 43rd Division was landed on New Georgia. The two battalions of the 148th Infantry and two battalions of the 145th Infantry were ordered to ship out to Rendova Island. After great effort and many unanticipated problems, these four battalions of the 37th Infantry Division reached Rendova Island in a piecemeal fashion.

Most of the 145th had landed at Zanana Beach by the 16th. The 148th came in on the 18th. We immediately encountered casualties who told horrifying tales of Japanese cruelty and cunning. Many soldiers with knife wounds and others with mental disturbances were being evacuated from the Zanana beachhead.

It was soon apparent to all concerned that, in this type of combat, the medical detachment had to be an intimate part of the battalion at all times. This was necessary for the safety of its men and for the quick care of the sick and wounded.

Battle casualties started immediately and continued daily. Because of the close fighting, at times offensive and at other times defensive, I was able to keep careful records. These records were later to be invaluable in a wound ballistics study I would make in the fall of 1944.

On the second day of combat we came to an isolated area where the enemy had massacred seventeen wounded and their litter bearers. This barbaric act, and others of which our men were aware, tended to convince them that they were fighting uncivilized animals. This did not bode well for the Japanese.

During the battle that (for my unit) ended on 5 August, many inexcusable situations and problems developed. A tactical error resulted in my battalion being trapped for four days. Two companies of the Second Battalion were also involved. We came out with many dead and 127 wounded soldiers.

The bravery, endurance, perseverance, innovation, and mental ability required to ignore the odds and press forward to defeat the Japanese was, for me, beyond reasonable expectation.

One can imagine the great sense of joy mixed with sadness as we reached the beach and the Munda Airfield and watched a few Japanese attempting to swim to a neighboring island.

We now renewed work and training, deep in the New Georgia jungle, under primitive living conditions. Time was available to evaluate physical and mental illness and to thank whatever God we had for our survival. Many of us gave thanks to men no longer alive who had either saved our life or contributed to our survival. The time had come to move to other action, but the memories, which we were never to forget, would continue to disturb us.

Forty-six men in my battalion had been killed or died of wounds. One hundred and thirty-five had survived their wounds. Official reports obtained after the war would give figures of 1,121 dead and 3,873 wounded in the New Georgia campaign.

Before the 43rd Division was to start its drive toward Munda Airfield, a secondary action began on the northwest coast of New Georgia Island. This planned activity was not generally known in my unit, still located on Russell Island.

THE BEGINNING

This combat team, as we found out at the end of the campaign, was made up by the First Marine Raider Battalion, the Third Battalion of the 145th Infantry, and the Third Battalion of the 148th Infantry. The latter two units were part of the 37th Division. These three units landed at several different areas at Rice Anchorage, about fifteen miles north of Enogai Inlet and twenty miles north of Bairoko Harbor.

On 5 July 1943, a naval battle developed and the destroyer *Stark* was sunk. The infantry made it to shore with minimal casualties but with many problems due to poor planning.

The mission of these men was to eliminate several small Japanese beach units, capture shore batteries, occupy Bairoko Harbor, and block trails leading to the airfield at Munda, where most of the enemy were concentrated. Without adequate food and other supplies, they had to move about ten miles through rivers, swamps, and dense jungle. This operation continued until 1 September. During most of this period, the Third Battalion of the 148th Infantry was blocking the Bairoko-Munda Trail. This defensive area was soon called "Starvation Ridge" because of the weeks they went without food. Wounded were kept for days and ammunition was limited. All units suffered greatly and were near mental and physical collapse.

On 6 July, a naval battle took place in Kula Gulf near the landing site. The U.S. cruiser *Helena* was torpedoed and sunk. A second naval battle developed on 13 July. The Japanese lost one cruiser, and our navy lost the destroyer *Gwin*. The cruisers *St. Louis* and *Honolulu* were severely damaged by torpedoes. New Zealand's cruiser *Leander* also took a torpedo.

Very little information about this Rice Anchorage action reached our unit on Russell Island. Our information was obtained later from infantrymen who joined our group as volunteers.

We never obtained information about the number of American dead and wounded men. Several hundred Japanese were eliminated, and the aggressiveness of the Japanese navy was reduced.

This operation was not over until 1 September, when the 37th Division units joined the rest of the division on the southwest corner of the island. It was apparent to everyone that this mission, even though it had been poorly planned and inadequately supported, had been of great help to the major force driving toward the Munda Airfield.

CHAPTER I

I was among the group that welcomed the men in the Third Battalion as they came from the northwest area on 1 September. The first patrol to contact our group was under the command of First Lt. Logan Weston. His friendly but all-business attitude immediately made an impression on me. His tall, commanding presence was made more striking by his thinness. He explained that his weight had dropped from 185 to 119 pounds. This was the result of seven weeks of defensive trail blocking and many patrols, all without adequate food and other supplies. He was also suffering from chronic malaria.

This brief account of my military career has been told in an attempt to help the reader understand why I volunteered for the "dangerous and hazardous mission" proposed by President Roosevelt. My description of the progress of the war in the Pacific gives some of the reasons for my decision to move on. The following are some of my most important reasons:

1. The battles of Coral Sea and Midway had neither stabilized the situation in the South Pacific nor produced conditions in which the military had adequate time to plan, train, and assemble military equipment sufficient to overwhelm the Japanese.

2. The significance of this lack of stability was ignored. Guadalcanal was invaded in spite of poorly trained and equipped army, navy, marine, and air forces.

3. Our navy failed to realize that the Japanese were better trained and equipped for naval warfare than our forces, and their torpedoes were much better than ours.

4. Not enough planes and pilots were available.

5. The lack of planes and pilots produced a situation in which the marines on Guadalcanal were virtually abandoned for over a month.

6. There was little evidence of intelligent planning or action concerning the prevention of illness and injury and the care of sick and wounded.

7. Army troops in the South Pacific were very dependent on decisions made by persons of high naval authority.

8. The New Georgia Campaign was planned and carried to conclusion in spite of all of these negative factors. One could easily argue that the entire campaign was unnecessary and only sacrificed men and material.

Those of us who gave thought to the future conduct of the war favored better cooperation between the army and navy. One command for the Central and Southwest Pacific would have been a better way to conduct the Asiatic Pacific Campaign. The men favored island hopping with a strategy of isolating Japanese-held islands.

When we realized that only four or five thousand front-line infantrymen were attempting to occupy New Georgia Island, we were shocked and found such a tactical error to be inexcusable. This action of the navy command resulted in the emergency use of four battalions from the 37th Division and three understrength battalions belonging to the 25th Division. During the campaign, many items had been in short supply. These included food, water, combat clothing, entrenching tools, and heavy equipment of all types, such as bulldozers, ambulances, tanks, and armored vehicles. Medical supplies and medical support had been inadequate.

A division commander was replaced, as were several battalion commanders. The Americans took more than five thousand casualties while eliminating fifteen hundred Japanese out of an estimated ten thousand. I concluded that future combat in the South Pacific, under navy command, would offer more of the same. I wanted a new start under new command.

New Georgia to New Caledonia

Passage from New Georgia to Guadalcanal

On 15 September 1943, the 37th Division headquarters ordered the 132 volunteers to report to the 6th Replacement Depot. I, my medic Dan Hardinger, and six riflemen from the First Battalion immediately left by jeep for the beach over a rough jungle trail. We passed the new cemetery, where over one thousand of our former comrades were buried. I was deeply disturbed by the many wooden crosses.

The airport had been greatly enlarged since its capture, at such great sacrifice, on 6 August. Several acres of surrounding jungle had been cleared. A large forward base was now in use. The service troops in this area had constructed comfortable quarters. An extensive beachfront was available for many landing craft of all types. For the first time, we saw the massive and cavernous Landing Craft Tank.

With little time to reflect further about what had taken place on this island, we were aboard and on our way to Guadalcanal. The first large island to come into view was Rendova, which had been our staging area before combat. As we sailed by, I viewed it in a more relaxed way than when I had first seen it. I wondered what historians would say about the New Georgia campaign. History books would probably have a brief discussion giving credit to Admiral so and so for his brilliant tactics. No one would be interested in the sacrifice of men and material that had taken place. The only ones who would understand ground combat would be the infantry veterans. Poor decisions, haphazard planning, and inadequate support from superiors could and at times would lead to unnecessary misery, illness, wounds, and even death.

As we continued on our 175-mile trip to Guadalcanal I took the opportunity to meet and talk with some volunteers. This ship had not been designed to carry troops on long sea voyages. The best way of passing time was to walk about or sit on whatever piece of equipment was available.

CHAPTER II

The list of the 37th Division volunteers brings back many memories. Most were outstanding individuals who had made or would make great contributions to their comrades and country. Many were to become disabled or lose their lives. Survivors would have the personal satisfaction that they had been loyal to their comrades, had served their country well, and had been part of a great military unit. As we continued toward Guadalcanal we were surprised to learn that other passengers included about 150 volunteers from the 43rd Division and 100 from the 25th. As the landing craft continued down the "Slot" toward Guadalcanal, my thoughts shifted to the ten thousand or so men, both American and Japanese, whose remains lay deep in the ocean beneath our route of passage.

Return to Guadalcanal and Shipment to New Caledonia

Shortly before dawn, the great mass of Savo Island loomed to our right. We soon anchored off Tulagi Island, as an air battle was in progress in the Guadalcanal airspace. This was to be the last large air strike in this area. I estimated that more than seventy Japanese zeros were shot down.

After the dense jungle, the coral, the air raids, the miserable living conditions, and the mud of New Georgia, even Guadalcanal looked presentable to the battle-weary volunteers. Our group was soon set up in a tent camp at Lunga Point. Henderson Airfield was nearby and with its great activity provided us with reassurance. Life was now good. We had survived with reasonably good health, no serious wounds, and the prospect of an uncertain but exciting future.

As the only medical officer with our group, I had little time for rest and recreation. In spite of orders that every man was to swallow one atabrine daily, recurrent malaria was a problem. I recall one man being stung by a scorpion. He was in severe pain and developed temporary kidney failure. Several injections, using morphine surrettes, were necessary to control the agony. The next day I was stung on a finger and more than ever understood his problem.

After recovery from the injury I took a brief sightseeing tour by jeep. Near Henderson Airfield I encountered a fallen mule suffering from heat exhaustion. Salt solution—for intravenous use—was soon obtained, and a veterinarian arrived to help, but the animal died. The mules had just arrived and were not adjusted to the hot climate of Guadalcanal. None of us would have guessed that we would soon depend upon many of these splendid animals in combat.

As I continued on the dusty road, I saw a large cloth banner stretched across the dirt tract between two palm trees. On it was printed, "THE LITTLE YELLOW BASTARDS MURDERED 17 OF OUR WOUNDED." This effective, poignant, and truthful banner referred to the Medical Collecting Group that had been destroyed by the Japanese on New Georgia Island.

I had first met Lt. Logan E. Weston when his patrol from the north side of New Georgia had reached our unit in late August. Now I was happy to meet him again here on Guadalcanal and to learn that he also had volunteered for this mysterious mission. I now had an opportunity to get information concerning the almost impossible situation the Third Battalion had encountered on the north side of New Georgia Island. Their two holding actions on the Bairoko-Munda Trail had been accomplished against high odds. They had had little food or rest for almost six weeks. Weston's weight had gone from 185 to 119 pounds, but except for recurrent malaria he was otherwise healthy. He and I talked about our and others' reasons for volunteering. He said that some had a score to settle with the enemy. Some felt that the future in their outfit had little to offer them and were willing to take a chance with a new unit. After much thought and prayer he had decided to offer his service and combat experience in any way that might shorten the war and save the lives of American servicemen. He had been jilted by his fiancee and had no home to look forward to. He was in a better position than many men to do the task at hand. The future would show that Lieutenant Weston was to contribute more to the volunteers than any of the group. I came to know him well, not only as a colleague, but as a very good friend. Despite his outstanding efforts, he would be the first to deny that his contribution, on many occasions, had been beyond the call of duty.

Our pleasingly simple way of life was soon disrupted. We were informed that our stay on the island would end the next day when we would leave for unknown parts. The volunteers departed from Guadalcanal in small groups packed into landing craft. Climbing up cargo nets onto the deck of the troopship now seemed easier. This vessel, the U.S.S. *American Legion,* had been doing great service in the Pacific and was a welcome sight. It was to provide a very satisfactory voyage, taking us about twelve hundred miles to the French possession of New Caledonia. In spite of the need to attend to many minor medical problems in cooperation with the ship's medical staff, I had time, during this two-day voyage, to meet many officers and men. Good food and fellowship made this a happy ship. The men and officers with whom I talked impressed me as outstanding individuals.

Arrival in New Caledonia and the Formation of a Special Infantry Unit of Combat Veterans

Most of us had never heard of New Caledonia. As we approached the island, its appearance was most impressive. The coastline was said to be 850 miles long. We saw that mountain ranges extended the entire length of the island. Plateaus and much fertile soil provided many areas for farming. Mines provided the island's chief exports of chromium and nickel. The population of friendly people exceeded 100,000. Our forces had begun to protect the island and build up a base here in April of 1942. The sea battles of Coral Sea and Midway, as well as the sea and land conflicts of Guadalcanal and New Guinea, had prevented the Japanese from occupying the area. From the ship we were immediately transported about ten miles by truck to an isolated tent camp. The site was on a high bluff facing the Pacific to the South.

Shortly after we had settled, approximately two hundred volunteers from the Americal Division joined our group. The force now came to about six hundred combat veterans and was named Casual Detachment 1688 C.

I soon got to know the noncommissioned men who would join the six from the 37th Division to make up the medical detachment. Dan Hardinger had been at my side during the New Georgia campaign. His courage, compassion, strength, and efficiency had been known to all. Dan, a Seventh Day Adventist, had come from a farm in Ohio. At well over six feet and 250 pounds he was an imposing figure. His demeanor was as gentle as a lamb with the sick and wounded, and I knew that he would always be first to show the way in difficult combat situations. He was a conscientious objector and would not carry a weapon.

The 37th Division had been activated and Federalized in late 1940. Part of the division, the 147th Infantry, had served on Tonga and Samoa Islands and later fought on Guadalcanal from November 1942 through May of 1943. Infantry Regiments 148 and 145 had served in New Zealand, Fiji, Guadalcanal, and the Russell Islands. Their part in the New Georgia campaign has been discussed.

Among those who came from the 37th Division (along with myself) was Pat Perrone. He has given an account as to why he joined the Marauders:

> My name is Dominic A. Perrone—Pat Perrone. I am a regular army enlisted man who made the army his career and retired as a major. I was born in Connecticut and served a tour overseas in Panama originally.
>
> I got out and went to school, and when they called regular army reservists again I came back in and had a desire to go to the Philippines. Pearl Harbor occurred, and I took a reduction to buck private trying to get to the Philippines. The convoy was rerouted back to the states and ended up going first to Australia and then over to the South Pacific. I was made first sergeant six months after I went overseas. I was commissioned six months later and then made first lieutenant at New Georgia.
>
> On New Georgia it seemed like my desire to go to the Philippines would finally materialize. They asked for volunteers for a commando outfit to go back into combat immediately, and I thought immediately, "This is headed for the Philippines," so I volunteered (Perrone, videotape).

New England sent the 43rd Division overseas in October 1942. This National Guard Division had served in New Zealand, New Caledonia, New Hebrides, and Guadalcanal. The division occupied the Russell Islands in February 1943. They made the initial landings and took very heavy casualties on New Georgia. The division suffered over twenty five hundred casualties, including 555 killed in action, died of wounds, or missing in action.

CHAPTER II

On New Caledonia I soon met and began to admire Second Lieutenant Abie Weingartner from the 43rd Division. He tells how he became a Marauder:

> My whole battalion volunteered from New Georgia. We had been in combat for about thirty days, and out of a battalion of eight hundred men and approximately thirty officers we got four hundred replacements. Fifteen replacements were officers. Less than a hundred men and fifteen officers were let go. We figured nothing could be worse than this, so everybody volunteered. I was among the least valuable, I guess—because they picked me and sent me off. I became a platoon leader in Orange Combat Team and with the rest of the second lieutenants was promoted to a first lieutenant (Weingartner, videotape).

The regular army sent the 25th Division from Hawaii. Many men in this outfit had been at Pearl Harbor on 7 December 1941. Regiments 27, 161, and the Second Battalion of the 35th Infantry had arrived on Guadalcanal during the first week of January 1943. They had played a major role in the offensive action to eliminate the last of the Japanese from the island. This action resulted in the death of 216 men. The 161st came in late to New Georgia but had been very active on Guadalcanal.

Two months after landing on Guadalcanal, the First Marine Division was in desperate shape. In October the 164th Infantry Regiment was sent from New Caledonia to contribute toward their survival and victory. The American Force was reinforced in mid November by the arrival of the 182nd Infantry Regiment. The situation on Guadalcanal was now much better, and the survivors of the First Marine Division were sent for rest and reorganization. This situation had been greatly helped in November when the navy destroyed much of a Japanese landing force. Out of ten thousand enemy troops, six thousand were killed or drowned. Soon the 132nd Infantry Regiment came in to reinforce the victorious survivors of the 164th and the 182nd. These three regiments were named the Americal Division. Next, the 25th Division and the Second Marine Division were brought in. In early January we had forty-three thousand men on the island, and the Japanese had twenty-one thousand. The Japanese were strongly entrenched and well fortified on and about Mount Austen. Some then—and others in retrospect—would have allowed the Japanese to die of starvation and disease in and about their strongly defended positions. General Patch and his staff decided that they should be eliminated. The riflemen of the Americal Division and the 25th Division paid a heavy price because of this decision. Five hundred and sixty-two soldiers lost their lives on Guadalcanal. One thousand two hundred and seven marines were killed or died of wounds. Four hundred and twenty air personnel and four thousand and eleven navy men were lost. American dead totaled over seven thousand.

Japanese ground forces, including navy personnel on the island, lost approximately twenty-five thousand. At sea, the Japanese Navy lost about three thousand sailors. Their navy air force lost upwards of 880 planes and 2,362 pilots and crewmen.

The men assembled on New Caledonia had remarkable esprit de corps. There was a sense of accomplishment and purpose. The fact that they had survived and remained in good mental and physical condition in spite of combat with a barbaric enemy seemed to produce a sense of exhilaration. There was little thought or discussion about the danger or hardships of the future. The past had presented about the worst that an infantry soldier could take.

They were looking to the future and expected to defeat all enemies with the aid of superb leadership, brilliant planning, and every possible modern weapon and support service. We all hoped that more effort would be made to prevent disease and battle casualties and provide better care of the sick and wounded. This group was counting on the rumored information that President Franklin Roosevelt was backing this as-yet-unnamed mission.

After a brief period of confusion while settling in at this new camp-site, the group was happy to welcome Col. Charles Beach as commanding officer. He had been with the 37th Division (Ohio National Guard) during their long training period and had seen combat. Enthusiastic, personable, experienced, and well-trained sergeants, technicians, and other medical men were among our volunteers. Three other battalion surgeons were now with the unit.

Major Horton Camp had been a surgeon with the 25th Division and was the senior member of the group. Capt. Philip J. Cecala had been with the 132d Infantry on Guadalcanal. Capt. Milton P. Ivens came with men of the 43rd Division. He had been with the medical collecting company that had been overrun on New Georgia Island. There was reason to agree that the members of the medical detachment were ready, willing, and trained to give the best possible medical care in and out of combat. The future would show that the detachment would live up to expectations.

The few days available gave little time to enjoy the beauty of this South Sea paradise. Colonel Beach and the senior officers and noncommissioned officers organized the framework of an infantry battalion. The medical officers and men, under the supervision of Major Camp, began to process the volunteers with medical histories and physical examinations. Immunizations were also attended to. During World War II, needles and syringes were not disposable. This equipment had to be sterilized and used again. A big problem was the care of needles. They often had barbs on the point that required removal by careful sharpening with a whetstone. I still remember finding needles on New Caledonia with bent tips supposedly ready for use. During a period of immunization injections, a chain reaction develops if one man is hurt. Others become very apprehensive. Some men faint or perhaps break out in a cold sweat. Some begin to have doubts about the need for the injection. Even today, with sharp disposable needles, much trouble can be avoided by having the recipient sit or lie down at the time of their injection.

The men were given every opportunity to explain physical and emotional problems. The men in the Americal Division had been on Fiji Island for six months. Here they had access to two general military hospitals and many other medical facilities. In general they were in good physical and mental condition. A different situation existed for the men from the other divisions. They had been through recent combat with high casualties. Living conditions and diet had been far below standard for many weeks before, during, and after combat. Malnutrition, chronic malaria, gastroenteritis, chronic diarrhea, skin rashes, chronic bronchitis, joint problems, and muscle disturbances were all very common. One could easily have justified the need for further diagnosis and treatment in many men. At that time and place such an approach was not possible.

NEW GEORGIA TO NEW CALEDONIA

After much deliberation, approximately twenty men were declared unfit for infantry duty and were eliminated from the unit. The need for eye refractions and dental care was largely ignored. Every effort was made to treat all medical problems that had a chance of improvement while on duty. Prophylactic atabrine had been discontinued, and about fifty cases of clinical malaria developed. These men were treated in quarters. One daily atabrine per man was then ordered for the entire group, with satisfactory results.

Much dissatisfaction soon spread among the men and officers. Our camp was very isolated, and passes were not freely given. Living conditions were not satisfactory: poor food, no electricity for reading and writing, and poor kitchen and latrine facilities made basic functioning difficult. Men and officers were not promoted. No effort was made to give Purple Hearts to men who had been wounded, and there was no recognition for demonstrated performance. On my own initiative I was able to contact my friend and former teacher, Colonel Benjamin Baker, who was on the Central and South Pacific Staff. This action resulted in some promotions, especially among the lower ranks. Fortunately we were ordered to prepare for shipment on or about 1 October 1943. At the time I was of the opinion that discipline could not have been maintained much longer. Trucks carried the men and their belongings to Noumea Harbor. The once-luxurious *Lurline* was docked, and we prepared to board. To the surprise of all, the rails were lined with about eighteen hundred clean-shaven, enthusiastic, robust infantrymen.

Transfer from barges to the ship was rapid. Our men were now quite expert at climbing cargo nets. There was no need for or sign of any formal welcome aboard. I do not recall any announcement or speeches. The usual banter between one group of G.I.'s and another filled the air. Our six hundred yellow-skinned, bedraggled men were welcomed with apparent admiration and some awe. Our hosts were amazed at our sudden arrival.

As the *Lurline* was approaching Noumea Harbor in New Caledonia, Ray Lyons was at his desk as a clerk on Colonel Hunter's staff. For several days he had been hearing the men complain of the absence of arrangements to send letters home. Lyons describes what he did:

CHAPTER II

I went to the colonel and said, "Colonel Hunter, the men are complaining to me that they want to write letters home and there is no provision for it. There has been no arrangement for censorship or anything else." Hunter was very receptive to ideas, and you did not have to worry about military rank and so forth. "OK," said the colonel, "I'll take care of it." He set up an officers' meeting to assign the officers a method of censoring the mail, and I started collecting it (Lyons, videotape).

Ray Lyons also recounts a related incident:

The next thing that happened occurred when we got to Noumea, New Caledonia. At this point I said to Colonel Hunter, "I have had postal experience before the war. We need to take this mail that has been collected to the post office." He said, "You stay where you are, and I will get somebody else." So a lieutenant—I have no idea what the guy's name was—was given the responsibility of taking the letters and money to the post office at Noumea. He starts walking to the post office, and on his way he runs into a couple of friendly G.I.'s. They begin talking to him, and in the course of the conversation one of them asks him where we are headed. He tells them we're going to India. I had no idea where we were going, but this officer did. He had apparently been at meetings where they discussed where we were headed. When he revealed to these guys—who turned out to be CID agents in the intelligence department—a military secret, he never returned to the ship. That was the last we saw of him. (Lyons, videotape).

CHAPTER III
NEW CALEDONIA TO INDIA
3–29 OCTOBER 1943

Getting to Know Each Other

As the land mass of New Caledonia gradually faded from view, many friendships were beginning. Rumors were readily available, but at this stage we were given no definite information about our destination or mission. The men on the *Lurline* were infantrymen. They soon shared with us the minimal knowledge they had of their origin and possible mission. Pamphlets had been provided and were titled "Long-Range Penetration Units." This newly written literature talked about the operation of small units behind enemy lines. It described how they generally used mule transport, were supplied by air, and used radio communication, and stated that their purpose was to harass the enemy. We were told that the British had sent small units of this type into Burma during the current year of 1943. They were said to have been very successful. The originator and commander of these units was said to be a famous General Wingate. By now we had become convinced that our units were headed for India or perhaps Burma or China. Any further information the senior officers had was not passed on to the men.

Our fellow travelers consisted of two loosely organized groups. They were listed as Casual Detachment 1688 A and B. Each was battalion-size, with about 950 men. Our combat veterans were labeled Casual Detachment 1688 C. Most of the men in the B and C detachments had been overseas two or more years. Draftees and National Guard men were in the majority. Common to all was a love of country and the need to defeat a ruthless, aggressive enemy. Self-confidence was universal. Without question in the minds of the men, the enemy would be defeated in all engagements. None doubted the courage of their comrades. As time went on, one could sense that the men had great confidence in their commissioned and noncommissioned officers.

Life was good on the ship. Even without escort there was little thought of torpedoes. This vessel could outrun enemy submarines. Since the *Lurline* was an official navy vessel, food was much better than it had been on the other ships most of us had traveled on. Medical care was given by the navy doctors. Adequate space was available for training classes and entertainment. Interesting films and news bulletins were available. Control of the three units remained with their respective officers and noncommissioned personnel.

After a few days of the voyage, our men realized that Col. Charles N. Hunter was commander of the force. Unofficial information suggested that he had been given the opportunity to volunteer for this "dangerous and hazardous mission" the same as the rest of us. Unlike the other volunteers, he had been informed about many aspects of its secret organization and movement.

Colonel Hunter was a West Point graduate, class of 1929. He had served in the Canal Zone and the Philippines. When he volunteered, he was Chief of the Rifle and Weapons Platoon Group of the Weapons Section at the Fort Benning Infantry School. The colonel was about five feet seven and very muscular with no excess fat. His athletic appearance and firm facial features created an aura of authority. Everyone understood that no nonsense would be tolerated, and perfection was the only answer.

Casual Detachment 1688 A

The formation of Casual Detachment 1688 A began on or about 17 September 1943, when volunteers from many units arrived either alone or in small groups at Camp Stoneman, San Francisco. In early September a directive was read to army troops stationed in the states. Men trained for jungle warfare were being asked to volunteer for "a dangerous and hazardous" mission. Members told different stories about what had been explained and promised and why they had volunteered. Some said they were guaranteed promotions, others that the mission would only last ninety days. Few had been told of the possible risk. None were told where they would be fighting. The average man was free spirited and willing to do his duty.

Approximately nine hundred stateside volunteers had arrived at Camp Stoneman by 18 September 1943. These men soon learned that they were members of a group called Casual Detachment Shipment 1688 A. At dockside, the senior officers and noncommissioned officers asked the men to complete qualification cards. With this information they set up the personnel requirements and organizational outline of an infantry battalion.

On 20 September the group, under tight security, boarded the USS *Lurline.* This vessel had been converted from a luxury liner to a troop-ship. In spite of its unusual beginning, this casual detachment made rapid progress. Their future was to be brilliant under the leadership of Maj. William L. Osborne. The major (later a colonel) had been a reserve battalion commander in the Philippine army. He had avoided capture after the fall of Bataan and with another officer had escaped from the island. The two had arrived in Australia after a fifty-six-day voyage in a twenty two-foot sailboat. When the request for volunteers came to his attention, he was on duty at Fort Benning. An affirmative response was immediate. He was soon on his way to San Francisco with Colonel Hunter.

Maj. Melvin A. Schudmak was the senior medical officer in the First Battalion, and Capt. Winnie Steinfield and Capt. John J. McLaughlin were the junior members of the medical detachment. The unit was fortunate to have an outstanding group of doctors.

Casual Detachment 1688 B

In late August 1943 the 33rd Infantry Regiment received a request from the War Department to furnish nine hundred volunteers for a "dangerous and hazardous mission." The men had to be in good health and trained for jungle warfare.

The request, when read to the infantry troops, brought a very enthusiastic response. This regular army unit had been shipped from the Canal Zone to Trinidad in December 1941. Their new mission was the defense of the Caribbean. During the twenty-one months that followed, a large turnover of personnel had taken place. The ranks had been renewed by draftees, reserve and newly commissioned officers, and regular army noncommissioned officers.

CHAPTER III

Col. George A. McGee Jr., the Commanding Officer of the Second Battalion of the 33rd Infantry Regiment, received the War Department directive with enthusiasm. The response was so strong that the senior officers were given the opportunity to pick the most qualified men and officers. The result was a well-organized battalion of well-qualified volunteers. The men and officers knew each other and had trained together.

The record is not clear about how much of the War Department request was passed on to the men. From time to time some of the men and officers were to complain that the true facts of the request for volunteers were not given to them.

Practically all medical personnel in the regiment volunteered. Four battalion surgeons were in the unit. Maj. Bernard Rogoff was the senior medical officer, and Capt. A. Lewis Kolodny, Capt. Henry G. Stelling, and Capt. Horace C. Gardner were all members of the medical detachment. Their presence guaranteed a great unit. 1st Lt. George F. Hickman was the veterinary officer. The unit was to have a dental officer, 1st Lt. James W. Parker. The doctors had selected outstanding medical technicians from many volunteers. Volunteers for the Pioneer platoon came from an engineer unit in Puerto Rico.

I soon learned that Lewis Kolodny was from my home town, Baltimore, Maryland. Naturally we had a lot in common, and as time passed became very good friends and have remained so over the years. I soon learned that his lovely wife, Mildred, was my most admired and favorite nurse at Johns Hopkins Hospital, where I had interned in surgery the previous year.

Between 6 and 10 September, the newly organized battalion was moved by air to Miami. The unit arrived, after crossing the continent by train, at Camp Stoneman, San Francisco, on 16 September. Here the men were surprised to find another battalion. Headquarters at Camp Stoneman recognized the need for tight security. Because of the lack of previous opportunity to contact family and friends, the men were allowed to make individual calls and mail letters. Total observance of security regulations was to be maintained. Since the men knew nothing about the mission, it was unlikely that any harm to the war effort would come from this intelligent and humanitarian action.

New Caledonia to Brisbane

Maj. Melvin Schudmak, the senior physician of the units, became the unit surgeon. In this capacity, he became the one member of the three units in a position to acquire information and keep the surgeons informed about all medical problems. An officer in this position has great responsibility. He is expected not only to have the ear and cooperation of his immediate superiors but also that of the chain of command leading up to the theater surgeon. Without his aggressive approach, many aspects of the infantryman's welfare can be expected to deteriorate. He should have a voice in all aspects of the men's physical and mental well-being. He should constantly be working on sanitation, adequate food, proper care, mental health, and evacuation of the sick and wounded. This medical officer should have a voice in decisions that are apt to produce unnecessary casualties from accidents, illness, and combat.

Little time passed before it was generally known that fourteen very important men were part of shipment 1688. The War Department had wisely recruited fourteen Nisei. These Americans of Japanese ancestry were to be with us from beginning to end. Their loyalty and bravery would save many American lives. From the beginning, these infantry soldiers were treated with great respect. At no time did I see any evidence of discrimination.

The future would show that the three units could be counted on to overcome all obstacles and complete the most difficult tasks with brilliance and bravery. They faced the enemy, the hostile environment, unusual diseases, confusion in higher command, and the possible prospect of death or debilitation with unusual equanimity.

The ship passed at maximum speed toward Australia. Our course was somewhat south of the Coral Sea. Few of the men knew much about the sea battle in this area that had taken place 7–8 May 1942. This crucial naval battle forced the Japanese to abandon the invasion of Port Moresby and the probable attack on Australia. In this battle we lost the aircraft carrier *Lexington,* and the *Yorktown* took heavy damage.

Two enemy carriers were put out of action, and the Japanese lost many planes and pilots. The crucial battles of Midway and Guadalcanal followed. Early defeat of the enemy at Coral Sea probably played some part in the victory at Midway.

CHAPTER III

Brisbane to Freemantle, 270 Volunteers Join Detachment 1688 C

On the day after leaving New Caledonia, land was sighted midway between north and south Australia on the east coast. The prospect of leave at the important port of Brisbane resulted in many plans for a day or so of freedom and pleasure. The reason for docking, however, was more important: Here Casual Detachment 1688 C was to welcome aboard 270 men from the command of Gen. Douglas MacArthur. Several of these men told me that Gen. Walter Krueger had been very frank when he explained the request for volunteers. The horrible slaughter of our troops during the New Guinea battles had apparently made many reluctant to risk their lives on an unknown mission. Five outstanding officers were with the new group. Lawrence L. Lew and Edwin J. Briggs were to become very important members of Shipment 1688 C. They had been with the 32nd National Guard Division from the West Coast. One hundred and fifty of the enlisted men came from the 32nd Division and 125 from the 98th Pack Artillery. Many of these men had no combat experience. Most were waiting to be assigned (Stone 1969, 300).

One of the privates who came to us from the 32nd Division, Tony Colombo, soon became known to most men in Unit C—later to be called the Third Battalion. He tells how he got into the service and then into the Marauders:

> I came from Brooklyn, I guess I should say drug up in Brooklyn. Anyhow I was seventeen in 1943, and when I asked my mother if I could go into the service she refused to sign the papers. So what I did was I falsified my baptismal papers and registered for the draft. About two weeks later I won the lottery, and anyhow I ended up in Camp Hood, Texas. There I continued to be the same old guy that I was, and I got into a crap game and won thirty-eight hundred dollars of my first sergeant's money and his automobile. He put that automobile in hock to me for a few bucks when cars were hard to come by, but I proceeded to keep gambling and wound up losing the automobile. I was supposed to stay in this cadre, and I realized that since I had lost all this money and he was going to be my first sergeant, I was in trouble.

I went and volunteered for the paratroopers, which was the only way you could get out of there. My C.O., when he got the papers, said, "I thought you were going to stay in this cadre." I said, "I just want to get out of Texas." He said, "I can arrange that. If you want to get out of Texas, fine." So he put me on a train with a bunch of other guys with gas impregnated clothes and shipped me up to New York. The curtains were down, but we got to Orangeburg, New York, Camp Shanks, where I went AWOL. My family only lived about six or seven miles away. I then got the word that the men were leaving and got on a ferry boat. I said, "I am going overseas on a ferry boat." We met troop transports outside the harbor there, proceeded to load up, and wound up in Australia.

I got into in a weapons depot, and the first thing you know I got assigned to the Thirty-second Division. I got into Port Moresby and got an attack of malaria. They sent me back with this malaria attack. What happened then was this: The Thirty-second came back a beat-up shambles, they got to talking about what they were going to do next, this volunteer thing came up, and I volunteered. I had to fight my way in because I had flat feet and had had malaria. There were not many volunteers, and MacArthur didn't want very many people to go. So anyhow I got by the doctors, but it took a little fighting. I said, "Gee, I think I am going to Italy where at least I can speak the language and go around with the senoritas and have a ball." They put us on a boat and we wound up in Bombay, India (Colombo, videotape).

Our stay was brief before we sailed. Time would show that Unit 1688 C had been given outstanding men and officers from MacArthur's command. The *Lurline* left Brisbane minus several men who had gone AWOL. Needless to say, no men or officers were allowed shore leave while in port.

The weather grew cold as we rounded the southern tip of Australia. Without winter clothes, most of our time was spent in our cabins. A Dutch destroyer had joined us when we left Brisbane. An occasional glimpse of this small vessel gave me some reassurance as we sailed through more dangerous waters.

After two more weeks of rest and good food we docked at Freemantle on the southwest tip of Australia. The three shipments were each allowed ashore, but only one at a time. First, A marched through the town. Next went Casual Detachment 1688 B. Finally C was allowed ashore. Some men from C had very skillfully left the ship with A. They gained freedom for a brief period by slipping away from A and returned with unit B. They then left the ship for a second time with their unit. Again they slipped out of the parading column. While exploring the town, they were picked up by the military police and thrown in jail. This group of three or four included Dave Hurwitt.

David Hurwitt told me this story of his background and escape from jail:

I was originally from New York, the good old USA. I enlisted a short while before Pearl Harbor. I was one of two crazies in my outfit who decided we would volunteer for the Marauders after one year of the Solomon Campaign. I wasn't promised anything. All we were promised was what we were told, "a dangerous and hazardous mission." They said there would be a lot of combat guys in it. That I appreciated. One thing about combat people, experience may expose you more and more to the ultimate fatality, but at the same time you want that experience next to you. I tell you, I appreciated the men and officers because they knew what they were doing. They showed you the way. They didn't tell you how to do it—they showed you how to do it. At Walawbum that became very apparent, and it became more and more apparent as we went up the hill at Nhpum Ga. I think that those who went on to Myitkyina learned that. I don't think it could have happened without the kind of guys we had all around us.

In Freemantle, during our second leave from the ship, we had no trouble in slipping out of the column of soldiers and entering a pub. We were soon picked up by M.P.'s and thrown into a jail cell. Being in jail, we were now in a very difficult situation. The rather small, broken-down jail room was on the ground floor, and we quickly concentrated on a small and rather high window. I could barely look out of the top, but in doing so I saw a pickup truck parked just under the window with the owner standing nearby. We had a friendly conversation, and he soon understood our problem. Perhaps he needed money for gas or a drink, but he soon agreed to accept a few dollars to help us. He quickly threw us a rope. One end was attached to the window and the other to his rear axle. He raced his motor, and the window came right out. Our escape was successful, and we made it back to the ship without being discovered (Hurwitt 1980, personal communication).

The men who had been left in Brisbane were returned to the ship in Freemantle. The friendly ladies of Freemantle were free with beer and kisses to the marching Americans. This outing in Freemantle was the closest the units would ever come to a parade during the entire time of their existence, with one exception while training in India.

Freemantle, Australia, to Bombay, India

The men's spirits were uplifted by this brief visit to western Australia. Their outlook became more serious as the ship steamed westward. Word was passed out that the destination was Bombay, India. I don't recall that anyone produced maps or gave simple geography lessons, but the men seemed satisfied. Calcutta would have been the logical port for our group, but the harbor would not accommodate such a large ship. A few more days at sea gave more rest and rehabilitation, greatly appreciated by the combat veterans.

The medical staff in charge of the sick bay on the *Lurline* insisted that they and they alone were responsible for all medical care on the ship. One of the first decisions they made, presumably with the concurrence of senior medical officers of Unit 1688 C, was that prophylactic atabrine be withheld from the men. It would seem that the idea was to determine how many men needed atabrine (to prevent the recurrence of malaria) before arrival in India.

The well-equipped and well-staffed sick bay provided invaluable service. Approximately 150 recurrent malaria attacks were treated. Twenty or more men were found to have amoebiasis. Numerous chronic problems were evaluated. The navy physicians expressed considerable concern over the general condition of the men in Casual Detachment C. Because of this, a letter was given to the senior medical officers stating that, in the opinion of the physicians, the unit as a whole was not fit for combat. Needless to say, the junior medical officers—including myself—were not involved with many decisions or privy to much information.

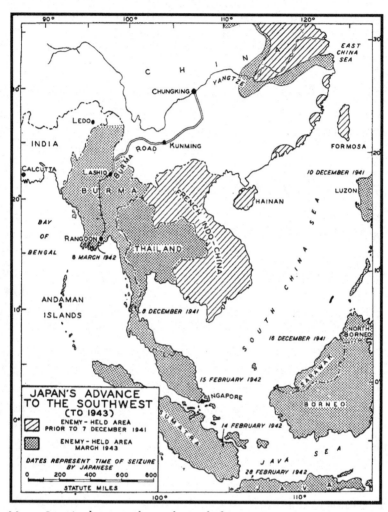

MAP 1. Japan's advance to the southwest, before 1943.

CHAPTER IV

TRAINING AND ORGANIZATION

Bombay to Deolali

Thirty-nine days out of San Francisco, 29 October 1943, the *Lurline* docked in Bombay Harbor. Few of the men had any knowledge about the people, geography, history, government, religions, or other important facts concerning India. Most knew that the country was an ally under British control. All were surprised to learn that Bombay was the most important port of this Asiatic country. We found the city located on an island that surrounded the fourteen-mile-long and five-mile-wide harbor.

After docking, about twenty men were transferred by the navy medical officers on the ship to the 181st U.S. Army Hospital, located in Karachi. Maj. Horton Camp did not return from treatment at the hospital. Maj. Bernard Rogoff and Lieutenant Hickman, both from the Trinidad group, were treated and eventually joined the unit.

For reasons unknown to us, shipment 1688 C remained on board until 31 October. Shipment A had debarked on 29 October and B on 30 October. No passes were given. The only entertainment was provided by watching the Indian dockworkers. Clad in loincloths, these men slowly went about their work. British military personnel smartly clothed in tropical uniforms would occasionally smack one of them with a swagger stick. This was apt to cause unkind remarks from the soldiers who lined the ship's rail. The attitude of the men was further disturbed by the heat, not only on the inside but also on the outside of the poorly ventilated ship. On 31 October 1943, we marched from the dock area to our waiting train. The small, wooden cars were different from any passenger cars we had ever seen. Their wooden seats resembled weathered park benches. Facilities for personal hygiene were primitive. The floors were dirty and provided a race course for many large roaches.

CHAPTER IV

After much jerking and banging, we were under way. Our troop train stopped at many small villages. There was much to see and hear. Scantily clad children, skinny adults, and beggars were frequently seen. Hawkers of fruits, knives, jewelry, and other products were active. These peddlers and others were present at every train stop.

Some areas of countryside were verdant with grain, foliage, and grass. Other sections of the passing panorama were swampy, but mostly we saw arid land. The first day we saw small plots of land with crops and cattle. Many workers were in the small fields.

During the day-and-night trip we welcomed the American-style sandwiches our mess sergeants had provided. We looked forward to a good meal at the end of our journey.

Camp Deolali

After a trip of 125 miles northeast of Bombay, we arrived at Deolali, near the town of Nasik, where more than 100,000 people lived. Deolali was now a military transient camp. For a hundred or more years it had been a major British military camp. A brief march along dusty roads brought us to the imposing gate of the camp.

The enlisted men were directed to long brick barracks with drafty windows and doors as well as dirt floors. Furnishing consisted of wooden beds with ropes crisscrossed for springs. The long-awaited meal was the first of several days' feedings that were accepted with disappointment and revulsion. The quality and quantity were poor. Flies were always present, and during daylight hours vultures hovered overhead, ready to grab a morsel. The situation was compounded by primitive outdoor stoves and the unwashed cooks and helpers. Preparers and servers of food and drink seemed to have no knowledge of sanitation. Flies traveled directly from the waste buckets to the food. Our cooks soon took over food preparation, yet the poor quality of the available food still presented insurmountable problems.

Fortunately, the regimental staff soon learned that Tony Colombo had been a butcher's apprentice in New York. As Colombo recounts, "The natives were cutting the meat for the camp. What they would do was to take the side of a bull and plant their feet on it and hack away at it. I became the butcher for the outfit. I knew how to cut meat without the flies around it and make roasts and everything to eat instead of squares and cubes and so forth. I did that for a while and then we went up to Deogarh and I joined the Third Battalion kitchen. I would clean the deer and skin the deer that we would shoot to eat" (Colombo, videotape).

Officers found long, low buildings with double rooms and more comfortable beds. Even in the enlisted quarters, the wash houses and latrines were in separate structures without screens. Buckets were present for the collection of human waste. Men and boys of the lowest untouchable cast were present for waste disposal.

The officers' mess was in a large, well-screened building, but the preparation and quality of the food was still substandard. With the knowledge that we were only temporary guests of our British hosts, we tolerated the situation.

The units were allowed to hold sick call in a small medical dispensary. The men in shipment 1688 C kept our medical detachment busy. Unfortunately our medicines and supplies were not available. We were dependent on many liquid mixtures, contained in large bottles, which our allies used. Because of this situation, many of our sick were sent to the British base hospital. This group was kept busy treating more than one hundred recurrent cases of malaria, as well as such conditions as chronic bronchitis, dysentery, dermatitis, and chronic and acute back problems. The hospital food and service was very satisfactory. This service took away some of the apprehension associated with the possibility of going into combat under control of British command. Again for undetermined reasons the men of 1688 C were advised to withhold the use of atabrine.

Fortunately the men had two sources to supplement their diet. Natives freely circulated through the camp selling oranges, coconuts, bananas, and other fruits. During their free time the men could walk to the town of Nasik, where food could be obtained. This town was ancient and typical of many towns in India. Dust was everywhere. Sewers were open. There was little grass or foliage during this, the dry season. The streets were narrow and poorly paved. Traffic was mostly people, carts, and horse- or bullock-drawn vehicles. Trucks and automobiles were scarce. Almost every type of shop could be found. These occupied the first-floor front, with the living quarters in back or above. The entire front of the shop would be open to the street during the day. A customer could easily see the activity and bargain with the owner. At other shops it was more convenient to enter to inspect the many types of goods and haggle over price. Shoes and any type of clothing could be made to order and delivered on short notice. The natives were friendly and very persuasive. Children suggesting sexual liaison with various female members of their families were very much in evidence.

On one hot, dusty day I walked the two miles to Nasik with the purpose of checking out the local hospital. The building was small, old, and dilapidated. It seemed clean but did not sparkle. Patient accommodations were on the plain side. Departments of X-ray, pharmacology, surgery, and pathology lacked many essentials but were staffed by dedicated people. The pathology department displayed a large collection of bladder stones. The pathologist explained that bladder stones were very common in this section of India. One of the hospital surgeons was noted for surgical correction of this condition. The visit to this hospital was a very moving experience for me. I began to think about war and peace. How wonderful it would be if we and the Japanese were in Asia to help these people instead of killing each other. Education, management, and money could bring health and happiness to millions in Asia.

Ray Lyons, the regimental clerk attached to Colonel Hunter, describes an interesting episode:

> One of the things I remember is this: The Indians had a daily practice of selling hot tea. "Hot tea walla," they would holler. They would make a big pot of hot water and put tea in it and sell hot tea for one ana, about one cent. The American G.I.'s soon got the idea of "Hey, we can improve on this." So they convinced these guys that instead of hollering "hot tea walla," they should holler, "Lana Turner hot tea," and other phrases not for family reference. They thought up some very nasty phrases, and these guys were going all over the camp. The American G.I.'s thought it was hilarious. When the guys got to the British Army headquarters, where families were, the families complained about this stuff. They informed Colonel Hunter, and that was the end of the coolies selling hot tea (Lyons, videotape).

TRAINING AND ORGANIZATION

Another interesting episode, this one related to our mail, was cleared up by Ray Lyons:

We got a message from Bombay that they had mail for us. I quickly volunteered to Colonel Hunter to take care of the problem. I said, "I have had postal experience, and if you would like, I will get the mail." "No," he says, "You stay here and watch the store, and I will get someone else to take care of it." So he got some sergeant from the First Battalion to go down to Bombay for the mail. He came back and he had four pouches with LA locks on them. An LA lock is a lock that fastens by a spring lock onto the hasp and you have to have a key to open it. I said to this first sergeant, "Did they give you a key to open it?" "No," he says, "I don't know anything about it." They should never have given us the pouches with the locks on. They should have put a seal on them. The post office has a system where they put on a seal that can easily be broken. I said to Colonel Hunter, "If we don't get these pouches open, we will have a mutiny." I said, "Colonel, I know what we should do because I have been in the postal service. Every year I have to put up a postal examination. If you can't open up a lock for some reason, what you do is cut along the seam, get the mail out and distribute it, and then sew it up again." He said, "Are you sure?" "Yes," I said, "I am positive, and we need to do it." So I cut it open and we distributed the mail. Everybody was happy they got mail. I guess it had been months, particularly for those guys in the Third Battalion, since they had got mail. Now they had mail at the first stop. I sewed up the pouches and put them on the train.

The next day, up comes an officer from the army postal service, and he wants to know who cut open the pouches. Colonel Hunter says, "Sergeant Lyons said it was okay to do," and I said, "I have worked in the postal service. You should never have sent those pouches up here with locks on—you should have used seals. It would have made more sense than what you did. In any event, I did what was appropriate at the time." This Captain went off with Colonel Hunter into the inner headquarters to tell him what a wise guy he had for a sergeant. Many years later I had been promoted in the mail service, and they sent me up to a regional office in Syracuse, New York. When I went, here was this Captain White. I said, "Captain White, do you remember me?" "No," he says, so I repeated the story. He had no idea how to react or whether or not he should smile, because now I outranked him. I really enjoyed telling him that story (Lyons, videotape).

In spite of the problems with health, food, sanitation, general living accommodations, and recreation, this period of relative inactivity and freedom did a lot for the physical and mental outlook of the men. I do not recall any criminal activity, significant complaining, or fights among the men or with the natives. The minimal classroom-like training and organized marches were completed with good humor.

One day, many of us who were resting at camp noticed a line of people following four men who were carrying a crude throne on which the body of a man was tied. The procession was on the way to a tower at the top of a nearby hill. Here they spent time chanting to strange music. A few days later some of the men visited the tower. They found the remains of the body resting on a slab at the top of the tower. The bones had been picked clean by vultures. These same birds were very active about the camp during meal time when they attempted to swoop down and steal food from the men's mess gear. A few days later, while on an organized march, we came to an isolated grove of trees. Baboons were screeching as they climbed in the trees. Nearby we found an unattended but active wood fire with a body on top slowly being consumed.

After a week or so at Deolali, the group was joined by Colonel Hunter, Colonel McGee, and Colonel Osborne. They brought with them Colonel Brink. Our men gradually learned that Colonel Brink was a U. S. Army officer attached to the CBI headquarters. He had been designated by General Wingate to supervise our training. We were told that we had been and would remain under British control for a campaign in Burma at an unspecified time and location. Soon we would move to a more suitable location for training. These, our senior officers, had gone directly from Bombay to visit a British headquarters in Agra and also General Wingate's headquarters in Jhansi. They had been told that we would get our food and other necessary support, during our training period, from British supply. Our training would be under the supervision of General Wingate's headquarters.

Fortunately, the above information was leaked slowly. The knowledge that we would continue under such tight British control was difficult for most of us to accept. In a few days General Wingate arrived at Deolali. I was present when he talked to the assembled officers in the mess hall. He told us, briefly, of his long-range penetration of Burma in the spring of 1943. He had commanded three thousand Indian, Burmese, Gurhka, and British troops. They were divided into six columns of about four to five hundred men each. They had used mules and horses and had been supplied by parachute-dropped supplies. After harassing the Japanese for three months, they had withdrawn. Among the pearls of information he offered us, he explained that it would be wise to use garlic every day. He further stated that "dysentery can be controlled by wearing a tight band about the waist." I don't recall that anyone took this advice seriously.

First Lieutenant James H. Stone, in his "United States Army Medical Services in Combat in India and Burma, 1942–45," tells how Wingate "informed the troops that if they fought under Stilwell they would not be withdrawn in three months, and they would be used to spearhead the Chinese drives to prove Stilwell's point that his Chinese Divisions, trained and supplied by Americans, could be inspired by this means to fight" (Stone 1945).

Conversations with many Indian and British enlisted men and officers suggested that the success of Wingate's Chindits was somewhat exaggerated. Two-thirds of his men had been lost to combat and disease. His evacuation system had been hopeless. Some seriously wounded had to be killed to put them out of their misery. Others were abandoned. Yet the world press had backed him in his daring raid, and it was said to have boosted British morale.

It soon became apparent that the three battalions had been promised to Wingate to operate as three separate units. When we eventually came under Stilwell's control, he determined to use the entire force to form a spearhead that would lead the Chinese attack— or, by successive operations in the Japanese rear, serve as an anvil against which the Chinese hammer would beat.

Colonel Brink's first significant decision was not liked but was accepted. Apparently with General Wingate's backing, he decided to put a few experienced men and officers from the Pacific into the other two groups. C group then accepted a like number in trade. Six officers and 160 enlisted men were moved from C to A and B. This move resulted in great dissatisfaction, but it had to be accepted. The long

CHAPTER IV

association of the men and officers on the Lurline and the three weeks at Camp Disloyal, combined with the transfer of men, probably paid dividends. Great camaraderie developed among the personnel in the three units. The men and officers were better able to understand problems as they developed in the different units.

As three weeks at the Deolali Transit Camp approached, the junior officers had discussions concerning many unanswered questions. Why was so much training time being lost? After all, it had been one hundred or more days since the men had been removed from any significant contact with infantry tactics or study and use of infantry weapons. Why were they not given descriptive material and maps about the area where they were to meet the Japanese? What was the overall situation in this, the China-Burma-India (CBI) theater of operations? Who was really in charge, and what were they accomplishing? Why was the War Department allowing them to waste time after declaring this such an important operation? What had happened to those who had authorized this mission? Had our welfare and the importance of the mission been forgotten by the War Department? All of these and many more questions were unanswered. Our men knew they were facing death, injury, and illness. Word had been leaked out that the War Department expected about eighty percent casualties. No replacements were planned for men lost due to battle deaths, wounds, and sickness. In spite of the unanswered questions and the dismal outlook, there was no whining, only doubts. The general attitude was *let's get the job done.*

The junior medical officers and the medical detachment personnel had many questions. How would the health of the combat veterans hold up? Many of them were suffering from chronic recurrent malaria. Others had not recovered from the physical and emotional distress of combat. Conditions for many in and out of combat in the Pacific had been intolerable. When, if ever, would the senior staff present a plan for evacuation of the sick and wounded? Was any plan in the works for the proper delivery of medical supplies, food, ammunition, and so forth? Was the proposed animal transport going to be available and adequate for our needs? If we could get the sick and wounded out of the combat area, would adequate care be available in the rear area? These and many other important questions remained unanswered.

Deolali to Camp Deogarh

On 16 November 1943, a movement order was transmitted to the three unit commanders. Unit 1688 C was to entrain on the 17th, Unit A on the 19th, and Unit B on 20 November. No destination was given. Rations were not to be provided by the camp. The train that had transported eight hundred tons of our supplies from the USS *Lurline* had never been unloaded. It was to leave on the 18th. Unknown to the rank and file, Maj. Edward T. Hancock of the regular army had been appointed as supply officer to the three units. Shortly after the Lurline had docked on 29 October, he had come aboard to accept and guard the supplies that belonged to the units. Many other shipments were to arrive during the next three months.

The departure of the three units proceeded without any significant problems. Preparation only required that our few belongings be loaded on trucks for transport to the train. We marched in columns and were soon on our way late in the day. As before, our accommodations were primitive but adequate. We were beginning to understand that we were guests in a country that was providing us with the best equipment and help available in the area. Our group now definitely knew that we were under British command. The men in our units had been given no information about this new location near the geographic center of India. The nearest village was Jahklann station, eight miles from our destination. As we arrived, we learned that our camp was one-half mile south of the Rewa River and twenty miles south of the nearest town, Lallitpur, located in Bengal Province. Gen. Orde C. Wingate's Chindits were based near the city of Jhansi about eighty miles north of our new camp. Agar, the home of the magnificent Taj Mahal, is one hundred miles south of the great city of New Delhi, the capital of India. Our new training area was located about three hundred miles south of this city.

The seven-hundred-mile train trip took three nights and two days. Each unit arrived about six thirty in the morning and then marched about ten miles across dry, rugged land, irregularly covered with spine-producing bushes about six feet high.

Our speed between the many train stops seemed to be about twenty-five miles per hour as the small engine pulled the many boxcarlike coaches. Thoughtful planners in Washington had supplied large quantities of combat rations with our freight. When it became known that the British command was not providing rations for our trip, the shipment of freight was searched and found to have a very generous supply of rations that we were not familiar with but were happy to discover. A distribution of 10-in-1 and K-rations provided a welcome change from the monotony of British rations. Small gasoline burners were also discovered among the items of freight. These allowed the men to have hot food and liquids.

Enthusiastic merchants, clothed in everything from cloaks and turbans to loincloths and skirts, peddled hot tea, peanuts, bananas, and various dishes of chicken, rice, and grain at every stop. Merchants of every age offered monkeys, ferrets, chickens, rabbits, knives, jewelry, and every imaginable article for sale at negotiated prices.

At these stops we saw beetle-nut chewers, with red lips, expectorating into the dust of the streets among the naked and skinny legs and feet. Mongoose and cobra fights, carefully monitored by mysterious men, were frequently staged. At some stops we saw unattended dead bodies lying in the dust.

During daylight hours we marveled at work crews of women moving great masses of dirt along the railroad. Baskets filled with excavated material were perched on their heads and carried in this manner to disposal sites. Other women, men, and children seemed to spend all daylight hours cultivating small fields of rice, wheat, cotton, beans, and peas. These people lived in mud and straw huts with dirt floors and no running water, inside plumbing, or electricity. Roads were mostly dirt tracks traveled by bullock carts. We rarely saw telephone or electric lines.

Camp Deogarh, Home of Shipments 1688 A, B and C

19 November 1943–28 January 1944

During the late afternoon of 19 November 1943, the men of Unit 1688 C caught sight of white tents in the distance. The long, hot, dusty march had brought us to a carefully laid-out tent camp. Brush had been cleared from the dry and dusty plain at four closely related sites. At the smaller area, tents were present for the headquarters personnel. A site had been set aside for each of the three infantry units. Each site had a row of single-occupant tents for the officers. Company areas were laid out with squad-size tents. Kitchen and storage tents were well placed and roomy. Each battalion's medical tent was large enough to accommodate ten cots and an area to dispense medicine and examine and treat patients. The camp was not electrified; we depended on scarce gasoline lanterns. There was no running water or indoor plumbing. No telephone system was in place.

We soon realized that our camp had been put in the middle of a wilderness area. Being three hundred miles south of New Delhi and in an isolated brush- and small-tree-covered wilderness, there would be little to distract the men from intensive training.

Near our tent camp the British had provided and staffed a small tent hospital, the 80th British General, which was set up to provide about one hundred beds. The always exceptionally competent English nurses and several doctors were in residence for our emergency needs.

The tents of our camp were well constructed and had a blue-lined flap over the roof to reflect heat and give ventilation. Tent sides could be easily opened and closed. Furniture consisted of folding standard army cots. Major Edward Hancock was now our supply officer, and he had created this camp with the cooperation of General Wingate's staff. Unfortunately, he had not provided the camp with screened kitchens, latrines, or slit trenches. Drinking water, brought from the Rewa River, was of questionable quality—even after chlorination in Lister bags. The unit's freight began to arrive on 20 November, soon to be followed by the men of Units A and B. Kitchen and medical supplies were soon located. At our first battalion-prepared meal we knew, for certain, that we were still under British control. The vegetables and meat were of poor quality and in inadequate supply. Volunteers from our infantrymen were now preparing our food. They did the best they could with what was provided, but the men continued to go hungry. This situation improved when our British hosts increased our rations to fifty percent more than they usually allowed. The men became even more tolerant when the British liquor ration began to arrive. All men were supposed to get an ounce of ale per day, and the officers a fifth of whiskey per month. Perhaps the unit was fortunate that the supply soon ran out.

CHAPTER IV

The Units Are Reorganized and Training Begins

Sgt. Ray Lyons explains the headquarters setup during the early days at Deogarh:

> When we first got there, we had a big tent. As you came in the front, we had a long table. I sat first at the door and Joe Doyer was behind. From there we had the subtents where Colonel Hunter sat as the operations operator, and so on. A Major Still showed up. He had experience in jungle training and took over as a training officer. Colonel Hunter was still, for all practical purposes, in command of the three battalions. He was still putting out orders under his name and would do so until General Merrill unexpectedly took over (Lyons, videotape).

At the time of our arrival at Deogarh, the organization of the units was fairly firmly fixed. As directed by General Wingate, each battalion had been split into two equal infantry units that were called columns. The battalion commander would operate with one or both at the same time.

The overall command situation of the three units continued to be very confusing. Colonel Hunter was in command by right of seniority only. Col. Francis G. Brink continued as director of training. From a practical standpoint, Colonel Hunter assumed the job of administrator of the camp. He took care of all problems that concerned the three units—such as contact with General Wingate's headquarters, food supply, greeting of visitors, and need for outside medical care. Col. Daniel E. Still, Cavalry, U.S. Army, was brought in to help Colonel Brink. Colonel Hancock remained in charge of supply.

As the units detrained at Jahklann, the nearest stop to Deogarh, Colonel Brink presented each battalion commander with a training exercise to be carried out on the ten-mile march to the camp at Deogarh. Speed, realism, and efficiency characterized the training program from the start.

Colonel Brink was said to be one of the foremost authorities in the U.S. Army on jungle training and tactics for fighting the Japanese. Junior officers soon learned that he believed in giving them every opportunity for individual ideas and work. It did not take him long to understand that the members of Unit 1688 C had acquired a great deal of practical information and individual confidence from their participation in one or more Pacific-island campaigns. He had prepared the training program to last ten weeks. The methods and actual plans and training became the responsibility of the battalion commanders.

Apart from many problems related to sickness, absence-without-leave episodes, supply and sanitation deficiencies, and transfer of men from one unit to another, the training program went forward on schedule. Unfortunately, communication personnel and equipment—as well as our animals—did not arrive until a few days before the departure date for combat. There was no training in delivery of supplies by air or in the evacuation of casualties. Particular attention was given to individual, squad, and platoon tactics, including movement at night by celestial navigation. All officers were required to learn cipher and radio operating procedure. The objective was to perfect sound tactics first; then unusual variations could be developed. Critique was held on completion of each exercise, no matter whether it was day or night. Long maneuvers, sham battles with the British and each other, and river crossings were carried out with enthusiasm.

Unit 1688 A was fortunate to have as its commander Colonel Osborne, a veteran of the fighting in the Philippines. As explained previously, the men in his unit were volunteers from many units based in the states. Their training would allow them little time except for sleep. Some claimed that they barely had time in the morning to wash their faces and brush their teeth. After dark they would have discussions of the day's training activities. Many of their daily exercises were extended to last overnight. They had many long marches.

Unit 1688 B had a different origin from A and C. Most of its members came from the well-organized and jungle-trained 33rd Infantry Regiment. As explained earlier, most of the men had been in the regiment, located in Trinidad, for more than a year. They came to India as a well-organized unit under their commander, a West Point graduate, Col. George A. McGee, Jr. Some said that their training at Deogarh had been much more rigorous than that of the other battalions. Their marches were very long, at times covering more than twenty miles in twenty-four hours. The heavy weapons section was at times forced to hand-carry their heavy mortars. They were pushed especially hard in learning river-crossing technique.

CHAPTER IV

Since the men in Unit 1688 C were, for the most part, veterans of the vicious Pacific-island conflicts (as was their commanding officer, Col. Charles N. Beach), their training during this period at Deogarh was somewhat different from that of the other two units. Unit C seemed to concentrate more on squad and platoon activity and use of weapons. Colonel Beach avoided grueling and exhausting long marches.

Whatever the differences in their training, none of the units—no matter how great their experience—failed to stress all aspects of basic infantry combat.

Training was somewhat limited in all the units by sickness. There was never an opportunity to practice delivery of supplies by parachute. Radio equipment and additional communication personnel would not arrive until shortly before departure for combat.

While at Deogarh—and before our three battalions had a several-day serious maneuver against several of General Wingate's brigades—the famous general visited our camp. Ray Lyons was at his desk in the headquarters tent when the general arrived:

> When he came in the front tent, at the time I was the only one there. I jumped to attention and said, "Yes, sir! What can I do for you?" He told me he was Brigadier Wingate and he was there to visit Colonel Hunter. He looked like a crazy man. I must say that I instantly got the impression that his eyes were very wild looking. When you looked at his eyes you got the impression that there was something wrong with this guy. He didn't seem to be a normal person. Eventually, when we were taken from under his command and put under Stilwell's, I for one was very happy—and I know a lot of other people had the same reaction. He went in and had a chat with Colonel Hunter. He later had an informal meeting with our officers (Lyons, videotape).

About the middle of December, a ten-day maneuver was held with units of General Wingate's forces. They were to infiltrate and attack the area occupied by the U.S. force in an attempt to capture an airstrip. One of our groups soon captured the headquarters of one of the British combat teams. Maneuvers stopped when the units came into contact before reaching the field. It then appeared that physical contact might determine which side would win the maneuver. On one area of the front, our British opponents retreated to be taken prisoner in order to share our plentiful field rations. Actually, there were no hard feelings toward the British forces. We admired them for their ability to train and live from day to day with less food, less pay, harder training, and a smaller chance of returning to their homes as soon as we had a right to expect (Hunter 1963, 5).

During the Third Battalion's training period, we raided the combat-inexperienced battalion's kitchens so frequently that the unit was nicknamed the "Chow Raiders." We were very proud and flattered, and soon found use for the small collapsible can opener supplied with 10-in-1 field rations. For the group—with no logical name, no flag, no colors, no history, no chaplain, no dentist, no recreational facilities, no post exchange, no leave, inadequate transportation, inadequate facilities for personal hygiene, poor general health, and many months without female companionship—this small can opener provided a prized insignia. It was worn with pride, pinned to the lapel of our fatigue jackets.

While at Deogarh, two groups of our officers were sent to a British intelligence school at Agra. At the end of the course these men were sent into the brush country with the mission of surviving for three days without help. They were to hunt game and live off the land. Few fell back on the five-pound can of beef they carried for emergency use.

At Deogarh we were supplied with several officers from General Wingate's unit. They were greatly admired for their spit and polish, which presented to us an attitude and way of life that we could never seem to fit into our training period or later combat experience.

Several Ghurkas from Wingate's troops spent time with us during this training period. These men came with a history of being fabulous fighting men. They carried a heavy, curved knife that was razor-sharp. We were told that if they drew the knife from its sheath they were duty-bound to draw blood. Because of this rule, while demonstrating the knife, they had to prick their own finger before replacing it. Many of us soon realized that the Ghurka knife had advantages over the machetes that had been supplied. Through his magical methods, Major Hancock was able to obtain a plentiful supply.

CHAPTER IV

Special attention, during the training period, was given to the intelligence and reconnaissance (I & R) platoons. The men were carefully selected by their respective platoon leaders. Intelligence, strength, endurance, enthusiasm, leadership, loyalty, common sense, health, and past record all played a part in the selection process. Above all, the men had to volunteer to become members of these important units.

The I & R units were made up of one officer, a first lieutenant, and fifty-four enlisted men. The platoon had two or more animals, one for transport of radio equipment and one for other equipment. At times it was necessary to carry a mortar with ammunition.

Headquarters was made up of eight men, one platoon sergeant, four radio operators, one Nisei (Japanese interpreter), and two muleskinners.

Three sections consisting of fourteen men each were commanded by a sergeant. Usually no machine guns or mortars were carried. These men were superbly trained infantrymen. In addition, they were expert in scouting, patrolling, use of all weapons, and map reading.

The I & R platoons had three SCR 300 radios for communication within the platoons and one SCR 280 for contact between the platoon and the battalion headquarters. In jungle warfare the I & R platoons are the eyes and ears of the combat unit. They precede the unit, feeling out the enemy, selecting the best trails, picking bivouac areas and airdrop fields, and usually make the first contact with the enemy. While on reconnaissance they only fight the enemy, if necessary, to feel him out, spot his automatic weapons, and try to figure his strength, then break contact after perhaps leaving one or two men to keep an eye on the enemy's position. They precede the unit from one to fifteen miles and know that they are liable to contact the enemy at any time. They move swiftly but with alertness that enables them to react to every sound or sign of the enemy. The moment a shot is fired and the enemy is contacted, the tenseness breaks and the men operate like clockwork, fixing the enemy and feeling him out. Every man has an assigned duty and position.

Lieutenant Logan Weston, in his book *The Fightin' Preacher*, tells about the formation and function of the I & R of Orange Combat Team:

> Our battalion, the only one with previous combat experience, was being prepared to head up the drive into Burma. The

battalion commander was ordered to organize an I & R platoon. This platoon of fifty-four men was to blaze the trail into Burma from near the Tibetan border, operating between four and twenty-four hours' marching time in advance of the main body of the lead battalion. This I & R platoon was to locate enemy camps, outposts, and radio stations and see what types of weapons they had. They were to locate trails over which mules could travel, and find jungle areas where supplies could be dropped by parachute. If they ran into the enemy, they were supposed to knock out the opposition, then continue to advance. If unable to knock out the opposition, they were to maintain contact with the enemy and delay action until the main battalion arrived to help. Each night the platoon was to establish radio contact with the battalion headquarters, inform the battalion commander of the day's events, and give the current map location of the platoon.

It was a tall order, and the officers of the "Chow Raiders" battalion were deemed the best ones capable to fill the bill. From the group of officers, a call for a volunteer to command this I & R platoon rang out. Not a hand was raised. We had already volunteered for a "dangerous and hazardous mission," and they were looking for volunteers for something even worse.

The battalion commander, a lieutenant colonel, looked around. Although I was merely a first lieutenant, I stood head and shoulders taller than the rest of my fellow officers, and he focused his attention on me."Preacher, you are it," he said. "You have just volunteered to command the I & R platoon." From that moment on, I & R stood not for "intelligence and reconnaissance" but for "ignorant and rugged."

"You have excessive combat patrol experience, according to your personnel files," the colonel continued. "I need a unit up there that will tell it like it is. You will have the option of selecting your fifty-four men from the battalion for this job and then of preparing them for this mission."

I interviewed about two hundred men from the battalion and selected my platoon of fifty-four from that group. Each man was carefully screened and thoroughly checked, including his combat record from the South Pacific.

Among other qualifications I was looking for in my men was a requirement that they at one time or another had experienced a combat situation in which they realized their need of supernatural protection and help. These men, with very few exceptions, had trusted the Lord to deliver them under combat conditions. I have no reservations in declaring them one of the best all-around platoons in the United States Army—ever. It was an honor to be in command of such a unit (Weston 1992).

Before our campaigns were over, we would have many reasons to be proud of and grateful for all of the I & R units.

In Unit A, Sam Wilson was made commander of and organized and trained an outstanding I & R unit. At the age of 16 he had enlisted in the National Guard. Soon after he was commissioned as a second lieutenant at Fort Benning, he volunteered at the age of 19 for our mysterious mission. Just as Logan Weston, he picked his men with great care. In his case he looked to the guardhouse for recruits. It has been said that he got the cream of the crop and that he was a hard taskmaster during training. From the results obtained, he was proven to be a born leader. A critical time came when one of his men drowned during a practice crossing of the Betwa River.

In Unit B, the I & R commander within Blue Combat Team was 1st Lt. William C. Grissom. He had been with Colonel McGee in Trinidad and was to do an exceptional job in combat.

Unit training suffered a serious setback just before Christmas. From the time of formation, no leaves or recreational passes had been offered the men. At Christmastime the volunteers from the Pacific took matters in their own hands. About half of Unit C left Deogarh AWOL. After a truck ride to Jhansi, they commandeered an express train and disappeared into Bombay and other cities of India. Military police spent a busy week or more following their adventures and encouraging them to return to duty before their self-directed leave was over (Hunter 1963, 5).

One of our most innovative and courageous Pacific veterans, an enlisted man, spent a month in Calcutta wearing captain's bars before he returned to duty—just in time to head for action in Burma. Tony Colombo briefly describes the unprecedented action that was taken by many of the Pacific veterans:

> Then came Christmas. Around Christmas we all went AWOL. I won about twelve hundred dollars in a crap game, and we had been paid and had no place to spend any money. So somebody

decided we would get a bunch of trucks and go down to the railroad station—I forget the name of the town, it was a little town. And then we flagged down the Bombay Express. Well, we didn't exactly flag it down: We took railway ties and started burning them across the tracks; took the flagman's flag, and stopped the train. We jumped on the train and filled up every bit of space. Up the road a bit they made us stop, and somebody tried to collect tickets, and somebody hit the ticket collector with a bottle of beer, and so rather than see somebody killed I signed for the tickets as Captain Colombo of some army. I told them to take it to the quartermaster and that they would pay for the transportation since these guys were going on leave.

We got into Bombay, and I had myself a ball. I stayed at the Taj Hotel. We all became officers. You could not get anything if you were a private or corporal. The British cantonment there was for officers and better, so I became a captain and others became lieutenants and colonels. They had never seen anyone in the American army infantry. Most of the guys left a little early. I stayed there thirty days. Finally I decided I'd better get the heck out of there because I got news—because there was guys coming in and out anyhow—that the Marauders were taking off.

I spent Christmas eve, by the way—Christmas eve and New Year's eve—with "Smoky" Gomez and an another of the flying tigers. They were on their way home. We were out drinking and having a lot of fun. We took one of those tongas and were shooting at the horses' ears to get them to go faster. On our New Year's celebration we hit a Chinese restaurant, and Gomez, who had false teeth, upchucked and lost his teeth. He came up to sleep in my room, and the next morning we took another tonga and got into this Chinese restaurant and the Chinaman goes "clackety-clack." He says, "Here's his teeth." Gomez got his teeth and went on home. I never heard from those guys again.

Well, thirty days later I turned myself in. I went down to a British camp three miles out of Bombay and told them that I needed transportation. I got in a little trouble there from a colonel who was riding by. He wanted to know what kind of an army I was in. I had a pith helmet, split toed sandals, and British K.D.'s. The only thing American were my dog tags. They got me out of that camp pretty fast. I got back to Deogarh and there they were—the mules were all packed up and ready to go. I went in to see Johnson, who was a combat team commander. I said, "I am back," and he said, "Did you just get in?" I said, "Yes," and he said, "Get in with that group over there and march," and off we went (Colombo, videotape).

The men who stayed in camp exhibited a free and boisterous spirit. Large quantities of rifle and machine-gun ammunition were available. Christmas and several days after were celebrated on a more-or-less twenty-four-hour basis. The crack of rifle fire and the bright streak of machine-gun tracer bullets created a free and festive air. The situation was like an uncontrollable fire—it had to run its course.

Pat Perrone tells of some of the interesting events at Deogarh:

> A number of happenings occurred there. I incurred the wrath of Colonel Hunter, who was the regimental commander before General Merrill arrived. I was the first duty officer of the Third Battalion, and he came in and found us in the middle of his headquarters cooking stew. He was not very happy about that. We were riddled with malaria and dysentery, and I was really unfortunate—I had both bacillary and amoebic dysentery and malaria at the same time. They figured three days and I would be out. We had a blanket treatment for the malaria, and I was the only officer. There were four other men of the unit with malaria, and the medical officers accused us of not taking the medicine—which was not true. I was boarded by a combined American and British medical board at the 80th British General Hospital, which was attached to the unit at that time. I was considered unfit for field duty and sent to the Karachi General Hospital in Bombay. I soon went AWOL from the hospital and joined the outfit. If I could not get to the Philippines, I figured I might as well go along. I had a man in my outfit who came from the islands, and I figured I could not trust him. So I thought I would just go along for the walk and be there (Perrone, videotape).

Lieutenant Perrone was to go the whole way.

Organization, Deogarh

Shipment 1688 A:
White Combat Team and Red Combat Team

Shipment 1688 B:
Blue Combat Team and Green Combat Team

Shipment 1688 C:
Orange Combat Team and Khaki Combat Team

Each combat team was composed of:

1. Headquarters and headquarters company
2. One and one-half rifle companies
3. Intelligence and reconnaissance platoon
4. Pioneer and demolition platoon
5. Heavy weapons platoon
6. Medical detachment

- Lt. Col. William L. Osborne remained as the First Battalion commander, Red Combat Team, which included Hq. and Hq. Company and Company A.
- Maj. Edward Ghiz was in command until 6 April, when Capt. Tom P. Senff took over.
- White Combat Team included Company B and Company C, with Major Caifson Johnson in command.
- Lt. Col. George A. McGee Jr. remained in command of the Second Battalion.
- Blue Combat Team, with Hq., Hq. Company, and E Company, was under the command of Maj. Richard W. Healy.
- Green Combat Team included Companies F and G and was under command of Capt. Thomas E. Bogardus.
- Lt. Col. Charles E. Beach, a veteran of the Solomon Island campaigns, continued in command of the Third Battalion.

- Maj. Lawrence L. Lew, who had come from MacArthur's command, was appointed commander of Orange Combat Team, which included Companies K and L.
- Maj. Edwin Briggs was the commanding officer of Khaki Combat Team, which included Hqs. and Hq. Company, as well as I Company.

Battalion and Combat Team Table of Organization

(This does not include the supply-base detachment that was gradually formed and later permanently based at Dinjan in Assam.)

	Bat. Hqs.	Team #1	Team #2	Total
Officers	3	16	16	35
Enlisted men	13	456	456	928
Aggregate	16	472	475	963
Animals (horses & mules)	3	68	68	139
Carbines	6	86	89	181
Machine guns, heavy		3	4	7
Machine guns, light		2	4	6
Submachine guns	2	52	48	102
Mortars, 60mm		4	6	10
Mortars, 81mm		4	3	7
Pistols		2	2	4
Rifles, Browning		27	27	54
Rifles, M-1	8	306	310	624
Rockets		3	3	6

Medical Organization, Facilities, and Problems

Shipments 1688 A, B, C at Deogarh

During the training period at Deogarh, each battalion's medical detachment worked out of its individual ten-bed tent. Administrative and senior technicians were based here for duty. One of the battalion surgeons was always on duty. At all times a medical technician (aid man) was with each platoon. He was expected to give advice and help while in camp, during training exercises, and in combat. These men understood that the combat surgeons were available twenty-four hours daily.

Each medical detachment was authorized four physicians, to include one major and three captains. A captain in the veterinary corps was also a member of the medical detachment. The roster of the enlisted men listed one technical sergeant, two staff sergeants, and a variable number of technicians of grades three, four, and five. Fifteen to twenty privates completed the roster.

Unit 1688 B went overseas with a unit dentist, 1st Lt. James W. Parker. This service was greatly missed in the other two units.

Medical Detachment, First Battalion

Maj. Schudmak, Melvin A., M.C. (regimental surgeon)
Capt. Steinfield, Winnie, M.C.
Capt. McLaughlin, John J., M.C.
Other records not available

Medical Detachment, Second Battalion

Officers

Maj. Rogoff, Bernard, M.C. 0-357969
Capt. Gardner, Horace T., M.C. 0-435739
Capt. Kolodny, Abraham L., M.C. 0-1634051
Capt. Stelling, Henry G., M.C. 0-1634051
1st Lt. Hickman, George F., V.C. 0-507610
1st Lt. Parker, James W., D.C. 0-1587894

CHAPTER IV

Enlisted Men

Technical Sergeant
Scherkenbach, Robert J.

Staff Sergeant
Jordan, Ernest W. Jr.

Technicians Third Grade
Dittfach, Albert H.
Englert, Howard N.

Technicians Fourth Grade
Benedetto, Michael R.
Reever, Clyde E.

Technicians Fifth Grade
Johnson, George W.
Cromer, Dean M.
Durhan, Lewis W.
Binder, William J.
Enright, Thomas
Roth, Franklin P.
Vainko, George

Privates First Class
Byers, Peter C.
Cipolla, Daniel
Clinton, James O.
Creeden, Gerard
D'Apice, Nunzio
D'Arcy, John P.
Defillippo, Joseph G.
DeMilo, Jerry
Dezotelle, Myron
Feschine, Edward
Goin, Edward P.
Lonas, Blondell H.
Martinez, Mardeqeco
Rumore, Alfonzo
Wagner, William R.

Medical Detachment, Third Battalion

Officers

Maj. Camp, Horton, M.C. (left unit in Bombay)
Capt. Cecala, Philip J., M.C 0418418
Capt. Hopkins, James E. T., M.C. 0-462235
Capt. Ivens, Milton J., M.C. 0-1700473
Capt. Bell, William T., V.C. 0-368760 Veterinary Officer
1st. Lt. Armstrong, Paul E., M.C. (joined unit after Jan. '44)

Enlisted Men

Technical Sergeant
Wheeler, Whitney E. 20134126

Staff Sergeants
Hascal, Ralph, Jr. 6149340
Simpson, Wilbur B. 31023542

Sergeants
Camera, Frank E. 20134358
Stevens, Chester 3l7085493

Corporals
Beauchesne, Ernest E. 31023968
Lyles, Frank 18031096
Sibley, Guy R. 36358111
Ratcliff, Charles E. 35214555
Toporoski, Michel 31023955

Technicians Fifth Grade
Hardinger, Daniel R. 35016106
Teague, Frank 34011303

CHAPTER IV

Privates First Class
Anderson, Eric 36358108
Arnold, Eugene F. 20519596
Bates, Richard D. 20151358
Beach, Robert E. 20519495
Byers, Robert W. 205190495
Conklin, Albert N. 32005311
Curl, Vivian O. 36184419
Gearhart, Glenn, T. 20519523
Gomez, Joseph N. 18016284
Haws, Vance L. 39831275
Higgs, Ernest N. 17076068.
Mitchell, Russell J. 37422330
Perdomo, Louis O. 34209171
Shilling, Theodore R. 14024544.
Smith, James A. 37370267

Private
Campbell, Newman P. 19021375

One of our medics, Daniel Hardinger, had been at my side during the Battle of New Georgia, when and where he proved to be a very brave, caring, and capable medical technician. I have previously mentioned that he volunteered, but the battalion would not let him go. After I left the area, he talked his battalion commander into permitting him to join those of us who had been released for participation in the so-called "dangerous and hazardous mission." Lt. Pat Perrone gives an account of his meeting with Dan:

> I was with the Third Battalion, Orange Combat Team, and I was one of the individuals who interviewed the men in connection with the positions they would hold within the organization. I had a handsome, strongly build man come to me, and as I sat there to interview him he said to me, "Lieutenant, I would like you to understand one thing: I am not going to kill anyone. I don't believe in killing." Now here was one of the original men from the Guadalcanal, New Georgia complex, and I was sort of nonplussed. I couldn't understand. Here was a man volunteering for a commando

unit, and he wasn't going to kill. He looked at the expression on my face and said, "I want you to understand I am a conscientious objector." I said, "What in hell are you doing here, if you are an objector, volunteering for a commando unit?" He said, "Well, I am a medic." That put everything back into scope (Perrone, videotape).

It should be pointed out that each battalion's medical detachment was divided in half during training and while in combat. One half supported each combat team. All medical personnel were very busy during the training period at Deogarh. As the Orange Combat Surgeon, I spent about half of my time in the battalion medical tent. Sick call was on a fairly continuous basis. When in the field, I was the only doctor with Orange Combat Team. Captains Cecala and Ivens handled the problems of Khaki Combat Team.

Unit 1688 A (with Red and White Combat Teams) and Unit 1688 B (with Blue and Green) operated in the same way. Shortly before we left Deogarh, I was joined in Orange by a replacement surgeon, Lt. Paul E. Armstrong. From the beginning, he was an outstanding medical officer and human being. He was tall and muscular and fit in well with any group. He could always be counted on in any emergency, whether medical or nonmedical. In combat he was to be proven outstanding in every way.

From the very beginning, malaria was a significant problem. For reasons unknown to me, the policy set up on the Lurline—to withhold prophylactic atabrine—was continued until the situation became intolerable in Unit 1688 C. It should be remembered that over fifty percent of the men in this unit had been infected during the previous year. During the first five weeks at Deogarh, between two hundred and three hundred cases of recurrent malaria were treated. We were managing between seventy-five and one hundred cases in the small 80th General British Hospital, the medical tent, and the men's quarters. Some men in Unit B were having problems with recurrence of malaria they had acquired in the Caribbean area. Unit A was having little trouble. It should be noted that the prophylactic use of atabrine was not widespread in the CBI area at that time. Some Pacific veterans, including myself, ignored the order to withhold atabrine and continued its use with good effect.

The acting theater malaria specialist, Maj. F. A. Mantz, was summoned after we had been at Deogarh three weeks. He wrote, "It was incumbent upon any medical officer surveying a unit with a current malaria rate of 408/1,000 annum, with 7.4 percent of the men noneffective each week because of malaria, and 57 percent of the remainder infected during the past year, to consider that unit as unfit for operations before adequate rest, treatment, and replacement were provided." He expressed the opinion that if it were possible to replace the infected men, all soldiers who had had three or more malaria relapses, and whose last relapse had occurred since 1 September 1943, should be removed. He then proposed that the remainder of the malaria victims should be put on rest for a long period and given a therapeutic malaria treatment. He explained that if the three-relapse policy was adopted, Unit 1688 C would lose 12.8 percent of its men. No men were released, but training was put on hold for two weeks while the men of Unit 1688 C rested and were given a full course of treatment for malaria. Prophylactic action was then ordered, and the men started taking one atabrine daily. Needless to say, the findings of Major Mantz were carefully guarded. If the command had actually offered to transfer the men who were suffering from chronic malaria, it is doubtful that many would have gone willingly. It should be again pointed out that the men had volunteered for this dangerous mission knowing full well what combat was like. They were the few men out of six divisions who had signed up for a "dangerous and hazardous mission." Had they left, they would have believed that they were letting down their comrades (Stone 1969).

As an example of the loyalty of these Pacific veterans, Dominic A. Perrone's story is typical. Because of a serious medical problem, he had been admitted, shortly after the Bombay landing, to the 181st General Hospital in Karachi. He was scheduled to be shipped home. Shortly before we took off for Burma, he went AWOL from the hospital and worked his way back to the outfit. He lasted until the end of the campaign, when he was hospitalized with a case of cerebral malaria that almost cost him his life.

Our unit was not alone in its struggle with malaria and other medical problems. At the time, we had little knowledge of the number of American service personnel in India. After the campaign, figures showed that thirty-one thousand Americans were under SOS control when we arrived and forty-two thousand when we left for Burma. Even fewer facts about their disease incidence were available. Unbeknownst to our group, medical problems in India and Burma were potentially grave. We were given no indication that scrub typhus, a serious illness with a very high mortality, was to be expected to appear among our men. No one informed our medical officers that this condition was present and had already struck American soldiers. Later figures showed more than eight thousand admissions for malaria, over six thousand for alimentary disorders, and numerous admissions for other disorders during 1943. Approximately one-fourth of all military personnel had been sick with one or more attacks of malaria in 1943. Prophylactic atabrine was not generally used by military personnel stationed in the CBI area until late 1943.

Before the end of December the malaria problem in our units was well under control. The occasional recurrent attack strongly suggested that some of the malaria parasites carried by the men who had come from the Pacific area were becoming resistant to atabrine. Malaria is a deadly disease. Our men who came from the Solomons (Guadalcanal and related islands) were in an area that has the world's highest recorded incidence of malaria. This single-celled, mosquito-borne parasite has been and continues to be difficult to control and treat. The World Health Organization (as of the 1990s) estimates that three hundred million people carry the parasite.

The attacks—whether primary or recurrent—occur every twenty-four, forty-eight, or seventy-six hours, depending on the strain of the parasite. Anopheles mosquitos, when infected at the time of their bite, inject the parasite into the blood stream. Plasmodia soon lodge in the liver, where each multiplies forty thousand times. Red blood cells become invaded, more multiplication occurs, and chills and fever develop. The victim has recurrent flu-like attacks, with aching bones, fiery fever, icy chills, loss of appetite, nausea, vomiting, and weakness. There are four different types of these vicious parasites. If untreated, all can cause great debilitation and death. Under ideal circumstances, the individual with an acute attack of malaria should be put to bed, tests should be done to determine the type of parasite, and treatment should be started and continued with bed rest until a cure is obtained.

CHAPTER IV

The most dangerous form, Falciparum or cerebral malaria, will result in death if not carefully managed. After a course of treatment, a recurrence can occur even though the individual is not again bitten by an infected mosquito. Over the years since our campaign in Burma, worldwide studies have shown the parasite's ability to develop resistance to numerous drugs. The drug atabrine, used by us in Burma, is no longer used because of this gradual loss of effectiveness. Quinine was not available to our men.

The three battalion medical detachments, while at Deogarh, treated many cases of gastroenteritis. These men had multiple symptoms such as weakness, fatigue, nausea, vomiting, abdominal pain, and loss of appetite. This problem seemed to be worse in Units A and B than in C.

Many men in Unit 1688 B had developed diarrhea while at Deolali. At Deogarh, from time to time, ninety percent of the men had attacks of dysentery. These were mostly found to be bacillary dysentery, but a few were amoebiasis. Their ten-bed unit was kept busy, and many were treated in quarters or at the 80th British General Hospital. During the latter half of December, Unit A had many men sick in quarters with severe dysentery.

Shortly after we arrived at Deogarh, one of our lieutenants, a veteran of the Solomon Island campaigns, became ill and died within two weeks of acute leukemia.

As a result of the necessity to train all personnel in the proper way to make a river crossing, a tragic accident occurred. Lt. Sam Wilson had chosen, for his I & R platoon, a narrow but deep spot on the Betwa River. A line was strung between the banks. One of the men protested that he could not swim and had a fear of the water. He was halfway across when one platoon member said, "It's breaking!" The line did break, and in spite of all rescue efforts he drowned. It was estimated that fifty percent of the men in the three casual detachments could not swim. Shipment 1688 B had several episodes of near drowning. It should be remembered that our promised mules and horses were not available to take part in these river crossings until early January 1944.

At Deogarh many chronic medical problems required treatment and disposition. Unit 1688 C had records of thirteen chronic backaches, thirty chronic gastritis cases, ten severe psychoneurotics, eight psychotics, thirty chronic bronchitis problems, ten hernias, thirty chronic malaria patients with enlarged spleens as well as anemia and weight loss, nine men with chronic recurrent attacks of pleurisy, five with perforated ear drums (some with draining ears), eleven severe chronic tonsillitis cases, and five pilonidal cysts.

Unit 1688 C transferred 115 men considered not fit for combat to the supply section that was being organized and trained by Major Hancock. Their job was to prepare and load our supplies on planes, from which they would push the required items to our men in combat. Unit 1688 C sent about seventy men to the 181st General Hospital at Karachi and thirty-six to the 97th Station Hospital at Agra (the location of the Taj Mahal).

The medical officers of Unit B sent twenty-five men to the 181st General Hospital and the 97th Station Hospital. About fifty men were sent to the rear echelon for various medical and nonmedical reasons.

Unit A also lost a few men to hospitals and to the rear echelon.

My guess would be that about fifty percent of the men who had been admitted to hospitals other than the 80th British General during the training period eventually returned to duty. Needless to say, the chronic and acute health problems caused considerable disruption of the training and organization of the units. Chronic illness, acute illness, and poor sanitation and living conditions combined to put many of the men in poor mental and physical condition by the time the training period ended.

I know of no direct commands or official orders restricting the actions of the medical sections. All medical officers were aware of the need to keep the men on active duty. No effort was made to do careful and complete physical examinations to eliminate individuals who would not be able to meet army standards such as those followed on induction into the service. Those of us who had been in combat knew that the military situation frequently required that good medical practice and humane action had to be ignored in order to keep infantrymen at the front. We had seen no evidence of replacements in the Pacific battles, and our small, isolated unit had no promise of any in Asia. We were the only infantrymen in a vast area at the extreme end of the supply line. We depended on the regimental surgeon for liaison with higher authority. It is a fact that during our period in Asia, before and during combat, we were never visited by any representative of the surgeon general or the theater surgeon. We would later have reason to censor higher medical authority as well as those who offered our services to the Southeast Asia command. The lack of medical and replacement planning was to have grave consequences. The loyalty, courage, ability, fortitude, self sacrifice, and determination of these men was to be an inspiration to the home front as well as to our allies.

An attempt was repeatedly made by myself and other members of the medical detachment to gain information about the details of a plan to evacuate combat casualties. No plan was ever presented to the shipment units by our U.S. Army superiors or by General Wingate.

Recreation and Entertainment at Deogarh

From the time the men volunteered through the end of December 1943, I can recall no official effort to provide recreation or entertainment. Post exchange supplies did not exist. I don't remember any period in which candy, soft drinks, or beer could be purchased, and tobacco products were limited. No recreational leaves were given, and movies or other forms of entertainment were not provided.

In the limited time available, some of the men used their weapons for hunting deer and other wild animals. One time several of the hunters shot and cooked vultures, thinking they were turkeys.

On several occasions I spent time exploring a red sandstone temple said to have been constructed in the fifth century A.D. It was home to a group of very unfriendly monkeys. One of our younger medics, Pvt. Walter B. Owensby from Ashville, North Carolina, soon brought a sickly young one back to his bunk and nursed it to good health. Among other problems, its intestine was loaded with small roundworms. After treatment the little monkey became a great pet of the medical section. Because of a chronic disability, Owensby was transferred out to the rear echelon, where he became a member of a crew that delivered our supplies in C-47s. Unfortunately, the plane he was working out of disappeared into the Burma jungle near the end of the campaign. The plane was located approximately fifty years later.

Supply Arrangements of Shipments A, B, and C in 1943

Units 1688 A, B, and C were very fortunate that Maj. Edward T. Hancock was appointed as unit supply officer. As I have stated, he met the units as they arrived in Bombay. He immediately took charge of the eight hundred tons of supplies that had accompanied the troops on the *Lurline.* He was responsible for the erection of the tent camp at Deogarh and the three long train trips, including the final one, yet to be described, to Assam north of the combat area.

His greatest accomplishment during 1943 was the development of a superb supply section. Most of his enlisted and officer personnel came from men who for one reason or another were considered not physically suitable for the job of an infantryman. Their physical condition and lack of experience was no barrier to classification and preservation of our supplies and the development of plans for delivery by air to our units in combat.

It must be remembered that, until early January 1944, we were scheduled to fight in north central Burma under the command of British General Wingate. Ground transportation, storage, security, parachute packing, replacement, air transportation, and communication—as well as many other factors—had to be considered. Many officers and men had serious doubts as to the way supply would work out if we went into combat as planned while still dependent on the Southeast Asia Special Forces supply section. We were still, in early January, under General Wingate, the commanding officer of special forces. His representatives had continued in a liaison capacity with our three units. Major Hancock's plans had been based on information that we would be part of General Wingate's force of twenty thousand men who were to have their supply base in India on the western or Manipur front. Our men, up to this time, had been given no information of the size of this operation, where it would be, or how long it would operate. Our medical section had not been able to obtain information about evacuation or hospitalization of our expected sick and wounded. The uncertain situation had severely limited the ability of the supply group to plan and function.

CHAPTER IV

Transportation at Camp Deogarh Until 1944

During the nine-week period that battalions were at Deogarh, very few vehicles were available. These were only used on urgent missions. The absence of animal transportation severely curtailed the training mission. General Wingate had loaned a few mules for training, but near the end of December these were withdrawn. One can only guess that he knew he was losing command of the Americans and therefore acted to recover his valuable property. He also withdrew a detachment of the North Burma Rifles, who had been assigned as guides and interpreters.

Information 1944

At all times very little information was made available to the men and officers. Again it must be remembered that the men in Unit 1688 C had been isolated in the Pacific since early 1942. They rarely got information about the progress of the war beyond their immediate area of activity. Units A and B were much better informed, up to September 1944, of the history of World War II. Few of the men had significant knowledge of local or world geography.

As January 1944 approached, the units were still under the command of General Wingate. The British made no effort to teach us anything about the proposed operation in Burma. No books or maps were available, and no instruction was given about the political situation in China, India, Burma, or any Asian country. To most of the infantrymen, Burma was a total mystery. They knew nothing about the mountains, borders, rivers, jungle, natural resources, railroads, diseases, history, or people. Most did not know that President Roosevelt and General Marshall had made the decision to organize and supply the three thousand-man unit and then turn it over to the British in India for use during the attempted reconquest of Burma. We had no knowledge of the great buildup of American service, air, engineer, and railroad personnel in Asia. We were to learn, after our campaign was over in August 1944, that as of January 1944 the strength of U.S. Army forces in the China-Burma-India theater totaled 105,073. While in India, our men had absolutely no contact with any of these American military personnel.

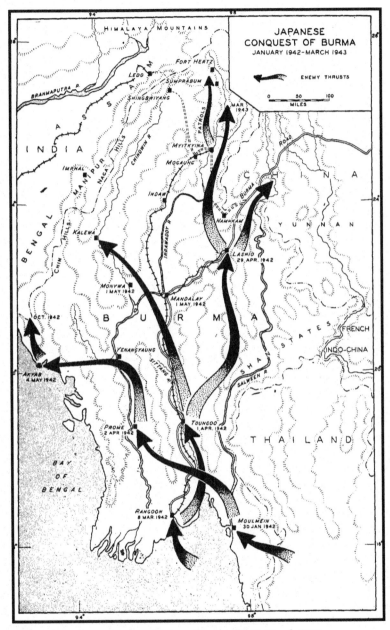

MAP 2. Japanese conquest of Burma, January 1942–March 1943.

CHAPTER V

BECOMING THE 5307TH

Introduction

On 1 January 1944, Colonel Hunter was authorized to issue General Order Number One. The new name of the organization was the 5307th Composite Regiment (Provisional). As far as we knew, we were still under British control and would go into combat under General Wingate. General Order Number Two followed in a day or so and made Colonel Hunter commanding officer. General Order Number Three soon changed us from a composite regiment to a composite unit. This order came out just after Brig. Gen. Frank D. Merrill arrived on the scene. There had not been any hint before this that he would arrive as our new commander. Shortly before Merrill's arrival, Colonel Hunter learned that we had been removed from Wingate and turned over to Stilwell (Hunter 1963, 9).

Records would later show that Stilwell had been notified by General Marshall on 1 September 1943 that our group of American troops would operate under General Wingate (Stuart 1984, 4). Stilwell promptly wrote the following in his diary:

> What's the matter with our people? After a long struggle, we get a handful of U.S. troops, and by God, they tell us they are to operate under WINGATE! We don't know enough to handle them, but that exhibitionist does! And what has he done? Made an abortive jaunt to Katha, got caught east of the Irrawaddy, and came out with a loss of forty percent—net result, cut the railroad that our people had already cut [by air attacks]. Now he is an expert. This is enough to discourage Christ (Stilwell 1948).

On 7 September 1943, a second communication from General Marshall reached him:

CHAPTER V

It is visualized that the three battalions will be employed separately—probably two in Assam and one from Yunnan—and they will operate in front of the main efforts. They will have pack transport and will be resupplied by air. Although operating separately, the three efforts should be coordinated by one 'group' headquarters composed of personnel who will train with the battalion and thus become familiar with their capabilities, personalities, communication and supply problems, and other vital factors, as well as to maintain liaison and coordinate with other friendly troops in the area (Stuart 1984, 1).

Stilwell did not like the plan. His national pride was offended. He wanted a regiment to fight in close cooperation with the Chinese main advance. He wanted the Americans to fight as a spearhead or flanking weapon. Wingate resented Stilwell's claims. The Marauders had already started toward Burma before Stilwell's authority over them was assured (Stone 1969, 293) (Romanus and Sunderland 1956, 62).

Stilwell had been requesting that Lord Louis Mountbatten turn the Marauders over to him for some time. The CBI theater surgeon, Col. Robert P. Williams, told a theater historian that Mountbatten had said, "For God's sake, take them off my hands" (Stone 1969, 294).

James H. Stone, in *Crisis Fleeting*, expressed the following opinion about the Marauders:

> The Marauders fitted the traditional image of volunteer, expeditionary troops in their slouchiness, touchiness, and air of rascality. The fact that they had many grievances did not show. But the time had been and would come again when their recollection of real or imagined promises of special amenities and prerequisites would surface and fester (Stone 1969, 295).

By General Order Number Four on 4 January, Brig. Gen. Frank D. Merrill assumed command of the 5307th Composite Unit (Provisional}. We could only conclude that the 5307th was now a unit instead of a regiment, because it was improper for a general to command a regiment (Hunter 1963, 6).

Word soon spread that we were to go into North Burma as part of General Stilwell's forces instead of General Wingate's. No attempt was made to educate the men about the military situation in the China-Burma-India area. Absolutely no information was given about the mission, geography, or the Chinese Army operating in Burma under the command of General Stilwell. This change in plans raised the spirits of the men. There was a general feeling among the men that they wished to get on with the job. History would record that General Stilwell had been making every effort to get our infantry unit away from General Wingate's control since the time of our origin. Mountbatten had offered British troops to spearhead the Chinese, but Stilwell had refused them. (Romanus and Sunderland 1956, 131). He had no desire to accept British troops when Americans were available to lead the Chinese against the Japanese in North Burma (136).

The transfer of the 5307th Composite Unit (Provisional) from British command to General Stilwell put a severe burden on his advance operations in Assam and North Burma. This move was a last-minute decision made two months after the Chinese, with American support, had begun the second Burma campaign. Our unit had been sent for one three-month operation by the War Department. Tactical and supply air support had not been planned. No arrangements had been made for the evacuation of the sick and wounded. Hospitals in the area had no plans or facilities to set up additional beds to take care of the additional sick and wounded. Arrangements by Stilwell's command had been improvisations, and many of these were useless. The situation would be so bad that Stilwell at times feared that the whole operation would be abandoned.

Normally, planning precedes logistical preparation, and logistical preparation precedes fighting. One of the noteworthy aspects of the North Burma campaign of 1943-44 is that the logistical preparations, the planning, and the fighting proceeded simultaneously. The troops moved forward before the commanders had agreed on their plans, and the logistical preparations were months in being completed (Romanus and Sunderland 1956, 10).

The word soon spread among the men that General Merrill was the right man for the job. He had a very open and friendly type of personality. Here was a man who knew how to talk to the men and officers. His friendly smile—and his ability to listen and move among the men giving sympathy and practical advice—quickly won them over. He had a way of making his audience think they were important. When speaking, which he did forcefully and frequently before a few or many, he delivered his message in a clear and pleasantly authoritative way. All gained the impression that he had the total backing of General Stilwell and would do all possible to wisely guide us into and through all assigned missions. The general let us know that we had been neglected and unappreciated and promised improvement. A noticeable difference appeared in the quality and quantity of food. More time was available for rest and individual tasks. Equipment, which had been carefully guarded, was soon distributed where it was needed.

Few of the officers or men knew much about General Merrill's personal life or past military record. Most of what is recorded here was learned after the Burma campaign. There was no briefing about the coming campaign or General Merrill's background. After the campaign was over, I obtained the following facts from Charlton Ogburn's *The Marauders* and other publications. General Merrill had risen through the ranks from private to win an appointment at West Point, from which he graduated in 1929. This date of graduation made him a classmate of Colonel Hunter. As an engineer with a love for horses and an intense interest in military affairs, he was from the start of his career a man to watch. While serving with cavalry regiments in the U.S. during the 30's, he was sent to Japan as a language student. There he learned the language and also the nature of the people he was later to fight. He cultivated the army class and spent much time in the field with the Japanese army on maneuvers.

On 7 December 1941, he was on a flight from the Philippines to Rangoon. He remained in Burma and joined General Stilwell, who had been sent over by General Marshall on 4 March 1942 to take charge of two Chinese divisions fighting in Burma. President Roosevelt had asked Generalissimo Chiang Kai-shek to take over the job of commander of the united nations in the China theater, and Chiang had agreed. He requested, in accepting the position, that a United States officer serve as his chief of staff in the theater. General Stilwell spoke Chinese and had spent years in China. He arrived just before the Japanese captured Rangoon and closed China's lifeline, the

Burma Road. Within a week he was in Burma to take command of two Chinese divisions.

The Japanese advanced against heroic Chinese and British resistance. General Stilwell escaped with a party of about one hundred individuals. This group walked about 140 miles from the Chindwin River over the Chin Hills into Manipur State, India.

Many Chinese infantrymen were lost during their attempt to escape to India and China. Some made their way into Manipur State, while others crossed the northern Burma mountains to Assam. These men made the nucleus of the two Chinese divisions that General Stilwell later trained at Ramgarh Training Center in northwestern India. We now learned of the presence of these two divisions on the North Burma border. We guessed that our mission would be to help them in an advance into northern Burma. General Merrill had retreated from Burma with General Stilwell's group. On the march he had a heart attack and barely survived.

Our men and officers knew little about the Chinese retreat, the fate of the refugees, or what General Stilwell had been doing since the retreat. I, as a doctor, did not know that General Merrill was known to be a very poor risk with a history of heart attack. If any of the men were known to have a similar history, they would not have remained in the 5307th Composite Unit (Provisional).

Some Facts Important to the Record

General Stilwell never visited the 5307th during our training period or during our period of combat. It is likely that, if our battalion surgeons had seen and examined him, we would have been shocked by his general health. His wife, in the foreword to *The Stilwell Papers*, explains that because of a World War I injury he was almost totally blind in his left eye. The vision of his other eye required a very thick lens for correction. He died of a debilitating disease in 1946.

In retrospect one has the right to condemn not only these two generals for accepting the great responsibility of commanding infantry troops in combat, but also those who appointed them. Anyone who has given any thought to jungle warfare or actually taken part in it would know that the superb physical condition of the officers, as well as the men, is essential. The medical detachments did all they could to get the men ready for battle but were defeated by lack of interest from higher command. During the entire existence of the 5307th they were never visited by anyone from the surgeon general's office or the office of the theater surgeon.

Recordkeeping

Before and after General Merrill arrived, the small regimental clerical staff kept excellent records. The rear echelon continued their careful work during the combat period. The regimental roster was kept current. Records of the sick, the wounded, and the dead—as well as promotions, demotions, decorations, and all other important items—were recorded. At the end of the campaign, these rear-echelon records disappeared and have never been located.

Major John M. Jones, who can be considered coauthor of this history, joined the 5307th at Deogarh and became a member of General Merrill's staff. General Merrill asked him to keep a record of the 5307th in addition to his other duties. His "War Diary of 5307th Composite Unit (Provisional)" was started on 15 January 1944. As stated in the preface, this very accurate and informative history, with some minor changes made by John and myself, makes up a very important part of this record.

Sgt. Russell F. Hill kept the record titled "S-3 Journal, Third Battalion 5307th Composite Unit (Prov.)—Merrill's Marauders" from 1 September 1943 through 1 June 1944.

Master Sgt. William C. Collins, battalion sergeant major, and Sgt. Joseph C. Magnate, battalion clerk, kept a record of the activities of the Second Battalion.

Sgt. Ray Lyons, the Marauder who understood recordkeeping better than anyone else in the unit, was to be frustrated before we entered Burma. Ray, who was the chief clerk, was told by General Merrill that no records were to be kept in combat. Ray Lyons for many years has been the Executive Secretary of the Merrill's Marauders Association and has been an invaluable source of information. Ray explains the recordkeeping situation as follows:

> I had just arrived at Ledo, Assam, India, when Merrill called me into the tent he was using for his office and said he was going

to promote me to staff sergeant. I said, "Thank you very much," and he then says to me, "What do you want to take down the road?" I am thinking, "What does he mean by this?" At this point I had not been in touch with the headquarters of the outfit for at least a month while we were traveling to Calcutta by truck and then to Ledo by train. I tried to figure out what he meant by this: Does this mean that Joe Doyer is not going to be the sergeant major and he wants me to be the sergeant major? I tried to think what would the sergeant major take? Well, I started scratching my brains and I am saying to myself and to him that I would need a typewriter, onionskin paper, bond paper, morning reports, and all the other forms I could think of that would be turned in from the battalions to the regimental headquarters. The next thing I know he blows up. "What the hell do you think is going on here?" he says. "We are going down in back of the Japanese lines, and I don't want you keeping any records, any documents, any diaries, nothing." He says, "If they capture you and you have all this stuff written out, that will be valuable information to them. I don't want you to keep any records whatsoever." I said, "Okay, yes sir, yes sir." This was my first war—I didn't know what the hell was going on in the first place. That was what I got out of him. He did not want me keeping any records, any paper, any documents whatsoever (Lyons, videotape).

Lyons states that the general seemed to look on him as his personal secretary, giving him letters to type and many other unexpected duties. This worked out, since he had been trained in high school as a secretary but never worked at it. Ray describes an episode that took place while he was working for Merrill—one that could have caused him a lot of trouble:

When the mail would come in I would open it and distribute it. We got mail one time, and there was a brown envelope on which was written, "for eyes alone." I didn't know what it meant, so I opened it up to see. It was some kind of special orders from the headquarters in New Delhi to General Merrill. I went in and told him, "Here is your mail, general." He never said, "Hey, you are not supposed to open that." I don't think he cared any more than I did. I soon got the impression that he was the kind of guy who liked to operate verbally. I think he got this from Stilwell. I believe Stilwell was the same kind of guy. Merrill would call up on the radio phone to people in New Delhi and say he needed this or that. It was a case of calling his friends to get something. He wasn't too keen on documentation and putting things in writing. I do remember that I had to make up blue tables of organization for the six combat teams (Lyons, videotape).

The Staff, 5307th Composite Unit (Provisional)

General Merrill selected his staff primarily from the men who had trained the 5307th and who had volunteered for the mission in the early fall of 1943. Col. Charles E. Hunter became second in command. Colonel Hunter had been selected by the Infantry School and the War Department from a group of high-ranking officers who had volunteered for this mission. He had been an outstanding instructor at the Infantry School, specializing in jungle problems and problems dealing with close combat and combat firing. He had also served as a junior officer and a company commander in earlier years in Panama, where he had operated on extended jungle maneuvers.

In the states, John Jones had just completed a period of machine-gun training when the call for volunteers for a "dangerous and hazardous mission" was announced. He was immediately accepted and sent directly to the CBI area. Admiral Lord Louis Mountbatten had recently been appointed supreme allied commander in Southeast Asia. Among his plans for the reconquest of Burma, a sea invasion of the southwest boundary was foremost. Then a captain, John was assigned to be part of this operation. He eventually got his assignment to the 5307th to take part in the operation for which he had volunteered.

G-1 was Maj. Louis J. Williams, a veteran of the fighting in New Guinea.

G-2 was Capt. William A. Laffin, a former resident and business-man in Japan for almost twenty years. Speaking Japanese fluently, he knew the Japanese in peace and war; he had been a Japanese prisoner until exchanged in the early months of the war.

G-3 was Lt. Col. Daniel E. Still, a cavalry officer who had recently arrived from the states and was assigned to the 5307th from the Chinese Training Center at Ramgarh, India.

G-4 was Maj. Edward T. Hancock.

Supply, 5307th Composite Unit (Provisional)

With General Merrill's arrival five weeks before we were to march into Burma, Major Hancock had to drastically change the plans of the supply section. The unit would no longer be coordinated with that of General Wingate's eighteen thousand troops. It would be on its own, and the supply section would have total responsibility for meeting all the needs of the three battalions soon to be deep in Burma, far beyond the Chinese and at the rear of the Japanese.

Warehouses had to be located in Assam. Our eight hundred tons of supplies, as well as many other items, had to be transported twelve hundred miles over several different-gauge railway systems for storage in the warehouses. The freight cars would have to cross two great, unbridged rivers, the Ganges and the Brahmaputra, on barges. The battle zone would be over 150 miles from the storage area and would—it was hoped—advance deep into Burma.

Parachute packers were trained, and other men learned to throw or kick the loaded chutes from the transports without damaging the plane or killing themselves. Others were taught how to pack every conceivable type of load that the unit in the field would require. Most important of all, the men were imbued with the spirit of not letting down those men in the field by failing to supply the least little thing they asked for. Most of the men in supply had been transferred away from their infantry buddies because of some disablement. Close coordination was worked out with the Second Troop Carrier Squadron at Dinjan, Assam, which was to airdrop the supplies. Warehouses, parachute drying and packing sheds, a communication system—in fact, anything that dealt with supply—were centralized at the air base near Dinjan from which the 5307th was to be supplied during their operations in Burma.

By the middle of February, everything was ready at the air base to supply the unit by airdrop. A careful precombat plan of supply was set up. Records were to be kept of the strength of each unit. A prearranged ammunition set would make it possible to call for ammunition drops simply by requesting a "unit of fire" or a half-unit of fire, as the case might be. An accurate situation map—and records showing exactly what ammunition and rations each battalion had on hand—would allow approximate prediction about its needs on a certain date at a certain location.

In the field the battalion supply officers were to send daily requests as necessary to the regimental supply officer. His job would be to consolidate these lists. He and Colonel Hunter were to mark off any items considered unnecessary, after which they were to notify the unit involved. The drop was then to be requested. Twenty-four hours before a drop was to be made, every effort was made to select a drop area. After evaluation of information gathered from maps, the I & R units, and (at times) aerial maps and/or natives, a drop area was picked. It would now be the duty of regimental headquarters to contact the supply base at Dinjan, listing the drop area of each battalion or combat team and outlining their requirements. There could be many variations of the same message to meet the individual requirements. Shortly after the message reached the air base, it was to be plotted on schedules and maps. Capt. M. E. Lowell, commanding officer of First Troop Carrier Squadron, would then begin to schedule the planes. Capt. Robert C. Gardner, the air supply officer, was to draw the rations, ammunition, and supplies from the warehouses scattered around his packing shed. Rations and ammunition were to be kept ready for immediate drop at all times. Each C-47 load was capable of running about seven thousand pounds.

Air and ground coordination was to be maintained by the squadrons who would be transporting and delivering our supplies. An air liaison officer was to be assigned to each battalion and to the command group.

The next step was to place the packed chutes on a platform where a truck could pick up the proper number for one plane load.

Two hours before takeoff time, Captain Gardner's loaded trucks were to drive to the airfield for quick loading of the assigned C-47. Loading was to be under the supervision of the Marauder in charge of "kicking" the loads out of the plane door. He was to arrange the load for quick removal at the proper time and location.

The planes were to take off so that only three to five would be over the drop field at any one time. The unit on the ground was to lay out markers on the drop area. Air-ground radio communication was to be maintained to avoid any mistakes during the drops.

BECOMING THE 5307TH

The combat team assigned to defend the field would be ready for trouble from any direction. The sky was to be searched for enemy aircraft. Work details would be ready to rush onto the field, cut the parachutes off the loads, and carry them into the jungle for concealment. Other groups with animals were to go on the field and quickly haul the loads to a more protected area for distribution.

The supply officer's job was to control the clearance of the field using an SCR radio to contact the supply officers of the individual combat teams stationed about its periphery. Speed was to be the first consideration, as each combat team collected its food, ammunition, and supplies at its concentration point. Whenever possible, records of the amount collected were to be sent by radio to the regimental supply officer. After the planes had finished the drop, from one to two hours after starting (for a big drop), any extra supplies were to be broken down and any shortages evened out among all the combat teams.

In the air, the "kicker" and his helpers—usually two or three other men—were to stack the grain sacks in the doorway for the first delivery of the drop. These sacks of food for the mules and horses were to be kicked out without any parachute attached. Each time the plane circled the field it was suggested that six to ten bags be kicked out. The pilot was to judge the exact time to kick the load and then signal the "kicker" by lowering his arm. At that moment, the pilot was to lower the nose of his ship, bringing the tail up to give extra clearance to the loads. After the free drop, the parachute-dropped loads were to be taken care of—usually three to five parachute loads at a time. These loads were to weigh between 100 and 175 pounds.

Experience suggested two big dangers facing these troop-carrier and drop-plane pilots, aside from the weather and normal flying hazards. First, they would have to contend with Japanese fighter planes. The C-47's were unarmed and would be "duck soup" for the enemy fighters. It would not always be possible to have fighter cover, and it would be very hard to sit and be shot at when you could not shoot back. The second big danger would be that a parachute would catch the tail of the plane.

Shortly before our departure for Burma, the battalion surgeons learned that our chief source of food would be the K- ration. We were told that whenever possible this would be supplemented by either C or 10-in-1 type rations. From what we could learn, the K-ration contained three thousand calories and was designed to be light in weight, to be carried in the soldier's pack, and to be consumed only under emergency conditions when no other food was available. This decision to send the men into combat with the prospect of inadequate daily caloric intake was not sanctioned by the doctors and was to play an important part in the poor strength and general health of the men.

A day's supply of K-ration consisted of three waxed boxes, each about eight inches long, two inches wide, and one inch thick. In the breakfast unit there were four graham crackers, four hard biscuits, a two-ounce can of an egg-meat mixture, several dextrose tablets, a packet of soluble coffee, three lumps of sugar, a stick of chewing gum, and four cigarettes. The luncheon box contained two ounces of cheese, a fig bar, lemonade powder, and several crackers. For supper we were given two ounces of canned meat, soluble bouillon powder, and a two-ounce chocolate bar. As at breakfast, there were also the biscuits, a stick of gum, and four cigarettes.

At Camp Deogarh the men trained in summer uniform: light-tan cotton shirts and pants. They continued to wear the standard army shoes, socks, and underdrawers. After General Merrill arrived, equipment suddenly began to appear. Green twill fatigue jackets and pants were issued, together with a plentiful supply of socks and underdrawers. The men were offered high-top canvas jungle boots. Each man was given his choice of three types of packs. One could select the pack board, the standard infantry pack, or the jungle bag. I found the standard infantry pack to be most satisfactory, as did most of the men. As long as a man could carry his quota of ammunition, he was allowed other useful items of his choice. Some of the men were able to obtain a small thin blanket as well as a poncho. General Merrill made it clear that a man could discard equipment he did not think necessary. The Ghurka knife was a much-sought item. The handle was made of wood and fit the hand in a very comfortable fashion. The blade was a foot long, curved, and heavy. The knife came with a leather sheath, which allowed it to be carried in a comfortable fashion when slipped beneath the rifle belt. The men soon would find it much better than the standard-issue machete. We had learned of this knife from the few Ghurka soldiers who visited our unit when it was under General Wingate's control. They hesitated to draw their knife from its sheath unless they were ready to draw blood.

No provision had been made for individual-issue equipment for the men to carry medication, vitamins, and so forth. General Merrill immediately responded to the request from the Third Battalion for a small canvas container to be attached to the rifle belt. Each man was required to procure, keep available, and use atabrine for malaria prevention and halazone for water purification. He could also store vitamins when they were available. Several snakebite kits were supplied to each squad. All men carried standard wound dressings and sulfadiazine tablets.

Transportation

During the training period, truck transportation was very limited. The unit was dependent on borrowed vehicles. We had arrived at Camp Deogarh after marching about fifteen miles from the railway station. Transportation did not improve under General Merrill's command.

The unit had been scheduled to have about six hundred mules and horses for training and then combat use. At the end of December 1943, three hundred large, healthy, very active mules arrived at camp. Their long voyage from New Orleans had been delayed. As the liberty ship was leaving the mouth of the Mississippi River, it was torpedoed by a German submarine. Besides the mules, the ship was carrying a large supply of steel matting used on airstrips. This cargo took the greater force of the explosion and saved the ship, men, and animals. The vessel was towed into port and the damage repaired while the mules stayed aboard. Two weeks later they were on their way for the long trip to Calcutta. They arrived at Camp Deogarh, with their mule-skinner handlers, the eighty men of the 31st QM Pack Troop, during the last week of December. In spite of the long ocean voyage, during which they had not been able to lay down, and the train trip in tight quarters from Calcutta, they arrived in wonderful condition. Their presence created great excitement among our infantrymen, most of whom had never been close to a mule or horse. They soon learned that each animal would have to be cared for and led by designated men in each combat team. Each battalion had been scheduled to have approximately two hundred mules and twenty-five muleskinners. The decision was made to have each animal led by a soldier.

Perrone was one of those who had the job of assigning men as combination muleskinner and infantryman. More than four hundred infantrymen and other specialists would have to care for and lead animals. Lt. Pat Perrone has this to say:

> We learned we were going to have mules, and unfortunately many of our men had never had contact with these animals. My job was to assign a man for each mule. Some I picked because they had seen photographs of mules. The potential muleskinners were from the Bronx, Brooklyn, Pennsylvania, and New Jersey. There was no other way to go (Perrone, videotape).

Plans changed when tragedy struck the ship bringing the second group of mules. The 33rd QM Pack Troop had left New Orleans on 1 November 1943 with three hundred mules and eighty men. Lt. Albert Higgins was in charge of the troop. All went well until the 57th day, when the ship was torpedoed at 0415 on 27 December, 1943.

Harold L. Bengston of Comanche, Iowa, tells his story in an unpublished manuscript:

> When the torpedo hit I was sound asleep in the top cot (five high). I lit on my feet between the cots. I could smell burning oil. As I started up the ladder I realized I had no shirt. I ran back to my cot and got it. As I was running on the deck to my station, which was down a well in the back of the ship, I ran through smoke and fire, and slippery oil. My job was to put shells on a hoist for a gun in the stern. Oh how I hated to go down in that hole as the ship was sinking. The torpedo knocked out the partition between #1 and #2 hold. There are five holds in a liberty ship. You cannot imagine the relief when they blew *abandon ship*. I came up that ladder a lot faster than when I went down. I can still almost smell the burning oil as when I hurried along the ship looking for a life boat. I slid down about six ropes of a pulley that was used to lower the boat to the water. I cut all the ropes to release the life boat from the ship, as I was the last one in the boat. After daylight I saw that there was a pin which I could have pulled to release all the ropes at once.

BECOMING THE 5307TH

There were about 40 sailors, 40 merchant marines, and between 80 and 110 soldiers. You can imagine what it was like with sixteen-foot-long oars with some in oar locks and others not. One time the oars would be ten foot in the water and the next time would miss altogether, because of the high waves. That same evening they put another torpedo into the ship and sunk it. We could hear the torpedo going under our life boats.

We then split up so they could not machine-gun us. I don't know how long we were separated, but we were back together the next morning. There must have been a prevailing wind that brought us back together, because we did not know what we were doing. I think there were about eight life boats. I remember seeing sharks. One with a little pilot fish near its head swam under our boat. I also saw a swordfish.

One of our life boats had a motor. So they headed for an island, but the motor caught fire and made it useless. That may have been a good thing because it was a leper island. I never got sea sick all the days on the ship, but it was all I could do to keep from heaving in the life boat. What it felt like to me was some one shoving the boat up the roof of a house and then all of a sudden pushing it off the end. Then just as we were about to hit bottom something would slam against the bottom of the boat and start pushing us up again over and over and over again. A person has a lot of things go through your mind when you are in a situation like this. I think many of us thought this was the end. We were at a time when our country could not spend much time looking for us. The tide of war was not in our favor at this time.

My early thoughts turned to prayer, as did most of the others. A lot of my life went through my mind as we drifted along. At 23 I thought I had seen more of life than most people. This was in the Arabian sea that we were sunk. The sharks must have had a good meal over the three hundred mules (Bengston 1987, written communication).

Shortly after the initial attack, planes appeared and were overhead for a few minutes. They were not seen again until 28 December at 1000 hours. A British Corvette, the *Rajputana*, picked them up on 28 December at 1530 hours. There was very little room on this boat, and the deck was packed with the survivors. A twenty-millimeter antiaircraft gun came loose from the ship's gunners and sprayed the deck. It was a miracle that no one was hurt (Hunter 1963, 14).

CHAPTER V

The men arrived at a British rest camp at Kooshin, India, on 30 December. They remained here until 15 January when they left for Camp Deogarh. The eighty men arrived five days before A Battalion was to leave for Burma. In spite of the fact that they had lost all of their belongings and were dressed in unconventional clothing, they were in good mental and physical health and were ready to get more replacement animals into shape for D day in Burma. Concurrent with the arrival of the Navarro survivors, word came to Colonel Hunter that replacement animals were in Calcutta.

Lt. Albert B. Higgins was the commanding officer of the 33rd Q.M. Pack Train Unit, while his twin brother Elbert V. Higgins was with the 31st. Q.M. Pack Train Unit. These two officers and a detail of mule-skinners were soon in Calcutta to pick up the one hundred horses sent as replacement for the three hundred mules lost at sea. The loading of eight animals to each small boxcar was soon completed. The Americans had not, at this time, taken over this rail line on which they were to travel. Movement of the train was very slow, and the G.I.'s knew the urgency of the situation. When the Indian engineer could not understand why he should work beyond his scheduled eight hours, action was taken. The engineer was put out of action after freely accepting enough alcohol to become intoxicated. One mule-skinner acted as engineer and the other as his assistant. They soon reached Lallitpur, twenty miles north of Deogarh. Unfortunately the horses were of poor quality and in poor condition.

The horses had come from Australia to New Caledonia, where they were used by the United States Army. They were next sent to General Stilwell's Chinese training camp and staging area at Ramgarh, India. The veterinarians soon determined that they had been on a picket line for about six months with little exercise and no grooming. They were emaciated and unconditioned, with loss of strength and endurance. Many of the pack saddles would not fit. Instead of having six hundred mules, we would enter Burma with three hundred wonderful mules and approximately one hundred horses, most of which were in poor shape.

The saddle problems were made worse by the lack of metal pack saddle hangers. These had to be ordered and fabricated to carry fixed loads. They had to accommodate fixed ammunition, radio equipment, medical supplies, machine guns, mortars, and other equipment. The mules could each carry approximately two hundred pounds and most of the horses somewhat less. The horses were said to require twelve pounds of oats per day. If bamboo leaves were available, the mules would eat this vegetation and get by on ten pounds of oats per day. Proper care, feeding, and mechanical ingenuity soon produced a brighter outlook for the run-down and weakened horses.

During the few days remaining before departure for Burma, those of us who had arrived earlier and trained so hard soon developed admiration and respect for the 160 men of the 31st and the 33rd Q.M. Pack Train units. They were demonstrating that they were not only exceptional muleskinners but also great riflemen and teachers. They quickly began to pass their skills to the 240 riflemen, medical technicians, heavy weapons men, and others who had been assigned to care for and lead an animal during the coming campaign.

Few of the men had any previous contact with mules or horses. The camp area soon became a beehive of activity, with men leading their charges to water, measuring out oats, tying and untying their animals at the picket line, packing and unpacking loads of equipment, and using curry combs and brushes. It also soon became common knowledge that one had to avoid the mules' back legs because their kick packed a powerful wallop.

Because of the delay in arrival of our animals, the very important exercise of river crossings remained. With great effort and considerable excitement and danger, all animals and their handlers crossed the wide and deep Betwa. The trick was to send a bell-mare over first. The handler would then lead his animal into the water and try to steer the creature toward the other side of the Betwa. Once the animal got in deep water he could no longer kick, and it was safe to hold on and push the head in the right direction. This operation did a lot to correct any fear of the river or the animals.

Communications

After arrival in India, careful evaluation turned up very few men who were trained in communication techniques. Lt. Charlton O. Ogburn, Jr., had volunteered from the 99th Signal Company of the 99th Division. In his book *The Marauders* (Ogburn 1959) he explains that, even though he was the commanding officer of a communication platoon, he had no training in radio—though such training was expected of communication officers in the infantry. His specialty was field wire and telephone. While stationed at Deolali he could not find a single item of radio equipment. He only had visual communication supplies, which would be worthless in the jungle environment. A similar lack of radio equipment and specialists prevailed in the other units.

The communication situation improved greatly in December when First Lt. William T. Bright arrived from the United States, bringing most of our authorized radio equipment. Lieutenant Bright was appointed battalion communication officer in the First Battalion, and Lieutenant Ogburn continued in charge of the communication platoon. By the end of December the radio communication situation had improved for the soon-to-be 5307th Composite Unit (Provisional).

The Second Battalion brought with them 2nd Lt. Alexander E. Glaves, who was a well qualified communications officer and became the communications section leader in Blue Combat Team. He was fortunate to have, as his section chief, Joseph F. Purjue—who was appointed to T5g. Joe had been in Trinidad for two and a half years before joining the 5307th. Lieutenant Botts later joined the Second Battalion as a radio man, as did other well-qualified enlisted men.

The Third Battalion was fortunate to have from the beginning Lieutenant Vernon Beard from Ohio. He was an extremely well-qualified communications officer who had fought with the 148th Infantry Regiment of the 37th Division on New Georgia and had come with us from the Pacific. Albert L. Midyette—who had trained with the 233rd Operating Signal Company, gone to the Solomon Islands with this unit, and was in action on Guadalcanal and New Georgia Islands—was with Lieutenant Beard. Among other well-trained men, the Third Battalion was fortunate to have T.Sgt. Jim Ballard, Corporal Bernard Martin, Bill Smaley, and Jack Egan. Lieutenant Filiak was in charge of communications in Orange Combat Team.

A detachment of the 835th Signal Battalion arrived in late December 1943 and early January 1944, as did the radio equipment. The SCR 300 or walkie-talkie was used for intra-battalion, combat team, company, and platoon communication. The SCR 284 had a range of twenty miles. It was frequently used to contact regimental headquarters. The An-Pac-1 had a range of up to two thousand miles. This unit was used to contact the rear echelon headquarters in Assam, India.

Communication between air bases and supply points was set up to be maintained by the command group radio. During January 1944, Col. Milton A. Pilcher joined General Merrill's staff as unit communications officer. A command net between the command group and each battalion was arranged. Another command net between the units of a battalion or combat team was to be maintained, while plans were made for contact with and between the smaller combat units. Pigeons, liaison planes, and air-ground communications—with transport planes dropping to the unit and runners both mounted and on foot—completed the plans for the communication picture.

Ray Lyons has this to say about Captain (later Colonel) Pilcher:

> I remember his name from the initials I was putting on his documents, M.A.P. Of all the officers we had, he kept me the busiest. He was forever putting out instructions, orders, and special deals for his communication people. That's the kind of a guy he was, making sure everybody knew what he wanted them to do and making sure they would do it. I never forgot him (Lyons, videotape).

Medical Detachment

Under the new setup, the three separate medical detachments were now answering to the regimental medical detachment. Maj. Melvin Schudmak of Unit 1688 A was now on General Merrill's staff as the unit surgeon for the 5307th Composite Unit (Provisional). The arrangement in each battalion remained essentially the same.

Daily Activities at Deogarh after General Merrill's Arrival

As has been pointed out in the discussion of communications, transportation, supply, record keeping, and staff, many changes occurred after General Merrill was appointed.

The training was cut down and the men were given more free time. Men were allowed to fire all types of weapons. Target practice and hunting of wild game was encouraged. All types of ammunition were made freely available. New green cotton twill combat jackets and pants were issued. The men were allowed their pick of three different types of combat packs. High-top canvas rubber-soled boots or standard combat shoes were offered. Food improved somewhat.

Major Petito, Captain Bogardus, and Lieutenant Sievers Visit the North Burma Battlefront

A few days after General Merrill arrived, Major Petito, Captain Bogardus, and Lieutenant Sievers were ordered to visit the North Burma front. They were to collect information about the terrain, weather conditions, and progress of the Chinese so they could advise their respective battalion commanders. After flying to Ledo, in Assam, they traveled on foot and by jeep the 105 miles over the rutted dirt road that American engineer battalions had been carving out of the mountainous North Burma jungle since the fall of 1942. They learned that this dirt, two-lane road had been advancing rapidly since Col. Lewis A. Pick had taken over the job on 17 October 1943. The bulldozers finally reached Shingbwiyang headquarters area on 27 December 1943. The road at this time was far from being finished, but jeeps and trucks were beginning to roll into the base.

The three arrived at Shingbwiyang, where General Stilwell had his headquarters in a dank, bamboo-and-grass basha (house). They learned that Stilwell had arrived here on 21 December with his musette bag, bedroll, carbine, and a change of clothing. He still wore canvas leggings, an old field jacket with no insignia, and an old World War I hat held on by a shoestring.

The three officers from the 5307th soon learned that allied forces were in a position that roughly conformed to the natural defenses of North Burma. They had breached the mountain barriers, which formed a Gothic arch across the top of northern Burma, stretching form west to east. The forces on the west or Indian side were under the command of Admiral Mountbatten. The eastern boundary was protected by the Chinese Expeditionary Force occupying Chinese territory along the Chinese portion of the now-closed Burma Road. The British also had stationed three divisions on the Burma-India border, Bay of Bengal area. These divisions faced the Japanese 55th Division. Three hundred miles to the north, SEAC (Southeast Asia Command) had three more divisions. They faced three Japanese divisions.

BECOMING THE 5307TH

The three British divisions off the Bay of Bengal had been fighting the Japanese since November, with little success, in an attempt to gain a foothold for an amphibious attempt to capture the port of Akyab on the Arakan coast of Burma.

On the Salween River or China side, the Chinese Expeditionary Force had eleven divisions facing one Japanese division.

During September General Stilwell had sent the American-trained, equipped, and supported Chinese 38th Division into Burma over the Ledo Road, which was still under construction. By 30 October they were at Shingbwiyang to begin their attack into enemy territory. The enemy at that time was located twenty miles to the south, in and about the junction of the Tarung Hka and the Tanai Hka. The 22nd Chinese Division was gradually arriving at Shingbwiyang and was to be held in reserve. The 38th was supported by a Seagrave hospital unit and American engineer and quartermaster troops.

At first the Chinese made progress against lightly held outposts. During late October the Japanese had in place a company of veteran troops from the 56th Regiment of the 18th Division. A company from the 112th Chinese Regiment was soon annihilated. The chief U.S. liaison officer, Lt. Col. Douglas G. Gilbert, was captured. The Chinese soon had troops in action at Yupbang, Ningbyen, and Sharaw Ga. Yupbang is located at a ford where the primitive but only road in north central Burma crossed at the Tarung Hka. Shortly before this date the Second Battalion of the 112th Regiment hit Japanese outposts at Ningbyen and Sharaw Ga. Both small villages are located to the northeast. Each is at an important ford on the Tarung Hka. Sharaw is ten miles from Yupbang Ga, and Ningbyen is midway between the other two.

Another Japanese outpost had been located in a twenty-by-twenty-mile valley, the Taro Plain, five miles to the west of the Hukawng Valley. The Third Battalion of the 112th Regiment was sent to deal with this problem. In order to advance to the south, the 112th, the 113th, and the 114th Regiments of the 38th Chinese Division had to cross the three fords and encircle the Japanese forces.

In a short time all the Chinese battalions were surrounded and cut off by the Japanese. The Chinese could no longer be supplied by land, so air drops had to be used. General Stilwell rushed to the front to take over the advisory function from Brig, Gen. Hayden L. Boatner.

CHAPTER V

By 31 December the Chinese had broken out of the traps and had driven the Japanese across the Tanai and the Tarung rivers. The battle of Yupbang Ga was over on 31 December, and the Chinese had their first victory in Burma—but the Second Battalion of the 56th Regiment and other elements of the 18th Division had escaped to form a new defensive line ten miles to the south at Taihpa Ga. Over a three-month period the Chinese had driven the Japanese five miles to the south. The front was now about thirty miles south of the expanding supply base at Shingbwiyang.

On 1 January General Stilwell had on hand the 38th Division, the 66th Regiment of the 22nd Division, and the Chinese 1st Provisional Tank Group (less the Second Battalion), Col. Rothwell Brown, U.S.A., commanding. He knew that the Japanese had the choice of either resisting with what they had or canceling other operations in order to reinforce.

General Stilwell estimated that the Japanese had six divisions in Burma. The 56th and the 55th were tied down on the Arakan and Salween fronts, respectively. The 33d and the 31st faced the British in the Imphal area between the northern half of the Burma border and India. The 54th was protecting against invasion from the south. He calculated that the Japanese 18th Division had only five battalions to face his four regiments.

The three officers from the 5307th arrived in mid-January just as General Stilwell was beginning a new offensive straight down the road toward Taihpa Ga about ten miles to the south. They divided their attention among the various battalions as they fought the Japanese. After a week or so of observation, they prepared to return to the 5307th at Deogarh. General Boatner heard of their plans to leave as scheduled. He met and treated them like delinquent teenagers and more or less called them cowards. These responsible, courageous, intelligent, patriotic American volunteer officers were disgusted and shocked by his behavior. Major Petito and Captain Bogardus returned immediately to our base at Deogarh. Lieutenant Sievers was not able to leave in time to return to Deogarh, but joined the First Battalion in Ledo in February. Before leaving Shingbwiyang he had a cordial visit with General Stilwell, who gave him a carton of cigarettes. He had an opportunity to travel the new Ledo Road with Capt. C. E. Darlington, who before the war had been district commissioner of the Hukawng Valley for the government of Burma. Captain Darlington was currently attached to the Chinese Army under General Stilwell's command. He was very knowledgeable about all of Burma and was on friendly terms with the primitive tribes of North Burma. He was later to be of great assistance to the 5307th and especially to Lieutenant Sievers's First Battalion (Romanus and Sunderland 1956, 28, 32).

General Merrill and Colonel Hunter were shocked over the treatment of their representatives. Within days the name Boatner was well known in the 5307th. Little did they know that later this individual would have control over their lives for a brief period, which would contribute further to their dislike of him as a man and lack of confidence in him as a general (Romanus and Sunderland 1956, 4).

Colonel Hunter was later to state that the officers had brought back no important information. Unfortunately, no effort was made to present what they had learned to the men. I as a combat team surgeon was unable at this time to get any significant information about the CBI theater of operations. Data about past, present, or future operations was not available to any but the higher-ranking officers. Maps were not available, and most knew little about the geography of the CBI.

During and after my experience with the Solomon Island campaign in the Pacific, I had decided that trunk protection was essential in combat. Obviously there was no way to get authorization for the use of body armor or even procure it, since the U.S. Army did not believe in its use. In spite of this, I suggested to General Merrill that he procure from local sources standard entrenching shovels made out of ballistic-type steel with detachable handles. These would be carried on the front of the chest in a cloth pouch. Unfortunately, he did not consider the suggestion practical or feasible.

He did, however, consider a part of my suggestion—the pouches. He quickly procured, from local sources, small cloth pouches to attach to each man's rifle belt to store atabrine and vitamin tablets as well as other small useful items. This new equipment was to prove very valuable in combat.

CHAPTER V

Awaiting Mountbatten's Arrival

11 January

Shortly after General Merrill took over, word was received that Admiral Lord Louis Mountbatten, the Supreme Allied Commander, Southeast Asia Command—accompanied by Maj. Gen. Orde C. Wingate, Commanding General, Special Forces—would arrive on the 11th to inspect the 5307th and bid us farewell. The regimental staff decided that this momentous occasion required the procurement of a bathtub, since the guests would be spending the night. Major Hancock was given the difficult job of obtaining a tub in this isolated section of India. As one would expect, this development was soon known throughout the camp and resulted in many comical and caustic remarks among the rank and file. A tub was soon in place, with a heater unit and large container to heat the water. After his arrival, when he saw the tub, he expressed gratitude and stated that he hoped that this type of luxury under field conditions was not a sign of softening among the troops (Romanus and Sunderland 1956, 3).

Before the admirals arrived, an instruction sheet had been circulated calling for spontaneous demonstrations by the men. Fortunately, this was recalled. I can only speak about the welcome that the Third Battalion gave to our visitors. When they arrived at the Third Battalion area on 12 January, they found a spacious platform in the open, near a brush-covered area. The entire battalion was concealed in the brush. When the guests were on the platform and all was ready, the concealed group ran screaming into the open area. After this thunderous and terrifying welcome, Admiral Mountbatten gave a very brief and sensible talk. He praised the men, their patriotism, courage, and enthusiasm. His remarks suggested that, under Stilwell, the units would be used to spearhead the advance of the Chinese troops who were advancing very slowly in Burma. He further explained that he did not approve of this type of mission for the units. The men appreciated his friendly attitude and candor. The loud applause truly expressed their opinion (Jones 1944).

Admiral Lord Louis Mountbatten made an effort to meet some of the men. He was especially interested in the bazooka. Sgt. Salvadore Rapisarda, a heavy-weapons expert from Headquarters Company,

Khaki Combat Team, Third Battalion, was asked to demonstrate the function of the bazooka. He has this to say about Lord Louis Mountbatten:

> I think one of the most memorable things that happened to me was my meeting with the Supreme Commander, Lord Mountbatten. I was pretty good with the bazooka, and somehow I was picked to demonstrate it with my men. He was a very very good gentleman and an outstanding person. I spent a little time with him, and he was all right. He was right down to earth asking me questions about America and everything. I really liked the man. He did not high brass me or anything like that (Rapisarda, videotape).

Sergeant Rapisarda had come from the 37th Division and the Solomon Islands. He volunteered to get away from the terrible mess he had been through in combat there. He decided that no campaign could be worse and one might easily be better. This attitude was shared by many of us.

By now the men clearly understood that we would be entering the Burma conflict under the command of General Stilwell. Everyone felt good about the fact that General Wingate and Admiral Mountbatten had made the effort to see and talk to the troops, even though we were no longer under their control. Many men were disappointed and expressed criticism that General Stilwell had never found time to visit their units. General Merrill soon spread the word that we would not be used to spearhead Chinese troops.

15 January

Shortly after dawn a burst of BAR fire, followed by a few rifle shots, jerked newly arrived visitors in Camp Deogarh out of their sacks in a state of alarm. A discussion of when, why, and at what the shots were fired brought forth an explanation from a sleepy staff officer. He assured the visitors that no Japanese were around and advised them to hit their sacks for a little more sleep—explaining that "a few of the boys are just celebrating the break of the dawn." For the past few weeks, rifle and tommy-gun shooting—and, in fact, all types of range firing—had been going on at an accelerated pace, and men had

CHAPTER V

been holding on to some of the ammunition to fire at odd moments and to hunt deer for fresh meat.

Col. Roy Boylin, CBI ordnance officer, Col. Mason Wright, and a number of other officers from the rear echelon CBI were visiting Camp Deogarh to help General Merrill in his final preparations before leaving for Assam and also because most of them wanted to see the first American infantry to arrive on the continent of Asia. All day the sound of firing filled the air. Rifles, machine guns, tommy guns, mortars, bazookas, and rifle grenades all firing at the same time gave the impression of a major battle.

During our training period, while under control of General Wingate and the Southeast Asia Command, there were few visitors. Now that we were under General Stilwell and General Merrill, numerous visitors came in. A couple of well-known airmen arrived to visit General Merrill. Ray Lyons tells about their arrival:

> One of them was famous in the comic strips—"Flip" Cochran—and the other, Allison. The two of them flew in—each had their own L4 plane. They landed on a strip alongside the road. General Merrill said to me, "Go out and get the jeep and pick up these two fliers." I went down. One of them had cracked up his plane, which was a big source of embarrassment to him. The two of them came back in the jeep with me to talk with Merrill, Hunter, and other officers (Lyons, videotape).

The weather continued good—hot in the daytime and cold enough at night to sleep with all available clothes plus several blankets. The terrific changes in the temperature were said to be due to the fact that our camp was in the bend of the Betwa River. A few miles away the marked changes in the temperature were not noticeable.

Morale was good—men were eager to get on with the job. In General Merrill's command post, a brief officers meeting was held at 1900 hours. When the business of the day had been taken care of, General Merrill and some members of his staff adjourned to the adjoining tent to talk over some detailed plans for the train movement to Assam, only a week away.

A few minutes later, a somewhat confused sergeant brought in a box full of junk jewelry that had been in the initial shipment from the United States. He asked if the general wanted to pack the stuff with the equipment to be carried to Assam. The general most certainly did, as he planned to use it to barter with the natives in Burma. A tiny bottle of perfume was quickly seized by one of the officers and emptied on the head of a newly arrived officer in a sort of baptism. A spirit of fun and good feeling prevailed in every corner of the camp and added to the friendly cooperation with which each job was done.

16 January

General Merrill learned of several Pacific veterans who had never been notified that they had won decorations while in the Pacific. A formation was held for the purpose of awarding two of these men Silver Star decorations and Purple Heart decorations to six others. After the presentations, the three units—for the first time—passed in review before General Merrill and his staff. It was perhaps the strangest review any American unit had ever put on. In jungle clothing without colors or a band, the men marched over a rough field on the side of a hill as if they were on the grassy parade ground at West Point. I proudly marched with the other two Third Battalion surgeons, Maj. Philip J. Cecala and Capt. Milton J. Ivens, as well as Capt. William T. Bell, our veterinarian, and the twenty enlisted men who were members of the medical detachment. Shortly after the regimental review, Colonel Hunter informed me that the decorated veterans had been issued orders to spend one week of leave in Calcutta. I was to travel with them, on official leave, in order to see that they returned, as planned, in good condition.

Orders had been cut, and we left on the 16th, traveling by truck, rail, and plane to arrive in good order in Calcutta. Fortunately I had accumulated some money, which I could lend to the men. Needless to say, I did not expect that it would ever be repaid. I had not had more than a few hours' leave during the seventeen months in combat areas. This was the first leave for these young men for an even longer time.

CHAPTER V

We found Calcutta located on ten miles along the eastern side of the Hooghly River, a branch of the Ganges River. The metropolitan area of the city was vast, with a population of six million people.

My base was soon in the Great Eastern Hotel. The men went their various ways. They knew where they could reach me for emergencies and the arrangements to return after one week to our camp.

I spent my time exploring this great city, visiting two sections—the rich and the poor. The British and wealthy Hindus and Moslems lived in a large tree-lined section with attractive homes. The others, the vast majority, were distributed in the industrial, shop, and slum areas. Dead, dying, and starving could be seen on the narrow streets, in the railroad station, and in almost any area I visited. Small, open-front shops were found on all streets in the old city area. All types of goods were made and sold where the merchants worked and lived. Sanitation was terrible in this city, located on low-lying ground. Many areas had no electricity, running water, or telephones. Cattle and other livestock roamed freely on the streets. The odor of jute, grains, and vegetable products was mixed with that of poor sanitation and filth. Flies and dead rats were everywhere. Cloth, silk, leather, precious stones, jute, and every product imaginable were available in many areas at negotiable prices. Many fascinating government buildings, palaces, museums, and factories could be easily toured. Every vice known to man was available for a price.

For me the end of each day was greeted with considerable relief, and I found refuge in the magnificent old-fashioned hotel with the poor plumbing, rickety ceiling fans, and elaborate meals prepared and served with questionable sanitary methods. My intake was strictly limited to well cooked foods and bottled liquids.

The men returned with increasing frequency for conversation and—at times—loans, and all were ready and willing to return, after one week of freedom, to the rigors of combat training and camp life.

On our arrival at Deogarh we learned that, on the evening of our departure, the show "Assam Poppin'" had been put on by the ATC for the men of the unit. They said the show was great. Perhaps the high point was the imitation of the three Andrews sisters singing "Chattanooga Choo-Choo," or it may be that it was the scene of a girl arguing about whether to sit on another park bench because the last one had wet paint on it. They agreed to look further, and when the girl turned her back, the stripes of wet paint down the back of her dress indicated she had done more than sit on a freshly painted park bench.

A few days before the Second Battalion was to depart for Burma, Major Johnson, the commander of Green Combat Team, and Captain Benfield, F Company commander, were both hospitalized. Captain Bogardus replaced Major Johnson, and Captain Sanford replaced Captain Benfield. Major Hestad, who had recently joined the battalion, was appointed battalion executive officer.

Everyone now seemed to understand that we would be going into combat without plans for replacements. Our volunteers would have to make out the best they could as our ranks were reduced by disease, death, and injury. I could not help but wonder what would happen when our ranks became so limited that we would no longer be an effective fighting unit. The idea that we were expendable seemed to be a logical conclusion.

As time ran out I became increasingly shocked that the unit had no clear-cut plan for the evacuation of the sick and wounded. We had heard rumors, later substantiated, that General Wingate's long-range penetration unit, which had operated in Burma in 1943, had abandoned some wounded and killed others.

17–19 January

All three battalions continued their range firing. The muleskinners were practicing their animals in river crossings, and the intelligence and reconnaissance platoons were putting the finishing touches on their review of map reading, sketching, and patrolling. Each afternoon some of the men managed to get a swim in the Betwa River and occasionally a shot at a deer. Many men got up an hour before daylight to get in a couple hours of deer or bird hunting before breakfast. This frequent addition to our diets was greatly appreciated.

20 January

The correspondents took a jeep ride with General Merrill to watch the First Battalion mules swim the Betwa River. The route to the river was over a rough trail that would try the ability of an expert jeep driver—and that is just what General Merrill proved to be. He took the jeep over places that seemed impossible to cross. On one occasion, all but the general got out of the jeep, believing that progress was impossible, but he drove down into a deep ditch and out with the greatest of ease. When we finally returned to camp—after two and one half hours of vain searching for where the First Battalion was swimming their horses—we were convinced of two things: the general was the best jeep driver we had ever ridden with, and the jeep can go any place a Missouri mule can go (Jones 1944).

At 1700 hours a horse race was held on a dusty little road between Lt. Col. Daniel E. Still and a British major, one of the doctors in the small British field hospital that was helping with the care of the sick in our unit. The course was nine-tenths of a mile, and the race was even until the last quarter mile, when the British major gradually pulled ahead to win by several lengths. Quite an exchange of money took place. At a dinner a few nights before, the merits of our animals— shipped from the States and from Australia—had been compared with the general run of Indian riding horses, and the race was the result of the discussion.

24 January

A convoy consisting of about ten vehicles and forty officers and enlisted men under the command of Captain Laffin departed for Margherita, in Assam, by way of Calcutta at 0830. Most of the personnel were from the rear echelon and the command group.

The First Battalion swam its horses across the Betwa River. The Second and Third Battalions were engaged in small-unit combat firing problems.

Lt. Col. Still, Major Schudmak, Captain Embree (air liaison officer) and Mr. John Learson of the State Department left by air for Dinjan and Ledo, both located in the flat Brahmaputra River Valley of Assam, just north of the mountainous North Burma area.

The Third Battalion had an officer's party at 0800 in a little basha loaned to them by the 80th British General Hospital Unit. A number of "sisters," or British nurses, were present—including one fair-looking one. The officers had obtained some Indian gin, rum, and liquor. By mixing the combination with fruit juice, the concoction became drinkable. It was a good party, climaxed by the mock trial of an officer who had failed to cut his hair to the prescribed length of one-half inch. The prosecution asked for "The Chair," and the defense claimed he was the only officer fit to be seen in public and therefore was of inestimable value to the outfit in case of any emergency dealings with the public. As the jury was drunk, the judge threw the case out of the court after his chair collapsed, spilling his drink, and he had to leave the courtroom in search of another.

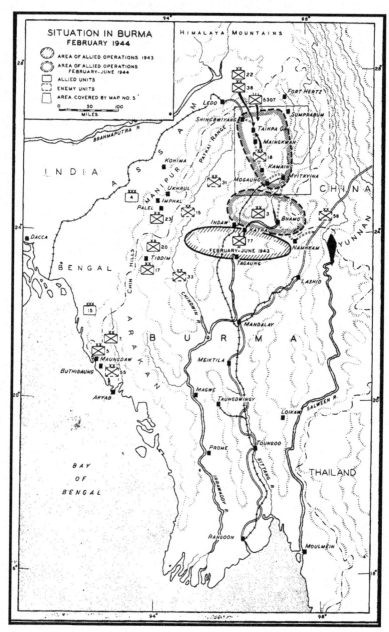

MAP 3. Situation in Burma, February 1944.

DEOGARH TO LEDO

Leaving Deogarh

On 22 January 1944, exactly on schedule, the rear echelon (less approximately forty men) left Deogarh for Jahklann at 0830, and pulled out on train number one at 1130 hours for Ledo, in Assam, India. Included in this party were all correspondents, observers, and liaison officers. Some members of General Merrill's combat staff were also present. Captain John Jones, unit historian (and collaborator with me on this history), was in this group. General Merrill came down and walked through the train, inspecting the accommodations and bidding the troops goodbye.

On this day, the First Battalion swam its animals again and the Second and Third Battalions continued to work on small-unit firing problems.

Shortly before our departure, a platoon of military police from the 502nd M.P. Battalion was attached to General Merrill's Headquarters.

23 January

Train number one reached Jhansi the night of the 22nd, then on the 23rd moved on following the route through Manipur, Allahabad, Mirzapur, Mugal Sarai, and Pildarnager. At Camp Deogarh, preparations were under way for the movement to Assam. The final bit of training was concluded, and equipment was checked and packed for the train transport.

24 January

Train number one reached Mokaraah Ghat and was ferried across the Ganges River. The troops were greatly surprised to see the bodies of a woman and child floating in the river, and also to see large fish, resembling porpoises, which were reputed to come up so far from the sea to eat the human bodies thrown into the river by Hindus.

The three battalions at Camp Deogarh continued the same program as on 23 January. Minor difficulties over some laundry arose between some men of the Third Battalion and some Indians in the vicinity of the Field Supply Dump. M.P.'s raided a fruit stand near the Indian labor camp and confiscated several bottles of whiskey.

25 January

Train number one moved very slowly the night before and at a snail's pace all this day. An investigation revealed that eight hundred Indian laborers, or WOG's, as they were commonly called, had been hooked onto the end of our train. The train now had forty-five cars and one small engine.

The rear-echelon soldiers on the train were buying pets wholesale. Dogs, monkeys, parrots, and even small snakes had joined the party. The unit staff suspected that the combat troops who were to follow would not attempt to follow their example.

At Camp Deogarh all three battalions continued to make preparations for the move to Assam.

26 January

The First Battalion, less its animals, started marching for Jahklann at 1430. The trains departed at 0130 on 27 January.

At 2130, headquarters at Deogarh was notified by the 80th General Hospital headquarters investigative unit (British) that there had been a shooting earlier that night. They reported that three Indian Dhobis had been wounded by thirty-caliber cartridges while in their tents. The empty cartridges were found outside the Dhobis' tent.

27 January

A muster was ordered by General Merrill, and all men in the camp were inspected to find the men involved in the shooting. Indian soldiers who had been at the scene during the shooting were present to identify the men involved. Privates Gumm and Nichols of L Company Third Battalion were identified as the men who had been at the scene of the shooting. They were placed under arrest and confined. An immediate investigation was ordered by General Merrill. Captain Hestad and Lieutenant Rothchild were appointed the investigative officers. This board obtained full confessions from Privates Gumm and Nichols. Gumm admitted doing the actual shooting. As the unit was on the eve of departure from Camp Deogarh, men and evidence were turned over to the Provost Marshall of American troops at Agra for action.

The Second Battalion entrained at Jahklann for Margherita, in Assam, on the same schedule the First Battalion had followed the day before. The Third Battalion and the remainder of the camp made preparations to move the next day.

By this time, train number one had passed through Simria Ghat, Kathihar, Parvatipur, and Lalmonir Hat, and at dawn arrived at Amingaon on the Brahmaputra River, one of the largest rivers in Asia. The men were ferried over to Pandu at noon and quartered at a British-operated transient camp. British, U.S., and Chinese troops were all quartered together. The camp was overcrowded and poorly run—the mess was bad, and sanitary facilities were run down. A U.S. Transportation Corps camp was across the road. This was one of the railroad battalions that had recently arrived in India and were beginning to take over the operation of the Bengal and Assam Railway.

28 January

Tony Colombo arrived at the Third Battalion area on the day it was to depart for Assam. He tells of his arrival and trip toward Burma.

> I got back to Deogarh, and the mules were all packed and ready to go. I went in to Johnson, who was a combat team commander, and I said, "I am back," and he said, "O.K, you just get with that group over there and march off." Off we went. Well, I got down the line a little bit, and all I had was a pocket knife—no weapons, no nothing. We got on to the boat, and there was "Bull Head" Mead, we called him. (His name was Mead. He was a lawyer from Indiana, I think.) He was in command and the officer of the day. He tried to put me on guard. He said, "Colombo, you are on guard." I said, "I can't be on guard—I am under arrest, and I don't have a weapon." He said, "Well, you are still under arrest. I'll get you a weapon because you are on guard—there is security on the beat anyhow (Colombo, videotape).

CHAPTER VI

After walking in the dark about fifteen miles with full equipment, the men of the Third Battalion reached the railhead and boarded the dilapidated coaches with the hard benches. With the rest of the camp personnel, we were on our 1,200-mile trip from Jahklann to Margherita using the same schedule and route that the First and Second Battalions had followed. I was in this group since I was the surgeon for Orange Combat Team of the Third Battalion. Our group had been joined by another surgeon, Lieutenant Paul E. Armstrong, who has been previously mentioned. Doctor Armstrong was a well-trained surgeon who, before volunteering for military service, had been in practice in Chicago. He had gone overseas with a hospital unit that had recently arrived in India. When the call went out to fill a vacancy in a combat unit, he quickly volunteered.

The personnel of train number one awoke amid the arrival of a large unit of Chinese fliers on their way to the 14th Air Force in China. They had recently trained in the U.S. and were extremely good-looking soldiers.

While looking for a canteen to purchase some shaving cream, John Jones asked a burly soldier in a British uniform where he could buy some. The soldier replied, "Speak no Anglish." An investigation proved that he was one of a labor battalion of Italian prisoners among us. They had been captured in 1941 and had volunteered to go to India to work. They were all skilled mechanics and healthy, jolly, strapping fellows. Their morale was good and their discipline tops. They seemed eager to talk to Americans and all day there was trading of coins, bills, and souvenirs. They despised Mussolini, but many thought the king was O.K.—though some called him a little nobody and a stuffed shirt.

At 1900, train number one pulled out of Pandu on narrow-gauge tracks, but it was a different train from the one we had left. This train was dirty—full of enormous roaches—and the finest car was a broken-down third-class coach. Not much sleeping was done for the next few days; poker games continued day and night in every coach.

29 January

The first animal train, consisting of the First Battalion and headquarters pack train, left Jahklann at 1300.

General Merrill, Colonel Hunter, Major Hancock, Captain Hestad, Master Sergeant Doyer, and a photographer left Camp Deogarh at 0800 and departed from Lallitpur by staff plane at 0900. They lunched at Gaya and arrived at Dinjan at 1800, where they were quartered in the transient camp.

Train number one arrived at Lunling, a beautiful little town as Indian towns go. The troops on all trains were eating 10-in-1 rations, which at that time were generally considered to be the best field ration that the army supplied. The seats were getting hard, and the men were getting tired from the long trip. While eating breakfast, one officer said to another, "Is there any more jam?" The second officer replied, "Not until we get to Dinjan." That was the sad state of humor on the train.

30 January

The Second Battalion animal train left Jahklann for Margherita at 1830.

Train number one arrived at a siding near Dinjan Air Field, where we unloaded at 1400 in the rain. No camp could be seen, but a few hours later the men had set up tents and were ready to bed down for the night.

31 January

The Third Battalion animal pack train left Jahklann for Margherita on the same schedule that all the other trains had followed. The entire command, with the exception of the rear echelon group on train number one, was now en route to Margherita by train.

1–5 February

All trains were still en route to Margherita. All personnel and equipment on train number one and all animals had to be ferried across the Brahmaputra River from Testamuch Ghat to Pandu. From Pandu they were transported by narrow-gauge rail to Margherita. At Testamuch Ghat, a different route was taken by the First, Second, and Third Battalions. In each case the men left the train at Testamuch Ghat without crossing the river and took an overnight trip up the great Brahmaputra River to Gauhati. Each battalion spent part of two days and one night on a paddlewheel boat such as one might have seen on the Mississippi River a hundred or more years ago.

CHAPTER VI

While at Gauhati, free time was available before the troop train was to leave for the end of the line. Logan Weston and I decided to investigate a nearby Leper Hospital. This did not prove practical, but we were told of a nearby Baptist Mission Hospital. This seemed a good alternative. We found a neat, well-constructed, small hospital building located on well-cared-for acreage and surrounded by large shade trees. We were greeted and conducted about by a Doctor Seagrave, who explained that she was a sister of the well-known Burma missionary surgeon Gordon Seagrave. She had established her missionary hospital about the same time her brother had moved into Burma, around 1927. Her staff consisted of several dedicated women doctors and student nurses from the Naga hill people of North Burma. After four years of training, they were qualified nurses. One of the staff doctors had gone on to medical school and was now a surgeon at the hospital. We were told that an American had recently been treated at the hospital for meningitis and had survived. As we drove back to the railroad station, we both agreed that this break in our travel had taught us much about self-sacrifice and what can be done by one group of people for another. How refreshing it had been for us to shift our thoughts from the filth, poverty, disease, and ignorance of the many areas we had seen to this oasis of efficiency, sanitation, and sacrifice by one group for another. We had at last had a brief respite from the eighteen months we had been either in a combat zone, in combat, or vigorously training for the destruction of others.

The rear echelon (supply) group at Dinjan had blossomed into a full-sized camp, and work was going on night and day, setting up tents and loading warehouses with food, ammunition, and supplies destined to be dropped to the unit when it finally hit the combat area in Burma.

6 February

At 0030 the First Battalion trains arrived at the staging area near Margherita and were unloaded at dawn. The troops were soon marching to the dirt-floored, reed-and-bamboo buildings they would use during their short stay here. They had had a hard, rough trip but were in good spirits and were glad to have their feet on the ground—even though it was wet ground. This trip from Deogarh in north central India to Margherita, Assam, India, had taken ten days and spanned about twelve hundred miles. The troops had traveled on two different railroad gauges, crossed the Ganges on barges, and traveled overnight up the Brahmaputra River on an ancient, overcrowded paddlewheel riverboat. When they disembarked at Gauhati they found a train on another gauge track, which was to carry them another 250 miles to their destination.

During one of the stops several men had taken possession of two wandering ducks. A passer-by soon claimed ownership in a very vehement fashion. Unfortunately, the train pulled out before the argument could be settled.

Fortunately for the men of the First Battalion, they were only to remain in mildew-coated bamboo structures for about forty hours of confusion and misery before they were to depart on foot for Burma.

At 1600 Mr. Harold Young, a Baptist Missionary born and reared in northern Burma, gave a talk to the officers and men of the First Battalion on how to live in the jungle. He demonstrated how to get water from bamboo and banana trees, how to build an insect-proof bed, and gave many other practical suggestions on what to do and not to do in the area we were to operate in. At the conclusion of his talk, the Office of War Information distributed a booklet on how to get along with the Kachins and Burmans. This booklet proved most helpful to the command headquarters in their later dealings with the Kachins.

From the train transporting the Third Battalion from Gauhati to Margherita, we were entertained at numerous points by watching baboons swinging in the jungle trees along the railroad right-of-way. At another time I got a clear view of a tiger slinking through the jungle vegetation.

It was here at Ledo, just before we started the march into Burma, that General Merrill emphatically told Ray Lyons that no records were to be kept during the Burma campaign. Instead of being assigned to General Merrill's forward advance group, Ray states, "I was reassigned to what was called the Command Post Group. This section was commanded by Major Louis J. Williams, and I was the sergeant. We had a couple truck drivers, a jeep, a cook—a handful of people, actually. (I am trying to think.) Yes, we had radio people, and we had cipher people" (Lyons, videotape).

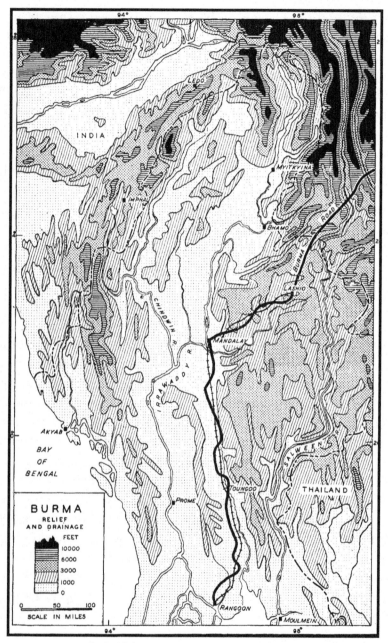

MAP 4. Burma relief and drainage.

TO THE BURMA FRONT

7–22 FEBRUARY 1944

Over the Kumon Mountains

On their day of departure, the men of each battalion put all equipment and personal belongings not carried on their backs in large barracks bags with each man's name painted on his bag. These personal belongings were then placed in a bamboo warehouse at the staging area. All were assured that the bags would be carefully protected and quickly available if they survived combat and returned.

Each battalion's kitchen crew had been set up at Deogarh. They were to remain in this capacity until the combat area was reached or the road was no longer available for trucks. They would then return to their combat assignments. This kitchen crew left by truck with all necessary equipment and supplies, as well as a billeting party. They were to make arrangements for each bivouac site and have hot meals ready for breakfast and supper. At the noon break, a chocolate bar was usually issued. Breakfast and supper were prepared from canned foods and were most satisfactory.

In the beginning, the battalions marched at night. This was soon abandoned—since Tokyo Rose soon announced that an American division was marching into Burma over the Ledo Road.

At 2200, the First Battalion marched out of the staging area at Margherita and hit the Ledo Road for Burma. They soon learned, as they walked fourteen miles the first night, that the dirt road was far from completion.

Those who knew about such things were worried about the condition of the mules and horses. They had been inactive for a long period, and the pack saddles had never been properly broken in for heavy loads and a long campaign. The Quartermaster Pack Troop personnel knew how quickly an animal will develop saddle sores—and become useless—if the pack saddles are not properly broken in. This long march into Burma would help to avoid this problem. I was very glad for the opportunity to break in my foot and leg muscles. We had had a lot of inactivity on the long boat and train rides and had done no hiking over mountainous terrain. When the long and difficult hike of about 150 miles was over, I sensed that the men felt good about what they had accomplished (Jones 1944).

Shortly after the First Battalion departed, the Second Battalion—followed by their animal train—arrived at the staging area. They were also to have their share of confusion and misery as they struggled with supply and animals, and attempted to get adequate food and rest before their departure. Lieutenant Hickman and the muleskinners did a good job as they turned over animals to their assigned keepers, who were soon struggling with the proper loading and care of their charges. It was necessary to constantly remember that the kick of a mule or horse could be fatal.

These men, like those of the other battalions, had welcomed the change of scenery and rest that came with the twelve-hundred-mile, eleven-day trip. The hard benches, cramped quarters and filthy coaches, and slow travel were taken as a matter of course. Like the battalions before and after, they enjoyed the C rations and 10-in-1 more than the food they had been getting at Deogarh.

At 2030 hours on 8 February, the Second Battalion and the command group followed the First for their long night and early morning march. The few service-of-supply personnel still awake along the road at this late hour looked with amazement as the 5307th marched by. This is understandable when it is realized that, for months, the rumor that American infantry were coming had only been a rumor, and most of them had given up the idea that the doughboys would arrive. The men of the unit were equally surprised that there were so many military units in the Dinjan-Margherita-Ledo area (Jones 1944).

The Third Battalion train, followed by its animal train, arrived before the Second had departed. We followed their procedures and had the same problems but were ready to start the march toward Burma at 1800 hours on 9 February.

Down the trail, shortly after we left Ledo, Tony Colombo was in luck:

> A while after we had left Ledo, I ran into some colored quar-
> termaster troops and got some boots and clothes and became a

Marauder again. I don't know how, but I was assigned to Lieutenant Ted Hughes' Platoon. He would later became Lieutenant Colonel Hughes and is now dead. This was just before the big Battle of Walawbum. We had been in a few skirmishes before the big battle. Beach, the battalion commander, wanted somebody up as a runner so I was chosen because the other kids did not want to go. Anyhow, I was chosen (Colombo, videotape).

During our travels and training periods, many thoughts about my past and possible future military experience kept my mind alert. At no time had we ever been given any significant briefing on the reason that the United States had sent what appeared to be a vast amount of supplies and number of men to India and China. Few if any of the men or officers had the slightest knowledge of the political ramifications involved in the relationship between Great Britain, India, China, and the U.S.A. The men had never received any information about why they had been asked to volunteer. No one ever explained how it was decided that this small token group of infantrymen should be sent like mercenaries to a theater where the British had more than one million men under arms and the Chinese a vast number.

No reason was ever given as to why this group of volunteers, when turned over to British command, were totally abandoned by the United States Army Force's China-Burma-India theater of operations. They had been organized in an express fashion and then put in a totally inadequate British transient camp in India for three unproductive weeks. Their permanent camp, where they were still under British control, was in an isolated area with inadequate sanitary facilities, religious support, food, and organization. There was no running water, electricity, telephones, or adequate facilities for washing our bodies or our clothes.

The three units had no significant headquarters until three weeks before combat. Significant hospital help was at a great distance, with slow and questionable transportation. No arrangements had been made for essential personal hygiene supplies such as tooth brushes and paste. No insect repellent was available. Simple luxuries such as candy and beer were only available to a few. Mail service was very bad, and entertainment was largely nonexistent. The few brief leaves that were given were of little use, since transportation was not available and distance was great.

CHAPTER VII

Few—if any—representatives of any branch of the United States Army visited the units until three weeks before departure for combat, when it was taken from British control and given to General Stilwell. The general never inspected the unit before or after the unit left the camp. The well-trained, highly qualified senior member of the unit, Colonel Hunter, was bypassed, and General Merrill was appointed commanding officer. His first visit to the unit was made before adequate contact with the mules and horses had been made and three weeks before the move was made toward Burma. General Merrill was qualified from a military standpoint, but no one was told that he had coronary artery disease and had had a heart attack in 1942. No effort was ever made to explain to the men why we were suddenly taken from the British and returned to our army.

In spite of the great effort of the medical officers to remedy health problems, some men left for combat in poor physical condition. Again it is worthwhile to point out that the Third Battalion men were infected with the malaria parasite and could be expected to have ongoing problems with the disease. It must be remembered that the medical officers had never been informed of the results of the evaluation of the theater malariaologist, which I recorded earlier.

The medical detachments were still troubled that no system of casualty evacuation had been worked out by the combat group. We were confident that the air-supply system that Major Hancock was still working on would fill our needs for plasma, intravenous fluids, dressings, and medications. Penicillin had not been available to our unit, and we thus would depend on sulfadiazine for wound infection prevention and treatment. We had sulfaguanadine for bacterial dysentery but no satisfactory treatment for amoebic dysentery. We would be depending on halazone tablets, dissolved in our canteens, to purify our drinking water. After the campaign we learned that halazone tablets would not kill the amoeba ova and thus not prevent the infection of the men. We hoped to prevent primary attacks of malaria as well as recurrent malaria with one tablet of atabrine taken by each man daily.

Those of us who had been in the Pacific wondered why the battalions had not been supplied with pack artillery. We had the animals and men—why not give us the readily available guns? It was inconceivable, after our combat experience, that an infantry unit should be asked to enter combat without artillery—especially when the enemy was a master of its use. In the Pacific jungle, fighter planes and light air bombardment had in many cases been of little help because they could not locate the troops below. Most of us were of the opinion that planes would not do the job of artillery.

The men, as they marched toward the enemy, had no previous conception of the terrain or the part they were to play in the Burma operation. We knew nothing about the previous battles between the Chinese and the Japanese. Our men were not aware that our unit would be entering Burma to fight before British troops moved into combat. No one had told us that over a million troops were available on the eastern border of India or that General Wingate's units had not been sent into combat. It is likely that the men would have been more confident had they known the above, as well as what they were to face in the way of mountains, rivers, jungle, and valleys when they crossed into Burma.

We had been told nothing about the Japanese conquest of Burma or the part the British and Chinese had played in the past, were attempting now, or could be expected to do in the future. No one had given the troops the slightest information as to how many Chinese or British troops were in Burma or what they were doing.

Like the two other battalions, at first we marched at night. The air was fresh and cool, and the road was well packed, with few ruts. The men seemed to enjoy their first good hike since leaving Deogarh. Some were beginning to realize that they would have to eliminate items from their packs.

On the 9th, their third day on the road, a tragedy occurred in Lt. Charlton Ogburn's First Battalion communications platoon. One of his men, who had been trained as a radio technician, did not quite make the grade and was given a Tommy gun. On this evening he could not be located. When the body was found, the cause of death was ruled suicide. In retrospect, as in so many civilian deaths, warning signs had been present.

10 February

The Second Battalion was awakened at dawn by the sound of grenades bursting in a nearby river and screams of laughter coming from Chinese service troops as they grenaded fish and then scrambled in the water to recover the stunned fish.

CHAPTER VII

Word was passed along the columns of marching men that Colonel Hunter had been promoted to full colonel and that a number of other officers had been promoted.

The road was wet for all the battalions, and walking was difficult. The Naga hills here would have been called mountains at home, and most of us noticed fatigue as we followed the winding road, sometimes up and sometimes down. In the distance the Patkai Mountain Range reached for the sky.

At times we saw short-waisted, sturdy natives who were obviously great hill climbers. Only men were seen, and they wore breech cloths and kept their hair long and straight. Their skin was light brown in color. The word spread that they were Nagas—one of three tribes in this part of Burma. These people, we learned, had until recently been very active as headhunters. Instead of hand-held freight, they carried their load in a bamboo basket that rested on the upper back and was held in place by a band, which went just above each ear and across the forehead. Further along the way we were to see members of the Kachin tribe. The Nagas were being hired by various American service units as bearers and laborers. They had left their wives and children at their individual villages, which were well hidden deep in the jungle.

11 February

The Third Battalion marched ten miles on this day in the rain. The road was slick and difficult for men and animals both. The men sang a great deal as they marched. This action seemed to impress Chinese service troops, who loudly expressed their enthusiasm from small camps along the road. A good breakfast was greeted with gratitude on the morning of the twelfth. The mobile kitchen crew was doing a great job as we moved along the road.

The Second Battalion had a short hike of three miles and stayed near an engineer outfit that was constructing a pipeline into Burma. It had rained all day, and the men were ready to enjoy the engineers' hospitality—which was accompanied by a movie.

The First Battalion also saw some movement on this day, crossing the line from India into Burma.

12 February

The march of the Second Battalion up Hell's Gate was tough—eight miles on an uphill grade, most of it very steep. Eventually the battalion reached Pangsau Pass at five thousand feet elevation. The panoramic mountain view was inspiring. To the northwest a snow-capped mountain of nineteen thousand feet was visible at the Burma-China border. The early arrivals could look down to the north and see the winding column of men and animals extending three miles as they slowly ascended the steep, crooked, dirt road. At this bivouac they were treated to a stage show by Captain Melvin Douglas. After he put on this show, Douglas took his group down a rain-slick road to put on a show for the Third Battalion.

13 February

Rain continued intermittently, and the Third Battalion had a rough thirteen-mile climb to Pangsau Pass. This proved to be my worst day in Burma. When the Third Battalion was about one mile from the five-thousand-foot summit, I developed a severe chest pain—which persisted in spite of several self-imposed rest periods. I eventually struggled into bivouac, barely able to put one foot in front of the other. Immediate sleep on the cold, wet ground soon eliminated my fatigue and pain. In the early morning I was thrilled by the magnificent panorama, with the snow-capped mountain, the green forest, smaller mountains, and finally mist-shrouded valleys on all sides extending far into the distance.

14–15 February

The units were now from fifty to seventy miles from the American forward base at Shingbwiyang, which had been constructed and kept stocked to support Chinese troops under General Stilwell's control. Supply trucks had been traveling the road as we marched. When we hit dry stretches of the road, men and animals were covered with dust. Now many of the steep grades were downhill, and those with heavy packs began to complain of pain in the thigh extensor muscles and the knees as we learned more about hiking in mountain country.

At mile ninety, a battalion of black engineers spent most of three nights demonstrating their happiness to see the arrival of American infantry troops. They played music as long as we marched by. "Dixie" and "God Bless America" were our favorites, and produced loud cheers from the marching men. Their hospitality lifted the spirits of the 5307th, and the engineers seemed to get a lot of pleasure out of their greeting. It was a fine gesture of goodwill and good luck, and the men of the 5307th appreciated it.

The Saigon (Japanese-controlled) radio announced that two divisions of American troops were marching down the Ledo Road and warned them to get off the road or they would be bombed off. The troops got a big laugh out of that.

At rest breaks and bivouac the men were seeing increasing numbers of skeletons. In India we had learned that many refugees had died in an attempt to get out of Burma during the Japanese invasion and occupation. The immensity of the great Burma tragedy was to become known to me in 1971 when I read the book *Walkout with Stilwell in Burma,* by Brigadier General Frank Dorn. He states, "I wondered how many in that endless stream of stricken humanity would manage to save themselves through their will to survive, and how many were walking to their death. Weeks later we learned that only about one-tenth of the nearly 900,000 who left Burma for India reached safety" (Dorn 1971, 148).

16 February

James Shapley, *Time* and *Life* correspondent, had been calling the 5307th Composite Unit (Provisional) "Merrill's Marauders" for some time. When the unit reached Shingbwiyang, everyone was referring to us as Merrill's Marauders—and so we were at last named.

A Marauder's girlfriend in the States had written to him just before he left Deogarh and said, "The name of your organization sounds like a quartermaster unit. I am glad to know that you are not going to be in the fighting" (Hunter 1963, 16).

17–18 February

General Merrill's command post group arrived at Shingbwiyang by truck and soon moved fifteen miles below this base to Ningam Sakan, where General Stilwell had recently set up his headquarters.

The First Battalion reached Shingbwiyang early on the 18th. During the previous two days the road had grown narrower, with more turns and steep grades. It needed much more construction work.

Overhead the men heard planes bringing in supplies. They heard, as we were later to hear, the distant roar of artillery as the Chinese and Japanese dueled each other in the distance. The weight they were carrying, including packs, weapons, and ammunition—combined with the very steep grade on the final few miles to Shingbwiyang—caused many of the men to have a problem with pains in their knees.

The village of Shingbwiyang, at the head of the Hukawng, was a village in name only, as far as we were concerned. Anything that looked like a base or village was bypassed as the First Battalion made a forty-five-degree turn to the southeast and headed into the wild and rugged but reasonably flat jungle of the Hukawng Valley. The trail skirted the mountains on the left as they advanced toward another name in the jungle, Ningam Sakan, located fifteen miles southeast of Shingbwiyang.

Because of approaching darkness the First Battalion bivouacked on the trail just south of Shingbwiyang. Here they received their last hot meal until the campaign was over—or until they were killed or evacuated because of sickness or injury.

The Second Battalion had a serious misfortune on 18 February. A kitchen truck was transporting its crew as well as a group of soldiers who, for one reason or another, had to drop out of the marching column. Just as it reached the crest of a very steep grade and gears were shifted to descend, the brakes malfunctioned. After a wild passage, the vehicle overturned and hit a pile of logs. One rifleman was killed and twenty were injured. Most had severe lacerations and fractures, and some had concussions. Doctors Rogoff, Kolodny, and Stelling took charge, and after emergency treatment the injured were admitted to Co.D of the 151st Evacuation Hospital. Some were evacuated to Ledo by air the next day. One Marauder remained at the evacuation unit for several days. He was suffering from a fractured spine with paralysis of his legs. He was told by the medical staff that he would be permanently paralyzed. Two weeks later, one of medical technicians fashioned a crutch out of a forked stick, and he started getting about with great difficulty. His records were lost, and in spite of the serious nature of his injury he was returned to combat duty when the paralysis and pain cleared.

20 February

Since General Stilwell now had his headquarters at Ningam Sakan,

CHAPTER VII

Colonel Osborne had anticipated that he would make an appearance as the First Battalion passed by. All men were ordered to shave, wear their helmets, and make every effort to make a good showing for the general. Unfortunately, the general did not show.

They continued on, over a very difficult trail, and came near Ningbyen just as darkness approached. Here, by the trail, they were greeted by General Merrill and Colonel Hunter. The two officers had been able to drive a jeep into the area. Their presence was appreciated by everyone. The men reached their destination in total darkness to bivouac near the Tarung Hka. They were hungry and tired, and faced the chore of picking a spot to sleep in unfamiliar terrain and total darkness.

The day was very late when the Second passed through the Shingbwiyang area. They were grateful that the accident had not been on this day because they were beyond the point where supply or evacuation by vehicle was possible. Each man was issued two days of K-rations and several grenades, and was advised to shed all unnecessary equipment.

The march was long and difficult, and even though the Second Battalion kept marching beyond sundown, they failed to reach Ningbyen. They went into bivouac about four miles from the proposed unit assembly point at Ningbyen.

21 February

With the onset of daybreak the men of the First Battalion were amazed to find much evidence of recent prolonged combat in and about the area where they had spent the night. Debris was everywhere. Destroyed Japanese equipment was much in evidence, and hundreds of little clay and wooden idols were scattered on the ground. Numerous trenches and foxholes, as well as dismantled log-covered pillboxes, stretched over several acres. Few if any of the men were able to learn about the circumstances of the battle that had obviously been fought in this area.

During the morning, the first air drop of supplies was carried out under the supervision of Colonel Hunter. Just before the drop, the battalion had waded the broad and now shallow Tanai Hka. An area of several acres on the south side was free of jungle growth and was picked for the drop. Fluorescent cloth panels were placed on the ground to designate the center of the drop area, the surface wind direction, the direction the aircraft should approach, and the direction they should follow on leaving the area. The color of the panels also identified the receiving combat teams. Most of the later drops were less complicated, since they would be directed to individual combat teams of the battalions. Here the drop was for the entire regiment. The pilots had been trained to come into the wind at an altitude of four hundred feet or less and at near stalling speed to lower the front of the plane and raise the tail. At this time the pilot would wave his hand, and the "kickers" would shove out a pile of freight. Most of the soldiers doing the delivery duty had for one reason or another been separated from the battalions and placed in the rear echelon. Throughout the campaign they were to carry out this dangerous duty of delivering freight to their former friends and buddies in a courageous, efficient, and timely way.

Just before each drop the SCR (Signal Corps Radio) 284 would be tuned to the proper frequency used by the C-47. An attached speaker would allow the operator to hear the flight leader's report as his planes neared the drop area. Often it would be necessary for the radio operator to talk the flight leader into the location of the drop area.

Free drops were made for animal food, clothing, and gasoline. The grain for the animals was placed in a burlap bag. This bag was then placed in another bag. The first would often break, but the second would hold. The mules got nine pounds of grain per day and the horses twelve. The mules made up the difference by eating bamboo leaves, which the horses would not touch. All personnel near the drop field had to be very careful to avoid being seriously injured or killed by an object delivered without a parachute.

The pilots, planes, and personnel of the First and Second Troop Carrier units were to do a fantastic job during the entire campaign. From beginning to end, the combat troops on the ground expressed admiration, gratitude, and thanks for the courageous and timely work of all concerned.

At all drop areas everyone on the ground knew his duty—be it security or rapid removal and distribution of the supplies. Drops were always to be in enemy territory, and ambushes and sudden attacks were to be expected.

Rain had been a bother all night, and the Second Battalion was glad to go into bivouac during the morning of the 21st. The day was dry and clear, and clothing and supplies were rapidly dried. As they joined the First Battalion in a common area to await D day, the prospect of a few hours of rest in sunshine, as well as a generous supply of 10-in-1 rations, was welcome.

CHAPTER VII

On this day the men of both battalions were pleased when they saw General Stilwell and General Merrill wandering about the assembly area. General Stilwell looked well beyond his 61 years. He had on a soiled field jacket, baggy khaki pants, leggings, and a cap. He lost a lot of respect when he failed to address the men in large or small groups.

On the night of 21 February the Third Battalion bivouacked after dark in an area recently occupied by Chinese troops. As I was finding my way to what was to be our last hot meal, I accidentally walked into a pit about ten feet deep. I had numerous strains and bruises, but only my pride was seriously hurt.

At Shingbwiyang the Third Battalion started on the jungle trail to Ningam Sakan. The trail was muddy and difficult, especially between Ningam Sakan and Ningbyen. Late in the day we passed a loaded jeep, which had pulled off the trail to let us by at a very narrow point. It was hot and the men were tired. As a particularly belligerent muleskinner was passing the jeep, he stopped. Looking squarely into the face of three American officers wearing Chinese Army caps, he spluttered, "My God—Duck Hunters!" He did not know that the men in the jeep were Lt. General Stilwell and several of his staff. In the story written by Jim Brown of International News Service, it was reported that General Stilwell got a hearty laugh out of the muleskinner's comment. The general was on his way back from Ningbyen where, earlier in the day, he had been with General Merrill at the D-day assembly area. Orange Combat Team's medical detachment passed the jeep, but the general never took the trouble to stand by the trail, and few of the men had any idea who he was.

The men were very happy to be provided with an adequate supply of 10-in-1 rations before they sought suitable spots on the rough ground to spend the night.

22 February

The entire unit was now at the assembly point. Some were resting while others bathed or washed their clothing in the clear, fast-flowing river. Men with more urgent tasks—such as receiving air drops, dispensing food and other supplies, and looking after the animals—had little time to rest or attend to their own needs.

Since I was supported by a well-organized and very competent group of men in the medical detachment, I took the time to review the medical aspects of the twenty-five days each battalion had taken to reach the area beyond which contact with the enemy would be expected.

Health problems had been minimal. As has been stressed, our passage had taken us twelve hundred miles—by foot, three different gauges of railway, and a paddlewheel boat up the Brahmaputra River—and had culminated in a 150-mile trek over very high and rugged mountainous terrain into North Burma. For all but ten days we had field-combat rations. Caloric, protein, and vitamin intake had been inadequate. Colonel Hunter was to explain in his book, *Galahad,* that Colonel Ravdin, the commanding officer of the 20th General Hospital (University of Pennsylvania unit) had asked him what we would be eating in Burma. When told that our food would be mostly K-rations, the colonel responded in no uncertain terms that the K-ration would not supply the necessary calories. Of course we knew this, and the War Department knew it, but—unknown to many of us—they considered the unit expendable and unlikely to continue as an effective force for more than three months. I have often wondered if this negative attitude was the reason the general's staff and our unit leaders failed to supplement our diet with frequent air drops of adequate vitamins and high-protein and high-caloric food, which could have been used when we were not actually in battle or on forced marches. Drinking water had been provided with questionable evidence that it had been adequately treated. At that time we did not know that halazone tablets, issued for our use as the latest chemical available for water sterilization, would not kill the amoebic ova. Insect repellent was rarely available, and at no time did we have screening or other protection from insects. No running water was available for body or hand washing. Filthy surroundings were always associated with train and boat travel. Sleeping and personal hygienic accommodations were unspeakable at all times. The hot weather in India and Burma and the cold during rest periods in the mountains of North Burma were not unexpected—and could not be avoided—but were rarely followed by adequate rest or attention to one's personal needs. In Assam and Burma, high humidity and frequent showers and occasional heavy downpours were expected (Hunter 1963, 16).

During the twenty-five-day trip, few episodes of recurrent malaria were reported, and these were treated in transit. Since arrival in Bombay on 28 October 1943, the men had been in areas where cholera, diphtheria, starvation, amoebic and bacillary dysentery, tuberculosis, malaria, dengue, and other obscure fevers and alimentary disorders were endemic. *Stilwell's Command Problems,* by Charles F. Romanus and Riley Sunderland, became available in 1956 and outlined the incidence of some of the diseases present in the CBI. Among American noncombat personnel there in 1943, medical records recorded 8,136 admissions for malaria, 6,744 for alimentary disorders, 2,637 for venereal disease, and 1,150 for dengue fever. The CBI malaria rate among the American forces was 206 per thousand per year. The high disease incidence among non-combat rear-echelon soldiers—living and working where preventive medicine and optimum medical care were readily available—suggests that combat soldiers living under field conditions would be faced with a very difficult problem in attempting to keep their illness rate to a minimum (Romanus and Sunderland 1956, 286). The prophylactic use of one ata-brine daily had kept malaria attacks to a minimum, and they—up until the beginning of combat—had usually been controlled by rapid ambulatory treatment while remaining on duty.

Security had not been tight since the march from Marg-herita had begun, but now we were on the edge of Japanese-held territory. Patrols were increased, security posted, and the camp was on an alert status.

General Merrill jeeped to Taipha Ga to see General Stilwell and returned with final instructions late at night. A Japanese plane flew overhead at about 1600 but was too high for positive identification.

All day long on 22 February, C-47's flew over the area dropping equipment, rations, and other supplies.

Lt. Col. Chun Lee of the 38th Chinese Division, fighting on the east side of the Hukawng Valley, joined General Merrill's command group as liaison officer. A graduate of Norwich University in the United States, he was a friendly and cheerful officer, on the job twenty-four hours a day.

An air liaison officer joined each combat team. Their job would be to handle radio contact with airdrop aircraft, informing the pilots as to wind conditions, hazards, approaches, and technical problems. They would also deal with supporting fighter aircraft.

As the day of departure into combat approached, no answer was given as to what plans had been or were being made to evacuate the sick and wounded.

CHAPTER VIII
THE MARCH TO WALAWBUM
23 FEBRUARY–3 MARCH 1944

General Merrill Outlines the Tentative Plan of Attack into Japanese Territory

At 0800 General Merrill held a staff conference at which all members of the staff were present, as well as the battalion commanders, combat team commanders, and intelligence and reconnaissance platoon leaders. The general turned to the group with a smile and made the following speech:

> Well, gentlemen, here is what you have been waiting for. We move in the morning, with our general objective to cut the road between Jambu Bum and Shingban and get into the 18th Division [Japanese] Command Post. The enemy situation is shown on this map. The Japanese are located at Mungwam, Taipha Ga, Kaduja Ga, Lanem Ga, Tanja Ga, and on the west bank of the Tawang Hka in the area around Maingkwan, Mashi Daru ferry and Makaw, Lalman Ga, and two Makaws where there is another company dug in.
>
> There is a possibility of artillery at Sina Gahtawng; there is one platoon of Japanese at Shamyan Ga—one battery of artillery south of the Makaw-Wa Gahrtawng area, one platoon of Japanese at Nytem, and some Japanese south of Nytem.
>
> Troops of the 55th Japanese Regiment of the 18th Division, the seasoned jungle division that took Singapore, are east of the main road, and the 56th Regiment is west of the main road. A captured Japanese order indicates that the new defense line will run from Yawngbang Ga to Lakyen Ga.
>
> The Japanese in the Sumprabum area are now practically surrounded by the Kachin levies.
>
> The Japanese are said to have been using balloons for observation in the general area we are entering. We are using no balloons of any sort.

CHAPTER VIII

Lately the Japanese have formed some new battalions consisting of three rifle companies and a machine-gun company.

All that this information does for us is to give us the general picture. We must depend on our own resources for information to make our plans. Therefore, I am taking the intelligence and reconnaissance platoons from all three battalions and placing them directly under my command for our first move.

The First Battalion intelligence and reconnaissance platoon will move by 1130 today on a reconnaissance of Nchang Ga, Ndawng Ga, Nding Ga, Nchaw Ga, Tingreng Ga, Tanja Ga, and Pup Ga.

The Second Battalion intelligence and reconnaissance platoon will make a reconnaissance to Ngukoan Ga, Warong Ga, then north to Nchaw Ga, Ndawng Ga, and Nding Ga. One-half mile east of Nding Ga, turn south on the trail to Lanem Ga to Nruar Ga as far as Maba Tinkrang Ga (south of the First Battalion I & R platoon).

The Third Battalion intelligence and reconnaissance platoon will make a reconnaissance of the trails to Warong Ga, Nchaw Ga, Ndawng Ga, Ngang Ga south to Nkhang Ga, and Kayang to Tingahan Ga.

All intelligence and reconnaissance platoons are to operate under regimental control, communicating through their own battalions until they reach Ngukun Ga. [You are] not to fight unless necessary—your mission is purely reconnaissance.

Each battalion will furnish personnel to leave behind until 26 February to build fires at night in their present battalion areas, as we are practically sure that the Japanese know that we are in this general area. The men left behind will be given the route plan and will rejoin their units after the 26th. I estimate that we will make contact with a sizable force of Japanese on March 2nd. The general route of march will be Ngukun Ga, Warong Ga, Nchaw Ga to the Tarung Hka. The First Battalion will lead out at 0600 hours on 24 February, followed by the Second and the command group at 0800 and the Third Battalion at 1000 (Jones 1944).

No further information was given out as to what route would be followed beyond the Tarung.

A discussion of the troop movement followed, and the meeting broke up. Orders had previously been issued for Lt. Laffin, G-2, to contact the Chinese 38th Division and let the Chinese know our general route, as well as to obtain any late information on trails, Japanese locations, and locations of Chinese patrols and outposts. General Merrill had not at this time been supplied with satisfactory air photos of the area.

Information on more than a day's plans rarely reached the combat teams. In spite of the fact that a battle would soon develop, few of us had any conception of what would be involved. We were not aware at this time that Stilwell's 38th Chinese Division could no longer be called on to face the enemy. Stilwell only had available five Chinese battalions from four regiments plus our force of twenty-four hundred infantry men with fewer than two hundred medics and other support personnel. Few of the officers and none of the rest of the men had any knowledge of what we were to do or where the Chinese would be. The rumor that we were to get in back of the Japanese and attempt to annihilate them would prove to be true. We would be spearheading the Chinese.

The command knew that we would be facing sixty-five hundred men of the Japanese 18th Division plus the Japanese 114th Regiment. The enemy forces were known to have twelve 70mm mountain guns and four 105mm guns. The Americans had no artillery. The Chinese had adequate 75mm pack artillery.

History would later show that, while we were preparing for our first major battle, Lord Louis Mountbatten had a mission in Washington attempting to cancel the Burma Campaign. The Chinese were also against the campaign (Romanus and Sunderland 1956, 162).

There was an air-raid alert at 1900, but the plane could not be seen because of its high altitude.

The Day of Departure

24 February

The First Battalion, carrying two days' C-rations and one day's K-rations, moved out on the trail to Ngukun Ga at 0600, followed by the command group at 0630, the Second Battalion at 0900, and the Third Battalion at 1100.

At this time the reader should clearly understand that many of the officers and men, including the personnel of my Orange Team medical detachment, had only a vague idea of how many Chinese or Japanese were in North Burma or where they were in relation to our regiment. Few if any of our unit knew where the British were or what they were doing or planned to do in the future. This situation was to prevail during the entire campaign. Our information was mostly obtained by rumor.

General Merrill, carrying a musette bag and map case, was leading his command group across the river when a temporary bridge broke as a mule was crossing, throwing the mule into the water on its side. The animal was carrying radio equipment, and it was imperative that the load be salvaged. The muleskinner jumped into the river and held the floundering mule's head above water while several men and an officer removed the load and pack. The mule and load were both saved. A lesson was learned, but such occurrences were to happen frequently.

Just before the unit left Ningbyen, the last mail was turned in for censorship. One letter from a private, who had volunteered from the southwest Pacific, gave his current attitude to his family. He wrote, "My pack is on my back, my gun is oiled and loaded, and as I walk into the shadow of death, I fear no son-of-a-bitch."

After a rather easy march of about fifteen miles, the entire unit had arrived and was attempting to get settled for the night at the abandoned small village of Ngukun Ga. All combat precautions were being taken. I noticed a very definite change in the actions and attitude of the men. The combat veterans understood and the others knew that D day had passed, and the enemy could be encountered at any time. We were now in a situation where an instant's hesitation or wrong move could mean life or death. Each man had a supply of suppressive atabrine that would be replenished as necessary, and he knew that he must take one tablet daily to prevent his first attack of malaria—or a recurrence, if he had been infected before.

This was a great night for sleep, with good weather, and all not on duty rested on the jungle floor. The fatigue of most was too great for arousal as a green flare lit up the sky nearby. Some said this was a signal from a Japanese patrol that Americans were on the march.

The First Battle Casualty

25 February

The battalions moved out in the same order as on the previous day and took a two-day ration drop at Warong Ga.

General Merrill and Colonel Lee rode horseback several miles to the west on safe jungle trails to Tumphang, where they contacted troops of the 38th Chinese Division.

At 1115 the Third Battalion Orange Combat Team I & R platoon, under the command of Lt. Logan E. Weston, turned to the right at Ndawng Ga to check for Japanese activity at Nzang Ga. At Ndawng they were about twenty miles southeast of Ningbyen and five miles ahead of the unit. After four miles they neared the small village of Nzang Ga. The lead scout, Corporal Werner Katz, just ahead of Weston, motioned halt and stopped to listen. The jungle was very thick on each side of the foot path. Weston and Katz had a quick meeting as Katz explained that he had heard sounds ahead. Weston had great confidence in Werner Katz's judgment. Both were veterans of Pacific combat, and Katz had become a naturalized citizen since he had fought in the Spanish Civil War. We all knew him to be one of Weston's hand-picked men.

Werner had every right to say, "It could be Chinese." Everyone knew that the Chinese had been and were fighting somewhere to our right. The rumor was that the fighting was twenty miles or more to the southwest. Logan advised him to be careful and not to shoot unless he was certain they were not Chinese or natives. Two scouts joined Logan, and they moved into firing positions. A few steps further, at a bend in the trail, Werner said, "They're Chinese. They are waving us to come on." A few yards ahead he had seen a smiling soldier motioning for him to come on. A moment later the man lowered his arm and two machine guns opened up. Katz went down into a slight depression as he fired. As he continued to fire, a rifle bullet grazed his nose. The fire of Katz, Weston, and the scouts either drove the enemy off or eliminated them. One could be seen sprawled in the dirt of the trail. The men estimated that four dead were in the jungle growth.

When they became disengaged, Weston and his men fell back to prevent the Japanese from cutting them off. At this time their job was to locate the enemy and not engage in extensive fire fights.

The platoon arrived back at Ndawng Ga just as I was passing through with the Orange Combat Team's medical detachment head-quarters, which on the march and in combat consisted of one or two doctors, two or three aid men (medical technicians), and two pack-horses. The I & R aid man, Sgt. Gomez, had done a good job not only in attending to Werner's wound but also steadying the nerves of one or two of the men. Katz was somewhat embarrassed by the wound but ready to continue with his platoon. He was soon informed that he had the dubious honor of being the first Marauder wounded in combat and also the first to kill one of the enemy. It was also a fact that this skirmish was the first American infantry action against the Japanese on the Asiatic continent during World War II and the first since the Boxer Rebellion in China in 1900.

The Death of Private Robert Landis

About the same time Weston's platoon engaged the Japanese, Lt. William C. Grissom's platoon was about seven miles from the deserted village of Lanem Ga, located three miles to the right of the trail that the unit was scheduled to advance on. The platoon came near the village at 1400 hours. Pvt. Robert W. Landis of Youngstown, Ohio, a veteran of the New Georgia battle, was the lead scout. Suddenly an unseen Japanese machine gun opened fire from about fifty yards. Bob Landis was instantly killed. The I & R patrol engaged the Japanese and found that a platoon was well dug in on high ground in the village. Since the Japanese had several machine guns covering the spot where this gallant scout had been killed, they were not able to recover his body. A messenger was sent back to the main body, and they set up an ambush along the trail.

During the day, artillery, mortar, machine-gun, and rifle fire could be heard several miles to the west, where the Chinese and Japanese were engaged in a battle.

26 February

Lt. Grissom and his men returned to Lanem Ga after his scouts determined that the Japanese had left at dawn. There was now no need to attack the village. The body of Private Robert Landis was recovered. His clothing and equipment had been taken. While a prayer was said, he was buried on a green hill near the center of the village.

The word of his death soon reached the other battalions. When he volunteered he had been assigned to the Third Battalion before being sent to the Second, in order to give them a cadre of battle-wise men. The mood of the men in my group changed noticeably when they learned of his death. He had been well liked and highly respected. In combat the front-line men are linked as brothers, and the death of one always leaves a void. There is sadness for the loss of a friend, deep feeling for his family, and the thought that *it might have been me.* Some develop an inner rage at the system that forces men to kill each other. Why did this happen? Could it have been avoided by better training, more fire power, better equipment, or more intelligent orders from higher authority? Was this particular military move necessary?

Bob was a veteran of the Pacific fighting, where he had been an infantryman in the 37th Division. I had met and talked with him several times. He was a good-looking, well-developed, intelligent, cooperative, patriotic young man who, like most of our men, was going all-out to serve his country. In combat, the riflemen—and especially the scouts—end up comprising the greater percentage of the dead and wounded.

The Marauders Reach the Tawang Hka

At 0700 General Merrill met the battalion commanders on the bank of a small stream at Warong Ga for a brief conference. The Third Battalion moved out in the lead, followed by the command group at 0740, the Second at 0900 and the First at 1030. The three battalions, traveling single-file, together stretched out over a distance of about six miles. The entire unit marched eleven miles through rain and over muddy trails to the village of Nchaw Ga. There was still a noticeable change in the men. Eyes that, a few days before, had looked wearily at the ground during the hot, musty march were alert, searching every tree along the trail for signs of the enemy. The entire unit was security conscious, and each route of approach was blocked by ambush and booby traps while the column was passing through. From time to time, I tried to imagine the thoughts of the scouts and the men in the I & R platoons, always leading.

During the march we passed a number of abandoned Kachin villages. Near them were built-up grave mounds where they buried the bodies of their dead. A ditch around the mound was dug to keep the spirit in, and offerings of roots and leaves were placed in the little Buddhist shrine close beside the mound. If several people died, a buffalo would have been killed and the uneaten portion offered as a sacrifice for the dead.

The command group arrived at Hchaw Ga at 1400, and shortly thereafter two pigeons were released with drop messages for the air base. A staff meeting was held at 1800, at which time orders were given out for the next day's march.

All I & R platoons were reporting by radio, by messenger, and in a few cases by their leader. Their activity was giving General Merrill a picture of the enemy situation on all sides and on the important trails. The probing fingers of the reconnaissance patrols were becoming increasingly important.

Lt. Samuel V. Wilson's intelligence and reconnaissance platoon had penetrated to the Tawang Hka, a distance of thirty miles from Ningbyen. On the 25th, while advancing toward their destination of the Tawang, they had first heard machine-gun activity when Katz was wounded and later the noise of the fire fight when Landis was killed. This was their second day on the trail. At that time they instinctively knew that Japanese were between them and the main unit. To many, this was as if they had been struck in the gut. When you suddenly realize that you are cut off from supply and friendly forces, a temporary uneasy sensation usually develops. It is something like the feeling one gets after being involved in an auto accident or when a pistol is thrust into your ribcage at the onset of a holdup.

It is certain that many in Wilson's platoon wished they could abort their mission of checking the trail to Tanja Ga and the nearby Tawang Hka. The platoon went forward, however, and—in spite of the personal tension, the fatigue, and the humid, hot weather—they reached and cautiously entered the village, which was deserted. Defensive emplacements were plentiful but empty. The surrounding area, including the river, was scouted, and the time came to report to General Merrill. The SCR 284 was set up and contact was made at the proper hour for the regimental net to open, but it was lost before a message could be passed.

Sam Wilson knew that the message had to reach General Merrill. In spite of having been two days on the trail, he mounted a splendid black horse, Pride-and-Joy, and in company with another rider took off at 2200 hours on what would prove to be a twenty-two-mile ride. All went well until the horse lurched while crossing a small creek. This loosened the girth, and the saddle turned—throwing him beneath the animal with one foot still in the stirrup. Just at this time, snarling and spitting broke out down the trail: Two creatures—possibly leopards or tigers—were fighting, Fortunately his horse was calm, and he was able to extricate himself and remount. With more bad luck he could have been trampled and dragged or attacked by the wild creatures.

Miles later, as the horses reached a clearing, his helmet fell off. He dismounted to retrieve the helmet and decided to inspect the clearing. Suddenly he found himself at the end of a gun. He had run into Lt. Grissom's platoon. They were dug in, awaiting a possible attack from the enemy who had killed Landis. They could have easily mistaken the two American soldiers for the enemy.

Four miles further on, the visibility was better—and Logan Weston stepped onto the trail to unexpectedly greet him. Weston's platoon had been blocking the trail leading to the village where they had a fire fight.

Merrill and Hunter were now ready to plan for further advance toward the Taja Ga and the river. The two men soon mounted their horses for the ride back to their platoon.

27 February

The Third Battalion left Nchaw Ga at 0700 and arrived at Tanja Ga at 1100, where a drop of rations—three days' K-ration and one day C-ration—was taken. Colonel Hunter continued to put into practice the extensive plans he had drawn up earlier to cover all aspects of a perfect air drop.

One of the regiment's carrier pigeons committed suicide by hanging himself in his cage during the night.

All concerned were beginning to clearly understand the rules to be followed during and in bivouac as well as during any contact with the enemy. It was now apparent that the bivouac area would extend three to six miles. Sometimes a section of the unit would be able to bivouac in cleared village area; at other times most—if not all—of the men had to find a place to eat, rest, and sleep beside the trail. One battalion would be ahead, one in the middle, and one in the rear. They would protect each other. All flanks and trails had to be blocked at rest and on the march.

The command staff had to try, at all times, to determine where the Chinese and the Japanese were located. Much of the responsibility was placed on Lt. Laffin. He had a very close call on the 27th while contacting the 38th Chinese Division.

At 1500 hours, the lead units had reached the Tawang Hka—but, because of the late hour, crossing was delayed until the next day.

General Stilwell Alerts the Marauders of Possible Mission at Walawbum

28 February

Much of the day of the 28th was for rest and organization. A liaison plane flew over Tanja Ga in the morning and dropped messages but had no hook to pick up messages. The Second Battalion pioneer and demolition platoon was ordered to prepare a landing strip out of a cleared area in the village. The L-4 plane returned several hours later with messages. The pilot, Technical Sergeant William G. Coleman of Fort Worth, Texas, made a safe landing on the rough field. Before we left the area the plane cracked up twice, but during the following weeks was repaired successfully. The passenger on the first flight was Major Williams. He brought orders from General Stilwell for the unit to move as fast as possible on Walawbum and block the retreat of the Japanese along the main road to Kamaing. The message further stated that the Chinese were putting heavy pressure on Maingkwan. As far as the battalions were concerned, they knew nothing about whatever information General Merrill had been given.

Eating their K-rations before dark, the men of the Third Battalion—followed by the Second and then the command group—crossed the Tawang Hka. The First was in reserve and was scheduled to cross in the morning. From bank to bank the river was about a mile wide. Since this was the dry season, the crossing was not difficult—but it did mean that we would sleep in wet clothes.

29 February (Leap Year)

With the Third Battalion leading, the Second Battalion and the command group—followed by the First Battalion—left the vicinity of the Tawang Hka at 0900, marching to Ngalang Ga and on to Owisu Ga for the night. We had crossed the Pabyi Hka at Ngalang Ga. This was as far east as we would go on this, our first mission. At that time few knew what the mission was. By air we were twenty-eight miles from Ningbyen, but far more by the route we had followed.

At one time during the day, Orange Combat's communications section was resting beside the trail as General Merrill and members of his command group came along. David Hurwitt was sitting with the radio communication section of Orange Combat Team and met General Merrill. He explains how this happened:

> I didn't get to meet General Merrill when he first arrived with our outfit because I was sort of absent—a sort of unauthorized absence, usually known as AWOL, in Bombay. When I got back I saw Merrill occasionally—you know, it was a rather unsocial type of arrangement—but I really didn't get to know him until we were marching through the Hukawng Valley and were entering the mountains. We were taking ten one day, and I had a little messenger on the radio team by the name of Benny Silverman. Benny was very small but a tough guy. We didn't know where in the hell we were going. Benny turned to me and said, "Hey, Sarge, where in the hell are we going?" So I looked at him and said, "Why in hell are you asking me—why don't you ask the general?" I'll be damned if little Benny Silverman doesn't yell out, "Hey, General! Where the f--- are we going?" Well, you know, if the earth could have swallowed me up or I could have dug a foxhole then and there, I would have been tremendously pleased. In any case the measure of the man showed up then and there. He smiled at us, came over and sat down, and said, "Sergeant, where are you from?" He could see the shadow of the stripes that had been pulled off. I said, "Oh, I have been to Guadalcanal and New

Georgia," and he nodded. He then questioned a couple of other guys, and then he pulled out his map case and pulled out some maps. He then started telling us where we were going. And the more he related to us the whiter I got. He was telling us we were going to attack the Japanese headquarters. I kicked myself and said to myself, Why did I ask this dumb little bastard to ask the general, and why didn't he keep his mouth shut? Well, after the general got done with his briefing he got up and said, "Okay, fellers?" We had about enough strength to nod. You know no general acts like this to a couple of enlisted men. I just shook my head in amazement and looked at Benny and said, "You little son-of-a-bitch, if you ever do that again I'll belt you," and he looked at me and said, "Well, you are the sergeant—why the f--- did you let me talk like that to a general?" I tell you that was a measure of our guy. He was the kind of man you could get to love, and I did—all the way up to Nhpum Ga, when I got it [wounded].

I guess it's the kind of thing you never forget. I remember him [Merrill] coming to reunions every year and telling us that we had the greatest outfit in the world, and you know, I think we got to believe him. Our officers were the best in the world—and I guess that's what made us the best. I tell you what I do remember, and I guess it's a little funny because it was in the midst of the heat of battle. You go into a war and I suppose before the war you have a kind of an intellectual opposition to war. You know you are going to meet the enemy and I suppose it's kill or be killed. At Walawbum, what I remember was the banzai charges from across the river and watching in amazement as I fired my carbine at these little soldiers coming across and they kept on coming. In the heat of battle—I don't know how many guys remember this, but a lot of Japanese knew English—I distinctly remember them shouting insults by yelling, "Eleanor eats C-rations" or "Eleanor eats powdered eggs," and I remember Blackjack, that's one of our majors, Major Petito, rushing out in the middle of this battle and making us laugh like hell as he yelled, "Tojo eats shit." But it was no laughing matter as we started running out of ammunition. That's what I remember—these guys coming across and yelling these obscenities at each other (Hurwitt, videotape).

Bob Bryant, international news photographer, flew in with Sergeant Coleman and landed on a rocky sand bar one mile south of

Nbang Ga. The sergeant said it took fifteen minutes to fly from Taipa Ga, General Stilwell's headquarters.

1 March

On the 1st of March, the unit marched into the area around Nytem, where the Third Battalion set up a defense preparatory to receiving an airdrop and made a feint toward Hakaw to deceive the Japanese. The other battalions rested along the riverbank. The march had been long and difficult for the men and animals. We had made eight river crossings in the crisscrossing route along the Pabyi Hka.

Captain Evan Darlington, British liaison officer from the Government of Burma, was welcomed by the villagers around Nytem with gifts of rice beer, chickens, eggs, and rice wine. He was a political officer for the area before the war, and that entailed being lawyer, doctor, preacher, and judge to the people of his area. They apparently thought very highly of him, for he was welcomed as a long-lost friend. These villagers had been badly treated by the Japanese and the Burmans. There was evidence of Japanese atrocities, and one of our patrols found several Kachins hanging by their necks in an abandoned village nearby. The villagers were glad to see the Americans, and the chief or headman was greatly impressed by General Merrill and told him that some of his men would join him if they had guns and some of those with guns (ancient muzzle loaders) would join if the general would take them.

General Merrill persuaded the headman that he would need all the people to protect their village and to plant the rice crop, but that they would do a great favor for the Americans by caring for two American soldiers who were too sick to march, and bring them to the unit in a week or so when they were notified that the trail was free of Japanese. The headman was overjoyed to have the Americans and moved them into his own basha.

Much good information about recent Japanese activity was obtained from the Kachins.

The bare-breasted women made quite a hit with the Marauders, and the naked little children quickly lost their fear of the soldiers and were soon munching K-ration crackers given them by the men.

CHAPTER VIII

Late in the afternoon a liaison plane came over and dropped a message saying that the day's airdrop was off and that it would be made on 2 March at a sand bar where the trail crossed the Tanai Hka. The mixup was due to radio code misfiring, and steps were being taken to find the reason and eliminate it.

When the Tanai Hka was reached, two platoons quickly crossed and secured the area where the drop was to take place. The rest of the battalion then crossed. The hour was late before the Second Battalion, the command group, and the First Battalion could reach the river. They continued late into the night, but after slow progress in the dark they were forced to bed down for the night along the rough trail where the jungle was dense on all sides.

The command staff knew that we were now approaching Walawbum, the area where a battle might take place.

First Mission: Block Japanese Supply Road and Escape Route at Walawbum

2 March

The men of the Third Battalion had until the late afternoon to rest and bathe in the Tanai Hka. All battalions were assembled at this, the drop area, by 1300.

Just before the expected drop, General Merrill met with the battalion commanders and issued the orders for the first mission. The plan was that the Chinese, now just north of Maingkwan, would attack down the road in conjunction with the First Provisional Tank Group. The 5307th would establish two roadblocks on the Kamaing Road in the section from Kumnyn Ga to Walawbum.

Colonel Beach had orders to move via Sabaw Ga and Lagang Ga to Walawbum, seize the high ground on the east side of the Numpyek Hka, and dig in, covering the main road to Kamaing with mortar and machine-gun fire and preventing the Japanese from retreating southward along the main road. Colonel McGee was ordered to move the Second Battalion to Wesu Ga about one-and-a-half miles north of Lagang Ga and three miles north of Walawbum. He was then to cross the Numpyek Hka and cut a trail through the jungle to the main road two-and-a-half miles west of Walawbum, which would put his battalion five miles west of Wesu Ga. At the road, he was to construct and hold a block.

Colonel Osborne's First Battalion was to block trails at Sana Ga and Nchet Ga to prevent Japanese movement southward, with one platoon along the Nambyu Hka between Shimak Ga and Uga Ga and the remainder of one combat team held in reserve at Wesu Ga. This combat team would be committed if a suitable opportunity presented itself.

Just as the conference was over, the first drop plane arrived with three days' K-rations and three days' grain, plus ammunition and equipment. While the airdrop was in progress, the Third Battalion was suddenly ordered to pull out. Rations were still being dropped, and as the single-file column passed, one day's ration was given out for each man and animal. This was obviously not enough, but speed was suddenly said to be essential—and the battalion departed at 1600. As we crossed the river toward the west, a soldier slipped on the steep riverbank, severely injuring and perhaps fracturing his shoulder. He was left behind for the regimental surgeon, Major Schudmak, to arrange for evacuation or rest with the Kachins. Up until this time, the Third Battalion had lost few to injury or illness. At Ningbyen a young lieutenant had to be sent out because of emotional problems.

Lt. Logan Weston's I & R platoon was soon far ahead, scouting the route. Lagang Ga was about sixteen miles, and the night march would take us across two rivers and numerous small streams. The battalion commander kept us moving in spite of total darkness. In six hours the column moved about eight miles. The men grew increasingly angry with what they considered the stupidity of marching on a difficult narrow jungle trail without light. After three or four hours, many complained of great fatigue and extreme desire to sleep. I remember falling asleep during several fifteen-minute rest periods. Decaying vegetable matter from the jungle floor, which tended to glow in the dark, was placed on many men's packs as they led the way. After six or seven hours the order was finally given to stop and sleep beside the trail.

The Second Battalion pulled out at 1645 and marched with great difficulty in the dark. They, like the First Battalion and the command group, were oversupplied with food and ammunition. Some extra ammunition and special equipment was hidden in the jungle to be picked up later. The command group crossed the wide Tanai Hka (Chindwin) in waist-deep water and walked five miles to Gum Ga, where they bivouacked for the night.

CHAPTER IX
THE BATTLE OF WALAWBUM
3–11 MARCH 1944

Skirmish Before Lagang Ga

3 March

Orange Column's I & R, under Lt. Logan Weston, was approaching Lagang Ga as the early-morning mist was clearing. Suddenly a huge elephant appeared. The platoon's mules bolted, as did the elephant. The platoon lost several hours rounding up the mules with their precious cargo of weapons and ammunition. Then, a half-mile from Lagang Ga, there was a burst of fire from up the trail. The standard operating procedure of the platoon went immediately into action. The lead scout took cover, and the lead squad plunged to the right, establishing a base of fire. The two following squads entered the jungle, one to the right and one to the left. With this set-up, the platoon moved forward to outflank the enemy. The squads gradually converged toward the trail to catch the Japanese at the far end of the so-called Japanese S-shaped machine-gun ambush. Since they were being outflanked, the enemy moved further down the trail. At each contact the Americans would go through the same outflanking procedure. The Japanese soon knew that they had more than met their match and broke off the engagement.

Orange's Ambush at Lagang Ga

Orange Combat Team led the Third Battalion in at noon shortly after the I & R had dispersed the enemy. The men in the Third Battalion were in a better mood than they had been during the first part of the night march because they had finally been allowed to get a few hours' sleep. The eight or nine miles were covered rapidly. As dawn was breaking a strange occurrence took place. Charles E. Beck,

CHAPTER IX

a BAR (Browning automatic rifle) man in Orange Column, reminds me of it in a letter. He was born in Circus City (Peru, Indiana). This was the home of Hagenbeck, Wallace, and Sells Floto Circus. When he was ten, his mother took him to see their spring rodeo. Several elephants were doing their act, and one got spooked and started running through the crowd toward the circus barn. He had been terrified as the elephant ran close by. Here on the trail to Walawbum, in the early and foggy morning, his BAR was leaning on a tree and he was mixing his powdered coffee. Suddenly he heard a clang, clang, clang and grabbed his BAR. When he looked up there was a spooked elephant, with a big gash on its head and broken chain on its leg, running through the camp. The elephant was coming directly for Charley, who was surprised and frozen in place. Suddenly the elephant veered off to the right and disappeared into the jungle. The experience—being the second of its kind in his life for this man—was as strange as it was unforgettable. A second elephant was also seen here.

The main body of the Third Battalion, with Orange in the lead, arrived several hours later, marching in single file. We were soon strung out along the left border of the deserted village of Lagang Ga, where all was quiet. To our right was a ragged two-acre area cleared of jungle growth. This could be called the village green. In the right far corner were several typical structures, made of bamboo and reed and elevated four feet from the ground on stilts. Dense jungle was on the left flank. The river ran directly north and south on the opposite side of the village. Straight ahead and to the south our trail entered the jungle just to the left of the river, where it continued two miles to reach Walawbum. Orange I & R was now leading, followed closely by Colonel Beach with a small group from the Third Battalion headquarters, one-half of Company I, medical detachment, pioneer and demolition, heavy weapons platoon, and the other half of I Company.

The column was moving very slowly since Colonel Beach and his staff were having a conference with Lieutenant Weston a few yards into the trail, which led south from the village and ran along the east border of the river toward Walawbum.

Word came along the column to stop and get the animals into the jungle. Dan Hardinger, one of my favorite aid men, and I suddenly spotted seven men trotting along a north-to-south trail running

144

between the village green and the river. They were carrying a litter. They suddenly stopped, and a Japanese in front raised a Nambu light machine gun. All hell broke loose. Many men fired, and five of the enemy were instantly killed. Two disappeared toward the river but were later shot. Most of the column stayed in place in a firing position, but Colonel Beach and his intelligence officer Capt. John B. George, a noted marksman, came to inspect the bodies. George states in his book, *Shots Fired in Anger*, that he and others were sitting on their packs surrounded by hip-high grass when they observed enemy soldiers approaching and had carefully identified them at seventy yards. As they came closer he identified the shoulder patch and the Nambu M-1922 as unmistakably Japanese. He stated that his first shot got the lead man and the others were hit by many missiles. All had weapons and none red-cross arm bands. A leather medical bag was found in the area, and there on its side was a red cross. The bag was brought to me, and I was surprised to find that it contained some Xeroform powder and a few ampules of medicine, emetine hydrochloride, used to treat amoebic dysentery and manufactured by Hynson, Wescott and Dunning of Baltimore, Maryland—my home town.

Lt. Pat Perrone, a veteran of the New Georgia Island campaign, has provided me with his account of the demise of the Japanese patrol at Lagang Ga on 3 March 1944.

Prior to the Japanese patrol having been taken under physical observation at the time it left the cover of the opposite brush line and entered the Lagang Ga clearing, Perrone had sensed its presence and had informed the men near him that Japanese were in the area. No one, including Perrone, could locate any Japanese, and some of the men started to laugh. There were a few crude remarks until Dave Hurwitt said, "If Perrone says that there are Japanese over there, there are Japanese over there—he can smell them." Perrone, Hurwitt, and the air liaison officer—possibly Buzz Seward (2nd Lt. John L. Seward, Air Corps)—used a set of binoculars to check the opposite side of the clearing without success. Finally, Perrone had to accept that his sixth sense for impending danger might be wrong for once; but it wouldn't go away. Perrone could see the joke following the rest of his military career—"Perrone and the Japanese who weren't!" Since lives were at stake, Perrone decided to go across the clearing and reconnoiter the area. He had taken two or three steps when Buzz Seward excitedly said, "There are people over there, probably Japanese." Seward, who was undergoing his first experience with the infantry, had continued to observe the opposite brush line with the binoculars and therefore was the first person to sight the Japanese. He gave the binoculars to Perrone, who immediately identified the one individual who could be seen as Japanese. There were others in the brush who could not be seen clearly, and there was no way to determine the strength or composition of the Japanese. Perrone took command and ordered the Marauders on the trail to take ambush positions directly in the brush behind them. He directed that word of the Japanese presence be passed up and down the line to alert the Third Battalion headquarters and the Orange and Khaki Combat Teams and to permit the battalion commander to take over command and control the situation.

About eight or nine mules had come out of the brush to enjoy the grass and had to be moved back under cover. Perrone ordered the pick-up ambush group to remain in position, and said there would be no firing until he gave the command.

Perrone had the binoculars and kept the Japanese under observation as they finally broke cover and left the brush to take the trail leading to the Walawbum trail, which would put them behind the Third Battalion headquarters. After the patrol left the brush it was under the direct observation of Perry Johnson, 1st. Lt. Vernon Beard, Tony Colombo, Paulson, Hurwitt, and Perrone, and continued to be under that observation until Perrone gave the order to fire at the secondary ambush site.

At the primary ambush site Perrone gave a preliminary order to fire on his command, and someone in the line, identity unknown, said, "Pat, let them come closer so we can get a better shot at them." Because Perrone was concerned about possible other Japanese units following the patrol and because killing the patrol at the secondary site would allow the opportunity of determining the strength and composition of any other Japanese troops, Perrone agreed.

At the secondary ambush site, when the Japanese armed with the light machine gun became aware of the danger, Perrone gave the order to fire. No shots were fired prior to that order. There was one blast fired from the ambush group, followed by some shots to our left up the Walawbum trail. Perrone ordered the ambush group to remain in position, since other Japanese troops might follow the patrol.

The ambush group was still in position when Lieutenant Colonel Beach, George, two others, and Sweeney ran out of the Walawbum trail into the clearing to the Japanese bodies. They ran so fast without stopping to check that we had no opportunity to warn them of the potential danger of a counter-ambush. We remained in position to provide covering fire.

Finally, when it was apparent that they had been lucky and were still alive, Perrone got up to report to the battalion commander and to suggest that the Lagang Ga clearing probably was not the healthiest place to stand around discussing the situation. George intervened and informed Perrone that they didn't require his assistance. Disgusted, Perrone left them to their own devices, crossed over to the opposite brushline to check for any sign of Japanese, and returned to his ambush position. This was the only combat action that took place at Lagang Ga during the afternoon of 3 March.

Perrone was thankful that the Lagang Ga ambush ended as a minor combat incident. Here was an improvised ambush that resolved the situation within the ambush group's capabilities. It could not be considered a fire fight, since the Japanese force was only a small unit, was taken completely by surprise, and was unable to fire one round in its defense. The primary objective of an ambush—to destroy the enemy without any threat of casualties to the ambushers—had been accomplished.

Orange Combat Team Advances toward Walawbum

The Third Battalion had been alerted for an airdrop at Lagang Ga during the afternoon of the 3rd. The drop was necessary prior to the battalion's moving into a blocking position at Walawbum, as the men needed more ammunition and only had one meal left. The planes arrived and circled, but for some reason the drop was aborted. Pat Perrone had been put in charge of the airdrop detail and, when it was aborted, was ordered to remain with a detail of men and animals for a rescheduled drop on 4 March.

In the late afternoon, Khaki Combat Team, Third Battalion, was left to occupy Lagang Ga and guard the trails while remaining in reserve. Weston's I & R, Colonel Beach, and Orange Combat Team advanced about a mile along the trail to Walawbum as it wound along the east side of the Numpyek Hka. Just before dark, Colonel Beach sent Logan Weston's I & R platoon across the river in order to gather information and protect the right flank of Orange. The I & R men found themselves in a swampy area where they had to spend a restless night.

Men of the Third Battalion consumed the one meal remaining in their packs. For Orange Combat Team it would be the last meal until the morning of 7 March.

On this day Tony Colombo had been chosen by Lt. Ted Hughes to be Colonel Beach's runner. Tony states:

> I went up to be Beach's runner. Well, the job—for the most part what I was doing—was just hustling along the trail to see if anything was happening. He really didn't need a runner. There was no place to run too far. He would send me up to see Logan Weston, and at that time there was not that much distance between us. I operated between the two combat teams, hustled food, and wound up as more or less a body guard for Father Barrett (when he finally came in) and Doctor Armstrong and Doctor Hopkins. Sometimes they were sent out on the job where the bullets were flying. I would be in there with them. One guy was there to preach, one guy was there to tend to their wounds, and I was there to protect them. Well, anyhow it worked out (Colombo, videotape).

Lieutenant Duncan's I & R from Khaki Combat Team Meets the Enemy

Near Lagang Ga, Lieutenant Duncan and his men came upon a group of Japanese who tried to get a machine gun into action. The Americans opened fire and advanced rapidly. They picked up three Japanese bodies and took over several hunks of raw beef the Japanese were preparing to cook.

Second Battalion Blunts an Ambush

The Second Battalion moved out in the early morning. They had ten miles to go over a rough trail before reaching Wesu Ga. At 0945, the point was fired on by an undetermined number of enemy, who then pulled out. At 1400 hours the Second passed through Green

Combat Team's I & R platoon, which had outposted the night's bivouac, and proceeded toward Wesu Ga. Shortly before Wesu Ga, the
point received enemy fire but the enemy soon withdrew. Blue Combat
Team's I & R was in the lead and continued on to meet more enemy at
1400. Just before Wesu Ga, a Japanese patrol opened fire from the
opposite side of a small open field. The lead scout fell to the ground,
and the Japanese— thinking he was killed—rushed forward. The scout
raised up and fired a full magazine from his tommy gun, killing two of
the Japanese and putting five others to flight, and the Second Battalion
moved on. Some evidence of enemy presence was found in the village.
An attack was organized in the late afternoon, and Wesu Ga was overrun. The enemy had fled.

No one except the men of the intelligence and reconnaissance platoons had seen any live Japanese up to this time, and the men behind
were itching to see something. Planes flew overhead, off and on, during
the day—and on two occasions all men and animals got off the trail, as
enemy planes were overhead. At times such as this, we really heard
cursing from the muleskinners. A Missouri mule—or any mule, for that
matter—doesn't like to be pulled off the trail where he can't see the
other mules, and when a mule with three hundred pounds on his back
says no—well, it's plenty tough to change its mind. Finally a system of
taking the mules off in pairs solved the problems, and the animals readily took cover.

The Second Battalion pulled out of Wesu Ga at 1930 and, after
crossing the Numpyek Hka, bivouacked at 2300 on the other side of
this small river in tall elephant grass (McGee 1987).

First Battalion Takes Its Position Near Wesu Ga

As night fell on 3 March, the First Battalion and the command
group bivouacked in the vicinity of Sabaw Ga with plans to move to
Wesu Ga in the morning. Their mission was to block all trails leading
into Lagang Ga and Wesu Ga. They would also control the airdrops,
receive and distribute supplies, start casualties through a chain of
evacuation, and remain in reserve.

CHAPTER IX

Colonel Beach Has a Close Call

4 March

During the early morning the colonel's small group was suddenly confronted with an armed Japanese on the trail. Sweeney, his orderly, reacted quickly and blew his skull away from his brain. This gruesome sight was on the trail for all to see.

Orange I & R and the Battle across the River

At dawn, Lieutenant Weston's platoon was still located in the swampy area on the west side of the Numpyek Hka. The fog was dense, but he was able to quickly move the platoon to higher ground three hundred yards southwest of the previous location.

Logan Weston tells what happened that morning in *The Fightin' Preacher:*

> Although we had faced the enemy quite frequently in the South Pacific, we were always part of a larger unit. Now we were on our own. We were isolated, and in the process of accomplishing our mission we had been surrounded. The lives of the men with whom I had trained, and for whom I felt responsible, were in jeopardy. To honor them, I feel that it is appropriate to use their names in the following document:
>
> The men began to dig in as soon as we reached the knoll. Half an hour or so later, Pete Leightner, one of the scouts, was in front of the perimeter collecting branches to camouflage his foxhole. Suddenly, a rapid burst of machine-gun fire split the eerie silence. Leightner was hit in the middle and crumpled to the ground, severely wounded. Before anyone could put a fix on the Japanese machine gunner, he disappeared in the dense jungle. Sergeant Paul Mathis, the platoon guide, and I crawled out and dragged Leightner back to the perimeter for safety. The men jumped into their slit trenches and braced themselves for a Japanese attack. They didn't have to wait very long. Through the brush, we could see the tan uniforms of the Japanese coming toward us, some with twigs sticking out of their helmets for camouflage. They were crouching, walking slowly toward our position. As soon as they were in range, we opened fire. The enemy soldiers hit the ground and fanned out, crawling closer and shooting ferociously. They

chattered among themselves; some seemed to be giving orders. Then came the hollow snap of knee-mortars being discharged from behind their front-line troops. Seconds later, the mortar shells exploded in the trees over our men. The mortars started coming in salvos, showering shrapnel throughout the entire area.

"Watch for five Japanese coming around the right flank!" somebody yelled. Sergeant John Gately spotted the first one and killed him. Private Harold Hudson glimpsed the other four and started his tommy gun at the rear of the quartet, mowing them down in a row. The main Japanese attack was coming in the center sector of my platoon's defense. A squad of enemy soldiers moved in closer, crawling, running a few steps, hitting the ground, creeping closer, and shooting.

Sergeant William Grimes added to his New Guinea record of twenty-five enemy by pumping shells into each Japanese who lifted his head within sight. Private Raymond Harris sprayed the attacking squad with his Browning automatic rifle. An enemy soldier managed to creep within fifteen feet of his position, shooting at Harris just as he ducked his head to put a new magazine in his Browning. The bullet dented his helmet.

Inside the perimeter, my platoon sergeant, Alfred Greer, relayed a message to me from the radioman, Private Benny Silverman. The main body of the Marauders, he said, had driven the enemy from the opposite bank of the river and had reached their position near Walawbum. "Fine," I told Greer. "Let's get them to help us over here with their mortars."

I had Silverman radio back our estimate of the Japanese positions based on the grid map. Soon the crack of a mortar discharge answered from across the river. An 81-millimeter mortar shell burst with a hollow boom behind the Japanese. I gave Silverman new elevation and azimuth figures. The next one burst a little closer, but was still too far from the first one.

"Anybody got a compass with mills on it instead of degrees?" I shouted over the noise. Near me, aid man Corporal Joe Gomez had just finished pouring sulfanilamide powder into Leightner's stomach wounds. He was working on the mortally wounded Sergeant Lionel Paquette, who had been hit in the head by a mortar tree blast. Unfortunately he had previously lost his helmet and had not been able to replace it. Gomez opened a pouch at his belt and handed me his compass. "We medics have got everything," he grinned.

CHAPTER IX

Greer told the mortars to lay in a smoke shell, then he took an azimuth reading on the new compass. I gave Silverman a new set of figures, which he radioed to the mortar crew.

Meanwhile, across the river, Lieutenant "Boomer" Woomer and his mortar crew set the figures on the mortar sights and lobbed over another shell. Using my observation and calculations, the mortars were soon right on the target. I would then vary the figures every few rounds to cover the enemy from flank to flank, surrounding three sides of my perimeter defense.

"Nice going, boys!" I yelled after a series of six bursts. "We just saw some Japanese blown out of their position less than twenty yards from our men."

As fast as the mortar men could rip open shell cases, they poured fire across the river. Still, the Japanese kept coming. They edged into positions on all three sides of our platoon perimeter, and were even trying to get between us and the river. Their machine gun and rifle fire intensified. We tried to keep up with an artillery barrage that had developed, but our ammunition supply was getting pretty low. I estimated that there was a company of at least two hundred Japanese troops opposing us.

Suddenly Silverman got an order on the walkie-talkie for our platoon to withdraw and join the battalion on the other side of the river. Our mission, it seemed, had been accomplished. While we had been distracting the Japanese unit, the main body of the Marauders (Orange Combat Team) had moved into position to our south and was prepared to make a direct attack on Walawbum.

Greer, Silverman, and a couple of the others buttoned fatigue jackets over bamboo poles to create some makeshift litters with which to carry the wounded back across the river. Under cover of mortar fire, our I & R platoon withdrew to the riverbank and prepared to cross.

The Japanese had been following us, attempting to maintain contact and attack when we were exposed during the river crossing. Across the river, BAR gunners and riflemen from our battalion opened fire to cover the river crossing of our men. Bullets whined over our heads. I told Silverman to radio that the Japanese were at our flanks, ready to knock off our men as they crossed the river. Two of my men then peeled off their white undershirts, and one was put on a tree at each flank of our platoon to serve as firing guides. I ordered the mortar men to throw smoke shells to the rear and both flanks to screen our move, and one by one, the members of the platoon splashed back across the river (Weston 1992 and videotape).

152

The dramatic story, as related, does leave out some important additional information. As the Japanese officers shouted orders, Sgt. Henry H. Gosho, Nisei interpreter with the platoon, was able to translate this information in time for shifting automatic weapons to meet each attack successfully. The Japanese made five significant attacks before the withdrawal at 1100 hours. During the fifth attack, Lt. William E. Woomer fired 235 rounds of light, heavy, and smoke shells according to Lieutenant Weston's directions. One of Weston's men, Sioux Chief Janis, a full-blooded American Indian, picked off seven Japanese after he had crossed the river and taken up position to help the others. The crossing was completed without any more casualties. Weston was the last man to cross the river.

Chief Janis had been sent across the river by Logan Weston to give covering fire of the flanks. He tells what happened:

> Weston said, "Janis, go across the river and protect our flanks so we can bring these guys out," so I grabbed my rifle and walked across the river and got on the far bank. Katz and this other fellow were bringing Leightner back. I saw a Japanese getting behind a machine gun, so I shot him through his head. He disappeared and another got in his place, so I shot him. There was a total of seven of them. One would go down, and there would be another one. The last one, I hit him and he crawled back, and I said, "You are not getting away, I am going to get you and keep you there." I shot him twice. By that time the boys got across (Janis, videotape).

Lt. Thomas Chamales, Company L, Orange Combat Team, was in charge of a squad to form a skirmish line with the purpose of helping Weston's I & R get across the river out of the trap it was in. Charles Beck, of Riverside, California, recently told me that he was a BAR man in that squad. With two or three other BAR men and the riflemen, everything worked perfectly. Robert Cole left the line and went down to the riverbank to be more effective. This man was a veteran of the 164th Infantry Regiment on Guadalcanal, where he had distinguished himself. On Guadalcanal he had spent the night in a tree surrounded by Japanese.

Lieutenant Woomer's mortar squad, while assisting Weston, was not without great danger and took three casualties. Sgt. Clarence J. Bruno, during a brief rest period, was sitting on the side of a foxhole he had been digging. A Japanese knee mortar shell burst in a tree fifteen yards away. I was a few feet away and immediately saw him. A shell fragment had entered through his left shoulder blade and penetrated his heart. His death was instantaneous from a massive hemorrhage. The same shell hit Pvt. George W. Wright, a muleskinner attached to the sergeant's heavy weapons company. The fragment entered his right lower abdomen and lodged in fatty tissue. I had the pleasure of telling him that the wound was not serious and he would be able to return to duty. At the time of the attack he was prone in a shallow fox hole. The wound became infected and drained until I was able to remove the shell fragment one week later. Another man, Frank R. Giandonato, was sitting on the ground without a hole. The fragment from a tree burst, at about five yards' range, lodged in the soft tissue of his right flank. He also returned to duty.

Corporal Dan Hardinger, from Orange's medical detachment, and several riflemen from Logan Weston's platoon carried Pete Leightner and Lionel Paquette several hundred yards back to Lagang Ga, where Khaki Combat Team had been patrolling and protecting trails. They had also learned that light planes, L-4's and L-5's, were available and could land on small, rough strips. Because of this, they had in the morning cleared an area in the village for planes to land with the idea of using them as small ambulance planes. General Merrill had previously said that he had no plans to evacuate the wounded, and there had been no evidence that anyone in authority had come up with an answer until this time. With imagination and ingenuity, the planes were soon rigged up to carry one litter case and one or two sitting wounded.

Unfortunately, even though Major Cecala of the Khaki medical detachment, Dan Hardinger, and others did all they could, Paquette died before he could be evacuated. He was buried at La Ganga, where his gravesite was marked by a bamboo cross on which a helmet rested and one dog tag was attached.

Leightner was given several units of plasma and evacuated ten hours after his injury. He died in the plane shortly after takeoff. Thomas E. Parren had also been hit while fighting as a member of the I & R unit. A shell fragment had severely damaged his left arm with considerable hemorrhage, which was controlled at the time by a tourniquet. He went out by small plane and made a good recovery.

After the wounded had been treated and returned to duty or evacuated, Sergeant Bruno was buried near the spot where he had been hit. His comrades and friends paid their last respects while a prayer was said at the gravesite. I thought, and I am sure that others did, but for the grace of God it could have been I. Many of us had been through the tragic experience of witnessing the death of a comrade from enemy action. The feeling is always the same. Why did it have to happen? Will I be next? We would begin to think of their loved ones at home and their reaction to this tragic occurrence. What will be the reaction of *my* family and friends if they are notified that I have been killed in the vast jungles of Burma? Will this be the end—my remains becoming part of the soil of Burma to nourish growing bamboo or perhaps a teakwood tree? These benign thoughts would often veer off to thoughts of anger against politicians, generals, and the whole system of government and world order. I would always end my line of thought by being thankful that we were fighting for the survival of democracy and freedom against madmen and slavery.

Years later, Pat Perrone—then a major with many years of military experience—was discussing his Marauder experience in the following words:

> There are only a few important things I could talk about. I was tremendously impressed by the medics. I can remember at Wesu Ga, this side of Walawbum, where Paquette was hit in the head, and Doctor Cecala and the conscientious objector [Dan Hardinger] worked on him for over an hour and a half. They were on their knees working while we were laying down because of mortar fire coming in. There were numerous other things that our medics did for us in a tremendous way. I would have gone anywhere with the men. We had probably the best discipline at that time that anyone else had. It wasn't the stateside discipline, it was a self-discipline. They might go AWOL because they couldn't go any other way, but when it came to the real thing they were there all the time (Perrone, videotape).

Colonel Hunter writes in his Marauders history, *Galahad,* "I intended to recommend to General Merrill that Lt. Logan Weston be

given the Silver Star for his conduct during that hectic morning"
(Hunter 1963, 19).

Colonel Beach received a Silver Star for gallantry in action at
Walawbum some months later, after he had returned home. Weston,
for some unknown reason, did not. Numerous officers and men were
of the opinion that Lieutenant Weston, by his brilliant leadership and
willingness to ignore almost certain death, deserved to be given the
Congressional Medal of Honor for leading his men and controlling the
enemy onslaught. This record will show that he distinguished himself
many other times during the Burma campaign.

Weston was a deeply religious man and a minister by profession,
although not ordained at the time. Later, in Korea, he was again to distinguish himself many times and receive wounds in action.

Orange Shows Its Muscle

During the afternoon of 4 March, the rest of Orange Combat Team
was establishing a perimeter along the east bank of the Numpyek Hka
on high ground directly opposite Walawbum. We were at this location
about thirty miles south of Taihpa Ga, where the 18th Japanese
Division had been locked in combat with two Chinese Divisions since
the first of January.

At our new location, digging in was and would be a continual activity. Our men had learned from combat in the Pacific that, when in any
position where there was the possibility of enemy activity, it was absolutely essential to dig in as well as possible. The mortars and machine
guns were soon in position to give good defensive and offensive capabilities. During the afternoon, Orange threw about a hundred mortar
shells into the Japanese positions in and about the village. Our fire
largely eliminated traffic on the road. The Japanese replied by sending in approximately twenty rounds of mortar. Sporadic artillery fire
was being directed against Khaki Combat Team, located in reserve at
Lagang Ga. In our riverbank position, on this day we had only one
battle casualty, thanks to the safety provided by the vigorous digging.
Pvt. Nellis D. Barclay had a bullet pass through his right forearm
while he was walking. The wound was immediately bandaged, and he
was given oral sulfadiazine and returned to duty.

Late in the afternoon everything became quiet at Walawbum, and it
appeared the Japanese might have evacuated their positions in and

about the village. Lt. Colonel Beach, nicknamed the "Old Ranger," decided to find out—so he waded across the river with his orderly, Sweeney, and walked up the west bank toward the village itself. He had reached the center of the village, and as he turned south about fourteen Japanese ran toward him from the north. Colonel Beach turned and pulled the trigger of his carbine, but the gun misfired. Both he and Sweeney ran for the east bank of the river. Across the river a machine gun opened up on the Japanese and covered the two men's quick return. It is thought that the reason the Japanese didn't fire when they crossed the river was that they were determined to get a prisoner. We spent a quiet night with no further disturbance from the enemy. We had been short on our K-rations on the 3rd. On the night of 4 March, most of the men had no more food. The men not on duty slept well because of mental and physical exhaustion.

Lieutenant Ted Hughes's Company I, Khaki Combat Team, Meets the Enemy at Lagang Ga

Back at Lagang Ga, the men of Khaki were just beginning to move about on the morning of 4 March. They had spent the usual uncomfortable night in enemy territory. Most were out of food and were looking forward to a much-needed supply drop scheduled for this day. Security was not very tight. A large group was examining the bodies of the five enemy killed by Orange the previous day. Fortunately Lieutenant Hughes, commanding officer of I Company, had his men deployed on the east side of the village open area (dropping field and proposed airstrip) here at Lagang Ga. Some of his automatic weapons covered a slightly used trail from the north leading to the river, which ran to the west of the drop field. About 0930 a platoon of twenty or thirty Japanese with one Nambu (light machine gun) attacked the field from the north along the trail his company was covering. Lieutenant Hughes's guns opened up, and the Japanese returned his fire with knee mortars. After the first burst of fire, Pfc. Theodore P. Thibodeaux was hit. He was in a defensive prone position with his machine gun in a protecting gully. His wound was a severe one, made by a .25-caliber bullet that caused a compound fracture of the radius of his right arm. Treatment was immediate by the aid man and later by Major Cecala and Captain Ivens. Shortly after this injury, Sgt. Jack V. Mayer was hit by knee-mortar fragments. He presented with multiple fragment wounds (about a hundred) in both legs and a fracture of the lower third of his left femur (thigh bone). Both men were on the same gun. They had continued to fire until others could get to them. Sergeant Mayer's assistant, Pfc. Adam J. Lang of Baltimore, was hit by another knee mortar burst shortly after he took over the gun. He remained at his post until the attackers were driven off, twenty minutes later, in spite of many knee-mortar fragments in each leg. One Japanese raised up in front of his gun to throw a grenade. Lang riddled him with a long burst from his gun.

Lieutenant Hughes used an SCR 536 to direct mortar fire on the Japanese for five minutes, before they pulled out— leaving ten dead on the field.

The platoon had three other casualties. S.Sgt. Jack D. Grigbsy had been near the machine gun, giving rifle protection. Unfortunately, he had not been dug in. A small grenade fragment tore a hole in the flesh over his left shoulder blade. He was treated and returned to duty. S.Sgt. Harold Schumaker was in charge of the rifle squad protecting the machine gun. He had been prone in the same gully as the gun. A knee-mortar burst threw a fragment into his face at the left corner of his mouth. He returned to duty. Pfc. Horace C. Finley was a rifleman in a defensive area in back of a tree. A knee mortar burst in the tree. One fragment lodged against his skull on the right and another went into the right chest wall. Unfortunately, he was not wearing a helmet—which would have prevented the head injury.

After the action was over, Lt. Ted Hughes took a small patrol forward to search further from the perimeter. They found five bodies. A few minutes later, others found only four bodies. As three separate men had counted the bodies, it appeared that one Japanese playing dead had gotten away. The word got around the perimeter, and all determined that it would not happen again.

The experience, preparation, alertness, and courage of Ted's men had prevented a great tragedy. With Americans moving about in a open area, one undetected Nambu (machine gun) could have killed many men.

An Answered Prayer: Air Evacuation Is Discovered

From the time of our arrival in India, the combat surgeons had been pressing the regimental surgeon for some plan for evacuation of the sick and wounded. No answer had been forthcoming. When we were under the control of General Wingate and knew that we were to be part of the British Army, fighting as a long-range penetration unit behind enemy lines in Burma, we had received no answer. All available information indicated that our wounded and sick would be left with natives or would have to accept the vague promise that they would get whatever help was possible. It was a well-known fact that Wingate's long-range penetration with three thousand men into Burma during the spring of 1943 had been a disaster. Sick and wounded had been left to their own resources, and some mortally wounded had been killed by their own men. We knew of no better plan for 1944.

General Stilwell and General Merrill seemed to have no answer to this extremely serious problem. The medical officers were not told that a plentiful supply of American L-4 and L-5 planes with pilots were available in the CBI. We had not heard that these planes could land on rough, short runways, sandbars, and other imperfect terrain. No one had explained that they were available and could be used as ambulance planes. Col. George A. McGee, the Second Battalion commanding officer, states—in his privately published personal historical account of the campaign—that he had talked to General Merrill about this problem. On page 42 he offers the following information:

> He [Merrill] told me that General Stilwell had asked him what his evacuation plan was and that he had replied, "I don't have one." The crux of the matter facing him was that the size and the nature of the problem with which we might be confronted could not be resolved to a planning figure of any validity, and further, our capability to deal with the problem in the field could not be increased or otherwise improved. There was no previous experience available as a basis for planning other than Wingate's, and I have outlined his thoughts on the matter. In summary, there could be no meaningful evacuation plan or policy laid down at this time. We would have to see what developed and in the meantime do all that we reasonably could to care for the sick and wounded. This was one of the conditions which volunteering had entailed (McGee 1987, 42).

In spite of the enemy ground activity and intermittent shelling of Lagang Ga by the Japanese artillery located near Walawbum, good progress was made on the clearing of an area at Lagang Ga for an airstrip to be used by liaison planes. With casualties beginning to collect at Lagang Ga, something had to be done. Major Cecala took advantage of the airstrip and the enthusiastic pilots, and they started sending the wounded out late in the day. Although Lionel Paquette and Pete Leightner died before and during evacuation, six wounded men who could not return to duty were successfully evacuated. The knowledge that our sick and wounded could be taken out by plane from improvised airstrips was a big boost to the morale of the men.

Lagang Ga Airdrop Cancelled Due to Artillery Fire

The much-needed airdrop was scheduled for the early afternoon of 4 March under Colonel Hunter's direction. The makeshift airstrip, where L-4's and L-5's were beginning to land, bring in messages, and evacuate the wounded, was five hundred yards to the east of the entrance to the jungle- and river-bordered trail that led to Walawbum. The drop area was between the strip and the river. General Merrill and his staff had set up headquarters in the jungle at the southern edge of the Lagang Ga clearing where the trail to Walawbum and the jungle began. Most of the First Battalion were also distributed about the Lagang Ga area, as were the men of Khaki Combat Team of the Third Battalion. Very few of the men had dug foxholes.

In the early afternoon just before the airdrop planes were due to arrive, the enemy artillery began to zero in on the Lagang Ga area. They were mostly hitting the airdrop area where the small planes were slowly removing the wounded. The pilots ignored the artillery and got out all the wounded.

Tanaka now knew that he was outflanked. He was throwing the bulk of the 55th and 56th Infantry Regiments against the Marauders. He knew from previous experience that he could contain the bulk of the Chinese with a few men. On 2 March he had begun to withdraw the bulk of his division and had begun to concentrate the 55th from the north against Galahad, which was now to his south. He had started to send most of the 56th Regiment against McGee's battalion, which would soon be astride the road (Hunter 1963, 34-35).

The C-47's were in the air but had to be sent back to base until new arrangements could be made. The situation of Orange Combat Team was getting critical because of the high expenditure of ammunition. They had to be resupplied. General Merrill had moved his staff north to Wesu Ga, and the men were converting a rice paddy into an airstrip and drop area. General Merrill called for a drop in that area. A new drop could not be set up until dark. Sure enough, after dark the message came through from the lead plane. The rear-echelon air corps officer, Lieutenant Lowell, had volunteered to lead the way—even though he was not a member of the 2nd Troop Carrier Squadron. It was his voice that was heard saying, "Old Crow calling Zipper Six." Merrill quickly answered back, "Zipper Six to Old Crow, I read you two by four, how do you read me? Over." The planes were at that time five minutes from the drop area. In the afternoon, dry wood had been gathered in order to start several bonfires to guide the planes in the darkness. The fires were now lit. Everyone wondered if there would be any enemy reaction. There was none in spite of the brilliant glow of the fires diffused into the heavy mist overhead. Because of the mist the lights of the planes could not be seen, but the pilots now knew exactly where to make the drops. The success of this night drop, the first for the regiment, was a good omen and created a sense of confidence among all men in the area (Hunter 1963, 38).

All evening, firing could be heard coming from Orange's position at Walawbum. Their need for more ammunition was urgent. A mule train from Orange was anxiously awaiting the completion of the drop, and before this dangerous operation was over they were on the drop field collecting mortar shells and other ammunition for the four-mile haul, in darkness, over a very dangerous trail. Because of the urgency of their mission they left before the K-rations could be unpacked and distributed. Orange was to go another day without food.

The First Battalion at Wesu Ga

The First Battalion had arrived at Wesu Ga on 4 March as scheduled and was continuing to block all trails and remain in reserve.

General Merrill Has a Close Call

General Merrill had set up his command post with the First Battalion at Lagang Ga, where he was protected by a platoon of military police that had recently arrived. At the command post everything was running smoothly until a soldier shouted, "Get that Jap"; then about four shots were fired. A Japanese was setting up a machine-gun position on the main trail to Walawbum within a hundred yards of General Merrill's command post. A wild chase followed, but the Japanese escaped with his gun into the thick Kunai grass (elephant grass). Five minutes later, less than fifty yards from the general's command post (where Merrill was then sitting), a soldier looked up from his search to see a Japanese smiling not ten feet away. The Japanese ran, and the soldier fired several shots—but the enemy escaped. The trail of blood on the grass, however, indicated that the soldier had at least winged him.

The Second Battalion Moves into Position to Block the Road North of Walawbum

The Second Battalion was about four miles west of Wesu Ga when they moved out at 0745 with the mission of blocking the road one mile east of Kumnyen Ga. As they were leaving, Sgt. Leo G. Click from headquarters company was wounded while removing booby traps that had been set up during the night. He was sent back to the First Battalion.

Progress was very slow as alternating groups took turns in cutting a trail through tall elephant grass and jungle growth. Visibility was very limited through the dense vegetation. The I & R platoon supplied security for the advancing battalion. Some of the animals were left at the bivouac area to prevent confusion and casualties among them. At about 1800 hours the advance scouts, protecting the main chopping detail, saw a movement through a little bamboo grove and immediately signaled the choppers. They found a single basha (bamboo grass house) occupied by an old man and a sick child. The man told Captain Darlington that he had not seen any Japanese recently. When it was explained that the child would be treated, he agreed to act as a guide.

Just before the road was reached, the battalion went into bivouac with tight security. The chief problem was mule anxiety. Those without their buddies tended to bray. Since Japanese had been heard yelling in the distance, this was a problem. The muleskinners got their charges paired, and this problem was eliminated.

Airdrop at Lagang Ga Canceled by General Merrill, Command Headquarters Moved North to Wesu Ga

At Lagang Ga, incoming artillery fire became a very troublesome problem. The airdrop had to be canceled, and General Merrill moved the regimental headquarters to Wesu Ga, four miles north of Walawbum. The airdrop was now scheduled for after dark at Wesu Ga. Khaki Combat Team remained at Lagang Ga.

Second Battalion Blocks Road

5 March

At dawn the Second Battalion was astride the rather unimpressive road. Surprisingly, they found telephone poles with an intact line. Sergeant Matsumoto, a Japanese-American Nisei intelligence sergeant, tapped the wires and found that he was on the mainline from Maingkwan to the Japanese 18th Division headquarters in Kamaing. The line was very active, and he passed the information to Colonel McGee. One message was from a Japanese sergeant at an ammunition dump a thousand meters from a bridge, which was later identified. This Japanese sergeant asked his commanding officer for help and advice—he told his commanding officer that he only had three men and no weapons other than their rifles. This message was relayed through to General Merrill for action and he sent it to General Stilwell requesting a bombing mission for the ammunition dump. In spite of enemy mortar fire and ground activity, Matsumoto remained at his job of wire tapping. He reported that the Japanese were surprised and confused by the blocks at Walawbum and north of Walawbum and were calling for help all along the line. One message was intercepted from Japanese headquarters ordering a general withdrawal. Matsumoto also learned that the Japanese had constructed a road that allowed them to bypass the fords at Kumnyen Ga and Walawbum. Late in the day he learned that the Japanese planned a very strong attack on the battalion's roadblock.

Lieutenant Dallison, the attached air corps officer, contacted a passing flight of P-38s and got them to hit the Japanese supply dump, which had been located by a patrol from Blue Combat Team.

CHAPTER IX

The road was in flat territory and was surrounded by jungle growth. The Second Battalion's position was about two miles west of the Third Battalion at Walawbum. The Japanese soon reacted to the American presence. All day the Japanese shelled and attacked the perimeter of the Second Battalion and suffered losses estimated by Colonel McGee of more than one hundred dead.

Blue Combat Team was on the north or Kumnyen side, and Green Combat Team faced Walawbum. The two I & R platoons were used on the periphery, as necessary. The entire outfit was well dug in before the enemy reacted.

Both sides used mortars, machine guns, and rifles. One Marauder was killed, and Pfc. R. W. Burnett sustained a serious abdominal wound. Because of the impossibility of rapid evacuation and treatment, it was certain that he would not survive without immediate surgery. Capt. A. Lewis Kolodny, my good friend from Baltimore, and Major Bernard Rogoff, from New York City, did emergency life-saving surgery. They placed him on a litter resting on two ammunition cases and operated in spite of heavy firing. His perforated intestine was protruding from the wound. They stopped the bleeding, sewed the holes in the intestine, and closed the wound under the most primitive conditions. He made a good recovery. Six other men were wounded during the roadblock. At 0800 a platoon of enemy soldiers was ambushed by Blue Combat Team. Intermittent activity, according to Colonel McGee's history of the Second Battalion, continued all day on the north side, but the south side was never much of a threat.

Captain A. Lewis Kolodny has recorded some of his thoughts about the medical situation and the care of the sick and wounded:

> I was with the Green Combat Team as combat surgeon, and when we first entered Burma we found a rather startling thing from the standpoint of medical problems. We had been given no medical intelligence by the rear-echelon medics and knew nothing about diseases we were to face, such as tsutsugmachi fever or scrub typhus. We also found that no method had been arranged to evacuate the wounded, which was rather shocking. Our first battle at Walawbum we found rather disturbing, but I think all the medics handled themselves rather well. The big wounded one we had was a young man who was eviscerated, and while he was lying on a litter and we were leaning over and trying to get everything, a

Japanese machine gun opened up and began hitting the trees behind us—at which point chips of wood were hitting us on the backs of our necks. We were a wee bit nervous. He was cleaned up and the wound was closed, and he was hand-carried for two days and evacuated. A number of years later I saw him still living, which was rather surprising (Kolodny, videotape).

Cpl. Warren T. Ventura, who was in F Company, gives an interesting account of his part in the battle on the road:

Our light machine gun, under the command of S.Sgt. Abe Bushman, was ordered to cover the road to our southeast, facing the position of the Third Battalion. One gun was on each shoulder of the road, which was not over twenty feet wide. As we were digging our positions, a heavy machine-gun section started to dig in not over twenty feet to our rear on each shoulder of the road. These guns would have no field of fire other than directly through our light machine-gun positions. Sgt. Abe Bushman, our section leader, said that he had his orders—and to my knowledge offered no protest to superiors. As we continued to dig in, one of the men on a heavy M.G. behind my position on the right shoulder yelled, "That's a Jap." He was referring to a man leaning against a tree at a bend in the road twenty-five yards to my southeast on the right shoulder. We dived into our holes like startled prairie dogs. Immediately that heavy machine gun opened fire directly over my position. Sgt. Bushman, Pfc. J. D. Young, Pfc. Lester Weddle, and myself were pinned down, unable to fire on the enemy, because of the expertise of the genius who ordered those heavys dug in where their field of fire was through our positions. We came within a breath of the distinction of being the first Americans in Southeast Asia killed by our own troops. My fatigue jacket lying on the left of my machine gun was riddled with holes. The heavy fired perhaps a hundred rounds. There was no return fire from the Japanese. About fifteen minutes after this action, a patrol of platoon strength was sent southeast on the road to reconnoiter. At the bend in the road just beyond the tree where the one Japanese had been observed, they found thirteen dead Japanese in the road. The only firing of any weapon from this roadblock by the Second Battalion was by the same heavy machine gun. That was supposedly in enfilade to support the Third Battalion in their roadblock two miles to the southeast. That fire did not consist of overexpending the rest of the 250-round belt which that gun had fired through my position. There was no other action of the Second Battalion from this position. My light machine gun had ten boxes of 250-round belts on entering this position, and the other light machine gun of my section had the same. Neither of these guns had fired a shot from the roadblock. Both gun crews withdrew with our full supply of 2,500 rounds, which we had on arrival to the position (Ventura, videotape).

The roadblock had been set up very close to Nambyu Hka, but the record does not show why this source of water was not used. There is also no indication that an airdrop of food and mortar ammunition was considered in the area. The men and animals had had no additional source of water since they had crossed the Numpyek Hka, just west of Wesu Ga, where they had bivouacked just across the river at 2300 on 3 March. The need for water and mortar ammunition, as well as the welfare of seven wounded men, made the situation critical. They had held the block since early morning on 5 March and had not received food since 3 March. Because of the unfavorable supply situation, the wounded, and the questionable need for the block to be maintained any longer, General Merrill ordered the battalion to return to Wesu Ga. They withdrew at 2400 hours.

Third Battalion Continues Battle on the Riverbank Opposite Walawbum

The Japanese attacked several times during the day, but not energetically. Our automatic weapons took a heavy toll as each Japanese platoon swept to the riverbank—only to fall back under a withering fire, leaving its dead.

Orange's mortars broke up numerous concentrations of Japanese, who appeared to be forming for an attack. Orange fired about a hundred mortar rounds and the Japanese about twenty-five.

All day several bombers had been overhead, bombing and strafing Japanese positions as pointed out by our air liaison officer over the radio and by smoke shells from our mortars. Late in the afternoon, they directed the bombers and fighters to two Japanese field pieces, about 150 feet apart, which our patrols had located. These guns had been firing on Lagang Ga and the trail leading to Orange on the riverbank. It is believed these guns were knocked out, for they were not heard again on 5 March.

All day, trucks pulled up south of Walawbum unloading Japanese reinforcements. The planes took a toll of some—as they strafed everything that moved—but just after dark, the trucks started moving again, and tailgates slamming against the back of the trucks could be heard all night, indicating reinforcements were arriving. Our mortars had taken a heavy toll on the enemy.

Captain Armstrong and I stayed at our position with the medical detachment near the center of the perimeter. Most of our aid men were dug in with their platoons on the firing line. We were constantly ready with blood plasma and dressings to care for the wounded. By some miracle, there were no dead or wounded among the men of Orange Combat Team on this day. We in the medical station spent our time digging our foxholes deeper. I made mine deep enough to stand upright and aim a shotgun, which I had been carrying since the start of the campaign. In the situation we were in, I could not help but think about the possibility that our position might be overrun by the enemy.

When I was not busy, there were brief periods of doom in my thoughts. Thank God these did not last long. After all, I had been in worse situations on the Island of New Georgia, where my battalion had been surrounded and totally lost and cut off for four days. The men in Orange Combat Team had my total confidence. I knew that we would come through. The chief problem was not knowing what was going on a few yards ahead.

Aside from the noise of combat with the periods of rifle and machine-gun fire and the bursting of mortars, as well as the whistling of artillery shells as they passed over the area, we were free of much noticeable activity. Once in a while the voice of an infantryman shouting obscenities at the enemy could be heard. When darkness came we had been forty-eight hours without food and began to think about what type of plant growth we could boil up. The muleskinners had made every effort to get their animals in as protected an area and as far into the jungle as possible. In spite of this, several were killed. We had brought one mule into the aid station to unload some supplies and lost him to shell fragments. The men were too busy and under too much tension to consider butchering any of the dead animals for a quick meal.

CHAPTER IX

Khaki Combat Team Backs Up Orange by Keeping Trail Open and Lagang Ga Free of the Enemy

Khaki was kept busy delivering ammunition to Orange, holding roadblocks on all trails leading into Lagang Ga, and protecting the landing strip. Having learned from their combat experience in the Pacific campaigns, they were very aggressive in digging foxholes. This paid off, since during this day Khaki only suffered three casualties. Pfc. Richard J. Chaffins, Jr., headquarters company, was in a defensive position—but not in a foxhole—guarding the supply line to Orange when he was struck by a Japanese artillery shell fragment. It produced a jagged two-centimeter wound of his left chest wall but did not penetrate the lung. This was a serious wound, and he was evacuated by air not long after he was hit. The same shell wounded Pfc. Ferdinand N. Stauch, Jr., from headquarters company. While in a defensive prone position without a foxhole, he got a laceration over the left shoulder blade but was able to return to duty.

Khaki Combat Team on Patrol

1st Lt. William L. Duncan, headquarters company, Khaki Combat Team, was leading his platoon on an open trail when a Japanese sniper at two hundred yards' range shot him. The bullet passed through skin and fat on the left chest wall. The wound was dressed, and he returned to his platoon.

Red Combat Team Narrowly Escapes

Lt. William C. Evans, the commander of the Red I & R, was on a patrol with Sergeant Hawk, one of the best scouts in the outfit, and another man. They were on horses, riding up a shallow river, about four hundred yards northwest of Wesu Ga, when they were suddenly surprised by rifle fire from a distance of about twenty feet. Both Lieutenant Evans and Sergeant Hawk rolled off into the water, where they crawled on the bottom while the Japanese fired about forty shots into the river where they had gone under. Lieutenant Evan's horse was killed, and he was shot in the hand. Sergeant Hawk got a crease across his cheek and a bad bruise on his back where a bullet had hit the saddle. When they finally came up for air they saw no evidence of the Japanese. Their companion had been behind them when the shooting started and had been able to gallop off without being hit. All three got back to their platoon a half-hour later. A heavy patrol was sent out but found no enemy.

White Combat Team I & R Encounters Enemy

Lt. Samuel Wilson was leading two of his sections on a reconnaissance and combat patrol, two and one-half miles from Shinak Ga at about 1000 hours, when the platoon scout saw something resembling a horse's tail move near a small stream parallel to the trail. Lieutenant Wilson quickly crept up to the riverbank. When he got about fifteen feet from the riverbank, two Japanese opened fire with rifles and threw hand grenades. One grenade landed within five feet of Wilson. His helmet was blown off and several fragments hit his pack but did not injure him. One of his section leaders reacted quickly, firing at the two riflemen, killing one. The other one escaped into the jungle growth. Lieutenant Wilson heard a noise to his left and saw one Japanese trying to get away on a horse. He shot both man and horse with his carbine. By this time, the patrol had closed in and was spraying the bushes. The enemy fled, leaving two dead—including a Japanese major. Blood on the bushes indicated that some of those who had escaped were wounded. Lieutenant Wilson gave a critique on the spot. He showed the tommy gunners that they could have got the other two horses if they had moved faster.

Second Battalion Begins Withdrawal from Kamaing Roadblock

Late in the evening of 5 March, General Merrill decided that the Second Battalion had accomplished its mission and ordered Colonel McGee to return if possible to Wesu Ga and then march toward Walawbum.

There had been no attacks on the perimeter after dark, and they were able to clear the area by 2300. The moon was favorable, and they found a route for the return that was not as difficult as the approach march had been. The men were hungry, thirsty, nervous, and completely exhausted from lack of rest, sleep, food, and water. As always in such a situation, where uncertainty and danger is faced, some had a feeling of emotional uncertainty that could be called fear. A rumor was spread, according to Charlton Ogburn Jr. in his book *The Marauders,* that "thousands of Japs were coming after them." This rumor was not without foundation, since the bulk of the Japanese 18th Division was withdrawing in order to tackle the Americans and annihilate them before turning to defeat the despised Chinese.

6 March

Despite darkness, fatigue, and anxiety, the column made very good progress with no panic or confusion. At one period during the march, booby traps were suspected and a mule was given the honor of being the lead scout. This wise move paid off when the mule gave its life, setting off a booby trap.

Anyone who has helped carry a wounded man on a stretcher knows what torture the carriers had this night as they covered about seven miles on this return trip. The battalion reached the Numpyek Hka at 0930, where they joined the rear echelon and stopped for water. A short trip put them at Wesu Ga, where the wounded were left to the care of Captain A. Lewis Kolodny M.C., who continued to care for them until they were evacuated from the rough airstrip at Wesu Ga. Green Combat Team stayed to protect the airstrip and cover the trails while they awaited a much-needed airdrop. The rest of the battalion moved about one and one-half miles to Lagang Ga to protect the flanks and rear of the Third Battalion. They arrived at Lagang Ga in time to be hit by the Japanese artillery, which opened up in the mid-afternoon. Some shells hit near the battalion command post as well as part of Blue Combat Team. Lieutenant Evans's P & D Section and Lieutenant Houghton's platoon took some casualties.

Without any explanation, late in the afternoon, the Second Battalion headquarters and Blue Combat Team were ordered to move from Lagang Ga to join Green Combat Team at Wesu Ga. This move was very hectic. It was getting dark, some of the animals were still at Wesu Ga, and the men and officers did not know why they were pulling out. They had heard that a large force of enemy were advancing on the area. Many seemed to believe that the Third Battalion was in very serious trouble and the Japanese might break through. Once they arrived at Wesu Ga they had to send several teams with animals back to Lagang Ga to pick up equipment which they had left. Any unguarded personal belongings or battalion equipment was fair game for the Chinese, who were due to arrive.

Colonel Hunter's Mission to Contact the Chinese

Colonel Hunter, Colonel Lee (Chinese liaison officer), and a few scouts left Wesu Ga at dawn for Ninghku Ga. The mission was to meet Colonel Brown and his tanks (Chinese crews), which had been placed under General Merrill's command, at about 1200 at the small village on the Nambyu Hka.

At about 1100 they were in sight of the river, where they expected to find the village and the tanks. Colonel Hunter at this time saw a Japanese Nambu platoon jogging down a trail on the other side of the river. From a jungle area they watched the busy enemy soldiers for several minutes until they disappeared.

While consulting his map the colonel was startled when he heard the slap of a scout's hand on a rifle butt, indicating *look out*. An all-clear came when Lt. Sam Wilson's I & R was identified. They continued on their way back to report to General Merrill.

The village was reached and found to be deserted. Firing to the north led the colonel to believe that the tanks had been held up. He decided to take the patrol further to the north. At a bend in the trail he lost sight of his two scouts, but heard the sudden fire of one's rifle and the other's tommy gun. They soon appeared and motioned *go back*. The patrol pulled off the trail into the Kunai grass and set up an ambush. The scouts had run into a large group of Japanese and hit three of them.

The Americans returned to the small village and, while there, observed another platoon of enemy under heavy pack, jogging down another trail. Colonel Brown's tanks failed to show up, and the group returned to Wesu Ga—where they arrived shortly after Colonel McGee's Second Battalion.

Hunter learned at Wesu Ga that the Chinese 22nd and 38th Divisions had captured Maingkwan during the day. He had been encountering various Japanese units withdrawing from that area north of our Walawbum operation (Hunter 1963, 41).

General Merrill Moves His Combat Headquarters Back to Lagang Ga

General Merrill had moved his command group back to Lagang Ga on the morning of the 6th in order to better follow the action of his troops. He had not anticipated the renewal of Japanese artillery fire that began at 1430. The artillery appeared to be 150mm. The Japanese were shooting two at a time, indicating they were using two guns. The shelling was heavy for fifteen minutes, and then there would be a fifteen-minute break. Many did not have foxholes, and between rounds the dirt flew as they dug with helmets, bayonets, and mess gear. Few men had shovels. Any available would have sold for a least a hundred dollars. As I have stated, part of the First Battalion was in the area, and they were taking the brunt of the shelling—losing not only men but also animals. About twenty-five shells exploded in the Lagang Ga area, producing six casualties including one death.

Pfc. Crawley L. Myers was hit in the head and face and died in about ten minutes. T.Sgt. David V. Clark took a shell fragment from a tree burst into his left shoulder blade area. He was sent out the next day and eventually made a good recovery. T5g. Clyde H. Smith was hit by a fragment in the left leg and returned to duty, as did S.Sgt. Joseph E. Bridgehorse, who was hit in the right shoulder blade area.

T4g. Joseph B. Groves was severely wounded in the left thigh and left face. Pfc. Dewey F. Diggs was hit in the left upper chest wall. Both men were sent out by small plane the next day.

Later on this same day, 1st Lt. William C. Evans of A Company of the First Battalion was walking on patrol when five Japanese suddenly appeared on a trail. A .25-caliber bullet at fifteen yards' range struck the lieutenant in one of his fingers. The wound was dressed by the platoon aid man, and he remained on duty. The Japanese disappeared.

In the middle of the shelling, about 1500 hours, a pfc from the First Battalion was digging a foxhole near the riverbank at Lagang Ga, about fifty yards from General Merrill's command post. As he turned to dig in the opposite direction, he saw two Japanese peering from some bushes about six feet away. They threw a hand grenade. He ran, then rolled to the ground as the grenade rolled over the riverbank and exploded. He got up and again escaped. Other men who were nearby quickly came to the scene. Pvt. Frank Weber, of the pioneer and demolition platoon, Second Battalion; Pvt. Gerald Perma, a Brooklyn M.P. who scorned a helmet, wearing only a wool cap through rain or shine; and Pvt. George Walulon, a muleskinner, attacked the two Japanese with M-1 and tommy guns and riddled them before they had a chance to get their rifles up. The excitement caused by the Japanese near the command post was electric. Other men started firing at supposed snipers. However, no other Japanese bodies were found in the area.

At 1600 General Merrill had to go through the artillery area to see Col. Rothwell G. Brown, who had arrived at Wesu Ga with some of his tanks operated by Chinese crews. It took an hour to go a half mile, but the general and his party finally made it. A conference was held at the command post of the Chinese battalion commander, who had just arrived to relieve us at Walawbum. Late intelligence information indicated that the Japanese were falling back rapidly from Maingkwan but were trying to bottle up our force with a regiment to the north and large reinforcements from the south. General Merrill did not know that the bloodiest engagement of the Walawbum Battle was beginning to break out in the Third Battalion area. Khaki Combat Team had been sent through the jungle in the late afternoon to assist Orange on its left flank. The battle was under way when the general issued his withdrawal orders. We, in Orange and Khaki, knew nothing about General Merrill's plans, as we were engaged in a life-and-death struggle. General Merrill decided that we would pull out of Walawbum at 2400 and try to cut the road south of Walawbum near Chanmoi.

The tanks would continue to operate north and west of the Nambyu River against the main Japanese forces to the north, as they could not cross the river and work directly with us. Orders were issued to the Third Battalion to pull back to the south of Wesu Ga at 2400 hours. The First Battalion was to hold the drop field at Wesu Ga and the area to the northwest of the town.

General Merrill and his party moved back to his command post at dusk. The shelling continued. He ordered an immediate move to Wesu Ga, and all moved out in the midst of scattered artillery fire ranging in all over the Lagang Ga area. Many of the men were critical of our lack of artillery to compete with the Japanese.

At 0900 the order was given for both the First and the Second Battalions to pull out of Lagang Ga and fall back to Wesu Ga. Shells were still falling in the Lagang Ga area. The men had to pull themselves together, gather up their packs, leave their foxholes, and pack equipment on the horses and mules. There was a great congestion of men and animals in this activity—what many thought was a hurried retreat. This was the first time that the whole battalion had been under fire, and it created some fear and much doubt and confusion as the shells continued to fall and the men and animals continued to move north. As I have explained, the Second Battalion was also involved in this movement, and here again many thought that the Third Battalion had been defeated. The Second Battalion had to wait until 7 March to learn of the great victory of the Third Battalion.

Orange Combat Team Remains at Walawbum

On the riverbank across from the Japanese at Walawbum, the early morning of 6 March had been quiet. Many of the men had had little sleep since we had arrived during the late afternoon two days before, and we were now trying to get as much rest as possible. There was a lot of grumbling about the fact that there had been nothing to eat since the evening of the 3rd. We were discussing the possibility of eating some of the jungle vegetation that the mules seemed to like. They and the horses were also hungry. We were grateful for the ammunition that had been supplied but could not understand why no food had arrived. None of us had any knowledge that the 18th Japanese Division was concentrating troops in our area with the idea that the Americans on the river must be destroyed. Above all, we had no knowledge that the First and Second Battalions had pulled out of Lagang Ga and were relocating four miles in back of us at Wesu Ga. The fatigue, the lack of food, and the lack of information caused me— and, I am sure, others—to have a deep sense of insecurity, which seemed to come and go. Above all, however, we had a deep sense of pride in Orange Combat Team and never doubted that we could withstand anything that the Japanese might throw at us.

The Japanese opened fire on Orange Combat Team just after dawn. By 1015 hours they were throwing medium artillery and a constant stream of mortar fire into the perimeter. Orange was well dug in, with logs over the foxholes and some trees cut down. The animals, however, were not so fortunate, and the shelling took a toll of eight killed and several wounded by 1200 hours. They should have been moved out of the area shortly after we took over the defensive position. Orange answered the fire with a heavy barrage of mortar fire on the Japanese concentration area behind the village and took a good toll of casualties from among the Japanese still unloading from trucks. One 81mm H.E.

light was seen to burst in the bed of a truckload of Japanese, throwing bodies in all directions.

Sgt. Andrew Pung of Malden, Massachusetts, climbed thirty feet into a tree located in his platoon perimeter. Using a 536 radio, he directed mortar fire and told his platoon leader exactly what the Japanese were doing, enabling him to warn the men before an attack. Finally a tree burst stunned him, and he dropped his radio. His canteen was blown off his belt, but he got down safely—though he was somewhat deafened for a few days. Sergeant Carl Hammond of Cleveland, Ohio, hit a land mine just outside the Orange perimeter. It blew him several feet into the air. He had powder burns and couldn't hear for an hour or so, but otherwise he was in good condition. He said, "I was really scared. It made a crater as big as a foxhole."

At 1430 the Japanese started shelling the airstrip at Lagang Ga, and the shells were passing directly over General Merrill's command post. This artillery appeared to be either 105 or 155mm. The shelling was heavy for fifteen minutes, and then we would get a fifteen-minute break.

At 1300 the guns had been located by a patrol and were dive-bombed as directed by General Merrill's command group. After this they opened up on Orange's perimeter. Orange expected this to be followed by an infantry attack, and was all set. Our automatic weapons were silent, as were those of the Japanese, but both sides kept up a mortar barrage. The Japanese had tried to get us to fire our automatic weapons all day, but Major Lew knew what they wanted.

At 1715 hours a reinforced company, followed by another company of skirmishers, tried to cross the river under cover of everything the Japanese could throw. There was much shouting of "banzai, surrender" and a lot of Japanese words as officers prodded the men forward and, in some cases, led them waving swords. Not a shot was fired by the Marauders until the first wave was about forty yards away and had reached the water. Then all hell broke loose from across the riverbank. Machine guns opened full automatic; tommy guns, BAR's, mortars, everything that would fire was turned on the Japanese. The river was suddenly full of bodies, and still the Japanese charged on, only to be cut down. The Marauders—in the face of the blistering Japanese mortar, artillery, and machine-gun fire—kept calm and fired until the gun barrels were hot. It seemed the Japanese had decided that they must storm our position or die, and that is just what they did. Our men were waving their arms and yelling, "Come and get some more of it, you yellow sons of bitches!" Someone said a Japanese yelled, "Roosevelt eats shit!" in reply to a Marauder who yelled, "Tojo eats shit!" Then the Marauders yelled back, "Tojo eats corned beef!" The Japanese replied, "Eleanor eats powdered eggs!"

The two heavy machine guns low on the riverbank swept the river with numerous bands of fire. Corp. Earl E. Kinsinger, who had been a gunner on Guadalcanal, and Corp. Joseph Diorio were the gunners. They fired five thousand rounds each in the course of the attack. Diorio's gun's water jacket was perforated by two bullets, and he and his assistant Clayton E. Hall poured water from every available canteen into it in an attempt to cool the gun. Shortly after the gun was disabled, the attacking force became more cautious and greatly slackened their effort. All types of ammunition were running low as sporadic attacks were renewed. I recall Lieutenant Hogan coming to the aid station and rounding up all weapons and ammunition. I gladly gave him my shotgun with the extra shells. About 1800 hours an eerie silence settled over the perimeter.

When asked by Dave Quaid what his most vivid memory of Walawbum was, Lt. Abie Weingartner answered with the following:

> I had the second platoon on the bank across the river. They kept coming—it was classic. They just kept coming across the field across from the river, and we kept shooting at them, except we were running out of ammunition. I believe I was in a foxhole with a BAR man, Inman Avery. At that time I was carrying a pistol, a .45 automatic. I remember vividly saying I have eight rounds in here and will fire seven and kill myself. We didn't want to be taken prisoners at the time. Down in the foxhole Avery poked me and said, "Save two and kill me before you kill yourself." We were serious at the time. It would have been pretty hard to be taken prisoner. They did bring us some ammunition, and they stopped coming. It was a good fire fight (Weingartner, videotape).

During the entire campaign, Abie had refused to wear a helmet. He later explained this continued failure to comply with regulations and standard practice:

I have a small head and it's a little thick, and the helmet used to be uncomfortable on me. I just said, "I am going to wear a mechanic's cap instead." Colonel Beach and Colonel Hunter said, "You will wear a helmet," and I guess—being an officer—it wasn't the right thing to do, to disobey an order. I said, "What the hell, I might get killed anyway, and I might as well get killed in comfort." I was fined—they fined me for disobeying an order—but I never did wear a helmet (Weingartner, videotape).

The Japanese continued to attack our flanks. Fortunately Khaki Combat Team had moved to our left flank just as darkness descended. We were able to control the right flank.

The spirit of the men was awe-inspiring. They seemed to ignore the bullets, the artillery, and the mortar rounds. Some stood up and shook their fists, imploring the Japanese to come on.

Pvt. John L. Gross, Jr., had distinguished himself by telling the machine gunners where to fire when dirt started coming in on them from ricochets aimed at their position.

Sgt. Louis Oliver of Princeton, Kentucky, fired only twenty-seven shots from his M-1 and was certain that he had eliminated nine of the enemy. Another rifleman who did a good job was Peter Forty. His friends called him P-40. Some said that he had been shot at by his own men because he was short and looked like a Japanese. He got several in the big attack—in spite of a bullet through the heel of his shoe, which tore his sock.

Shortly after the attacks began, Sgt. James E. Ballard volunteered to go to Lagang Ga for supplies. The battalion radio had failed, and no one knew that the supplies were at Wesu Ga, four miles away through no-man's land. Ballard and his men brought the pack train back through the darkened jungle, arriving shortly after all attacks ceased and most ammunition had been expended. They were greeted like heroes, and a great weight seemed to be lifted from our anxious minds.

After the attack, artillery shelling started again but finally petered out by 2200 hours. General Merrill's orders got through, and the Third Battalion evacuated their positions at 2300 hours and withdrew, in the darkness, to the Wesu Ga area four miles to the north.

A number of the men who were on Guadalcanal, New Georgia, and in the New Guinea area said that it was the heaviest attack they had ever seen before. The official estimate was that we had killed at least four hundred Japanese, not counting those eliminated by mortar fire beyond the riverbank. Japanese dead and wounded were everywhere on the ground and in the river. None came close to our line of defense. Captain John George is said to have stopped counting after he recorded 350 dead enemy. Many others perished on each flank, some of whom had met the guns of Khaki to our left.

During this intense battle, as in other attacks here on the river, I could not understand why the medical detachment had no work to do. Only three of Orange's men were wounded. T5g. Millard N. Health was in a foxhole when a Japanese mortar shell burst about twenty yards away in a tree. A fragment entered his left thigh. He went back to his firing position and was not later evacuated. Pvt. Clarence J. Crumb was in a partly covered foxhole with Pvt. Clarence G. Gillespi. A Japanese mortar shell hit a tree and burst directly over their hole. Crumb was without a helmet and was struck on the right temple. He walked to the aid station and, after treatment, returned to duty. Gillespi was not so lucky. The same shell wounded him in the left leg and, after treatment, he was evacuated by air on 9 March. In the hole, his legs had been exposed. In retrospect there were several reasons for the few wounded and no dead Marauders. First, the Marauders were on the high bank of the river, about ten feet above the Japanese. Second, we were dug in on the outer curve of the U bend in the river. Third, we had practiced what our men had learned in the Guadalcanal, New Guinea, and New Georgia campaigns: you must dig in and get as much protection as possible whenever there is any possibility of an attack by an enemy. Fourth, our officers knew from experience how important it was to take every advantage of the terrain and every weapon in setting up a defensive perimeter. Fifth, all possible ammunition had been obtained. Sixth, the men had to be knowledgeable, ingenious, courageous, and have the ability to cooperate with their buddies. Every man had to be willing to face the enemy and fire his weapon. The results showed that all did and would continue to do what was expected and required of them.

Khaki's Story: Movement to Orange's Left Flank

As darkness approached on 6 March, Khaki Combat Team, which had been on the trail and at Lagang Ga backing up Orange, was ordered to move through the jungle to protect Orange's left flank on the riverbank.

With great difficulty they reached their objective in time to blunt some of the enemy trying to hit Orange from the left flank. They had no casualties.

Khaki was ordered to withdraw at the same time Orange got their orders. On the way in, they had set up some booby traps to cover their rear. On the way back, in the dark, there was some confusion about direction. The column ran into their own booby traps; one was killed and four were wounded.

T.Sgt. George B. Clark walked into a booby trap near midnight as Khaki was leaving the riverbank position. He was hit by shell fragments, which penetrated the muscle of each thigh. After medical attention he was able to remain on duty.

1st Lt. Ted Hughes of Company I was near Clark. Small fragments hit him in the right knee, right elbow, right gluteal region, and right shoulder blade area. Fortunately, the metal lodged in the fat and muscle. He continued walking and remained on duty.

The Commanding Officer of Khaki Combat Team, Major Briggs, was hit later in the evening by another booby trap explosion. He had multiple fragments in the soft tissue of the right thigh.

Major Briggs's radio operator, Sgt. William T. Hoffman, ran into and exploded the shell that injured the major. The sergeant took the full force of the explosion and, because of the dark, was not missed until the next day. Burial took place several days later after a search party found his body. The same explosion sent a piece of metal through Pfc. Robert A. Boiteaux's lung and lodged in the left chest wall. He was also wounded in the right arm and both thighs. Under emergency treatment his condition was stabilized, and he was sent back to American care on the road by L-4 and later to the 20th General Hospital at Ledo by a C-47. He made a good recovery in the hospital.

Sgt John A. Acker tells his story about Khaki Combat Team and how it got lost during the withdrawal from Walawbum:

> As we came into Walawbum we met with some Japanese at Wesu Ga. While there, after being hungry for four or five days, we were able to obtain some rice. It still had the husks on it. We boiled it in our helmets and made a feast of it. Orange Combat

Team was on the front down by the river in deep combat with the enemy.

Major Briggs called for a group of us with a bunch of our mules. When I went into India I became a member of the pioneer and demolition platoon, with assignments to set booby traps and so forth. When we received horses to replace the mules that had been lost when the ship was sunk on the Indian Ocean, I was assigned to go to down and train the horses and to fit our pack saddles for our weapons and equipment. After that assignment I worked with the animals and those good men who helped care for them. As we went into Walawbum, Major Briggs came back to us and said we had an assignment to go around to the left in back of Orange Combat Team, cross the river, and catch the Japanese as they tried to cross the river to hit Orange's left flank.

On our advance to the river we hit the ground several times because of mortar and artillery shells coming in on us. The Japanese were trying to hit Orange, but while in back of them we were getting the effect of that firing. As we went into bivouac down by the river and dug in, it had taken all day. As we waited there we heard the Japanese, just across the river, bringing in reinforcements by truck. Late at night on 6 March we had just laid down to rest when we got orders to get out of there.

Major Briggs led, trying to get us out of there. We made a trip all around that place while we heard the bombardment of mortar and artillery. I know the Japanese had found our position. We wandered around and were lost. Major Briggs admitted he was lost and passed the word back that he was trying to find the trail. As it happened, I was sitting right by our old picket line, which we had made earlier. I let him know that I knew where the trail was, and we started out again on the trail. When we came back to our previous area we found that our position had been torn apart by the artillery and mortars (Acker, videotape).

First Battalion at Wesu Ga

7 March

At Wesu Ga, dawn broke on a foggy morning—and the men in the First Battalion were glad to see it, since the Japanese artillery wouldn't have much observation. There was sniper fire sporadically in almost every direction, and everyone moved with caution. Once a Nambu light machine gun opened up on a small column. When Marauders opened heavy fire, the Japanese withdrew. The situation was confused by the enemy wandering about trying to find their own forces.

A little later, at 0600 hours, as the Japanese artillery opened up on the drop field at Wesu Ga, the First Battalion moved out to a paddy field three and one-half miles east of the village. A fairly large open space, which had at one time served as a growing area for the native Kachins, was taken over. A strong defense was set up around and about the area, and a landing strip was prepared for the L-4's and L-5's to land and take out our casualties.

First Battalion Fired on by Chinese

Earlier, the first platoon of C Company, Red Combat Team, First Battalion had dispersed along the Nambyu Hka east of Wesu Ga. At 0700 hours they were fired on by unknown troops. They returned the fire using mortars. The noise of the conflict brought Lt. Sam Wilson and a Chinese interpreter who was nearby. They called out to the troops across the river, and they answered that they were Chinese. Our men ceased firing, as did they, and crossed the river to check on casualties. Four Chinese, including a Chinese major, were badly wounded. The Chinese lieutenant told our interpreter that they fired on us when they saw our helmets, which were so much like the Japanese helmets. We had no casualties. Our doctors and aid men were on the scene in a few minutes, and the American soldiers who had done the shooting volunteered to carry the wounded to the airstrip where they were evacuated before any American wounded. The Chinese and the Americans regretted the incident, but it could have happened to two platoons of American troops almost as easily.

The Bulk of the Chinese Arrives

All morning, units of the Chinese 38th Division had moved through the First Battalion toward Walawbum. The trails were jammed with troops. They had advanced rapidly when Japanese resistance on the northern front collapsed after the blocks were placed on the main road just north of Walawbum. At 1400 hours the Division Artillery section passed by the Marauder drop field. A cheer went up from every Marauder as they saw the pack artillery pass. They had been pounded for several days by Japanese artillery without anything to retaliate with, and were mighty happy to see that the Chinese had the means to even the score. The Chinese went into Walawbum without much resistance. The Japanese back was broken after its battle with Orange, and resistance to the American and Chinese forces was greatly weakened in this area.

Message from Generals Merrill and Stilwell

At 1845 hours on 7 March, General Merrill had a staff meeting at which he told the senior officers the following:

> The first phase of our operation is over. Our move to Chanmoi is off, since we would get jammed up with the 38th Division, which is heading that way. General Stilwell has sent a message that he is pleased. Between us and the Chinese, we have forced the Japanese to withdraw farther in the last three days than they have in the last three months of fighting.
>
> Our new mission will be made known to us soon. Please convey to your men General Stilwell's and my congratulations for a fine piece of work. Get rested and reequipped as soon as possible, and be ready to move on our next operation in three days.

Some of the Chinese bivouacked on the trail near our drop field, and before long it seemed as if a Chinese occupation force had taken over the American camp and an American force taken over the Chinese camp. Trading K-rations and cigarettes for bully beef and rice and exchanging souvenirs—from Chinese money to battle flags—was the order of the day. Many a Marauder ate a delicious Chinese-cooked meal. One group got together with some Chinese who had some meal and cooked flap-jacks in their entrenching shovels over a bamboo fire. Other modifications of K-rations were to be seen on all sides, such as making rice pudding by using a fruit bar chopped up in a bowl of rice and adding sugar. Chocolate rice pudding was produced by scraping the D bar into sweetened rice and allowing the whole thing to simmer. Rice with meat and vegetable stew from C-rations, or egg yolks from the K-rations, made a tasty dish. A great delicacy was the cheese ball made by crumbling K-ration crackers, rolling them in K-ration corned pork loaf, coating with cheese, and roasting over a fire until brown. For supper every night during the campaign I took the K-ration meat unit, crumbled the crackers into it, added the dehydrated bouillon, and heated the mixture over the wax-coated K-ration box as it burned gradually from top to bottom. For dessert a favorite was chocolate bread pudding made by crumbling the crackers into boiled sugar water and adding the D bar. The whole mixture simmered until thick.

The Three Battalions Rest and Await Orders

8 March

The next day, 8 March, the First Battalion moved to the banks of a stream near the deserted village of Shikau Ga, where they remained until they departed on their second mission on 12 March.

At Shikau Ga they rested, washed their clothes, and bathed in the stream. Here they had an opportunity to barter cigarettes for tea and rice with the Chinese. Some of the men were able to feast on fish that had been removed from the river after grenades had been used to stun them.

On 7 March, the Second Battalion had moved through Wesu Ga to the newly opened drop area, where they were supplied with two days' rations and bivouacked for the night. The next day they evacuated some sick by L-4's and, after watching more Chinese pass by, marched three miles to Chawka Ga to spend the night. T.Sgt. Joseph Freer, because of outstanding contributions and ability, was given the command of Blue Combat Team's I & R platoon. Recommendation was prepared for his promotion to second lieutenant.

The Second Battalion made a third move on 9 March, when they marched to Nachkaw Ga near Shikau Ga. They were to get much-needed rest before the start of a second mission.

After an uneventful but joyful march in the dark, Orange had made the four miles to Wesu Ga on 7 March. We were surprised to find Lagang Ga deserted as we passed through. Some abandoned equipment suggested that evacuation from this area had been rather rapid. At Wesu Ga we were given the answer that the hurried move had been made in order to get out of the way of the Chinese, who were to occupy the area. Khaki soon joined us, bringing Robert Boiteaux, who had been injured and was soon evacuated by an L-4.

The first thing on the agenda of Orange was to rest and obtain some food. The men had been without food since the evening of 3 March.

CHAPTER IX

Boxes of K-rations were soon distributed and enjoyed. We learned that members of the other units had been under the impression we had been chewed up and defeated by the Japanese. Those who were still unaware of the great victory at Walawbum were amazed by the happy-go-lucky, carefree attitude of the men of Orange. Needless to say, this attitude soon spread to all of the combat teams.

While eating, resting, and waiting at Wesu Ga for an airdrop of ammunition, a tragic event befell Pfc. Carter Pietsch. He and another Orange rifleman were engaged in conversation while sitting on a log a few feet from the aid station personnel. The parachute delivering a case of ammunition failed to open, and the heavy object was thrown wide of the drop area, striking Pietsch. He was killed instantly.

After the Marauders had defeated the Japanese at the Battle of Walawbum and the Chinese had captured Maingkwan, Major Williams's combat command group moved to the latter area. Ray Lyons, conducting business at the new location, describes the scene:

> At that location we were across a creek from Gordon Seagrave's hospital, and he had these Burmese nurses. They would come down to take a bath in the creek, and all of us were delighted— but when they went in to take a bath they didn't take their clothes off. They would just have these long gowns they wore, and they would just walk into the water with them on—but we were there. It finally dawned on me that I should chase these characters away and let them take their bath in peace, which I did—with a lot of grumbling, I might add, from our troops.
>
> At this hospital there turned up about a half-dozen Marauders, one of the first gang of the wounded. They were complaining, and I was it. I was the ranking person there. It seemed to me that Major Williams was always gone. They complained that they were looking for shaving kits, toothbrushes, and combs and brushes. After they had been wounded, all their gear had been left behind. When I went over to talk to them, that was what their complaint was. They wanted something that would get them into decent shape again as far as washing, shaving, and so on was concerned. So I sent a message to the rear echelon that we needed these kits to take care of the personal needs of the wounded, and sure enough they flew them in the next day. We got all these guys their little kits, and they were happy and stopped complaining.
>
> The next thing that happened at Maingkwan was this: We had a

Sgt. Ronald Pickett, with a pigeon detachment, assigned to us. I knew one thing about pigeons, because when I was little I had a friend who had pigeons as a hobby. In order to do what they call "hold," you have to keep the pigeon in one location for so many days, like four or five days or a week, before they are oriented. Then you can take then out, and they will fly back. They had been moving down the road all along, and this was the first stop. We had been here about a week. One day this officer who was in charge of the Northern Combat Area Command called me and asked me if I wanted to fly over the forward-echelon troops in an L-5. I said no, but that I had a guy who should fly, and that was this Ronald Pickett because they had a setup, a little parachute, that they hooked to the pigeon after tying its wings. A message would be attached to its leg, the parachute would open, and the pigeon would drop down. Sure enough, the parachute opened and the message was delivered. They put on a message, and the pigeon came back just like clockwork.

The message they sent to me was a request for three days' rations dropped at such and such location. I sent this radio message back to the rear echelon, that the forward troops had requested three days' rations delivered at such and such a place. I got a nasty message back, which really frosted me. Major Williams was back there. That's what got me. They sent me a message asking who had authorized me to drop three days' rations to the troops in the forward area. None of it made sense. We didn't have rations to drop to them or means to drop to them. Obviously, when the guys had transcribed the message they had changed the rations to something else which did not make sense. They didn't try to make sense—instead they gave me a nasty order not to do this anymore because I was not authorized to do it.

After Maingkwan, we continued with what we had been doing. My problem, which had gradually developed, was that in those days you had to make a copy with a piece of onionskin paper, and this is nothing like today's transparencies. For some reason, known only to the people in headquarters, it was always at night that they would call. All work had to be done under a gasoline lantern. Light was poor, and I was busy trying to make overlays showing the location of the Japanese troops and the Chinese troops and where the Americans were supposed to be, and after I had done all this with all the numbers on it I had to send a radio message. My eyes kept growing worse and worse. I had worn glasses before the war but not since I had joined the service. All of a sudden I couldn't read anymore. They flew me back to the rear echelon to get glasses. I wound up staying there until Myitkyina had been captured (Lyons, videotape).

By 9 March, all units of the Marauders were together at or near Shikau Ga. The members of the Second and Third Battalions began to enjoy the rest, bathing, and extra food.

The medical detachments were available for evaluation of the sick and noncombat injured. Many men had sprains, bruises, skin rashes, dysentery, fever, nausea, and vomiting. One man in Orange had a violent toothache, and—since no dentist was available—I extracted his tooth with a pair of pliers.

Regimental casualty records available for the Walawbum battle list six wounded and no dead in the First Battalion. The Second had one killed and seven wounded. The Third suffered five killed and nineteen wounded. Fifteen wounded returned to duty. The Second Battalion may have had several other wounded of which I have no record.

The next four paragraphs are quoted from *Crisis Fleeting*, a book compiled and edited by CBI historian James H. Stone. This clearly explains the medical evacuation and treatment system that had been set up to care for Chinese sick and wounded during the Burma Campaign. Our combat team surgeons had no knowledge of these arrangements. Some information was gained by conversations with pilots of the small evacuation planes. I do not recall any directive or visit from any higher-ranking medical personnel during the entire campaign. Stone's description follows:

> During the three-day rest, the Marauders could accept with justifiable pride the congratulations Stilwell sent them. After their brisk hundred-mile march they inflicted several hundred casualties on the enemy, and they passed their first battle test with aplomb and determination. They had lost only eight killed and thirty-seven wounded. Yet it might have sobered them to reflect that their strength was nearly ten percent less than it had been when they started for Walawbum. Thirty-three of the 250 men they evacuated had suffered nonbattle injuries. The rest of the evacuees (battle casualties excepted) were sick. Many of their disorders were either preventable or were conditions of long standing, with which the Marauders should not have been burdened.

THE BATTLE OF WALAWBUM

Nineteen men who should have been protected by atabrine suppressive control went to the hospital with malaria. Eight were sick with other serious fevers; dengue was the most common. Ten displayed neuropsychiatric symptoms. The remaining 109 invalids— almost the equivalent of a company—were evacuated with a miscellany of illness and disabilities. It is safe to conjecture that less-seriously afflicted men stayed with their comrades, and that many of those who were evacuated and those who remained had diarrhea, dysentery, and various chronic disorders. A few of the evacuees had scrub typhus, which they had probably picked up while crossing the northern edge of the Hukawng Valley.

The medical support of the Marauders was like that which the Northern Combat Area Command had devised for the Chinese army in India (and which Wingate's special force would adopt). Battalion medical detachments marched with the columns, established aid stations during battle, collected and gave emergency treatment to casualties, and cared for the sick. The sick and wounded walked, rode, or if necessary, were carried with the columns until they recovered or an air-evacuation point became accessible. One of the most essential points which the Third Battalion performed in the Walawbum engagement was to secure an airstrip at Lagang Ga. Communications with the rear regarding medical matters, supply, and evacuation mainly were the responsibility of the regimental surgeon. Through him, the battalion surgeons arranged to get their casualties to the airstrip and aboard the light planes sent down to serve as combat-area ambulances.

The L-4 and L-5 planes carried casualties to the nearest landing field that could accommodate C-47 planes. For the Walawbum engagement, such a field opened up on 29 February at Taihpa Ga; planes also continued to fly to the older and more distant airfield at Shingbwiyang. At these two points the patients were transferred to the C-47 ambulance planes of the 803d Medical Air Evacuation Squadron. In this way 135 Americans were brought to the 20th General and the 73rd Evacuation Hospitals at Ledo after the battle of Walawbum.

Air clearing stations were essential links in the chain of evacuation. Those in the most forward zone were improvised by local troops until detachments of the 13th Mountain Medical Battalion moved in. At the larger fields in the rear, the 151st Medical Battalion, a service of supply unit, provided clearing stations. A typical ACS, such as that which the 151st put at Taihpa Ga in

March for the Chinese and the 5307th evacuees, consisted of a medical officer and from ten to twenty-five men—nursing orderlies, drivers, loaders, and laborers. It had a ward tent and facilities for an average patient census of thirty; first-aid supplies on the scale of a divisional emergency unit; a few trucks or ambulances; and housekeeping equipment for the ACS personnel. The ACS could be opened or closed on short notice, or it could become the nucleus of a major evacuation center (Stone 1969, 322–23).

The system as set up had advantages and disadvantages. Those who were not critically wounded or ill did reasonably well. Many wound infections and delays in healing of fractures would result from delayed definitive care. Critically injured and ill patients would at times lose their lives because of delays in the chain of evacuation on the way to an expert medical or surgical team that could give life-saving treatment.

At Walawbum the Marauders did not have the benefit of any medical or surgical backup in the area until the battle was over and the Chinese arrived, to be followed by elements of the 13th Medical Battalion. Only one death during the battle of Walawbum might have been prevented if surgery had been available during the first two or three hours.

The Marauders had no information about the activity of the Chinese 22nd and 38th Divisions in Burma other than that they had advanced a few miles against the Japanese 18th Division during October, November, and December 1943, and January and February of 1944.

In 1956, *Stilwell's Command Problems,* by Charles F. Romanus and Riley Sunderland, explained that General Stilwell had under his command the 22nd and the 33rd Divisions, with a total of 2,626 officers and 29,667 enlisted men. To work with the Chinese, the Northern Combat Area Command had 331 American officers and 1,956 enlisted men. Through 18 March 1944, the Chinese on the Burma front had 802 killed and 1,479 wounded, plus 530 undifferentiated casualties (Romanus and Sunderland 1956, 32).

At Walawbum the Marauders did not know that they and the Chinese were the only allied troops fighting in Burma. In India, 1,654,094 British and Indian troops were available. General Wingate opened his campaign of 5 March 1944 with 18,000 men (Romanus and

Sunderland 1956, 159). The Japanese army at this time is estimated to have had 242,000 troops in Burma.

On 8 March a joint perimeter was set up by the American and Chinese forces around the Sana Ga-Shikau Ga area, and the camps became merged into one Chinese-American camp.

General Merrill, on the 9th, arranged for General Sun to see the correspondents who had arrived. On the way to General Sun's headquarters, the group passed many Chinese and Americans bathing in the small stream that paralleled the trail and also many Chinese chopping bamboo to make bashas. Everywhere they dug foxholes, slept, and set up an excellent perimeter. Once their foxholes had been in place for a few days they would be apt to construct trenches and pillboxes, which they would improve daily. Logs were laid over the pillboxes, and they had good protection from mortar and artillery. They had learned quickly about the need for protection.

General Sun's aide met the group at his headquarters basha, and a few minutes later General Sun appeared wearing riding breeches and leather leggings. He was tall and slender for a Chinese, with sharp aquiline features and brilliant black eyes. He greeted General Merrill warmly and talked to the correspondents mainly in English, though sometimes through an interpreter. He told them, "We need the Burma Road badly," and "This is fine work you fellows [Marauders] are doing." He told General Merrill, "You've got tough men who want to kill the Japanese." General Merrill replied, "Well, we haven't done much." General Sun said, "I think you are very modest." Forty-four-year-old General Sun had risen from the grade of private to that of lieutenant general in the Chinese Army. He was educated in China, and in 1927 graduated from Virginia Military Institute in the United States. He took some additional engineering training at Purdue University and returned to China to enter the army. He was aide-de-camp to the Generalissimo Chiang Kai-shek in 1930 and 1931. In 1937 he received nine wounds from shell fragments during the fighting at Shanghai. In 1942 he had risen to a brigadier general and came into Burma as the commanding officer of the 38th Division. Shortly afterwards General Stilwell was appointed commander of the two Chinese divisions fighting the Japanese invaders. In January 1942 he was awarded the C.B.L. by the British Government when one of his regiments saved seven thousand British soldiers trapped near the oil-field of Yananlgyaung, Burma. He was able to get most of his 38th Division out of Burma during the retreat in 1942 and went with them to the Chinese Training Center at Ramgarh, India. He remained as their commanding officer during this reorganization and training period conducted by General Stilwell's staff. His division left Ledo for Burma in April 1942. On 26 October they started the move to Shingbwiyang, captured it on 28 October, and took Ningam Sakan on Christmas Day. He captured Taipha Ga on 1 February, and his forces occupied Walawbum on 8 March.

General Sun said, "Frontal attack is no way to defeat the Japanese. In this case the long way around is the short cut." Col. Chun Lee, General Sun's liaison officer with General Merrill, took great pride in introducing the members of General Sun's staff, including American liaison officers attached to the 38th Division headed by Col. Edward J. McNally, another classmate of General Merrill's at West Point.

At Shikau Ga, patrol activity was being maintained in a six-mile radius. A Kachin patrol reported that three hundred Japanese had been seen a few miles down the river on 6 March.

10 March

General Stilwell ordered General Merrill to report to his headquarters on 10 March. The general, on this day, rode to Maingkwan with a party of about twenty-five. The route took them through a sixteen-mile section where scattered groups of Japanese were still milling about, but they encountered no problems. The general was given orders for the next mission, and the party returned to Shikau Ga. Here the Marauders continued to enjoy swimming, fishing, and resting. The mules joined in the rest and fun by rolling on the sand bar. An airdrop of two days' K-rations and two days' grain ration took place in the afternoon.

At 1400 hours Chaplain Lawrence A. Dickson, from Waco, Texas, held a memorial service for the First Battalion. Unfortunately no chaplains were available for the other two battalions. Under a cloudy sky, with C-47's flying overhead, the hard, unshaven men—resting their rifles on their knees—sat and prayed in this service. Mules and horses were grazing nearby, and twice our patrols passed by on their way back from reconnaissance. The sound of artillery landing only two or three miles away vied with the heavier thud of an aerial bomb released by a fighter bomber. The sharp rolling crack of strafing drowned out the chaplain's voice at times. After a prayer, Chaplain Dickson talked about the friendship of God. The men hung on every word as he talked briefly about salvation and the deliverance that Christ offers us. After the service I noticed a blue flag with a white cross and commented on the fact that he was lucky to have a church flag out here. He told me some of the men had made it from a parachute.

Lt. Logan Weston, during the brief period his I & R was not on patrol, held a memorial service for the five men from the Third Battalion who had been killed. Many of us, who had come safely through the Battle of Walawbum, said our own prayers and kept our thoughts to ourselves. Our mission had been successful. The American victory at Walawbum had allowed the Chinese to advance more in five days than they had been able to advance in five months. The enemy was now on the run. Unfortunately, they had not been cut off and trapped in North Burma. A rumor spread that the Chinese could now finish the job. Many of us hoped that we would wait out the rainy season before going further into Burma.

It has been stated that General Stilwell sent a message of congratulations to the Marauders for the great victory at Walawbum. Few Marauders knew of the message. General Merrill and General Stilwell could have easily visited the individual battalions and sincerely explained the significance of the victory and the appreciation of the American people and President Roosevelt. Such a visit would have given incentive and encouragement to these loyal American volunteers who were about to depart deep into enemy territory to show the way for advancement to Chinese troops who had little idea of where they were going or what they were fighting for. Many of the Marauders, with limited information, were beginning to suspect that they were facing more misery, sickness, injury, and death to save General Stilwell's reputation before retirement. Even with no personal line of communication to staff knowledge and decisions, those of us who tended to want answers to obscure orders, plans, action, and lack of action were beginning to have serious doubts about the overall ability of General Stilwell and his staff. One aspect of the campaign that we could count on was Major Hancock and his control of our own source of supply and delivery. We also knew, after Walawbum, that the pilots of the L-4 and L-5 planes would get our sick and wounded out if at all possible.

CHAPTER IX

The British foreign secretary, Anthony Eden, in late February told the House of Commons, "If any of us had the choice, we would say that of all the ordeals to which the military could be put, warfare such as the troops are now engaged in on the Burma frontier is perhaps the toughest of all." One of the Marauders, a veteran of Guadalcanal, on hearing this statement far behind the Japanese lines, asked, "What does he mean 'perhaps'?" The men were proud and grateful that the three battalions had performed so well in their first major battle. There had never been any doubt in my mind that Orange would defeat any enemy unless they were very heavily outnumbered. They had more than met all expectations. After the horrible experience that I and most of my comrades had endured in the Pacific, we tended to continually express gratitude that the battalion had only had five men killed and nineteen wounded. Very few of the two hundred men lost to combat, mostly due to disease and nonbattle injury, were from the Third Battalion.

Preliminary Plan for the Second Mission

11 March

Most of us had not looked forward to this day. General Merrill held a staff conference at which he explained the second phase of our operation, which would start the next day. The units would be split for a part of this new mission. This is the plan he outlined: The First Battalion of the 5307th would march out and would be followed at one day's march by the 113th Chinese Infantry Regiment from the 38th Chinese Division. The Marauder battalion would strike almost due south over the mountains until they were past Jambu Bum on the right flank. They would then turn west to strike at or near Shaduzup, throwing a block on the main road south of the village. When the block was firmly in position the Chinese would occupy it, allowing the First Battalion to regroup and await further orders.

The Second and Third Battalions of the 5307th would march almost due south to Pabum, then south at Pabum, and would be prepared to strike at Shaduzup or below Shaduzup, establishing a block on the main road to Kamaing ten miles or so below the block of the First Battalion. The object was to draw as many enemy as possible to the blocks, where they could be trapped and defeated. The Chinese would then break through any problems they had and would take over the American positions as necessary. No definite statements were made as to what the plan would be if the mission was successful or unsuccessful. We knew that high casualties were expected and no replacements were available.

No records have ever shown that General Stilwell had any plans or expectation to advance more than a few miles south of the entrance to the Mogaung Valley during the campaign of 1944. At the outset of this second mission, members of General Merrill's staff were beginning to discuss the probability of spending the rest of 1944 in the Mogaung Valley.

General Merrill showed his diplomacy in handling the 113th Chinese Regiment, which had been given to him for this next operation. Naturally, General Sun, division commander of the 38th Division, didn't like giving up a regiment—so General Merrill gave it back to him and said, "You keep it under your command, but have it cooperate with my battalion. I will lend you my G-3 and G-2 and also a radio team to move with the 113th so that the proper liaison can be maintained between them, the First Battalion, and my headquarters." General Merrill's ability to work with the Chinese was apparent on every side. He did not give them orders; he asked their cooperation, and they never failed him.

Colonel Hunter's Mission to General Stilwell

Colonel Hunter was given the mission of traveling to General Stilwell's headquarters to brief him on the plan as it was developing. In his history of the campaign, *Galahad*, he tells his story in the next several paragraphs:

> I was to fly to Maingkwan the next day, brief General Stilwell on the plan, and get it approved. The memory of that day is very clear. I was to be met by a L-4 aircraft the next morning in an open field in the middle of nowhere.
>
> Early on 12 March, riding Merrill's horse and accompanied by a mounted soldier to return the horse to Merrill, I set out for the improvised airstrip. The plane landed, I trotted onto the field, and within minutes I was airborne. But for the pilot, myself, and my

orderly, the area had been deserted. Landing at Maingkwan, I eventually located Joe Cannon, Stilwell's right-hand man and acting chief of staff in the absence of Haydon Boatner.

There was criticism of the plan with respect to our routes of advance. Cannon contended that the country was such that we would be forced to carve out the jungle to receive our airdrops. In rebuttal I stated that our experts were of a different opinion. After some wrangling, Stilwell commented caustically, "If the terrain is like that, how come I don't know about it?"

After lunch, which was a cold affair (not only had I brought my own K-ration, but I ate it alone), Stilwell reluctantly gave his approval to the plan, muttering something to the effect that he had confidence in Merrill. While at Maingkwan, I received the distinct impression that it was not a happy place.

Merrill's withdrawal from Walawbum on 7 March apparently was unknown to Stilwell. In *Stilwell's Command Problems,* the following statement is made: "After Galahad was withdrawn from Walawbum and on its way to cut the road again further south, communications between Merrill and Stilwell were finally reestablished late on the evening of the 8th. Stilwell recorded in his diary that he learned of Galahad's maneuver only after issuing orders for a coordinated action by the 65th, the 113th, Galahad, tanks, artillery, and the rest. Weighing this situation, Stilwell decided that his orders to Merrill had not been clear enough; in saying 'use your own discretion,' he meant to keep the casualties down and not go roaming. Stilwell's conclusions and his willingness to assume responsibility for not making his orders more clear deserve respect, but the communications difficulties that kept Stilwell in the dark as to the movements and location of the several units, plus the extreme caution of the Chinese 22nd Division, seem major factors in Tanaka's successful withdrawal from the Walawbum area."

After all these years, the paragraph quoted above and the questions it poses tell as succinctly as possible the story of the man's failure to achieve his greatest ambitions. When interviewed in India at the end of his famous "retreat" (in 1942), Stilwell was quoted as saying in substance, "I say we took a helluva beating, and we ought to find out why and go back."

Not accurate in its entirety, this illustrates, however, some of General Stilwell's operational methods as a commander. Why was he in the dark, and why did he have communication difficulties?

Army communications doctrine at that time placed responsibility for communications between a higher and lower headquarters squarely on the shoulders of the commander of the higher headquarters. With respect to the unclear orders and instructions, was his staff incapable of translating his plans, instructions, and desires into clear, concise written form? Why couldn't he get the 22nd, a Stilwell-trained division, to move?

With the plan reluctantly approved, I flew back to join Galahad. On arriving over the bivouac area, I was surprised to see Galahad extending in a long column, marching to the east. I was quite puzzled. Where was the outfit headed? I had no idea that Merrill would move until I should return with his plan approved. Yet there was Galahad moving snakelike along the trail, winding through the thick cover with the tail of the column already clear of the bivouac area.

We circled for a few minutes while I pondered the answer to the pilot's question, "Where do you want to land, Colonel?" On the next pass over the area at tree-top level, we passed over the sand bar in the river where my poncho on a bamboo frame could be seen with the freshly laundered, and by now dry, socks and underwear hanging alongside. "How about the sand bar?" I answered. "I'll try it," was his answer, and with that he went downriver, banked sharply, and set his aircraft down neatly on the downstream side of the sand bar.

After watching the pilot's beautiful takeoff, I gathered my equipment together and set out to catch up with the tail of the column, indignant that a guide or messenger had not been left behind to enlighten me concerning the reasons for this precipitous departure from the bivouac area.

The trail was not hard to follow, and by foregoing any rest periods, I eventually reached Merrill's position. I reported that the "boss" had approved his plan and explained to him the attitude of the staff back at Maingkwan.

The real reason for Merrill's sudden departure from the area was the sudden rise in the incidence of amoebic dysentery among the troops, caused by the pollution of the streams and the area by our Chinese Allies. Three hundred and fifty cases had been reported by the doctors at sick call the previous evening. The bulk of the cases were in the First Battalion, which had been longest in the area and more closely associated with the Chinese. A few of the evacuees had scrub typhus, which they probably picked up

CHAPTER IX

while crossing the northern edge of the Hukawng Valley (Hunter 1963, 49).

Sgt. Ray Lyons has interesting memories of the Northern Combat Area Command shortly after the great victory at Walawbum:

> General Merrill sent a message back when we were first set up at Maingkwan with the NCAC, and he recommended people for medals—Silver Stars, Bronze Stars, et cetera—for their actions during the Battle of Walawbum. I took his message and just forwarded it the way I got it. Four days later, back comes a message from the NCAC people in New Delhi. They said, "In accordance with army regulation 625-5 it is necessary for you to provide the following information ... There was a long list of stuff. It asked the weather conditions, our positions, the enemy positions, our strength, the enemy strength, and a whole bunch of data that General Merrill had no intention of providing. His idea was that he could just call up his buddies back there and say, "Hey, I got guys that should be given medals," and it would come to pass. It didn't come to pass because between him and those buddies were a lot of guys sitting in personnel offices who followed the military practices. I thought to myself at the time that he was wrong, but he said we shouldn't keep records and keep notes. Today we still have guys who were promised promotions and medals but didn't get them because we didn't keep records (Lyons, videotape).

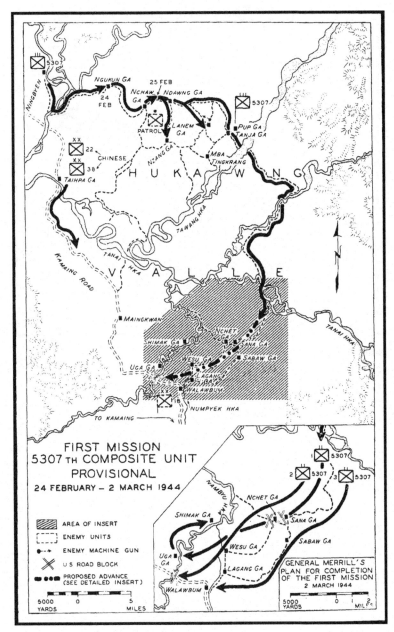

MAP 5. First mission, 5307th Composite Unit (Provisional), 24 February–2 March 1944.

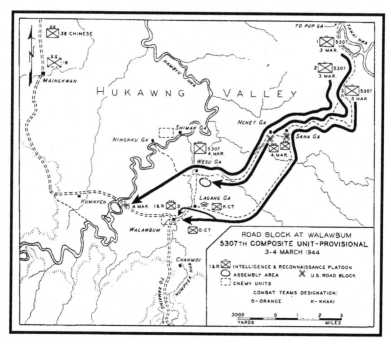

Map 6. Roadblock at Walawbum, 3–4 March 1944.

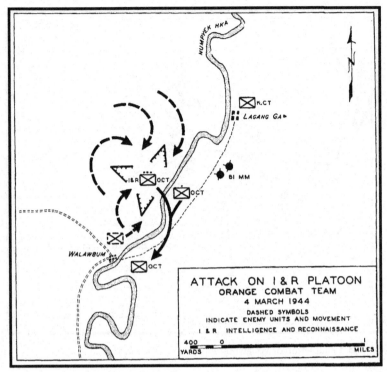

MAP 7. Attack on I & R platoon, Orange Combat Team, Walawbum,
4 March 1944.

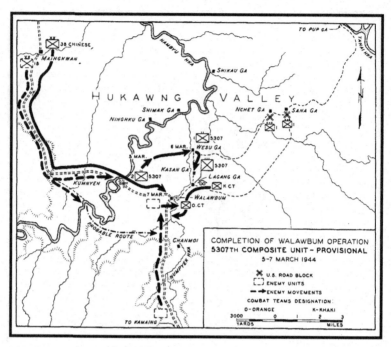

MAP 8. Completion of Walawbum operation, 5–7 March 1944.

CHAPTER X

THE SECOND MISSION

THE FIRST BATTALION: 12 MARCH–7 APRIL 1944

Into the Mogaung Valley

12 March 1944

At 0830 the First Battalion marched out of Shikau Ga on a narrow jungle trail. They were followed by the Chinese 113th Regiment and their 6th Pack Artillery Battery. They were to proceed according to the plan that had been approved by General Stilwell. This called for a fifty-mile movement from north to south over jungle-covered mountains. They would be traveling single file over any available native foot paths from five to ten miles east of the Kamaing Road. As they advanced along the southwestern slopes of the Kumon Mountain Range they would pass from the Hukawng Valley into the Mogaung Valley. Their mission would be to block the road a few miles south of Shaduzup, a small accumulation of grass, reed, and bamboo houses. This village straddled the Japanese-held Kamaing Road. At or near this location the Japanese were said to have supplies and troops. The men and supplies were supporting the 18th Japanese division, which was preventing the Chinese from advancing south. They were the same troops we had defeated at Walawbum.

Unfortunately our encirclement movement had not trapped the major part of their division. The retreating enemy had moved to Jambu Bum pass at the southern end of the Hukawng Valley, where they hoped to prevent the Chinese from advancing into the Mogaung Valley.

General Stilwell's plan called for the First Battalion to hit the road either at Shaduzup or at a suitable location on the road just south of the village on 24 March. At the same time, the Second and Third Battalions, under the command of Colonel Hunter, were to block the road ten miles to the south near the tiny settlement of Inkangahtawng, This double block on the supply line from the Japanese stronghold at Kamaing to their 18th Division would draw them to us like flies to honey. The Chinese could then advance into the Mogaung Valley to help the Marauders wipe out the enemy. As always, the Marauders had only limited knowledge of their mission.

On this first day the terrain was flat to rolling, the temperature was hot, and the air humid. The men were glad to be moving again. Most of the men enjoyed the easy walk through the dense forest.

As usual, the stress of advancing into enemy territory was borne by the I & R platoon, which was well in advance of the long column. The lead scouts knew that one false move or failure to detect the enemy before being detected could mean sudden death. The strain on them was always far worse than that on the men who followed. When marching through the dense forest, we usually had a feeling of security on our flanks. Everyone dreaded the possibility of the sudden sound of gunfire and the call for the mortars and the medics. Before bivouacking at Shingboi Ga, the battalion had covered nine miles.

13 March

The battalion moved out at 0800 and arrived at Makry Bum at 1630, having covered a distance of about twelve miles. The Chinese 113th Regiment, less one battalion, followed at a distance of one day's march.

The Battle at Tingkrung Hka: Multiple Skirmishes on the Trail

14 March

Lieutenant Wilson's Intelligence and Reconnaissance platoon, advancing ahead of the main column, saw fresh Japanese shoe prints on the trail. A few minutes later they slipped up on a group of Japanese sitting around a fire just off the trail about four miles north of Tabauyang. Creeping up as close as possible before opening fire, they completely surprised the Japanese—killing four of them and one Burmese. The surviving enemy ran, abandoning everything. The action had developed so quickly that the men had not had time to develop pre-battle anxiety. After the initial contact, they had the steadying influence of Sgt. Clarence E. Branscomb and several other veterans of fighting in the Pacific.

The firing stirred up about 150 enemy further down the trail. Lieutenant Wilson dispersed his platoon and began a slow withdrawal back to the main column. Lt. William C. Evans, the commander of Red Combat Team's I & R platoon, soon joined them. A message was sent back to the main column for help. Lt. John P. McElmurray's rifle platoon came to help. The three platoons, with the aid of mortars from the main column, soon drove the Japanese across the Numpyek Hka. Lieutenant McElmurray and his men followed, and soon occupied and held high ground.

The Japanese were using two light machine guns, knee mortars, and rifles as they slowly backed down the trail. The thick jungle made flanking of the enemy impossible, and McElmurray's riflemen had to move forward on a narrow front. This practically guaranteed that some of his gallant men would become casualties.

Pvt. Edward E. Foronoff was prone, in an offensive position, when a Japanese bullet struck him at 1700. The missile entered just above the right eye and passed through his brain. Death was immediate. Few of his comrades had seen one of their own killed in battle, and most were profoundly affected.

Sgt. James L. Lennon was moving alongside the trail and toward the enemy when at 1800 hours a bullet passed through his left arm. After the platoon medic dressed his wound he was sent back to Capt. John McLaughlin and Capt. Winnie Steinfield, two of the medical detachment doctors.The next morning he was helped up the trail to the Chinese, who passed him along to a Seagrave surgical unit.

Lt. Col. Osborne, commander of the First Battalion, quickly realized that the Japanese now knew that a large force of Americans was in the area. All signs pointed to the fact that the Japanese would mount a strong defensive position to bottle up the Marauders and attempt to destroy them. Only one sensible decision was possible. He had to keep the enemy occupied while he took half of his battalion around the block by cutting through the jungle. No alternative trail was available. This course of action looked almost impossible, but it had to be attempted. Any significant delay in blocking the Kamaing Road near Shaduzup could bring about serious problems with the

expected action of the Second and Third Battalions on the road farther south.

15 March

At dawn the White Combat Team started cutting a trail along the
river to Kumshan Gahtawng—a distance of about five miles. Red
Combat Team remained in conflict with the Japanese until late in the
afternoon—when, after multiple courageous and brilliant skirmishes,
they broke contact with the stubborn enemy defenses. The 113th
Chinese Regiment had now caught up and followed Red Combat
Team when they started out on the freshly cut trail through the dense
jungle and over mountainous terrain.

During the night the Japanese had regrouped and set up a strong
defensive position further down the trail. Lieutenant Evans's platoon
from Red Combat Team led off the morning advance. In a half mile
they met the Japanese, who had been driven across the river. The
enemy were armed with both light and heavy machine guns. They
were using six machine guns set up in an S-shaped fashion to make an
impenetrable block. The Marauders would use heavy Browning automatic rifle fire, M-1 fire, and mortars. With the enemy held in check,
they would infiltrate the thick growth to surround them. The enemy
would pull out and set up a new block just as they were about to be
surrounded. During the day, various platoons of the combat team
fought eight such engagements in less than two miles. Approximately
one company of Japanese was operating against us on the trail. Our
scouts reported that the enemy had brought up supplies from Jambu
Bum, a few miles to the west. The scouts estimated that they had sent
out about thirty wounded during the night, after which they had
brought in supplies.

Because of the dense jungle vegetation, only one platoon could
operate at a time. Lieutenant Evans's Platoon, made up of men who
had little previous offensive combat experience, repeatedly advanced.
In spite of the heavy fire they had no casualties but eventually became
exhausted because of the extreme exertion and the hot, humid climate.

Maj. Caifson Johnson now sent Lt. William Lepore's platoon into
action. The same offensive tactics were used, but two men were killed
and one man wounded. During this action Red Combat Team was

preparing to disengage. One senior officer became agitated, and his action caused considerable confusion and uncertainty as to how Lepore's platoon could be assisted in the disengagement action. Lt. Sam Wilson and Lieutenant McDowell, accompanied by a radio operator carrying an SCR 300, made their way to the engaged platoon. They soon had mortar fire directed on the Japanese, and with Lepore's aid turned possible defeat into victory. The wounded were sent back, and Pfc. William E. Clark and another man were buried by the trail. Clark had been struck in the head and arm by machine-gun bullets. Three minutes later his last words were, "Oh my God, mother." Both Wilson and Lepore said a prayer at the gravesite. Shortly after the platoon had left the area, the Japanese directed a heavy artillery barrage to that location. The bravery, aggressiveness, and emotional stability of these young infantry volunteers had been tested here in offensive combat against the best that Japan could offer. The battle of the trail at Tingkrung Hka was over, and had resulted in a considerable reduction in the number of enemy to be met in the future.

The First Battalion Cuts Its Way toward Jaiwa Ga

15 March

At dawn, White Combat Team started cutting a trail along the river to Kumshan Gahtawng. Red Combat Team broke off its action in the late afternoon and was soon advancing on the new-cut trail. Red was followed by the 113th Chinese Regiment. White reached its destination at 1515 hours and bivouacked for the night. The other units camped along the trail.

The cross-jungle route presented many obstacles. Much of this new trail was only developed after the men had cut a tunnel through dense bamboo growth. Some mature bamboo was six inches in diameter and had to be left in place, since the machetes were not adequate for this size. Frequently, cutting was necessary high up the bamboo in order to have room for the mules with their loads to pass through.

The work required great energy because of the toughness of the bamboo, the hot, humid air, and the steep up-and-down slopes of the mountain ridges. The men blazing the trail had to be replaced by others frequently. The unit had not been resupplied with food for the men and animals since 11 March. Some of the men were without food. The mules supplemented their diet by eating bamboo leaves, but the horses had to depend entirely on oats, which were no longer available.

16 March

The First Battalion had an air drop scheduled for this day. At dawn the men started clearing the most open space available to receive the drop. Planes came over but, due to the mountainous terrain, could not find the First Battalion until they had expended too much of their gas, so they reported they would come back on the morning of the 17th.

All day the men improved the drop area, cutting trees, clearing creepers and thick underbrush—but, being on the side of a hill, it was a poor field at best. It had to do, however, since no other area was available and the supplies were urgently needed.

17 March

Our patrols had located some Japanese in the area near where the battalion was bivouacked. Colonel Osborne, smelling a rat, moved the battalion to another location. At 0730 the drop planes came over, and as they started dropping the Japanese opened up with mortar fire on the bivouac area from which Colonel Osborne had just moved the battalion. The Japanese withdrew before we could get to them. No trail was found on which they could have escaped, so apparently only a few had cut their way through and then had withdrawn by the same route. The airdrop was only partially successful due to nearby hills, and the planes had to stay up pretty high. Consequently, quite a lot of grain, which was free-dropped, went over the side of the hillside and was lost. Some parachute loads also went over the side of the hill, but they were recovered.

In the afternoon the battalion started cutting its way again over the rough, mountainous countryside. Officers and men alternated at cutting the trail. By nightfall the battalion had moved two miles in the direction of Jaiwa Ga before they bivouacked for the night.

18 March

As on the previous days of this phase of the current mission, the march had been very difficult. Because of the slow progress being made by the fatigued cutters, the long column of men and animals was constantly stopping. One had the option of standing with resultant weariness or flopping on the jungle floor and running the risk of being stepped on by a restless mule or horse.

Men and animals were equally susceptible to the large, blood-sucking leeches. They fell from vegetation onto their victims. Their attachment apparatus was very efficient and allowed them to attach to any part of man or beast. During daylight hours they would attach to a part of the body where they could not be seen. Their small bodies would quickly become swollen with blood. Frequently their presence would not be recognized until the Marauder inspected his body at rest periods or at night. At times the leeches would rupture, and the blood sucked from the men would soak through their clothing. The leeches were removed by touching them with a match or lighted cigarette. The area where the leech had been attached would tend to bleed for several minutes, since the leech had injected an anticlotting chemical into the area of attachment. Frequently the leech would ignore easily accessible skin areas and would attach in the ear canal, in a nasal passage, or on an eyelid, scrotum, or penis. The mules and horses were not immune to these blood-sucking worms. They were apt to attach themselves to the ankles of the animals.

The men were beginning to show signs of weight loss and malnutrition. The combat team surgeons were seeing and treating an increasing number of men with diarrhea and stomach disturbances. Many of those who had had problems with dysentery back at Walawbum were still seeking treatment.

By nightfall the men bivouacked for the night at a position two miles northwest of Jaiwa Ga.

19 March

The campsite included a small open area, and drop planes were called in. Several days' food was supplied for the men and animals. Colonel Osborne decided to take time to rest the men and animals and to gather information. Captain Tom P. Senff, Battalion S-3, was sent to Jaiwa Ga with the mission of reaching General Merrill, approximately twelve miles to the east at Weilangyang, where the Second and Third Battalions were resting and patrolling while awaiting final orders. He made General Merrill aware of the reasons for the First Battalion's delay and carried instructions back to Colonel Osborne.

On the trail to Jaiwa Ga, Captain Senff was surprised to meet Lieutenant Tilley of the Office of Strategic Services. This meeting was a total surprise to Colonel Osborne, since he had not been told that the OSS had any men in Burma. Lieutenant Tilley had a force of fifty armed and organized Kachins in the area. He had known the Marauders were coming but had not had a way to contact them. His force had been in back of the Japanese who had been fighting the Marauders on the 13th, 14th, and 15th, and had caused some Japanese casualties.

Colonel Osborne and some of the officers and men joined Lieutenant Tilley at his safe area in Jaiwa Ga. They spent the evening being entertained by several Kachin elders. The natives enjoyed smoking opium while the Marauders smoked cigarettes.

Trailblock and Death at Nprawa Ga

20 March

The First Battalion marched over difficult trails a short distance to Nprawa Ga, where the lead platoon hit a Japanese machine gun blocking the trail. One Marauder was killed and two were wounded before our mortars wiped out the gun crew. I do not have the name of the dead Marauder. T5g. Paul M. Glova was wounded by a machine-gun bullet. He was treated by the medics for a severe wound with a compound fracture of the right foot. Pfc. Julius Goldman was hit a few minutes later, also by the machine gun. This resulted in a compound fracture of the left femur. Both men reached the 13th Medical Battalion in about twenty-four hours and were sent out four days later.

Other enemy in the block apparently withdrew, and our platoon moved forward in hot pursuit. These were the first casualties we had suffered that could be traced to language barriers. As we had moved out of Jaiwa Ga, with Kachins accompanying our lead scouts, the Kachins started muttering some unintelligible lingo. Our interpreter was not around, and the men tried to feed the Kachins or give them cigarettes when they started jabbering. Actually they were trying to tell us that the Japanese had a block somewhere along the trail we were using. Before the interpreter came up, the scout ran into the Japanese ambush. We were lucky to have only one man killed. If the Japanese had waited a few more minutes they would have had a much bigger target. The men had learned a costly lesson, and from then on when a Kachin had something to say, we got an interpreter.

21 March

The battalion received a five-day drop at the paddy field near Htingnankawng, about six miles west of Nprawa Ga. After the drop the Red Combat Team moved on to Hpauchye Ga and bivouacked for the night.

22 March

The First Battalion left Hpauchye Ga with Lt. Harry B. Coburn's platoon leading. About four miles southwest of Hpauchye Ga its lead patrol hit a Japanese ambush. T5g. William A. Stitt was mortally wounded and died one-half hour after injury. When the machine gun opened up, he had quickly assumed a prone offensive position behind a clump of thick bamboo. For some reason he was sent to the rear. He started running down the trail and was hit by a machine- gun bullet, which entered his right lower leg and exited in back of the knee. Hemorrhage was severe due to laceration of the main leg artery. The platoon medic applied a tourniquet, but he for some reason could not keep it in place and soon died in spite of all possible help.

Four men were slightly wounded by fragments from a mortar fired by the Marauders. T4g. Peter P. Guzaites, a medic, took a flesh wound in his right flank. T5g. Ralph G. Smith, also a medic, had a minor mouth wound with a fractured tooth. S.Sgt. Gerald Feathergill had a minor wound in the chest wall and thigh. Marion McNabb was hit in the left arm. T5g Richard S. Murphy got a minor wound of his right thigh from a Japanese grenade. All five men returned to duty.

The Japanese retreated and began delaying actions. Lieutenant Coburn decided to leave the trail and bypass the enemy. The rest of Red Combat Team and White Combat Team followed. The bypass route led down a streambed for about four miles and required cutting a trail most of the way. The going was very tough, but prog-ress was being made. Lieutenant Coburn's advance scouts smelled out a Japanese block at a stream junction, crept silently up on it, and killed seven Japanese resting near foxholes while the rest of the Japanese ran into the jungle. Lieutenant Coburn took the Japanese position intact and rested his men. While the platoon was resting in the enemy position they came back in strength, and four more were killed. A reconnaissance down the streambed showed the Japanese had a block with a dug-in perimeter and machine guns. Lieutenant Coburn led his platoon down the river and around the block. Late in the afternoon they bivouacked along the riverbank.

Colonel Osborne had been following with the rest of the battalion. The Chinese were not far behind. As the Japanese seemed to have blocks on all trails leading to the area, Colonel Osborne decided to cut his own trail, for he considered it extremely important that we have as little contact with the enemy as possible. He estimated that the unit would have ten miles of trail cutting over the jungle-covered mountain ranges before reaching the Chengun River. They would then have ten miles of travel, in and out of the river, until they reached a suitable area, four miles below Shaduzup, to block the road. When they reached the entrance into the Chengun, the Japanese-held road would be about five miles to the west.

24 March

Colonel Osborne and his men marched and cut a trail two miles over the mountain terrain. In some places the loads had to be taken off the animals and manhandled up the slippery mountainside. The unit bivouacked for the night on the side of a mountain. There had been no more contact with the enemy.

Colonel Osborne was aware that the First Battalion had missed its appointment to block the road on this day. He knew that this failure was very serious. The mission of the Second and Third Battalions required them to block the road about ten miles farther south on 24 March. Simultaneous blocks would have caused much confusion among the Japanese, and they would have had to concentrate their troops against two American forces instead of one. The failure of the First Battalion to meet its deadline could defeat the purpose of this end-run around the 18th Division. The possibility of putting the Second and Third Battalions in extreme danger was very likely. They would be alone, without any chance of assistance, about ten miles north of the Japanese base at Kamaing. The Japanese would have an opportunity to surround and cut them off deep in enemy territory.

25 March

The men continued to cut a trail for three hours, covering only one and one-half miles. This day was the hardest, most tortuous part of the march since we had entered Burma.

Colonel Osborne ordered a brilliant plan to confuse the Japanese. He sent Lieutenant McElmurray's platoon to the west, directly toward the road, which was five miles away. The colonel had learned from Lieutenant Tilley that approximately three hundred Japanese were at Shaduzup and six hundred near Jambu Bum to the north.

Lieutenant McElmurray led his rifle platoon to the northwest along a trail that led to Hkahku Gahtawng. Near the village they surprised two Japanese, who were carrying maps and sketching equipment. One escaped into the jungle. Soon after the platoon had passed through the village, the Japanese began to shell the area. This activity continued all night. The feint probably caused the Japanese to shift their defenses to handle the movement, thereby weakening their defenses on the main road south of Shaduzup where the block was to take place.

Lieutenant Coburn's platoon had accomplished miracles on 22 and 23 March, but the time had come for absolute secrecy of movement. Contact with the enemy while advancing toward the road block had to be avoided. Colonel Osborne had decided to strike the enemy about five miles south of Shaduzup, where the Chengun River joined the Mogaung River.

Free from enemy attention, the battalion cut through several miles of jungle-covered ridges and then began a ten-mile, tortuous hike down the bed of the Chengun River. Wading in the ankle- to knee-deep water over the rocky bed was difficult but better than hacking a passageway through the jungle.

At 1400 hours on 27 March, Lieutenant Wilson reported to Major Johnson of White Combat Team that the I & R had reached the objective where the Chengun joined the Mogaung River. Many Japanese were seen in the area. It appeared to Lieutenant Wilson that there was a Japanese camp between the river and the Kamaing Road. Major

Johnson ordered him to break his platoon into two sections. One group was to reconnoiter down the Mogaung River and the other up the river. Lieutenant Wilson personally led the patrol that reconnoitered the area north of the river junction. After careful investigation along the riverbank, he decided to cross the fifty-yard-wide river, taking one man with him, to get a better idea of the size of the Japanese camp and the location of their defenses. He also had to determine if the river was fordable. Slipping quietly into the water about two hundred yards up the river from the Japanese camp, Lieutenant Wilson and Sergeant Purlee Tintary held their weapons—a carbine and a tommy gun—over their heads and rapidly waded across the swiftly flowing river. As they waded up to their necks in the middle of the river, a signal from Sergeant Branscomb, left on the riverbank, brought their attention to an armed Japanese patrol walking toward the bank they were approaching. They strained every muscle trying to reach some bushes on the bank before the enemy spotted them. They succeeded in crawling into the bushes only a minute before the patrol passed. When the patrol members had filled their canteens at the river's edge they departed by the route they had come. With the coast clear, the two men worked their way into the Japanese camp, which was spread out in jungle between the road and the river. They estimated that a Japanese company was in the area and another company was located just to the north. Large quantities of food and clothing were stored in bamboo and grass shacks and tents. The two men worked their way back to the river and were able to get back to their men on the east bank just as another patrol came down to the riverbank.

After evaluating Lieutenant Wilson's information, Major Johnson made a personal reconnaissance at midnight on 27 March. He waded the river about seventy-five yards north of a lone Japanese sentry, who was walking up and down the riverbank carrying a smudgy lantern. Major Johnson was now convinced that the river was shallow enough at his point of inspection and would do for the main crossing of the attacking men.

The Battle of Shaduzup

With the full authority of Colonel Osborne, Major Johnson now issued orders that his White Combat Team would cross, with bayonets fixed, at 0300 on 28 March. The coordinated attack would begin at daybreak. Six platoons would cross the river in column initially, and, on reaching the west bank, the first platoon would move two hundred yards north along the river while the second would move on a 270-degree azimuth and hit the road. The third would tie in with the fourth and sixth platoons to remain in the vicinity of the point where the crossing had been made. After the attack swept through the Japanese camp, a perimeter would be dug on the road. Major Johnson's command post and aid station was to be at the river-crossing point on the west side of the river.

Colonel Osborne was coordinating the units. Red Combat Team was to remain on the east bank of the river. The Chinese 113th Regiment remained bivouacked on a jungle-covered hill about a mile northeast of the river in readiness to occupy the positions when the First Battalion pulled out. Seagrave's small portable surgical unit was well in back of the Chinese. This would be a long distance to bring the wounded.

28 March

At 0300, with Lt. Philip S. Weld's platoon leading and Lieutenant Weld the lead man, White Combat Team moved out silently, and slowly waded across the river. By some stroke of luck not a Japanese sentry was encountered, and the platoons slipped into place before daylight. Radio contact by the SCR 300 and SCR 536 was maintained. As dawn began to break and little fires began to pop over the Japanese camp, the signal for the attack was given, over the radio, by Major Johnson. The Marauders swept through the Japanese camp. Consternation and confusion do not halfway describe the scene. Half-dressed Japanese without guns ran amuck; some with guns fired wildly. The Marauders used their rifles, automatic weapons, and grenades very effectively. The first Japanese seen were at a semipermanent Japanese latrine, and they broke and ran shouting wildly. They were mowed down by a tommy-gunner.

Lt. Meredith Caldwell's platoon was at the southern end of the advancing Americans. They were the platoon closest to the road and the first to reach it. A Japanese sentry was seen eighty yards up the road. He was quickly killed by one shot from a sniper's rifle. They were hardly on the road before a Japanese truck arrived from the south.

The three Japanese in the cab started to jump when they saw four tommy guns aimed at them. A second later they and the cab were riddled. The Japanese truck proved to be loaded with uniforms and underwear, with a few sacks of rice thrown in. The truck was a copy of a 1935 Ford. The Japanese in the bivouac area by this time were in full alarm and were beginning to offer some resistance. The Marauders later ate the cooked rice and fish that some of the enemy had left cooking on small fires. The new Japanese underwear was also quickly used by some of the smaller men. The camp proved to be well supplied with guns, equipment, and food—but the Marauders didn't have time to inspect it, as they had orders to dig in a perimeter on the main road, to block all supplies from Kamaing to Shaduzup, and to withstand the inevitable counterattack, which was not long in coming.

Phil Weld's platoon was advancing on the north end of the attacking Americans. In front of them the river took an S-bend that required his platoon to cross the river three times to reach the road. They had advanced fifty yards into the forest, toward the second crossing, when the attack signal came. They quickly made the second crossing without serious problems. The location for the third crossing was soon found to be much less favorable. First it was necessary to cross a dry, rock-strewn secondary channel, followed by a brush-covered knoll. Beyond the knoll the river did not look difficult to cross, but the twenty-foot embankment on the far side was another matter.

Lieutenant Weld and Sgt. Allen H. Overby advanced over the knoll and observed a squad of enemy with a machine gun near the road. The platoon was immediately under enemy fire and answered with every weapon they had. The lieutenant, the sergeant, and four others were in an exposed position. One of the group, Pfc. Norman F. Page, had been hit by machine-gun fire. All of those in this advance group were exposed to enemy fire. At this time only a foolish officer would order his men forward. Weld ordered Overby to make a dash for the crest of the knoll. He had orders to get Red Combat Team to throw mortars on the two machine guns. By some miracle Overby made it to safety, and the mortars were soon zeroing in on the enemy.

Under the covering fire of his platoon, Lieutenant Weld dragged and carried Page to a depression, where in relative safety they both rested and gained some composure. With the aid of covering rifle fire and well-directed mortar fire, Lieutenant Weld found superhuman courage and strength to half drag and half carry Page to the east side of the knoll and safety.

The lieutenant was explaining that he was pulling the platoon back for further instructions when he was told that the three men who had followed over the knoll had been hit. While he was attempting to visually locate the wounded, the first one to be hit dragged himself to safety. Private Anthony N. Dinardo had a machine-gun bullet in his right leg. The two other wounded were still in the line of fire and in grave danger of more hits. Both men had gone to help Dinardo. Overby and Ernest Banks immediately volunteered to make a rescue attempt.

While the rescue plan was being outlined, Overby spotted a sniper in a tree above the two enemy machine guns. One shot from his rifle took care of this man, who would have been in a position to kill the exposed men.

Under the cover of rifle and mortar fire, Phil Weld and Ernest Banks first dragged Pvt. Milton Susnjer and then Pfc. Lambert Olsen to safety. The wounded were immediately carried to the aid station, where they got emergency treatment. A machine-gun bullet had fractured Olsen's skull and exposed his brain. He also had compound fractures of his left upper leg bone (femur) and left foot, and was unconscious. Susnjer had a compound fracture of his left femur and a severe flesh wound of the right thigh.

Olsen was given six units of plasma and gained consciousness after two hours of treatment in the battalion aid station. Susnjer was given four units of plasma. The wounded men reached the Seagrave surgical unit on 29 March. Olsen died on 2 April while still in Burma. Susnjer reached a platoon of the 113th Medical Battalion on 1 April and the 20th General Hospital on 4 April, seven days after he was wounded. Page arrived at the 20th General ten days after he was wounded and Dinardo seven days.

As time passed, Caldwell's platoon continued to do well. Colonel Osborne had sent a section of light machine guns to him. The guns were placed at a slight curve and pointed straight down the road to the south. They soon caught a company of Japanese marching in columns of twos. When the dust settled, one man counted sixty dead Japanese.

While the enemy was being occupied by Weld's platoon, McElmurray was on the road and setting up strong defensive positions. His men had watched while Coburn's men had mowed down the Japanese.

After Weld's wounded had been sent back, he took a new route and set up just north of McElmurray on the road. Here he was joined by Lt. Charles Scott. After an enemy attack, Scott killed a Japanese officer, whose body lay on the road. Over a period of an hour or so the men killed twelve Japanese who tried to recover the body.

Within two hours after the battle had begun, Japanese artillery opened up on Red Combat Team on the east side of the river. Apparently, at this time, the artillery was too close to fire on the perimeter dug on the road. By mid-morning, Japanese 150mm and 75mm guns were keeping up a steady barrage. Later, another battery opened up at point-blank range on the Marauders dug in on the road. The Japanese were turning their attention from the Chinese to the north at Jambu Bum to the Marauders, who were threatening their rear. The Chinese were taking advantage of this and were slowly advancing south toward Shaduzup. All during the afternoon and night the Japanese directed artillery and mortar fire at the Americans. Three Marauders were killed and ten wounded. Numerous Japanese frontal attacks were stopped by our mortar, rifle, machine-gun, and grenade fire. Miraculously, only two of our men were hit by Japanese bullets and only one by a grenade.

After the roadblock was established, a platoon from B company advanced north on the road. A Japanese truck rounded a corner before cover was available. Nine Japanese were killed, and Cpl. John L. Tulli was wounded in the right arm by a grenade fragment. He remained on duty. One hour later Pfc. Joseph E. Lynch had his head creased by a Japanese bullet. He also remained with his platoon on duty. About two hours later, during another enemy attack, T5g Joseph Asker was wounded when a bullet passed through his left thumb. At the time, he was in a prone defensive position but was not dug in. Asker was able to make his way across the river to the battalion aid station for emergency treatment. Next, he made his way several miles up the Chengun River to the small Seagrave surgical team that traveled behind the Chinese. He reached the 2nd platoon, company D of the 13th Medical Battalion on 2 April and the 20th General Hospital on 5 April. Passage to the medical battalion was by a small L-4 plane and to the general hospital by a C-47.

The location of the Battle of Shaduzup was such that the wounded could not expect to get any more than front-line emergency care for a variable and usually unreasonable period after injury. Men were to die who under better arrangements would have had a good chance of survival. Few of the wounded reached the surgical team in less than twenty-four hours. The average time to reach the medical battalion was five days. Few arrived at the general hospital in less than one week.

Private John Frigulti was digging a foxhole at 1100 hours when he was cut down by a 90mm mortar shell fragment, which tore into his right forearm. At the same time, Pfc. Ralph N. Cummins was resting in a shallow foxhole. He also was struck by a mortar fragment, which entered his right neck, fractured his collar bone, and lodged in the second rib. Two of his arm muscles were paralyzed. During the same barrage, one other man was wounded. 2nd Lt. Nathan Goldstein presented with a severe disabling injury of his right arm and wrist. The three men were evacuated with essential treatment along the route of passage, and all reached the 20th General Hospital in Assam, India, on 4 April. Frigulti was eventually able to return to duty, but the other two men were sent to the U.S. for further treatment.

C-47 supply planes showed up after the Marauders of Red Combat Team had established a very effective roadblock. The mortars of White Combat Team had been doing and continued to do a great job, but they were no match for the enemy artillery which was trying hard to knock out the roadblock. The supply planes brought fighter escort, and these effectively silenced the Japanese artillery while they were active in the area. Without this replenishment of food and ammunition, the Marauders would have probably been forced to abandon the block. As usual, the supply unit had done a great job.

One serious injury and one death from artillery fragments struck the unlucky soldiers of C Company at 1500 hours. T5g Richard S. Murphy was sleeping prone in a shallow foxhole. He died in less than thirty minutes from massive abdominal wounds. Pvt. Robert G. Bresse was resting in the same hole as Murphy when a fragment tore into his right buttock and right pelvis. After extensive treatment, Bresse made a satisfactory recovery.

At 1710 hours a Japanese platoon struck one sector of the defensive positions on the road. The enemy were supported with mortars. Pfc. Elbert V. McKinney and S.Sgt. Thomas N. Matney were both in foxholes when they were wounded by 90mm mortar fragments. The former was wounded in the lower back and sacrum. The latter presented with injuries to his right arm and leg. As usual, there was great delay in treatment beyond the aid station. Volunteers who carried the men back had to contend with darkness, extremely rough jungle terrain, artillery and mortar fire, trigger-happy Chinese troops who were distributed in an irregular way in the jungle, and the distance to the surgical team. The several-day period to get back to the medical battalion and later the general hospital involved the usual hit-or-miss arrangements.

During the entire period that Red Combat Team carried out the roadblock, White Combat Team remained on the east side of the Chengun river. While in reserve in this position, they gave mortar support, delivered replacement ammunition, and received the wounded. The battalion medical aid station was set up in a dug-out area beside the Chengun River. The doctors worked behind an inadequate screen of ponchos. When darkness came on, their only light was provided by candles. The mortally wounded and those who had come in too late for evacuation up the Chengun to the Seagrave portable unit lay in shallow ditches for the night. The battalion headquarters and communication section were close at hand.

During the early evening, with nothing to fear from air attack, Japanese artillery became very active and devoted their attention to the Chinese and American units on the east side of the river. They were using 70mm howitzers, with their arched projection, and 77mm guns that had a flat projector fire like a rifle. The former could be heard coming before they exploded, while the latter came with a sudden shriek. The howitzers went up and came down to explode in trees or on the ground. The men soon found that both weapons were terrifying and effective. Because of these weapons and the need to attend to the dead and wounded, few got sleep during the night. The men of headquarters and A companies also had to contend with mortar fire.

29 March

During the predawn hours, according to plans, the Chinese 113th Regiment moved, platoon by platoon, into the perimeter established by White Combat Team. By 1000 hours the move was complete. White Combat Team had moved to the east, across the Chengun River, to locate a mile to the north along the river, near the Seagrave portable hospital unit.

Red Combat Team was to remain for the night in their position across the river from the roadblock. Numerous artillery shells struck their bivouac area during the night. Adequate rest and sleep were impossible. Two men from headquarters company were killed, one was to die of wounds, and a third survived. Lt. Sam Wilson's platoon had been taking an especially heavy pounding before a shell made a direct hit on the foxhole where Pvt. Dervis J. Allen (Big Allen) and Pfc. Eugene Allen (Little Allen) were trying to sleep (they were not related). Sgt. Clarence Branscomb and the platoon medical aid man T5g Anderson immediately went to their aid. In the pitch-black darkness they determined that Big Allen was dead and Little Allen was mortally wounded. The platoon soon moved to a safer area, but Branscomb very courageously stayed with Little Allen until he died at dawn, shortly after calling for his mother. Sgt. Branscomb was later to be decorated with a Silver Star. He had shown great mercy and bravery in supporting a dying comrade while remaining under heavy fire. His unit had been moved to a safer area. Pvt. Grady B. Clayburn had also been wounded in the left leg. He was successfully evacuated early in the day.

At 0300 Pvt. James R. Welch had moved with his platoon to a safer area—but had forgotten his pack. In spite of continued shelling in the old area, he went back in the dark, without a helmet, to recover it. A shell fragment fractured his skull and penetrated his brain. He was found three hours later and immediately sent through the chain of evacuation. He never regained consciousness and died four days later.

Shortly after daylight on 29 March the Marauders heard a new sound, which soon had a quieting effect on the Japanese artillery. The men were thrilled to learn that a Chinese pack artillery unit with four 75mm guns had been following the 113th Chinese Regiment, had arrived, and was in action. The Chinese were soon settled at all important locations.

The Japanese army had been dealt a severe blow. They had been driven away from Jambu Bum and Shaduzup. Those who remained would have to fight through the Chinese on the road or bypass through jungle terrain. Many had been killed and wounded to the north. The Marauders had left many dead enemy on the road.

We always considered any dead or wounded far too many and thanked God that there were no more. Each of us in our own way mourned our dead comrades and hoped for the best as far as the sick and wounded were concerned. As our dead were buried at scattered places in the jungle, their friends would say a prayer in their own way. The mission to Shaduzup had resulted or would result in the burial of brave and dedicated American volunteers. The bodies of some, we knew, would never be removed from foreign soil.

30 March

The First Battalion rested along the banks of the Chengun River all day. The Chinese and Japanese artillery fired on and off nearby. More than three hundred Japanese were estimated to have been killed by the Marauders during the Battle of Shaduzup. Unfortunately, no information was available to the men concerning the fighting, north of our battleground, between the Chinese and Japanese. We could only hope for the best. By military standards, eight dead and about thirty-five wounded Americans during an approach through enemy territory for eighteen days, followed by a thirty-six-hour battle, does not seem high. Whether the casualties are high or low they seem unnecessary and tragic to their comrades in battle. The waste of life is even harder to bear when, as is the case of infantry soldiers, they have little or no knowledge of the plan of battle, the total number of dead and wounded, or the significance of what they have accomplished. Failure of higher command to show appreciation for the dedication, courage, and sacrifice of all concerned further compounds the temporary depression that often afflicts those who continue to put their lives on the line. During periods of rest there is a tendency to wonder why tactical mistakes were made, why more troops were not used, why replacements were not available for sick, dead, and wounded before the next mission, why better medical facilities were not available, why more air power was not used, and why pack artillery was not always available. Most of the men considered it inexcusable to send us against Japanese artillery when we had none to counter this deadly weapon.

When the First Battalion had left Shikau Ga for Pabum on 12 March, the muleskinners noticed that a cow and heifer were following the mule train. Over steep, slippery mountain trails and through jungle streams, they were soon sharing the animals' food. The word soon spread through the column like wildfire that the victory feast after the Battle of Shaduzup was walking along with the mule train.

There was considerable difference of opinion among the Marauders as to whether it was best to keep their dinner until the Shaduzup fight—some said a bird in the hand was worth two in the bush—but the muleskinners persisted in keeping their cow and heifer. Both animals survived the artillery shelling and the Battle of Shaduzup. When the Chinese took over the perimeter there was some confusion in the early morning hours, and—to the bitter disappointment of all—the cow and heifer could not be found.

The March to Join the Second and Third Battalions

Early on the morning of 31 March an order, transmitted by radio, directed the battalion to move to the east of Mupaw Ga to protect the rear of the Second and Third Battalions, which were engaged with the Japanese in the Manpin-Auche-Nhpum Ga area. The one day of rest had been helpful to the men from a mental and physical standpoint. The fact remains, however, that they had just completed one of the most difficult sixteen-day marches that any American battalion had ever made. Their march had taken them over little-used, narrow mountain trails. They had been forced to cut their way through miles of virgin jungle and had struggled along eight miles of a narrow, twisting, jungle-clad river gorge. Food had been inadequate. Casualties had resulted from numerous enemy ambushes. Many of the men were sick with dysentery and diarrhea. Animals and men suffered from continuous leech attachments to their bodies. The sick had to go forward, and the wounded were treated and evacuated with delay and difficulty. Fatigue among the men was severe and chronic. Sixteen days of physical and mental torture were followed by further battle with a brutal enemy.

With no change in their inadequate diet of K-rations, they were now faced with an even more difficult eight-day march over several three- and four-thousand-foot mountains. Their new mission was to assist the rest of their unit, which was locked in a life-and-death struggle with a regiment of the conquerors of Malaya, Singapore, Burma, and Nanking.

The first day's march took the battalion up the bed of the Chengun River. Their orders had not explained that there was an urgent need to reach the rest of the unit. Because of the tortuous river, with its rocky bed and overhanging jungle, as well as the condition of the men and animals, progress was slow. They were also looking for a suitable area to take an airdrop. Three horses had to be shot because they collapsed on the trail. Fatigue, diarrhea, and dysentery were major problems among the men.

1 April

The battalion's long-range radio had been out of commission for several days, and Colonel Osborne remained very concerned. He temporarily solved the problem of being out of touch with the command by riding a horse over jungle trails to Shaduzup.

During the colonel's absence the battalion took the muchneeded airdrop. The men waited and rested, as best they could, in the rain. He returned without mishap. As Charlton Ogburn states in his book, *The Marauders:*

> Then Colonel Osborne returned with the news. The Japanese had invaded India with three divisions. While the offensive had been foreseen by the British, it had never been expected to have such power and momentum. The main Japanese force had surrounded a British corps in Imphal; and one division had cut through to Kohima, where only a small British garrison stood between it and the Brahmaputra valley, which was the sole avenue of communication with Assam, from whence all the supplies for the 5307th and all those for the Chinese were flown. About the same time that Osborne got back—our long-range set having

been meanwhile repaired—we received a message from Merrill's headquarters saying our other two battalions had run into a Japanese offensive aimed at out-marauding the Marauders and flanking the Chinese advance. Our assistance was needed as fast as we could bring it (Ogburn 1956).

Shortly after Colonel Osborne returned, the First Battalion began the thirty-mile march over the mountainous jungle to aid the Second and Third Battalions. The terrain was extremely difficult, and they made only one thousand yards on 3 April.

2 April

During the afternoon, when the column was cutting a trail over a tortuous mountain, the animal train got separated from the end of the column. The word, "There is a gap in the column," was passed around. When it reached Colonel Osborne at the head of the column, it was "There's a Japanese in the column." Colonel Osborne, tired and sweating, turned his head slightly and said, "Well, get the bastard out of the column!" That message was passed to the rear—but the men were too tired to laugh.

Marching over the trail they had previously cut, with rain pouring down and every step forward only half of a step because of sliding back in the mud, the battalion reached the Shadu River. The climbing was very difficult, some of the horses couldn't make it, and several collapsed and died on the trail.

3 April

An airdrop was received at 0800, and the battalion departed at 1400. The trail cutting this day was very difficult, and the mountain climbing seemed to require more effort than it had in the past. Many of the men had bad feet, as well as extreme fatigue due to inadequate diet, dysentery, and the effort they had to make on this march. On this day they covered one and one-half miles.

4 April

After a hard march of seven miles, the First Battalion reached Kadungdukawng. They were now about a third of the way toward their goal.

CHAPTER X

5 April

The men and animals arrived at Singtawngkawn Ga at 1545 after an all-day march. They had covered seven miles, and the going was still tough. Some friendly Kachins, part of the OSS force, came to the bivouac area and provided information on the Japanese in the vicinity. The battalion's radio had been out of order for three days, and the weather had probably been the chief cause.

6 April

Radio communication was reestablished, and most of the day was spent resting and waiting for a much-needed airdrop. In the afternoon an urgent message was picked up. The Second Battalion was having a big fight at Nhpum Ga about fifteen miles to the west. The Third Battalion was fighting to open the trail to the encircled Second Battalion. Help was urgently needed. Colonel Osborne ordered the battalion to move out at 1845 without the airdrop. They marched under the worst possible conditions for five and a half miles to the southeast—still cutting and improving an old trail so that the men and animals could pass through.

The Exhausted Relief Force Arrives

7 April

After a very hard, forced march, the First Battalion arrived at Hsamshingyang at 1700. This spot consisted of a ten-acre rice paddy, nestled between mountain ridges on all sides, at an elevation of 1500 feet. This location served as the rear base for the Third Battalion, which had been fighting an offensive battle since 28 March. They had advanced approximately four miles up a razorback ridge that led to the Second Battalion, whose men were surrounded at Nhpum Ga at an elevation of twenty-four hundred feet. To reach the Second Battalion, the Third Battalion still had to advance about two hundred yards through jungle protected by Japanese machine guns, mortar, rifles, grenades, and artillery.

The Second Battalion's mountaintop location covered an area about a hundred yards wide and two hundred yards long and was surrounded by ravines covered by dense jungle growth. A trail passed through the area running north to south. The Third Battalion was advancing to them from the north, and the Japanese were blocking the trail both on the north and the south. The jungle-covered terrain on both the east and the west sides of the battlefield fell steeply one thousand feet to a river on each side.

Conditions on and about this battlefield were horrible. The Marauders in this battalion had been subjected each day to rifle, machine-gun, grenade, mortar, and artillery fire—as well as numerous banzai attacks. Their wounded were lying in foxholes, their dead were buried in shallow graves, bloated and decaying mule and horse corpses remained unburied, and the foul-smelling air teemed with thousands of flies.

As the sick, hungry, and exhausted men of the First Battalion arrived at the improvised airstrip, supply area, drop area, and evacuation location of Hsamshingyang, they found the area protected by a few muleskinners and friendly Kachin natives. All available Third Battalion men were fighting the offensive battle on the trail leading to Nhpum Ga. The men of the First were happy to see the remarkably optimistic spirit of these men, but were even happier to find 10-in-1 rations waiting for them. They had had no food in thirty-six hours.

Colonel Hunter soon outlined their combat mission. Capt. Tom P. Senff, now commanding officer of Red Combat Team, was ordered to select as many able-bodied men as possible and to lead them on a long and difficult march down the river to the west on a flanking movement to the left of the enemy. At a point south of Nhpum Ga they were to work their way up the thousand-foot mountain to attack the Japanese from the rear. Captain Senff was able to round up 250 men considered to be in good enough physical condition for this mission, which would begin on 8 April.

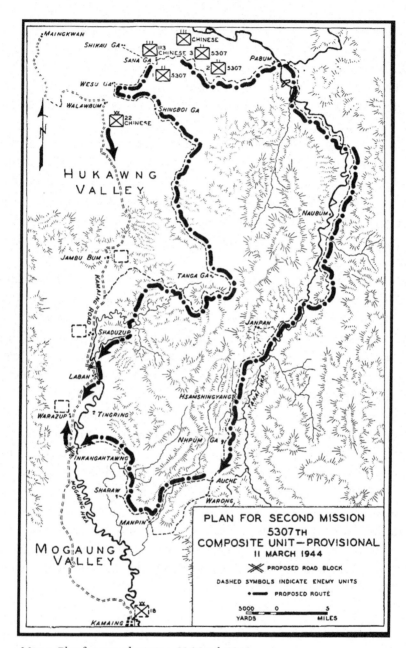

MAP 9. Plan for second mission, 11 March 1944.

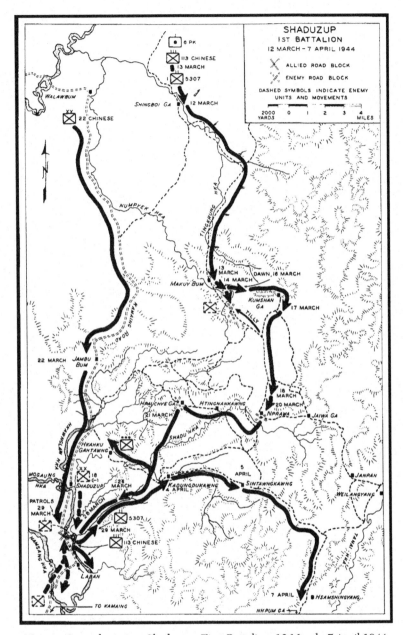

MAP 10. Second mission, Shaduzup: First Battalion, 12 March–7 April 1944.

CHAPTER XI
THE BATTLE OF INKANGAHTAWNG
THE SECOND AND THIRD BATTALIONS:
12–28 MARCH 1944

Forty Miles to Janpan

12 March

At 0700 hours the Second Battalion pulled out of the Shikaw Ga area, traveling south for a few miles and then due east. The command group followed at 0800 and the Third Battalion at 1000.

As the column passed by General Sun's headquarters, he came out to speak to General Merrill. There were "ding hows" and "habu hows" on all sides as the Marauders passed through the Chinese camp.

The Chinese general had every reason to be optimistic and grateful to the Marauders. By mid-March, two thousand Japanese had been killed and forty Burmese villages freed. The Japanese were leaving the Hukawng Valley (Chan 1986, 44–45).

The Marauders were not aware that a serious problem was shaping up on the boundary between India and Burma. On 3 March, the Japanese launched a massive attack on the Burma-India border about two hundred miles from our area of operation. During the next four months they almost cut Stilwell's railroad supply line into Assam and just missed an invasion deep into India. By the time of their defeat in early July, they had lost seventeen thousand horses and sixty-five thousand men (Romanus and Sunderland 1956).

About three and one-half miles southwest of Sana Ga, a sandy crossing gave difficulties and slowed down the animals. One mule, mired up to his belly, was straining and jerking, trying to escape from the mud and the water, which was almost up to his nose. The mule-skinner leading the mule had made the crossing successfully. When his mule got stuck, he plunged back in, being careful to stay away from the front of the animal. He knew that when a mule is in the mud it tries to climb anything solid—and a standing man is often a favorite stepping stone. The muleskinner quickly grabbed the mule's head, holding it above the water, and two other muleskinners dashed in to help. They loosened the rope holding the load and lifted it off the mule, carrying it across the stream. The mule was still unable to get out, so they lifted the heavy pack saddle off its back and carried it across the stream, later pushing and pulling the mule across. A corduroy crossing had to be made with bamboo poles further up the stream to get the remaining mules across. This is cited as an illustration of the many problems encountered by the animals during the campaign.

At 1600 hours, after a fourteen-mile march, the command group arrived at Glum Ga, with the Second Battalion ahead and the Third Battalion behind it. Glum Ga had recently been occupied by the Japanese. Most of the village had been burned when they departed suddenly on our arrival in the Walawbum area a few days before. Their foxholes and little semicircular slit trenches near the entrance to the village still looked fresh.

The march had been on relatively flat ground, and the men had stood the march well. The medical sections of the two battalions had few problems to treat.

13 March

The command group followed the Second Battalion at 0700 hours and arrived in the vicinity of Pabum before lunch. The first battalion of the Chinese regiment was stationed there. The entire place was a mass of trenches and trailblocks. The Chinese soldiers, as usual, grinned and said "ding how" to every American, and the reply was always "ding how."

As the lead scouts of the Second Battalion arrived at Pabum they carried small red and blue flags on their helmets and caps as an identification sign. This isolated action had been thought necessary, since the Chinese had a habit of standing silently behind a tree until you got about ten feet away, then yelling *Halt!*—or something that sounded like "halt"—in Chinese. At that moment you would see a barrel pointed in your direction and a finger on the trigger. A quick "ding how" usually did the trick, but it made the recipient of this type of greeting mighty jumpy.

At this location the Chinese had just finished a little bamboo bridge capable of holding our animals as we crossed the swift-flowing Tanai Hka—much to our surprise, without getting wet. The trail turned southeast from Pabum around a mountain and wound up and down over low hills along the Tanai Hka.

During the late afternoon I was marching in my position with the medical section of Orange Combat Team of the Third Battalion. One of the riflemen was resting on the trail because of nausea, vomiting, and general malaise. I dropped out of the column of marching men to help him. The column soon cleared the area, and the two of us were alone. The man was miserable, weak, and very sick, but we hurried after our comrades. After a few hundred yards the trail branched, and we took the right fork. We walked, with considerable anxiety, about one mile. Much to our surprise we were suddenly in the midst of a small American portable surgical unit, a mile or so in back of the Chinese, who were attempting to advance on the road to our right. I was amazed to find James Whedbee, M.D., an old friend from Baltimore, Maryland, and Johns Hopkins Medical School. We made a turnaround, and were soon struggling along what we hoped was the right trail. Two frightened Kachins passed us, muttering "Japs" and pointing back along the trail. Needless to say, my sick patient and I immediately became very apprehensive. Our chance of survival seemed limited. What should we do? Our best option seemed to suggest that we move as fast as possible. Our crisis was soon solved. We had finally been missed when the battalion bivouacked at Kalun Ga after the day's march of thirteen miles. I had learned my lesson. Never stop alone on a trail in enemy territory. After rest, medication, and food, my sick comrade was able to continue in the morning.

Up until the time I made the wrong turn I had been unable to obtain any maps of our planned area of operation. The maps of the unadministered area, in which we were to operate, had been printed after this isolated part of Burma had been surveyed between 1916 and 1920. Very few copies were available to the Marauders. After my potentially tragic mistake I was able to successfully beg copies of this rare item.

At a staff meeting at 1800, General Merrill told the officers that the 22nd Chinese Division was five miles south of Cain but that the Japanese resistance was stiffening. In that area and also in the Taro area,

Chinese units had been driven back slightly. In spite of these setbacks their advance was still continuing. As usual, such information rarely reached the men and, when it did, usually meant little—since few of the men or officers had significant knowledge of General Merrill's plans or those of General Stilwell that concerned the Marauders, the Chinese troops, or the China-Burma-India area of operation.

14 March

The column moved out of Kalun Ga at 0800 hours and marched to Nlam Ga, where a defense was set up around a large sand bar that was scheduled to be the airdrop field on the bank of the Tanai Hka. A three-day K-ration and animal grain supply was received at 1600, and the column bivouacked in the area for the night. We were now about twenty miles directly east of Walawbum.

The day's march had been different in that the trail was getting steep and rough. The mountains to the east and west of our march, along the narrow valley of the winding Tanai Hka, had elevations of from three to sixty-five hundred feet. Fresh elephant tracks were seen in a banana grove, and Captain Jack Girsham estimated that a hundred elephants were in the herd.

Jack Girsham, an Anglo-Burmese, had been a government worker and hunter before Burma fell to the Japanese. He was traveling up the Tanai with the Second Battalion and serving as an advisor, scout, and interpreter. He had joined the Kachin Levies when the Japanese invaded the country. His family had died with thousands of other refugees as they tried to flee the Japanese by attempting to enter India from north Burma. He hated the Japanese, as well as the many Burmese who had starved, stolen from, and murdered the refugees.

Everyone continued to be grateful that no enemy had been encountered on this mission to the expected battle on the road at a point about fifty miles to the southwest. General Merrill had been wise in planning our advance many miles east of the enemy. The terrain was indeed proving terrible for both the animals and men, but the route allowed us to avoid many small skirmishes and the sacrifice of many of our men.

The men had been, up until now, fairly free of sickness and exhaustion. Some of the Second Battalion men were suffering from amoebic dysentery, and a few recurrent attacks of malaria plagued the Third

Battalion. All continued to march; there was no evacuation. This situation was beginning to change for numerous reasons. The extreme physical exertion, inadequate caloric intake, and lack of sleep and rest all combined were leading to an explosive health situation. Increasing loss of fat and muscle mass was becoming more apparent among the men. All were showing weight loss and decreasing energy.

While visiting the 20th General Hospital in Ledo, before the march into Burma, Colonel Hunter had been asked by Colonel Ravdin, C.O. of the hospital, about our plans for food. Colonel Hunter had explained that our chief source of food would be the army's new K-ration. This would be supplemented by C- and 10-in-1 rations whenever possible. Colonel Ravdin explained that K-rations, as a routine diet, would not supply the necessary calories to provide energy and prevent weight loss. The medical officers—and all who gave the problem thought—knew that the food would be inadequate. The War Department had planned for a three- month operation under General Wingate's command and chose this new three-thousand-calorie diet because it was light, and a three- or four-day supply could be carried in each soldier's pack.

As time passed, hunger, weight loss, weakness, and privation became increasing concerns of the men. Up until this time, rain showers had been frequent but usually brief. On this night we had our first heavy downpour. Those who had ponchos tied the corners to bushes to provide shelter for the night. The less fortunate slept in the rain. Large leeches and black ants were becoming increasingly troublesome. The former would attach themselves to almost any part of the body and, if unnoticed, would soon be engorged with blood. The sores they left on the legs frequently turned into "jungle sores," which festered and had to be lanced and drained by the doctors before a cure would begin.

At 1700 hours a liaison plane flew over and dropped dispatches. General Merrill held a brief staff conference at 1800, at which he told us that the Chinese were continuing to forge ahead toward Shaduzup and that our trail to the south was thought to be free of Japanese for the next two days' march. Our progress had now taken us about thirty-five miles southeast of Walawbum. The Second and Third Battalions had now marched about 210 miles from Ledo, Assam, India.

CHAPTER XI

15 March

The Second Battalion departed from Nlam Ga at 0700 and was followed by the command group at 0900 and the Third Battalion at 1000. The trail was fairly good, but it went up and down steep little hills as it wound along the Tanai Hka. Daily showers were continuing, the trail was muddy, and the leeches were active. Clothing was wet, and equipment was damp.

The command group arrived at Naubum late in the afternoon after a twelve-mile march. This was the first village we had passed through that had not been deserted. Here we found a small but well-organized community of primitive, illiterate, friendly people who hated the Japanese. Shortly before arrival, General Merrill informed his command staff, for the first time, that the U.S. army had recently formed an OSS (Office of Strategic Services) to operate in small groups in Burma. The name of the parent unit was OSS Detachment 101. He knew that we would encounter an American officer who had set up a safe area in and about Naubum. Captain Vincent L. Curl of Palaxious, Texas, the commander of the Office of Strategic Services unit in this North Burma area, met us at the entrance to the village and led us to the bivouac area previously selected for the command group.

The Second Battalion had preceded the command group into Naubum. Lieutenant Grissom's Blue Combat Team I & R platoon was leading when they located the OSS team and an improvised small airstrip. The OSS detachment consisted of Captain Vincent Curl and Sergeant Jack Pamplin, both Americans, and a small detachment of Kachins. General Merrill had failed to tell either Colonel Beach, the C.O. of the Third Battalion, or Colonel McGee of the Second Battalion that any OSS personnel were in Burma.

Captain Curl had organized a force of Kachin boys and men into an organization known as the Me Pro Pumor Lightning Force. They wore green shirts and shorts and carried rifles, tommy guns, J.D. guns, and a variety of weapons of their own. The soldiers ranged in age from thirteen to sixty, and they saluted, stood at attention when reporting, and formed for inspection with smartness. They used guerilla tactics—ambushes were their specialty. Their job had been to keep the Japanese out of the area within a forty-mile radius of Naubum, to gather information, to rescue flyers forced down in the area, and to do as much damage as possible to the Japanese army wherever they could find them. They had been extremely successful and proved invaluable to us in the coming weeks. The OSS fed and cared for many Kachin refugees forced out of their villages by the Japanese.

Lieutenant Grissom's platoon ran into Father James Stuart, an interesting and helpful person, as they arrived at Naubum. He was a short, stocky man dressed in olive drab clothing and wearing an Aussie hat with a plume. Several Kachins were traveling with him. The men in the command group were to get to know him well and learned of his work as an Irish Catholic missionary. He had the respect and complete cooperation of the Kachins throughout North Burma. The OSS and (later) the Marauders were greatly helped by his decision to become attached to General Merrill's staff (Romanus and Sunderland 1956).

The radio information net from Naubum to combat headquarters was superb. Small groups of ten to twelve Kachins would gather information right in Japanese lines and installations and then send or bring it to their tiny radio transmitter hidden in the jungle for relay to Naubum.

Captain Curl's success had been largely due to Father James Stuart, who had lived with the Kachins for seven years. In 1942 he stayed and faced the Japanese whenever other white men left and, strange to say, had lived to tell the tale. He had been responsible for recruiting the Kachins and establishing friendly relations, without which the OSS's function would have been almost impossible.

Shortly after Father Stuart met General Merrill, he said, "Some *boys* [he always emphasized that word] asked me to hold Mass and confession for them in the morning. Will your unit be here, or do they move away at dawn?" General Merrill replied that the command group would move about 0800 and the Third Battalion would be in the area until about 1000. The battalion still had no chaplain, and his services were much appreciated by the men.

Both battalions camped at or near Naubum. It rained for a few hours, but almost all of the men had mastered the technique of constructing a lean-to or basha of banana leaves—or joining together two ponchos—for shelter, so very few of us got wet.

CHAPTER XI

16 March

Major Williams arrived by small plane at the improvised airstrip the OSS had built. He brought dispatches from General Stilwell and took away film and more dispatches.

The Third Battalion pulled out for Weilangyang earlier than planned and arrived there after a fourteen-mile march over a rough, muddy trail that got continually steeper and more difficult. The animals had rough going, and many slipped off the trail and down the slope due to treacherous footing and exhaustion. This caused many delays and put great strain on their handlers. One of the Third Battalion muleskinners got his mule bogged down in the mud, and—in his effort to pull it out—the mule rolled over on him. He was injured, but not fatally. If not for the soft mud, he would probably have been killed.

The Second Battalion followed with equal difficulty and took five hours to reach the crossing of the Tanai Hka after moving only five miles. The Kachins had constructed a bamboo bridge over the swiftly flowing river. We were all grateful that there was no need to struggle across this waist-deep river. The mules and horses seemed to enjoy the cool water.

At 1700 hours a transport plane flew over the Third Battalion at a paddy field one-half mile northeast of Weilangyang and circled several times. Our air-ground radioman, Lieutenant Paulson, asked to whom it was dropping; the pilot said, "Americans." Lieutenant Paulson said, "You must be looking for the First Battalion. We aren't expecting a drop until tomorrow." The pilot kept circling and said, "Are you Americans or aren't you?" Lieutenant Paulson said, "We are Americans," whereupon the plane dropped several loaded chutes which, on examination, proved to be marked for White and Red Combat Teams of the First Battalion. The plane took off in the direction that the First Battalion was thought to be in.

This air-to-ground episode illustrates what a difficult task the young pilots had and what a great job they usually did in locating and supplying our small units in the vastness of the jungle-covered mountain ranges of North Burma. The First Battalion was, at that time, about twenty miles to the southwest. Several three- to six-thousand-foot mountain ranges separated our unit from theirs.

Information was received, by radio, that the First Battalion was continuing to advance toward an expected battleground on the Japanese-held road a few miles south of Shaduzup. They had had several skirmishes with the enemy and had taken casualties. They expected to continue to encounter terrain difficulties and enemy trailblocks.

Father Stuart had now been unofficially adopted by the Marauders and was traveling with the command group. On this day he held confession and Mass for the Catholic men early in the morning. He baptized one man who had been prepared by two of his friends. Father Stuart said he had been well prepared and was remarkably well versed in doctrines.

The command group left Naubum about 1000 hours and marched four and one-half miles to the crossing of the Tanai Hka, where it bivouacked for the night. Rain started at 1700 hours, and everyone got wet before makeshift shelters could be put up; but it didn't matter much, as the water cooled us off. Intermittent rain continued all night, with a thunderstorm at about 1750.

The Second Battalion bivouacked in a banana grove on the west side of the Tanai Hka about two and one-half miles northwest of the command group.

During the day's march, Jack Girsham identified tiger and elephant tracks at several of the small streams we crossed. Elephant dung had been seen on the trail for several days, but only a few elephants had actually been seen.

Sitting around the command group campfire, Father Stuart told several officers a few of his experiences with the Japanese. In June of 1942 he was caring for a group of refugees in Sumprabum at the extreme northeast tip of Burma. Earlier, the Chinese had retreated through that part of Burma and had taken almost all the food the Kachins had. Consequently the Kachins hated and feared them, for at that time few of the Kachins had guns (and those who did had muzzle-loaders that fired homemade powder). When the Japanese came toward Sumprabum, they capitalized on the Kachins' hate of the Chinese and treated the Kachins kindly—but only in the country through which the Chinese had passed; elsewhere they were crueller and harsher than the Chinese had been.

CHAPTER XI

As the Japanese advanced toward Sumprabum, the Chinese withdrew from there, leaving Father Stuart and his group of refugees alone to face the Japanese. Father Stuart decided the best thing for him to do would be to go down the trail, meet the Japanese, and surrender the town to them. If he could avoid a fight, they might let him care for the refugees.

About four miles south of Sumprabum, he came upon an officer sitting on a horse in the middle of the trail. At first he thought the officer was Chinese. Father Stuart said, "Chinese?" The officer on the horse spat out of the side of his mouth and barked, "No! Japanese." Then the Japanese officer looked squarely at Father Stuart and said harshly, "English?" Father Stuart, without batting an eye, spat out of the side of his mouth and snapped "No! Irish." The Japanese major smiled wryly—and, in broken English, asked if any planes had flown over Sumprabum lately. Father Stuart replied, "Yes, one of yours flew over yesterday." The Japanese major said, "No, it couldn't have been Japanese." Father Stuart replied, "It had a white star on its wings." Father Stuart had never seen an American plane before and didn't recognize our insignia.

The Japanese major apparently was convinced that Father Stuart was simple-minded and couldn't do any harm, so he told him to lead the way to Sumprabum. On the way in, the Japanese major asked him when the Chinese had left, where they had gone, how many there were, and how they had treated him. Father Stuart told him that a large number had passed through a few days before and had taken all the food—that his refugees had only a little rice left. The Japanese major seemed pleased at this, and his manner warmed perceptibly.

When they arrived at the village, Father Stuart took the Japanese major and a group of his men over the entire village and asked the major if the Japanese couldn't occupy one part of the town and that the major give orders for no Japanese to go into the area where the refugees were staying, except for inspections. He showed the major that there were only old people and children, and that many were sick and terrified for fear the Japanese would harm them. The major assured him that none of his men would harm the refugees and that Father Stuart could remain with them. He lived up to his agreement through the weeks that the Japanese held the town.

THE BATTLE OF INKANGAHTAWNG

17 March

The command group and Second Battalion departed at 0730 hours and 0930 from Tate Ga. The Third Battalion received a large food drop at 1000 and used elephants supplied by Captain Curl and his Kachins to clear the drop field. The elephants had to be kept clear of the mules, as their mutual distrust of each other created a panicky situation if either was driven close to the other. The mules had to work at one end of the large field and the elephants at the other.

Colonel Hunter became very enthusiastic about the value of the elephants, and the command group used them for several days. Meetings between the elephants and mules could not always be avoided and resulted in much staff amusement. These meetings were not funny to the mahout riding on the back of the elephant, for the creatures would run through bamboo groves and thick jungle until they felt safe. Nor were they funny to the muleskinners, who were towed in the opposite direction and could be heard swearing at a rate never believed possible—even for a muleskinner. After a few almost disastrous experiences, a system was worked out whereby the mules or elephants were led a few yards off the trail separately and faced so one species couldn't see the other pass by.

During the morning I was resting on the ground with other members of Orange Combat Team. S.Sgt. John Zokosky of K company was cleaning his rifle while sitting on the ground. Suddenly an M-1 rifle shot rang out from an accidentally fired weapon. After a momentary pause to recover from the sudden unexpected explosion at near range, we were horrified to find Sergeant Zokosky prostrate and bleeding profusely on the ground. Our medical technicians and myself, as well as my two medical colleagues, Captains Cecala and Armstrong, immediately went into life-saving action. First, massive bleeding from a torn femoral artery in the left groin was controlled by a very high tourniquet and forceful pressure. Wounds included a severe calf laceration, a wound of entrance in back of the left knee with exit in the right groin, and a severe wound of the right elbow joint. After exiting the right elbow, the bullet had entered the right lower quadrant of his abdomen, passed through blood vessels and intestine, and lodged under the skin in his posterior left flank. Even with the liberal use of blood plasma, it was obvious that he had a mortal wound unless heroic surgery could save his life. There was no way to evacuate him, and he was bleeding internally. We also knew that he had many bullet holes in his intestine. Unless immediate corrective surgery was done to stop the internal bleeding, he would quickly die. Unless the many holes in his intestine were quickly repaired, he would die of peritonitis. Rapid intravenous administration of blood plasma stabilized his blood pressure. In his semiconscious condition he gave permission for immediate operation. Our few instruments were rapidly boiled. He was placed on a litter, which was placed on two ammunition cases. Drip ether anesthesia was given by Major Cecala. Lt. Jack Armstrong and I repaired the torn artery. While we were attempting to control the internal bleeding, his pressure fell—and we knew that we had lost him.

Even though our men had seen many comrades die during the Pacific Campaign, we and they were profoundly disturbed. He was one of us, and we could only think that but for the grace of God any of us could have been the one whose comrades were fighting for our life. I saw no evidence that the men gave any significant thought to the possibility of their death in battle—except perhaps while waiting to attack the enemy. Yet the death of their comrades was not taken easily. They expressed sympathy for the family and his buddies. They were free in their criticism of what they considered to be stupid orders and mistakes by their superiors. Rarely would there be any complaint about the action of their squad, platoon, or company commander.

The sergeant was buried near the site of his death. A simple cere-mony was conducted by Lt. Logan Weston, the leader of the Orange I & R platoon. Many of his comrades gathered to pay their last respects.

The day's march was extremely difficult because of the rough trail and many steep grades. We passed by a poppy field. Few men seemed to recognize that the crop was grown to satisfy the opium requirement of some Kachins. They used it for pleasure and for money.

A muleskinner was trying to get his mule out of a mud hole where it was stuck and lying on its side. The muleskinner was kicking, pushing, and cussing at the mule for all it was worth. Finally, fed up with the mule, he gave him a terrible kick in the ribs and said, "Git up, you son-of-a-bitch! You volunteered for this, too!"

THE BATTLE OF INKANGAHTAWNG

The Second Battalion, at the end of their march, arrived during an airdrop, and each man received three days' K-rations as well as some rice.

At the end of the march, both battalion commanders, Colonel McGee and Colonel Beach, were told that their men would rest at their campsites on 18 March. Major Williams flew in to Weilangyang with orders from General Stilwell. The orders were for the Second and Third Battalions to stay at Weilangyang and not to follow the original plan to attack Shaduzup, as it was believed the First Battalion would throw a block behind Shaduzup in a few days and the Chinese to the north were making good progress toward the town. General Merrill was also informed that the First Battalion was, at this time, only ten miles northwest of us near Tanja Ga—and was preparing to move toward Shaduzup to the southeast in the morning. The plan General Merrill had in mind, until ordered to stay at Weilangyang, was to strip the Second and Third Battalions of heavy equipment and all but eighty animals, then force-march the battalions over tortuous mountain trails into Shaduzup so as to arrive there on the twenty-first.

In spite of my position as the battalion surgeon of Orange Combat Team of the Third Battalion, I had no knowledge of the information given in the previous paragraph. It is unlikely that any but the most senior of General Merrill's staff were given any of the information General Merrill had just received. At this time no one in the two battalions had any idea of what our mission was to be. During a very rainy night, Colonel Beach and Colonel McGee were informed that they should be prepared to move out in the morning to march to the First Battalion's assistance. Merrill explained that they were running into serious trouble. No definite plan was given these officers. Later in the evening they were informed that a move would not be necessary. No explanation was provided.

As explained in the previous chapter, dealing with the First Battalion's march to Shaduzup, Lt. Jim Tilley of Denver, Colorado—one of Captain Curl's lieutenants, who had a force of Kachins to the northwest in the Jaiwa Ga, Tanga Ga sector—arrived in the afternoon at Weilangyang with Captain Tom Senff, S-3 of the First Battalion. In a confidential report to General Merrill, they confirmed reports that the Japanese were northwest of Weilangyang in a number of trailblocks.

CHAPTER XI

This information gave good reason for the action both battalions had taken in blocking all trails leading to Weilangyang.

18 March

The Second and Third Battalions and the command group remained in camp all day. Our patrols were active to the north, west, and south but had no contact with the enemy. The men rested all day, swimming, fishing with grenades, washing clothes, and swapping rumors—some of which were: "mail will be dropped today; we are going back to Assam to activate a new division; 10-in-1 rations will be dropped today; we are moving south to Kamaing: the First Battalion got badly shot up today; we are going home when the next phase is over."

Captain James W. Parker, a dentist, came in by small plane and immediately went to work with his foot-cranked drill. The captain brought dispatches, the gist of which came out in the staff meeting at 1700 hours. Here's the essence of the report: "The Chinese are having tough going in the Jambu Bum area. South of the main road at Chisidu, one thousand fresh Japanese have dug in, apparently expecting an attack from the west. One Japanese platoon has been located south of Mogaung near the main road; also in the same area are three hundred Japanese, two anti-aircraft guns, a large ammunition depot, and a large gasoline and oil depot."

Just at dusk a liaison plane flew over and dropped a message for General Merrill from General Stilwell, explaining that our help might yet be needed at Shaduzup and that for the present we were to block approaches up the Taenia from the south. General Merrill decided to do this by moving to the line of Kaulun Ga-Mupaw Ga and awaiting further orders. At 1730 we received a ration drop, and at 1900 all drop planes had cleared.

19 March

At 1300 the command group left to march to Janpan, preceded by the Second Battalion. The Third Battalion was ordered to stay in the Weilangyang area, protecting the airstrip and blocking all trails with patrols and ambushes.

The move to Janpan was extremely difficult. We were leaving the narrow valley of the Tanai Hka, which ran from south to north. The altitude here in the river area was about thirteen hundred feet. Our march to the west would force us to climb a narrow trail that led two miles to Janpan, which was at an altitude of about twenty-five hundred feet. The trail at times approached fifty degrees, which caused the men to touch the ground with their hands as they climbed. As the men and animals passed, the trail became more difficult to advance on because of recent rain. Most animals and men reached the village in two hours, but some took twice that time. We were now on a mountain ridge line that ran from north to south for about twenty-five miles while maintaining an altitude of from twelve hundred to to three thousand feet. At the southern end, the mountain dropped quickly down to flat country at five hundred feet. Two miles to the west, the elevation dropped twelve hundred feet to the Nampana River, which ran from north to south to join the Mogaung River. The mountains were covered by massive hardwood trees, bamboo, and other tropical vegetation.

About midway up the steep mountain trail, the head of the column was taking a break when a little MP came puffing up to the head of the column. One of his fellow MP's, in a Brooklyn accent, said, "Where ya goin' in such a hurry?" The first MP, in an even stronger accent, said, "Cheez, guys, I'm going up with the big shots where they take breaks." General Merrill, sitting ten feet away, got a hearty laugh out of that.

The MP unit had joined General Merrill's command group shortly before we started the march over the Patkai Mountains into Burma. Few of the men knew that MP's were a part of the command group.

Unbeknownst to the men of the two battalions, Captain Curl of the O.S.S soon arrived with an estimated five hundred Kachin guerilla. They were said to be intelligent, energetic, and good fighters who hated the Japanese. The few that any of us saw carried bandoliers of ammunition slung over each shoulder and wore earrings and bamboo leg bracelets below the knee. They wore odd pieces of British and American equipment and carried ancient as well as modern weapons. They were capable of marching fifteen miles or more per day in the mountainous country. These guerilla were used for patrolling and local protection of the command group. At no time were they a part of the missions of any of the three battalions of the Marauders.

Shortly after arrival at Janpan they built a basha for General Merrill. This twelve-by-fifteen bamboo-and-reed structure was completed in four hours. The room had flooring, a fireplace, windows, a porch, a candle holder in the wall, a sliding door, a rain-proof roof, and walls. It was the first building the command post had been in, and it was dedicated with a bottle of rice beer the village chief presented to General Merrill.

20 March

The Third Battalion began to arrive at Janpan early in the morning as the Second was preparing to move to the south. The water situation was very bad—with only one spring, producing about fifteen gallons per hour. Obviously the area could not accommodate the Marauders for more than a few hours.

While at Janpan I first learned that General Merrill had available a ball of raw opium about four inches in diameter. This was to be used in place of money to pay for certain services rendered by the local population. After the war I learned that some of the workers from the hill tribes accepted opium from British government personnel before the war for services rendered. This practice had been continued by the Northern Combat Area Command staff. Won Loy Chan was the central intelligence figure on Colonel Joseph W. Stilwell Jr.'s staff during the Burma operations. He states, "By rough estimates the Allies in Burma and India must have dispensed at least twenty kilos a month for at least twenty-four months of the second and third Burma campaigns. That's over a thousand pounds or $240,000" (Chan 1986, 25).

Merrill Gives Orders for Orange, Khaki, Blue, and Green Combat Team Missions

At 1030 hours General Merrill had a staff meeting at Janpan and gave the following information and orders. He estimated the enemy to have three hundred men at Shaduzup, five to six hundred at Jambu Bum, and about two thousand men to the south and west.

He described the general situation thus: Tasu Bum, halfway between Taro and Lonkin, had been captured by the Chinese on the 18th. The First Battalion, now in the vicinity of Jaiwa Ga, was moving southwest to put a roadblock below Shaduzup, followed by the Chinese 113th Regiment and the 6th Chinese Pack Artillery Battery.

It had contacted the enemy at 1200 the previous day one mile south of Tanga Ga. The enemy appeared to be using delaying tactics.

The general gave orders as follows: A unit composed of the Second Battalion and Khaki Combat Team of the Third Battalion, under the command of Colonel Hunter, was to secure the trail south of Warong, reconnoiter the trails south toward Kamaing, and move a portion of the force, as the situation permitted, to a block on the main road between Warazup and Nalskawng. A supply drop had been arranged at Auche for the late afternoon of the 22nd.

Orange Combat Team of the Third Battalion was to remain in the vicinity of Janpan, prepared to move on short notice. Two reinforced platoons would be kept ready to polish off any Japanese filtering into this area. Extensive patrolling of the trails to the north, south, and west would be maintained. One radio team from the Third Battalion was to report to the command group with SCR 284 radio to work the OSS information net. Captain Curl's Kachin guerilla would also aid in the patrolling of this area—and guides would be furnished from among them to go with Hunter's force. The general's command post would be at Janpan temporarily. Communications would be maintained by radio, runner, and liaison planes. As was the custom of General Merrill and General Stilwell, no orders were put in writing.

The Forty-Mile March Begins Toward a Probable Battle on the Road

The staff meeting was over at 1100 hours, and Blue Combat Team of the Second Battalion marched along the mountaintop trail leading south to Nhpum Ga and bivouacked for the night. Green Combat Team of the Second Battalion and Khaki Combat Team of the Third followed the same route, but stopped for the night at Hsamshingyang, four miles short of Nhpum Ga, where they received an airdrop. Our ancient map gave Hsamshingyang an elevation of 1,532 feet and Nhpum Ga 2,779 feet. The former had no huts or inhabitants but was the name given to a flat, cleared area bordered on the east by headwaters of the Tanai Hka. Over the centuries, it had apparently been used by several villages as a rice-growing area. The trail passed through the middle of this four- or five-acre area. One or two bamboo shacks were standing at Nhpum Ga. This well-shaded mountaintop area measured about three hundred yards from north to south and one to two hundred yards from east to west. The north-south trail continued along the top of this razor-backed mountain for fifteen miles until it descended into the flat, broad Mogaung Valley about seven miles north of the Japanese stronghold of Kamaing.

General Merrill's Headquarters Remains at Janpan

The command group got to know Janpan quite well. It was the first real Kachin village, pursuing a normal existence, that the Marauders had seen. The Kachins, a Mongolian type, had slowly immigrated for hundreds of years from central Tibet into the mountains of northern Burma. This typical village of 150 contained about twenty large bashas, each basha housing a family consisting usually of three generations. During the several days the command group remained at Janpan, they were royally serviced and entertained by these primitive people. Unfortunately the men of the battalions had more important things to do as they advanced to meet the enemy. Major Melvin A. Schudmak, regimental surgeon, and his medical aid men took time off from their duties to give medical care to the people. Captain James A. V. Girsham, of Maymyo, Burma (and also of the Kachin Levies and the British Army), who was liaison officer and trail adviser to General Merrill, gave assistance as interpreter. Major Schudmak set up for business near the head man's basha. The first patient was a woman with dozens of infected leech bites on her legs. Major Schudmak won her confidence quickly as he treated each sore, and her face was wreathed in smiles and giggles as he bound them up. The next patient was a ten-month-old baby with scabs, secondarily infected. The mother with the screaming baby grasping her exposed breasts watched every movement the doctor made as he removed the scabs, cleaned the sores, and applied sulphur ointment to them. A stream of patients followed, with ailments from enlarged spleens—due to chronic malaria—to simple sore throats and colds.

At the village of Janpan there was no suitable spot for an airdrop except in the village itself. General Merrill told the village head man that we were moving down the mountain to a large paddy field close to Mupaw Ga to get our drop the next day. The chief protested, saying his people would rather have the chutes and take a chance on damage to their homes than see the residents of Mupaw Ga get the supplies.

Movement on the Nhpum Ga-Auche-Kauri-Warong-Poakum-Kamaing Trail

21 March

Green Combat Team arrived at Auche, five miles south of Nhpum Ga, in the afternoon. Blue Combat Team remained at Kauri, where a small spring was available. The spring at Auche would not supply the needs of the three combat teams. Khaki Combat Team was along the trail in back of Blue Combat Team. When the Second Battalion moved through Kauri they saw fifteen elephants, ranging in size from a five-month-old baby to an enormous bull. The elephants checked out quickly as the men passed through the area.

At Kauri the combat team set up outposts on a trail leading southeast to the Tanai Hka as well as on a trail leading down one thousand feet to the Hkum Hka to the west. The main north-south trail was also blocked.

The Marauders Get New Plans

Colonel Hunter arrived late in the afternoon at Auche. The airdrop had not yet taken place. Shortly after Hunter arrived, Lieutenant Botts brought in a radio message from General Merrill. Merrill had changed the plan of attack. The new plan ordered the three combat teams to move with all possible speed to put a block on the main road in the vicinity of Inkangahtawng instead of Warazup. This would require a march of about thirty more miles.

Orange Combat Team would move immediately from the Janpan area to block the trails to the south around Auche, Warong, and Manpin by 24 March.

The message further stated that the Chinese had pushed the Japanese out of Jambu Bum.

The hour was late, and the planes had not arrived for the proposed airdrop. As there would not be time to complete the drop and get an early start in the morning, Colonels Hunter and McGee decided to take the drop at Manpin on 22 March.

22 March

At Janpan, where General Merrill still had his command post, Captain Curl of the Office of Strategic Services reported that he had been ordered back to his base in Assam but would leave his assistant in charge of the Kachin guerrillas working for us.

General Merrill and his staff spent much of the day enjoying a celebration that was put on in their honor by the village. They marveled at the ceremonial dances and had an elaborate feast.

The March to Inkangahtawng Begins

In an attempt to avoid detection by the Japanese and reduce marching distance, the most direct route to Manpin was selected. This march of ten miles to the southwest would take the unit from an elevation of three thousand feet to six hundred feet. The first two miles of the march followed a very steep, ill-defined trail through bamboo and other jungle growth to descend a thousand feet to the Hkum Hka. Here the route took them in and out of the bed of this rock-strewn river to continue in the same fashion in and out of the Nampana River. The eight miles of river travel in the deep gorge required twenty-five river crossings. The exhausted men and animals of the three combat teams had assembled at Manpin by 1500 hours. Fortunately Colonel McGee had left several sick men and animals at Auche rather than forcing them over the difficult trail. They were ordered back to the command unit. Manpin was found to be a small, cleared area on the northern edge of the Mogaung Valley about ten miles north of the Japanese base at Kamaing. The scheduled airdrop was very risky because of the nearness to the enemy, but the combat teams were out of food. The four C-47's arrived very late in the day, and the drop got under way. As each combat team left the area on the way to Sharaw, the marching men were each given three days' K-rations. Colonel McGee had no information about the progress of the fighting on the road and no knowledge as to where the enemy were located in the Mogaung Valley.

In spite of the late hour and a steady rain, Colonel Hunter pushed the three combat teams on toward Sharaw. After a very difficult and slow night march, the combat teams bivouacked at 2100 hours just short of Sharaw.

THE BATTLE OF INKANGAHTAWNG

Orange Combat Team had an easy march to Auche, where—after blocking all trails and setting up a perimeter defense—they spent the night.

While at Auche on the 23rd, one of Orange's patrols picked up a tired and hungry aviator. He was Lt. Irvin E. Jenkins, of Longview, Texas, from a fighter squadron that had been working for us.

This is his story: On Sunday 19 March he was strafing at a hundred feet just north of Kamaing, with his P-40, when the Japanese blew up a land mine. His plane exploded and caught fire, and he bailed out. The remainder of his squadron circled the place where he had landed—strafing parties of Japanese who were trying to hunt him down. They also radioed back to base for a liaison plane to come and attempt a pickup in what looked like a fairly level field.

Lieutenant Jenkins had landed safely and quickly cut out of his parachute and headed due east to try to escape. He walked three miles before dark, at which time he became stuck up to his waist in a swamp. He worked his way out of the swamp with great difficulty and decided to wait until daybreak before going on. Moving cautiously on the 20th, he followed streambeds and stayed clear of trails. For two and one-half days he walked to the northeast, eating only bamboo shoots. On the morning of the 23rd he saw empty K-ration cartons. A few hours later he hit the patrol that was on the way to Manpin. He reached Manpin with Orange on the 24th. An hour later, word came down that Kachins had picked up another American aviator.

This aviator was Lt. Hugh McFarland from a fighter bomber group of Lubbock, Texas. When word was flashed to Maingkwan that Lieutenant Jenkins was down, McFarland, on liaison duty there, jumped into an L-4 and took off at 1700 hours for the field where Lieutenant Jenkins was reported down. From the air he saw a chute lying in the field and something brown lying beside it that looked as if it might have been Lieutenant Jenkins. The field was covered with elephant grass, but it looked smooth. He touched his wheels on the ground to test it and it seemed okay, so he came in and landed, keeping his tail low. When he landed he found the field rough under the grass, and when the plane stopped his wheels were mired in mud. He jumped out and ran to the place where he thought Lieutenant Jenkins was lying, only to find a patch of darker-colored grass.

CHAPTER XI

He shouted, fired his pistol, and searched the field and surrounding ground carefully. Next morning he was convinced that Lieutenant Jenkins was either a prisoner or had escaped, so he started to prepare for a takeoff. He was pulling grass, on his hands and knees, about sixty yards from the plane when he looked up to see a Japanese face peering at him over its wing. He crawled quickly away through the tall grass, then walked to the northeast around a mountain, where he found a deserted village and some yams that tasted like green persimmons. He found a trail the next day and reached the Mogaung River the next night. Without a map he was lost. On the 23rd, having had no food for four days, he saw some Kachins down by the river about a hundred yards away. He ran, but they followed—and he realized they would catch up. When they first approached, he noticed that one carried a piece of cardboard. Lieutenant McFarland was looking squarely at his own name. On the board was written, "Lt. Jenkins and Lt. McFarland, follow this man." He followed him to Tingkrukawng and about an hour later was told that Lieutenant Jenkins was safe at Manpin. The OSS soon arranged for three Kachins to bring him by elephant to Weilangyang, where both men were sent out by L-4.

The men of Green, Blue, and Khaki Combat Teams moved into the rough, grass-covered clearing called Sharaw. They found only one ramshackle bamboo building, which Colonel Hunter took over as his headquarters. The colonel was to remain here while Khaki Combat Team, commanded by Colonel Briggs, and Green and Blue, commanded by Colonel McGee, carried out the assigned mission. He was provided with an SCR 284 radio and team under Lieutenant Glaves and a rifle platoon commanded by Lieutenant Lindgren. At this base, his plan was to keep the line of communication open and to clear the area for L-4 and L-5 planes to land in order to evacuate wounded and sick men.

Colonel Briggs and Colonel McGee knew their verbal orders as given by General Merrill at Janpan and later supplemented by radio. Their combat teams were to attack the road at or near Inkangahtawng and hold for twenty-four hours or longer. They were to move as fast as possible. No information was given about the progress of the Chinese or the progress of the First Battalion, which was working its way toward Shaduzup. No Kachin or British guides or interpreters were with the unit (McGee 1987).

THE BATTLE OF INKANGAHTAWNG

Preparation for Battle

23 March

Shortly after dawn, Colonel McGee and Colonel Briggs coordinated their plans and issued orders. Green Combat Team I & R platoon, followed by Blue I & R, moved out immediately—followed by the main column one hour later. Khaki Combat Team brought up the rear. From Sharaw the muddy trail ran up and down, on a winding route over foothills, northwest about ten miles to Tigrawmyang. Here a minor trail to the west led to Ngagahtawng and then to Inkangahtawng, a distance of about ten miles. The I & R platoons set up trailblocks at Tigrawmyang.

By the time the task force had reached the trail junction at Inkangahtawng at noon, Grissom's and Freer's I & Rs had scouted Ngagahtawng and found no evidence of occupation by inhabitants or enemy. The Marauders immediately advanced over the marshy, brush-surrounded trail leading to Ngagahtawng. While they advanced, Green Combat Team I & R scouted three-quarters of a mile to the riverbank. No enemy were seen.

The Mogaung riverbed, at a point one mile north of Inkangahtawng, was 250 feet wide. The river was 150 feet wide, with banks ten or more feet high. It appeared to be fordable at his point. The road was approximately one mile to the west. The three combat teams were now about ten miles south of Shaduzup, where the two combat teams of the First Battalion were supposed to hit the Japanese at the same time. Colonels Hunter, McGee, and Briggs were not aware that the First Battalion would not be able to meet their deadline or that the Chinese had made little progress since Jambu Bum had been taken. The combined lack of progress would allow the Japanese of the 18th Division to hit McGee's and Briggs's forces from the north and south rather than from the south alone.

By the time the Marauders were closing in on Ngagahtawng it was 1600 hours, and since there was no evidence that their presence had been detected, the prudent action would have been to rest and regroup (McGee 1987).

CHAPTER XI

The Battle of Inkangahtawng

23–24 March

Action had to be taken during the late hour on the 23rd since an unexpected event took place. Reconnoitering a small stream near Ngagahtawng, scouts from Lieutenant Joseph Freer's I & R platoon heard a noise down the stream: *tic, tac, tic, tac.* The sound of voices was barely audible. Soon the American lead scout saw an elephant coming up the shallow streambed with a man on top; the man on top saw the scout at the same moment. A moment later the lead scout, Sergeant George L. Fike, opened fire with a tommy gun. The elephant was so close that he had to lean back to hit the man on top. As he fired he looked squarely into the eyes of the startled Burman, who shouted a warning and tried to turn the elephant to escape—but Fike's first burst hit him and he toppled into the stream. A moment later the man next to Fike opened fire on three Japanese walking behind the elephant. He killed two. The third Japanese and the elephant ran back down the stream and escaped before further action could be taken.

At 1630 they were fired on by three Japanese, who then ran. The patrol cautiously crossed the river and drew close automatic-weapon fire. The chance that the unit had been or soon would be detected was likely. The unit had to cross the river and set up a defensive perimeter on the west bank. Blue and Green Combat Teams crossed after the I & R platoons had blocked all approaches along the north and south flanks on the west bank. The mortars and animals of the Second Battalion were left on the east bank. Khaki also remained on the east bank to protect the rear and provide mortar fire as necessary.

As darkness came on, the tired, wet, and hungry men immediately set up a strong perimeter with strategic placement of weapons and extensive digging in. They spent a miserable night because of anxiety, discomfort, and intermittent rifle shots by the Japanese. During much of the night the Marauders heard truck motors and tail gates slamming as enemy reinforcements arrived.

Khaki Combat Team secured the bridgehead on the east with a very strong perimeter defense. 60mm and 81mm mortars were in strategic positions for cover of the road and all areas of approach to the Second Battalion's position.

THE BATTLE OF INKANGAHTAWNG

As dawn came, all men of Blue, Green, and Khaki knew the small skirmishes were over and that a major battle was imminent. They had defeated the enemy and seen their comrades killed and wounded at Walawbum. Some were veterans of the Solomon Island Campaigns and others of New Guinea. All were volunteers. They, in spite of being deep in enemy territory, had confidence in themselves, their officers, and their weapons. Few of the men and officers had any significant knowledge of the relation of their mission to the military plans of the British, Americans, or Japanese in Burma. The Marauders knew basically nothing about the history of the Burma campaign. They were fighting to defeat an enemy who had taken the lives of fellow Americans and who were considered to be barbaric and utterly ruthless individuals.

No one needed to tell the men what the situation was. They knew they were dug in on a perimeter about one-quarter mile north of Inkangahtawng and three hundred yards east of the main road. On the road, at least a company of enemy were getting ready to attack. As usual, they did not understand why higher command would send them against enemy who had artillery while they had none. After all, there was such a weapon as pack artillery—which had been available to infantry troops for many years and could be readily transported on mules and horses. They had seen the Chinese well supplied with this weapon. They knew that if the weather cooperated and communications were satisfactory, Colonel McGee would call on the air corps for strafing and bombing of the enemy. Some wondered what would happen if the battle were prolonged because of some tactical reason or overwhelming enemy action. In a tight situation, could food and ammunition be airdropped successfully?

The doctors were well aware of the tragic situation that would exist if casualties were excessive. Even if the Japanese were totally defeated, wounded would have to be carried about fifteen miles back to Sharaw. If they could be carried by litter to that location, would it be possible to get them out one at a time in the small planes?

The worst possibility would be that the three combat teams would be trapped by a superior force of Japanese who had unlimited reinforcements, food, and ammunition available by truck transportation from Kamaing fifteen miles to the south.

CHAPTER XI

Colonel McGee, by now, knew that the First Battalion would not be able to hit the road ten miles to the north for at least four days. Unknown to the Marauders, the Chinese troops were not advancing. If the Marauders became surrounded, there was virtually no chance that they could escape from a superior force well supplied with artillery and adequate food and ammunition.

No matter what their training or experience, most of the men had periods of doubt about what their reaction would be during the various phases of the approaching battle. My experience suggests to me that they worried most about what would happen if they were wounded. There is a tendency to block out thoughts of the possibility of death. When a battle gets under way, men tend to concentrate on carrying out their duties and using their weapons.

An hour before dawn, Colonel McGee's situation looked like this: His block was dug in on a perimeter north of the town about a quarter mile and about three to four hundred yards east of the road. His east flank rested on the river covering the crossing. Shortly after dawn, the Japanese began moving about. They could be heard to the north, the south, and the west. Colonel McGee sent two reinforced platoons out to envelop the village, but they hit heavily fortified positions to the north and to the south of the village and were rapidly becoming involved in heavy action. The colonel ordered them back into the main perimeter by radio. Lt. Hessel D. Whitten, platoon leader of F Company on the west flank of the perimeter, was attacked heavily from the road at about 0700 hours. The Japanese crept up through the eight-foot-high Kunai grass and seemed to assemble in small groups about fifty yards in front of the perimeter; then there was much shouting and loud talking, and you could hear them charging through the underbrush straight for our perimeter. Enemy mortaring had been heavy for fifteen minutes, but now firing slackened as the enemy got closer. All of a sudden you could see one man here, another there, through the brush. Then they burst upon our lines about twenty yards from our perimeter. Everybody was calm. Then one shot rang out and the whole perimeter opened on them. Corporal James Phillips was on the extreme west flank of the perimeter—the closest man to the Japanese. He saw three Japanese—one a first lieutenant—heading directly toward him yelling "banzai" and waving a sword in one hand

and a pistol in the other. Phillips fired a burst into the Japanese at fifteen yards, but he kept coming, so he let him have what was left in his magazine. The Japanese lieutenant did not stop until his body was almost cut in two. His head fell on the parapet of Phillips's foxhole. His sword was in two pieces, shot in two by the .45-caliber bullets. Phillips reached for another magazine, only to find all of them empty. Carrying a hand grenade with the pin flattened so it would almost fall out, he ran about ten yards to his squad leader's foxhole, grabbed some ammunition, and ran back to his position. There was only scattered rifle fire as he returned to his hole, but when he got there, the Japanese officer's sword, pistol, and pocketbook had disappeared. Another Marauder almost fifteen yards away had seen them and risked his life dashing to pick them up for souvenirs. A few moments later another attack hit the same spot. This time Private Gerald A. Bryant, a Browning automatic rifle man, was firing when his gun jammed and failed to eject. Bryant said he was "scared as hell," as the Japanese were yelling like thousand-tongued horses and were running in every direction. Dropping his automatic rifle he threw three hand grenades as his assistant rifleman, Pvt. Julian Bell, fired his M-1. Bryant took his gun, ran to the rear, knocked the empty cartridge out with the cleaning rod, slipped in another magazine, tested the gun, and ran back to his hole.

The Japanese next attacked Sergeant Willy's pioneer and demolition platoon from the north. His platoon was attacked hard and often for almost three hours but repulsed each attack. Lieutenant Phillip Piazza was badly wounded in one attack by a bullet in the head and a shell fragment in his foot while he was moving back to the battalion command post with information he had gathered around the perimeter. He fell during the hottest part of one attack.

Lieutenant Piazza yelled, "Stay back—I'll crawl to you." Corporal Berry Foshine, a medic, ran back and got a stretcher, and two men then ran to where Lieutenant Piazza was lying. Disregarding his own safety, Foshine dragged him into the perimeter and bandaged his wounds. He was carried across the river by willing riflemen for further care and treatment.

Sergeant Rapisarda has this to say about the evacuation of Lieutenant Piazza. "I remember carrying him across the river. I happened to be there, and I brought the stretcher up. He was bleeding like a sieve, with blood coming out from all over. While carrying him I thought I would never see him again (Rapisarda, videotape)." Over the years we have all been delighted to see him alive and well after a long period of hospital care.

Major Cecala and Captain Ivens of Khaki Combat Team were accepting all wounded from the Second Battalion doctors who were on the west side of the river, where they gave immediate attention.

At 0830 hours the Japanese opened up another artillery battery at very close range. It sounded like a dual-purpose antiaircraft and anti-tank gun. It was really bad because you heard two explosions almost as one. The Japanese by now were throwing an almost continual artillery and mortar barrage into the perimeter. We answered with mortars but felt the need for artillery support. The only possible answer to the enemy artillery was to get help from the air with bombing and strafing. A message was sent by radio at 0945 requesting help from the air. This message had been sent to Colonel Hunter, who—it was later learned—could receive but not send. At 1245 another request was made for fighter support, this time to regimental headquarters. Four P-51's came over at 1545. Our air corps air liaison officer was on the radio with them and directed bombing and strafing of the artillery positions for an hour and fifteen minutes. During this period Colonel McGee took steps to get all animals well out of artillery range.

Khaki Combat Team had remained on the east side of the river to provide mortar fire, accept the wounded, take care of supplies, protect the flanks east of the river, and provide patrol activity. During the early morning a very tragic event took place. Pfc. Raymond L. Bratton was on a five-man patrol from the Khaki I & R platoon. They had just come out of dense jungle along a narrow trail when they saw a patrol from the Second Battalion about fifty yards away. Bratton saw one of the Americans raise his rifle. He yelled, "Don't shoot—we are Americans." Private Bratton was wearing light tan British type coveralls, which caused some confusion. The man fired, and Bratton was killed instantly, with a bullet through the heart. Later in the morning Khaki's only other casualty occurred when Sgt. Murray P. Clayton was struck by fragments from a defective propelling charge that exploded while he was loading a 60mm mortar. He received numerous puncture wounds in his right thigh. After medical attention he remained on duty.

THE BATTLE OF INKANGAHTAWNG

The Japanese had attacked from the north, south, and west almost continuously from 0700 hours, making a total of sixteen charges. Only one had gotten into the perimeter, and this took place during one of the early-morning attacks. This was when the Second Battalion lost one of its best-liked Marauders, Pvt. William S. Thornton. Known as "Smiling Jack," he served as an assistant machine gunner in Company E of Blue Combat Team. He had come from Trinidad with the 33rd Infantry. A Japanese had jumped into a hole occupied by Pfc. Leonard S. Wray of F Company. Wray could not get to his gun quick enough, so he grabbed the Japanese's. He jumped out of his hole twisting and turning the rifle and bayonet with the Japanese on the other end. Wray snatched the gun and the enemy soldier fled. Jack Thornton fired his machine gun, as did Pfc. James L. Waldron of Republic, Kansas. The enemy died under a hail of bullets. The activity caused the enemy to direct intense fire to the area, and William S. Thornton was killed.

During the afternoon the Japanese slipped as close to the river as they could and attacked from the south. They hit Lieutenant Robert Shearer's platoon hard under a heavy mortar and machine-gun barrage following a heavy artillery barrage. They were repulsed, but the sound of trucks indicated they were getting replacements.

Ammunition was running low, and Colonel McGee sent a radio message to Colonel Hunter, who was still at Sharaw, requesting that one unit of fire be put on standby to be dropped upon request at Inkangahtawng. No reply was received, suggesting that Hunter's equipment was out of order. Colonel McGee then sent Captain Hickman and a patrol back to Sharaw with request for ammunition and information. At this time, he communicated only with General Merrill—who informed him of Hunter's breakdown in radio communication. Ammunition was put on standby. Interception of another message explained that the First Battalion was still not close enough to Shaduzup to carry out its mission. Colonel McGee had orders not to withdraw under any circumstances and had received a message from Colonel Hunter that at least a battalion of Japanese appeared to be moving north from Kamaing. By this time his ammunition supply was low. He was being attacked from all sides and was in danger of being cut off. The usefulness of continuing the block was lessened by the slow Chinese advance in face of fierce resistance on the approach to

Shaduzup. He was now aware that the First Battalion had not established a block below Shaduzup. At 1630 hours he received orders to withdraw toward Manpin.

General Tanaka's forces had suffered many casualties, including an estimated two hundred dead, but they had not been trapped in a pincer movement. Those who would have been forced to engage Colonel Osborne's force had been available in an attempt to destroy McGee's Marauder unit at Inkangahtawng. With the enemy still engaged and the lateness of the hour, it appeared that the Marauders could not get delivery of food and ammunition on 24 March. With the probability of cloudy conditions and rain daily, McGee knew that he could not count on the fire power of the air force at the time of his choosing. He had no way to counter the enemy artillery and lacked unlimited access to replacements, food, and ammunition. Sick and wounded had to be evacuated, and the men desperately needed rest and sleep. Colonel McGee had no information suggesting that he might be surrounded and cut off from Orange Combat Team, but since he was only fifteen miles by road from the Japanese main base at the town of Kamaing he had to expect the worst. Nothing could be accomplished by sacrificing the Marauders under his command.

Before pulling out, Colonel McGee sent two platoons ahead to block all trails to the east and to booby-trap everything in the perimeter. A count of casualties showed two killed and twelve wounded, and the Japanese known dead ran to over two hundred.

The withdrawal as ordered by General Merrill was accomplished successfully, and the Second Battalion pulled through Khaki, holding the bridgehead on the east side of the Mogaung River, and marched into Ngagahtawng, where they bivouacked for the night. Khaki and the Second Battalion medical detachments nursed the wounded through the night under the usual primitive circumstances. The bodies of Jack Thornton and Darrell Avery had been reverently buried near the river (McGee 1987).

George M. Rose, from Portsmouth, Virginia, gives an interesting account of the battle:

> Col. McGee gave the order to cross the river as quickly as possible knowing full well the Japanese would be ready for us the next morning. At 1730 we hit the water and got across as quickly

as we could. We then proceeded to set up our machine guns and dig in.

Where we took positions, the terrain was level—providing a clear range for firing. We were on the eastern edge of an open field about 175 yards across. It had been previously burned off and cleared all around. I could see the trees on the other side of the field and knew that was the direction from which the Japanese would attack. Our perimeter was formed in a half circle leading back to the river on each end. To our rear was the river and, on the other side, the mortars and mules and the Khaki Combat Team.

Nightfall was rapidly approaching, and we began digging in, but the ground was hard. We were completely exhausted after a few inches. Those of us on the machine guns did our best to get them in position. About eighteen feet ahead of us was a Nip shack, a native meeting house sometimes used for grain. I had dug in on one side of it, and about eight feet away Harry Hahn had dug in on the other side. The number one machine gun was positioned on the left side of the shack and the number two on the right side.

As darkness settled in, some of us were standing in the trail looking over the situation. Lt. Phil Piazza and his runner, Bob Mills, joined us. They had come up to observe for the mortars. While we were talking I took out my shelter half to spread in my foxhole. I gave the thing a snap to straighten it out, and when I did, from the corner of my eye I saw something move in the field. I whirled around to look when someone yelled, "There goes a Jap!" A Japanese was camouflaged like a green tree standing in the open field. Since the field had been burned off, he stood out like a sore thumb. I grabbed for my Thompson submachine gun but about thirty other men saw him move. Everybody opened fire. There was so much firing that I never got off a shot. The last I saw of that Japanese he was running for cover. He got at least one hundred shots fired at him. All through the night the Japanese fired scattered shots just to annoy us and keep us awake. Most of the firing appeared to be from the treetops across the field.

Throughout the night we heard noises that troubled us greatly. There were sounds of trucks coming and going, the banging of truck tailgates, the thud of feet landing on the ground, and Japanese chattering. It sounded like ten thousand of them. We knew we were in for it the next day. All we could do was sit at our guns and wait. Around 0200, word was passed that Colonel McGee was coming up to check out our positions. With him was my good friend Roy Matsumoto and two other fellows. I walked over and asked Roy if any of those Japanese were his kinfolks. He replied, "I hope not." No shots had been fired by us since the episode with the camouflaged Japanese just before dark, only single shots by the Japanese. When daybreak came, the Japanese were still firing random shots at us, but had not made a charge. About 0730 still no Japanese charge, but all at once I heard firing from trees across the field. The leaves in the tops of the trees were moving. It was a temptation to open up on them. However, we were trained that under no circumstance were we to open fire unless on a massive target. Suddenly someone yelled, "Fire for effect! Fire for effect!" All at once there was a blinding explosion right in front of us: an 81mm mortar shell hit the top of the Nips' shack. From the direction it came it had to be one of ours. No Japanese shell could have come from that direction. Those of us manning the machine gun were only a few yards from the shack. The ground around us shook like a giant earthquake, tossing us around in our foxholes and slit trenches. A thousand church bells were ringing in my ears. Before the smoke cleared away, Harry jumped straight up, yelling that he couldn't hear anything, that he was deaf. Grabbing him by the arm, I pulled him back into the foxhole. For a moment or two I was deaf, but not enough to keep me from hearing Ellis Yoder screaming for help. "The gun won't fire and Avery is dead!" he shouted.

I scrambled over to see what had happened, only to view a terrifying sight. Darrell Avery was dead, and his brains were scattered all over the place. A piece of shell had pierced his helmet and went right into his head. Ellis and I jumped into the emplacement and pulled him away from the gun.

While examining the damaged machine gun I discovered the bolt was binding and the water jacket around the barrel was leaking. It had to be repaired as quickly as possible, because at any moment the Japanese could come charging out of the woods and across the field after us. With the machine gun out of action we were dead meat.

It was my custom to always carry an extra bolt in my pocket, and that day it paid off. The most difficult job of my life was to disassemble the gun and replace the damaged bolt as quickly as possible. In less than three minutes I had it back together and ready for action. The leak in the water jacket was beyond repair. With all the tape we had, even our bandaids, we could not stop the leaks.

THE BATTLE OF INKANGAHTAWNG

The explosion had wounded the other machine-gun crew, Bernard O'Neill and Jessie Norton, on the number-two gun. Lt. Phil Piazza and his runner, Bob Mills, were critically wounded. Robert Thompson and Albert Wankel rushed in to replace our wounded on gun number two."

Lt. Richard Neidinger, Lt. Paul Bergman, and William Binter, our medic, rushed to our position to help evacuate the wounded.

Who fired the mortar—the Japanese or us? To this day there is uncertainty as to who did it, but from the direction it came, it had to be one of ours. No Japanese shell could have come from that direction. Apparently it was fired from our unit across the river back of us and was an 81mm mortar.

For a short time everything settled down and was quiet. About forty minutes later, all hell broke loose. The Japanese came pouring out of the woods, charging across the open field toward our position, a distance of about 175 yards. All day long they came in wave after wave. We would stop and attack, they would fall back into the woods, regroup, and suddenly come at us again. Someone said they made eighteen charges, but I believe it was more. On one of the banzai charges, they got within twenty feet of our machine gun—too close for comfort.

Each attack was made with ten to forty men, but never more than forty. If they had charged with all their men at once they could have overrun us. Only one Japanese made it to our line, and that was to our right. He jumped into a foxhole with a kid named Leonard Wray. The two wrestled and tugged until Leonard was pulled from his foxhole. He finally managed to twist the Japanese rifle away. With no weapon the Japanese made a dash for his life. He never made it. A hail of bullets brought him down. Leonard's squad leader was Melvin Potter from West Virginia.

I was gunner on the number-one machine gun, the one damaged in the mortar explosion. During the charges, I fired about ten boxes of ammunition. The gun failed to fire about nine or ten times. Every time it got hot it would misfire. But thank God it held up through the day.

During a brief break in the charges, Lieutenant Bratloff and his runner moved to the slit trenches Harry Hahn and I had vacated. Following one of the charges I looked back and saw Lieutenant Ken Bratloff shaking his carbine in the air. It had been demolished by a Japanese bullet.

Over to my left, James Breeden was dug in and lying in a slit trench. As he pulled his right leg up to prop himself up for a better view, a Japanese bullet struck him in the front part of his right thigh. It penetrated the thigh, came out of the back of the thigh, passed through the left calf breaking bone, and then wounded a toe. He received five wounds from that one bullet, but Jim made it back to Orange, Virginia.

The Japanese made several charges after Breeden was wounded. He began yelling to me for help, but there was no way I could get to him. The Japanese kept firing away at us. Every time he yelled, a Japanese machine gun would fire in his direction. The bullets came zinging over my head, cutting down straw a few inches above me. Of course I saw how small I could draw up! He had to lie there in his foxhole for over an hour. I kept talking to him and telling him to use his belt as a tourniquet to stop the flow of blood. Lieutenant Alvin Effron moved up to our position and got someone out to him when there was a break in the charge. He was dragged back to safety—another Virginia boy saved!

Throughout the day, as I twisted and rolled around on my belly firing the machine gun, I had been lying in Darrell's brain matter—but I was so busy I never gave it a thought. Then around 0530, with our ammunition running dangerously low, we were ordered to fall back across the river. The water was a welcome relief as it washed away the mess that covered my clothing and me (Rose, videotape).

End of the Battle and Withdrawal to Ngagahtawng

The entire combat force was set up with perimeter defense at Ngagahtawng by 1900 hours. Fortunately for all, especially the wounded, there was no rain until the morning of the 25th. During the withdrawal no wounded had died, and all—including Lieutenant Philip Piazza, Bernard O'Neill, Jessie Norton, Bob Mills, K. C. Kelly, Minewski, Bushman, McGee, Hiscar, Nakada, and C. H. Thompson—spent a satisfactory night under the care of the medical detachments.

Later in the night Colonel McGee received a message from General Merrill that three hundred Japanese were moving north on the trail leading from Kamaing toward General Merrill's Headquarters at Nhpum Ga. He was told that Orange was blocking all trails leading to the ridge running from Auche to Nhpum Ga, the route his force would have to reach as soon as possible.

The Battle of Inkangahtawng was over. The men had carried out their duties to perfection. They had fought in a way to call for great credit to their unit and to America. General Stilwell in his journal never mentions the action. The miracle was that the Marauders suffered so few casualties. Unfortunately, the superhuman effort of the men and the death and wounds of their comrades did not produce the desired result. If General Stilwell had followed the advice of Colonel Hunter and General Merrill, the First Battalion would probably have been able to block the road at Shaduzup when the three combat teams of the Second and Third blocked it at Inkangahtawng. The best route for the First Battalion and the Chinese regiment would have been to travel with the Second and Third Battalions and then turn west over much easier trails to Shaduzup. If the end runs had been coordinated, the battle would have probably have opened up the road to Inkangahtawng and caused a general retreat of the enemy.

The March to Nhpum Ga

25–27 March

At dawn the Second Battalion, followed by Khaki Combat Team, moved out in a pouring rain that continued all day. Holes had to be cut in the litters to let the water off the wounded, and the muddy, sloppy trail became a quagmire for man and beast. After a march of about a mile they reached Tigrawmyang, where most of the animals, under the care of muleskinners, were waiting. Total security was soon obtained, and the men were able to rest and eat their K- ration breakfast. Colonel McGee had planned to attempt air evacuation of the wounded from an improvised strip here, but little progress could be made because of the rain. He also needed an airdrop. The weather and tactical situation soon caused him to change his mind. The rain continued here at Tigrawmyang. At 0700 a radio message from Colonel Beach to General Merrill was intercepted. Five Japanese had been seen looking for a downed pilot, who was now with Orange. Later in the day Colonel McGee received a message from General Merrill, which explained that he could see no help coming from either the First Battalion or the Chinese for several days. He advised Colonel McGee to pull back to Warong, midway between Poakum and Auche, on the trail leading from Kamaing to Nhpum Ga. Khaki and the Second Battalion started to move toward Sharaw, about five miles away.

During the day, with the few men under his control, Colonel Hunter had cleared the small available open area at Sharaw to be used to bring in small planes. Having no knowledge that the Battle of Inkangahtawng was over and the group was headed toward Sharaw, Colonel Hunter asked a pilot to fly him over the battle area. He soon saw the long column of troops moving toward Sharaw. From the air he could see some wounded walking and others on litters. With this information, he immediately returned to Sharaw and called for litter-bearing L-4's to come to evacuate the wounded. On the arrival of the casualties, two planes were ready to fly. Because of the late hour and the rain, only Pvt. K. C. Kelly and Lt. Phil Piazza were flown out. Fights were also limited because of the bad field and a strong wind.

At 1730 hours Colonel Hunter received word from Office of Strategic Service guerrillas that two Japanese battalions were moving to the north from Kamaing, possibly to cut off the Marauders at Manpin. He passed this information to General Merrill. Late in the day, regiment sent this message to Colonel McGee, ordering him to withdraw to Nhpum Ga. The Second Battalion pulled out in the morning, after the men not needed for security spent a restful night— in spite of the rain and their great fatigue.

Orange at Manpin, 24–26 March; Khaki Passes through Manpin for Nhpum Ga, 26 March

Orange Combat Team remained at Manpin, where tight security was maintained. They had arrived late in the day on 24 March and were wet, hungry, and exhausted after the march from Auche and a night spent in the gorge of the Nampana River. Lieutenant Weston's I & R platoon had arrived at Manpin late in the day on 23 March. By radio he had requested that Colonel Beach allow him to block the trail from Kamaing to Nhpum Ga. When the request was granted, his platoon immediately marched five miles northeast to block the trail.

During the morning of 25 March, radio contact was lost with Weston. Lieutenant Smith's platoon was sent to check his progress and to block the trail from Kamaing to Tatbum. This trail was several miles further to the east. Both trails joined at Warong five miles to the north and two miles south of Auche.

During the morning of 25 March, I had made a round-trip from Manpin to Sharaw. Colonel Hunter had sent a message to Orange, then at Manpin, requesting that a doctor come to Sharaw to check several incapacitated men. A sergeant and I immediately rode horseback five miles to evaluate the men. The small group had been having trouble because of bad backs and sprains. I saw no reason to evacuate them, and they later joined their unit. On the way back to Manpin, even though we were moving slowly, the horse I was riding fell dead in the trail. The animal had shown no previous evidence of any problem. We could only conclude that it was a combination of overwork and poor diet. Many of the animals were beginning to lose weight, as were the men. The trip, though difficult, took me away from wasting time in the jungle and worrying about the consequences of a possible Japanese attack on Orange Combat Team.

When I arrived back at Manpin, I was told that a radio message had been received explaining that Lieutenant Weston's I & R platoon had been hit hard by what was thought to be at least a reinforced company and perhaps a battalion of Japanese. No further details were known.

As I waited at Manpin with my medical detachment, I developed a sense of uneasiness. The possibility of being surrounded and cut off in enemy territory seemed to be likely. The jungle was wet, and the atmosphere was foggy and humid—all of which helped to create a sense of anxiety and depression. Fortunately no enemy appeared. During the night a false alarm occurred when some wandering water buffalo came near the perimeter. The night of 25 March was otherwise uneventful.

26 March

Mills, Minewski, Bushman, O'Neill, Breeden, Hiscar, Thompson, Norton, and Nakada were evacuated from Sharaw by L-1's and L-4's in the early morning.

An airdrop of food and ammunition had been planned but was canceled because of the need to reach Nhpum Ga before the advancing Japanese. The battalion and the combat team soon left for Manpin. Hunter and two riflemen remained, since two light planes were still scheduled to land. Hunter planned to use them to get himself and the riflemen to Manpin. The first L-4 came in without circling the improvised strip. The pilot seemed to misjudge the altitude and hit a ditch at the front end of the strip. The plane nosed over and had a broken propeller. The second pilot had an identical accident. The unfortunate pilots had to travel the five miles, on foot, with the three Marauders to Manpin. They would be guests of the Third Battalion until flown out from Hsamshingyang on 27 March.

The Second Battalion and Khaki arrived at Manpin at 1200 hours. Khaki returned to Third Battalion control, and Colonel McGee was now receiving orders from General Merrill. A three-day airdrop of K-rations, grain for the animals, and ammunition was planned for the afternoon. Because of the need for speed, the Second Battalion moved out before the drop and was soon in the streambed of the Nampana Hka for the ten-mile march to Auche. Captain Scott was left behind, with men and animals, to collect and follow with their share of the supplies. The Marauders had to move out as fast as possible to beat the Japanese to Auche.

The march up the rocky riverbed, deep in the mountain gorge, was much more difficult than it had been on the way down. The men and animals would climb over a thousand feet and cross the river about twenty-six times. At 1500 hours they stopped to rest and sleep as best they could, in spite of wet shoes and clothes, on the dank banks covered with dense jungle vegetation.

The supply party arrived at 1700, and the march was resumed under some moonlight until 2000 hours, when they bivouacked in the narrow river gorge as best they could.

During the night, garbled radio messages were received stressing the need to beat the Japanese to Auche.

Back at Manpin, meager information was received suggesting that Smith and Weston's platoons were having a running battle with four hundred or more Japanese. At 1630 hours a Chinese OSS agent, operating under the name of "Skittles," appeared at Manpin bringing information. He had been informed by radio that a large force of Japanese had left Kamaing at 1200 and was marching toward Auche. This information had come to OSS from a purveyor of milk to the Japanese officer's mess at Kamaing. While Colonel Hunter was studying a map, a flight of fighter planes came over. He gave the flight leader the information and requested that he search the trail. The Japanese were located and strafed. When the pilots completed the mission they buzzed Manpin to tell of their success.

The Second and Third Battalions Arrive at Auche

27 March

The Second Battalion left the riverbed at 0730 and reached Auche at 1000 hours in good order. The medical detachment had handled the treatment and evacuation of the wounded in a professional and humane way. Every effort had been made to give treatment and show consideration for the few men with anxiety, dysentery, fever, sprains, bad backs, sore feet, and general aches and pains. The doctors, who were older than the men and officers, had held up well during the battle and the four-day, seventy-mile round-trip over very difficult terrain. They had marched and fought in heat and rain with little rest and inadequate food.

Orange and Khaki had an uneventful but wet night at Manpin. We entered the river gorge, with Khaki leading, at 0630 hours 27 March. After an extremely difficult march, the last of the long column of men and animals cleared Auche at 1730 hours and bivouacked on the trail just north of Kauri for the night of 27–28 March. The men of the Third Battalion had held up very well while carrying out their part in support of the Second Battalion We had put up with tactical uncertainty, heat, humidity, and rain. All the men except those out on patrol had had adequate rest while at Manpin. We were all very fatigued from the ten-mile trip up the riverbed and the steep climb to Auche.

Lieutenants Weston and Smith's platoons were still holding the trail south of Auche and continued to do so until all the Marauders had reached that location on the afternoon of the 27th.

The Battle of the Trails between Kamaing and Auche

24–27 March

On 23 March, Lieutenant Logan Weston's I & R platoon was several miles ahead of Orange Combat Team. They had come from General Merrill's headquarters at Janpan, traveling south on the Janpan-Hsamshingyang-Nhpum Ga-Kauri-Auche-Warong-Manpin-Poakum-Kamaing trail. The trail runs south from Janpan on a ridge of the Kumon Mountains. Janpan is about thirty miles north of Kamaing, which at that time was the main base of the Japanese 18th Division.

CHAPTER XI

The trail runs over a series of razorback ridges, with elevation of up to three thousand feet. In some areas it varies as much as sixteen hundred feet within four miles. At Poakum, seven miles north of Kamaing, the vegetation is shrub and the elevation about seven hundred feet.

The platoon was delayed in leaving Auche when, as they were passing through, one of Weston's men lost his nerve and hid in the jungle. He had planned to turn himself in when the rest of the battalion arrived and explain that he had been lost. An hour was lost before the deserter was found.

At Auche they left the trail and turned to the west, descending through rough terrain and thick vegetation to reach the Nampana river. During the two-mile march they had descended a thousand feet. They then traveled southwest in and out of the riverbed twenty-eight times during the eight-mile march from where they had come to the river.

The platoon was exhausted when they reached Manpin. In spite of darkness and fatigue, they dug in and set up a defensive perimeter. Contact was made, by hand-powered radio, with Colonel Beach. Weston recommended that a method be developed to keep the trail open for the return of Khaki and the Second Battalion after completion of their mission at Inkangahtawng. His plan called for a trailblock, by his platoon, four miles south of Poakum on the trail leading from Kamaing to Nhpum Ga. There was also a trail leading from Manpin to Kamaing, and Orange would be blocking it on arrival at Manpin during the afternoon of 24 March. Weston's plan was approved, and he immediately put it into action. His unit left Manpin for Poakum at 1100 hours on the 24th, and in the early afternoon had a trailblock outpost set up a few hundred yards south of his block at Poakum.

Even though Khaki and the Second Battalion had passed through Manpin and taken an airdrop there late in the afternoon of 22 March, they had made no effort to block the trail leading into Manpin from Kamaing. Colonel Beach had previously been ordered to block all trails leading to Manpin and Warong.

Weston's platoon of about forty-two men and four mules, with a section of light .30-caliber machine guns and a section of 60mm mortars, was in position at Poakum by 1300 hours to ambush any enemy marching from Kamaing. The platoon outpost was made up of a half-squad placed in ambush three-quarters of a mile south of Poakum on the trail that led to Kamaing. Shortly after the outpost was set up, they were hit by a Japanese patrol of twelve—all of whom were killed. Weston then ordered the outpost to return to his platoon perimeter and complete their defensive positions.

Shortly after the outpost returned, the platoon was hit by lead elements of a larger force. The Japanese had a scout dog, which was used to locate the platoon's machine gun. Three separate probes were made, during which the enemy tried to outflank the I & R platoon. Each probe was preceded by mortar shells. Fortunately the Americans were dug in well. Unfortunately, they had not had time to camouflage their foxholes. Weston had picked his location with great care so that he was on high ground with dense jungle on each side and high ground to the rear. The location was ideal for flank protection and slow withdrawal if necessary. Each of the probes was turned back, with a known enemy loss of twenty-eight men.

There was little firing during the night, but the enemy was heard attempting to get around the platoon. It was necessary to throw a few grenades. On mule was hit by mortar fire, but no men were wounded.

At dawn on 25 March the enemy hit the platoon from the west and south. Weston estimated that he was being hit by a company of Japanese. At 1030 hours the platoon radio was destroyed by a Japanese knee mortar that made a direct hit. Just before the radio was destroyed the enemy had withdrawn, presumably to return to Kamaing to regroup. Enemy losses were estimated to be eighteen dead. Shortly after the action, Lieutenant Weston took a patrol out to determine if any enemy had moved around his platoon to Manpin. He saw no evidence that they had, but he found eleven enemy bodies on the trail.

While awaiting the next enemy action, Weston took three men and moved northeastward on the trail to Warong to locate his next defensive position in case such action was necessary. The trail followed a razorback ridge crossing consecutive terraces. The flanks of the terraces were steep, precarious, and difficult to negotiate—in addition to being covered with dense jungle overgrowth. A good defensive area was located a few hundred yards up the trail, and the three men returned to the platoon at 1630 hours.

Shortly after he arrived back at Poakum, Lieutenant Warren Smith and his platoon from K Company, Orange Combat Team, arrived from Manpin. When radio communication had gone out, Colonel Beach had dispatched Smith and his platoon to gather information and offer help.

Weston sent Smith and his men to dig in at the newly scouted location further up the trail. Here he could protect the rear and offer help in case of a withdrawal. Smith and his group dug in and spent the night at the new area.

Throughout the night of the 25th, Weston's I & R received harassing fire from miscellaneous weapons, including mortars. Patrols could be heard on both flanks. Shortly after daybreak three enemy soldiers stepped onto the trail between Smith's and Weston's locations. There was an exchange of hand grenades, and Weston was wounded in the left leg. The platoon aid man, T5g. Joseph Gomez, carefully dressed the wound, and the lieutenant continued his duties. The Japanese did not survive the skirmish.

At dawn on the 26th a loud frantic banzai attack immediately began from the southwest. Another mule was hit by mortar fragments. Enemy casualties were difficult to estimate. One knee mortar was knocked out, and one mule loaded with artillery was killed.

Withdrawal was necessary, since the enemy were both in front and in back of Weston's I & R platoon. He began sending his men in small groups up the trail toward Smith's platoon. The more heavily engaged were withdrawn last, moving back only as the enemy forced them.

The mules were led back, but the two wounded ones were unable to carry loads. The blown radio and generator were destroyed with fragmentation grenades. The men had to hand carry the decoding equipment, the machine guns, and ammunition previously carried on the mules. By late morning the platoon was dug in at the new defensive position.

At 1025 hours about a hundred Japanese ran into Lieutenant Smith's ambush on the Tatbum Trail. There were twenty-eight known enemy dead, and a knee mortar was knocked out. Shortly after the ambush the enemy withdrew to a small valley where Smith and Weston laid a mortar barrage on them.

By 1115 hours the main body of the Japanese began to outflank the Marauders on both trails. At 1130 hours the squads in each Marauder platoon began to leapfrog each other while they carried out a withdrawal toward Auche. Lieutenant Smith's platoon had an especially difficult and dangerous time as they withdrew under the protection of his tommy gun. Smith carried out an especially dangerous maneuver as he passed through an open area with his frequent bursts of fire controlling the enemy riflemen.

During the day's activity, Logan Weston had survived almost certain death when a Japanese grenade failed to explode as it fell at his feet. The thrower of the grenade was not so lucky.

The two platoons arrived at Auche during the afternoon and set up defensive positions on the trail south of the area to keep the trail open for the Second and Third Battalions. Weston had been informed by radio that they were en route up the difficult trail from Manpin. They continued to hold the trail until the Second Battalion arrived and set up a defensive perimeter on 27 March. Lieutenant Logan Weston, with the men of his I & R platoon, and Lieutenant Warren Smith and his men had held up a Japanese battalion for four days. If the enemy had reached Nhpum Ga, the Second and Third Battalions would have been cut off and isolated in the Burma jungle. In an inhospitable location, fifteen miles from the Japanese base of Kamaing, their situation would have been desperate. The Japanese in the area would soon outnumber them with veteran troops, supplies of food and ammunition easily trucked to the area, and plenty of available artillery. The Marauders would have no hope of relief by friendly troops. Supplies could be brought in, by parachute, if they became trapped in a suitable area. Fighter strafing and bombing would be hit or miss due to the rainy season. The First Battalion was locked in combat at Shaduzup. The Chinese could not have provided help.

Without the heroic and brilliant action of the two officers and their men, General Stilwell's campaign would have in my opinion been a total failure. The slow-moving Chinese units and their many brave infantrymen would have been stalled in the mud and rain of the monsoon. The record would show that by 15 April 1944 the cost to the Chinese of the North Burma Campaign was: 22nd Division, 800 men killed and 2,000 men wounded; 38th Division, 650 men killed and 1,450 wounded. Their number of casualties would suggest that they were making every effort to advance against a very powerful enemy.

The Battle of the Trails was over during the late morning of 27 March, and the valiant and victorious men of the two platoons rejoined Orange Combat Team.

CHAPTER XI

General Merrill and the Command Group Establish a Base at Nhpum Ga

General Merrill and the command group left Janpan at 0600 hours and arrived at Mupaw Ga on the way to set up a base at Nhpum Ga. It rained all day, which made the heat more bearable. Radio reception was very good on top of the little mountain. The clouds were below our bivouac location and created a beautiful sight. The headquarters now included eighteen Kachins to be used as messengers, guides, and soldiers. The men were carrying rice and chicken given them by the grateful people of Janpan, who now possessed more food, trinkets, cloth, and general equipment than ever before in their lives.

Another month behind enemy lines began on 24 March. Rain had started at 0430 hours and would continue all day. Headquarters was moved eight miles to Nhpum Ga over the up-and-down mountain ridges and along the narrow, muddy trail. Communications were quickly established. General Merrill learned that the First Battalion was being held up by numerous skirmishes with the enemy. Colonel McGee's Second Battalion had fought all day and then withdrawn after the successful operation. The Japanese had been dealt a severe blow and had taken many dead and wounded. The Marauders had few casualties. Communication with Colonel Hunter at Sharaw was not good.

At dawn on 25 March all units appeared to be in good order. McGee was on his way to Sharaw. Hunter had planes waiting to take out the wounded. Colonel Hunter reported that two Japanese battalions were on their way to cut off the Marauders at Nhpum Ga. Colonel Beach reported that Orange's two platoons were fighting the Japanese on the Kamaing-Auche trail.

At Nhpum Ga, John Jones—Marauder historian and collaborator on this history—was learning more of Kachin games and warning signals:

> At Nhpum Ga, the few children in this small village play the same games as they do in New York or Centerville. One game is something on the order of bowling. They dig two small holes a few inches apart and wet them with saliva, then stand two large brown nuts about three inches in diameter and one inch thick in the holes. The players stand at a line either four feet or ten feet away for the throw. They then hold a nut between the thumb and forefinger of the right hand against the second and third fingers of

the left hand. With a lunge forward, the nut is spun with the fingers of the right hand. It goes like a flash and pops as it strikes the nut in the hole. When some of the Marauders tried the game and fumbled the nut, the Kachin boys got a hearty laugh out of it.

The Kachins taught our men to build a little warning signal to place on trails they were guarding. It consists of a piece of bamboo chopped almost through from two sides and split back to the place where it was chopped out. A stick is placed in the opening to keep the two halves apart. A piece of root is stretched across the trail about thirty to fifty yards below the warning signal. The root is then tied with long pieces of vine or string to the stick which holds the clapper open. When a passerby walks up the trail he will hit the vine and pull the stick away from the clappers. The two halves of the bamboo will clap loudly. The warning signal is always put across the trail at a distance from the sentry's post— otherwise it might give away his position if it were heard by the man tripping the root.

On 25 March, at Nhpum Ga, the command group had a close call. At 1800 hours a Kachin woman came running into the village in a state of great excitement. One of the guerilla leaders talked to her. She told him that some soldiers had jumped from the trail and torn her basket from her back as she was walking from the paddy field to the village. The Kachin chief sent three of his guerilla to investigate. They returned fifteen minutes later with the report that about four hundred yards down the trail they heard voices that might be Chinese or Japanese and saw two gun barrels sticking out of the bushes a few feet from the trail. He took a party consisting of ten Kachins, Captain John Jones, Lieutenant Higgins, and two M.P.'s to investigate. General Merrill warned the group to be sure the soldiers were not Chinese before they fired. This particular Kachin chieftain, the greatest guerilla leader in Burma and a man who was reported to have killed more Japanese than any other man in India or Burma, was leading the patrol. He carried a tommy gun with a drum magazine, and his barefooted guerillas carried everything from U.D. guns to muzzle loaders marked "Harper's Ferry 1864."

Filing out in single-file without a sound, the column moved about two hundred yards before it stopped. Then the chief went into action. Quietly he indicated from a diagram drawn on the ground that he wanted three of them to slip around to the rear of the place the Japanese or Chinese were supposed to be located. He peeled off another group of three to go around the other side, then he motioned the Kachin who had seen the guns to lead the way down the trail. As John Jones describes it:

> We moved slowly and cautiously, every eye alert and every ear cocked for a sound that would tell us something. I heard a slight rustle in the underbrush to the right and swung my gun around to look face to face at a water buffalo. At least five people had that water buffalo covered. Crouching close to the ground, peering into each bush, we moved down a draw, then up over a little knoll. On the other side of this knoll our lead scout came back to tell the chief the guns were just over the crest of the knoll ahead of us and that the Chinese or Japanese were still there.
>
> We crept closer and could hear a twig snap and occasionally a voice, but it was quite dark now, and it was impossible to identify the voices as Japanese or Chinese. The chief decided that, in view of the difficulty of identifying them in the dark and the fact that we couldn't get closer to them without getting in their field of fire, we would leave four men to watch them. We were to come back at dawn, surround them, and have our Nisei interpreter determine whether they were Japanese. As we returned to Nhpum Ga we left most of the Kachins to block the trail between the unknown enemy and our command post at Nhpum Ga.
>
> It was dark when we reached Nhpum Ga at 2000 hours. We learned that another woman and her small child were working in that same paddy field where the first woman had been and had not returned. We spent a tense night, and just before dawn the next morning, the same patrol moved out in the same formation to surround the unknown people and deal with them according to plan. The tactical plan was the same. Finally, we got to the place we had reached the night before and crept slowly forward. At the crest of the knoll where the guns could be seen the night before, there was nothing to be seen. Not a sound was heard, so the chief guerilla sent one of his men down the trail to attract attention. Still, not a sound was forthcoming. The man walked into the position occupied the night before and signaled forward. Our party closed from four sides on the empty trap.

They had pulled out an hour before we got there. I thought the chief was going to kill the scouts he had left to watch them when they told him the Japanese, as they proved to have been, had milled about and got away before they could call him. There were two machine-gun emplacements and Japanese cigarette packages scattered about. Several .25 caliber rounds, scraps of cooked yams, and about five bivouac areas where at least ten men each slept during the night marked the place. Japanese shoe prints could be found on the soft, muddy trail leading toward the river, so we continued in that direction for two miles to no avail. At the paddy field we found the woman's jacket and a garment belonging to the child, which the woman's husband identified. A basha at the paddy field was torn up and the floor raised. Apparently the Japanese were hungry and were searching for food. They were traced to the river, where they turned had south.

As we had no force available at Nhpum Ga to follow them, we returned to Nhpum Ga and reported to General Merrill. He notified Orange Combat Team to be on the lookout for them.

General Merrill's command post was lucky, for there was at least a company in that area. We had about fifteen Kachins and eighteen Marauders at Nhpum Ga at that time, and no machine guns or mortars. The Japanese apparently didn't know that we were anywhere near them. The woman and child were never heard from again but were believed to have been taken for guides by the Japanese—or possibly killed.

At 2000 hours on 24 March, General Merrill received a message by runner that Orange's I & R platoon had been hit by a platoon of Japanese at 1600 hours below Poakum and again at 1800 hours. He now knew that Weston's radio was inoperative and that the Japanese were attempting to cut the Marauders off at Nhpum Ga. There was little he could do but wait and hope for the best.

The regimental headquarters remained at Nhpum Ga until the morning of 28 March, when General Merrill moved and set up his new headquarters at Hsamshingyang. He had pulled out of Nhpum Ga before the enemy attacked the area.

CHAPTER XI

Third Battalion Sets Up Base at Hsamshingyang, Four Miles North of Nhpum Ga

27–28 March

Khaki Combat Team and the Second Battalion had arrived at Auche, four miles south of Nhpum Ga, during the morning of 27 March. Orange Combat Team followed but marched through the area to Nhpum Ga. General Merrill with his small staff was still at Nhpum Ga. The general had been getting radio messages from Weston's I & R and knew about the approaching force of Japanese. In spite of all his anxiety about an approaching battle, he was in good spirits as Orange passed through late in the evening. He sent Orange Combat Team four miles farther north to set up a base at Hsamshingyang. The trail between the two areas ran along a razorback ridge, which descended from twenty-eight hundred to fourteen hundred feet in elevation. On all sides the mountain was covered with bamboo, some large trees, and other thick jungle vegetation.

The jungle at Hsamshingyang surrounded an open, grasscovered clearing about two hundred by one hundred yards in area. Colonel Beach immediately ordered the unit to clear brush and rice paddy ridges to turn the central portion into an airstrip large enough for the small planes to land and take off.

The medical detachment opened up a medical evaluation and treatment area on the edge of the clearing. At our location we had heard, on the morning of 28 March, the sound of artillery fire to the south. By noon, Khaki Combat Team had joined us at Hsamshingyang. They brought word that a battle had begun at Nhpum Ga and casualties were beginning to accumulate.

Weston's I & R platoon was the last group of the Third Battalion to arrive at the new base of Hsamshingyang. The men were sleepy, hungry, and tired, but otherwise in good condition. They were proud of what they had accomplished and convinced that they could handle the enemy under any circumstance. In my capacity as a combat surgeon I was amazed and very happy that they had no one killed and only one wounded during the four-day Battle of the Trails.

Up until the time the base was set up at Hsamshingyang, the Third Battalion had not had the service of a chaplain. All were gratified when Father Barrett came in on a liaison plane. Tony Colombo came to know him very well, as he says in an interview with Dave Quaid:

I got to be very friendly with Father Barrett. He joined us the first time we went into Hsamshingyang. He said he was going to say the first Mass, and he asked if anybody had ever served as an altar boy. I said I would serve the first Mass with him—I still remembered my Latin. He was from Chicago, and his plan was that I was going to be his chauffeur and we would go out and proselytize the Catholic religion and see that the Mafioso all went to church on Sunday. This was a big joke. We teased and kidded. Barrett died in the hospital, the 20th General. We were evacuated the same day with typhus. I guess he was overweight. He was a pudgy little guy, had never been in the infantry, was freckle-faced, and was a heck of a guy to have around you.

I remember one day climbing, and he was sweating and had this pack set on his back about three yards long, and I said, "Father, give me that pack." I made it inches long and put it on the top of his back. I taught him how to shoot a .45 because he had never thought of carrying a gun in his life. Stuart [the Irish missionary who was now traveling with General Merrill] talked him into carrying a gun. I taught him how to clean it. I used to borrow it from time to time when I was running up close to the line. He didn't know how to fire other weapons. One time I got back a little late, and I heard him calling, "Tony, Tony—give me my gun. I can't sleep." Anyhow, he got to fire the weapon one time. One day he said, "I fired my gun, I fired my gun." I said, "Did you get it?" He said, "No, I fired it into a tree. I just wanted to see if I could do it."

This kind of relationship kept up. He was kind of like an older brother. One other thing about Father Barrett. I had a bad mouth, and I guess I still have. Every time I would swear, he would say, "You owe me a scotch and soda." Well, I guess I owed him about two barrels of scotch before we got to Myitkyina (Colombo, videotape).

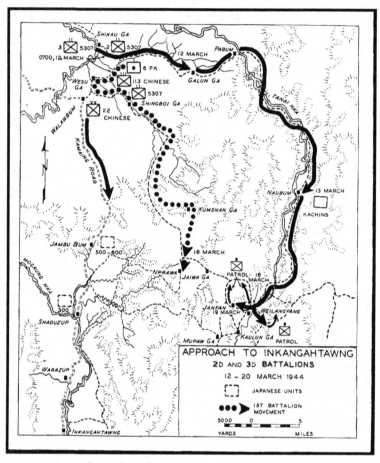

MAP 11. Approach to Inkangahtawng: Second and Third Battalions,
12–20 March 1944.

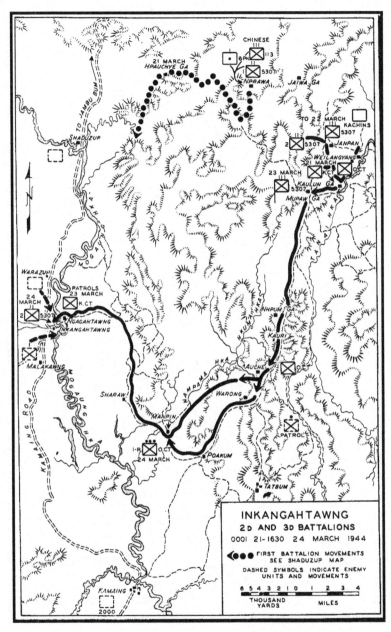

MAP 12. Second mission, Inkangahtawng: Second and Third Battalions, 21–24 March 1944.

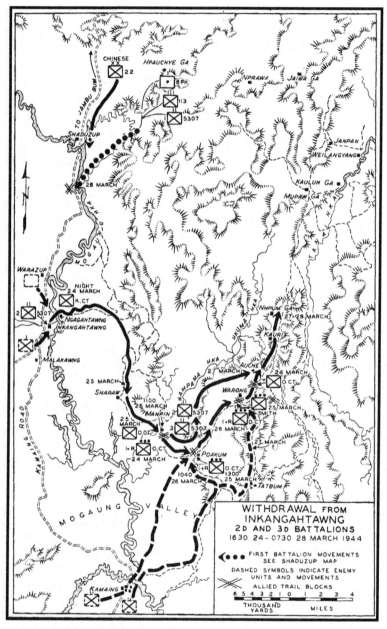

MAP 13. Withdrawal from Inkangahtawng: Second and Third Battalions, 24–28 March 1944.

Chapter XII

The Battle of Nhpum Ga

28 March–10 April 1944

Day One

28 March: The Second Battalion Reaches Nhpum Ga under Heavy Fire

At 0630 hours on 28 March, the men on the Second Battalion perimeter at Auche had not been hit by the expected enemy attack. The order came through from their commander, Colonel McGee, to prepare to move over the north trail four miles to Nhpum Ga. The spirits of the tired men were lifted as they prepared to move. They had been under great stress for four days and had seen plenty of fighting. What they wanted was rest, food, and sleep. Battalion headquarters, followed by Green Combat Team, was slowly filing out of Auche when two loud explosions were heard and, a moment later, a loud whistle as everyone hit the ground. Japanese artillery had opened up on them from the vicinity of Warong. The first two rounds were two hundred yards to the right of the trail but on the edge of the village. Moments later two more rounds came over a little closer. This time the men got up and started moving a little faster.

Lieutenant Witten's pioneer and demolition platoon and a machine-gun squad had been previously set up by Colonel McGee to cover the rear. The colonel used his SC 306 radio to encourage the Blue Combat Team commander to keep his men and animals moving. Just as the tail of Green Combat Team cleared the outskirts of Auche, a shell burst nearby, wounding one man and several animals.

Once the Japanese got their artillery barrage on the trail, all hell broke loose. They threw a steady stream of shells into the area. One shell made a direct hit on T5g. Hugh H. McPherson, who was instantly killed. Another hit a tree, and several men and animals were wounded. There was no protection for men or animals. The wet, slippery trail was narrow as it continued two or three miles up the razorback ridge leading to Nhpum Ga. The jungle-covered terrain on either side of the trail fell down one thousand feet on each side to a river. Only luck could save the men and animals from death or injury. There was no possible escape other than advancing as rapidly as possible toward the more open area where Nhpum Ga was located at twenty-eight hundred feet elevation on a mountaintop.

The exhausted men had marched seventy miles in five days, fought a battle, and made 114 river crossings. Food and sleep had been inadequate, the mountain trails had been difficult, and the heat, humidity, and rain continued to be oppressive.

Now they were caught in a situation no commander wants to be in—an artillery shelling in a narrow place where deployment is impossible and the enemy is apparently getting observation to adjust fire for maximum effect.

Khaki Combat Team of the Third Battalion had departed from Auche in advance of the Second Battalion. Colonel McGee radioed them to move as rapidly as possible so that Green Combat Team could get over a little crest that would give them some cover. The trail was hard climbing, slick as glass, and ankle-deep in mud. Animals slipped and fell. Some had to be unloaded to get them on their feet and then reloaded. It takes a brave man to do that during a shelling, but it was done several times.

Somehow up front the word was passed to "move faster," then a little later again, "move *faster*." Men were practically running uphill, falling to the ground only when a shell burst close to them. The word passed up the line: medics and horses to the rear.

The shelling increased in intensity and was amazingly accurate. Wounded men screamed out from the side of the trail for help—for it was easy to pass by and not see a man ten feet from the narrow jungle trail. Brave deeds became the order of the day: When one medic heard that there might have been a wounded man left by a tree just out of Auche, he walked back almost one-half mile leading a horse, calling out and searching for the Marauder. He found the body of Hugh McPherson.

On the return back up the trail, this same medic found a man limping along with a severe wound of both a leg and an arm. First he dressed the soldier's wounds and then put him on the horse for a ride back to Nhpum Ga.

William Pete Henderson was a BAR man bringing up the rear of Green Combat Team. During the shelling he was wounded in both legs by a tree burst. Because of his position in the column, he was left behind. Ed Kohler was quite a way up the trail when he looked back to see if any Japanese were in pursuit. He saw none, but he did see Henderson attempting to drag himself. Ed Kohler was suffering from malaria and had a high fever, but he threw Henderson across his shoulders and carried him for about a mile. A horse was brought to the rear, and he rode the rest of the way to Nhpum Ga.

Second Battalion Dead

Hugh H. McPherson 37160239, T5g., Co. F

Second Battalion Wounded

Kart G. 33293345 Assoc. S.Sgt., Co. F; Neutrino, Pa.
James W. Campbell, T5g., Co. H; Tottenville, Staten Island, N.Y.
Luther Hushes, T5g., Co. E; Relief, N.C.
Thomas A. Dabs, Pfc., Co. E; Port Huron, Mich.
Wilber R. Littler 37234696, Pfc., Co. E; Cass Lake, Minn.
Amos J. Smashed, 37212325 Pfc., Co. H; Hutchinson, Minn.
William P. Henderson, T5g., Co. F; P.O. Box 21, Warsaw, N.Y.

In order to avoid more casualties from the well-directed artillery fire, the men of the Second Battalion had come part of the way to Nhpum Ga walking as fast as the column would allow. On arrival all were exhausted. Several had shown evidence of severe emotional distress at Inkangahtawng, and their problem had continued. They would need evaluation and probable evacuation. A few new cases would need medical evaluation. One man, a big, burly fellow with a tommy gun, was shaking violently all over, tears running down his face. He cried, "Major Rogoff, I'm not afraid, damn it. I tell you I'm not afraid, I just can't stop shaking."

Others in worse shape jumped and screamed each time a shell went off, and the shells were getting closer all the time. Some were too exhausted to speak; others were carrying wounded or holding them on horses. One man passed out as he reached the aid station. With all the confusion and terror of a shelling they were unable to combat, the vast majority of the men were plodding along doing their jobs. It was those men who quickly whipped the top of the hill at Nhpum Ga into a veritable fortress that was destined to withhold two weeks of all the Japanese could dish out.

As the anxiety cases talked and the wounded were being attended to, Major Rogoff, Second Battalion surgeon, and members of the medical detachment quickly set up an aid station in front of a basha located between two hills near the center of the village area. Already four or five wounded lay on improvised stretchers where Captains Kolodny and Selling, as well as aid men, were attending to their needs. The doctors were all known to be very cool under fire. They showed this as they calmly started on the most serious cases, and an orderly line of patients was soon getting plasma and being moved to a more quiet place on the northern edge of the village awaiting evacuation. They were soon moved out by horse and stretcher over the ascending trail, four miles to Hsamshingyang.

When Colonel McGee reached Nhpum Ga at 0800, just before the rear guard, General Merrill ordered him to hold Nhpum Ga, with his battalion, while the Third Battalion constructed and held an airstrip at Hsamshingyang, four miles to the north.

Hsamshingyang was to be the supply base and evacuation point. The Third Battalion would support the Second in every way possible. Colonel McGee states in his history of the Second Battalion that General Merrill did not tell him that higher command had ordered the Marauders to prevent the enemy from advancing north up the trail through Nhpum Ga. General Merrill failed to state that the new mission was to protect the left flank of the Chinese. No mention was made of the location of the Chinese or Japanese forces.

Shortly after the meeting with Colonel McGee, General Merrill's staff learned that the general had not felt well for several days. He soon left Nhpum Ga on the four-mile hike to Hsamshingyang. His condition was such that he required assistance during the walk.

Colonel McGee called his combat team commanders together. They made a quick reconnaissance of the hill and decided the rough boundaries for the perimeter defense.

By 1200 hours the rear guard and the outer trail blocks had been withdrawn into the rapidly forming perimeter. These units included Captain Scott, Sergeant Marsh, and a detail from Green Combat Team's pioneer section, which had been placing booby traps at Kauri. The rear guard also included a rifle squad and a machine gun serving under Lieutenant Lynch. The machine gun section included Warren Ventura, J. D. Young, and Lester Weddle.

The village of Nhpum Ga sits atop a mountain at an elevation of twenty-eight hundred feet but is also surrounded by a knifelike mountain on the east and southeast. To the north the ridge continues up and down for one-half mile until a gradual descent, which runs four miles to the north to reach Hsamshingyang at an elevation of twelve hundred feet. Several plateaus are encountered as one passes along the trail. On all sides it is surrounded by dense jungle, which includes bamboo, large hardwood trees, and tropical underbrush. On the south side of Nhpum Ga the trail leads downhill for five hundred yards, and then it ascends five hundred yards to reach Kauri.

From Poakum to Hsamshingyang, the jungle terrain falls away rapidly to the east and west. A rapid drop in altitude is found when one fights through the jungle for two or three miles to the east or west. The Tanai Hka flowing from south to north is on the east, and the Hkuma Hka flowing from north to south is on the west. The drop from Nhpum Ga on each side is fourteen hundred feet.

The perimeter had to have a figure-eight-shaped boundary to hold the high ground and include a slow-flowing water hole situated under a promontory on the northeast corner. From east to west the perimeter varied from one hundred to two hundred yards in width. The length from north to south measured three hundred yards. The division of the perimeter roughly developed into Blue Combat Team taking 90 to 220 degrees and Green Combat Team taking the rest.

The terrain features included a long slope to the south, a central hill, a hill on the northeast and one on the northwest. The trail wound up the slope to the west of the central hill and then passed between the two northernmost hills as it passed on to Hsamshingyang. The northeast hill would be called Marsh's Hill and the northwest one would be called McLogan's Hill. Both were in the Green Combat Team sector. Both hills were in the widest section of the perimeter. A trail ran from the village hill and reached the Hkuma Hka a mile and one-half away to the west.

On 28 March about nine hundred men remained in the Second Battalion. They had available seven heavy machine guns, six light machine guns, seven 81mm mortars, and ten 60mm mortars. In addition to M-1 rifles there were about fifty Browning automatic rifles and a hundred Thompson automatic guns. Since the Battle of Inkangahtawng the battalion ammunition had not been replenished. There was no 81mm mortar ammunition and only a few rounds of 60mm mortar ammunition.

The 51st Fighter Group would be available for bombing and strafing, on a limited basis, when the weather permitted. They could also depend on the 2nd Troop Carrier Squadron and their C-47's for resupply from the unit's warehouses in Assam.

Water was going to be a problem, since the small spring gave a limited supply and was located in a spot that would be difficult to defend. The animals had not been removed from the perimeter, and this was to lead to the death of many of them. Apparently the command did not realize how quickly the Japanese would assemble a large and strong attacking force.

Supply would likely be adequate by air, but if the trail to Hsamshingyang became closed there would be no way to evacuate the wounded. Fortunately some of the wounded from this day had been sent to Hsamshingyang before darkness.

Blue Combat Team on the southern end of the perimeter was hit shortly before noon, with the enemy using light machine guns, knee mortars, and artillery. A flight of F-51's was contacted in the early afternoon and bombed and strafed the trail from Kauri to Warong. The planes gave the Japanese a second going-over later in the day. Eight animals had been hit on the trail to Nhpum Ga. Now more were hit in the perimeter. Fortunately few men were wounded during the afternoon and night, and none were killed.

The night was fairly quiet, and many men got a muchneeded rest. Most of the men were in two-man foxholes. One would sleep while the other kept watch. They would be ready for future attacks.

THE BATTLE OF NHPUM GA

28 March: The Third Battalion Supports the Second from Hsamshingyang

General Merrill, in spite of his sudden illness, worked with Colonel Hunter and the command group to advise Colonel Beach of the Third Battalion and Colonel McGee of the Second Battalion. Colonel Beach made maximum use of his patrols and trail blocks to prevent the Japanese from moving north by way of the Tanai and Hkuma river-beds. The Second Battalion men would be able to do little more than protect their own perimeter. A schedule was set up to send patrols to Nhpum Ga twice daily.

The command group was keeping the Second Battalion staff informed of all developments, and the Fighter Command and Colonel Hancock were made aware that all of the Second Battalion's needs would be urgent.

Major Cecala, Lieutenant Armstrong, Captain Ivens, and myself—as well as all members of the medical detachment—were giving every possible aid and comfort to the sick and wounded who arrived at Hsamshingyang during the afternoon. They were carefully nursed through the night, since we had not yet been able to bring in the small planes to land on the makeshift airstrip in this jungle clearing. Take-offs and landings would be very dangerous, since mountains loomed on all sides. A medical technician was with each platoon at all times, no matter what the activity of the unit. All medical personnel continued to carry arms for their own and their patients' protection. We had learned in the Pacific that the Japanese would show no mercy to the sick, the wounded, or the healthy who fell into their hands.

The wounded were placed on the ground. A spot had been selected near the clearing where trees gave protection from the sun and ponchos could be tied to branches to keep the rain from the sick and wounded. Now that we were not in long daily marches, men sick with dysentery, malaria, dengue, gastroenteritis, chronic headaches, arthritis, sprained ankles, chronic backaches, foot troubles, and problems such as chronic fatigue syndrome, anorexia, nausea, vomiting, anxiety, and depression were asking for help. Numerous types of skin problems such as rashes, ulcers, boils, small abscesses, and itching problems were seen. Insect and leech bites caused a lot of trouble and misery. Numerous malaria attacks were seen in spite of conscientious use of the daily atabrine tablet. Most dysentery was chronic, but an increasing number of cases were acute. Since we had no laboratory facilities, we never knew the cause. The cases that responded to sulfa-guanidine were assumed to be bacillary in origin. The others were probably amoebic in origin.

Our medical supplies consisted of sodium bicarbonate, sulfadiazine, sulfaguanidine, morphine surretes, codeine, aspirin, vaseline oint-ment, and blood plasma. No quinine sulfate or emetine was available. Combat dressings and adhesive tape were always available. Our only instruments were a few hemostats (clamps), a scalpel with detachable handle, crude pickups, suture scissors, and a needle holder. Some silk and catgut suture material was usually available. We also had ether and denatured alcohol in small amounts.

While on the march, two metal cases were attached to one mule's saddle. Boxes of plasma were carried on a second mule's pack saddle. Each animal carried stretchers and miscellaneous supplies.

By noon on 28 March, General Merrill was prostrate in our make-shift medical shelter. Major Schudmak, the regimental surgeon, sought consultation with several of us, and we all agreed that he prob-ably had had a heart attack. No one was aware that he had suffered a previous heart attack when he walked out of Burma with General Stilwell in 1942. The next day General Merrill refused evacuation until he was assured that all men who needed urgent evacuation had been sent out.

During the march from Auche to Nhpum Ga, two men from the Third Battalion, T4g. Elmer J. Kuczor of Company K and Pfc. Raymond Brown from I Company, were hit by shell fragments.

Day Two

29 March, Nhpum Ga: Second Battalion under Siege

At Nhpum Ga the Japanese artillery opened fire at daylight and continued off and on all day. There was also intermittent mortar fire. During daylight hours the enemy made three attacks against Blue Combat Team defenses on the southwest perimeter. The strongest attack came at 1750 hours. First, ten artillery shells hit the perimeter.

Under cover of mortar and machine-gun fire, the Japanese hit the perimeter again on the west. They were repulsed with heavy losses. All attacks were turned back with significant Japanese casualties. S.Sgt. Joseph F. Dunlevy from F Company, Pfc. Facundo C. Leal from G Company, Pfc. Willie Boutin from E Company, Pfc. Ralph B. Cooley Jr., Pfc. Roy E. Conway, and Pfc. Clyde E. Hawks were also wounded.

When one attack started, Corporal Samuel Stokes was digging to improve his foxhole. He had placed his helmet on the dirt at the edge of the hole. A Japanese grenade hit the edge of the hole and rolled in with Stokes. The helmet rolled into the hole and neatly covered the grenade, which exploded a moment later. The corporal was not injured.

The Japanese were close to the perimeter all day before each attack. They could be heard moving about before they would shove off. At nightfall they would pull back and start digging. One of our scouts found a note on a dead man, which said, "Cook rice at 21 hours at Warong and bring up to forward troops." Apparently the Japanese were feeding much like the Chinese did. That is, their cooks would prepare rice for a platoon or company, roll it into balls, wrap it in banana leaves, and carry it in baskets along a bamboo pole right up to the front lines.

There had not been a drop of food since 26 March, and those who still had food ate their meager K-ration meal for breakfast. They had finished and were improving their defensive positions and remaining alert for any enemy attack. A flight of P-51's soon came over and bombed and strafed the enemy at Auche.

C-47's were over at 1040 hours and, in spite of intermittent shelling, continued to drop food and supplies. The desperate situation of the two battalions was now known back at the base, and they went all out to deliver all requested items. Ammunition, food, and clothing came in as well as K-rations and some 10-in-1 food units. The men were also surprised and grateful to find fried chicken, bread, turnovers, jam, and some milk. No such luxuries had ever been delivered to the Marauders. The Red Cross was responsible.

In the battalion aid station, Major Rogoff had found a good job for the psychoneurosis cases, and it seemed to aid their recovery. He was having them dig foxholes—big ones with a place for two men to lie down feet to feet. He had evacuated only two of the eight cases he had, and he believed that in a few days he would have the other six back with their squads. The medical detachment was doing all it could to encourage reasonable attention to all principles of sanitation on the hill. They could do nothing about the disposal of the dead Japanese on the edge of the periphery or the dead mules. In the heat and rain the odor of decaying flesh and the annoyance of thousands of blue bottle flies could not be avoided. The area was soon to be called "Maggot Hill."

Second Battalion Wounded

Willie Boutin 34155605, Pfc., Co. E; Lafayette, La.
Ralph B. Cooley Jr. 33214137, Pfc., Hq. Co; Saltville, Va.
Roy E. Conway 13070057, Pfc., Co. E; Bard, W.Va.
Joseph F. Dunlevy 13027170, S.Sgt., Co. F; Philadelphia, Pa.
Facundo C. Leal 37341828, Pfc., Co. G; Springier, N.Mex.
Clyde E. Hawks 37200739, Pfc., Co. G; Heme, Mo.

29 March, Hsamshingyang: Third Battalion Continues Patrols, Receives Airdrop

Four liaison planes landed safely at Hsamshingyang and took out seven wounded to Maingkwan, from where they were flown in a C-47 to the 20th General Hospital (University of Pennsylvania Hospital Unit) at Ledo in Assam, India. One plane broke a prop on takeoff but was repaired with a spare flown in from Maingkwan. No one was injured.

The command group learned that a large group of enemy was moving toward Nhpum Ga from the east, and the Second Battalion was alerted. Available evidence indicated that this additional attacking force consisted of a company of infantry and a heavy-weapons group. The reasons for pulling back as far as Nhpum Ga and Hsamshingyang were gradually becoming clear. We had moved back in order to prevent Japanese forces from moving to the north, where they could cut off our unit and outflank the two Chinese divisions that were now just south of Jambu Bum on the Ledo-Kamaing Road. If we had stayed at Auche, the Japanese could have more easily surrounded us and outflanked the Chinese.

The Third Battalion continued patrols on all the trails, rivers, and streams in the area. We had already found some Japanese trying to move around us to the north, and had driven them back. In addition to this, the Kachins had ambushes in a number of places and were reinforcing our trailblocks. A Kachin report came into General Merrill's command post that two hundred enemy had been seen at Mupaw Ga, about eight miles north of Hsamshingyang, on 27 March. This might have been the party that had come so close to sleeping in General Merrill's command post at Nhpum Ga a few days before.

At 0800 hours an airdrop started, and a Kachin who had been warned to get away from the field got hit by a bag of grain that bounced into him after hitting the ground. No serious injury was suffered, but the Kachin didn't have to be told again to get off the drop field. Unfortunately, we did not get the luxury items of food the Second Battalion had received. We did not envy them, since water and K-rations were available, and we could rest and move about knowing that we were not surrounded and had confidence in our patrols and the trailblock units.

Our improvised medical treatment and receiving area was running well, and at this time there were few wounded to treat. Everyone was thrilled by and grateful for the unexpected but very reliable evacuation system that was developing. The sergeant pilots and their small planes had begun to demonstrate their ability, courage, and dedication to this phase of their flight activity. Our medical supplies had been replenished, and we were in a position to treat the sick and support the wounded. No facilities were available for any but the most minor surgery. We desperately needed a surgical portable hospital unit such as were available to the American-supported and trained Chinese divisions far to our rear. Any serious head, chest, or abdominal casualties who survived long enough to reach the aid station had little chance of survival without quick and definitive surgical help. Since no such help had been provided, only death awaited most of these wounded men. We would continue to have no access to the most basic laboratory studies or tests.

During the afternoon a small Kachin boy of fourteen marched proudly up to Father Stuart with his guerilla unit returning from patrol. Clothed in a green shirt and shorts, an ivory-handled dagger in his belt, a bandolier of ammunition over his shoulder, a heavy Lee-Enfield at his side, barefooted, smiling innocently, he greeted Father

Stuart as a long-lost friend. He was so young that Father Stuart was asked how the boy happened to be with the guerrillas fighting Japanese. Father Stuart told this story: This little fellow had come to him at a refugee camp at Sumprabum in the northern tip of Burma about two years before. The boy had said, "I want to go with the others [meaning the older boys in the guerrillas]." When Father Stuart asked why, he replied, "I want to fight the Japanese. I am not afraid of them, but there are only two of us here and I am afraid of the dark."

Day Three

30 March, Nhpum Ga: Second Battalion under Fire, Sanitation Problems Develop

At Nhpum Ga the Japanese artillery opened up at dawn, then the mortars, and finally the automatic weapons—and the enemy swarmed up the east slope of the perimeter. Everything available was thrown at them, and they fell back—only to try again a little farther to the north; but again they were repulsed. With each attack the morale of the men improved, for they knew the Japanese had had them at their worst the day before. However, they were still tired, for they hadn't had much sleep for the past three days. The Japanese seemed to know that they couldn't crack the perimeter from the south, and now they were concentrating all their efforts on the eastern flank.

In spite of intensive enemy activity on this day, the battalion got no fighter support. There was no explanation for this lack of support, and the Japanese used it to good advantage.

Colonel McGee sent a message to the command post asking that the trail be kept open between Hsamshingyang and Nhpum Ga, as he expected the Japanese to try to cut it. Headquarters told him that a daily combat patrol from the Third Battalion would be pushing through to him. They stressed that because the bulk of the Third Battalion was engaged in protection of the strip and supply base or out on patrols, he would have to do any other patrolling he felt necessary. The large size of the perimeter at Nhpum Ga left very few men available for patrols; however, all-day patrols from the Third Battalion and the Second Battalion moved over the trail, and the wounded and sick were evacuated to the airstrip late in the afternoon of the 30th.

THE BATTLE OF NHPUM GA

The Japanese seemed to have located our mortar position on the reverse side of the hill at Nhpum Ga, and they concentrated on knocking them out with their artillery. The Second Battalion distinguished between two types of artillery fire: The big gun, probably 105 or 90mm, was known as "Big Bertha." Its shell could be heard coming over with a whistle. But the one they hated and feared the most was the one they called "pet-pet." It was probably a high-velocity 70mm dual-purpose gun, and it was fired from a range of almost one thousand yards point-blank into Nhpum Ga. The two explosions were almost simultaneous, and on the 30th of March this gun proceeded to blow the top off the hill directly in front of the battalion mortars. This problem was partly solved by moving the mortars to a better position on the east side of the village.

Early in the morning, Lieutenant Brendon J. Lynch and Corporal Louis Black of Blue Combat Team were slipping back into the southern part of the perimeter after a reconnaissance. They made the mistake of not returning from the same section of the perimeter from which they had left. They gave no recognition or signal. The men in this section had not been told they might expect a patrol to return. By tragic action, they were hit by bullets from a Marauder machine gun. Black was killed instantly, and the lieutenant died the next day. From other action, Private George Jerry and Private John Locker also died.

The Japanese threw a few shells over at 2100 hours, and one, a tree burst, wounded one man seriously. Two aid men left their foxholes to bring him in. Japanese snipers fired a flare into the middle of the perimeter, and the two heroic medical technicians were wounded.

Snipers ringed the perimeter from the east, west, and south, and banged away off and on, day and night. Sometimes they fired at the sound of a shovel striking the ground. Many times they fired directly over the aid station on the reverse slope of the hill. Major Rogoff by now had excellent foxholes for the sick and wounded. Twelve litter cases had been received on this day and were awaiting evacuation on the morning of 31 March.

Sanitation was becoming an increasing problem. Men could not leave their foxholes at night for fear that their own men would shoot them by mistake. The men used their helmets as waste receptacles and buried their own waste in the morning near their foxholes. This was beginning to complicate matters, for the ground around the fox-holes was rapidly becoming covered with little piles of earth—some not completely buried. About seventy-five mules and horses had already been killed. Many others were badly shot up. Bodies of these animals lay all over the place, and the ones two days old had already begun to stink badly. Japanese bodies about the perimeter were also beginning to give off a foul odor. After thirty-six hours in this hot, moist climate a dead body is bloated and covered with maggots.

It was impossible to bury the animals, as the Japanese opened fire whenever they heard a shovel hit the ground. Colonel McGee's command post was also suffering. A large tree about twenty yards away had attracted at least four tree bursts, which had killed one Marauder and injured several others. Continuation of the hazard was eliminated by the pioneer and demolition platoon. They ringed the tree with dynamite for its quick elimination.

Second Battalion Dead

George Jerry 20127616, Pvt., Co. E
Louis Black, Cpl., Co. G

Second Battalion Wounded

Raymond Brown 34319560, Pfc., Co. I; Broadway, N.C.
Robert E. Clatterback 33127206, Pfc., Co. E; Culpepper, Va.
Victor J. Cizerwinske 36262985, Pfc., Co. F; Wausau, Wis.
Joseph P. Hutchinson 35401604, Pfc., Co. F; Columbus, Ohio
John K. Kast 32196444, Pfc., Co. I; Hamilton Beach, N.Y.
Arthur J. Richards Jr. 33353539, Pfc., Co. E; Scranton, Pa.
Robert O. Taylor 14151062, Pfc., Co. F; Star, Miss.
William L. Haney 17057599, Sgt., Hq. Co.; El Dorado, Kans.
Marvin K. Vickory 36044335, Sgt., Hq. Co., Moline, Ill.
Brendon J. Lynch 01301657, 1st Lt., Co. E

30 March, Hsamshingyang: Kachins Assist Third Battalion

The airstrip was very muddy, and only a few planes were able to land. No contact with the enemy was made to the east or to the south of Nhpum Ga, but in the southwest one of our Kachin patrols reported that Japanese had been seen one-half mile southwest of the airstrip. Father Stuart said that the Kachins had the Japanese confused with their variety of ambushes. In the past the Kachins had ambushed the Japanese many times, using punjis or sharpened sticks on the side of the trail, to impede them when they would run to the flanks to envelop the Kachins. Modifications of the ambush method had become necessary since the Japanese had become wise to the methods used. During a recent ambush near Warong, the Japanese patrol didn't run to the flanks as usual but fell down and hugged the ground along the trail and opened fire on the Kachins. Enemy superior firepower had caused the Kachins to withdraw. The next day the same ambush was laid further up the trail, and the Japanese hit the ground and opened fire. The Kachins withdrew, firing occasional shots as they withdrew up the trail. The Japanese, thinking the Kachins had withdrawn, got up and proceeded down the trail—but when they got a few feet, a Bren gun opened up on them from the rear. Now it was their next move in the battle of the ambush.

Later Father Stuart told us more about the Kachins. He said they were honest, moral, and just. He stated that few were thieves and that they were severely punished when caught. He told the following story: Not long before, two men had been sent by their chief with one hundred rupees to the leader of an outpost several days' march away. On the way, they pinched twenty rupees and turned over the rest to the outpost leader. The leader was expecting one hundred rupees, and he suspected them of taking twenty. He thanked them and gave them a note to take to the chief, in which he said, "Your men brought me eighty rupees. If you sent more, they have taken it." The men, simple and unsuspecting, took the note back to the chief. He read it and, turning to them, said, "I have a little job for you." He set them erecting, in the center of the village of Naubum, a large bamboo frame in the shape of a triangle, and had them anchor it firmly in the ground. While they were building the frame, he let the story of what they had done get around the village.

When the frame was finished, the chief's men seized the two thieves and bound them each to a foot of the frame. The entire village gathered around, and each person passed by and struck them with a switch or stick. A sign was placed overhead that read, "This is what we do to thieves." Needless to say, the men were badly beaten and would doubtless remember the punishment for stealing.

CHAPTER XII

Father Stuart told us how a murder case was handled. A Kachin killed a Ghurka. He was sent to prison for seven years. It seems that one quiet afternoon a Kachin and his Ghurka friend were pleasantly getting drunk on rice wine. Each was praising the merits of his native knife. The Ghurka showed his kukri, razor-sharp, and said he could kill quicker and better with it than anyone could with any other weapon. The Kachin, equally proud of his dah, denied that the kukri was best and made the claim for his dah. The argument got stronger as they got drunker, and finally they decided they would fight it out to prove which was the better weapon. The Kachin took the head off the Ghurka in the first few minutes of the fight, which, for the Kachin, proved the supremacy of his dah—even though it cost him seven years in prison.

Kachins have a unique method of sending messages, sometimes a hundred miles or more. If one Kachin wants to tell another Kachin in a distant village something, he will send a small package of salt or tea or some little gift, for he knows Kachins are honest and will send his gift on. A message always accompanies a gift, so they will give his message, too—whereas if he simply sends the message, it will never reach the one to whom it is sent.

Father Walsh, a Catholic missionary who lived for many years among the Kachins, was attending a conference once at which the subject of Kachin drunkenness was the topic of conversation. After a discussion of the evil that whiskey wrought, the chairman of the conference asked Father Walsh what, in his opinion, was the effect of whiskey on the Kachins. Father Walsh, without batting an eye, replied, "Whiskey is responsible for all their drunkenness and half of their children."

The men of the Third Battalion, in spite of the continued patrol and trail-blocking activity, were more vigorous and rested than they had been since D day back in February. As always, we were sleeping on the ground under the stars or in improvised poncho or jungle vegetation shelters. We had been getting a limited supply of the more nourishing and appetizing 10-in-1 ration, which fed ten men for one day or one man for ten days. Few wounded were arriving from the Second Battalion, and sick call was not large.

One can surmise that the command staff was very worried about the situation on Nhpum Ga Hill. The apprehensiveness did not stop there. We were all, in our own way, dreading the consequences of this latest development and the coming battle. Our thoughts and sympathy went out to our brothers in the Second Battalion. We knew that they had inadequate water and horrible living conditions but were mentally and physically able to turn back anything the Japanese could throw at them. We, from our daily patrols to Nhpum Ga, were learning of their increasing dead, sick, and wounded. Most of the men with minor wounds were staying at the perimeter with their squads. The unit was getting adequate food and ammunition by air. Unfortunately a few of the parachutes were landing in enemy territory.

Major Lew ordered Lieutenant Logan Weston and Lieutenant Abie Weingartner to take their platoons to the east in an attempt to get in back of the Japanese at Nhpum Ga. Abie discusses this operation:

> Major Lew told me to take my platoon and Weston his platoon to make a flanking movement down the valley to the left and come up to flank the Japanese at Nhpum Ga from their right flank and our left flank. We started and went down the valley. We looked at our maps, and the hills were so steep that the contour lines were all together. It was rather difficult to read those British maps. We started down in the morning. We didn't get up there until late in the afternoon, so we stopped and just went to sleep. We only had ammunition and arms and one or two canteens of water. We laid down that night on the side of the hill and tried to sleep. It's difficult no matter how you lay on a hill. The next morning we moved ahead, and we heard some murmuring ahead of us that sounded like Japanese talking. We stopped, and I said to George Henderson, "Sneak up a little bit closer and see if you can see." He went closer, and we didn't hear anything—then all of a sudden there was a lot of noise coming back through the brush and hollering, "Don't shoot." Here comes Henderson back with a five-gallon can of water on his shoulder. He said, "Those are our people. We went around in a big circle." We had come back right where we started after an eighteen-hour mission (Weingartner, videotape).

Near the end of the campaign, Abie was to be evacuated with Tsutsugmachi fever (scrub typhus and malaria). He states, "I use that as an excuse now. I am a little bit stout—and, according to the medical people, when you have scrub typhus your internal organs are all enlarged. People say, 'You eat too much,' and I say, 'No, my internal organs—including my spleen, my heart, and my liver—are all enlarged. I am not really fat—this is due to the fever I had'" (Weingartner, videotape).

Day Four

31 March, Nhpum Ga: Second Battalion Surrounded

At Nhpum Ga, just after daybreak, the Japanese artillery and mortars opened up as usual, and at about 0645 automatic weapons also opened and the Japanese attacked from three sides—south, east, and northwest—a few minutes apart. Their machine guns and mortars were raising hell with our animals. The Japanese principal effort was from the east in the vicinity of the waterhole. They attacked savagely and bravely, in some cases running directly up a slope that we were covering with a machine gun. An hour later neither we nor the Japanese could get to the waterhole, but it was more serious for us. We had no other waterhole. The enemy covered the waterhole with mortar fire, and snipers ringed the tall grass and jungle growth that overlooked the trail leading to it. We counterattacked to drive them off the little ridge, but they were firmly established. It was outside our perimeter, and we didn't have the men to occupy the ground if we had taken it.

Already, Colonel McGee was using muleskinners, photographers, and every available man in battalion headquarters on the perimeter. One hour later a radio message from regimental headquarters at Hsamshingyang said that the Japanese had blocked the trail between there and Nhpum Ga during the night. The Third Battalion was trying to dislodge them and thought they could get through to Nhpum Ga by noon.

The word that the Second Battalion was surrounded soon spread throughout the perimeter. This information, coupled with the loss of the waterhole, was a severe blow to morale. Japanese artillery continued to pound them, and they could not do a thing about it.

It would be necessary to bury the dead in temporary graves where they fell. From this day on, no wounded could be evacuated. They would be cared for in deep foxholes by the dedicated members of the medical detachment. Only minor surgery could be done. Severe flesh wounds of the extremities and compound fractures of legs and arms would be treated by placing the extremity in plaster casts. Fly eggs would hatch into maggots under the plaster and would eat the dead flesh without disturbing the living flesh. The chief problem was lack of water to mix with the plaster.

At 1000 hours a flight of P-51 fighter planes came over and were directed to the Japanese positions by our air liaison officer. As always when the planes were in the area, Japanese artillery and mortar fire ceased as long as they were overhead. They could not be used on the north trail since the location of Orange Combat Team patrols were unknown. The weather had been so bad for the past four days that we had seen very little of the P-51's. Even a brief visit from them always helped morale. The planes were over again at 1500 and were used for bombing and strafing the south trail.

Colonel McGee decided to try to push through on the north trail to the airstrip. He ordered the Blue Combat Team commander to exert all possible pressure on the trail without endangering the perimeter. He was given a reinforced platoon taken from the rest of the perimeter. They attacked under mortar and machine-gun support but struck strong Japanese dug-in positions and were repulsed, losing several wounded and one killed. The Japanese increased their pressure on all sides of the perimeter during the day. Apparently the Japanese commander figured he had this battalion trapped and would annihilate them in a few days.

The battalion received a heavy airdrop of food and ammunition, but the shortage of water had everyone worried. There was a muddy hole in a draw where several horses had been killed. A little water ran from it, so a squad from the pioneer and demolition platoon dug a pit, and it filled up with a brackish mixture of mud and water. It was enough to quench thirst, but that was all. The dead horses, only twenty-five feet above it, didn't add to its taste—or maybe they did.

On the south flank of the perimeter, Lieutenant Grissom's platoon was firing 60mm mortars at eighty to ninety yards range without bipeds or base plates and was hitting the target. All evidence at this time suggested that the attacking force was made up of a reinforced company with heavy mortars and artillery.

CHAPTER XII

Colonel George A. McGee Jr. clears up all speculation concerning the units of Japanese who were and would be attacking at Nhpum Ga. The first group of Japanese consisted of two companies from the 114th Infantry Regiment from Myitkyina. This was the group Lieutenants Weston and Smith had fought in a delaying action for four days on the trail leading to Nhpum Ga from Kamaing. The second group consisted of six hundred men and six 7.5cm infantry guns belonging to the First Battalion of the 55th Infantry Regiment. These enemy forces were soon joined by the rest of the battalion, which had sent the two companies plus a second battalion from the 114th Regiment. This new force was under the command of Colonel Maruyama and had a strength of eight hundred men, about twenty heavy machine guns, and eight 7.5cm guns.

The Second Battalion on this day requested an ammunition drop as early as possible. The list included fifty cloverleaves of H.E. light, fifteen heavy, five smoke, one hundred canisters of 60mm, ten G Bakerable Rogers, ten grenade containers, and two hundred pounds of TNT.

During the afternoon the men of the battalion were encouraged when they heard machine-gun, rifle, and mortar fire on the north trail where Orange Combat Team was attempting a break through the trailblock.

This night was the low point in morale so far, but every time a Japanese made the least move he drew fire. Any thoughts of annihilation or defeat were short-lived. In spite of the worsening situation, the general mood of the men was optimistic. They had not lost faith in themselves and the Third Battalion. After dark the Japanese opened up again with artillery and mortars. They did a lot of yelling, including, "Where's McGee?"

Sgt. Phil Christner, from Buffalo, New York, and a member of Blue I & R platoon, tells an interesting story in *The Burman News*. He and Sergeant O'Hara were leading Sid Savitt to the aid station after he had been hit in his left eye. On the way an artillery shell exploded nearby. Sid said, "O'Hara, are you hit?" O'Hara had released his hold on Sid's arm. He was unconscious on the ground. His helmet had been hit by a fragment of metal and was dented and cracked. He recovered, and Sid was delivered to the aid station.

Second Battalion Dead

Charles L. Varela, Pfc., Co. G
Willard C. Arnett, Sgt., Co. E
Brendon J. Lynch, 1st Lt., Co. E [died of wounds]

Second Battalion Wounded

Luther L. Bowman 15054484, S.Sgt., Co. F; Floyd, Va.
William R. Mortimer, Sgt., Hq. Co.; Lowell, Mass.
Sidney Savitt 13118277, Sgt., Hq. Co.; Philadelphia, Pa

31 March, Hsamshingyang: Third Battalion Patrols
Meet Japanese Trailblocks

During the early morning, Sgt. John Keslik's patrol from Orange Combat Team advanced south along the trail to Nhpum Ga with no enemy contact. On the trail they encountered a reconnaissance patrol from Nhpum Ga. This patrol had bypassed a Japanese trailblock just north of the Second Battalion's position. They were now in the process of directing mortar fire by radio to the Second Battalion. Shortly after the two platoons met, a group of Japanese set up two machine guns on the trail to the north of their position. The Marauders were brought under machine-gun fire. Private First Class Davis, of the Second Battalion platoon, shifted his position to the opposite side of the trail to get a better firing position. He opened rapid and accurate fire with his BAR on the machine guns and silenced them, enabling both platoons to withdraw. He then led a few isolated men, separated from the rest, through the jungle three miles to Hsamshingyang. The platoon from Orange withdrew through the jungle and entered the Nhpum Ga perimeter to spend the night.

Later in the day a patrol from the Third Battalion under Lt. Warren Smith ran into a Japanese trailblock and had to fight its way out. They returned to Hsamshingyang through the jungle. The enemy attempted to reach Hsamshingyang but were turned back after a hot skirmish. There were no American dead or wounded.

Colonel Hunter had for all practical purposes been in command since General Merrill's heart attack on 28 March. On this day (the 31st), he gave orders that a transportation train and supply dump would be formed under command of Lt. Dominic Perrone, supply officer of the Third Battalion. Starting in the morning a regular supply train of pack animals would begin operating from the supply dump to the troops fighting to open the trail. On the morning of 1 April, Orange Combat Team would use everything they had to push open the trail into the Second Battalion perimeter. Khaki Combat Team would take over all patrols. Colonel Hunter further stated that he had sent Captain John George as a representative to General Stilwell's headquarters requesting that the Chinese battalion at Pabum be sent down to block trails to the north. Starting in the morning all officers and noncommissioned officers were to wear or improvise insignia of rank and grade. The situation was extremely tense. Probably the best evidence of how tense it actually was is furnished by a little incident that happened only thirty yards from the command post.

During a church service at dusk a shadowy figure in an off-size suit and a G.I. helmet walked by. A few moments later a whisper of "Did you see that man? He looked like a Japanese in our uniform" swept through the audience. Automatically the audience began to peel off from the rear, but the figure had disappeared into the jungle. More and more men joined in the search. Finally, some ten minutes later, a Chinese soldier attached to the Marauders was found talking to a group of soldiers sitting in front of a lean-to. On investigation it was found that he was attached to the organization, but had got a bad fit in a uniform. The men were as relieved as the Chinese soldier when his story proved to be true, because they were expecting the Japanese to pull a smart stunt like this at any time.

Day Five

1 April, Nhpum Ga: Second Battalion Repulses Banzai Attacks, Water Shortage Critical

There was no enemy activity at Nhpum Ga during the early morning. Patrols found several areas occupied by the enemy. Effective mortar fire was directed to those areas. At 0900, artillery shells began to hit the hilltop perimeter. The guns now seemed to be located about two and one-half miles south, probably at Kauri, just north of Auche.

After the barrage the enemy pulled banzai attacks on the east and northeast. Both were repulsed. The 60mm mortars were worth their weight in gold. Our mortar men lay the 60's right in front of the Japanese perimeter only thirty yards away from our perimeter, and they hit their holes many times with tree bursts. All agreed that the 60mm mortar was perfect for close work, and a good mortar crew could actually put them down a stovepipe if they had a little ammunition to play with. They were always used when the Japanese attacked and were frequently fired at a range as short as seventy-five yards with good results.

When the drop planes came over they drew heavier-than-usual fire. One of the pilots reported that a bullet had passed between the legs of a kicker in the back of the plane. It should be noted that the planes had been and would continue to be hit by ground fire.

The Second Battalion had now buried seven dead Marauders and had accumulated seventy-five seriously wounded. The battalion had started with two hundred and twelve animals and was now down to one hundred and twenty, with some of these shot up badly. The stink of the dead Japanese and dead animals sprawled and bloated all around the perimeter was becoming unbearable. The water shortage was critical. Colonel McGee asked for a water drop in plastic bags to be made the next day. The medics did not have enough water to make a plaster cast for a fractured leg bone, and they were giving sulfadiazine without water. Everyone was rationed to half a canteenful—if he could get it down. The artillery shelling continued to be hellishly accurate, and mortar fire continued to be the chief cause of our casualties.

Colonel McGee sent two strong patrols out in the morning to try to feel out weak spots in the Japanese lines. They found Japanese every place they tried and returned with the information that there was one possible route to the outside: down an extremely steep and rough mountainside on the west of the perimeter. It would be up and down through some rough jungle for almost a mile to the river and then up the river to Hsamshingyang.

The platoon from the Third Battalion, which had entered the perimeter on 31 March and was now cut off, decided to attempt return to their parent unit by this route. The platoon leader divided his unit into two sections, one following the other by about twenty minutes. They started their tortuous journey through the Japanese lines and back to their battalion at the airstrip. The first section pushed its way through the thick jungle growth to a tiny streambed. Following the streambed they made better time and soon figured they were through the Japanese lines. They began moving faster and less cautiously. They were following a rough compass course of 210 degrees, but the roughness of the terrain made it necessary to vary their course as they went along. After five hours of struggling through the jungle growth they unexpectedly came upon the river and bivouacked for the night along its banks. The second section, which had started twenty minutes later, did not show up. The men in the first section were not worried about them, figuring they had turned off at a different place.

1 April, Hsamshingyang: Third Battalion Orange Fights through Trailblocks

At the airstrip, Orange Combat Team sent the usual morning patrol at 0600 to Nhpum Ga. On the trail four hundred yards south of the strip, on top of a ridge, the lead scout of the patrol was fired on by a Nambu light machine gun. The Japanese pulled a boner here—they fired at the first man, whereas if they had waited a minute or two, they could have had a better target.

Our patrol immediately engaged the Japanese and found that they had a small trailblock, probably no more than half a platoon, but they were dug in and would be difficult to get out. The lead scout left his patrol in contact and went back to report to his platoon leader. The firing had brought the platoon leader, Orange Combat Team leader Major Lew, and the battalion commander Colonel Beach on the run.

After a quick reconnaissance, Major Lew moved Lt. Logan Weston's I & R platoon up on the razorback mountain trail. Lt. Ted Hughes' rifle company C was also ordered up to help clear the trail. Clinging to the mountainside and working through the dense jungle vegetation, the Marauders pushed the enemy back up the steep trail. As soon as they were about to be surrounded, the Japanese would pull back to previously prepared defensive positions. Their selection of ground to defend was excellent. It appeared that a Japanese officer was some distance behind the front-line troops marking emplacements for automatic weapons. The Japanese used a clever S-shaped trailblock with Nambus on the humps and ends that could send crossfire usually both up and down the trail. A few riflemen were in foxholes between the Nambus, and some were scattered back along the trail. The Japanese truly used men and ground to maximum advantage and forced us to be extremely careful about our envelopment. In some cases they estimated where we would envelop and got a machine gun there to hit us in the flank. The Orange Combat Team had the most seasoned and experienced fighters in the command, and their ability to sense where the Japanese would be saved many a life.

On this day Orange Combat Team fought through two blocks and moved approximately two miles up the trail. During the long day of offensive fighting, Company L of Orange Combat Team suffered four wounded—one of whom later died of his wounds.

Private Robert W. Cole was the second scout in a group of five. The scout on the left moved off the trail to investigate a noise. Cole moved off to the right and was in a kneeling position in order to give crossover fire from his BAR. The Japanese were firmly entrenched on either side of the trail. Cole was hit by a rifle bullet at twenty yards' range. The bullet entered the right lower quadrant of his abdomen near the outer edge of the pelvic bone and passed to exit just above the top of his thigh bone. The Japanese machine guns then opened up. The rest of the patrol poured in a heavy volume of fire and made flanking approaches. The enemy then pulled back one-half mile to a previously dug position. Under the protecting fire, Cole was pulled back, and others carried him about two hundred yards to the Orange surgeons. His wounds were immediately dressed, and he was given two units of blood plasma to replace blood loss. After a litter carry of one mile, he was immediately evacuated in a small liaison plane. He returned to combat seven weeks later.

By 0900, Company L reached the second trailblock, which was much more heavily dug in and expertly defended. First the block was subjected to a heavy mortar attack. Next, flanking movements were made by the two platoons of L Company. These were carried out with great difficulty because of the terrain, thick jungle growth, heat, humidity, and poor visibility. Maneuvering, mortar fire, rifle

CHAPTER XII

fire, and machine-gun fire from the Marauders would continue until 1600 hours.

The first burst of Japanese machine-gun fire wounded two Marauders. Pfc. Leroy E. Brown was advancing up the steep, zigzagging trail flanked by large bamboo trees and other tropical vegetation that formed a canopy, blocking the sun. He was followed by Sgt. Aloysius Kazlousky. They were both pulled back by comrades under heavy protecting fire. The platoon aid man gave immediate help by applying pressure dressings and injecting morphine for pain.

Brown was dazed and tending to choke from blood in his mouth and nose. The bullet had entered the center of his chin and base of his tongue and passed through the angle of his jaw (mandible bone) that was fractured and visible through a large wound in his cheek. He was seen within five minutes by the Orange Combat Team surgeon, and pressure dressings were applied. He then walked with help two miles to the regimental medical section at the airstrip. Because of the late hour, no liaison planes were available, and he could not be evacuated. He died about eighteen hours later. If a mobile surgical portable operating unit had been attached to the Marauders, his life could have been saved. Such American units were in the China-Burma-India theater, but they were attached to the Chinese regiments under General Stilwell's command. These regiments were fighting many miles in back of the isolated Marauders.

Sergeant Kazlousky's wound was very disabling but not life-threatening. He had a severe open machine-gun wound of the left foot with fractures of all the metatarsal bones and damage to numerous muscles and tendons. He was quickly treated and sent to the rear. Thirty hours later, after lying on the jungle floor, he went out in an L-1 small plane and arrived at the General Hospital in Assam, India, on 3 April. The wound was severe enough to require further treatment in the States.

Later in the day Pvt. John V. Carbone was in a sitting position firing his Browning automatic rifle. A Japanese rifleman crawled through the thick jungle vegetation and fired at a range of twenty yards. The rifle bullet entered the front of his left thigh and passed upward sixteen inches to lodge in the soft tissue of his right buttock. Evacuation was quick, and his wounds were treated surgically at the general hospital on 4 April.

The numerous strong attacks of Orange had forced the enemy to withdraw up the trail by 1600 hours. All fighting ceased, and a very strong perimeter was set up at this area. The exhausted men of Orange Combat Team spent the night here at their furthest point of advance, which was approximately two miles south of the airfield.

In common with many of the men and officers, Sgt. John A. "Red" Acker of Khaki Combat Team had frequently mentioned the need for artillery. He knew what he was talking about, having volunteered with a large number of men from the 98th Field Artillery after their action in New Guinea. On 29 March, Major Briggs had come by his position on the perimeter. Acker brought up the subject and explained that he could easily round up several experienced and reliable gun crews.

A day or so after his talk with Major Briggs he was asked to assemble the gun crews. He selected Thomas Averred, from Khaki, to be gun chief on gun number one and George "Red" Lobe, from Orange, to be gun chief on gun number two. He soon had eight men per gun crew, plus muleskinners. "Hoot" Gibson was the radio man. Charles Thurman could speak Chinese, and he was to be useful if any of the Chinese arrived. The group of thirty men included gun crews, packers, ammunition handlers, and picket-line guards. John Acker would be the battery commander. They were given the jobs they knew regardless of their present grades. One of the best gunners in the 98th was found in Pvt. Isaac W. "Little Chief" Robs, a full-blooded Cherokee Indian from Cherokee, North Carolina. These men were all like school kids on a vacation—they were so happy to learn that they might soon have their hands on a pack howitzer again. The gun crews went through a dummy run, completed their organization, and were all set to receive the guns.

When General Merrill was taken out, the first thing he told Major Hancock, who met the plane at Ledo, was to get two howitzers and drop them to the Third Battalion at the airstrip. Major Hancock had two guns packed and ready to drop by 1000 hours on 1 April, and sent Colonel Hunter a message that they were available when he wanted them. Colonel Hunter radioed back to drop them on 2 April.

When news leaked out that we were to have our own artillery for the first time since we had been behind the Japanese lines, morale picked up all over the area. The cheering news was radioed to the Second

Battalion, which was told it would be out in short order when the artillery arrived. Morale also lifted there—but Major Rogoff was not so encouraged. His twenty-five wounded still remained in foxholes at the aid station. Some of them would not be able to survive another two days without hospital care, surgery, and—in one case—blood transfusions. The only way to get them out was over the trail.

At the evening staff conference, Colonel Hunter ordered Orange Combat Team to be prepared in the morning to renew the attack up the trail toward Nhpum Ga. They still had about two and one-half miles to go. Everyone knew that the Japanese defenses would grow stronger as they advanced over the remaining two miles of heavily defended trail between our position and Nhpum Ga. We would again face artillery, mortar fire, machine guns, and riflemen. The battle would continue along the mountain ridge ascending from an elevation of fifteen hundred feet at Hsamshingyang to one of twenty-eight hundred feet at Nhpum Ga. The route had several small level areas or plateaus, each preceded and followed by steep elevations in the trail. Most of this narrow dirt trail was blocked from the sun by towering bamboo and other trees. The mountain terrain on either side of the trail continued to be almost impassable because of thick growth and steep grades descending rapidly a thousand feet or more to the two rivers running two or three miles along each flank. We could expect continued heat, intermittent tropical showers, high humidity, and a dry, dusty trail alternating with a muddy trail. It had been raining all day.

Khaki Combat Team would send as many men as possible through the jungle to the Hkuma Hka a mile or more to the west, and then, after a four- or five-mile march, attempt to climb through the jungle to hit the rear of the Japanese on the Second Battalion's western border. They would have to hand-carry all equipment and would have no mortars.

Third Battalion Dead

Leroy E. Brown, Pvt., Co. L [died of wound on 1 April]

Third Battalion Wounded

John V. Carbone, Pvt., Co. L
Aloysius Kazlousky, Sgt., Co. L
Robert W. Cole, Pvt., Co. L

THE BATTLE OF NHPUM GA

Day Six

2 April, Nhpum Ga: Second Battalion Receives
Food and Ammunition

This day at Nhpum Ga started with heavy Japanese mortar and artillery fire that continued until noon. Several infantry attacks on Blue Combat Team were turned back with heavy enemy losses. Marsh's Hill was also hit, and there was some activity on the trail to the north. Just before dawn, one of the Marauders was sitting in a buddy's foxhole when he saw a Japanese approaching. The man appeared to be groggy and lost. He walked to the Marauder's location mumbling to himself, apparently believing he was in his own perimeter. The Marauder mumbled back while reaching for his gun. The Japanese walked away, apparently looking for his own foxhole, and the Marauder shot him dead with one shot through the head.

Water remained a critical problem for the Second Battalion. Colonel McGee radioed regiment to come up with a method of dropping five hundred gallons. This job was turned over to Major Hancock, and none doubted that he would find a method of dropping the water in. During the afternoon there was a heavy but short rain, which was collected on ponchos. The men were able to quench their thirst, and the few remaining animals got some out of small collections on the ground.

Someone started a rumor that the battalion had been told to fight their way out the next day with their wounded. Everyone knew that such an action was just what the Japanese wanted. Colonel McGee spiked the rumor by passing the word around that the Second Battalion was accomplishing its assigned mission of blocking a Japanese counterthrust on the Chinese east flank at Shaduzup. He further stated that we had plenty of food and ammunition and that the next day we would have water dropped. We would stick out the siege until the enemy were defeated and our two battalions were victorious. Colonel McGee was at all times able to communicate with the key points of the perimeter using field telephones and SC 300 and even SC 536 radios.

Under protection of a squadron of fighter planes, much- needed food and ammunition was parachuted to the battalion. After the drop, the planes strafed the enemy positions at Kuri and Auche. Some amusing items arrived. There was one book on office gynecology and a number of french novels. The men got quite a kick out of the books as they were passed around the perimeter.

Second Battalion Dead

None

Second Battalion Wounded

William Astle 32297042, Pfc., Co. E; Barking, England
Vincent J. Codamo 6841653, T.Sgt., Co. G; Philadelphia, Pa.
Marshall W. Hurlocker 14009121, S.Sgt. Co. G; Concord, N.C.
Milton Koff 19099761, Pfc., Hq. Co.; Hawthorne, Calif.
Glenn J. Maddox 35127871, T5g., Co. F; Hamilton, Ohio
Victor E. Mead 39376014, T4g., Hq. Co.; Hawkins, Wis.
Harold D. Wagner 35402941, Sgt., Co. E; Flushing, Ohio

2 April, Hsamshingyang: Third Battalion Receives Pack Artillery Guns

At daylight, Orange began to advance toward Nhpum Ga. We had covered about two miles and had arrived at a very steep incline of two or three hundred yards that led to another plateau in the jungle. The enemy had picked a strong defensive position at the end of the ascent in the trail on the edge of the plateau. Several other machine guns were in place along the east and west sides of the trail. All areas of reasonable approach over the steep, jungle-covered terrain were thus covered by enemy weapons.

L Company of Orange Combat Team had been leading the attack. Casualties started when they began to work their way around the machine guns on the steep incline. West of the trail, Cpl. Edgar Robertson was the lead scout, while Cpl. Frank L. Graham was second, and S.Sgt. John L. Ploederl was the third scout. These scouts ran into what was the third major trailblock to be encountered since the relief advance began. Graham was the first to spot the heavy machine gun, twenty yards ahead on the right side of the trail. As he jumped into a slight depression to the right, he warned the others. They dived to the left. The heavy—as well as a light gun—opened up. Frank Graham was able to fire a clip from his rifle before a bullet passed through the muscle of his right shoulder. Edgar Robertson was prone when hit. The bullet entered his right thigh and passed upward into his body. He was instantly killed. The machine gun caught John Ploederl in both thighs. He lay wounded for several minutes. A comrade crawled up under the supporting fire of his platoon and dragged him back. He was hit again in the chest and died instantly. The medical section, located a hundred yards back, got word that several wounded men were trapped. All firing ceased, and it was hoped that the enemy had withdrawn to another block. I went forward with a litter and aid men to help the wounded. When our little group had almost reached Graham, a Japanese machine gun opened up and we made a hasty retreat on our bellies. Frank Graham had continued to fire at the machine gun. He was soon able to crawl out and get treatment and then a trip for hospital care.

The Marauders made probing attacks and limited frontal attacks all day long with limited success. Fighter bombers were also available for limited use, but their efforts combined with the infantry did not dislodge the Japanese.

During a subsequent infantry attack, S.Sgt. Walter J. Mikolzcizyk was wounded in the right arm by a bullet. He remained on duty after the wound was dressed by the aid man. Further back from the skirmish line, Sgt. Kenneth Dewhurst was in a shallow hole with a mortar squad. A stray bullet wounded him in the left groin. He remained on duty.

Early in the morning a group of soldiers from Company K were resting on a bank very near the aid station. The men were soaked from a heavy rain at daylight. Among the group, David Hurwitt had found a spot where sunlight penetrated through the jungle vegetation. He had begun to dry off and was somewhat warmed up. T5g. Ryland Howard asked him to move in order that he could enjoy the warmth of the sunny spot. They changed places. A few moments later a mortar shell exploded. Ryland Howard died instantly when a fragment passed through his heart. David Hurwitt and six others were injured. Hurwitt, Pvt. Albert Agress, Cpl. Thomas W. Howard, and Pvt. David S. Berger required hospital care. S.Sgt. Chester N. Dulian, Pfc. Arvil Lewis, and Pfc. Martin E. Gardner were immediately treated by our forward aid station a few yards away. They then returned to duty.

CHAPTER XII

The attack on the steep mountainside trail continued until dark, but we were not able to eliminate the enemy. The lead platoons dug in at their point of furthest advance to spend their usual uncomfortable and anxious night.

Sergeant Acker continues to tell the story of the pack artillery pieces:

> During the morning of 2 April, the guns floated down under twelve parachutes—six chutes for each gun. These weapons could be broken down into six pieces, and one mule could carry one piece. Six mules to carry a gun. We had chosen our mules already, and when the guns dropped those fellows ran out. Colored parachutes identified each part of the gun. Within fifteen minutes each gun was assembled on the field. Right away we realized we did not have a maintenance circle. That was a little instrument used to make the guns parallel. We realized we had to go to a compass. I had a compass, but Gibson had a real mass compass, and I got him to let me use it.
>
> Colonel Hunter had asked me to come over and tell him as soon as I got the guns. As I went into the tent he was there with a couple of fellows at a card table with paper all over it. He said, "Here are the instructions on how to handle the guns." As soon as I made the statement, "Colonel, the guns are all ready to fire," you could see a delight in his eyes. He realized that he had more dependence on us than he had before. He got away from his desk immediately, and he got the biggest map I guess he had, and he opened that map up and he said, "This is what we would like to do." So he started giving us some points, and he agreed that we should move in a three-side angle. We realized that we would fire over the head of the Second Battalion up on Nhpum Ga Hill. We did not want to hurt anybody (Acker, videotape).

Colonel Hunter ordered the first rounds to fire at the maximum range of eighty-five hundred yards. The Second Battalion was notified that the first round from Sergeant Acker's battery of howitzers would be at extreme range west and south of Nhpum Ga. With the help of guidance from an observer at Nhpum Ga, the rounds would be gradually brought in. The howitzer adjustment fire worked well and soon registered on Kauri. It would continue to be effective and accurate, and would usually be directed on the same targets as the Second's 81mm mortars and the periodic fighter plane attacks.

As would be expected, the howitzers gave great emotional uplift to the men of the Second Battalion. The Japanese now tended to fire less at Nhpum Ga and frequently shifted to the north trail in an attempt to knock out Orange's infantry as well as the two pack-75 guns. The sudden appearance of the guns probably convinced the Japanese that the Marauders had received reinforcements. Our artillery did not seem to reduce the aggressive activity of the Japanese infantry, however. Acker continues:

> In our guns we could vary the elevation. We could up and over or whatever. Anyway, we went back and fired a few rounds, and we heard a lot of cheers. I was reminded that I had asked the fellows to all stand back when we fired the first round to make sure the gun didn't blow up. We fired several rounds there, and we were very thrilled. Colonel Hunter had a lot of confidence in us then. I did remind him that after firing those rounds we would have to move the guns. We needed a position that would be difficult for the Japanese to find. We moved the guns immediately over to a better location to avoid being hit by the enemy (Acker, videotape).

At dawn on 2 April, Maj. Edwin J. Briggs, Khaki Combat Team commander, led out a reinforced company of his men, leaving 81mm mortars and heavy machine guns at the airstrip. They marched west a mile or so and then down the river for about three hours until they estimated they were opposite the Second Battalion perimeter on Nhpum Ga Hill. Turning east they moved over the most difficult stretch of mountains and jungle they had encountered. As the day passed it became apparent that the mission could not be completed because of the terrain, the heat and humidity, and the long march through the jungle. Supplies were limited, and any wounded could not be evacuated. Colonel Hunter ordered them back to Hsamshingyang.

Third Battalion Dead

Edgar Robertson 3543040, Cpl., Co. L
John L. Ploederl 31620824, S.Sgt., Co. L
Ryland A. Howard, T5g., Co. K

CHAPTER XII

Third Battalion Wounded

Frank L. Graham 209l01551, Cpl., Co. L
Walter J. Mikolzcizyk 36012765, S.Sgt., Co. L
Kenneth H. Dewhurst, Sgt., Co. L
Albert Agress 1606532, Pvt., Co. K
David Hurwitt 32174963, Co. K
Thomas W. Howard 20133543, Cpl., Co. K
Chester N. Dulian 36217812, S.Sgt., Co. K
Arvil Lewis 35417451, Pfc., Co. K
Martin E. Gardner 33139150, Pfc., Co. I
David S. Berger 32494933, Pfc., Hq. Co.

Day Seven

3 April, Nhpum Ga: Second Battalion Sick and Wounded Accumulate

The Second Battalion opened up with heavy mortar concentrations on the enemy. Their fire was answered by a prolonged artillery and mortar barrage by the Japanese. During the day, six Marauders were killed and forty were wounded. On the perimeter the Japanese kept up the pressure with numerous probing attacks.

No letup in responsibility and danger was found in the medical detachment. They were having an increasing number of men with nausea, vomiting, general malaise, extreme fatigue, weakness, anxiety, and fever. The wounded, as well as all the Marauders, were suffering from thirst and dehydration. The location of the aid station was just as susceptible to mortar, artillery and gunfire as the rest of the perimeter. Sick and wounded were accumulating in an increasing number of deep trenches in this location. A significant number of wounded and sick returned to their positions on the perimeter.

Captain Hickman and Lieutenant Craig were dealing with the increasing number of sick, dead, and wounded animals. All the living were losing weight and were dehydrated.

The wounded were kept alive as long as possible in order to prevent the need for burial and minimize the breeding ground for flies and contamination of any rainwater collected in muddy holes. Only eighty animals were left.

An airdrop was successful, but no water was delivered. The fighter planes that covered the drop were used to strafe and bomb the Japanese.

Second Battalion Dead

Norman H. Lusardi 36456337, Pvt., Hq. Co.
John F. Carter 36368347, Pvt., Co. F
Perry F. Coltrane 34430074, Pfc., Co. F
Wayne Robinson, Co. G
Robert E. Noonan 13022665, Sgt., Co. F
Curtis Fountain 14064074, Pvt., Co. F

Second Battalion Wounded

Olin D. Askew 34200705, T.Sgt., Co. E, Birmingham, Ala.
Morris Auerback 33170181, Sgt., Co. G, Philadelphia, Pa.
John J. Barranco, 6719358, T.Sgt., Hq. Co., Salisbury, Md.
Raymond Bressler [See died of wounds 4 April]
James J. Carr Jr. [See died of wounds 4 April]
Max N. Cercelius [See died of wounds 4 April]
Joseph J. Codispoti 33335712, Sgt., Co. G, Philadelphia, Pa.
Joseph N. Cotton [See died of wounds 4 April]
George Cranston 12032007, Pfc., Co. F, Woodside, N.Y.
Jerry DeMilo 32634f557, Pfc., Medics, Ossining, N.Y.
Resee Drattlo 38l059869, Pfc., Hq. Co., Sealy, Tex.
Joseph G. Edwards 33211828, Pfc., Hq. Co., Winston, Va.
Ervin J. Frecks 37145549, Pfc., Co. G, Culbertson, Nebr.
Russell V. Fresh 13103618, T5g. Co. F, Cumberland, Md.
Edward F. Gallant 32428002, Sgt., Co. E, Bangor, Maine
Alvin Harrell 34357608, Pfc., Co. F, Folkston, Ga.
John F. Henry 35129329, Pfc., Hq. Co., Crittenden, Ky.
Gilbert H. Howland 11027325, Cpl., Co. G, Boston, Mass.
Bert E. Johnston 33159861, T5g., Co. E, Sharon, Pa.
Raymond W. Jones 36002803, P.Ofc., Hq. Co., Waukegan, Ill.
Harold F. Kallhof, 15010523, Sgt., G Co., Cleveland, Ohio
Glendon K. Kennedy 34428442, S.Sgt., Co. G, Philadelphia, Pa.
Henry C. King 428932, Pfc., Hq.Co.,Water Valley, Miss.

Frank J. Krasa 33270561, T5g., Co. E, Meadville, Pa.
Roscoe H. Meeks 16019591, T5g., Co. F, Colfax, Ill.
Etham E. Murphy 34428785, T5g., Co. F, Starkville, Miss.
Paul V. Michael 15010345, Pfc., Co. F, Fayetteville, W.V.
Robert C. Noel [See died of wounds 4 April]
John J. Onie 35423724, Pfc., Co. G, Shelby, Ohio
Robert Oxendine 34451527, Pfc., Co. F, Rowland, N.C.
Leon Pavloski 61981763, Sgt., Co. G, Yonkers, N.Y.
Ernest P. Reed Jr. 33240130, T4g., Co. G, Harrisburg, Pa.
George E. Reed 35492229, Cpl., Co. F, Springfield, Ky.
John L. Reed 34384807, Pfc., Hq. Co., Belton, S.C.
George W. Rhodes 34087998, T5g., Co. E, Hawkinsville, Ga.
Richard M. Schneider 33240146, S.Sgt., Co. E, Harrisburg, Pa.
James W. Spears 34038775, Pfc., Hq. Co., Lenoir, N.C.
James G. Sproat 36191542, Pfc., Co. G, Grand Rapids, Mich.
John T. Spurgeon 34428924, Pfc., Hq. Co., Coffeeville, Miss.
Edward H. Stine 12022224, S.Sgt., Co. G, Ozone Park, N.Y.

3 April, Hsamshingyang: Third Battalion Plans Attack

A meeting of the Third Battalion staff with Colonel Hunter resulted in plans for a strong offensive on 4 April. It was first planned to keep steady but cautious pressure on the Japanese positions with patrol activity, probing flanking movements, and frontal maneuvering during the day.

At dawn on this day, Orange Combat Team continued its patrol activity with cautious frontal maneuvering and probing flanking movements. In spite of the rugged terrain and dense jungle, combined with the fatigue of the men and the heat and humidity of the day, a lot was learned about the Japanese positions. During the morning our two pack-75's continued to harass the enemy but were limited because of scarce ammunition supply. T.Sgt. John Keslik was the only Third Battalion man wounded on this day.

Since Orange was not to become involved in strong offensive action on this day, many necessary actions could be taken by the men. Some were able to get a well-deserved rest. Others tried to clean up a little. They had been in the same clothing for six weeks with little opportunity to bathe or wash their clothing. Numerous men went to the aid station back at the airstrip to seek help for diarrhea, chronic indigestion, skin rashes, backaches, sprains, bruises, and other complaints. Most of the men in Orange had to remain on or near the trail at the front line. This continued to be the position of Orange's medical detachment. Medical care at the field was being handled by regiment and Khaki's medical sections. All wounded had been sent out by the early morning.

Back at the airstrip at 1900, Colonel Hunter called a staff meeting. He told his officers that the situation was bad. Reports had been confirmed that the Japanese were moving in strength up the Tanai Hka to the east, and we had been told not to expect much Chinese help for eleven days. The Chinese battalion at Pabum was supposed to move down to Tate Ga to block trails to the south. Colonel Hunter said he had given orders to Colonel Osborne to move the First Battalion as fast as possible from Shaduzup. The block on the road there had been successful but late. His message had been late in getting through to Colonel Osborne, and his battalion would need five days to reach us. Finally he said:

> Gentlemen, in the morning we start an attack that will drive through to the Second Battalion. It may take two or three days, but we will get through. All troops except the sick and the muleskinners will be withdrawn from the airstrip. Large patrols will be called and Kachins substituted where possible. Tomorrow, as soon as we can get ready, Orange Combat Team will attack due south along the trail. Khaki Combat Team will leave their heavy equipment here, march down the trail behind Orange until they are four hundred yards from the Japanese positions, then turn west down the mountain and attack the Japanese on their west flank.
>
> The artillery will be moved up to where it can fire point-blank into the Japanese bunkers. The attack will be set for 1200 hours tomorrow. Ruses, feints, and anything else we can do to fool the Japanese are in order. A fake message will be dropped from a plane so as to fall in the Japanese perimeter. The message will be to the Second Battalion and will say that a battalion of parachutists will be dropped between Kauri and Auche at 1700 on 4 April. If possible we will have a dummy airdrop in that area to fool them (Hunter 1963, 110).

CHAPTER XII

A brief discussion of the plan followed. Then everyone scattered to get his own job done. "Red" Acker encountered quite a problem involving the transportation of the two pack-75's to a location closer to the enemy. The pack saddles had been fitted to the mules for flat loads. In order to carry our gun pieces, the packing had to be adjusted, as the gun pieces were lengthy and didn't carry as well as a normal load. The gun barrel and tail pieces were long and would cause a rocking and swaying motion on the animal. Sergeant Anderson and Sergeant Thompson were given credit by "Red" Acker for solving this problem.

Sergeant Acker's guns were to be moved up as close as possible to the Japanese pill boxes. The sergeant continues his discussion of what actually took place:

> Two or three of us went up, George Harmon with me and Clemon—who is a Russian-born fellow who could speak Chinese. We found an ideal place for our guns—protected from the enemy, who had a flat trajectory gun (and, as you know, that is just one trajection, just up and down). They couldn't do things with their guns that we could with ours. The artillery group moving up the trail had twelve of our best mules to carry the guns. Eight mules were loaded with ammunition, and four with miscellaneous equipment and oats for the animals. Another animal carried our vital radio equipment for the artillery unit. A well-protected site was picked at the base of the steep incline that Orange had been attacking on 2 April and probing on this day, 3 April.
>
> Our two guns were set up by 1700. We were now in a position to fire directly at the Japanese strong points, which Orange would be attempting to eliminate on 4 April. We could also fire into any of the area between our location and Nhpum Ga. Whenever the Japanese guns would open up, our two guns could send shells over Nhpum Ga into their general area. This tended to keep them much quieter than they had been. Unfortunately, we had no observer to direct our fire for the area south of Nhpum Ga. The pack-75's had an advantage over the Japanese flat-trajectory guns. Our guns could fire over Nhpum Ga to hit them, but they could not hit our gun position. Their missiles went over our guns into the jungle beyond (Acker, videotape).

Third Battalion Wounded

John Keslik, T.Sgt.

Day Eight

4 April, Nhpum Ga: Second Battalion under
Continued Fire, Machine Gun Overrun

Throughout the night at Nhpum Ga, the perimeter had been hit by intermittent fire. In the morning this continued. Now there was artillery and mortar fire. The mortar fire, for the first time, was coming from the north side of the perimeter and hitting the aid station and the CP.

This was another day without the expected drop of water. The battalion was still depending on a very limited and sporadic amount of rainwater collected in ponchos and mudholes. Some was contaminated by seepage from dead animals.

Four men who had been wounded on 3 April died during the day: Pfc. Robert C. Noel, Pvt. Max N. Crecelius, Pfc. Joseph N. Cotton, and Pvt. Raymond N. Bressler. During the day Sgt. John M. McDevitt was killed, and eight men were wounded—including Captain Sanford.

As darkness was falling, the perimeter was hit on the north, east, and west. The attacks were beaten off, but during the night a machine gun on McLogan's Hill was overrun. This gun covered the trail coming up the mountain from the Hkuma Hka on the west. The courageous crew of this gun were killed. They were Pfc.'s Albert G. Wankel, Ellis C. Yoder, and Robert K. Thompson. After this terrible episode, this portion of the perimeter was pulled back for more favorable defense. At the risk of their own lives, the comrades of the eight dead buried them in shallow graves within the perimeter.

Only seventy usable mules were left; the rest were dead or wounded. The wounded were not shot because of the problems of odor and burial. Their presence also offered some protection to the muleskinners, who were in nearby holes. One dead animal had twenty-six bullet holes.

As on previous days, the Marauders on Nhpum Ga Hill had every reason to have periods of anxiety and depression. Morale had picked up considerably at about 1600 hours when the Third Battalion attack had started. The survivors were euphoric when they learned of the ground gained and the Japanese casualties.

Second Battalion Dead

Robert C. Noel
Max N. Crecelius
Joseph N. Cotton
Raymond N. Bressler
John M. McDevitt
Albert G. Wankel
Ellis C. Yoder
Robert K. Thompson

Second Battalion Wounded

Theodore I. Langlois 31170636, Pfc., Co. F, Putnam, Conn. Walter E. Lawhorn 7083986, S.Sgt., Co. F, West Palm Beach, Fla.
Emil P. Olenik 33302514, Sgt., Co. F, Mckeesport, Pa.
Harold B. Wentz 34172688, T5g., Co. G, Charlotte, N.C.
Edward A. Zaino 36333623, T4g., Co. G, Cicero, Ill.
John E. Ferguson 15521034, Pfc., Co. D, Bege, W.V.
William Z. Scott 03175971, Capt., Co. F, Lansford, Pa. Edward A. McLogan 0468313, 1st. Lt., Co. F, Flint, Mich.
James K. Sanford 0470288, Capt., Tucker Hill, Va.

4 April, Trail to Nhpum Ga: Third Battalion Stages Sham Battle, Mounts Full Attack

As the airstrip was to be left relatively undefended, Colonel Hunter moved his headquarters to Mahetkawng, two miles north of the airstrip, where a platoon of Chinese had just arrived from the Chinese battalion at Pabum. The unit was ordered to dig in and hold the trail junction at Mahetkawng. Colonel Hunter and his staff moved up with Orange Combat Team, which was attacking astride the trail. Planes were overhead, strafing and dive-bombing the Japanese all day. At 1100 hours, Colonel Hunter saw that the attack could not move off before 1600 hours, so it was set for that time. The delay was due to the time it took to move Khaki Combat Team into position. Colonel

Hunter wanted to wait until he could hit an overpowering blow before hitting at all. Major Lew, the commander of Orange Combat Team, had the following plan of attack: At 1530, his pioneer and demolition platoon would move down the east side of the mountain toward the valley below and have a sham battle among themselves. Carbines, which sound something like an Arisaka, would represent the enemy, while tommy guns and M-1's would represent the Marauders. It was hoped that the commotion would draw the Japanese attention and mortar fire while his main attack moved along the trail. The front was only one hundred and fifty yards wide. The men of Orange had to advance up the heavily fortified, steep mountainside for about two hundred yards. At the top of the steep incline, they would have to fight along a heavily fortified ridge, with the Japanese on the south end and the Marauders on the north end. The trail continued on the jungle-covered ridge, which gradually rose in elevation to Nhpum Ga about one mile south of our location.

Major Lew's mortars were set up to lay down a close-in barrage with 81mm heavy ammunition to try to penetrate some of the Japanese pill boxes, and also because the H.E. light would be hitting too close to our own front-line troops. Our artillery was prepared to fire point-blank into the Japanese defenses.

Captain Burch, commanding officer of the assault company making the attack, was employing three platoons in a U-shaped formation. The bottom of the U would be his center platoon with two flank positions echeloned out as close to the Japanese opposition as possible. Colonel Beach, the Third Battalion commander, planned to have his air liaison officer direct the planes on the Japanese strong points for fifteen minutes of bombing and air strafing and then open with the artillery at point-blank range at the same time his mortars were to pulverize the closed-in positions. At a signal over the radio, the artillery and mortars would cease firing, and Burch's company would rush the Japanese positions before they could recover from the shock of the artillery barrage. Then we would do the same thing over again, consolidating after each attack.

At 1700 hours, Khaki Combat Team informed Colonel Hunter that they were engaged with the Japanese and were temporarily pinned down by mortar and machine-gun fire.

CHAPTER XII

The ruse fight at the bottom of the valley to our west got under way at 1530. It sounded real, and five minutes later the Japanese started throwing mortar fire in that direction. At 1545 hours the planes were circling, and Lieutenant Paulson was directing them on the target not more than one hundred and fifty yards in front of our lines. They made several passes from east to west, and at 1555 hours strafed and bombed the target. At 1605 hours our artillery opened up at point-blank range, and the mortars followed in a moment. What happened next can best be told from the SC 300 radio net that was used to actually direct the attack. The force commanders were:

Yuma: Lt. Col. Charles E. Beach, Commanding Officer, Third Battalion

Luke: Lt. Col. George A. McGee, Jr., Commanding Officer, Second Battalion (surrounded in Nhpum Ga, one mile south of the Third Battalion)

Lew: Maj. Lawrence L. Lew, Commanding Officer, Orange Combat Team

Boston: Maj. Edwin J. Briggs, Commanding Officer, Khaki Combat Team

Burch: Capt. Clarence G. Burch, Commanding Officer, K Company (with the center platoon making the assault)

Tom: Lt. Theodore T. Camellias, Commanding Officer of Burch's right flank platoon

Vic: Lt. Victor Weingartner, Commanding Officer of Burch's left flank platoon.

"Lew from Yuma, Lew from Yuma. Come in, Lew."

"Lew to Yuma. Go ahead, Yuma."

"Lew from Yuma. The 'fatboys' [artillery] will open up at 1600, your mortars at 1605, and the jump-off your decision—roger on that."

"Yuma from Lew. Come in, Yuma."

"Yuma to Lew. Go ahead, Lew."

"Yuma from Lew. The 'fatboys' are raising hell with the pillboxes on the right slope of the hill—a direct hit on one— Japanese ran from another. Have the 'fatboys' hit that machine gun firing two hundred yards to the west of their present target and then swing their barrage up the slope of the hill. We are preparing to push off."

"Lew from Yuma. Roger, Roger."

"Lew to Burch. Come in, Burch."

"Burch to Lew. Go ahead, Lew."

"Lew to Burch. Shove off, boy—and good luck."

"Burch to Lew. Roger on that. Roger."

"Burch to Tom. Come in, Tom."

"Tom to Burch. Go ahead, Burch."

"Burch to Tom. Shove off—and be sure to cover that little draw on your right with at least one squad."

"Tom to Burch. Roger on that—the Japanese are running from that pill box to my front. Our snipers got one sure and lobbed a 60mm or two on them—believe we got some more."

"Burch to Vic. Come in, Vic."

"Vic to Burch. Go ahead, Burch."

"Burch to Vic. Did you hear my message to Tom? Same applies to you—shove off and keep your eyes open for each other."

"Burch from Vic. Roger—I understand you."

"Burch to Lew. Come in, Lew."

"Lew to Burch. Go ahead, Burch."

"Burch to Lew. Have shoved off—am now moving my command post forward with center platoon—no enemy fired yet."

"Lew to Burch. Roger on that—and close in fast."

"Yuma from Boston. Come in, Yuma."

"Boston from Yuma. Go ahead, Boston."

"Yuma from Boston. Have Luke fire three rounds of 60mm two hundred yards due west of perimeter. I am close but can't locate him."

"Boston from Yuma. Roger on that."

"Yuma to Luke. Come in, Luke."

"Luke to Yuma. I heard Boston will fire in three minutes—Japanese are pressing us from the north—ask the bombers to drop a few and strafe four hundred yards north of Nhpum Ga on that little ridge."

"Luke from Yuma. Roger on that."

A separate radio net worked the planes, and Yuma reached over and told his liaison officer what he wanted. The air liaison officer gave the planes overhead the target.

"Tom from Burch. Come in, Tom."

"Burch from Tom. Go ahead, Burch."

CHAPTER XII

"Tom from Burch. The Japanese are rolling hand grenades down on the squad near the trail—can you throw some rifle grenades on them?"

"Burch from Tom. We just threw three hand grenades on them. I don't believe those Japanese are throwing them—I'll tell Bill [squad leader] to watch out—we're almost to the crest of the hill, so don't fire on us."

"Tom from Burch. Roger, old boy."

"Burch from Lew. Come in, Burch."

"Lew from Burch. Go ahead, Lew."

"Burch from Lew. Your left flank is too far down the hill— the Japanese are moving out, so move that flank up fast."

"Lew from Burch. Roger on that."

"Lew to Yuma. Come in, Yuma."

"Yuma to Lew. Go ahead, Lew.'

"Lew to Yuma. How about that mortar ammunition—we need some 81 badly."

"Lew from Yuma. The supply train is passing my command post now—will be with you in a minute."

"Yuma from Lew. Roger on that. Roger-r."

"Burch from Tom. Come in, Burch."

"Tom from Burch. Go ahead, Tom."

"Burch from Tom. We're over the top of the ridge on our way down—three pill boxes are blown to hell—bloody Japanese uniforms all over the place and one Nambu machine gun blown up—looks as if the Japanese are in strength on the next hill. We're drawing inaccurate small arms fire and a little more knee mortar. Put some 'fatboys' on that hill for us, but be damn sure it's on the hill."

"Tom from Yuma. Roger on those 'fatboys'—good work, fellow— keep going."

"Burch from Lew. Are you on the trail yet?"

"Lew from Burch. We are one hundred yards past the trail—there are no Japanese on the east side of the trail. Japanese have moved out of their positions—will be at top of hill in five minutes."

"Yuma to Lew. Come in, Lew."

"Lew to Yuma. Come in, Yuma."

"Lew from Yuma. Have you moved anything up to occupy the ground you have taken?"

"Yuma from Lew. I am moving a platoon up now. How about the ground we are leaving?"

"Lew from Yuma. O.K.—I'll occupy it with muleskinners."

"Boston from Yuma. Come in, Boston."

"Yuma from Boston. Go ahead, Yuma.

"Boston form Yuma. You are coming in 3 x 3 [poor radio reception]. Have you contacted Luke yet?"

"Yuma from Boston. We've hit Japanese perimeter—they have machine gun covering this area—can't get at them with mortars—am trying rifle grenades now—looks like I might be held up here."

"Boston from Yuma. Tell Luke to put pressure on that spot—if necessary, try further south."

"Yuma from Boston. Roger on that—it's getting dark down here—we'll start digging in soon."

"Burch from Tom. Come in, Burch."

"Tom from Burch. Go ahead, Tom."

"Burch from Tom. I am pinned down by heavy machine- gun fire from west side of hill—artillery is hitting too high on hill to do any good—my flame thrower is way round on my right flank trying to knock that gun, but doubt if he can get close enough—am going to pull up a little knoll ahead and dig in, as it's almost dark."

"Tom from Burch. Good work—we may be able to help you when we get our mortars up—I see that machine gun—Roger on digging in."

"Burch to Lew. Come in, Lew."

"Lew to Burch. I heard Tom—over."

"Burch to Lew. I am held up by a position on the next hill like the position we just took—believe we will have to have those 'fatboys' in close again—it's almost dark. I am reorganizing and digging in."

"Lew to Burch. Fine work—I am coming up with the supply train now."

"Burch to Yuma. Have one and one [one killed, one wounded] that I know of."

"Yuma to Burch. Send him back—we'll notify a plane to stand by."

"Yuma from Burch. Lew hit by Japanese sniper—suggest you come down at once—our perimeter is set up and we are digging in."

CHAPTER XII

"Burch from Yuma. Roger—am on my way" (Hill 1944).

Considering the opposition and the firing of artillery, mortars, machine guns, automatic weapons, rifles, grenades, and flame throwers, the Marauder casualties were remarkably light. Our men had been advancing against an equal number of enemy who were well protected and had adequate weapons and supplies.

Pfc. Daniel V. Carrigan was the only Orange Combat Team Marauder killed in action. He was with 1st Lt. Logan Weston's I & R platoon of K Company near the center of the advancing company. Dan Carrigan was struck multiple times by bullets from a light machine gun at close range. The platoon had just advanced forty yards into an area where Japanese pillboxes were being destroyed. He and Pfc. Jean P. LeBrun, from Auburn, Maine, were covering Mueller, who was advancing with a flame thrower. Jean LeBrun was hit in the chest and right arm at the same time. His injuries were severe and required treatment in the U.S. after evacuation by L-1 and hospitalization in Assam.

T5g. Inman W. Avery was also in the I & R platoon. He had just killed six Japanese with his BAR. Visibility was about thirty yards since mortar and artillery had cleared much of the vegetation. Suddenly a Japanese grenade was thrown and landed nearby. He threw himself on the ground, but the explosion sent a fragment into the soft tissue of his left shoulder. He continued advancing with his platoon until the aid man could reassure him and apply a bandage. He remained on duty.

Orange took another great loss when our commanding officer, Maj. Lawrence L. Lew, was hit. The day's battle was over and the men were digging in for the night when he was hit by a sniper at a range of sixty yards. As was the case with all the wounded, he was seen immediately by an aid man and a few minutes later by myself. The bullet had passed through his right lower chest and liver. Because of the loss of considerable blood, five units of blood plasma were required to stabilize his condition. Since the hour was too late for air evacuation, I kept him at the perimeter. The next day he was carried by stretcher the four miles to the airstrip and was evacuated to the 20th General Hospital in Assam, where he made a good recovery.

Pfc. John W. Seegars was hit by a Japanese bullet while in a prone position. Fortunately the wound of his left arm was minor, and he remained on duty.

The Japanese were not so fortunate. Their casualties were estimated at two hundred. During the close and bitter fighting the Japanese had literally been blasted out of their holes. Our advance had taken us to within one thousand yards of the Second Battalion perimeter at Nhpum Ga. The long, steep grade up the mountainside, which we had not been able to take on the 2nd and 3rd, was now behind us. The four-hundred-yard plateau at the top of the mountain had been eliminated, and the battalion now faced a shorter grade that faced another plateau. Orange's offensive action of the past several days had regained approximately four of the five miles from Hsamshingyang to Nhpum Ga.

4 April, West of Nhpum Ga: Third Battalion Khaki Moves into Position

During the afternoon of 4 April, while Orange was preparing for its attack, the men of Khaki started working their way to the west through the jungle. All equipment had to be hand-carried, and 81mm mortars, heavy machine guns, and flame throwers had to be left behind. Near the appointed time, they were close to the Japanese perimeter west of Nhpum Ga. They located the perimeter by having the Second Battalion fire three rounds of mortar.

Early in the action three scouts were moving up the trail leading the first platoon of I Company. Pvt. Edward Nichols of I Company was the first scout. A hidden machine gun suddenly opened up, and a bullet passed through his helmet and brain. He was killed instantly. The bullet was defeated only by the back of the totally inadequate and antiquated M-1 helmet. Moments before, he had turned to his platoon leader and said, "We should not be doing this."

The second scout, Pvt. Paul Fields, was also hit by the first burst of fire. He fell into a ditch, which offered fair protection from this gun—located at a range of fifty yards. T5g. Luther E. Satterfield bravely maneuvered to reach and help him. After a careful approach, he was mortally wounded as he jumped into the same shallow depression. The bullet passed through the lower part of his skull on the right and made an exit over the left shoulder blade. After effective action by the Marauders, Satterfield and Fields were pulled out of the line of fire by Pfc. Harold C. Dibble of Cincinnati, Ohio, and Paul E. Bicknell of

Norwood, Ohio. Captain Milton Ivens, the combat team surgeon, gave Satterfield two units of blood plasma after dressing his wounds—though this, unfortunately, was not enough to save him. Corporal Satterfield was from Dunbar, Oklahoma, and Fields was from Franklin, Ohio. They were friends, and had both served with the 147th Infantry Regiment at Guadalcanal.

Pvt. Kermit "Tony" Bushur was hit in the right thigh by a machine-gun bullet. This twenty-year-old volunteer and BAR operator had joined the Marauders after we reached India. The wound almost cost him his leg. He reached the 20th General Hospital about thirty hours after the injury.

Pvt. Roland W. Rasmussen lost part of his right third finger to the same machine gun. He was sent out the next day.

Khaki set up a perimeter and dug in for the night. The wounded were made as comfortable as possible.

Third Battalion Dead

Daniel V. Carrigan 36605795, Pfc., I &R , Co. K, Orange
Edward Nichols 20609310, Pvt., Co. I, Khaki
Luther E. Satterfield 38022721, T5g., Co. I, Khaki

Third Battalion Wounded

Jean P. LeBrun 20144706, Pfc., I & R, Co. K, Orange
Inman W. Avery 1481840, T5g., I & R, Co. K, Orange
John W. Seegars 34097016, Pfc., Co. L, Orange
Lawrence L. Lew 0401329, Maj., Commanding Officer, Orange
Kermit A. Bushur 36742815, Pvt., Co. I, Khaki
Paul Fields 2050997, Pvt., Co. I, Khaki
Ronald W. Rasmussen 12179998, Co. I, Khaki

Day Nine

5 April, Nhpum Ga: Second Battalion Prepares for Japanese Attack on McLogan's Hill

During daylight hours, Japanese activity was scattered. Intermittent artillery barrages were answered by the Second Battalion's 81mm mortars. A few probing attacks were made at various areas of the perimeter.

Food and ammunition were getting low. By radio the battalion requested three hundred rounds H.E. light, one hundred H.E. heavy, thirty smoke, 250 fragment grenades, five cases of BAR, one case of .03, eight cases of .45 cal., five BAR rifles, five SMGs, three LMGs, and mags for TSMG and BAR. They also requested a medical A & B unit, one Vet A, twenty BA 70, thirty BA 37 and 38, four 536 radios, two sound-powered telephones, and one mile of W 130, as well as three days' rations.

The airdrop took place and was covered by P-51's. They were over twice and strafed and bombed the Japanese at Kauri. The drop did not contain mortar, BAR, or M-1 ammunition. As of this date, no water had been dropped. The water situation continued to be critical.

Major Rogoff, Captain Kolodny, and the rest of the medical detachment continued to carry out their duties in an efficient and heroic fashion. Since the onset of the Battle of Nhpum Ga they had recorded seventeen dead and ninety- seven wounded. Many men were sick and required observation and treatment. Much of the day was spent in digging new foxholes and moving weapons in order to confuse the enemy.

Colonel McGee had anticipated a strong attack on McLogan's Hill and during the day had sent additional machine guns and men to reinforce McLogan's platoon. His suspicions were confirmed about midnight when a noise was heard in the Japanese perimeter on the west. Sgt. Roy Matsumoto had, during the previous days of the siege, risked his life on numerous occasions by crawling into or near the Japanese perimeter to gather valuable information. He was not alone in this heroic activity at Nhpum Ga. Colonel McGee placed the Nisei at strategic locations about the perimeter. They frequently were able to hear the Japanese talking and shouting when getting ready for an attack. On this night Matsumoto was to hit the jackpot. He returned to the perimeter with the news that he believed the Japanese were getting ready to attack.

McLogan's sector of the perimeter stuck out on a nose of ground that sloped downhill. It was difficult to defend, but so far they had held it mainly because they wanted to deny the defile it would offer to the Japanese if the platoon pulled back to the crest of the little ridge. Sergeant Matsumoto said the Japanese plan was to creep up as close as possible to the perimeter before dawn, then rush the little nose, which about twenty men were holding. Lieutenant McLogan figured that it might be possible to give them a surprise. He decided to pull his men back to the crest of the ridge, concentrate tommy guns and Browning automatic rifles along the rise of the ridge, booby trap the foxholes they were leaving, and let the Japanese attack the nose of ground, take it, and then be annihilated by his automatic weapons.

At dawn on 6 April everybody was set. Sergeant Matsumoto was in a two-man foxhole overlooking the nose of ground with a tommy gun. Suddenly there were shouts of "Banzai!" "Death to the Americans!" "Die!" "Banzai!"—and a hail of hand grenades hit around the nose of ground as a reinforced platoon swept up the hill. A moment later they were sticking bayonets in foxholes, firing wildly, shouting, and grenading everything that looked like a gun emplacement. Their sudden occupation of the nose startled them. They hesitated in any further advance. Sgt. Matsumoto immediately stood up in front of their ranks and yelled an order to advance in Japanese. They then charged up the hill, an officer leading them carrying a sword (which later proved to be a beauty). Lieutenant McLogan held his fire until they got within fifteen yards of his perimeter. Then tommy guns, Browning automatic rifles, grenades—everything—opened at once. The Japanese were falling like flies. Another platoon or part of a platoon was following the first, and they started hitting the ground—jumping into the booby-trapped foxholes. Sergeant Matsumoto then shouted in Japanese, "Charge!" "Charge!" and they charged. Thirty minutes later, fifty-four dead bodies were counted on that slope—including two officers. Sergeant Matsumoto became a legendary character overnight.

THE BATTLE OF NHPUM GA

Second Battalion Dead

Gerald A. Bryant, Pvt.
Julian D. Belk, T5g.
Leo G. Godkins, Pfc.
Robert W. Henneburg, T5g.
Robert S. Evans, Lt.
Harold E. Asher, Pvt. [died later of wounds]

Second Battalion Wounded

Elihue Campbell 6647304, 1st. Sgt., Co. E, Hazard, Ky.
Warren T. Ventura 15069130, Cpl., Co. F, Cleveland, Ohio

5 April, Trail to Nhpum Ga: Third Battalion Orange Advances

The Third Battalion followed the same plan on the 5th that it had used the day before—blasting pill boxes with bombs, strafing, throwing artillery, mortars, and bazooka fire, and twice using flame throwers. The infantry followed closely, making maximum use of machine guns, automatic weapons, and rifle fire.

In spite of the great damage done to the Japanese on 4 April, their resistance was strengthened and resulted in extremely bitter and close fighting. Ammunition, food, water, and other supplies were packed up to Orange Combat Team, four miles from the airstrip, over the steep, slippery trail. Hurry-up calls for mortar shells were frequent and—in spite of the distance, the weather, and the terrain— were taken care of quickly. The animals carried wounded and sick back on their return trips.

The ground we had taken the day before was blasted bare along the trail. Every tree was either down or chipped all over with fragments or bullets, and the bamboo was cut as if by a huge knife. Japanese bodies were found in trees where a five-hundred-pound bomb had blasted them the previous afternoon.

As usual, all elements of the attacking force and the support groups spent the night at the furthest point of the previous day's advance. On 4 April, Orange had advanced up the steep mountain trail and gained about four hundred yards on the mountain plateau at and beyond its crest. Approximately one thousand yards of heavily defended jungle remained between Orange and the Second Battalion at Nhpum Ga.

Lt. Jack Armstrong and I, as usual, had our forward medical station as far forward as possible. When the infantry platoons were getting their early-morning instructions from Colonel Beach and their company and platoon leaders, they were assembled nearby. Our thoughts were somewhat similar to those of the men who were soon to begin the deadly serious business of advancing into the machine-gun, rifle, mortar, artillery, and grenade fire of the entrenched enemy. The men of the Second Battalion were facing possible annihilation. Some of their wounded and sick would die without early hospitalization. There was no chance of support from any of General Stilwell's four Chinese divisions. The First Battalion was at least three days' march from our area after their hard-fought actions in and about the Shaduzup region. It seemed unlikely that they would be able to reach us in time to give help. Colonel Hunter continued to ask for help from the Chinese, but he received no help or encouragement.

We, as members of the support groups to the advancing infantrymen, would never be able to say that we understood their courage—or their mental and physical strength—as they on this morning prepared to advance into almost certain death or injury. We had seen these incredible men in action before. Now we were seeing the survivors repeating their heroic actions as they prepared to meet the enemy without hesitation or complaint. Several of the platoons left their packs in a pile at our forward aid station. I had an opportunity to say a few words to some. I had previously advised the men to eat as little as possible of the breakfast K-ration. I was thinking that with their stomachs and intestines empty they would have a better chance of survival if they had abdominal wounds.

This morning Lieutenant Weston's intelligence and reconnaissance platoon was in the forefront of the attack. As the artillery lifted, his men rushed forward. Lieutenant Weston, running down the middle of the trail, suddenly came on a Japanese foxhole with a sack over the top. He jerked the sack off to see two terrified Japanese shaking all over from the shock of the artillery fire. Before he could stop, he shot both with his carbine, one shot for each. Later he regretted he hadn't tried to take them prisoner. With missiles flying in all directions and active Japanese in other holes, it is easy to understand his action.

During the day's advance the I & R platoon had three men wounded but none killed. T5g. Inman Avery had been hit by a grenade fragment on 4 April. He refused to leave his unit and remained in combat with his Browning automatic rifle. On 5 April at 1400 there was a lull in the advance, and he was crawling back to an old Japanese hole to take cover in preparation for a Marauder artillery and mortar barrage. A Japanese sniper hit him in the right shoulder at a range of forty yards. He immediately crawled to the aid station.

At 1500, T5g. Joseph N. Gomez, the aid man who had given Lieutenant Weston a compass at Walawbum, was hit. He was prone in a foxhole waiting for a Marauder mortar barrage to lift. A 60mm U.S. mortar shell fell short and hit a tree fifteen yards away. A fragment struck the left side of his helmet, tearing a hole in the metal. His scalp was torn and a fragment of bone driven into his brain. As usual, Logan Weston was extremely upset over another one of his men becoming a casualty. The word came to me, and I rushed forward and arrived just as he regained consciousness. Logan Weston was at his side, and I heard Gomez say, in response to a question from Weston, "Yes, I have faith." Weston said, "Shall we talk to him now?" Gomez said, "Thanks," and nodded. Weston prayed while I bandaged the wounded Gomez. He was then carried, as fast as possible, the four miles to the airstrip for evacuation. He survived. Another helmet had saved a life. Here, as in the past, I reminded myself that about fifty percent of men killed in battle die of chest or abdominal hits, mostly on the front part of the body. Metal or fabric with ballistic properties placed in the vulnerable area could be expected to save many lives. Even as with Gomez, we had seen numerous cases where the helmet had prevented either death or injury. Many deaths and wounds were being caused by low-velocity bullets, grenade fragments, and shell fragments. I continued to hold the opinion that the Defense Department was grossly negligent in not providing a better helmet and a trunk protector of the best available material to the men of our armed forces.

The same short mortar round that had wounded Gomez also wounded Lieutenant Weston. He had a jagged wound of the soft tissue of his right ankle. He refused to be sent out for further treatment. The wound took several weeks to heal, but he continued to lead his platoon. The medical care of his wound and his platoon was now in the care of Daniel Hardinger, who had been my right-hand aid man since the Battle of New Georgia in the south Pacific.

Captain Burch was right up with the lead platoon all through the day's attacks. His calm decisions whenever a Nambu machine gun opened up on a flank kept his company functioning like a deadly machine. He had taught his men the importance of moving fast in the jungle to keep from being hit by snipers and, unlike most troops when they are in combat areas after severe fights, Captain Burch's men tended to keep their heads up. Anyone who hit the ground and ducked was in for a severe reprimand. He had proved it is safer to see what is going on around you.

Lt. Abie Weingartner's platoon continued to do an outstanding job. He let all know that the Browning automatic rifle was the best weapon for jungle fighting, although most men swore by the tommy gun. Abie used his Browning automatic rifles right behind his attacking echelon. He had them spraying the trees ahead as the riflemen advanced. He had proved that the heavy fire from these weapons produces visibility by tearing open the jungle growth. The heavy fire also makes the enemy keep their heads down. Pfc. Claude L. Davis was advancing with his platoon when an enemy bullet tore a small piece of flesh out of his left leg. After the wound was dressed, he insisted on remaining at his post. Carroll D. Walsh, while advancing under fire and movement, took a bullet through his left forearm. After the aid man dressed the wound he remained with his platoon.

During the attacks, Lt. William E. Woomer, a veteran of the Pacific known as "Woomer the Boomer," platoon leader for Company L, worked his way forward to within twenty-five yards of two machine guns that had been holding us up for several hours. Using an SCR 300 radio he directed his mortar fire on them and had shells landing within twenty feet of his position. During this activity, he was heard to give this order over his radio: "Deflection correct. Bring it in twenty-five yards, and if you don't hear from me, you'll know that you came this way too far. Then shift it just a little and you'll know that you are right on it."

During the day a flight of P-51's gave the battalion valuable assistance by strafing runs on the trail between Nhpum Ga and our advancing battalion. Unfortunately on one pass they riddled the packs, which the infantrymen of L Company had left stacked in the front-line aid station. Two L Company men, waiting in shallow holes, were hit by .50-caliber bullets. Private Charles R. Bowen was grazed over the left wrist but returned to duty after the wound was dressed. Pfc. William W. Scott's wound was very serious. The bullet passed through his chest, stomach, liver, and kidney. He was immediately given five units of blood plasma and then rushed four miles by hand-carried litter to the waiting small plane. On the same day his chest was drained, the liver was packed, the kidney removed, and the stomach sutured. The doctors at the 20th General Hospital had done their best, but he died on 6 April. His chance for survival, and that of other seriously injured Marauders, would have been much greater if General Stilwell's headquarters had supplied us with a small unit of well-trained surgeons. At that time it was known that life-saving surgery can be successfully done very close to the front line.

Mounted messengers, supplementing radio and telephone communications, galloped up and down the trail. Aid men and litter bearers moved among the front-line troops. The wounded were bandaged where they lay. All credit should go to the aid men. Dan Hardinger, a Seventh Day Adventist and conscientious objector, had come with me from my battalion in the Pacific. His courage was frequently demonstrated and known to all. During this battle he carried several men out of danger, even though he was exposed to sniper and machine-gun fire. Although he would not carry a gun, he volunteered to crawl out and bring back tommy gun ammunition when the intelligence and reconnaissance platoon was pinned down by fire. Wounded were carried or made their own way to Orange's front-line aid station. Blood plasma and morphine were used freely. After the four-mile trip to the airstrip, the small planes were waiting to move them to more definitive but often inadequate care.

As always, the weapons platoons did a great job. They were ready at all times to carry out any mission requested. Those who handled the flame throwers were especially courageous and innovative. If a flame thrower wouldn't ignite, they solved the problem by throwing an incendiary grenade and then shooting liquid into it.

When darkness approached, Orange ceased all offensive activity. All units dug in at their furthest point of advance and began to plan for action on 6 April. Some patrolling continued, and each unit was prepared for any nighttime activity. As we bedded down we had every reason to be optimistic about further victory. Our infantry soldiers had, this day, advanced three hundred yards against the best that the conquerors of much of Asia and Indo-China could offer.

As the men were inspecting the battlefield and digging in for the night, 1st. Sgt. Robert H. Saunders, a New Guinea veteran, came up to the front to check on a friend, Sergeant Voltz. He was sitting on a log just off the newly liberated trail when a Japanese rifle bullet hit his hand and weapon and then the center of his chest. Father Barrett and I were close by, and he thus got last rights and immediate medical attention. He immediately collapsed, with loss of consciousness and rapid death. Minimal chest protection would have prevented his death.

One of our men had found a note torn into small pieces on the trail. A Nisei intelligence sergeant put it together, and it contained a very interesting message. It was a note from a Japanese platoon leader to his company commander. He was explaining that the Americans were attacking fiercely and had brought artillery up to one thousand meters from their positions and were shelling them continuously. He said that he was forced to withdraw to better positions on the hill. Search of a number of dead Japanese revealed a poem and a statement of policy by a Japanese company commander that is quite interesting.

The following is the poem that was found, written by Kiroshi Shimosaka, a Japanese soldier killed near Nhpum Ga:

World Unification (Conquest)

With the blood-stained flag of the rising Sun,
I'd like to unify the world.
As I urinate at the great Walls of China,
A rainbow rises above the great Gobi Desert.
At the Ganges River at the foot of majestic Himalaya Mountains,
Sons of Japan look for some alligator (crocodiles).
Today we are in Berlin, tomorrow, Moscow, home of snowbound Siberia.
As the fog lifts we see the city of London,
Rising high as the ceremonial Fish of Boy's Day does.
Now we are in Chicago, once terrorized by gangsters,
Where our grandchildren pay homage to our Memorial Monument.
O, Governor General of Australia and South America,

Only in Japan, sweet odor of Fragrant Blossoms permeates.
When I die, I'll call together all devils (ogres)
And wreath them in a three-inch Rivulet.
I've set my mind in making my home in Singapore,
For there my darling awaits my return.

Another captured document listed the policy of the Japanese opposing Merrill's Marauders at Nhpum Ga:

1. Abide by the Imperial Prescripts.
2. Strict and rigid discipline and courtesy.
3. Cooperation (highest).
4. Health.

5 April, West of Nhpum Ga: Third Battalion Khaki Repulsed

Major Briggs's Khaki Combat Team had spent a miserable and uncertain night on the jungle-covered mountainside. Here they continued to face the western perimeter of the Japanese, who were still besieging and attacking the Second Battalion at Nhpum Ga. Captain Ivens and his small medical detachment, working with the limited supplies they had hand-carried, nursed the wounded through the night. Because of the late hour and location there had been no way to evacuate the wounded.

At 0915 hours two squads of the fourth platoon of I Company opened the advance that had been stopped on 4 April. One squad advanced on each side of the overgrown trail. The light machine gun that had wounded Bushur the day before opened up. A baseline of fire was soon established. The squad on the right under Sergeant Dalmus, with six riflemen, one BAR man, and one tommy gunner, advanced up a draw. They were crawling up a steep bank to get closer to the enemy flank. When they were about thirty yards from the top of the hill, two heavy machine guns, one light machine gun, and a number of riflemen opened fire on them from the top of the hill. They were pinned to the ground, and Pvt. Heinz Sander was critically wounded in both legs. A machine-gun bullet entered his right leg below the knee, passed through the knee, and exited in his thigh. The bullet also tore the right popliteal artery. Because of his location in a fire lane, the aid men and his squad members could not reach him. Sergeant Dalmus crawled, leaped, and ran through enemy fire to a position where he could drag Sander out of the line of fire. When he reached Captain Ivens, Sander was in severe shock from blood loss. Blood plasma was given but could not save him. He died about thirty minutes after he was wounded.

T.Sgt. Alfred J. Curtin was wounded during the same advance. He was fortunate in that he had a minor flesh wound over his right shoulder blade and was able to remain on duty.

Pfc. Wayne N. Price was attempting to operate a defective flame thrower as he worked his way toward a machine gun. His advance was slowed, and he was hit by a Japanese machine gun at thirty yards. The bullet passed through his right upper arm. After hospital treatment and several weeks of rest he returned to duty.

Major Briggs and Khaki Combat Team, with their limited fire power and untenable position, withdrew late in the morning. An impossible and some might say ill-advised mission had cost them three dead and three wounded. They were urgently needed at Hsamshingyang and on the trail. The need for patrols and trail protection in back of Orange was critical.

Third Battalion Dead

Robert H. Saunders 20649662, 1st Sgt., Khaki
Heinz H Sander, Pvt., Co. I, Khaki [Died of wounds]
William W. Scott 206099211, Pfc., Co. L, Orange [Died of wounds]

Third Battalion Wounded

Charles R. Bowen 21031923, Pvt., Co. L, Orange
Carroll D. Walsh 20710750, Pfc., Co. L, Orange
Inman N. Avery 1481840, T5g., Co. K, Orange
Wayne N. Price 18116969, Pfc., Hqs. Co, Khaki
Joseph N. Gomez 18016224, T5g., medical detachment,
    I & R, Orange
Logan Weston, 1st. Lt., I & R, Orange
Claude L. Davis 35320357, Pfc., Co. L, Orange
Kermit A. Busher 36742815, Pvt., Co. I, Khaki
Alfred J. Curtin 20201150, T5g., Co. I, Khaki

Day Ten

6 April, Nhpum Ga: Second Battalion Receives
First Water Drop

On Nhpum Ga Hill, now called Maggot Hill (after the masses of maggots hatching on dead animals and Japanese flesh), the usual artillery barrage began at about 0600 hours. Another five rounds came over at 1500 hours and more at 1930 hours. As usual, many of the men found these barrages hard to take. The knowledge that Orange was able to counter the barrages with the two recently arrived pack-75's did give them a feeling of more security. Their morale was also helped by the first parachute delivery of five hundred gallons of water in five-gallon plastic bags.

The early-morning slaughter of Japanese on McLogan's Hill gave the men a lot of encouragement. The progress of Orange, water drops, adequate food and ammunition, dedicated care by the medics, and brave men on the perimeter tended to eliminate all thoughts of defeat. The feeling was that we would soon get out of this difficult situation and what appeared to be possible defeat would be a significant victory.

The medical detachment reported a total of one hundred wounded and twenty-one dead to date on Nhpum Ga Hill. Six men were wounded on 6 April, but none were killed. The stink of the dead mules, horses, and Japanese was growing worse daily. Four of the battalion aid men had been wounded. Three men that were wounded and were sent back to the perimeter after treatment had later been killed. Many of the wounded refused to stay in the aid station and insisted on returning to the perimeter where they were sorely needed. Lack of sleep during day and night was contributing to the exhaustion of the men. The dead animals could not be burned because the smoke would draw Japanese mortar and artillery fire.

The water drops were far from adequate but were a godsend nevertheless. The Japanese also seemed to be hurting for water. About six were killed when they were trying to use the small spring they had captured several days before.

The men and officers were beginning to praise the helmet that so many men had scorned before being under shell fire. There had been several instances where shell fragments had badly dented the helmet. All wished for a better helmet and trunk protection.

CHAPTER XII

By the end of the day they knew that Orange was within seven or eight hundred yards from breaking the siege of Nhpum Ga. The sound of artillery, mortar, machine-gun, grenade, and rifle fire from the north was getting closer each day. They knew that the men of the Third Battalion would never consider the possibility of failure. Only one option was considered. No matter what the price, they would continue their offensive drive until the Japanese had been eliminated or driven from the area. Good radio communication continued between the two battalions. The Second Battalion gave some help to Orange by supporting them with their mortars.

The afternoon drop of supplies seemed to stir the Japanese up more than usual. As they usually did during drops, the Second Battalion kept the encircling Japanese busy with heavy fire. On this day the enemy concentrated their fire on the C-47's, causing them to fly a higher delivery pattern. This resulted in the loss of some of the parachutes with their supplies.

Second Battalion Wounded

George M. Ball 35369370, Pfc., Co. F, Carthage, Ind.
David Bieler 37422776, T5g., Hq. Co, Ortho, Ill.
William M. Jefferson 34319742, Pfc., Co. E, Bath, N.C.
James F. Richardson 3437800, Pfc., Co. E, Jacksboro, Tenn.
Edward L. Stietzle 12014174, Pfc., Co. G., Brooklyn, N.Y.
Walter J. Walczk 33184311, Pfc., Hq. Co., Philadelphia, Pa.

6 April, Trail to Nhpum Ga: Third Battalion Orange Continues Advance

On this day the Marauders had reason for encouragement. Orange was within seven or eight hundred yards of Nhpum Ga. The Japanese on the trail were being eliminated slowly but surely. The pressure on Nhpum Ga had been reduced. The Chinese battalion that had been forty miles in the rear at Pabum had finally arrived at Weilangyang. This location was about ten miles north of our battle area. They were blocking trails and had eliminated Japanese who held one village to our rear. There was hope that they would eventually be able to help the Marauders if the Japanese were not soon defeated.

Colonels Hunter and Beach carefully prepared for the day's attack. All attacking units remained in place, and the artillery was moved forward for close firing. The plan was to use a one-hundred-round artillery barrage at Japanese strong points thirty yards ahead, following a dive-bombing and strafing attack. Use of the H.K. heavy at the same point was to be simultaneous. There would also be H.E. light shooting from two hundred yards out and working back toward our perimeter. In addition, 60mm mortars would be fired at a medium rate along the Japanese supply route.

After a fifteen-minute artillery barrage and a seven-minute 81mm mortar rolling barrage, the attack was to jump off under a heavy machine-gun support.

Our communications setup was a little different. We had sound-powered wire to each of the two flank platoons—radio net from company commanders, combat team commanders, battalion commanders, and also for mortars. Sound-powered wire to the forward artillery observer was to be used part of the time. The rest of the time he was to use the SCR 300. Flares were only to be used for an emergency—red for stop firing, green for lift firing.

The infantrymen were well informed about the day's plans and objective. They had reasonable rest in spite of a wet night. Adequate time had been available for them to eat their K-ration breakfast. Father Barrett had been available to counsel any who wished religious help. They had checked and cleaned their weapons and had plenty of ammunition.

The aid men were with their platoons, and they and the men knew they were supported by the nearby battalion front-line aid station. All sick men had been seen and treated. Medical supplies had been replenished. All the previous day's casualties had been evacuated.

At 0830 hours we zeroed in our artillery, a battery of four heavy machine guns, and a battery of four 81mm mortars using H.E. heavy. We pinpointed these thirty yards in front of our troops. Next we zeroed in a battery of 81mm mortars for H.E. light about two hundred yards in front of our positions and finally zeroed in a battery of four 60mm mortars firing for three hundred yards along the main trail, which was the Japanese supply route.

At 0930 hours the attack went off exactly as planned. In the first attack we only gained fifty yards, but by adjusting the barrages onto

Japanese strong points the total advance for the day was three hundred yards. Three of the dead Japanese found along the trail were using M-1 rifles, and one was wearing G.I. jungle boots.

The Japanese got smart after the first barrage and ran back up the trail fifty or sixty yards to prepared positions. Then, when the barrage was lifted, they ran back to their weapons and opened fire. Our lead scouts noted this, and after the next artillery barrage they picked off four running back to their guns.

Each Japanese strong point was set up with an all-around perimeter, and they were using high spots for strong points—not low ground, as they sometimes did in the Southwest Pacific.

T.Sgt. John Keslik of Chicago, with two scouts, crawled up a steep mountainside, slowly parted the tall grass, and peered directly into the eyes of two equally startled Japanese. One Japanese threw a hand grenade at Keslik as he and his companion fired and rolled downhill. The grenade exploded, wounding one slightly, but they all escaped safely.

Pfc. John D. Chopp had been resting in a shallow foxhole in the front-line aid station. One of our H.E. 81mm mortar shells fell short and wounded him and Pfc. Jess Scott from L Company. Chopp's wound was minor, and he stayed on duty. Scott was in a foxhole near Chopp. He was not wearing a helmet and was struck in the head. Several fragments of the shell lacerated his scalp in several places. He was also kept on duty after emergency treatment. Earlier in the day, Pfc. Peter Forty had been resting at the aid station, in a two-foot-deep foxhole. A Marauder 81mm mortar round fell short and exploded three feet from the edge of the hole. His helmet prevented a head wound, but he had numerous small flesh wounds. After the wounds were dressed he returned to his platoon.

During much of the several days' offensive battle Lt. Winslow B. Stevens, from Barton, Florida, had been serving as an artillery observer. Much of our success was due to his handling of this dangerous and extremely important work. On this day he was crawling with several others near a Japanese machine gun. S.Sgt. Salvadore Felix Rapisarda was a few feet ahead. He parted some brush and looked into the eyes of a Japanese machine-gun crew. One threw a grenade, which wounded him in the forehead. Bleeding was profuse: he was covered with blood and thought he had a fatal wound as he lay face-down, half buried in the jungle vegetation. The curious Japanese decided to strip the dead body and carelessly approached the still figure. Rapisarda suddenly lost all thoughts of a hole in his head and death. His tommy gun went into action, and he wiped out the six-man crew of the gun. With the thought of certain death on his mind he had screamed to the others to save themselves. As he got his weapon into action, Lieutenant Stevens crawled to him, grabbed his ankles, and the two got away together.

Fifty years later, Lieutenant Stevens tells what he remembers of 6–9 April:

> I was a second lieutenant and heavy weapons commander in Khaki Combat Team at the time. Colonel Beach was desperate to get the Second Battalion off of Nhpum Ga Hill. On 5 April, Beach called an emergency meeting because we were not having much luck dislodging the enemy. At this meeting he asked for any suggestions from his officers. He had placed Lieutenant Woomer of Orange Combat Team in charge of the battalion heavy weapons. He of course outranked me, so I was his assistant. At this meeting I proposed the idea that we conduct a mass firing exercise to not only clear out as much jungle as we could but also to eliminate as many of the enemy as possible. Unfortunately Lieutenant Woomer was not familiar with the mass-firing exercise, so— equally unfortunately—Colonel Beach turned the battalion heavy weapons over to me. I had to make some plans rather hurriedly and draw on my memory quickly, because it had been a long time since I had conducted such an exercise. We managed to make it work. We banked all the machine guns, and I gave each noncommissioned officer in the heavy weapons groups express orders as to what I wanted done and told them to be sure to check each and every gun and to make sure they were doing what they had been told to do. They were to watch the gun sights, in particular on the 81mm mortars.
>
> The thing worked out beautifully. One boy got excited and, luckily for all of us, he was firing H.W. heavy, which buries in the ground before it explodes, and he ran a string of those right back past my slit trench and through the aid station. A couple of "Doc" Hopkins' boys back there were wounded, and I thought Doctor Hopkins was going to come after me with one of his syringes, but we finally got him cooled down and he forgave me when he found

out what had happened. We dislodged the enemy and killed quite a number as we found out later. They fell back to a secondary position.

Sergeant Rapisarda (who had just been promoted to top sergeant to take the place of Sergeant Saunders, who had been killed the day before) and I were following the two lead scouts up the trail. We were winding through the jungle and trying to find where the secondary Japanese position was. We found out with a bang. We walked right into their two machine-gun nests on either side of the trail. The two lead scouts jumped over the left side of the trail, and Rapisarda blew away all the machine-gun crew we could see as we went over the right side of the trail doing our level best to get out of there. All hell broke loose. Fortunately the ravine into which we were falling was so steep that they couldn't depress the muzzles far enough to get us, so they started throwing grenades. One of them burst and gave Rapisarda a superficial wound of the forehead and disorientated him. He hollowed for help, and I went back. I thought he was killed. He was all covered with blood, so I had to crawl back and told him to grab my ankle and we crawled out of there. I told him we would make it together or would both stay. We got back safely (Stevens, videotape).

Our Orange Combat Team aid station was, as usual, within less than fifty yards from the front line. The men knew they would be seen and treated quickly, by Captain Armstrong or myself, after being wounded. They constantly expressed their gratitude for the guaranteed quick professional medical attention they knew would always be there. The men knew that if a battle resulted in their death, their comrades would not surrender their body to the enemy. The men were assured that they would always have the immediate service of an aid man or medic and immediate removal for the best possible treatment.

The well-organized and well-conducted offensive battle on the trail had been extremely successful. Casualties had been few, and Orange had gained about three hundred yards. Only five hundred yards or less remained between our forward positions and the Second Battalion on "Maggot Hill."

An unfortunate accident occurred after we had settled in our foxholes for the night. Pfc. Thomas Nichols sat up in his hole when he was changing guard with the other occupant. The battalion veterinarian mistook him for a Japanese soldier and shot him in the head with a .45 pistol. Death was immediate.

From 1 April through 6 April, the Third Battalion had lost eight men—six killed and two who died of wounds. Fourteen wounded had returned to duty, and fourteen wounded had been sent out for hospital care.

Orange Combat Team fired the following ammunition in support of Khaki Combat Team during 6 April.

Rounds	Type
220	81mm H.E. light
210	81mm H.E. heavy
322	60mm
136	75mm
12,000	.30-caliber machine gun

The Japanese had taken clothing off of some of their dead, suggesting that they were short of clothing.

Third Battalion Dead

Thomas P. Nichols 35686178, Pfc., Co. K, Orange

Third Battalion Wounded

John D. Chopp 36657573, Pfc., medic, Orange
Jess W. Scott 6988926, Pfc., Co. L, Orange, Portsmouth, Ohio
Peter Forty 12182121, Pfc., Co. L, Orange, Culbertson, Nebr.
Salvadore F. Rapisarda 35009154, S.Sgt., Hq. Co, Cleo, Ohio

Day Eleven

7 April, Nhpum Ga: Second Battalion Awaits Release

The night had been quiet at Nhpum Ga. During the morning there was sporadic artillery and mortar fire. The Japanese artillery had been moved farther south in an obvious attempt to get out of the range of our pack-75's. Their heavy mortars were no longer active. No more attacks were made on the perimeter. Our Second Battalion was now able to give mortar assistance to the Third Battalion as it advanced along the trail from the north.

C-47's came over to drop our supplies. Our communication with them was poor, and some bundles were dropped outside our perimeter. Because of this and intense fire on them by the Japanese, we called off the drop.

The rapid offensive movement of the Third Battalion, and the strafing and dive-bombing, had caused the enemy to move in closer on our northern perimeter. Because of this we had to pull the fire of the 60mm mortars closer to our northern line.

Major Rogoff and his medical detachment were ready to move their wounded as soon as the Third Battalion opened the trail. They had hoped this would be the day. Their wounded were doing reasonably well in and near the uncomfortable foxholes. S.Sgt. Glendon Kennedy, from Philadelphia, Mississippi, was their chief worry. He had been wounded in the chest and lung on 3 April and was desperately in need of better care. Sgt. John F. Magiowych was the one Marauder from the Second Battalion killed on this day.

Documents taken off dead Japanese this day indicated that we were fighting a reinforced Japanese battalion from the 114th Regiment, 18th Japanese Division, and also elements of the 55th Japanese Division.

Second Battalion Dead

John F. Magiowych, Sgt.

Second Battalion Wounded

Clifford E. Stiffler 35413966, T5g., Co. E, Jackson, Ohio

7 April, Trail to Nhpum Ga: Third Battalion Khaki Attacks

At the airstrip, Col. Henry L. Kinnison, Jr., G-3 of General Stilwell's forward echelon, arrived by liaison plane and joined Colonel Hunter, who was with the Third Battalion on the hill.

As we were stretching our stiff muscles, loosening up joints, and opening our K-ration boxes for a quick breakfast, we learned that

Khaki's turn had come to hit the Japanese head-on. Orange's new mission was to protect the airstrip and keep the trail open to Hsamshingyang.

Khaki had essentially the same fire-power setup as we had used on the previous day. They also had the same communication arrangement. During the day they were to fire about two hundred artillery shells and two hundred mortar rounds. The infantry platoons were to take advantage of the regular artillery and mortar barrages. After each they would advance as fast as possible on a front of about one hundred yards. They would move forward under overhead machine-gun fire. The Japanese held the high ground defended by riflemen and numerous machine guns.

The I Company platoon advancing on the left side of the trail soon had three men wounded. Pfc. Eladio A. Arias was hit by a machine-gun bullet. This caused a compound fracture of his left forearm. Sgt. Philip Tinsworth was wounded by the same burst of fire from a machine gun at sixty yards. He was hit in both arms and the left knee. The same gun stopped Pfc. John R. Meyers when a bullet lacerated the back of his left hand. He remained in combat. The other two were quickly attended to and moved the four miles to the airstrip.

By 1400 several machine guns had been knocked out or forced to take new positions. At this time, after several successful advances, the platoon of I Company was working its way on the right side of the trail up a steep incline covered with bamboo. Here they lost Pfc. Raymond J. Bokelman from the initial fire of a light machine gun at about a hundred yards' range. He had a mortal wound of his right chest. The men quickly carried him to the nearby front-line aid station, where he was given two units of blood plasma. In spite of all possible attention he died in ninety minutes. If a small surgical unit had been attached to the Marauders, his life probably could have been saved.

An hour after Bokelman was hit, Pfc. Peter L. Hervoyavich was wounded by a grenade fragment at a range of ten feet. At the time, he was throwing grenades at an enemy emplacement. The fragment fractured his right thumb. After hospitalization he made a good recovery.

The 3rd platoon of I Company had been making steady but definite progress in its central position along each side of the trail. During the late morning Sgt. Paul K. Tabbies was wounded in the chest by a rifle bullet at twenty yards' range. The missile passed through the soft tissue of his right chest without entering the chest cavity. By a miracle his life was saved due to the care of the platoon aid man, the front-line aid station, and the men who carried him four miles to the regimental and Orange medical detachment at the airstrip. He was in satisfactory condition when he was sent by small plane to the general hospital in Assam the next day.

Pfc. Leonard G. Porath of headquarters company was at his post as a radio operator about a hundred yards in back of the troops. He and his radio were in a log-protected hole that had been constructed by Japanese. At 1230 a machine-gun bullet at a range of 150 yards tore into his right leg, causing a severe flesh wound and fracture of bone. Attention was immediate.

Two men in the 3rd platoon of I Company were wounded at 1500. Pfc. John R. Darling, a BAR man, was advancing just to the left of the trail. A machine-gun bullet, at a range of fifty yards, tore up his face and fractured his skull just above the right eye. Due to the late hour he remained at the airstrip for the night but got to the hospital on 8 April. The platoon leader, 2nd Lt. William V. Murray, was near Darling and put his arm out to help him. A machine-gun bullet caught his fifth finger. He was able to remain with his platoon.

The platoon radio operator, Pfc. Leone R. Warlstead, was carrying his radio and slowly walking beside Lieutenant Murray at 1700. The enemy was suddenly located at forty yards. Philip Olsen was leading up the trail and motioned for Leone to move off the trail. As both men moved, the machine gun opened up, and Leone was killed instantly. The platoon regrouped and later tried another attack.

A short time later, Pfc. Charles A. Bias was about to move out of the line with his platoon to set up flank protection. He was prone when a bullet, fired at one hundred yards' range, passed through his chest. This potentially mortal wound was treated, and he was given two units of plasma. He lived for two hours. Here again we have a man whose wound could have probably been prevented by a trunk protector. A nearby surgical team might have been able to save his life.

The well-planned and heroic offensive action had pushed the enemy from the face and top of the steep mountain incline. A plateau of about four hundred yards on the razor-backed mountaintop remained before our comrades in the Second Battalion could be reached. The men were confident that victory would soon be theirs. In spite of the daily stress of battle, they were prepared to face the deadly fire on 8 April.

Lieutenant Stevens further comments about the part he played on 7 April:

> The next day I took my radio man and we went out, nearly to the bottom of the ravine, maybe thirty-five or forty yards outside of our perimeter—about halfway between the two perimeters. I started calling in the mortars, and after just a few rounds the Japanese sent an automatic weapons team down to take care of us again. They started firing and put twelve bullet holes through my denims without putting a scratch on me. They got my wireman, who was on the other side of me, and fractured his leg. I of course started firing immediately and killed or wounded some of them. At least they withdrew. They disappeared. I called Colonel Beach and told him that we had to have some flat trajectory weapons. We were not getting to first base with those fellows on the high side of that ravine. He ordered the use of the 75mm howitzers (Stevens, videotape).

Khaki, even as Orange had done, continued the attack from the north on the ever-rising north trail toward Nhpum Ga. They continued to meet heavy resistance, provided by Japanese machine guns, mortars, artillery, and riflemen.

Our planes dive-bombed and strafed the Japanese during the day. Artillery, mortar, and machine-gun fire were used as on 6 April, but we could not blast the Japanese off the ridge. We were approximately five hundred yards from the Second Battalion's perimeter.

7 April, Third Battalion Dead

Raymond J. Bokelman 32306750, Pfc., Co. I, Khaki
Leone R. Warlstead 6937940, Pfc., Co. I, Khaki
Charles A. Bias 35208149, Pfc., Co. I, Khaki

7 April, Third Battalion Wounded

Eladio A. Arias 32509474, Pfc., Co. I, Khaki
Philip H. Tinsworth 35160436, Sgt., Co. I, Buffalo, N.Y.
John R. Meyers 20609123, Pfc., Co. I, Middletown, Ohio

Peter L. Hervoyavich 33405649, Pfc., Co. I, Pittsburgh, Pa.
John R. Darling 6980548, Pfc., Co. I, Catskill, N.Y.
William V. Murray 01307736, 2nd Lt., Co. I, Chelsea, Miss.
Paul K. Tabbies 36429160, Sgt., Co. I, New Holland, Ill.
Leonard G. Porath 35015322, Pfc., Hq. Co., Curtis, Ohio
John J. Gross, Jr. 20744927, Pfc., Co. K, Cleveland, N.D.
Charles W. Maple 65d62709, S.Sgt, Co. K, Oakland, Calif.
Johnnie Smith 34398554, Pfc., Co. I, Warren, Ohio

7 April, Hsamshingyang: First Battalion Support Arrives

As explained previously, the eight hundred men of the First Battalion arrived at Hsamshingyang airstrip at 1700 hours after a forced march from the vicinity of Seola. Thirty-six hours before, they had learned that their help was urgently needed. At the time, they were out of food and were awaiting a supply drop. The drop was abandoned, and they marched day and night without food and with little rest. The terrain they had to cross made the march very difficult. On arrival at the airstrip, many of the men were in a state of extreme exhaustion. A third were suffering from severe dysentery. The new arrivals found the men of the Third Battalion in better shape than they had expected. Their arrival helped the morale of both the Second and Third Battalions.

Shortly after the arrival of the sick and exhausted men of the First Battalion, Colonel Hunter began to plan their use. At 1900 he called a staff meeting. Khaki Combat Team, on 8 April, was to continue the attack down the trail toward Nhpum Ga. Orange was to continue to guard the rear and keep the trail open, bring up food and ammunition, and evacuate the wounded. Captain Senff, of the First Battalion, was to use as many able-bodied men as he could muster from his combat team for a flanking movement to the southeast of Nhpum Ga. Patrols were to continue in all directions.

The attack would start 8 April at 1300 with dive-bomber, artillery, and mortar support. The regimental headquarters would be at the front, and the animals would remain near the front to be ready to evacuate the sick and wounded when the Japanese were defeated. Morale was high among the First and Third Battalion men.

Day Twelve

8 April, Nhpum Ga: Second Battalion

The Second Battalion spent a quiet night at Nhpum Ga. The Japanese artillery barrage in the morning was light. During the day the C-47's made two drops to supply adequate water, food, and ammunition. The battalion's patrols moved about more freely. During the late afternoon one made contact with the First Battalion, which was getting into position.

Major Rogoff totalled his casualties and found that he had 25 dead and 103 wounded to date, but it was possible others would be found when a muster could be held.

The Japanese activity was centered on the north, where the Third Battalion was steadily advancing. Colonel McGee was concentrating mortar fire on this area of about four hundred yards by two hundred yards.

Second Battalion Dead

None

Second Battalion Wounded

Norman E. Rice 7008031, Cpl., Co. E, Jasper, Ala.
Creight Smith 6985943, Pfc., Co. F, Zebulon, Ky.

8 April: Third Battalion Orange and Khaki Battle on the Trail

Orange's relatively safe location and mission of guarding the rear was short-lived. During the early morning of 8 April, Colonel Hunter ordered Orange to move east through dense jungle and to continue on to the southwest to outflank the enemy at Nhpum Ga.

Orange's two rifle companies and medical detachment, minus the heavy weapons, were soon on their way. Each man carried one day's rations and two canteens of water. All animals were left behind. Because of the dense jungle and the mountainous terrain, passage was very slow. By late afternoon the men were exhausted, and Major Petito was not certain of our position. We struggled with the terrain and dense jungle vegetation. The physical exertion, the heat and humidity, and the stress of a very dangerous mission presented insurmountable odds. With darkness approaching, the mission had to be aborted. Without water, food, heavy weapons, and a supply line, the mission was only supposed to last a few hours. It had been ill-conceived and quickly developed. There had been no reason for it to succeed. After their arrival back at the trail north of Khaki on the evening of 8 April, Orange was put in reserve and also given the mission of blocking Khaki's flanks and all possible areas of attack along the trail to the north. They were also to help with front-line supply and evacuation of the wounded and sick.

On the morning of 8 April, Khaki's turn came to continue the offensive battle on the trail in the desperate attempt to eliminate the Japanese and reach the Second Battalion.

Under the watchful eyes and ears of the front-line infantrymen sharing periods of watch, the night had been quiet. At dawn the men consumed their cold K-ration breakfast and prepared for battle. The heavy fire of the 7th had torn up an area of jungle about five hundred yards from north to south and about one hundred yards from east to west. The Japanese had not been driven from the southern half of this area, which was high ground. They thus held about three hundred yards of jungle north of the Second Battalion. At 1800 on 7 April, Major Briggs had withdrawn Khaki back from no-man's land. On this morning, two hundred yards separated the Marauders from the Japanese.

Colonel Hunter planned to make maximum use of the two pack-75 guns, his 81 and 60mm mortars, and whatever flights of P-51 planes he could call in. The heaviest part of the offensive battle would be assigned to the Khaki I & R platoon of headquarters company and the 2nd platoon of I Company. Four hundred mortar shells and one hundred artillery shells were available. All infantry attacks would be preceded by as much fire as possible. Before the day was over there would be five strong attacks, with good forward movement and destruction of many enemy and most of their machine guns.

The I & R platoon started with a strength of twenty-two. During the day, nine were wounded—but none were killed. Seven were wounded by grenades; six of this group were hit by grenade fragments during the first attack between 0930 and 1030.

Sgt. Gordon E. Mackie from Oshkosh, Wisconsin, was the lead scout of his I & R. The men were advancing up a forty-five-degree slope into and through bamboo and jungle growth near the south end of the battlefield. A Japanese grenade was thrown from twenty-five yards and exploded in a tree just over his head. He was wounded in the right thigh. Adequate treatment required evacuation.

Somewhat later, Pfc. Frank J. Hus of Piniconnini, Michigan, took grenade fragments to his head and nose but was not sent out. Pvt. David J. Burgoon was wounded in the leg and remained on duty. Pfc. Donald Darcey, from Houma, Louisiana, was a squad leader. He was standing when many small fragments struck him in his face. He remained with his squad.

As the attack progressed, Pfc. Wilford S. Locke was working his way, in a crouch, through the thick bamboo. A grenade fragment produced a severe injury to his left hand, and he had to make his way back to the front-line aid station. After a four-mile walk to the airstrip he got out the same day for definitive hospital care.

During another attack by the I & R platoon, about one hour later, two other Marauders were severely wounded. Pfc. Ralph E. Asbury, while prone on the ground, was firing at a Japanese machine gun thirty yards away. A machine-gun bullet fractured his left elbow and lacerated his left thigh. He was quickly carried to the aid station and then the airfield for further treatment and a flight out for hospital care. T5g. Edward A. Gilmore, from St. Louis, Missouri, was in a shell hole delivering fire from a BAR. He had just killed a Japanese machine-gun operator who had been firing at a Marauder making an advance with a flame thrower. A grenade thrown twenty-five yards exploded two yards or so from his position. He was hit by multiple fragments in the right arm, both legs, and the head. Shortly after the injury he called to his platoon leader Lieutenant Hearn, "Hearn, how about charging the yellow bastards?" The ulna nerve in his right arm was damaged and required prolonged treatment in the U.S.

Much later in the day, Pfc. Karl E. Parson was prone on the ground when a grenade exploded a few feet away. Multiple fragments entered his thigh, but he was able to walk to the aid station. He was sent out the next day after the long trip to the airstrip.

CHAPTER XII

The 2nd platoon, I Company, Khaki Combat Team, fought on the line to the left of the trail from 0900 until 1900. They, like the I & R platoon, encountered heavy machine-gun fire as well as many hand grenades. The fighting, as on the other side of the trail, was up steep terrain through closely growing mature bamboo and other jungle growth. The men advanced by fire and movement. They took every advantage of the supporting artillery, machine-gun fire, and mortars, which were used as much as possible before each attack. This platoon, like the rest of the attacking force, soon learned that the Japanese would run from the field of fire when the heavy weapons were used before an attack. On numerous occasions there was a race between the Marauders and the Japanese for the temporarily vacated Japanese defensive positions.

Four 2nd platoon men were wounded and one was killed. Pvt. Joseph F. Medeiros was crawling over a rise in the ground instead of around the area. He was immediately hit by a rifle bullet fired at a range of thirty-five yards. This caused a wound with a compound fracture of his coccyx. After several enemy were eliminated, he was able to crawl out and walk to the front-line aid station. He of course needed and got hospital care. Sgt. William D. Muller Jr., from Cincinnati, Ohio, was moving forward in a crouched-over manner. He had just worked his way through a clump of bamboo, where he had made excessive noise. His location and presence was immediately picked up by a hidden Japanese sniper. The bullet caused a ragged wound in his right forearm. When the action quieted down he walked to the aid station and then was sent on the long walk to the airstrip.

The platoon radio man, S.Sgt. Gilbert R. Shelton, from Prescott, Arizona, was crawling back to the platoon command post to get more ammunition. A grenade was thrown from thirty-five feet and exploded into a clump of bamboo. A fragment produced a laceration in his neck, which the aid man treated. He returned to duty.

A Tennessean and squad leader, Pfc. Monte H. Potter, was advancing in a crawl when a Japanese grenade fragment wounded him in the right thumb. The wound was dressed and he remained with his squad.

The 2nd platoon's good luck ran out at 1630. S.Sgt. Keith R. Carnes, a squad leader, was in advance on his knees in a clump of bamboo when he was caught by the first burst of a Japanese machine gun. He was hit in the right chest, the abdomen, and the right thigh. The machine gun was soon knocked out, and he was carried one hundred yards to the front-line aid station. Several bottles of blood plasma stabilized his condition. After the long trip to the airstrip he reached a collecting company about fifty air miles to the rear. Emergency surgery was done. Three days later he was in the 20th General Hospital in Assam, India. Further surgery was done, and during a two-week period he was given thirteen blood transfusions. In spite of heroic treatment he died twenty-four days after the battle injury.

On this day's advance an unfortunate accident occurred. A Marauder 60mm mortar shell scored a direct hit on a headquarters company heavy machine-gun crew. One Marauder was killed instantly, two later died of wounds, and one was seriously wounded but survived. Prior air and artillery barrages, when the Japanese had held this ground, had cleared away bamboo and other jungle growth for a hundred yards along the trail. Since this was the only area with overhead clearance, the mortars had been put in this location. The front of our perimeter was now two hundred yards in front of the mortars. Corporal Gnarling had set up his heavy machine gun at the perimeter in a shell hole just to the left of the trail. Across the trail was another shell hole, occupied by the battalion commander Colonel Beach and the officer directing mortar fire.

A mortar barrage was planned. The 81mm mortars were zeroed in. Next the decision was made to add the 60mm mortars. The initial range was 360–400 yards, which was calculated to put the mortar shells onto the enemy locations. One zeroing round was fired. Another was called for. This 60mm round fell short and exploded on the machine gun. Subsequent investigation proved that all precautions had been taken.

After this accident, the 60mm mortars were used only as a front-line weapon. In a way it was a freak accident, but in any event the likelihood of a short round in the future made it inadvisable to fire the 60mm mortar very far from the front line. It will be recalled that a short round had wounded two men on 8 April. On 6 April, an 81mm short exploded one hundred yards in front of the mortar and wounded Private Forty at the front-line aid station.

CHAPTER XII

Corporal Robert W. Norling was on the left side of the gun. The shell produced large, mutilating wounds of his head, trunk, and right arm and leg. Death was instant. Pvt. Paul W. LaPanne was located on the right side and two feet from the gun, which offered him some protection. His wounds were multiple, penetrating and perforating of the abdominal wall and intestine. Other wounds were in the buttock, both thighs, and the chest. At the front-line aid station he immediately got two units of plasma. The medics rushed him over the four-mile carry by stretcher to the airstrip. Six hours later, when he arrived at the Ledo medical facility, he received twelve units of blood plasma. A portion of his small intestine was resected, and the two ends were exteriorized. He died six hours after surgery.

Pfc. Bernard J. Marshall was resting on the left and in back of the heavy machine gun. Multiple fragments entered his left forearm, wrist, buttock, leg, foot, face, and abdominal wall. A very serious wound was caused by a fragment that entered his left chest, fractured several ribs, tore his lung, and passed through his diaphragm and his kidney. In spite of hospital care with gradual improvement, he suddenly died two months after he had been wounded in battle.

The fourth member of this unfortunate machine-gun crew was Pfc. Joseph D. Clement Jr., from Lawrence, Massachusetts. When hit he appeared to have very little immediate disability but was soon found to be seriously injured. Fragments entered his upper chest, neck, and thighs. He was sent out quickly and made a good recovery after hospital care.

During the period that Khaki Combat Team was advancing, Lt. Winslow Stevens was the artillery observer. He directed fire on the Japanese-fortified positions from thirty yards' distance, and the remarkable job the artillery did in knocking out Japanese strong points up to 8 April was due in large part to his outstanding work as an observer. On another sector, Sgt. John A. Acker had no designated forward observer from Khaki for the two 75mm guns. Major Briggs had explained to him in the early morning that all possible help from the guns was necessary for the day's battle. As the sergeant and major were talking, a Khaki muleskinner, Robert L. Carr, overheard the conversation and told Acker that he would like to go forward to observe for the guns. The conversation continued, and Major Briggs explained that thick jungle growth separated the Marauders from the Japanese. Acker knew the area well, since he could see the location from his gun pits. His crew had also taken small-arm fire from that location. Because of Carr's dedication and courage he was sent forward—in spite of lack of training and experience. Soon Carr came in, on the radio, explaining that he was in front of our forward lines and would like a few rounds to be fired. Acker's guns were ready to fire point-blank into the Japanese positions. A round was fired from gun #2. Carr reported that it had fallen just over their front. The next round burst in a tree and had little effect on the enemy dugouts. At this time Sergeant Acker decided to fire a fuse-delayed round, which he was fortunate to have. The shell would hit an object and explode a split second later. When it hits the ground it really tears up the area. Carr was told to watch for the effect of the delayed fuse.

When the fuse-delayed round hit, Carr said to move in a little closer. The next round went into a foxhole occupied by Japanese. This was confirmed by Major Petito, who came in on his radio and said, "You're on target! Fire battery one hundred rounds." Sergeant Acker had to correct him. To fire one hundred rounds he would have to fire into the same spot. Petito was talked down to fifteen rounds, which heated the gun up quite a bit. Carr got back on his radio and said to move a few yards closer to our lines. He said, "Move over ten yards, and if you don't hear from me you'll know that you got too close." After the salvo he told Acker that we were right on target and the Japanese were squealing and running around. Carr was called out, and the artillery and mortars pulverized the area.

About an hour later Acker was able to go up and check the damage. Two hundred rounds had been fired. The delayed fuse shells had done a great job. The area had been largely cleared of upright vegetation. Bamboo and other trees had been uprooted and largely cleared of leaves. Dead Japanese littered the area, and body parts were hanging from brush and trees.

The men moved up in a cautious mop-up operation and occupied many trenches and dugouts, which were now free of living enemy. The bodies of some of the dead animals from which the Japanese had cut meat were found nearby.

CHAPTER XII

On this day, 8 April, the time had come for the First Battalion to go into action. White Column of the First Battalion took over the defense of the airstrip, and Red Combat Team departed to attack the Japanese from the west and south of Nhpum Ga.

A selected group of two hundred and fifty-four men from Red Combat Team had food, sleep, and rest after their forced march to help the Second and Third Battalions. They departed on their mission at 1830 hours. Captain Senff and his men marched the four miles to Khaki's position. They then turned right to enter the jungle-covered mountainside. The two-mile struggle through the thick jungle required them to descend about eight hundred feet. When they reached the Hkama Hka, which drained the mountaintop on which Nhpum Ga was located, they made their way southeast. After a mile or so along the riverbed they had lost five men from exhaustion and one seriously injured from falling over a twenty-foot embankment. These men were sent back together. Along the river they saw Japanese tracks leading in the direction of Nhpum Ga. Captain Senff sent reconnaissance patrols to follow the tracks and to scout out the area. They found three old paddy fields on the mountainside, two clearings, freshly dug foxholes, and one dead Japanese. They figured, since the Japanese hadn't buried this corpse, they were not operating in this area. After sending a report back by SCR 300 to regimental headquarters, which was with Orange Combat Team, they moved south, guided by the almost continuous firing in the vicinity of Nhpum Ga.

At 1800 hours Senff hit a trail leading southwest. It appeared to have been freshly used by men and animals. He sent one Browning automatic rifleman and two tommy gunners two hundred yards in each direction to block the trail. He then turned his group to the north moving slowly and cautiously toward Nhpum Ga. At 1810 hours, when the group was about eight hundred yards from Nhpum Ga, they were fired on by three Japanese. A reconnaissance patrol was sent out and found several deserted foxholes. A platoon was left as a block on that trail. The rest of the unit moved to the southwest to get high ground for a bivouac. At 1815 hours Captain Senff bivouacked 850 yards from Nhpum Ga on an azimuth of 240 degrees. The stench from the dead animals and men near the perimeter was bad. He put in a perimeter defense and dug in blocks across a pronounced footpath leading through the bivouac area.

At 2230 hours a four-man Japanese patrol moving north on the footpath was fired on by a Marauder. Only three rounds were fired before the gun jammed. The Japanese threw a grenade and withdrew after a brief fight.

During the night, at 2200 hours 1st. Lieutenant Robert Allen Johnson got out of his defensive foxhole to investigate a noise. He was killed by a U.S. carbine bullet, which passed through his brain to cause instant death.

Third Battalion Dead

Keith R. Carnes 19000838, S.Sgt., Co. I, Aldrich, Mo.
Robert W. Norling 20504451, Cpl., Hq. Co.
Paul W. LaPanne 20150281, Pvt., Hq. Co.
Bernard J. Marshall 3112506, Pfc., Hq. Co.

Third Battalion Wounded

Gordon E. Mackie 20647323, Sgt., Hq. Co., Oshkosh, Wis.
Frank J. Hus 36524822, Pfc., Hq. Co., Pniconnini, Mich.
David J. Burgoon 37229218, Pvt., Hq. Co.
Donald P. Darcey 34154552, Pfc., Hq. Co., Houma, La.
Wilford S. Locke Jr. 33191042, Pfc., Hq. Co.
Ivan R. Dayton 32375242, T5g., Hq. Co., Wild Valley, N.Y.
Ralph E. Asbury, Pfc., Hq. Co.
Edward A. Gilmore 17030822, T5g., Hq. Co., St. Louis, Mo.
Karl E. Parson 20503381, Pfc., Hq. Co.
Joseph F. Medeiros 39152715, Pvt., Co. I
William D. Muller Jr. 20508060, Sgt., Co. I, Cincinnati, Ohio
Gilbert R. Shelton 19032761, S.Sgt., Co. I, Prescott, Ariz.
Monte H. Potter 34142334, Pfc., Co. I, Unicoi, Tenn.
Joseph D. Clement Jr. 11088980, Pfc., Hq. Co., Lawrence, Mass.
Ernest B. Beauschene 31023968, T4g., medical detachment, Manville, Rhode Island

CHAPTER XII

First Battalion Dead

Robert Allen Johnson 0422409, 1st. Lt., Co. A, Red

8 April, Nhpum Ga: How Much Longer?

In Colonel Hunter's field order for the day he said, "The siege of Nhpum Ga will fall by noon today." Although there had been heavy fighting all around them, the siege still held at 1830 hours. The men in the perimeter wondered, "How much longer?"

Lt. William L. Fleming, regimental air liaison officer, was directing some fighter bombers on their targets over the air-ground radio (SCR 284) when he thought he recognized the squadron leader's voice. He said, "Is this Roland J.?" The answer came back, "Is this William L.?"

It was his former squadron leader and old friend Lieutenant Roland J. Mignes doing the bombing. They carried on a little personal conversation, and Lieutenant Fleming asked Mignes to promise to write his wife for him. Mignes answered "Roger" and added, "Boy, you just give us the targets. We'll make this place the milk run."

From a historical and factual standpoint it should be noted that bombing by the air force played a very small part in our Burma campaign. Yet the presence of the planes, at the infrequent intervals they came over, did seem to cause the Japanese to hold their fire.

Day Thirteen

9 April, Easter Sunday: Third Battalion Breaks Through

At the airstrip all was quiet, and Father Barrett held Mass at 0700 hours. All along the trail, Orange was patrolling and preparing for another day of support to Khaki. An early-morning patrol from Khaki killed a lone Japanese and found that he had been carrying an arm cleanly cut from the body of a fellow soldier. Our artillery fire was again directed into the Japanese positions, and mortar fire hit every area where the Japanese were thought to be. Our infantry attack was strange in that there was little answering fire from the enemy. Tricks were expected, but they only answered with sniper fire. We continued to blast our way through, and at 1000 hours our lead scouts reported dead Japanese everywhere.

T5g. Alfred L. Finn was leading a five-man patrol at 1100 hours two hundred yards on the right or western flank of the advancing platoons. He heard a noise and motioned the men to stop. He was immediately hit by machine-gun fire at seventy-five yards. He died instantly by machine-gun bullets through his chest.

Shortly after Finn was killed, Pfc. Thomas J. Gross, while crawling, was wounded in the chest by a rifle bullet from a sniper. Fortunately this was a soft-tissue injury, and he returned to duty.

Fifteen minutes after the above action, T5g. Frank G. Romanosky, a squad leader in I Company, was wounded by a rifle bullet. Japanese had been contacted in his squad's area, and all his men had cover. His was not adequate, and the sniper hit him from a range of sixty yards. The bullet passed through the thigh and lodged in back of his knee. He of course had to be sent out for adequate hospital treatment.

At 1200 hours, 2nd Lt. Winslow B. Stevens was leading his platoon very close to the Nhpum Ga perimeter. Suddenly a large Japanese major appeared. Stevens thought he wanted to surrender and raised his hand for the men to hold their fire. The Japanese started to raise his weapon, and the men blew him away. The lieutenant knew he was close to Nhpum Ga and was cursing at the top of his voice to alert the men on the perimeter. Suddenly he broke through some brush, and there before him was Warren T. Ventura and his machine-gun crew of the Second Battalion. The siege had been lifted, and the Second Battalion was free.

In another sector Colonel Beach had, by radio, asked Colonel McGee to fire three spaced shots to be answered by Khaki. The shots rang out, and Major Briggs soon walked into the Second Battalion area.

The lead platoons walked through an area of desolation worse than we had ever seen on New Georgia or Guadalcanal. Hundreds of Japanese, dead for a week, were stinking everywhere. Dead mules and horses twice their normal size, covered with maggots and flies by the million, blanketed an area near the north perimeter.

Major Briggs soon reached Colonel McGee's command post, a series of two-man foxholes dug out of the rock and red clay in the side of Nhpum Ga. Colonel McGee, smiling, said, "Sure am glad to see you, Ed."

CHAPTER XII

The Japanese had all they wanted on the north side of the perimeter but were still in strength on the southern and eastern sides. Khaki Combat Team held the ground gained that day, and part of the team was moved into Nhpum Ga. The horrible stench of death that pervaded the place was appalling.

Contact with the Japanese was maintained to the south, and at 1630 hours the Japanese artillery opened up. Everyone got back in foxholes, but the shelling didn't last long. A few mortar shells were also thrown in. Unfortunately, Eugene Chancy, from I Company, was wounded in the left leg. He was sitting on the edge of a Japanese-dug foxhole a hundred yards north of Nhpum Ga when a shell exploded close by. He went out by small plane the next day.

At dusk Pvt. William N. Worstell was on patrol near the perimeter at Nhpum Ga. A well-hidden U.S. grenade booby-trap exploded and seriously wounded him. He had numerous wounds of his face, chest, abdomen, and legs. There was also a compound fracture of the main bone of his right lower leg, the tibia. He was evacuated on the following day.

Colonel Hunter made a reconnaissance of the Nhpum Ga area and ordered five hundred pounds of lime to be dropped early the next morning. The cleanup of the dead started immediately. The enemy dead were searched, thrown into foxholes, and covered up. The animal dead were very difficult to bury, but a start was made on it. Many men vomited at the sight and smell of the place, and the Second Battalion veterans of the siege simply smiled and said, "It sure is good to see you."

Third Battalion Dead

Alfred L. Finn 36306304, T5g., Co. I, Khaki

Third Battalion Wounded

Thomas J. Gross 35365918, Pfc., Co. I, Khaki
Frank G. Romanosky 31193304, T5g., Co. I, Khaki
Eugene Chancy 38321255, Co. I, Khaki
William N. Worstell 18019662, Pvt., Hq. Co., Khaki

THE BATTLE OF NHPUM GA

9 April: Second Battalion Leaves Nhpum Ga

The night at Nhpum Ga had been very quiet, and the usual Japanese artillery barrage was not present in the morning. Fighting soon broke out on the east side of the perimeter. T5g. Clarence E. Pyle, Pfc. William M. Brophy, and Pfc. James D. Prairie were killed. Sgt. John L. Marsh of Green Combat Team was wounded, as was Pfc. Oscar Walters.

When Khaki broke through at 1200 hours, Major Rogoff and his medical detachment were ready to start more than seventy patients on their way to hospital care. They and three medical officers started the five-mile trip to the airstrip. Others who were mostly ambulatory would follow. As the sick and wounded slowly wound their way northward along the trail to Hsamshingyang, Sergeant Acker gave the order for his gun crews to fire two rounds from the two pack-75's in honor of the courageous stand of the men of the Second Battalion.

When the siege began, the Second Battalion had over 150 healthy mules and horses. Eighty weak, thin, and dehydrated animals remained. The muleskinners continued to look after them as if they were their best friends.

During the afternoon the Japanese artillery fired about twenty rounds, which went mostly overhead into the jungle. Our two pack-75's soon quieted them forever.

1st Lt. Edward A. McLogan, of McLogan's Hill, showed Captain John Jones fifty-four dead Japanese in front of his platoon and also two dead Marauders that the Japanese wouldn't let them get out. They were so badly decomposed that they were buried on the spot. A total of 212 dead Japanese were counted in the area they had withdrawn from. Aside from what they had buried themselves, at least four hundred Japanese were killed around this village. All over the area were unexploded duds—mortars, artillery, grenades—both Japanese and American. There were also several bazooka shells unexploded because they had not hit anything hard enough to make them explode. Aimed at a pillbox, they had missed and slipped into the jungle. Patrols were sent out to mark or explode all duds in the perimeter. Two days later, duds were still being found. On a trail leading up to the village was a Japanese body that looked normal except that it had three arms—a piece of body nearby showed where the third arm had come from.

CHAPTER XII

The First and Third Battalions were made responsible for the defense of the trail and Nhpum Ga, and the Second Battalion moved to Hsamshingyang to protect it and the airstrip.

Second Battalion Dead

Clarence E. Pyle, T5g.
William M. Brophy, Pfc.
James D. Prairie, Pfc.

Second Battalion Wounded

John L. Marsh 38056042, S.Sgt.
Oscar Walters 35123050, Pfc., Hq. Co.

9 April, First Battalion Engages the Enemy

Captain Senff's column was up at dawn expecting some action, but no Japanese showed up. He sent a patrol one hundred yards south on the footpath to investigate the firing during the night. They returned with a Japanese trenchcoat and four boxes of cooked rice balls, each box holding enough to feed a platoon. The rice balls looked like baseballs. At 1730 hours, a Japanese patrol hit the perimeter from the south. Lieutenant McElmurray quickly set up a machine gun. Captain Senff worked two squads forward with rifle grenades because it was too close in for mortars. A fire fight developed, and two Marauders were wounded.

The first man hit was T5g. Salvatore C. Garcia. At the time, he was out of his hole rolling his pack. A Japanese rifle bullet caused a mild flesh wound of his posterior chest wall. The Marauders had fired first, but Garcia did not have time to get back to his foxhole. He was not disabled.

About thirty minutes after Garcia was hit, a rifle bullet got Pfc. Stanley Erris in the right foot as he was advancing with his squad. The foot was badly shot up, and several Marauders had to carry him six miles to the airstrip.

When the Japanese attacked the perimeter, Pfc. Floyd V. Hayden suffered a compound comminuted fracture of the lower third of the chief forearm bone, the radius. The M-1 in his foxhole got him accidentally. Shortly after this accident the Japanese were driven off.

THE BATTLE OF NHPUM GA

At 1855 hours, Captain Senff moved his Company five hundred yards southwest across an old paddy field grown high with elephant grass. He left his intelligence and reconnaissance platoon in position at the bivouac area to block the trail and evacuate his wounded.

After a brief period at the new perimeter, harassing fire opened from the northwest, northeast, and due south. It seemed to be coming from the direction of the main trail between Nhpum Ga and Kauri. Colonel Hunter called Colonel Osborne on the SCR 300 radio and ordered Captain Senff back to the bivouac area where he had left the intelligence and reconnaissance platoon. This area was eight hundred yards from Nhpum Ga.

The move was made without delay, and the company dug in and set up strong defensive fire. His orders were to hold the block and contact the enemy from the north. At 2100 hours the block drew harassing fire from the north and northeast. It was not aimed fire, and the Japanese threw in some mortar fire covering the approach to the main trail. At 1100 hours one of Senff's combat patrols (one squad), moving to the north to contact the Japanese perimeter, was fired on by six dug-in automatic weapons. The patrol suffered no casualties.

At 1230 hours the intelligence and reconnaissance platoon reported that they had been able to deliver all the wounded from the first block back to Hsamshingyang for medical care. It took them five hours, whereas they had walked it without the wounded in one hour.

Captain Senff decided not to push north, as he would have suffered bad casualties from the Japanese automatic weapons and the evacuation route for the wounded men was so difficult. Also, there were Japanese positions 150 yards from his perimeter.

He sent three reconnaissance patrols to the south, east, and southwest. The patrol to the southwest reported the trail to the waterhole was open, so he let one squad from each platoon go after water. It took one hour and fifteen minutes for each round-trip. The patrol to the southeast reported no action but returned with two loads of rice balls, each load weighing about fifteen pounds. At 1345 hours his men fired on four enemy near the southeast side of the perimeter—killing two—and drew no return fire. It appeared that the Japanese, however, followed our reconnaissance patrol back.

At 1400 hours Lieutenant William Lepore's platoon reported movement, talking, and animals neighing 250 yards to the northeast, in a

CHAPTER XII

deep draw. Captain Senff checked with the Second and Third Battalions over the SCR 300 radio to see if they had anything in that position. The answer was negative, and Captain Senff gave orders to mortar and machine-gun the draw. A half-hour later, Pfc. Norman G. Sutton was sitting in a foxhole cleaning his carbine. The weapon accidentally discharged, and the bullet passed through his left foot.

At 1620 hours Captain Senff pulled his guns back after mortaring and machine-gunning the draw, and at the same time a Japanese mortar barrage from the ridge to the east opened on an area two hundred yards to the northeast of his perimeter on the approach to the draw. Japanese screamed and hollered, so it looked as if the Japanese figured we were attacking. They mortared the area, hitting their own troops. At about this time the Japanese artillery opened fire from Kauri on our artillery position north of Nhpum Ga.

Colonel Hunter was anxious that Captain Senff's men locate the exact position of the Japanese guns at Kauri. This would give Sgt. John Acker and his two pack-75 howitzers a better chance of knocking them out. Captain Senff located the probable site of the guns. He then moved his radio to a clearing on high ground where he could observe our artillery fire dropping four hundred yards short of the target. He reached Acker by radio and said, "I'm sitting along the trail between Kauri and Nhpum Ga and I can see the Japanese artillery guns. You are firing about four hundred yards behind them." Acker asked him if he knew anything about artillery fire, and he said he did not. He was then asked to watch for the effect of the next round. He reported that the fire was two or three hundred feet short but was right in line. The captain radioed back that the next shells were right on target and the Japanese were squealing and running around. The area was pulverized, and the guns were knocked out.

Captain Senff's White Combat Team set up strong defenses for the night. The Japanese did not bother them, and they hoped to be recalled in the morning. They had wounded men to get out and were low on food, water, and ammunition.

First Battalion Dead

None

First Battalion Wounded

Stanley Erris 36044864, Pfc., Co. C, Chicago, Ill.
Salvatore C. Garcia 39263575, T5g., Co. C, Oceanside, Calif.
Floyd V. Hayden 35621182, Pfc., Co. A

Day Fourteen

10 April: First Battalion Repositions

Colonel Hunter ordered Captain Senff to bring his company into the Second Battalion perimeter. He was to send a patrol to a clearing northeast of the perimeter and fire four well-placed shots. The patrol made contact with the Second Battalion at Nhpum Ga in about an hour, but the route was too bad to evacuate the wounded. Lieutenant McElmurray took a platoon and moved up a little-used trail to Nhpum Ga. In thirty-five minutes his platoon hit the Second Battalion perimeter and sent back a patrol to bring in the rest of the column. The patrol was fired on by a Japanese Nambu machine gun but took no casualties and reached Captain Senff and his company. From there, the company got to Nhpum Ga without opposition, then proceeded the five miles to Hsamshingyang and went into bivouac.

White Combat Team of the First Battalion, which had been protecting the airstrip, moved up to the Second Battalion's old position at Nhpum Ga. They were greeted by enemy mortar fire directed to the waterhole at Nhpum Ga. A brief fire fight developed, but the Marauders continued to hold the waterhole. The Japanese had pulled back between Nhpum Ga and Kauri and were consolidating their position on an easily defended ridge.

CHAPTER XII

First Battalion Dead

None

First Battalion Wounded

Norman G.Sutton 34150912, Pfc., Co. C

10 April, Hsamshingyang: Second Battalion Evacuates Wounded

The makeshift medical facility at Hsamshingyang had now been taken over by the Second Battalion medical detachment in cooperation with the other medical detachments. On this day, eighty-seven wounded were carefully checked and prepared for evacuation by the small L-4 planes. The evacuation process was slow but otherwise efficient, and all were taken out by the end of the day.

Green Combat Team, as well as the battalion headquarters, moved from Nhpum Ga to Hsamshingyang. Blue Combat Team still remained at Nhpum Ga.

Second Battalion Dead and Wounded

None

10 April: Third Battalion on Patrol

The Third Battalion was kept busy patrolling around Nhpum Ga, Hsamshingyang, and the five-mile trail between the two areas. They also pushed the enemy south and east of Nhpum Ga.

The End of the Battle of Nhpum Ga

The Second Battalion had moved to Hsamshingyang, where Blue Combat Team of the First Battalion was now located. The Third Battalion and White Combat Team of the First Battalion were now operating from Nhpum Ga.

All significant fighting had stopped, and the Japanese would not advance north of Kauri. A Chinese battalion was expected to arrive in a few days to occupy Nhpum Ga and block all trails to the north.

THE BATTLE OF NHPUM GA

The Battle of Nhpum Ga was now officially over, but two men were to be killed and several injured before we left the area. On 13 April Captain Senff was notified at 1600 hours that his patrol from B Company had run into a Japanese ambush on the trail south of Nhpum Ga. Pvt. Deck B. Grant had been instantly killed by a light machine gun at close range. His body was not recovered for several days. At the same time, the platoon leader, 1st Lt. Anthony H. Clark, had been wounded. He was disabled by a compound fracture of both bones in the right lower leg and was not to reach the 20th General Hospital, in Assam, India, until 14 April. When hit, they were in sight of the former Japanese artillery position at Kauri. A previous patrol had run into Japanese in this area the day before. This taught the entire command a lesson they had known but let slip: never use the same route twice while in enemy territory.

Our artillery continued to fire a few rounds daily in order to discourage the Japanese and keep them out of our area. Captain George G. Bonnyman, an artillery officer, was flown in about 10 April. He praised Sergeant Acker for the way he had conducted himself and handled the two howitzers. The Captain put Acker in charge of firing the guns. He took the responsibility of observing fire. Liaison planes were ordered to fly over the Japanese positions at Auche and Warong. They gathered valuable information from time to time, and Captain Bonnyman passed this information to Sergeant Acker. This very successful team worked well until 14 April, when Sergeant Acker accepted Captain Bonnyman's invitation to observe the fire from a liaison plane.

Sergeant Acker had never been in a plane, but he was trained in artillery fire observation. On the morning of Friday, 14 April, he walked four miles back to the airstrip and climbed into a Piper Cub. The pilot normally flew in the rear cockpit, but because of Acker's weight he decided to put Acker and his radio there and fly from the front cockpit.

The plane took off without any problem. As they approached the surrounding mountaintops the pilot gave Acker a worried look. Acker saw they were headed into a mountainside. They crashed, and the pilot was killed instantly. Acker regained his senses and climbed out of the plane. In due time he was able to patch up the radio and contact a patrol that had been sent out. In the dense jungle and the mountain terrain, the patrol took several hours to reach him. He was soon in another liaison plane on the way to a hospital for the care of a fractured clavicle and other injuries.

He tells how he was found:

> When I woke up I was climbing down out of the plane. I reached back and looked at the pilot and realized there was no hope. You could tell he was gone. I moved away from the plane for a little while to make sure the Japanese did not converge on the plane. Anyway, I moved back to the plane and got my radio in action. I called in, and they said, "We are going to fire one time, and you answer with three rounds." I said, "I don't have much ammunition. You fire three rounds, and I will fire one." By the time they got there I was sore and I could hardly move. My left arm was out of place. Old Steve Camber—we called him the mad Russian—and some others saw the plane go down. He grabbed his rifle and took off to try to find me. Sometime before, I had borrowed seven rupees from him. As he came up to me, you could see that the bamboo had cut him and he was bleeding all across his chest. When he looked at me, he said, "You are not going to get by with my seven rupees" (Acker, videotape).

An accidentally self-inflicted wound on 14 April caused Pfc. John W. Like of L Company, Orange Combat Team, to lose his right leg. He had been cleaning his M-1 rifle when the gun slipped and accidentally discharged. He had removed the clip but forgot a cartridge in the chamber. The leg was so badly damaged that an amputation had to be done after evacuation two weeks later.

Lieutenant Winslow B. Stevens, Third Battalion, Khaki Combat Team, heavy weapons section, had just been promoted to the battalion S-3. Colonel Beach had been ordered to send a patrol to contact General Stilwell and a unit of Chinese about fifty miles to the north at a Naubum. As the patrol traveled north, one member, a regular army man, got them very disturbed and unhappy by expressing in a very strong manner his lack of desire to go on another mission. They seriously debated as to whether they should fail to cooperate—not only on this current patrol but also on any future mission. Lieutenant Stevens had been and continued to be sick with chronic dysentery. His weight was down to one hundred pounds, and he was weak. Because of his poor condition, Colonel Beach had ordered him to ride a horse during the mission. On the first day this did not help matters with the men.

When they were about ready to bivouac for the night they had reached the bamboo bridge at the Tanai Hka. The lead scout spotted movement on the far side of the river. Stevens decided to scout out the possible enemy himself rather than ask for a volunteer. He hoped that this action would help to calm the men down and cause them to have more confidence in him. Fortunately, friendly natives were found. As he was preparing to cross the river he had put a round in the chamber of his forty-five. He was still holding the pistol in his hand when the rest of the patrol came over. As he called the men together for a meeting he put the gun on half-cock and shoved it into his hip holster. The hammer slipped off the edge of the holster and the gun fired. The slug went through the bottom of the holster into the calf of his left leg, following the Achilles tendon to the heel bone. Much of the tendon was destroyed and the bone severely fractured. The men wrote out a sworn statement that the wound was an accident, but the leader of the troublemakers later spread the word that the injury was not an accident. Lieutenant Stevens did not hear of the false accusation until after the war, when at a reunion one of his former platoon leaders heard the man telling the story. The troublemaker was confronted and admitted that he had lied about the cause of the accident. His excuse was that he had always hated officers.

During the Battle of Nhpum Ga Lieutenant Stevens had, as previously mentioned, saved the life of two wounded men. He was recommended for the D.S.C. While in the hospital recovering from the accidental pistol wound, a Silver Star metal was unceremoniously thrown on his cot. One can only conclude that the false story of the lying regular army man had affected the thought process of those who passed on the justification for his decoration.

What had started on 27 March as an operation by the Second Battalion to block the trail at Nhpum Ga had turned into a siege. The Second had fought for survival. In the process, they—with the help of the Third Battalion and finally the First Battalion—had won a great victory. Three battalions of Japanese had been defeated in their own territory. The Japanese trailblock separating the Second Battalion from the rescuing Third Battalion was deep in enemy territory, with no possibility of reinforcements or supporting units. This epic battle had been fought for fourteen days on the top and sides of a jungle-covered mountain at twenty-four hundred feet elevation. The Marauders' victory had been decisive and complete. The enemy had vanished, leaving more than four hundred dead.

Total Marauder Casualties, Battle of Nhpum Ga

	Dead	Wounded
First Battalion	2	4
Second Battalion	31	92
Third Battalion	19	67
Total	52	163

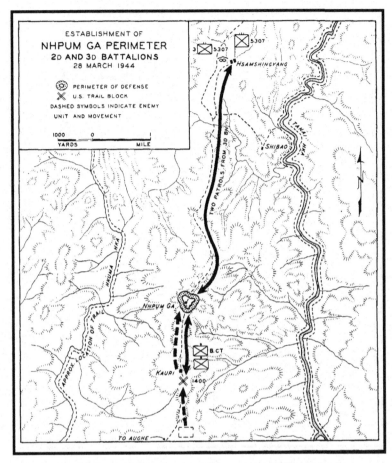

MAP 14. Establishment of Nhpum Ga perimeter: Second and Third Battalions, 28 March 1944.

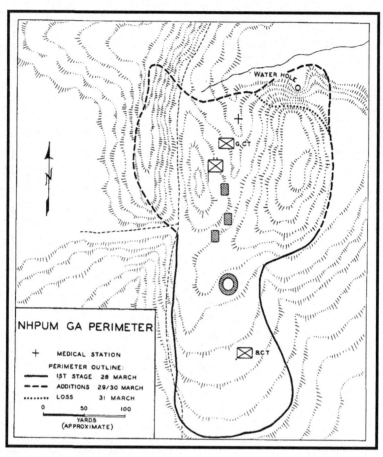

MAP 15. Nphum Ga perimeter.

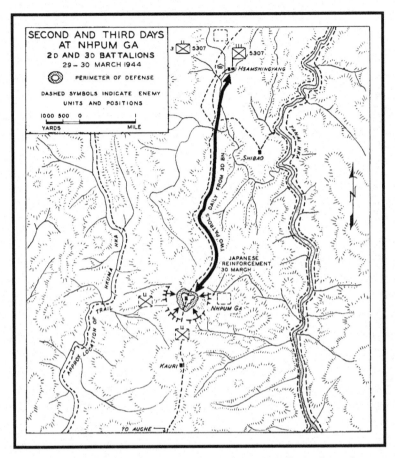

MAP 16. Second and third days at Nhpum Ga: Second and Third Battalions, 29–30 March 1944.

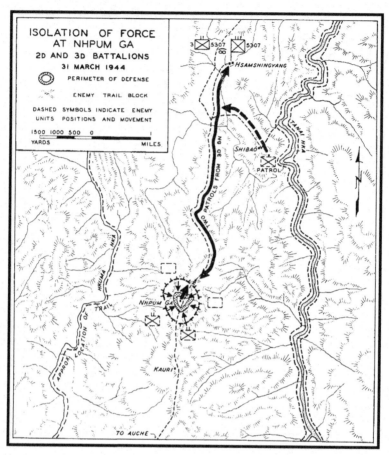

MAP 17. Isolation of force at Nhpum Ga: Second and Third Battalions, 31 March 1944.

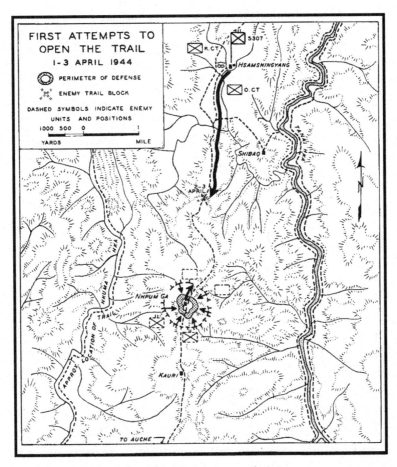

MAP 18. First attempts to open the trail, 1–3 April 1944.

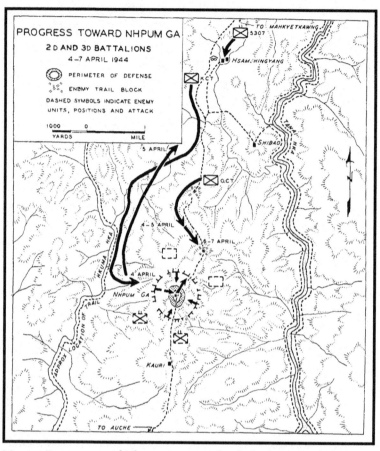

MAP 19. Progress toward Nhpum Ga: Second and Third Battalions,
4–7 April 1944.

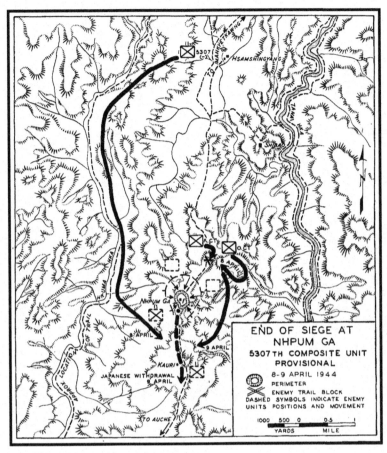

MAP 20. End of seige at Nhpum Ga, 8–9 April, 1944.

CHAPTER XIII
AFTERMATH AND PREPARATION

Colonel Hunter Plans for Rest, Reorganization, and Probable Future Mission

With the Battle of Nhpum Ga behind us, Colonel Hunter announced a temporary reorganization. Colonel Still became the executive officer, Major Williams S-5, Captain Michaelson S-1, and Captain Laffin S-2. A staff meeting was held, and jobs were assigned to plan another mission in case General Stilwell called on us again. Trail studies were being made in the Myitkyina area and a thorough survey of our own strength and condition was also planned. All these activities and plans were confidential information, and the battalion officers and men knew nothing about the actions and conversations going on at regimental staff level.

The Third Battalion and White Combat Team of the First Battalion Relieve the Second Battalion

The Third Battalion, with my medical section, and White Combat Team were to remain at Nhpum Ga until 19 April, a period of nine days. Within three or four days all the Marauder dead had been reburied and a small cemetery set up with crosses made from thick bamboo. Lime and covering dirt disposed of the seventy-five or so dead animals. The foul odor on the mountaintop soon cleared. The numerous foxholes, many lined with nylon parachutes, provided safe and reasonably comfortable sleeping areas. Our first mail—since we had left our training area during January—arrived. We were allowed to send out two V-mail letters. These were also our first since late January. Earlier we had been told that the War Department had notified all next of kin that they would not hear from us for several months. Our K-ration diet was somewhat improved by an occasional drop of the more acceptable 10-in-1 ration. No effort was made to send in significant supplies of toothbrushes, toothpaste, soap, or razor blades. No candy, soft drinks, cookies, or beer was dropped to us. Somehow the men seemed to make out with what they had.

During this period at Nhpum Ga the men in the infantry platoons of the Third Battalion and White Combat Team of the First Battalion had little time to rest. Constant patrol activity was necessary during daylight, and guard duty and defensive work at night. Headquarters, communications, and heavy weapons men were able to get much-needed rest. Muleskinners were kept busy tending to their sick and debilitated animals and bringing in supplies over the five-mile trail to Hsamshingyang.

Father Barrett, the Catholic priest who had joined the Third Battalion just before the Inkangahtawng mission, did a superb job during that operation and the Nhpum Ga battle. During this brief period at Nhpum Ga he officiated at the reburial of the dead, counseled some Marauders, and held religious services.

On Nhpum Ga Hill my Third Battalion medical detachment worked with the medical section of White Combat Team to give all possible medical care. Thanks to few mosquitoes, little contact with the Kachins, and prophylactic atabrine medication of one tablet per day, malaria had not been an unmanageable problem since we had been in Burma. When the men came in with temperature elevations, we had no means of doing malaria smears for a proven diagnosis. We made the clinical diagnosis based on bodytemperature and symptoms. Their condition was in some cases undoubtedly due to other causes such as dengue fever, amoebic dysentery, bacillary dysentery, dehydration, and exhaustion. Many of the men were suffering from chronic fatigue, weight loss, and/or numerous other vague complaints. I saw no acute psychiatric problems or war neurosis. Many of the men had a chronic cough due to chronic recurrent bronchitis. Numerous varieties of dermatitis were seen. Numerous men came to the medics with small, deep-seated ulcers on their legs. These seemed to be the end result of leech bites, which tended to become infected. A few of our more difficult problems were sent down the mountain to Hsamshingyang for evaluation by the regimental surgeon and possible evacuation.

During this eight-day period at Nhpum Ga, no one from any higher medical authority paid us a visit. Our much-admired rear echelon supply officer, Major Hancock, flew in and took the trouble to visit the group at Nhpum Ga Hill. He had done a superb job on supply, and every officer and man in the unit was grateful for his untiring work in getting rations, ammunition, and supplies in whenever asked for. During the first few days in this relatively safe area, it seemed strange that General Stilwell did not fly in to congratulate the Marauders. There was a rumor that he might be worried by the possibility of personal harm from a disgruntled Marauder. By this time the men had every reason to be unhappy with numerous actions and problems that had seriously touched the unit since our arrival in India. Some of us were flattered when Colonel Hank Kinnison, Stilwell's G-3, flew in and took the trouble to hike the four miles uphill to see the sights of Nhpum Ga. No effort was made to meet any of the unit's enlisted men or junior officers. A few days later, Col. Robert M. Cannon appeared at the airstrip—but did not take the hike to Nhpum Ga.

Another Mission for the Marauders

A rumor reached us at Nhpum Ga Hill that General Merrill would be back in a few days to form a special task force. The force would consist of three combat teams, two of which would have one battalion of the Marauders and one Chinese regiment. One battery of Chinese pack artillery would be part of one unit, while the other would have the Third Battalion's two pack howitzers. The Second Battalion would be formed as the reserve. The men and officers, and especially the medical departments, were very disturbed by this rumor. We were soon to learn that this information had come from Colonel Hunter and was probably authentic. I assumed that he had obtained this information from Colonel Kinnison—who, on his visit to Nhpum Ga, had spent the night there with Colonel Hunter. Those of us who knew the condition of the men could only hope that we would get medical help and some delay before the start of another mission. Previous information gave us even more reason to be disturbed by this apparent change in the Marauders' future. Some weeks before, it was generally known that General Merrill had told Colonel Hunter that when the Chinese occupied Shaduzup the campaign would be over until the end of the monsoon or rainy season. Shaduzup had been taken over by the Second Battalion of the 65th Chinese Regiment shortly after the Marauders' First Battalion had turned over the roadblock just south of Shaduzup to the 113th Chinese Regiment.

If this new mysterious mission were ordered, it meant that the greatly understrength Marauders, many of whom were either in poor condition or chronically ill, would be called upon to do the job. The expected weather conditions during the monsoon season in this jungle-covered, mountainous area would present many problems. The men and officers were very troubled that Generals Stilwell and Merrill cared so little for American troops that they would contemplate and perhaps plan an operation that, if successful, would accomplish little and cause much hardship and death. The majority of the medical officers and infantry officers freely expressed their opinion that the men should not be used for another mission until they had been given adequate rest, rehabilitation, and replacements to fill up the ranks of the men we had lost.

A few days after the rumor spread that we would have another mission, it was learned that our commander, Colonel Hunter, had been working on his own plan to determine the best route to Myitkyina. He had reason to believe that this city and its all-weather sixty-five-hundred-foot airfield was General Stilwell's objective. With the aid of maps, the missionary Father Stuart, Kachins, and others, he decided that a long-unused trail over the Kumon Mountain Range into the Irrawaddy River area was the best route to Myitkyina. There was considerable difference of opinion as to whether or not men and animals could get across the numerous mountains, including the sixty-four-hundred-foot pass, Naura Hkyat.

In a few days Colonel Hunter was ordered to send a staff officer to General Stilwell's headquarters. He sent Major Louis Williams, the adjutant. Colonel Hunter had written his plan for the mission to Myitkyina in pencil on scraps of paper. It was incomplete but gave the best route for the Marauders to take.

The news soon spread that General Merrill, now back on his feet, had eagerly taken the staff study. Merrill soon presented his plan for the march to Myitkyina and the capture of the airfield to General Stilwell. Colonel Hunter's plan had worked. He had caused General Stilwell to send us over a route that had been studied, rather than over a more dangerous and difficult route. Major Williams was given the orders for the deployment of the fourteen hundred Marauders who, in spite of fatigue, weight loss, and chronic illness, were expected to go into their third mission. No replacements were available for the other twelve hundred men lost to combat, and there was little time for rest, rehabilitation, and treatment of chronic illness, weight loss, and debility.

The Third Battalion at Hsamshingyang

The Tanai Hka was nearby, and we had our first chance in several weeks to properly bathe. New clothes were issued from the skin out, as the old clothes were filthy and worn out. Numerous sleeping areas had been prepared by other Marauders in and about the airfield perimeter. Maximal additional use was made of parachutes, ponchos, and banana leaves to keep each area dry.

It was now raining one or more times practically every day. Fortunately, mosquitoes were not very active—even though we were now at an altitude of fifteen hundred feet instead of the twenty-eight hundred feet of Nhpum Ga.

Some of the more alert men saw a Japanese soldier run through the area. Four Marauders fired at one hundred yards and missed. Colonel Hunter jokingly said that if this continued we would set up a range and zero rifles again. Most of the men had their sights set for firing at a distance of fifty yards.

As soon as the Third Battalion medical detachment arrived back at Hsamshingyang, we joined forces with the regimental surgeon, Major Schudmak, and his small staff. Major Cecala and Captain Ivens had been evacuated sick. Lieutenant Jack Armstrong and I were now the only medical officers in the Third Battalion. The sick and wounded were still being sheltered by parachutes draped over bushes and poles. The patients continued to sleep on the ground. The Marauders were being treated for diarrhea, dysentery, obscure fevers, acute and chronic arthritic problems, bad backs, foot problems, and skin conditions. Weakness, fatigue, giddy spells, anorexia, weight loss, and mild cases of depression were seen daily at the twenty-four-hour sick call.

During the Battle of Nhpum Ga the regimental medical section had done a marvelous job as they treated and evacuated over 150 wounded. The Marauders lost a total of 436 dead, wounded, and sick as a result of the Battle of Nhpum Ga. The evaluation and treatment of the sick in this location continued until we left for the next mission. At the beginning of the battle, Colonel Hunter had asked the Northern Area Command to send in additional medical personnel, but we had been told that such an action was not practical. The explanation was that the men would be better treated if they were removed from the combat area.

A few days after the Battle of Nhpum Ga ended, the Northern Area Combat Command flew in four junior medical officers from the 14th, 48th, and the 73rd Evacuation Hospitals near Ledo, Assam. They expressed horror over the conditions under which the doctors had been working. They were pleased over the work of the battalion surgeons. While they were with us, an average of seventy men were kept under the medical lean-to as patients. These doctors were very helpful in treating the sick and wounded and in assisting in the evacuation of men not fit for combat. Two would remain to help on our next mission.

Stone quotes from the annual report of the 73rd Evacuation Hospital, appendix 3, "Brief Resume of Detached Service with the 5307th Prov. Unit":

> Terribly exhausted, suffering extensively and persistently from malaria, diarrhea, and both amoebic and bacillary dysentery; beset by festering skin lesions, infected scratches and bites; depleted by five hundred miles of marching on packaged rations, the Marauders were sorely stricken. They had lost seven hundred men killed, wounded, disabled by nonbattle injuries, and most of all sick. Over half had been evacuated by the Second Battalion alone. Many remaining in the regiment were more or less ill, and their physical condition was too poor to respond quickly to medicines and rest (Stone 1949, 331).

AFTERMATH AND PREPARATION

Some officers who were familiar with the facts pointed out that General Stilwell had been very critical of General Wingate when he lost one-third of his brigade in Burma in 1943. The Marauders had, up until this time, lost almost as many—and, like the Chindits, had many sick and dazed in their ranks. Now, in spite of his statements about the British general, we were forced to believe that he was prepared to sacrifice his own troops.

Shortly after the Third Battalion moved to Hsamshingyang, Colonel Hunter decided that a rehabilitation and training program should be started. Much to the amazement and amusement of the men, daily close-order drills were started in the jungle clearing. At first they were pretty sore about it, but soon they were counting in cadence and doing fancy drill. One old sergeant said, "Now I've seen everything, but it's a damn good thing to whip men back into shape."

On 20 April a mule race on the airstrip brought practically every man on the field. "Old Jake" and "Old Puss," two of the best riding mules in the regiment, were the contenders. "Old Jake" won by two lengths when "Old Puss" took a little detour off the race course. He knew where the oats were kept. Not much money changed hands, as there was not much in the regiment.

At 1145 hours a C-47 of the Second Troop Carrier Squadron was dropping rations on our drop field. As it turned to make another run, it hit an air pocket, which threw several parachute loads out the door. One chute opened and hit the tail of the plane, locking the elevators. The pilot fought to get it off but it wouldn't come off, and he was rapidly losing altitude. Circling the field at treetop level, he belly-landed the ship on the edge of the airstrip. It was a beautiful job of setting the plane down gently by cutting both motors. There was no fire, and the pilot, copilot, and navigator were not injured.

The kickers, however—from the Marauder's supply base in Assam—*were* injured. They had no safety belts and were slammed against the walls of the plane when it hit the ground. Salvage work began immediately. Fifty years later, as this history goes to print, a native family is probably living in the fuselage.

A picture was taken on this day, and twenty-five different nationalities were represented. This means that these men were either at one time citizens of another country or their parents were. At least half of them were not American citizens at one time.

On 22 April the First Battalion of the 112th Infantry Regiment of the 38th Chinese Division appeared at Hsamshingyang to take over the defense of Nhpum Ga. This regiment had been in combat since early November 1943. They had taken very heavy casualties during their numerous battles. Colonel Hunter had sent Captain John George to determine when they might arrive at Nhpum Ga to offer help during the siege. No answer had arrived. No further contact was made with the captain, who did not return because of illness.

Considerable excitement developed at Hsamshingyang during the afternoon of 22 April. Numerous explosions were heard, and flares were ignited in a bamboo-and-grass hut where the regimental communications and supply sections were located. Everyone went on a rapid alert, ready for a Japanese attack. It was a false alarm. A small fire had been accidentally started and had caused all the trouble.

The First Battalion had two unfortunate accidents. Pvt. Harmine Johnson had emerged from his foxhole on 19 April at 0100. When he returned he was mistaken for a Japanese soldier and shot by a comrade. The bullet from a Thompson submachine gun killed him instantly. At 0400 hours on 22 April, Private Joseph T. Lunsford was wounded when a bullet passed through his left foot. He had just traded a Thompson submachine gun for a carbine and was cleaning the carbine. The weapon discharged accidentally.

From 14 April the Marauders had the service of an L-1 liaison plane used by Cochran's air commando unit. It could take out four passengers at a time and had greatly helped the airstrip evacuation operation. From the pilots of these planes we learned that a great battle was still in progress between British and Japanese forces on the India-Burma border. The Marauders had been given no information about this operation and were surprised to learn that the Japanese had almost entered the Brahmaputra Valley, in an attempt to cut the Bengal and Assam Railway, early in April. This would have cut off all American and Chinese forces, in Assam and Burma, from overland supplies. After our campaign was over, some of us learned other important facts. Three Japanese divisions had attacked the India-Burma border on the southern or Arakan front in February, and had been defeated—with considerable loss of Japanese. The British had saved the day by flying in additional troops.

On 8 March the Japanese launched a drive hundreds of miles to the north, on the Manipur-Kohima section of the India-Burma frontier, in an attempt to enter India. They concentrated on the Kohima and Imphal area. By moving numerous divisions using C-47's borrowed from transportation duty over the Hump, the British and Indian troops gained a great victory near the end of June. The Japanese lost seventeen thousand horses and sixty-five thousand men.

We also learned of the operation, between 5 March and 8 March, in which 9,250 of General Wingate's Chindits, a force of 18,000 men, were flown into central Burma by the small American air force known as Cochran's No. 1 Air Commando, AAF. This group included fighter bombers, medium bombers, transports, and liaison craft. Gliders were also used during the initial landing to carry American engineers and small bulldozers. Three strongpoints were set up about two hundred miles southwest of the Marauder's operating area. General Wingate was killed in an air crash on 24 March.

One of the Chindit missions was to cut off the supplies going to the 18th Division—which, with other units, was opposing General Stilwell's forces in North Burma. This operation, if successful, would have made little difference since the 18th Division had stockpiled all necessary supplies for one year. They proved very helpful, however, in harassing some of the Japanese engaged on the western Burma front during the attempted invasion of India. In early April the Chindits were ordered to turn their attention to the north to work with and help General Stilwell's forces. This decision was to cause much friction between General Stilwell and the Chindit staff.

The First and Third Battalions Prepare for the Third Mission

As the date approached for the beginning of the third mission, there was some confusion as to how many men were available and able to make the hundred-mile trip that this mission would require. To the best of my knowledge, somewhat fewer than six hundred men remained in each battalion. Even during the past fifty years, the exact number has not been determined. The medical staff all agreed that the majority were chronically ill and in very poor physical condition.

Colonel Hunter received the following message from General Stilwell's headquarters on 21 April: "General Sun, Commanding General of the 38th Division, desires to convey to all officers and men his sincere appreciation of the fine spirit of cooperation with his men. General Liao, commanding the 22nd Division, sends the message that his division has admired the fine job done by Galahad [the Marauders' official name, not known to the officers and men] and hopes that in the future he will have the chance to work with us" (Stone 1949).

During the late afternoon on 21 April, Colonel Hunter informed Colonel Beach that the Third Battalion was to depart Hsamshingyang at dawn on 22 April and march northward toward Naubum. We covered about twelve miles, over a very rough up-and-down trail, and bivouacked for the night. On 23 April, after a march of several miles, we arrived at Weilangyang. A large airdrop was awaiting our arrival. Three of our men were very ill and had to be left for evacuation by the Second Battalion. In spite of their high temperature, weakness, fatigue, general aches and malaise, their clinical picture was not that of malaria. Unfortunately, they had to wait three days for evacuation.

After a restful night at this area, we departed for and arrived at Tate Ga. Here we spent another good night in spite of intermittent rain. On 26 April we completed the last stage of the thirty-mile march from Hsamshingyang and camped about two miles south of Naubum. We now learned that the 88th Chinese Regiment was to follow, as part of the K Force, and was now camped at Naubum.

The First Battalion was now located two and one-half miles north of Naubum. The Chinese 150th Regiment, which was to be a part of the H Force, was bivouacked at Taikri, five miles north of Naubum.

We had been having intermittent rain all week, and it continued as the Third Battalion pushed off for Taikri on the morning of 27

April. I was ordered, with several other officers, to report to Colonel Hunter at Naubum. We left the Third Battalion as the men continued their wet, muddy march to Taikri. I reported to Colonel Hunter, and he told me that I had been appointed K Force surgeon. I would march with the Third Battalion, but was responsible for the medical and surgical care of the entire unit. By rumor I heard that an American portable surgical unit would be marching with our attached 88th Chinese Regiment. Before our departure date there would be no opportunity the see or meet anyone in the Chinese unit or the surgical unit.

At Taikri during the afternoon of 27 April, some of the officers met Colonel Kinnison for the first time. We were given a very minimal amount of information about our route of passage over the Kumon Mountain Range and our objective. The difficulty of the mission was minimized. Few had any conception of the enormity of the task we were being asked to carry out. At this time the word had gotten out that General Merrill was to command the task force in spite of his recent heart attack. In a conversation, Colonel Hunter had explained that when the airfield at Myitkyina was captured, the Marauders would be flown out. The other four regiments of the 50th and 30th Chinese Divisions would be immediately flown in to defend the airfield and capture the town of Myitkyina. The Marauders would be taken to a predetermined area for rest and recreation.

At this late date men continued to get sick, and a few were evacuated during the several days before D day, 28 April.

The First Battalion and the 150th Chinese Regiment were to remain in the area until 1 May before they began to follow the difficult, steep, and muddy trail in the footsteps of the K Force.

The Second Battalion—Now M Force—Prepares for the Third Mission

Shortly after the Second Battalion had sent out their sick and wounded, they were assigned the job of patrolling the numerous trails that led from Nhpum Ga, Hsamshingyang, and much of the jungle in and about this southern portion of the Tanai Valley. This required numerous combat patrols to travel many miles and be away from the

Second Battalion for one or more days. The stressful and fatiguing work frequently deprived them, for several days at a time, from adequate food, medical care, rest, and sleep. They had to travel in jungle-covered, mountainous terrain where they had to be constantly on the alert for enemy ambushes.

Colonel McGee and his Second Battalion had required considerable reshuffling of men and animals, as had the other two battalions. His animal loss had been much greater than the others, which shared their remaining animals with the Second Battalion. The medical detachment lost Captain Gardner because of illness. He was replaced by Lieutenant Congdon, who was one of the four doctors brought in to help with the treatment and evacuation of sick and wounded at Hsamshingyang.

After the Battle of Nhpum Ga, the Second Battalion had evacuated 114 wounded and 33 sick by 14 April. On 15 and 16 April, an additional 66 sick were sent out. Among the sick, malaria was not a significant problem. They were suffering from chronic diarrhea and dysentery (mostly amoebic), unknown fevers, severe skin diseases, emotional conditions, critical weight loss, malnutrition, and unexplained exhaustion and weakness. Up to this time, no cases of scrub typhus had been diagnosed in the battalion.

The Second Battalion was north of Hsamshingyang on 26 April at Weilangyang. At this location they were able to evacuate, by light plane, eight men from their battalion, five left by the First Battalion, and three who had been left sick by the Third Battalion. On this date Colonel McGee informed General Merrill by radio that he had 27 officers, 573 enlisted men, and 108 animals. The battalion's original strength had been about 984 men and officers and 140 animals.

Colonel McGee was finally called to see General Merrill on 30 April. Here he learned that the mission to capture the Myitkyina airfield had already started. The general explained that K and H Forces had departed Taikri in that order, and were headed for Myitkyina. His job was to travel by a more difficult, but 30-mile-shorter, route. His force was to be called the M Force and would include a variable number of Kachins, as well as the Second Battalion. Their route would also take them southeast over the numerous mountains of the

Kumon Range. It lay about ten miles south of the route that, at that time, the main force was struggling to get over. They would be going through the Naura Hkyat Pass at sixty-one hundred feet elevation. The M Force would cross the Hpumsimaru Bum at 5,923 feet elevation and the Sharaw Kawng at 4,928 feet as they pulled themselves and their animals over the Hka Ga-Muta Ga trail.

The general gave Colonel McGee very little information about the Myitkyina task force or the plans for the capture of the airfield. He did not discuss the logical next step, the capture of the town of Myitkyina. Colonel McGee was given no written orders.

General Merrill did not contact Colonel McGee again until 6 May, when he ordered him to report to his headquarters at Naubum. The colonel was informed that his mission was to move over the Kumon Mountain Range starting on 7 May toward Myitkyina. He was told to explain to the troops that their destination was Ritpong. The route would be the Hka Ga-Muta Ga trail. Maps showed few suitable areas for airdrops. General Merrill implied that this problem could be worked out. He explained that he might be able to arrange for the Second Battalion to be airlifted from Arang to Myitkyina. If this movement of part of the Second Battalion had been possible, forty miles of difficult marching in the hot, humid Burma climate would have been avoided. Yet the surprising offer would not be carried out. This was the last time McGee would see the general during the campaign. Merrill said that thirty Kachins and an interpreter would join the battalion at Hka Ga.

At this time the battalion was tailored to a battalion headquarters, two rifle companies, a heavy weapons company, an I & R platoon, and one P & D section, as well as a medical section. They would be supplied and ready to go on 7 May.

From the time the battalion was rescued at Nhpum Ga, Colonel McGee was to have little opportunity to meet with the other battalion commanders, the staff of the Myitkyina task force, or any ranking visitors. General Stilwell had been at Naubum, but Colonel McGee had not been given the opportunity to meet him. No effort had been made to have the general meet or speak to any of the men. Colonel McGee had one brief visit with Colonel Kinnison and a short visit with Colonel

CHAPTER XIII

Marcel Colombez from Army Field Services. They discussed the value of various infantry weapons and equipment. Colonel McGee told of numerous men whose lives had been saved by the steel helmet (McGee 1987).

CHAPTER XIV
THE THIRD MISSION

Since the Japanese had been defeated at Nhpum Ga, much of the information acquired by the men and officers was in the form of rumors. We had only vague information about the new mission and about the new regimental headquarters being set up at Naubum. We had passed through the area on our way to Inkangahtawng and remembered it as a cleared area, thirty miles to the northeast, in the foothills of the Kumon Mountain Range—which we were to cross in our new mission.

The day-to-day activities and orders of the three separate battalions were not shared. Each was operated separately under control of the new headquarters. The plans and activities of the new headquarters were carefully guarded. Few of the men or officers had any significant knowledge of the overall situation or of the headquarters activity or setup.

General Stilwell and his son, Lt. Colonel Stilwell, arrived at Naubum by L-5 at 0900 on 26 April to meet with General Merrill. They visited the headquarters staff officers and stayed in the area until 1400 hours, when they departed. General Merrill did not arrive on this day, as his plane could not get over the mountains due to low clouds. He was able to come in by L-5 at 1000 hours on 27 April. In compliance with previous orders, the combat team commanders had made the long hikes, from the various locations of their combat teams, to Naubum. Colonel Hunter was present as the commander of the newly created H Force and the newcomer, Colonel Henry L. Kinnison Jr., as the commander of K Force. The senior officers of the Chinese 150th and 88th Regiments were also present. General Merrill stated that our mission was to capture the airstrip at Myitkyina. He then gave the officers a rough plan of operations. K Force, under Colonel Kinnison and consisting of the Third Battalion of Marauders and the 88th Chinese Infantry Regiment, 30th Division, would be leading out from Taikri, then over the sixty-one-hundred-foot Naura Hkyat Pass down to Ritpong. H Force, under Colonel Hunter and consisting of the First Battalion Marauders and 150th Chinese Infantry Regiment, 50th Division, would follow. H Force would break to the west at Ritpong, and a two-pronged drive would be made to the south toward Myitkyina. M Force, under Lt. Colonel McGee and consisting of the Second Battalion of Marauders and some Kachin guerrilla units, would remain at the Senjo Ga-Hkada Ga area for a few days to block any Japanese advance from the south. They would later join the First and Third Marauder Battalions. After General Merrill had briefed the battalion and team commanders, he met with the force and regimental commanders to give them detailed verbal instructions.

Either by design, accident, or impracticability, little knowledge about the makeup of the various units of the forces, the commanders, the terrain of the route of march, the distance, the location of enemy, supply of food, water, and ammunition, and evacuation of sick and wounded reached the Marauders. The one thing that all men understood was that they were to reach and capture an airfield about one hundred miles to the southeast. When the field was captured, they were to be flown out of Burma on the planes that would be bringing in supplies and Chinese troops. Our mission was definitely the airfield. No information was given about the nearby town of Myitkyina. The town was the principal base for the defense of Burma from the north. Located 170 air miles southeast of Ledo, it was at the head of navigation on the Irrawaddy River and the northernmost point of the railroad from Rangoon. It lay 170 miles north of the junction of a railroad with the Burma Road at Lashio. Capture of the airfield and town would eliminate the base for the Japanese aircraft that had been attacking American planes as they flew over the Hump between China and India. Loss of the airfield would paralyze all Japanese operations in North Burma. The capture would allow the planes that had been flying over the Hump to take the route over Myitkyina at a much lower altitude. Oil pipelines were already being installed from Calcutta into Assam, and would reach Myitkyina a few months after successful capture of the airfield and city. The tonnage of supplies going into China would then be greatly increased.

Before and during the campaign, the men and officers had been able to learn little about the war in Burma other than their own part in it. This pattern was to continue in this, the third mission. After the battle of Walawbum, bits of information allowed some of us to conclude that when we entered Burma the country was occupied by eight divisions of Japanese troops. A few days after Walawbum, General Wingate dispatched six brigades of English troops to fight about two hundred miles to our south. Two days later the Japanese army launched a massive attack on British troops who were guarding the India-Burma border on the west. Some of us were also aware that the Chinese 22nd and 38th Divisions were still in Burma fighting the Japanese to our west, under General Stilwell's command. The Marauder men and officers had learned little about the progress these troops were making. As time passed we learned that we and the Chinese had been the only allied troops fighting in Burma at the time of the Battle of Walawbum.

If the following information had been passed on to the troops, they might have had more enthusiasm for the new mission and respect for General Stilwell and his staff. The Chinese 22nd and 38th Divisions were now at Inkangahtawng, twenty miles north of Kamaing. General Stilwell planned to continue his drive down the Mogaung corridor toward Kamaing. In the Irrawaddy Valley, forty-five miles north of Myitkyina, small units of Gurhka forces and Kachins led by British were fighting for a large Japanese supply dump. They had driven the enemy out of Sumprabum at the northeast tip of Burma. Across the Irrawaddy River, southeast of Myitkyina, the Chinese were massing troops in a planned attempt to cross the Salween River. Their next step would be to attempt to drive the Japanese down the Chinese section of the Burma Road and eventually hook up with the troops in Burma at Myitkyina. General Wingate had been killed in an air crash, but his twenty-six columns of four hundred men each were still operating in Burma. Their operations about eighty miles south of Myitkyina had blocked the Japanese-held railroad, which had been used to supply the Japanese who opposed the Americans and Chinese to the north. Unfortunately, the Japanese had already built up heavy supplies. The

Japanese could still supply their troops by water transport on the Irrawaddy River. Two hundred and fifty miles to the west the Japanese had massed, in mid-March, 155,000 men to invade India. This crucial battle was to rage until mid-July, when the Japanese were defeated. They would lose seventeen thousand horses and sixty-five thousand men. The casualty rate in combat units would be eighty-five to ninety percent.

If the Marauders had known how badly the Japanese were being defeated at Kamaing and Mogaung and of their total defeat on the Burma-India border, they would have been even more resentful that General Merrill and General Stilwell failed to keep their promise to send them out of Burma on the same planes that would bring in the Chinese.

General Merrill's staff at Naubum consisted of his communications officer Captain Pilcher; G-2, Major Louis J. Williams; G-3, Major George Hestad; and G-4 at rear echelon, Major Edward Hancock. Captain John Jones, collaborator on this history, continued as historian but was also assisting with G-1 work. Lieutenant Colonel Warner and Captain Oakley from CBI were also working with the staff.

Now that the day of departure approached for what appeared to be a foolhardy mission, the men and officers were prepared to do their best for the honor of the unit and their own survival. As usual, what little information was available was obtained mostly from rumors and distorted facts. There was little opportunity to discuss the day's events with any but the few men in your squad or platoon. On the trail and in bivouac, the combat teams were stretched out in long single lines of men and animals, usually extending several hundred yards. When the men were not on patrol, hiking, looking after their animals, or doing their assigned tasks, they were trying to get some rest. Those of us who knew of General Merrill's recent heart attack had anxiety about the motives and intelligence of those in higher authority who were responsible for allowing him to return to duty. They should have known that any individual who had suffered a recent heart attack had no right to be commanding troops in the field. The medical officers of the Marauders were very disturbed over the decision to return him to duty. They would have been even more apprehensive and critical if they had known that he had had a previous heart attack the year before.

Another important fact was not known to the medical officers of the Marauders. General Stilwell's wife states in the foreword to *The Stilwell Papers,* arranged by Theodore H. White and published in 1948, that he was almost blind. She states, "The explosion of an ammunition dump during World War I, at Belrypt, caused a severe injury to the left eye. There was a deformity of the pupil and the growth of a cataract. The vision of the eye was so impaired that he could not distinguish the fingers on a hand at three feet. The vision of the other eye required heavy correction and constant use of glasses." At age 61, Stilwell admitted that he was in poor physical condition when he stated in his diary on 3 May 1944: "Hot 1:30-to-3:30 hike up to 114th Command Post near Nawngmi Kawng. Hill 2,000 feet high. Damned near killed me. All out of shape. No wind, no legs. Swore off smoking then and there. Felt like an old man when I staggered in." Stilwell never appeared before a large group of Marauders, but the few times he was seen, remarks were made about his apparent poor physical condition.

My opinion in April 1944 was that, because of his heart attack of 29 March, General Merrill should not have been in command of the Marauders on their mission to capture the Myitkyina airfield. If I had known of his earlier heart attack I would have strongly objected to his command of the unit. We were not told that Merrill was too sick to march and would only be available to supervise the few areas he could land in by small plane.

Until the time of departure for Myitkyina, some of the medical officers and junior officers continued to express dismay because of the irrational decision to send sick and debilitated men over mountainous terrain—terrain known to present extreme obstacles to passage by heavily loaded men and animals. Even more irrational was the decision to ignore the fact that only 1,400 Marauders out of the original 2,997 were left in Burma for the proposed mission.

No evidence has ever been presented to show that General Stilwell or General Merrill gave any serious thought to the consequences of their decisions to command troops in the field when neither of them were in proper physical condition to carry out their responsibilities. Many of us assumed that General Stilwell was seeking to obtain the "crown jewel" of his military career. By modern-day standards he would have been setting himself up for court-martial. The numerous poor command decisions and overall operations from General Stilwell's forward headquarters and the Northern Area Command were to cause many serious problems. The lack of a commander who could operate with his troops in the field would result in a prolonged operation with many tragic consequences. Much unnecessary misery and excessive illness would plague the troops, and many would be unnecessarily killed and wounded.

During the march of the three forces over the Kumon Mountains and the battles of Ritpong and Tingkrukawng, radio communication was poor. General Merrill flew once over the Ritpong battlefield. He landed once at Arang and saw Colonel Hunter.

At no time during this epic and all-important march did any of his or General Stilwell's staff fly in. I know of no records that would indicate that they were worried about the condition of the men.

In spite of weather conditions, the Myitkyina task force arranged for and worked with the troop carrier group for the delivery of supplies. The system worked very well for Hunter Force. K Force and M Force were each dealt a serious blow when the system failed to supply food for the men and animals when they were out of food and forty-eight hours from the airfield. The men and animals had not eaten for more than forty-eight hours when they arrived at Myitkyina. On arrival they learned that General Merrill's promise to have food and ammunition delivered as soon as planes could land had not been kept. Food and ammunition did not come in until 20 May. When the food finally arrived, it was learned that the Marauders' food and equipment had been combined with the Chinese supply system.

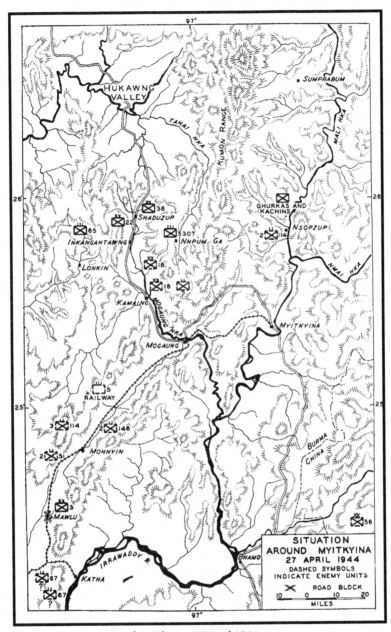

MAP 21. Situation around Myitkyina, 27 April 1944.

CHAPTER XV
K FORCE CROSSES THE PASS
28 APRIL–6 MAY 1944

Monsoon and Mountains

When I returned to the Third Battalion late in the day on 28 April, I learned that it was to pull out in the morning for the Myitkyina airfield. The assistant Third Battalion medical officer Lt. Paul Armstrong and the enlisted members of the medical detachment were organized, equipped, and ready to depart in the morning. The men had learned that we were to attempt to cross the Kumon Range on the Chinglazptu Trail. This was the route that led from nearby Taikri over numerous smaller mountains and then over the Naura Hkyat Pass at sixty-one hundred feet. On the eastern side of the pass it would be necessary to hike approximately thirty miles before rolling jungle and brush-covered land would be reached. Our final objective would then be about forty miles through brush-covered flat terrain. This was the northern route that Colonel Hunter had gathered information about when he heard the rumor that General Stilwell was thinking of sending the Marauders on the mission he called "End Run." Father Stewart had questioned Kachins about the possibility of men and animals passing over the trail. They had said, "Men, yes—but horses and mules, no." Native ponies had never been over the trail. Further information was obtained from Captain Quinn, Det. 101, who had a small group of Kachins in a safe area near the passage to Myitkyina. The word was out that Captain Laffin (who had lived in Burma before the war) and Lt. Paul A. Dunlap, both from task force headquarters, were already on the trail. With them went thirty Kachins and thirty coolies who would attempt to improve the trail.

The several doctors who had been flown into Hsamshingyang after the Battle of Nhpum Ga was over had done their best to help treat and evaluate the men of the three battalions. Approximately sixteen hundred Marauders were left in the regiment for the quickly planned campaign. The First and Third Battalions each mustered about 550, and the Second Battalion about 500 men. Many medical problems still troubled the survivors. Weight loss varied from ten to fifty or more pounds. Incipient problems were present—from chronic diarrhea, which later proved to be mostly amoebic in origin, to skin diseases, foot problems, back aches, stomach and abdominal pain, anorexia, nausea and vomiting, and general malaise. Constant fatigue was a common complaint. Most of the men were troubled by severe morning stiffness, and many had aching joints, muscles, and bones. Malaria was well controlled by atabrine, but brief periods of chills and fever and weakness were frequently seen—some of which were probably caused by dengue fever. It should be mentioned that the medical detachments had no means for doing laboratory studies to diagnose diseases such as malaria or amoebic dysentery.

General Merrill's promise that the Marauders were to be flown out of Burma as soon as the airfield was captured was now common knowledge. This promise from a general who had their confidence and trust went a long way in boosting their resolve to accomplish the impossible. Little did they realize how difficult this last mission would be. The so-called trail, running up and down steep grades, would be far more difficult to move over than any we had encountered before. No one suggested that we would face lack of food, water, and rest as well. The sick would have to struggle on for forty or more miles, since there was no area where planes could land. We hoped that men could be evacuated from a small, rough airstrip that, we were told, was located about fifty miles north of the Myitkyina airfield. Walking had been difficult for the past ten days because we had rain each day. Since few of us had any knowledge of the devastation brought about by the monsoon season, the daily rain did not alarm us. After all, we had had eighteen days of rain in February, ten in March, and almost daily rain in April.

While I was meeting with Colonel Hunter at Naubum, several men from the medical detachment had located the Chinese 88th Regiment and talked to Americans assigned to the unit that belonged to the 30th Chinese Division. They learned that these troops had been flown from China to the American training base for Chinese at

Ramgarh, India. They had arrived at wide intervals beginning in July 1943. They had arrived at Shingbwiyang on 1 March 1944. By 24 March their forward elements were at Pabum, about fifty miles north of Hsamshingyang. This was the group that Colonel Hunter had been hoping would arrive at Hsamshingyang to help defeat the Japanese at the Battle of Nhpum Ga. Captain George of the Third Battalion had been dispatched north to request their help, but his mission had been unsuccessful. The medics were surprised to learn that a newly formed surgical portable hospital was attached to the regiment as a part of K Force. The 42nd Portable Surgical Hospital's table of organization called for four doctors and about thirty enlisted men. Equipment was carried by horses and mules. We later learned that the 42nd, 43rd, and 46th Portable Surgical Hospitals worked with the 22nd Chinese Division. I had no opportunity to meet any of this group until the K Force reached Ritpong. The knowledge that, for the first time, a unit was available to do limited emergency surgery near the front line was a big booster of morale.

The men of the Third Battalion had spent a miserable night in the rain and awoke on the day of departure, 28 April, for passage over the mountains to the east. The weather was fairly clear, and some progress was made in drying themselves, their equipment, and the animals. By noon all patrols had been called in, packs arranged for men and animals, and units consolidated. Khaki Combat Team was to lead the battalion. Each combat team had its I & R platoon out front. The medical detachments—with one officer, three or four men, and two pack animals—marched near the center of each combat team. Each platoon had, as usual, been supplied with an aid man for evaluation and treatment of the sick and wounded. Our pack-75 artillery guns, which had served so well at Nhpum Ga after being dropped by parachute, were following at the rear of the column of marching men, carried by the ten best mules that could be found.

The column of marching men was not as impressive as it had been when we entered Burma and General Stilwell was reported to have said, "They are a tough-looking bunch of men." The men had been reduced to half of the original number and the animals to two thirds. The men's ruddy complexions and muscular appearance had vanished. Their skin was yellow and sallow from the chronic use of atabrine and the lack of sunlight. The dirty fatigue jackets and pants hung on their bodies due to chronic loss of weight, which could be estimated at from twenty to fifty or more pounds per man.

Each man carried twelve boxes of K-ration (enough for four days). The infantrymen were burdened with extra ammunition and grenades, as well as two canteens to be filled with water at every opportunity. Some of the heavy weapons group were carrying mortar shells, and machine-gun crews carried extra ammunition. The radio men were carrying extra batteries and tubes and guarding their cipher machines. The stronger animals were carrying heavier loads. Each animal also carried thirty or forty pounds of grain—enough to last three days. Many men were carrying shovels and other digging tools. Every man in the battalion had a weapon, which he had kept in top-notch shape by loving care.

The monsoon had arrived, and the Marauders and Chinese would pay a severe price in pain, fatigue, sickness, wounds, and death as they as they moved over mountains, across rivers, and through jungle to reach the Myitkyina airfield. The men of the Third Battalion, with the experience of the Solomon Islands and New Guinea campaigns, knew their duty to the army, their unit, and their comrades. Their thinking was that the job would be done as assigned. There was absolutely no indication that any of the men thought they would gain anything but victory. They knew they were being called upon to accomplish a mission their British allies considered impossible. They were not aware that the mission had not been authorized by the Joint Chiefs of Staff until it had begun. Most guessed that General Stilwell had planned it at the last moment with the full knowledge that use of the troops at this time would take the lives of many Americans and Chinese needlessly. Subsequent events would show that the price paid by the men was not worth the effort.

The men's pride and loyalty would guarantee a smooth operation. Their morale was, however, strengthened by General Merrill's promise that, should we succeed in capturing the airfield, Galahad personnel would be relieved and flown to an already selected site where a rest and recreational area would be constructed. General Merrill even told Colonel Hunter that money had been put aside for this purpose. None thought that General Merrill would fail to keep his promise.

K FORCE CROSSES THE PASS

The day was late, the air was hot and humid, and the trail was narrow, rough, and up and down steep hills as we climbed about a thousand feet to bivouac along the narrow, steep trail about two miles east of the small village of Taikri. Rain was intermittent during the night and guaranteed a slippery trail in the morning.

On the morning of 29 April the difficult climb began almost immediately. The column moved with many stops and starts. Word would be occasionally passed back that an animal had been lost or steps had to be cut to proceed. At times we could hear the noise of brush or bamboo being cut by machetes. Loud cursing was frequent. The many delays were very helpful to our lungs and legs, but enough is enough. We all wanted to get this misery out of the way. The nightmare was to continue on 30 April and 1 May when, late in the evening, the last of the Third Battalion reached the Naura Hkyat Pass at sixty-one hundred feet. In three days we had climbed several mountains of three or four thousand feet before the climb to Naura Hkyat Pass. The entire route was through virgin jungle on a trail that had been rarely traveled by natives on foot and never by pack animals. Khaki Combat Team lost fifteen or more animals, and Orange lost eight. They simply slipped and fell a few or hundreds of feet below. Many could not be recovered. Much valuable equipment was lost. Numerous men had sprains, bruises, and lacerations. Due to complete exhaustion, many fell by the trail and had to follow as best they could. By some miracle, no lives were lost. Fever, pain, exhaustion, gastrointestinal complaints, and emotional distress were kept as personal problems or, in some cases, treated by medication as we marched. We ate our cold K-rations braced on the mountainside. The men slept, in many cases, in an almost upright position. As usual the men were constantly reminded to take their one atabrine tablet daily and use a halazone tablet in each canteen of water. We were muddy, wet, and sweating during the entire mountain passage. As we approached the Naura Hkyat Pass, towering peaks could be seen on either side. The vegetation began to change near the top. The trees were not as tall, and many had moss-covered limbs. The air was humid but much colder. We now had adequate clear, cold, uncontaminated mountain water. A steady stream flowed through the pass from higher peaks. During our ascent, water had been very limited. The water points before this had been few and far between and required that the men descend a hundred feet or so down the side of the mountain to reach them. Men and animals were dehydrated. Sitting, standing, or crouching beside the trail we had time to make small fires out of bamboo to warm up the last of our rations. Mule meat was cooked and available to all who had strong teeth and plenty of time to chew.

Lt. Logan Weston's I & R platoon from Orange had started to climb the mountain a day before the battalion. He discusses some aspects of the march over the Kumon Mountains in his book *The Fightin' Preacher*:

Once again we marched about twenty-four hours ahead of our battalion. This particular march was quite terrifying in places. In one area we climbed from thirteen hundred feet to over six thousand feet in about a half-mile of map distance.

The monsoons were upon us, and we were attempting to do the impossible. The enemy didn't think that we could get across the mountain range, but we were determined to maintain the element of surprise. With our entrenching tools we dug steps into the mountainside so even the sure-footed mules could get enough footing to negotiate the steep, slippery slopes. There were occasions when the hills were so steep that we had to unload the mules, manhandle the heavy loads to the next mountain terrace, coax the mules across, then reload the animals and proceed onward.

On one occasion a mule balked and simply refused to go another step. Two soldiers pulled on the reins, while two more pushed from the rear in an attempt to get the stubborn mule moving again. Suddenly, one of the men in the rear yelled and leaped about six feet straight up, changing direction in mid-air. A split second later the other soldier followed suit. It seems the men were pushing the mule with their shoulders while bracing their feet on some fallen trees that crossed the trail when one of the trees began to crawl. At that moment they realized they were flirting with death by antagonizing a twenty-five-foot python. They shot upwards as if they were being followed by General Tanaka himself and stood there panting breathlessly. Not wanting to chance giving away our position, I ordered them not to shoot the huge beast, and we watched it slither silently into the jungle.

Our battalion lost twenty-three mules over cliffs on that climb. Our best radio equipment, guns, medical supplies, emergency food, and ammunition also tumbled over the edges. We could do nothing but grasp a bamboo pole or jungle vine, look out over the precipice, and watch our valuable possessions as they crashed on the jagged rocks hundreds of feet below.

At one of the escarpments, I called for a rest break while steps were being cut into the last steep slopes so our mules could get a footing. Torrents of monsoon rains continued to complicate our progress. The platoon, exhausted and out of breath, sank to the ground. I decided to check out the next steep incline we would face. To our left there was a sheer cliff. Jungle undergrowth spilled over the edge. Vision ahead was limited, but it seemed we were on a relatively level plateau. I moved into the brush a few steps when suddenly there was no ground beneath me. I threw my hands up and tried desperately to grab a vine as I crashed through the foliage, which had concealed the drop-off. A weathered old snag halted my descent. I lay there on my back hugging the vines, uncertain in my confusion whether the slightest movement would send me plunging downward to join lost mules on the jagged rocks nearly half a mile below. Some of the men in the platoon, hearing the commotion, suspended a rope and pulled me up to safety.

Progress was slow. On one occasion, we found ourselves expending all our energy on vertical slopes, using whatever tropical vegetation we could find to pull ourselves up the embankments. More than once I lay on my back, pushed my battle pack over my head, and with my heels digging into the slimy, spongy soil, I wormed my way up the steepest slopes. The extra exertion made up for the decrease in temperature in the higher altitudes."

Mist clung to every vine and leaf, giving a hazy unreality to our surroundings. In addition, the intolerable elephant leeches would attach themselves to any part of our bodies as we passed their leafy hiding places. A native guide even crafted a pair of tweezers from bamboo to help dislodge a leech from inside the nose of our lead scout.

When we reached the pass we had to bivouac for the night. The flat area of trail was very narrow and would not allow the men and animals to spread out. As during many nights before, the men and animals of K Force bivouacked as they marched in a narrow column extending several miles. All spent a cold, wet night, with little room for movement of the men or animals. Our extreme fatigue made everything unimportant except sleep (Weston 1992).

CHAPTER XV

Sgt. Bernard Martin, from Orange's radio section, has this to say about the passage over the Kumon Mountain Range:

> I remember the worst experience of my life, and that was that climb. I think it was one of the saddest experiences. I never experienced anything like that before, and neither had any of the men—the grueling climb that we made and the way the animals suffered. Some of them had to be shot, and I remember the way they fell down and had to be unloaded and manhandled up the path. Sometimes the path wasn't even wide enough for a mule to get by, and we had to chop the side of the mountain so we could get by. We would unload the mules to get them by, and then— after they had been manhandled—the load had to be lugged up the mountain and the mule reloaded. To me that was a trail of sadness all the way through. It took us all day and half of the next day (Martin, videotape).

At daybreak on 2 May, the 550 men of the Third Battalion, followed by the twenty-five hundred Chinese of the 88th Regiment, began the five-mile march to Salawng Hkayang. The neglected trail took us up and down over several smaller mountains. Rain came and went, and the air was hot and humid. The steep climbs and descents were especially hard on the animals and men who had heavy loads. During the early evening, the elements of the column gradually arrived at Salawng Hkayang. Several grass-and-bamboo shacks resting at four-foot elevations on posts were centered on several acres of grass-covered land. The open area was on a steep hillside. This so-called village was deserted.

The medical section bivouacked on the grass near the center of the area. Few of the Marauders presented themselves for medical treatment. Most of the men were out of food and very tired. Units set up security, and with the rapid onset of darkness all lay on the ground for rest and sleep. Colonel Kinnison and some of his staff took over the native huts, as did the radio section. Communication by radio was established, and a drop of food, ammunition, and replacements for other vital supplies lost during the climb was set up for 4 May. A radio message was passed to me explaining that several men who had been evacuated from Hsamshingyang were found to be sick with a form of typhus fever. No other information was given. Little did we realize that this disease was to cause much misery and many deaths among our men. At no time had the medical officers been informed that the condition, scrub typhus, had made its appearance as early as November 1943 among Americans and Chinese in the Hukawng Valley. The serious nature of the disease was well known to the army physicians in the rear areas. It seems incomprehensible that medical officers in command positions would fail to pass this information on to the Marauders as they entered the Hukawng Valley. We were soon to suffer from the consequences of this tragic mistake of our superior officers.

I awoke at daybreak to a fresh, clear morning. As usual, I had slept fully clothed, with my pants legs tucked tightly into the tops of my canvas jungle boots. One had to make every effort to prevent mosquito, bug, and snake bites, as well as the attachment of leeches. As I was readjusting my pants and boots I was alarmed to find a flea on my leg under the pants. My thoughts immediately turned to the information about the men who had been found to have typhus. Could the condition be Tsutsugmachi Fever, a condition not due to a bacteria or virus but a microscopic organism called rickettsia? Could fleas or rodents play a part in its transmission? While we were waiting for the airdrop I wandered about the area. Much to my amazement I found a raspberry patch. These prickly shrubs were loaded with ripe berries. They were delicious, and some of the men joined me in this improvised breakfast.

Our rear-echelon supply section and the C-47's of the troop carrier command did not fail us. In the early morning the sound of the planes could be heard, and the open area was cleared for the drop of vital supplies. The varicolored parachutes floated down, and the loads were picked up, distributed, and packed as soon as possible.

The Marauder Third Battalion moved out quickly to allow planes to supply the 88th Chinese Regiment. The trail was now better, and the I & R platoon had located a rather flat brush-covered area with good water supply about two miles beyond the drop area. Colonel Kinnison decided to bivouac here. The next village was Ritpong, located about eight miles to the southeast in rough, hilly, jungle-covered territory. Information gathered from Kachin scouts and Captain Laffin's party suggested that a company or more of Japanese had occupied the village. In order to be properly prepared for destruction of the enemy,

Colonel Kinnison decided to allow the Chinese to catch up to the Marauders. As darkness approached there was some mingling of the Marauders and the Chinese. The next morning, 5 May, the Marauders reported considerable equipment missing. Packs, shoes, knives, and even some weapons and ammunition had disappeared. This strange turn of events was taken up with the Chinese regimental commander. Under threat of severe punishment, many of the items were located in the Chinese area. Instead of returning them to the owners, the Chinese ordered all items destroyed. It seems that this was their method of saving face.

While in this area I was able to meet members of the 42d Portable Surgical Unit, which had been marching at the rear of the Chinese regiment. I learned that this type of mobile surgical unit, which the army had recently set up and standardized, called for four medical officers and thirty-three men. This unit—along with the 43rd and 46th—had arrived and been assigned to the Chinese 22nd Division early in the year. The unit's equipment was carried on about twenty mules. The 42nd had recently been assigned to the green troops of the 88th Regiment. These mobile surgical units were exactly what the officers of the Marauder medical detachments had been asking for. We had been given no clue that such units were available and had been assigned to the Chinese when we entered the combat zone in Burma. The personnel were expected to work under fire if necessary, though every effort was made to keep them in a defensive perimeter. They were to provide the prompt and definitive surgery that the battalion aid stations were unable to offer. They were expected to carry out all procedures their training would allow. Unfortunately, they were not prepared to do major brain, vascular, thoracic, or complicated abdominal surgery. The chief function of the unit was to do debridement of flesh wounds, amputations, and treatment of fractures. Shock was prevented and treated when present with plasma and intravenous fluids. Blood transfusions were not available.

On the march again, we found the trail wider but its twisting, turning, up-and-down character did not change. Khaki's I & R reached a trail junction one mile north of Ritpong late in the afternoon of 5 May. Colonel Kinnison decided to send Khaki through the jungle to the northeast to block the trail leading into Ritpong from the southeast.

He planned for Orange to remain in place for mortar support and reserve. The Chinese were to send two companies of infantry with mortars to attack the enemy at Ritpong from the front.

Khaki pulled into the jungle on the north to bivouac for the night. No trail was found, but by slashing and cutting the jungle growth they—and Orange, which followed—were able to prepare a bivouac area for the night. The long column of Chinese bringing up the rear fell out along the narrow trail for several hundred yards. It rained during the night, and, as usual, the hot and humid air enveloped all.

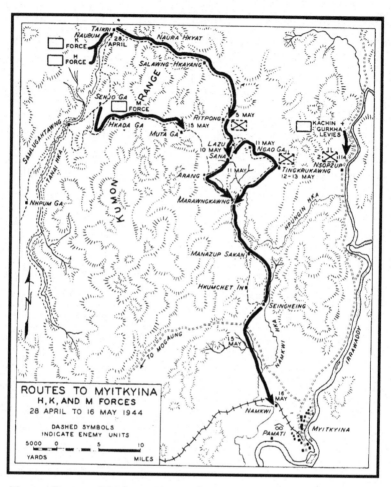

MAP 22. Routes to Myitkyina: H, K, and M Forces, 28 April–16 May 1944.

CHAPTER XVI
THE BATTLE OF RITPONG
6–9 MAY 1944

Lt. Logan Weston's I & R platoon left the bivouac area at dawn on 6 May to force its way through the dense jungle with the mission of blocking the Japanese escape route from Ritpong. They first followed a streambed, well to one side of Ritpong, for about two miles. They then struggled through the jungle growth another two miles and finally reached the trail. Their block was soon successful in that they ambushed a group of Japanese on their way to Ritpong with supplies of food and ammunition. They moved further south toward Sana and held a block until the battle to their north was well under way.

Early on the morning of 6 May, Khaki Combat Team began forcing its way through the jungle at a point approximately one mile northeast of Ritpong. The plan called for them to make a wide arc through the jungle with the objective of blocking the trail from the south in order to cut the Japanese supply and escape route. The combat team was preceded by a strong combat patrol, which was able to move through the jungle more readily since they had no heavy equipment or animals. They had to block the trail just south of the enemy and hold it until Khaki's infantrymen could arrive and set up a strong defensive block. Passage was extremely difficult because of the mountainous terrain, the dense jungle, and the humid, hot weather. A few pack animals bringing up the rear were greatly delayed because of the need to cut vegetation in such a way that they could get through with their loads of equipment. Persistence paid off, and they were able to get the much-needed 60mm and 81mm mortars and their ammunition to Khaki's location.

Mortars were used on the 7th and 8th to pound the enemy. Khaki was also able to direct mortar fire thrown in by Orange Combat Team. The mortar crews did a great job in coordinating their mortar fire with that of the Chinese. Khaki had some close calls from some of the Chinese mortar fire, which was well off target.

In spite of rain, low clouds, and the thick jungle, Major Briggs was able to call in a flight of fighter bombers, which opened up the battle early on the 7th by strafing the village. The appearance of the planes and their aggressive action was a big booster to the morale of the men.

Approximately two companies of Chinese infantry were gradually assembled at the area of departure on the trail one mile north of the village. During the afternoon of the 6th and the morning of the 7th they worked their way along the narrow trail and the surrounding jungle. The trail was very steep, and the altitude increased about five hundred feet over the last three hundred yards to the village's defensive perimeter.

Orange Combat Team's medical detachment was set up about four hundred yards north of the village. Orange Combat Team was dispersed in the jungle well off the trail. My plan was to have the 42nd Surgical Portable Unit set up about one hundred yards north of the medical detachment's location.

When on 7 May the 42nd was notified that they would soon be needed at the front, they were able to send medical personnel to assist Captain Zombro and myself with the care of the increasing number of Chinese wounded. Dawn came on the 8th before enough equipment could be hand-carried to the front, where it was quickly set up so the surgeons could begin their work.

When Khaki's combat patrol reached and blocked the trail on the 6th they made no effort to engage the enemy. Colonel Kinnison had ordered them to dig in and block the trail. The Japanese became aware of their presence during the early afternoon and did some random machine-gun and rifle firing. One of the youngest men in the unit, Pvt. Charles R. Page, waited alertly in a foxhole in a well-protected area. At 2230 hours a stray Japanese bullet entered his right posterior chest between the fourth and fifth ribs and lodged in his body. A sucking, open wound was produced in his chest. He was seen after a few minutes by the combat team surgeon, Captain Paul Armstrong. The sound was sealed by a tight dressing, and he was given blood plasma and sulfadiazine. The 42nd Portable Surgical Unit was at this time far in the rear. Their equipment, carried as it was on twenty-five horses, was very difficult to manage. They had been constantly in back of the Chinese due to the need to load, unload, and physically manhandle their equipment because of steep grades and a narrow trail. For most of the trip the equipment was wet because they had no waterproof coverings. As no crates or boxes had been made available to them, their supplies were wrapped in bundles covered by parachute cloth.

As had been done in past battles, Captain Armstrong had no option but to keep Private Page under his care while he and the several medics stayed at their post with the Khaki Combat Team. Lying there in the jungle he received tender loving care from his comrades, but unfortunately his condition gradually deteriorated, and he died after four days—on the last day of the action. He was buried at Ritpong while a simple prayer was said.

Anthony C. Colombo, working in his job as Colonel Beach's runner, knew and liked Page. Colombo was also one of the younger men in the unit. While his story of the Burma campaign was being taped by Dave Quaid fifty years later, he gave a very touching impression of Page's unfortunate situation and death. His remarks could apply to the way many of the men felt and acted at such times:

> We got word that Page had been hurt. I went up with Dr. Armstrong, and we set up a makeshift operation. I was no medic but was just helping. He was talking and was coherent, and then he started to fade away. We knew that he was going to die. I was 19 years old and he was 18, and from what I understand it was his birthday. I just sat and held his hand as he lay there (Colombo, videotape).

Late on the morning of 7 May the men of Khaki heard the sound of bugles as the two Chinese infantry companies began their frontal attack on Ritpong. This green troops had never been in combat before, but they pushed forward with remarkable courage during 7 and 8 May. Wounded soon began to filter back to the aid station, and about fifty were seen on the first afternoon. After dressings had been applied, bleeding stopped, plasma given as necessary, and sulfa drugs swallowed, the wounded were placed to rest on the jungle floor. A level area had been picked near a sharp rise in the trail about three hundred yards north of the advancing Chinese. My aid station was close by, but in my capacity as K Force surgeon I was to spend most of my time helping the surgical portable hospital and encouraging the Chinese to bring their wounded back for treatment.

When the portable surgical unit's equipment arrived on the 8th, the doctors and technicians quickly set to work. Serious surgery began under a bamboo lean-to. When the battle was over on the morning of 9 May, sixty litter cases and about forty walking wounded were ready for evacuation. A Chinese liaison officer estimated that approximately thirty men from the two companies had been killed. They were quickly buried in the jungle.

The Japanese had machine guns and knee mortars with plenty of ammunition. Fighting continued all day on the 7th and 8th. The Chinese fired intermittently all night long. When I was not busy helping with the care of the wounded I was appealing to the Chinese, through their English-speaking officer, to bring their wounded back for treatment. Strangely enough, we saw few living with chest, head, and abdominal wounds. Most of the wounded seemed to make their own way back to the medics. I remember thinking that the mortally wounded were being left in the jungle after their medics and litter bearers had decided they had no chance of survival. At any rate, few were seen at the portable surgical unit.

The two platoons of Khaki's I Company and its I & R poured heavy machine-gun, rifle, and mortar fire into the Japanese positions on both the 7th and 8th. Because of the Chinese machine-gun, rifle, and mortar fire the Marauders were ordered by Colonel Kinnison not to press their attack at close range. They were indeed in grave danger from the fire of the Chinese.

The Marauders' 1st and 2nd platoons of I Company each lost one man to wounds, while Khaki I & R had two wounded. S.Sgt. Frederick R. Chesbro was bringing up several men to support the light machine gun his platoon leader had set up on the 7th. He knew that Japanese snipers had been shooting into the general area for fifteen minutes. Just to the right of the trail, where the cover was poor, he turned to give a command. At this moment he was struck by a sniper's bullet. He was hit in a very bad area, the middle third of the neck on the right. The bullet traversed the soft tissues of the neck but did not injure any major blood vessels, nerves, esophagus, or trachea. This injury would ordinarily have been fatal. After simple dressings and sulfadiazine he did well and was able to walk about fifteen miles three days later for evacuation at Arang. Pfc. Richard Swanson, two hours later, was advancing in a crouched position when he was hit by a sniper's bullet. He was carried back to Captain Armstrong, who treated a wound of entry that had fractured his left tenth rib and a wound of exit that had fractured the eleventh. Severe hemorrhage was checked by pressure dressings. Captain Armstrong then gave blood plasma, which stabilized his condition. On the 9th he was carried to Arang with the other American and Chinese wounded.

During the 8th and 9th the Japanese made several attempts to break through Khaki's block, but all were turned back with heavy enemy losses. After one Khaki patrol advanced toward Ritpong and dispersed a group of Japanese due to a premature shot, no further offensive actions were attempted. Colonel Kinnison was satisfied with the job the Chinese companies were doing and decided to give them the job of annihilating the enemy. Khaki remained in place until the battle was over on the 9th.

The I & R platoon was ordered to set up a trailblock at Lazu, about two miles south of Ritpong. Near their objective they ambushed a small column of Japanese infantrymen who were supplied with one heavy machine gun and two light machine guns. Because of the suddenness of the encounter and the terrain, only one squad of the I & R could be used. They had no mortar support. The fight lasted about twenty minutes before the enemy withdrew.

Shortly after the I & R action began, Pfc. George E. Courtwright was wounded by a bullet from a Japanese heavy machine gun. The bullet passed through his left thigh. With the help of others he was able to walk one and one-half miles back to Captain Armstrong's location. He was treated with blood plasma and sulfa drugs and then remained with the medical detachment until time for evacuation.

During the fire fight, S.Sgt. Herman W. Kussro was wounded when hit by mortar fragments. This caused a fractured foot and numerous flesh wounds of his legs, chest, and abdomen. His condition was good after the long litter carry, and after treatment he continued to do well while awaiting evacuation.

The village was finally entered on 9 May. The Chinese had borne the brunt of the fighting. All agreed that these green troops had done a great job. They had bravely faced a well-armed and fortified enemy. They had pushed their attack to completion in spite of heavy casualties and a very tenacious group of veteran Japanese. I would estimate that in this one battle about one-third of the two companies of Chinese became casualties.

The Marauders had done more than had been asked of them. Their mortars had been very helpful, bottling up the Japanese so that they could not outmaneuver the Chinese or escape from their assault.

An enemy prisoner captured in the Ritpong area stated that the 6th Company had ninety killed and that only forty had escaped. It later developed that thirty-six of these forty were killed by our patrols. This man explained that he had originally been in the medics before being transferred to the infantry. His testimony further suggested that poor food, understrength units, and continued harassment by Kachins combined to make the troops very discouraged. His company got a new commanding officer in January who was a mean man and further discouraged them. Not long before, American planes had caught an entire truck convoy on its way to the northern base of Nsopzup. Only three trucks were left for supply, and gasoline was hard to get. The Nsopzup road was in bad condition because of heavy rain and poor maintenance. All Japanese troops had been recently warned that anyone caught listening to American broadcasts would be shot. They were told that the reason they did not see Japanese planes was because they were being held at Rangoon for a big offensive.

Colonel Kinnison's plan for removal of the wounded was worked out with the Chinese commander. One battalion from the Chinese 88th Regiment was to litter-carry the stretcher cases and help the walking wounded to Arang, an OSS-controlled area about fifteen miles to the south. From this area an attempt would be made to evacuate them by small liaison planes. Litters were constructed from bamboo poles and ground sheets, each to be carried by two Chinese. Of the one hundred wounded, forty-seven were litter cases.

Assigned soldiers carried fourteen rifles per man and eight packs per man. One officer from the 42nd accompanied them and supervised the operation. The long column of sick and wounded left Ritpong after H Force was on the way to Arang. It is not difficult to imagine the thoughts of the men as they were carried or walked toward Arang. Here they had hope of removal from the horror of battle and the fatigue, heat, humidity, wild animals, insects, rain, inadequate food, and other problems faced by an infantry soldier in a tropical environment. Those who believed they would survive their wounds or illness would think this the most memorable day in their lives.

Colonel Hunter's H Force had been stranded at the rear of the 88th Regiment for about two days waiting for the Battle of Ritpong to be over. On 10 May they had their chance to bypass K Force while the last of the enemy was being sought out and destroyed by patrols from Khaki. The trail previously developed by Khaki provided a means for H Force to bypass the battle area. They arrived at Arang on the 10th and 11th.

Before evacuation of the sick and wounded could begin, a suitable airstrip had to be constructed at Arang. Colonel Hunter's H Force had arrived shortly before the casualties from the Ritpong Battle. They quickly cleared a brush-covered area for a very rough landing strip. A downdraft combined with a rough field made landings and takeoffs hazardous for the small planes, which were called in on an emergency basis. One plane hit the trees just after takeoff. The pilot and passenger were not badly hurt and were put in another plane, which also cracked up. He became airborne on the third attempt.

As soon as the airstrip was ready, L-1's and L-5's began to arrive, and the hundred or so sick and wounded from K Force were flown out to Maingkwan. C-47's then took them to the 20th General Hospital at Margherita, near Ledo. Some would arrive in a few hours; others would take a day or more to get definitive hospital care.

The service of the 42nd Portable Surgical Hospital had been outstanding at Ritpong. They had saved lives and prepared those who could be expected to live for satisfactory later treatment and recovery. Without the wonderful professional help they were given at the front line, some wounded and sick would not have survived, and the late surgical treatment of others would have been far less satisfactory. They had indeed showed how combat casualties should be treated. My thoughts strongly censored those in higher command who could have provided the Marauders with equal support during the battles of our first and second missions. I thought of the men who had died unnecessarily and those who had suffered because of lack of care and delay of care. These units should not only be able to prevent and treat shock, do wound debridement and amputations, and treat fractures and uncomplicated abdominal procedures, but should be able to accomplish more advanced surgery. Chest procedures, brain surgery, and vascular surgery should be possible. Blood should always be made available and used as necessary.

I spent as much time as possible with the 42nd and observed most of the wounded. Our Chinese interpreter estimated that during the three-day battle they had lost between twenty-five and thirty dead. It has never been possible to obtain more information. Approximately 150 wounded were treated by the 42nd Portable Surgical Unit, located about four hundred yards north of the village. Local anesthesia was used in all cases but was supplemented by sodium pentothal for the two laparotomies.

Mortar and grenade accounted for at least eighty percent of the casualties, and machine-gun and rifle fire for the rest. A conservative estimate was that one-half of the casualties were due to their own mortar fire.

No skull fractures or brain wounds were treated. One soldier had a severe mortar wound of the right neck, with entrance on the middle-third lateral surface, which traversed the neck tissues and passed transversely through the distal third of the tongue. He died in seventy-two hours without surgery. The entire end of his tongue became necrotic before death, and he died with uremia the most prominent feature.

No sucking wounds of the chest were seen, and very few penetrating ones. One came with a wound six centimeters in diameter over the right scapula and no evidence of chest penetration. He died after wound debridement.

Three abdominals died of hemorrhage and shock a few minutes after arrival. Two abdominal cases had penetrating wounds, but no perforations were found. A sixth case survived a severe peritonitis on sulfadiazine and a liquid diet without operation. He presented with a foul wound of the left lower quadrant, with leakage from the descending colon.

No lower-extremity amputations and only one arm and one hand amputation were done. About fifteen compound fractures were treated.

After the battle was over, the wounded removed, and the dead buried, it occurred to me that this had been the first time in history that American and Chinese soldiers had been fighting side by side against a common enemy.

The delay in getting the 42nd into operation at Ritpong caused them to work out a new plan of movement. The essential equipment was pared down to an amount that could be packed on four animals. Four of the unit's men and the animals would march with the Third Battalion medical detachment. The rest of the surgical unit would march at the rear of the battalion. The secondary and reserve baggage would follow the Chinese. The men marching with Orange Column would go into action as soon as a battle began. By the time the main unit arrived, all would be ready for care of the wounded.

Marauders Dead

Charles R. Page, Pvt., Co. I, Khaki

Marauders Wounded

Frederick R. Chesbro, S.Sgt., Co. I, Khaki
Richard S. Swanson, Pfc., Co. I, Khaki
George E. Courtwright, Pfc., Hq. Co., Khaki
Norman W. Kussro, S.Sgt.

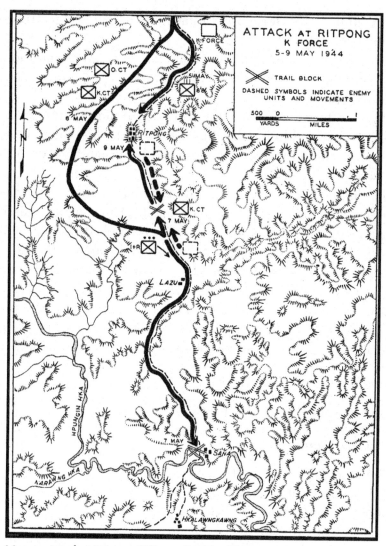

MAP 23. Attack at Ritpong: K Force, 5–9 May 1944.

CHAPTER XVII
H FORCE REACHES NAMKWI
29 APRIL–16 MAY 1944

Colonel Hunter's task force H began its march on a wet 29 April. The monsoon season had begun, with rain for the previous ten days. Showers—and an occasional downpour—could now be expected every day.

The First Battalion was in the lead, followed by the 150th Chinese Regiment. At the end of the long two- or three-mile column the heavily laden, two-gun Chinese pack howitzer unit was followed by the Seagrave portable surgical unit.

1st Lt. Milton A. Dushkin led this Seagrave team of three officers, sixteen enlisted men, an English civilian technician, and three Chinese orderlies. The medical officers included Lieutenants Carl J. Antonellis and Theodore Gurney. This group had been working with the Chinese New First Army for many months. Before the First Battalion departed, the medical officers learned that a few of the men evacuated from Hsamshingyang were found to have scrub typhus after they arrived at the 20th General Hospital. Twenty-five had come from the First Battalion, and two had died. Five of the men sent out by the Second Battalion had the disease, but none had died. Of the four men from the Third Battalion, one had died.

As the task force struggled up, over, and down numerous smaller mountains, they could see the Naura Hkyat Pass looming ahead at sixty-one hundred feet. Air distance from their starting point to the pass was said to be about five miles. Climbing up and down with full packs, the men felt it was more like twenty miles. The route was not only up and down but back and forth around mountain peaks and deep ravines. Each day brought showers and the occasional heavy rain. They had no need to find or cut a trail, as had been necessary with K Force, but mud frequently caused the men and animals to slip and slide. Two steps forward would often be followed by one or two backward. A few mules went over the mountainside to their deaths, valuable equipment going with them.

Sleep was difficult—and often impossible—on the steep grades with the animals close by. If a man could find a safe spot, his fatigue and the dark nights overcame these obstacles. As usual, the lack of bulk and caloric content of the K-rations did not eliminate hunger or the body's need for energy or muscle mass (Hunter 1963, 102–08).

General Stilwell recorded the following in his diary:

> May 1, rain (depression days), commander's worries; I start them off for Myitkyina, it rains. The resistance grows here [in the Mogaung Valley]. Why didn't I use them on our front [again in the Mogaung]? Is the gap too big? Will they meet a reinforced garrison at Myitkyina? Does it mean we will fail on both sides instead of only on one? Can I get them out? Are the Japanese being sucked toward Mogaung or is the new [Japanese] unit staying in Myitkyina? etc,etc. And nothing can be done about it. The die is cast, it's sink or swim. The nervous wear and tear is terrible. Pity the poor commanding officer (Romanus and Sunderland 1956, 131).

It is a shame that General Stilwell didn't make some statement about the condition of the troops he was sending on this poorly planned, ill-defined, and questionable campaign.

The daily struggle of H Force continued. An undetermined number of Chinese and Marauders fell by the wayside, some sick enough to return down the mountain for evacuation and others deciding to struggle on. It took three days for the lead elements of the long column to reach the Naura Hkyat Pass, at sixty-one hundred feet. At this elevation the trees were smaller, the jungle less dense, and the night air colder than the men with their light clothing wished for. The mountain stream with its fast-flowing, clear, and uncontaminated water was much appreciated by the dehydrated men and animals.

The cold night had aggravated the men's usual stiffness, aches, and pains. The sick and exhausted caught up to the column in the late evening, and all looked forward to a downhill march of about eight miles to Salawng Hkayang, the small village at which an airdrop of food and equipment was scheduled. Here the men and animals would have a brief period of rest and the inadequate but necessary K-rations.

The uphill and downhill march proved almost as difficult as that of the previous three days. Downhill pulled the knee caps and thigh muscles, and uphill caused great fatigue. After a full day's march, all units of H Force found room to bivouac on the open mountainside areas of this small village.

The various units of the force settled about the periphery of the village with the Chinese to the west and the Marauders to the east. Colonel Hunter and his staff took over the several small bamboo-and-reed bashas. These one-story structures, as usual, were elevated, with the bamboo-and- reed floor about three feet above the ground.

As frequently occurred in combat, on the trail, and in bivouac, accidents happened. Charlton Ogburn tells about the accident that was the cause of his injury. He was resting in a native basha at Salawng Hkayang, together with Colonel Hunter and several other officers. The stillness of night was suddenly changed by machine-gun, rifle, and mortar fire. The trigger-happy Chinese, who had never been in combat before, had cut loose with everything they had. The Marauders had every reason to think the Japanese were launching an attack against the Chinese sector, but held their fire. With bullets and mortar shells being fired indiscriminately, Ogburn and the others sought ground cover. Unfortunately, Ogburn had dived out of the basha without his shoes. He soon stepped on a K-ration biscuit can, which produced a biscuit-size defect in his heel. This caused him much misery, as he hobbled on a makeshift bamboo crutch for about twenty miles before evacuation at Arang on 13 May.

The Chinese officers soon stopped the unnecessary battle. Some pointed out that the trigger for the action was the sudden chattering of a group of monkeys moving about in the trees. The Chinese commander ordered bayonets only for the rest of the night. If anyone failed to follow his orders, they would be executed at dawn. Needless to say the rest of the night was quiet.

Another sad and unnecessary accident happened the next day in this bivouac area. We had seen this type of accident before, and it always seemed inexcusable. The orderly of the commander of the Chinese 150th Regiment had dashed onto the drop area while bags of grain were being free- dropped. His object had been to pick up several parachutes in order to line the bamboo bed and lean-to he was preparing for his boss. His neck was broken by a falling bag, and he died on the drop area. This death did not seem to cause any significant disturbance among the Chinese troops (Hunter 1963, 95).

While at this bivouac area the Marauders soon learned that their gear had to be carefully guarded day and night. Some of the Chinese seemed to believe that if personal belongings or equipment were not actually on an American they belonged to the first man who was able to take them.

Hunter Force got some well-deserved rest near Ritpong when it was held up by the battle in which K Force was engaged. The delay at Salawng Hkayang and Ritpong gave the medics an opportunity to evaluate the condition of the men. They were shocked to find several scrub typhus cases. Captain William Bright, the First Battalion communication officer, was very ill and had to be carried until he could be evacuated on 13 May. He died soon afterwards at the 20th General Hospital, in Assam. Many had critical weight loss, some with chronic dysentery were passing blood, and others had infected leech bites. Some had skin problems, low-grade fever, recurrent malaria, arthritis, bronchitis, muscle and joint sprains, and stomach and intestinal problems. Later events would show that they were in much better shape than the Marauders in the other two battalions. It should be remembered that they were in better condition when the 5307th Composite Unit had been formed. They had also had much less contact with the enemy and had taken fewer casualties.

Contact with the Chinese medics and the Seagrave portable surgical unit showed that the Chinese were holding up better than the Marauders. It must be remembered that the 150th Regiment had never been in combat and had joined the Hunter Force a few days after arriving in Burma. They had also had medical evaluation and treatment by the hospital of Major Gordon Seagrave (Hunter 1963, 96).

Colonel Hunter was able to bypass the Battle of Ritpong on 10 May and continue on toward Arang. The designated supply and evacuation area at Arang was reached on 11 and 12 May. The men immediately began to improve the rough and inadequate landing strip. Liaison planes had already begun to evacuate the more than one hundred wounded, of whom sixty were litter cases, who had been brought over mountain trail from Ritpong. Two planes had crashed, each without serious injury to pilot or passenger. The pilot of the first plane to crash in the trees got into a second plane to fly it out. He crashed again, and this time—because of minor injuries—was flown out in a third plane.

Approximately one hundred men from Hunter Force (including Chinese and Americans) were flown out with illness and accidental injury. The Seagrave surgical unit was left behind to help with the evacuation of about fifty sick and wounded litter patients and walking casualties who would soon arrive after traveling fifteen miles from K Force's Battle of Tingkrukawng. M Force was not expected to arrive until K Force had cleared the area. The surgical unit was to wait and help them (Hunter 1963, 96).

Arang was one of several isolated areas in the mountains and forests of Burma that the Japanese had not been able to enter. In each area an American officer and one or more noncommissioned men had been flown or parachuted in to organize and work with the primitive Kachins. These natives of isolated North Burma hated the Japanese, who had been very cruel to them. They were friendly to the British and, with aid from missionaries such as Father Stuart, trusted and cooperated with the Americans. Here the OSS (Office of Strategic Services) officer Lt. Bill Martin had their trust and cooperation. He had organized and controlled a group of about a hundred in his small army. They were armed, supplied, and treated well by the OSS. The Japanese had not been able to penetrate their area before or after the arrival of the OSS. Without their help, the Burma campaign would have been far more difficult (Hunter 1963, 100).

Shortly before arrival at Arang, Colonel Hunter had seen a plane flying over Ritpong. He could hear General Merrill talking to Colonel Beach but was unable to break in. When he arrived at Arang he was surprised to see General Merrill sitting on a bank beside a stream. He crossed over to discuss the plan of attack on the airfield and what was to be done after it was in our hands. The two officers agreed on certain important points about the attack on the Myitkyina airfield (Hunter 1963, 98–99):

1. There was to be radio silence except for brief important messages.

2. Forty-eight hours before the expected attack, the message would be "Cafeteria Lunch."

3. Twenty-four hours before the attack, the message would be "Strawberry Sundae."

4. When the attack started, the message would be "In the Ring."

5. When the field was secure and transports able to land, the message would be "Merchant of Venice." This message would automatically eliminate the need for engineers to clear the runway.

6. "Strawberry Sundae" would be used again as the next message. Here it would mean that five days' supply of ammunition and three days' supply of food was to be readied, with aircraft standing by and loaded.

7. At the message "In the Ring," the transports were to take off.

8. If information was sent out that the field needed repair, the engineers would be put in the air and landed by glider.

This information was only given to General Merrill and Sergeant Doyer.

Colonel Hunter next asked General Merrill, "After we take the airfield, what do we do?" The general said, "You don't have to worry. I'll be the first man on the field." The colonel said, "Shall I take Myitkyina? Shall I cross the river? What is the big picture if we are successful?" General Merrill replied, "Don't worry. I'll be there and take over."

Hunter Force left Arang well-supplied with food on 13 May. It was led by the I & R platoon and Lieutenant Martin, with seventy-five of his OSS-trained Kachins. Captain William A. Laffin, the Marauder regimental S-2 or intelligence officer, was with them. Seingheing was about twenty miles, and they reached that location on 14 May.

Kachins had reported that Japanese had recently been in Seingheing. As the village was approached, the Kachins and I & R were very careful and ready for action. Fortunately no Japanese were there. The area was quickly occupied. Time was available before dark for some of the men to bathe in a swift-flowing river. Others rested, worked on their weapons or looked after their animals, and worked out better methods of packing the unit's equipment. The many sick had an opportunity to consult with the doctors of the medical detachment. On 13 and 14 May, thirty men and two officers were certified to be so ill that they could not continue. Most were running high fevers and were thought to have scrub typhus. Liaison planes were called in to take them out, one at a time. Unfortunately, the available open space for a landing strip was very small, and the weather conditions were unfavorable. One plane tried to land but got hung up in a tree. The flights had to be cancelled. During the early part of the Burma campaign, two accidentally injured Marauders had to be left behind to be evacuated by Kachins. Here again the only option was to leave them under the care of the two sick officers. A squad of Kachins was provided to offer extra security. The Myitkyina task force headquarters, still at Naubum, was notified of the need for immediate help and evacuation, The sick men had three days' rations and no radio. Colonel Hunter was counting on immediate help from task force headquarters after Hunter Force had left later on 15 May. No action had been taken on the 18th, and Major Tom Senff, a combat team commander, was forced to act. He had injured his back and leg at the Naura Hkyat Pass on 4 May. His condition had become progressively worse. Now he could only move with the aid of a crutch made of bamboo, since one leg was paralyzed. His disablement was complicated by a persistent sore throat and ruptured throat abscess. No one had helped these desperately ill Marauders by 18 May. Tom decided to hobble to the airstrip at Myitkyina with the aid of Sgt. Frank S. Drolla, whose malaria had improved. Their epic two-day struggle through twenty miles of enemy territory ended at the First Battalion (Hunter 1963).

A message was dropped by liaison plane to the forgotten men. They were advised to return to Arang or go forward to Charpate. They elected to return to Arang—and, after a heroic struggle, with sick carrying sick, they reached Arang and were flown to hospitals. William Patton, a First Battalion medical technician, had been left to help the sick.

Before leaving Seingheing on 15 May, food for men and animals was received by airdrop. Ammunition was also supplied for the Chinese and Americans. The loss of some of the First Battalion's animals and the poor condition of others resulted in a surplus of ammunition. A grave was dug and the ammunition buried. The name "Joe Blow" was placed on the bamboo cross.

The commander of the Chinese pack-75 artillery decided to leave some of the artillery ammunition at Seingheing. He gave the excuse that his animals were in poor condition. This resulted in an animated argument with Colonel Hunter, who explained that artillery was no good without ammunition. The Chinese animals, like the Chinese soldiers, had been in Burma about a month and had not fought one battle. Our men and animals had been there three and one-half months and had fought many battles. Colonel Hunter won the argument.

Colonel Hunter now knew that he was approximately two days' march—or twenty miles—from Namkwi and four more miles to the airfield. If H Force left now during the early afternoon, they could halt for some rest at night and arrive on the Mogaung-Myitkyina Road at daybreak. He knew that the Japanese only used the road at night because the Allies controlled the air. Calculations showed that it would take the long column of men and animals two or three hours to cross the road. His decision was to cross the road at daylight and hope that the column would not be detected. They would then start on the ten-mile brush-and-Kunai-grass covered, flat terrain that led to the Namkwi Hka, south of Namkwi.

The time had come to flash, by radio, the forty-eight-hour notice "Cafeteria Lunch." One can well imagine the excitement this message caused back at Myitkyina task force headquarters. They probably uncorked champagne—or at least took a slug of scotch. On the 14th, Merrill had sent a message from Naubum to General Stilwell saying, "Can stop this show up till noon tomorrow, when the die is cast, if you think it too much of a gamble. Personal opinion is that we have a fair chance and that we should try." On the same day, Stilwell wrote in his diary, "Hunter expected to give us the 48-hour signal tonight. I told Merrill to roll on in and swing on 'em" (Stilwell 1948, 295).

From my memory of the approaching operation, I would say that the men and officers of the Marauders were more optimistic about the success of the approaching conflict than Generals Stilwell and Merrill. I heard no expression of fear or doubt from the men in the Third Battalion. As usual, the Marauders always assumed that they would defeat the enemy.

Hunter Force got under way in the late afternoon and marched until well after midnight with the usual ten-minute breaks every hour. One rest period just before dark was a little longer so they could consume the K-ration supper. The last stop was not on the schedule. They had walked about ten miles and had just crossed a branch of the Namkwi Hka, which should have been near the Mogaung-Myitkyina Road.

After a prolonged wait, the I & R platoon at the head of the column contacted Colonel Hunter by radio to inform him that the Kachin who was leading, by a route unknown to the Japanese, had been bitten by a snake. He was being attended by Captain (Doctor) McLaughlin, who was requesting that he be given permission to use a flashlight. Permission was granted. Minutes dragged on to what seemed like an hour or more. Urgent messages passed back and forth. Because of the darkness no one had seen the snake. They were afraid it had been the dreaded Hamadryad, the King of the Cobras. Captain Laffin and Lieutenant Martin had been sucking out the wound. The message came back that if the guide was moved it would probably kill him. The colonel radioed back that he was sending his horse forward. No matter what the man's condition, he had to continue leading Hunter Force.

The Kachin guide's knowledge of the area, now in spite of the snake bite, continued to be a major factor in the approach to Namkwi. He had formerly been employed as a forest ranger in the Pidaung National, which extended west from the Namkwi Hka. His help was essential in guiding the force undetected to the small village of Namkwi, located on the east side of the river and four miles northwest of the airfield.

The overheard messages were whispered throughout the column, and the men quietly waited for the result of this dramatic development. In spite of pain and the obvious toxic condition, the Kachin was placed on the horse, and the road was quickly located. The force continued to need his help. They had ten miles to go before the small village of Namkwi would be reached.

Colonel Hunter was called forward and given the honor of being the first to cross this two-lane, gravel-covered road. He accepted quickly—then one platoon was sent east and one west for several hundred yards to set up ambushes covering the road. Colonel Hunter had planned to give this duty to two Chinese companies. Just before they were to move into position it was learned that they had thrown away the batteries for their radios.

Colonel Hunter relates that he had time to think and go over many problems during this last night of the march. The First Battalion could not muster more than four hundred men. The Chinese were called a regiment, but they had fewer than 880 rifles. Their artillery battery was untried and very light. Fortunately, the Seagrave portable surgical unit was following in the rear. The job was to reach an assembly point and then cross flat terrain to attack a five-thousand-foot airfield, which had been bombed many times and was surrounded by numerous revetments.

General Merrill, at Arang, had given Hunter an aerial photo of the airfield. This showed many areas where machine guns and mortars, if in place, could wreak havoc on troops advancing over several miles of open terrain.

Neither he nor any of the officers, other than Captain Laffin, had ever been in the area or flown over any location in North Burma. Maps showed the wide and swift-flowing Irrawaddy River bordering Myitkyina on the east. After passing the town it formed a broad U and then turned northwest. After five miles it again turned south. He knew that Namkwi was just south of the railroad on the Namkwi Hka and four miles northwest of the airfield. Charpate was on the Mogaung-Myitkyina Road, two and one-half miles from Namkwi, two miles north of the railroad, five miles northeast of the airfield, two and one-half miles northwest of the river and Manpin. A north-south road ran along the river and branched two miles north of Manpin. The east branch ran three miles to join the road running southeast from Charpate at Radahpur. The map showed Radahpur to be four miles northeast of the airfield, while Manpin was five and one-half miles. I have not mentioned Zygun, situated on an island in the river, two and one-half miles south of Myitkyina.

The Marauders would come to know all of these locations. The Chinese would be confined mostly to the west and south of the town of Myitkyina. The Second and Third Battalions of Marauders would spend most of their time in the northwest sector and would remain there after the capture of the airfield. The Marauder First Battalion would return to the airfield, which they would guard until the battle was over on 3 August 1944.

Colonel Hunter had no idea what the condition of the airfield would be, or how many Japanese would be in any of the towns or on or about the airfield. He knew that Myitkyina had been the main base for the Japanese who were fighting the Chinese on the east side of the river on the Salween front in China. It was also the base for their forces fighting a small British outpost at Fort Hertz, two hundred miles to the north in the extreme northeast tip of Burma. The road along the river passed through Manpin, then through Nsopzup, and continued on up to Fort Hertz. The Battle of Tingkrukawng took place a few miles west of Nsopzup.

Hunter was totally dependent on General Merrill arriving immediately after the airfield was captured. His hands would be tied if food and ammunition did not arrive immediately. Someone had to quickly set up a complete communication system linking all the American and Chinese units with each other and a central headquarters. The town of Myitkyina should be taken before Japanese came in from all directions. His Marauders were loyal, experienced, and ready to do whatever was asked of them. He knew that, when all had arrived at the airstrip and the surrounding towns, they would number fewer than fourteen hundred men. They would have two pack-75 howitzers with limited ammunition.

He knew there was hardly a Marauder who was not ill with one or more conditions that, in other theaters of World War II, would require they be sent out of combat for hospital evaluation and treatment. Generals Stilwell and Merrill never seemed to understand, even after the battle for the airfield, that the always courageous, brave, loyal, and victorious volunteers were at the point where they were being defeated by tropical diseases and malnutrition.

Colonel Hunter continued to wonder why General Merrill had been so uncommunicative—why had he failed to share any of his and General Stilwell's plans for what would be done after the airfield was taken. He could only assume that they actually understood that they were sending sick men into combat and would honor their promise to send the survivors out for evaluation, treatment, and rehabilitation as soon as the airfield was secured.

Two to three hours after the road was located, the entire force had crossed. The leading elements of the Marauders had now reached the Mogaung-Myitkyina Railroad. Telephone wires were tapped, but no important messages were discovered. It seemed reasonable to believe that the Myitkyina garrison did not know of our approach.

Colonel Hunter knew that, with good luck, the force would attack the airfield before noon, within twenty-four hours, on 17 May. The First Battalion's depleted radio section sent off the code phrase "Strawberry Sundae."

CHAPTER XVII

The village of Namkwi was reached in the early evening. In order to prevent passage of a message to the Japanese, Colonel Hunter had our Kachin allies round up and keep the village residents as guests for the night.

Hunter Force continued along the east bank of the river for two and one-half miles. From this point a bivouac area was established and occupied another two miles of the riverbank. The Marauders were at the south end of the perimeter. The deep and fast-flowing river would prevent any of the green and poorly trained and equipped Chinese from going west instead of east. It was known that few of the soldiers in the 150th Regiment could swim.

On this night of 16 May, all knew that Colonel Hunter was working on plans for an attack on the airfield. It seemed only logical that it would be scheduled for 17 May. Food was still available for the men and animals, and there was plenty of water. The men had had little sleep for twenty-four or more hours. Those not on duty needed little encouragement to seek rest and sleep.

Lieutenant Sam Wilson, the I & R platoon leader, was weak with malnutrition, weight loss, and bloody amoebic dysentery. His second in command, Sgt. Clarence E. Branscomb, a veteran of the Solomon Island campaigns, was ordered to take a night patrol to the airstrip. His own story is told forty-four years later as part of a letter to *The Burman News* dated November 1989:

> Towards the end, our platoon—and, I guess, all of A [First] Battalion—wound up somewhere in the flats after several grueling days pushing and pulling mules over a very wet, slick mountain. We made camp, we were all bushed, we could hardly fix our K-rations. Then I got a call that Lt. Col. Caifson Johnson wanted to see me. He said, "After what your I & R has been through, we sure hate to ask you to do this, etc., but would you go over to see Colonel Hunter?" When I did, he informed me that we were somewhere near the Myitkyina airport. This is about 8:30 or 9 p.m. He didn't know exactly, but thought it was someplace northeast of where we were, and would I take a couple of men and a compass that you can see at night and go till we find the airport? It was imperative that we find it, and Caifson would give me the details.
>
> He also handed me what he said was his last fifth of Canadian Club. I went back to Caifson, and he presented me with one of

those old beat-up pack radios and said we were to go on a certain azimuth until we could either hear or see some action on the airport. As soon as we found it, we were supposed to investigate all the gun emplacements to see if they were manned—then walk the airstrip to see if all the bomb holes had been repaired. All this was a hell of an assignment, especially if the gun pill boxes were manned.

Then he says, "The radio is acting up. It seems to receive, but sometimes you can't send."

Well, anyway, I went back to the platoon and asked for a couple of volunteers. Finally, I got two—and I'm not sure if it was Clark and Frye—but anyway, we started off but didn't get too far before we had killed the Canadian Club and things got better.

After walking for what seemed like forever, probably two and one-half to three hours, we heard talking and, as we crept closer, finally saw lights from work crews. We were fairly tense, and as we crept around in the grass trying to get a better view and find some pill boxes, the Japanese started packing and leaving. I guess they were only working until midnight, but it seemed they didn't live on the field because they kept leaving via truck and the lights eventually all would go out.

We crawled around in the grass trying to work our way around the airport perimeter. After almost knifing each other a few times, at about 2:30 a.m. I picked up the radio and started walking down the middle of the runway, thinking if those emplacements were occupied we'd soon find out—besides, our time was up. I sat the radio down and called Caifson. I could hear him fine, but he couldn't hear me. So we invoked the code "one is no, two is yes." He asked me if there were Japanese on the field. I answered "one." He asked me if there were holes in the runway. I answered "one." Then he asked, should he call India and send the gliders in? I answered "two."

Well, we pulled back on some high ground, and as it got lighter the whole world changed. The sky was suddenly full of gliders and the ground was full of Chinese, which we sure didn't need.

Anyway, when Sam and the rest of the platoon arrived we walked across the airstrip and on into the town of Myitkyina and camped by the Irrawaddy. I asked Sam to call Hunter and see if we could take and hold the town, and we got a negative.

It seemed the Chinese were in need of accomplishing something, and everyone knows what happened then. We did pull back to the revetments at the airport and watched the Chinese shoot up plane loads of ammo, killing and maiming each other.

Finally, after most of our outfit left, I boarded a plane for Ledo. So I never met any of the Mars bunch or whoever replaced us. Never really met many of the men in A Battalion, much less B and C Battalions.

It's just an old man's rambling. Use it or lose it (Branscomb 1989, letter).

Other information helped Colonel Hunter formulate his plans. Two thousand Japanese had recently been in the town, a train left every day at 1100 hours, there was little cover west of the strip, the revetments were not fortified, no wire was around the field, and military police were at Pamati. Many oil drums were on the airfield.

CHAPTER XVIII
CAPTURE OF MYITKYINA AIRFIELD
17 MAY 1944

The 150th Chinese Regiment was ordered to form up in a broad front at the bivouac area. Two battalions would be in front and one in the rear. Maintaining this formation, they were to march the four miles to the airfield. Once the airfield had been overrun they were to dig in on the southeast side and hold against a counterattack (Hunter 1963, 112).

The First Battalion of Marauders was to move out in a formation of their own choosing. Their one-half mile front would extend from Pamati on the north bank of the Irrawaddy River to the south end of the airfield. They were to capture Pamati, where the Japanese had their police force, and then sweep along the river to take the Zygun ferry crossing. After this they were to advance as far as possible toward the town of Myitkyina.

The Chinese pack-75 artillery battery was to set up at the present bivouac area. The Chinese battery commander was sick, so his assistant took over to work with the American liaison officer.

The four-mile approach to the airfield started at 1030 hours with a red flare signal. No problems developed. As the units departed, Colonel Hunter's two-man radio section struggled to made contact with General Merrill's Myitkyina task force headquarters at Naubum. After considerable delay and a lot of cranking, the two radio men made contact and sent the message "In the Ring." An affirmative answer soon came through (Hunter 1963).

The OSS officer Lieutenant Martin and his small band of Kachins set off to blow the bridge at Namkwi. Their next job was to round up some men from the village and get them to roll the steel oil drums off the runway (Hunter 1963, 113).

The Chinese met little opposition and were soon dug in on the southeastern side of the airfield. No effort was made to advance on the town.

CHAPTER XVIII

The bridge was quickly blown and the drums soon cleared away. Colonel Hunter arrived and located his headquarters spot midway along the southwestern border of the airfield. He had no radio or wire communication with the 150th Regiment but was able to get messages to both M Force and K Force, ordering them to get to the airfield as soon as possible.

A flight of P-40's flew over looking for a target, and he advised them to look over the city. When they returned he released a smoke grenade to show the spot he had chosen midway along the southwestern border of the airstrip for his headquarters. They relayed the message "In the Ring" to General Merrill. The general now knew that the airfield was ready for use, and there was no need for engineers. Colonel Hunter awaited the arrival of food and ammunition. The troops would be without food on the morning of 19 May (Romanus and Sunderland 1956, 297).

Two liaison planes soon came in. One carried Colonel Moe Arsenio, of the engineers. The other brought in General Don Old of the troop carrier command, who was there to watch the new squadrons of C-46's that would soon start bringing in three Chinese regiments (Hunter 1963, 115).

Seven C-47's each soon cut loose a glider loaded with engineering equipment and a company of the 879th Engineer Aviation Battalion. No warning was given to numerous Chinese and Americans on the field, and there was no way to communicate with the gliders or planes. Gliders skidded in all directions, and fortunately no one on the ground became a casualty.

After the field had been cleared of gliders, the C-47's began delivering the Second Battalion of the 89th Chinese Regiment—but without its commanding officer.The regiment was followed by a battery of 50 caliber antiaircraft before the weather closed in. Colonel Hunter had no radio or wire communication with this unit (Hunter 1963, 115–16). No food or ammunition was delivered (Romanus and Sunderland 1956, 227).

Neither General Merrill nor any of the Myitkyina task force headquarters arrived on this day, 17 May. The complete absence of plans by higher headquarters was evident. Colonel Hunter had no way to communicate with the Chinese 150th regiment other than by runners.

As the regiments came in they operated their own communications, but there was no central network of communications (Hunter 1963, 117–18).

It was soon apparent that the attack on the airstrip would be successful, and Colonel Osborne broke away from the advance and turned the Marauder First Battalion toward Pamati. The men paid little attention to scattered sniper fire as they moved across the flat open country in a southwest direction for one and one-half miles toward their objective. The village and Pamati ferry crossing were soon controlled by the First Battalion. Red Combat Team remained to hold the ferry, and White Combat Team quickly returned to the airstrip.

They arrived back at the airfield to find that the Chinese had been able to sweep across the airfield to dig in on the east side. Sporadic rifle and mortar fire was continuing. The Marauders were able to watch the Chinese using their Lee-Enfield rifles with fixed bayonets and to move forward on the east side of the airfield in response to bugles.

Pfc. Harold Hamilton from C Company was wounded while at the airport by a Chinese-fired U.S. mortar. Fortunately the wound was minor, and he was allowed to return to duty. No record has been located to determine how many dead and wounded the Chinese had on this day. Stilwell had not made arrangements to send medical personnel or units to the airfield. Fortunately, the planes that had been delivering Chinese troops and freight were available to take any wounded back to India. The small portable operating team that had been attached to H Force would not arrive until 19 May.

Since operations were going well at the airstrip, Colonel Hunter decided to send White Combat Team two miles southeast to capture the village of Rampur. They would bivouac there and on 18 May would advance southeast four miles to attack and occupy the Zygun ferry crossing.

By late afternoon it was apparent that the airfield was secure. The Japanese had made no attempt to counterattack, and no reinforcements were known to be in the area. *Stilwell's Command Problems* was to state, "The brilliant seizure of the Myitkyina Airfield was the height of Stilwell's career and the grand climax of the North Burma campaign." Nothing was said of the sacrifice of the American and Chinese men. Stilwell never mentioned the brilliant work of the Marauders.

Nothing was admitted about the need for hospitalization of the majority of the men because of multiple tropical diseases and malnutrition. He failed to send a radio message congratulating the men for their great victory and explaining why he was not keeping his promise to send them out on the many empty planes returning to India.

The march to Myitkyina and seizure of the airstrip was a total surprise to Lord Louis Mountbatten and his Southeast Asia Command. Stilwell had not informed him of the mission. Churchill was also upset. He had been against the Burma campaign and knew nothing of the mission until the airstrip was captured (Romanus and Sunderland 1956, 228–29).

When Stilwell learned that the airfield was in the hands of the Marauders and Chinese, his comment was, "Will this burn up the Limeys" (Stilwell 1948, 296).

No explanation was given as to why Stilwell did not order the Marauders out of combat as soon as the airport and the surrounding villages had been captured, as had been promised. Captain Chan of Stilwell's staff states that the promise of such action was well known (Chan 1986, 59–60). Stilwell in *The Stilwell Papers* states on 20 May, "They [the Marauders] are to finish the job [at Myitkyina]" (Stilwell 1948, 297).

The Siege of Myitkyina Begins with No Designated Commander

K Force arrived at Charpate on 18 May after a forced march on limited rations. There was hardly a man in the Marauders' depleted Third Battalion who was not sick with chronic malaria, amoebic dysentery, and malnutrition. Some had died from scrub typhus, and many others had the disease. The Chinese 88th Regiment had followed them and was now positioned three miles northwest of the city between the southern boundary of the Marauder Third Battalion on the Mogaung-Myitkyina Road and the northern outpost of the 150th Chinese Regiment extending along the Mogaung-Myitkyina Railroad. The 150th was responsible for the siege line extending south to the airfield and along its eastern border, then east to the Irrawaddy River at the Zygun ferry crossing. The 88th was fresh to Burma and had been involved in the battles of Ritpong and Tingkrukawng, where a limited number of their men had been used. Most of the 89th Chinese Regiment had by this date successfully arrived by air and was attached to the 88th. In spite of the large buildup of three Chinese regiments, two Chinese pack-75 artillery batteries, a battery of heavy mortars, and an antiaircraft unit, there was no other tactical support on the ground on the morning of 18 May.

Records would eventually show that the Japanese had seven hundred able-bodied men available on 17 May. Colonel Maruyama had two understrength battalions of the 114th Regiment, 100 men in an airfield battalion, 318 laborers, and 320 hospital patients (Romanus and Sunderland 1956, 226).

Many of the men of the 150th Chinese Regiment had gone to bed without food, since the supplies that General Merrill had promised would be on the first planes had not arrived. This major error in logistics would not be corrected until 20 May and would cause general dissatisfaction among the Marauders and Chinese and serious tactical problems (Hunter 1963, 125).

The rest of the 89th Regiment came in and joined the 88th Chinese Regiment, which was getting into position to advance along the railroad toward the town. They brought with them a company of heavy mortars.

Pfc. Russell J. Plunkett of Company C was the first Marauder killed on 18 May at the airfield. He was wounded in the chest by a Japanese sniper at 0900 hours and died while en route to hospital care in Assam.

A few jeeps had arrived by air on 18 May. Grenville O. Couch, a T5g. in A Company, was wounded in the left chest by the ricochet of a .25-caliber bullet that had struck one of these vehicles. He was sent out for hospital care.

"Uncle Joe's Chariot"—General Stilwell's plane— touched down in the morning on 18 May, and Stilwell got out with about a dozen correspondents. Colonel Hunter greeted and briefed him but got no helpful information. There was no explanation as to where General Merrill was on this day or had been on the 17th. No explanation was given about the absence of food and ammunition. No mention was made about the previous promise that the Marauders would be sent out on planes as they returned to base after bringing in Chinese replacements. The general was very upset when he learned that Colonel

McCammon, who had come in earlier on 18 May, had been unable to get the Chinese to move toward the city. Colonel Hunter and the Chinese generals agreed that the chief limiting factor in the failure to carry out orders was lack of food and ammunition (Hunter 1963, 118).

Major Louis Williams, the Myitkyina task force adjutant, and Major Melvin Schudmak, formerly the Marauders' regimental surgeon and now the task force surgeon, arrived from Naubum.

The planes brought in a few men from the 69th Light Antiaircraft Regiment and the rest of the 89th Regiment, as well as a company of Chinese heavy mortars.

Colonel McCammon informed Colonel Hunter that Stilwell had asked him to put on the stars of a brigadier general, but he was going to keep them in his pocket since this was not a certified promotion. It seems that he was to be in charge of the Myitkyina operation, but orders would not come through until 22 May. It must be assumed that Stilwell had to have a general in command, since the Chinese divisions now in the area were commanded by generals. It had been obvious to all that Colonel Hunter was the best man available and should have been given the job. Colonel McCammon had just been released from a hospital and was still suffering from pleurisy. He had come into the airfield with no knowledge that he would be staying and had no previous briefing of the situation (Hunter 1963, 123–24).

He was not furnished with a signal section, a supply officer, an intelligence officer, or even a clerk. These vital men and sections would arrive gradually over the twelve days of his command (Hunter 1963, 171).

Colonel Hunter explains that he lost confidence in Colonel McCammon when he asked, "What are your plans for withdrawal if the stuff hits the fan?" From the time the Marauders had crossed the Burma border in early February, I had never heard any Marauder mention the possibility of any outcome other than victory. It is very easy for me to see how shocked Colonel Hunter was by this negative attitude (Hunter 1963, 126).

Shortly after General Stilwell arrived, the general of the 150th Chinese Regiment acted on his orders and sent a battalion on a combat mission to explore the defenses of the town. The unit failed to follow the proper direction and because of this mistake ended up northwest of the town. The American liaison officer Colonel Combs discovered the mistake, and they took the long, hot hike back to their jump-off location on the northeast side of the airfield (Hunter 1963, 119); (Romanus and Sunderland 1956, 229–30).

Late in the day they started again, this time following the road on the east side of the airfield for about one mile until they reached a road junction. They took the southeastern branch, which ran toward the city of Myitkyina. They soon had to dig in because of darkness and increasing Japanese resistance. I have been unable to locate a record of the number of dead and wounded Chinese during this advance. The Third Battalion's American liaison officer of this, the 150th Chinese Regiment, was shot from the back and killed (Hunter 1963, 119).

Back at the airfield, Colonel Hunter's orderly had located a recently flown in and unoccupied jeep. Colonel Hunter decided to take a ride out to the 150th's location to check on its progress. With Major Bell—a fighter group intelligence officer—as a passenger, they took off to locate the Chinese. As they reached the road junction, a lone Chinese soldier waved them on. They were soon fired on by a Japanese machine gun. As Coon frantically backed and turned, he discovered the lack of brakes. During the mad dash to safety, Coon was hit in the chest. Hunter took over while supporting Coon with one arm. Back at the airfield he was given plasma and soon put on a plane. As the C-47 took of it was strafed by a flight of Japanese Zero fighter planes. The plane got off, but a bullet from the Zeros killed Coon and wounded a nurse. Few of the men ever knew that American nurses had been allowed to serve on these C-47's, which were serving as freight and makeshift ambulance planes (Hunter 1963, 123).

From the same flight of Zeros, Colonel Hunter was hit in the face by many small fragments of metal. After a tetanus shot and emergency dressing of his wounds, he was going through Coon's belongings. He found two carefully wrapped front teeth, which had been knocked from Coon's jaw early in the Burma campaign (Hunter 1963, 123).

Ray Lyons was ordered to the Myitkyina airfield on 18 May. He tells what happened:

CHAPTER XVIII

The lieutenant who was in charge of the airdrop section came over to me and said, "Get your pack and rifle—Sergeant Doyer has been wounded, and Colonel Hunter wants you to fly in and take his place as sergeant major. I grabbed my pack and my rifle and went to the Dinjan Airfield. I wound up getting in a C-47 with two colonels. Two colonels and me in a C-47. One of the colonels was McCammon, who was being flown out to take charge of the Myitkyina task force. They weren't talking of the 5307th any more, it was now the "task force." He had a colonel with him who apparently was an advisor. During the time we were on this flight the two were sitting together, talking in low voices and obviously paying no attention to me all the time we were flying out to Myitkyina.

We got off the plane. I went looking for Colonel Hunter and told him I had been flown out to take Sergeant Doyer's place as sergeant major. They had revetments where the Japanese had parked planes, and he told me to put my gear in one nearby. He also said there was a Chinese guy and I should turn over my C-rations to him and he would take care of the food, which he did. He cooked up a meal in a helmet, and that is what we ate from. He was a Chinese soldier, not really a cook. He slopped everything together, and it tasted delicious.

The first night I was there I am in this sleeping bag with my blanket over me when all hell breaks loose. Somebody thought that they saw a Japanese patrol moving down the middle of the airfield. Troops on each side of the field were shooting across the field into each other's area. I jumped into a foxhole with somebody, god knows who, and there was water up to our heads. Well, we were soaking wet. After I was in there a while I thought to myself, "I am the sergeant major of this outfit—I shouldn't be hiding here. I'll get out to see what is going on." I crawled over the revetment to the headquarters tent, and when I got there, there was one guy there, Colonel Hunter. I said, "Colonel, is there anything I can do for you?" "No," he says, "I'll call the other side of the field." So he took the telephone and called the other side of the field. He says, "What are you shooting at?" They didn't know what they were shooting at. They were just replying to fire from our side of the field. "Suppose you stop shooting and we see what happens," he said. They did, and that was the end of it. Being under fire from American army troops with their automatic weapons was the worst thing in my experience. It was really something,

446

and I think most of it was probably coming from those .50-caliber antiaircraft guns on the airstrip.

The morning after I was in this foxhole getting wet, Colonel Hunter says to me, "You are all wet and muddy. I've got a can over there." He had gotten them to open up a fifty-gallon drum of gasoline. "Get yourself clean." So I dumped my clothes in the gasoline, took them out squeezed them, and hung them up to dry.

So about the second day that I was there, I decided what I should do was to make a record of it. I walked all around the field and asked people who they were, what outfit they were in. One was an engineer outfit that had flown in wire, so I asked the sergeant if he had a water-purification unit—most engineers have them. He said he did. So I said, "I want you to set up your water purification on the far corner of the field" where a little brook ran across. "It's not right that all these men don't have good water for drinking." He had no idea that I was a big staff sergeant. He thought I was a colonel probably, because there were so many colonels floating around. Anyway, he said he would take care of it. They did in the daytime, but at nighttime they tended to abandon the thing and did not come back but stayed where their positions were. We had Major Seagrave's outfit on the other side of the airfield. We had an antiaircraft outfit over there with .50-caliber machine guns. I wrote all this down in notes.

They were all, I am sure, West Pointers, and they had to get experience, combat command experience, in order to get further promotions. A lot of these guys came up for that reason, and they soon found that the situation was out of control and getting worse. They had very worried expressions on their faces. In fact I noticed one in Dave's pictures at Wakefield, Mass., when he showed a picture of General Stilwell getting off a plane and walking over toward our headquarters. Two officers intercepted him to get their two cents worth. They were all very much concerned because of what they had experienced the first day the Chinese were there. Two Chinese regiments got off the planes, and they refused to leave the vicinity of the field unless they were provided with three days' rations. It soon became apparent to me—and I am sure everybody else—that *we* fought the war as if the quicker we got it over with and got back to our homes and families the better. "Faster, better" was our way of fighting a war. The Chinese could care less. They had been fighting the Japanese for years, and they were not in any hurry. They were looking for any creature comforts they could get—like food. They were not interested in shooting the Japanese at the airfield. They were only interested in getting their rations and would move out afterward. So Colonel McCammon and whoever it was called on Stilwell as Stilwell comes off his plane, as I described, when he was besieged by these two officers. The next thing that happens, they get these two Chinese generals and I am standing alongside Stilwell when he is busy chewing these two Chinese generals out in Chinese. I had no idea what he was saying, but I could tell by the tone of voice and the gestures that he was really laying it on because of their refusal to move out.

It had been critical at that early stage to take the town of Myitkyina. It could have been captured fairly easily before the Japanese moved in in force. That was not the way it worked out. They could not get the Chinese moving, so Stilwell came in and chewed them out, and then they started to move.

Another thing that happened, about the second day. I flew in on the 18th with these two colonels. The next day, a Japanese Zero flew in over our side of the field, and everybody was stunned. I never thought of grabbing my rifle and trying to shoot at him—he zoomed right overhead. Major Laffin had just taken off the field in an L-5. He wanted to fly over the town and get an idea of the Japanese defenses. The plane had barely taken off from the ground when the Zero came along and shot him down. He was shot down within a hundred yards of the field. It was a shame both he and his pilot were killed (Lyons, videotape).

On the afternoon of 18 May, word went out that medical help was now available on the east side of the airfield. Major Gordon Seagrave tells the story in his book, *The Burma Surgeon Returns*. He had been told that he, his four U.S. Army surgeons, and thirteen Burmese nurses would be given duty at the Myitkyina airfield as soon as it was captured. His unorthodox field hospital had no official table of organization and was always ready to move on short notice to give medical care and whatever front-line surgery was necessary. Limited service was offered for brain, chest, and vascular procedures.

On 18 May he was notified that the Myitkyina airfield had been taken and his unit should move immediately to set up and offer all medical measures. He was told that medical needs had third priority, but that planes would soon be available. They finally flew to Myitkyina late in the day.

In spite of intermittent air and ground activity the three planes landed safely, and the hospital's supplies and personnel were soon located in a revetment midway along the five-thousand-foot runway on the east side. No bamboo poles were available to erect their tarpaulins, but they were able to cover all cases. Flares lit the airfield, and planes arrived all night in spite of intermittent mortar and rifle fire. Two casualties came in, and they were dead on arrival.

During this day Colonel Hunter had not been in contact with K Force. Attempts at radio contact had been unsuccessful. In order to ask them to get to the area as soon as possible he dispatched the Marauders' S-2, or intelligence officer, Captain William Laffin, as a passenger in an L-4 to locate and notify them. The plane had just become airborne as the flight of Zeros came over, and they shot it down. Col. William H. Combs, the liaison officer of the Chinese 150th Regiment, sent Major Thomas L. Kerley with a patrol to locate the crash site. The pilot was alive when found but died on the way to the airfield. Laffin's body was recovered for burial. Another officer in this group of liaison men was Major Fred Huffine with the Second Battalion of the 150th Chinese Regiment.

White Combat Team occupied Rampur without difficulty early on the morning of 18 May. Here they found warehouses that contained Japanese uniforms and little else of value. They moved on to the Irrawaddy River and the Zygun ferry landing, which they occupied after a small skirmish and the capture of several Japanese. Defensive positions were taken, and Colonel Hunter was contacted by radio. They were informed that a company of Chinese had been dispatched to take over their position. They were to return to the airfield as soon as the Chinese arrived and were in position (Hunter 1963, 123–24).

While waiting for the Chinese, Major Caifson Johnson decided to send a seventeen-man patrol north along the west bank of the Irrawaddy River to look for the ferry boat and check on Japanese defensive positions. After advancing 750 yards they were fired on by about ten Japanese with a light machine gun. After a brief skirmish, the Japanese retreated.

449

CHAPTER XVIII

This patrol's activity is described fifty years later in the *Burma News*, February 1992, by Ralph W. Polock of Mount Union, Pennsylvania:

Here is a little information on this incident. After the initial attack at Pamati, White Combat Team continued on to the Myitkyina airstrip. There they were ordered across the strip and up the river hunting the Japanese ferry boat. We continued up the river as far as Zygun and had not found the ferry. There a native came into the perimeter and was interrogated by Captain Ahrens. The captain was a medical officer who was from that part of the world and could speak the language. He learned that the boat we were looking for was upstream and hidden during the day. Major Caifson Johnson organized a patrol to go out and destroy it. Our machine-gun belts were loaded: one tracer, four armor- piercing, one tracer, etc. They stripped one of these belts and gave each member of the patrol a chip of armor-piercing bullets. They took the other machine gun from our section and left our gun inside the perimeter.

It wasn't long after they had left that we heard the shooting and explosions, and we knew that they had run into something other than just a boat. Jim and I rushed our gun over to cover the trail they had left on. Sometime later they came back carrying two and supporting a third. I left Jim and the rest of the crew covering the trail and helped get the wounded to the aid station. Stan Vruggink would not be quiet—he insisted on telling me what happened.

He and Chambers were the front scouts. They were crossing an open area when they saw Japanese. They signaled back but were ordered forward. When they did stop, the Japanese were just beyond a clump of bamboo, and they were afraid that if they laid down they would not be able to get up in time to defend themselves against a bayonet. They stood behind two trees, and the Japanese started lobbing grenades into the bamboo. A grenade hit the tree Stan was behind but rolled down the hill before it exploded. Then one landed between the two trees. When it exploded they were both hit in the head—but on opposite sides. Stan could still travel and took off running and stumbling back to the rest of the patrol. Pamplin went after the Japanese on a one-man tommy-gun charge. Dr. Hopkins's report says he was hit with a grenade fragment. Not so—it was a .25-caliber bullet that was removed later at the 111th Hospital. It had ricocheted off his tummy gun and entered just above his penis. It was badly bent.

Now let's get back to the aid station. When Chambers was brought back he was unconscious and had been vomiting. His teeth were clenched, the vomitus was in his nostrils, and he was having difficulty breathing. Captain Ahrens took a plastic tube from a plasma kit and inserted one end up his nostril and sucked the vomitus out with his own mouth. He was later loaded into an ox cart and sent to the airport (Polock 1992).

The record shows that Chambers was evacuated by air to the 20th General Hospital but died at 0210 hours on 21 May.

Pvt. Adrian R. Pamplin, Company B, was given no recognition for his heroic action. He probably killed some and wounded others. The enemy retreated, and his action probably saved the lives of the other wounded Marauders. He was sent to the airfield by oxcart and made a good recovery.

Stanley Vruggink of Company B was also evacuated by oxcart and recovered after hospital care.

Sgt. Raymond K Chambers, Hq. Co., had a mortal wound of the brain as well as numerous flesh wounds of his chest wall. It is unlikely that more efficient transportation and medical help would have prevented his death.

The Chinese company that had been dispatched to take White Combat Team's position at the Zygun ferry failed to arrive. The men of White Combat Team prepared to spend the night with empty stomachs. No food had, as of this date, been sent to the airfield—and their three days' supply of K-rations, taken at Seingheing, was exhausted.

At this time the complete absence of plans on the part of higher headquarters became evident. There was no unified command or other known plan. Each regiment, except those that marched in with the Americans, operated their own internal communications but had no communication with Colonel Hunter, who had assumed the job of the airstrip force commander (Hunter 1963, 128).

Sufficient wire, telephone equipment, and wire personnel were not available at first to provide wire communications to any of the units or the rapidly expanding headquarters installations. There were no radio, cipher, or message center personnel provided for handling communications, which had to be of radio alone from the airstrip to the rear, for what amounted to an army corps.

For one week this work fell on the shoulders of one officer and a skeleton section salvaged from the already exhausted communication section of the Marauders. This small group, one third the size of the group which at Naubum had handled fifty-nine messages per day, attempted to handle one hundred messages of abnormal length each day (Hunter 1963).

On 19 May, Lieutenant Sam Wilson's White Combat Team I & R platoon was ordered to cross to the village of Zygun, which is situated on an island in the Irrawaddy River. From here they crossed over to the eastern bank of the river. Their job was to search for and destroy Japanese, gather information, and forage for food. They found hospitality at a little village where the people gave them a small quantity of rice. Shortly afterward a flight of American fighter planes came over and strafed the village. They dove for cover in a drainage ditch. The air force bullets killed a small child, and they had the sad duty of offering apology and sympathy without verbal communication. Needless to say, some of these hardened veterans were emotional and upset.

They withdrew to White Combat Team with heavy hearts and empty stomachs. The Chinese company had not arrived, and they were forced to stay another night in the area.

General Merrill flew in on the 19th for a brief period. It seems likely that he consulted with some of the small headquarters staff, but Colonel Hunter had only the opportunity to wave to him as he was getting on a plane to leave. There is no evidence that he left any important plans or advice. He did not explain his late arrival, the absence of food and ammunition, or the forgotten promises. No message of encouragement and congratulations was left for the Marauders (Hunter 1963, 118).

General Stilwell in his diary dated 19 May states, "Merrill in—he has had another heart attack. Peterson gave him morphine and put him to bed (Stilwell 1948, 297).

Major Gordon S. Seagrave's surgical unit rapidly set up at its designated location midway on the eastern side of the five-thousand-foot runway. First the instruments were boiled, and then several litters were placed on packing boxes to serve as operating tables. He was assisted by a medical officer, two Burmese contract surgeons, three Burmese technicians, three American medics, eighteen Burmese nurses, five Chinese orderlies, and a Chinese-speaking Chinese-American corporal, who handled registration of patients. Seagrave states in *The Burma Surgeon Returns*, "The sun was blistering hot and our skins began to burn, for we were bare to the waist. Then a squall of rain blew up and a nurse held an umbrella over the operating field when I removed a man's shattered spleen" (Seagrave 1964).

The doctor further states, "At noon Dushkin and Gurney arrived with their detachment, the thinnest, dirtiest, weariest bunch of men I'd seen for a long time." Seagrave is referring to his small detached surgical unit, which had marched as far as Arang with H Force. They had been temporarily left there to help with the wounded who were being evacuated from the battles of Ritpong and Tingkrukawng as well as sick from H Force and K Force. The doctors included Lt. Milton A. Dushkin, Lt. Theodore Gurney, and Lt. Carl J. Antonellis. They now joined Doctor Seagrave (Seagrave 1964).

Parachutes were rigged up on bamboo poles to give a minimum of cover to the stretchers used for operating tables, hospital personnel, and patients resting on the ground, as well as to provide storage areas. The increasing showers made the ground a muddy mess. A portable generator provided light.

During 19 May numerous small skirmishes took place in back of and in front of the siege line. A limited number of casualties were taken to Seagrave's unit, where they were quickly treated before evacuation in the departing C-47 freight planes. No major offensive had been planned or carried out.

On 20 May, the ever-faithful and overworked pilots began bringing in the long-awaited K-rations in the morning. The hungry Chinese were close to the airfield and were able to eat early. The Third Battalion of the 42nd Regiment of the 14th Chinese Division also arrived by air on this day. They had flown from China to Maingkwan a few days before the Marauders and Chinese had departed on this mission to Myitkyina.

The Marauders' Third Battalion had a mule supply train awaiting the hoped-for delivery. The muleskinners quickly loaded and started the dangerous four-mile trip back to their unit. After the first food in two days, the men were much more enthusiastic about advancing from Charpate toward the road junction at Radahpur.

CHAPTER XVIII

On this day General Stilwell wrote in his diary, "Merrill passed by medicos. I let him go back—they [the Marauders] are to finish the Job [at Myitkyina]" (Stilwell 1948, 297). If any of the Marauders had known of his thoughts, it is likely they would have asked why he didn't return to move among the men who had paid such a sacrifice while under his command. They would have also wanted to ask him why he had promised to take them out of combat when the airfield was captured and then not followed through or explained why he could not keep his promise. General Stilwell's plan to let the Marauders finish the job at Myitkyina can only lead me to believe that he had no knowledge of what they had been through, how few men remained, and how—almost without exception—the men required hospital care for diagnosis, treatment, and rehabilitation before returning to combat. His attitude must therefore have been due to lack of knowledge, total indifference to the health and survival of his troops, or early senility (Romanus and Sunderland 1956, 183). The setup and actions of the personnel section of divisional staff, intelligence section, operations section, and supply section during the early phase of the Myitkyina operation suggests that the whole operation was not under the control of a competent individual. Hunter's opinion of Stilwell became progressively lower (Hunter 1963, 171).

After being supplied with food and ammunition, the 150th Chinese Regiment advanced toward the town from the position they had occupied on the 18th. Colonel Hunter discusses the action:

> The 150th moved out again on the 20th, and its attack was successful beyond imagination—carrying to the railroad station in the heart of the city.
>
> Colonel Huang characteristically selected and moved his headquarters into the tallest building opposite the railroad station. Fire from Japanese, dug in around the station and under railroad cars, began to pour in on the leading battalion. The battalion following, in column, received "overs" and some Japanese fire intended for the leading battalion.
>
> The battalions following stupidly opened fire on their own troops to the front. The entire regiment broke and ran, leaving close to three hundred of their comrades dead or dying in the city.
>
> This catastrophe, the result of inexperience, revealed a fundamental weakness of the Chinese as a whole. They were unable to

tell their own troops from the enemy. Their uniforms (British-supplied lease lend) were identical in color to the Japanese. Only the helmets were different. Without a helmet, no identification could be made if but a portion of the body was to be seen.

The Chinese motto seemed to be "Every man for himself," and that became each individual's guiding principle on the 20th for both officers and men. Stragglers were even collected by McGee, who by now had arrived at the village of Namkwi, four miles west of Myitkyina.

The first news of the fighting came from a villager who had witnessed the fight. However, he was as confused as the 150th: he reported two to three hundred dead Japanese lying all over Myitkyina.

This buoyed up our spirits to a new high. However, on the heels of the native, Colonel Combs arrived, completely out of breath and near exhaustion, to gasp out the horrid details I have just related (Hunter 1963, 119–23).

Official reports later showed that, as of the end of this day, the 150th Regiment had taken 671 casualties (Hunter 1963).

Doctor Seagrave reported that his group operated on 120 patients before turning in for the night. This information suggests that most of the casualties were killed and perhaps a few came back over the next several days. He further stated that "three light days followed, with only twenty or thirty patients per day." (Seagrave 1964).

The editor of *The Stilwell Papers*, Theodore H. White, has added a note to General Stilwell's 20 May diary entry:

> Within a week, the success at Myitkyina had transformed itself from a brilliant coup to a squalid, heartbreaking campaign.
>
> The 150th Chinese Regiment, which was the first flown in to consolidate, had but lately arrived from China and was unbloodied in war. In its first action, several of its battalions mistook each other for Japanese and succeeded in inflicting disastrous casualties on themselves before recognition was achieved. Panic spread. Before the troops at Myitkyina could be pulled together, the Japanese had had time to bring in all their outpost garrisons from the field, to rush supplies and reinforcements from the south, and to dig in for desperate resistance.
>
> The Japanese force, variously estimated at from five to seven thousand men, decided to make a suicide stand of it, and each

individual pocket had to be dug out in intensive fighting. Two full months dragged by while their stronghold was being reduced. Two American commanders were relieved. The Marauders, exhausted from their previous four months of fighting, were decimated with disease. The rains poured down, the battle area became a quagmire, and it was impossible to withdraw from the struggle through the jungle without disaster.

Although this was a period not unmarked with success—for the Chinese had captured Kamaing and gone on to Mogaung beyond—it was a period of bitterness and worry for Stilwell (Stilwell 1948, 297).

A rebuttal to some of White's statements is in order. It is true that the 150th Regiment had just been flown in from China. They had not, however, flown into Myitkyina, but had been flown into North Burma and then become part of H Force. As part of this unit, they had walked over the mountains with the Marauder's First Battalion and then helped them capture the airfield.

He states that it was impossible to withdraw through the jungle without disaster. Even though there was hardly a Marauder who was not sick enough to be eligible for hospital treatment, there was never any thought about the inability of the forces involved to defeat the Japanese. This sentiment was continually expressed by Colonel Hunter. The disillusioned, malnourished, and sick Marauders would have remained in force at Myitkyina after 1 June if Colonel Hunter had believed it essential to victory. At that time Stilwell had four American-trained Chinese infantry regiments and a few key men and officers from the Second and Third Battalions. He also had about two hundred men from the Marauder First Battalion who were in position, at the airfield, for its indefinite protection. Two battalions of combat engineers had just arrived, and a battalion of American infantry was in India and soon to be at Myitkyina.

In spite of the presence of an adequate number of Chinese and the understaffed and sick Marauders, Colonel McCammon, Colonel Cannon, and General Boatner all painted a dismal picture of the situation until General Boatner left on 25 June. Two battalions of American engineers and two battalions of untrained and unorganized American infantry replacements were also soon available (Stilwell 1948, 225).

The Chinese company that had been sent to relieve White Combat Team finally arrived, and the Americans departed for the airfield and food. They had dug in five times during the forty-eight hours it had taken them to advance through open flat country.

On this date, 20 May, the First Battalion had approximately four hundred men on its roster. Their general condition was not good, but was better than the other two battalions. Rather than have them hunt out outlying pockets of enemy and work at preventing Japanese reinforcements from entering the city, Colonel McCammon ordered them to guard the airfield.

Shortly after White Combat Team arrived at the airfield the battalion surgeons evaluated some of the sickest. Lt. Sam Wilson was known to have had bloody diarrhea for two weeks and was now very sick. He went out by plane and was soon in the typhus ward at the 20th General Hospital in Assam, India. He had scrub typhus, amoebic dysentery, and malaria. He soon learned that Lt. Bill Bright, the First Battalion communications officer, was critically ill in the next bed. Bill died the next night. Lt. Billy Lepore was in a nearby bed, which was soon empty. Sam and Billy had been together when two of Lepore's men were killed on the way to Shaduzup. Sam was still struggling with his own diseases when Colonel Kinnison, the K Force commander, and Sergeant Herbert Nelson, of Lt. Charlton Ogburn Jr.'s platoon, died.

The Second Marauder Battalion had arrived on the evening of 19 May and was holding Namkwi and controlling a Japanese pocket along the railroad west of the area and four miles from the airport. This battalion (M Force) was famished. As previously noted, the airdrop they were to take at Seingheing had been cancelled at the last minute. The First Battalion was able to give them enough food for one meal. They would get food from the airfield on 20 May. They had been so long without food that their physical condition was impaired by weakness and fatigue. In spite of all problems, they occupied Namkwi and patrolled to the west and southwest (Romanus and Sunderland 1956, 18) (Hunter 1963, 118).

By 20 May the situation had changed. An estimated three or four thousand Japanese had filtered in from Nsopzup, Mogaung, and other locations. Some even were sent from Bhamo. The 114th Regiment of the 18th Division was joined by the 18th Infantry Battalion, the 148th

Regiment of the 56th Division, the 15th Airfield Battalion, and the 56th and 58th Regiments. The Japanese had soon dug and occupied trenches on the three land-based sides of the town (Chan 1986, 100) (Romanus and Sunderland 1956, 91).

From 21 May until well into June, it was apparent that General Mizukami, the Japanese Commander at Myitkyina, was keeping pockets of troops in areas such as Charpate, Namkwi, and Radahpur in order to force the Allies to fight on two fronts and be less effective in blocking the arrival of replacements.

As has been previously stated, written orders were issued on 22 May 1944 giving Colonel John E. McCammon the rank of brigadier general and making him the commanding officer of the Myitkyina area and all units therein. The 88th and 89th Chinese Infantry Regiments were placed under the command of Brigadier Hu Si and the 150th and the 42nd Chinese Infantry Regiments under Brigadier Pan Yu-qun. A few days later the Chinese would add the 90th Regiment, the 148th Regiment, and the 41st Battalion. H Force, K Force, and M Force were dissolved. Colonel Hunter was given command of the First, Second, and Third Battalions, which again made up the 5307th Composite Unit (Provisional), better known as Merrill's Marauders (Hunter 1963, 126).

The six Chinese regiments plus one battalion would be responsible for preventing the Japanese from entering or leaving the city over an area of six miles along the west and south borders of an ill-defined defensive line west and south of the city.

The greatly understrength Marauders were to continue to patrol and protect an irregular five-mile line running along the northwest border of the town of Myitkyina to the village of Namkwi. They also had orders to advance toward Myitkyina from the northwest and north (Hunter 1963, 131).

The medical staff was struggling to deal with an increasing number of cases of scrub typhus. A conservative estimate is that they sent out 175 men with this condition, and between thirty and forty died. Adequate records dealing with this tragic situation have never been made available. Very few men, among the courageous Marauders who had arrived at Myitkyina, were free of significant disease. The great majority had amoebic dysentery, chronic malaria, malnutrition, and chronic stress syndrome. Many also had additional problems such as acute and chronic bronchitis, various degrees and forms of arthritis, skin problems, chronic sprains and backaches, miscellaneous gastrointestinal complaints, and other recognized clinical conditions. These men were making a last desperate effort because of pride in their outfit, respect for their comrades, and a general attitude that they had a responsibility to their country. At no time did I see any evidence of panic or admission to the possibility of defeat—or any suggestion that they would not fight until someone ordered them out for treatment of their multiple physical conditions.

The following several chapters detail the struggles of K and M Forces as they made their ways to Myitkyina.

CHAPTER XIX
K FORCE MARCHES TO TINGKRUKAWNG

During the morning of 11 May—when the sick and wounded were on the way to safety and evacuation from Arang—the bulk of K Force pulled out of the Ritpong area. A battalion of the 88th Regiment was left to stay long enough to eliminate any remaining Japanese. American patrols were dispatched to locate enemy stragglers. We were headed south to take an airdrop at nearby Sana. The planes came in over the mountains on schedule, and we now had three days' regular fare of emergency K-rations. Our ability to carry the usual amount of ammunition, especially mortar shells, was limited because of the loss of animals. As usual, the day was hot and humid, and we were developing an abnormal number of sick. There was little we could do for these men other than ask them to carry on.

Much to the surprise of the men, Lieutenant Weston's I & R platoon turned on the trail to the east. The word was soon passed out that Colonel Kinnison was attempting a diversion by moving east toward Nsopzup, which was a Japanese base about ten miles to the east of the village of Tingkrukawng. We soon learned that Nsopzup was a small village located on a tributary of the Irrawaddy River. A road runs from Myitkyina through Nsopzup, and continues northward about one hundred miles to Fort Hertz, still controlled by a small British force at the extreme northern tip of Burma. In order to give Colonel Hunter's H Force a better opportunity to capture the Myitkyina airfield, as many Japanese troops as possible had to be kept occupied elsewhere. Our command assumed that, after Ritpong, the enemy knew that they were outflanked.

The heat and humidity on 12 May was the worst we had yet encountered in Burma. The trail was very difficult, with lots of steep grades to climb and small rivers to cross during the ten miles or so before we were to reach the village of Tingkrukawng. We were now traveling at a lower altitude. Here, on the eastern side of the Kumon

461

Mountain Range, rainfall was greater than on the western side. Swarms of insects thrived, and leeches were continually attacking the men and animals by dropping from trees and bushes. Black buffalo flies were constantly present. Anopheles (malaria carrying) mosquitoes came out in hordes in the early evening and at dawn. For several months our men had been on one atabrine tablet per day in an attempt to prevent malaria attacks. Very few men in the Third Battalion had been unable to continue fighting because of recurrent malaria. We were now beginning to see more men suffering from attacks as the malaria organism was becoming resistant to the medicine. An increasing number of men were having episodes of fever with chills, body aches, and general ill-defined periods of illness.

As in the past, we had no method of doing blood smears to prove that malaria was the cause of their fevers. We also had to worry about dengue fever and scrub typhus, as well as numerous other infectious diseases. Almost without exception, every man had suffered from diarrhea or dysentery, at times bloody. An increasing number of men were being seen with problems such as chronic cough, skin rashes, foot problems, bone and joint problems, and chronic indigestion.

Before this third mission, the medical officers had made certain that the command knew about the medical problems as outlined. They were bad then—but much worse now. After passage over the Kumon Mountains and the stress of the Battle of Ritpong, disease, inadequate caloric intake, lack of rest, unfavorable environment, chronic fatigue, lack of tactical knowledge, and failure of the command to give any evidence of appreciation all tended to cause many of the men to lose faith in Stilwell's staff. They had never lost faith in their officers or their ability to meet and defeat the enemy.

The Battle of Tingkrukawng

The march to Tingkrukawng proved very difficult because of terrain and environmental conditions. The deteriorating physical and mental health of the men, as well as disease, took more time than expected. Logan Weston's I & R platoon left Sana on 11 May in order to scout the trail and pass through Tingkrukawng early the next morning. The march was difficult but uneventful. No action was expected in the village. At 0945 hours on 12 May, they had moved several hundred yards up a very steep section of the mountain trail. The first scout motioned for his platoon to halt. He saw about forty men bunched up on the trail about a hundred yards ahead. Their helmets were decorated with parachute cloth such as the Chinese frequently used. One hollowed the Chinese greeting "ding how." The scout replied, mistakingly thinking he had run into Chinese troops. The mistake was apparent when the strangers began to take firing positions. Our men could not deploy properly, since they were on a narrow ridge. A fight began, and T5g. Raymond Harris was instantly killed. After a temporary withdrawal, a defense line was built up. The enemy did not press an attack. The men dug in and strengthened their position while awaiting the arrival of K Force.

The lead elements of Orange Combat Team arrived in the area about 1030 hours. After a survey of the situation, they deployed on either side of the trail. An offensive advance was then set up on either side of the razorback trail toward the village, which was thought to be about three hundred yards to the southeast. Orange's mortars were in a position to be used as necessary. Because of the terrain, the hot, humid weather, and the uncertain location of machine guns, rifles, miscellaneous automatic weapons, and mortars, the advance was necessarily slow.

As usual, casualties were expected, and Orange's aid station was set up in the jungle on the left side of the trail in back of the mortars. The lead elements of the 42nd Portable Surgical Hospital, which were marching, as planned, in front of the Chinese 89th Infantry Regiment, immediately began to set up for their mission of doing emergency surgery. Their canvas shelter was strung up between dense clumps of bamboo, which offered some minimal protection against stray bullets and shell fragments. They were quickly ready for surgical care of the wounded.

Pfc. William F. Toomey of K Company was well off the left side of the trail while setting up his machine gun. An hour or so earlier this location had been within the Japanese field of fire. It was now 1100 hours, and the Marauders had been walking about the area. The men had assumed that the Japanese had withdrawn their weapons to a more favorable location. Such was not the case, however, and Toomey was suddenly cut down by light machine-gun fire. His death appeared to be instant from hits in the chest. T5g. Robert E. Beach from the medical detachment had been moving forward in back of Toomey in order to get a few yards closer to the body of Raymond Harris. He had been told by the battalion commander that the route to Harris's body was safe. The burst of machine-gun fire tore through his canteen and produced a flesh wound just above the crest of his left pelvis. After his wound was dressed, he returned to duty.

Just before he was hit, Toomey had noticed that Dave Quaid, Orange's cameraman, was on the trail and warned him to be careful. As the machine gun cut loose, bullets passed through a small tree just above Quaid's head.

Colonel Beach quickly maneuvered infantry platoons from Orange's K and L Companies so they could work their way forward on either side of the trail toward the village. The 60mm and 81mm mortars were ordered to support their advance.

As the advance progressed it became increasingly apparent that the tactics had to be modified to knock out the enemy. Subsequent events were to show that the area was held by a battalion of Japanese infantry (Stuart 1984, 32).

Colonel Kinnison, the K Force commander, sent a company of Chinese forward with orders to advance on the right side of the trail. They were to attempt destruction of all strong points and envelopment of the Japanese. After several hours and the expenditure of considerable American and Chinese machine-gun and mortar ammunition, it was apparent that all attacks had failed. The Japanese remained entrenched and showed no sign of withdrawal. They appeared to have plenty of machine-gun, rifle, and mortar ammunition.

As the Chinese wounded worked their way back or were carried, they were immediately accepted by the four military doctors. Captain Bone, the anesthesiologist, quickly had each man ready for surgery, which was done exclusively under nerve-block anesthesia. The freshly wounded lay on the jungle floor in one area of virgin tropical rain forest vegetation, and the treated wounded in another.

During the late afternoon, Orange's men worked their way to high ground on either side of the trail as they gradually approached the village. Before dark they had located and pinpointed the Japanese defensive trenches and dugouts on either side of the village. The entire battle area was covered by dense jungle with massive hardwood trees and dense low vegetation, including much thick and heavy bamboo. The Japanese defenses dominated all approaches.

As darkness approached, Colonel Kinnison outlined the action to be taken on 13 May. The Third Battalion's Khaki Combat Team was to make a wide circling approach around the north side of the village and attempt to cut off the enemy from the rear. The Chinese, who were in position, would move a little forward and block the south trail. The Marauders would have to work their way through about four miles of jungle to be in a position to fight for control of the east trail. The jungle was too dense to allow Khaki to take their heavy weapons or animals.

Khaki began their move at 0600 hours. By noon they were at a point where they could reach the east trail by climbing a steep slope. This action had been carried out with great effort, and the men were exhausted. At the crest of the hill they soon discovered a strong Japanese trailblock. The terrain was such that it was virtually impossible to outflank the enemy at the block.

Before the block was discovered, Pvt. John J. Osborne was near its location on a narrow ridge. There had been some Japanese rifle fire, and he was attempting to locate a sniper. He was soon hit by a Japanese rifle bullet at a range of about a hundred yards. The missile hit and caused a grenade, which was attached to his rifle belt, to explode. He was mortally wounded, with torn intestine protruding from his abdominal cavity. He also had severe thigh wounds and a compound fracture of the right leg. Captain Armstrong and his Khaki aid station immediately took charge. In spite of all supportive help, including several units of blood plasma, he died four hours later.

Fifteen minutes after Osborne was hit, a Japanese knee mortar exploded in a tree directly above the aid station, which was located a few yards away. S.Sgt. Layman Foundress was kneeling while administering blood plasma to Osborne. A shell fragment struck him on the left side of his chest, causing a flesh wound. After this was dressed he remained on duty.

Two men in the 3rd platoon, I Company, were hit by snipers at 1400 hours. They were hit when their squad was being moved across the trail in an attempt to get closer to the enemy. A bullet passed through

CHAPTER XX

William J. Panetta's thigh as he attempted to cross the trail. Pvt. Lee Mohler was sitting behind the bank on the side of the trail before crossing. His nose was wounded by what seemed to be a fragment from a rifle bullet. He returned to duty, while Panetta was carried back to Captain Armstrong. After treatment, several men carried him four miles back to the surgical team.

When it became apparent that Khaki was having trouble finding men to carry their wounded out, I requested help from the Chinese 88th Regiment. They quickly sent litter bearers to Khaki's location and carried out all wounded who needed help.

Late in the afternoon, the 1st platoon advanced toward the trail-block with little success against the well-fortified and entrenched Japanese. Before they were ordered to return to their last position, several were bunched up and not aware that they were exposed. Four were wounded by the tree burst of a knee mortar. Corporal Richard J. Hecht was not wearing a helmet. A shell fragment passed through the soft tissue at the back of his head and fractured the outer table of his skull. T5g. Paul R. Bickwell was without his helmet and was wounded over the left temple, the shoulder, and the chest wall. Pvt. Thomas J. Cross was struck over the right foot, where he had a severe injury. They all received surgical treatment and eventual evacuation. Sgt. George R. Hill was sitting without a foxhole. He returned to duty in spite of a flesh wound of the left calf.

Somewhat later, at 1530 hours, Pfc. Johnny Smith was mortally wounded at this same location. He was one of the younger Marauders and a veteran of the Solomon Island campaign. He was sitting in a well-protected spot and had removed his helmet. When he looked over a hummock that protected his position, a rifle bullet creased his skull. He immediately became unconscious. The bullet caused a fracture of the skull at the front. The wound was wide open, and brain was protruding. Captain Jack Armstrong saw and treated him immediately. Because of the late hour, he could not be carried to the surgical portable unit. All possible was done for this young Marauder who had a mortal wound. He was to die about forty hours later while being carried on a litter with the battalion medical detachment in attendance.

While at the same location as Johnny Smith, Pfc. Karl J. Torson was wounded by a bullet that struck his right arm. Surgery was done, and he returned to duty. He would later be evacuated from Myitkyina for further treatment.

Although Khaki was not able to take the village or cause the Japanese to pull a banzai attack, they did their part in keeping them confined to the village. From a rise to the north of Tingkrukawng, Major Briggs, Khaki's commander, was able to get and keep a good view of the Japanese-occupied village. He was able to direct the small amount of mortar available to Khaki but, more important, mortar from Orange. During the later part of the battle, the Japanese were also hit by some of the K Force pack-75 artillery.

By 1645 hours Khaki was low on ammunition and out of food. Colonel Kinnison's only option was to order Major Briggs to withdraw. Because of the late hour, darkness, terrain, and wounded, they did not leave the area until 0800 hours the next morning.

During the early period of Orange's advance on 13 May, Pfc. Carroll R. Molder was wounded in the right supraorbital region of the head by a rifle bullet. The missile caused serious damage to his right eye. He was immediately treated by his company aid man, then taken to Orange Combat Team's aid station and later to the nearby surgical unit.

Four other men from Orange became battle casualties on 13 May. Two were hit when Orange's 2nd platoon, L Company, was setting up a perimeter for the night of 13–14 May. They were on a jungle-covered ridge to the left of the trail. S.Sgt. William C. Noe and Emmauel C. Valderama had been assigned a spot in back of a small ridge, which offered excellent protection. Unfortunately, they both exposed themselves by standing. Valderama saw two Japanese behind a tree and fell prone as he warned Noe. The staff sergeant was killed at that instant. A bullet fired from seventy-five yards passed through his heart and lungs. Valderama, fortunately, only suffered a lacerated wound of the left buttock. He was quickly treated and held for evacuation.

Earlier in the day, Orange Combat Team had advanced well beyond their mortars, the medical detachment, and the 42nd Surgical Portable Unit. The four doctors were busy with surgery while the short trail between Orange's medical detachment and the surgical unit was protected by Chinese troops. High ground to the left of the trail had no protection. Five Japanese with a light machine gun occupied this area and began firing into the aid station and the surgical unit. The Chinese seemed confused and unable to handle the problem. In desperation and with considerable courage, several muleskinners took off to eliminate the machine guns.

Pfc. H. T. Pausch's heroic action cost him his life, and that of Pvt. Clayton A. Vantol resulted in his being wounded. These two and several other muleskinners worked their way toward the gun and, at about fifty yards' range, a burst from the gun caught Pausch in the chest, causing his instant death. Private Vantol was firing his Thompson submachine gun as he tried to reach Pausch. A bullet struck his weapon and caused multiple soft-tissue wounds over one hand, his right leg, and his arms. He made his way back to the aid station, where he was given blood plasma. The wounds were treated by the surgeons, and he was ready for evacuation.

A member of the medical detachment—our veterinarian, Captain William T. Bell—was walking on the trail about twenty yards in back of the area of the recent machine-gun attack when a small piece of metal lacerated his left shoulder. He remained on duty.

Orange sent back a heavy machine gun and crew. This weapon plus mortar fire soon eliminated the Japanese. Orange had no further casualties, and the surgical team was able to get back to work.

As the hour became late on 13 May, the two companies of Chinese had not been able to destroy the Japanese in their sector. Their men were becoming increasingly ineffective because of casualties. They were replaced by a battalion of Chinese that made no better progress, but they continued offensive action. They had cooperated with the Marauders in every phase of the battle.

Chinese casualties began to filter back in increasing numbers. They buried an estimated five dead in the jungle and sent back approximately twenty-five wounded. At least ninety percent of the wounds had been caused by mortar fire. In this group, few brain, chest, or abdominal wounds were seen. They were presumably among the dead. All surgery was simple debridement of soft-tissue injuries and treatment of fractures. Many of the extremity wounds were very severe. One Chinese soldier had his tongue largely destroyed by a bullet that had entered one cheek, passed through his tongue, and exited from the other cheek.

K FORCE MARCHES TO TINGKRUKAWNG

All indications were that a battalion of enemy were in the village. They were now receiving reinforcements from the east. Colonel Kinnison reached the decision that his mission of keeping this battalion of enemy from advancing toward Myitkyina was completed and had been successful.

It was logical to assume that severe damage had been done to the Japanese here at Tingkrukawng. There was no need for further engagement. The time had come for K Force to get to H Force's aid at Myitkyina as soon as possible.

Before the day was over, all the dead Marauders were buried. Invariably each grave was dug by close comrades. Religious services were conducted for some by Lieutenant Logan Weston of Orange's I & R platoon and for others by Father Barrett, the Catholic priest who had been flown in to join us at Hsamshingyang.

The Battle of Tingkrukawng was now over. The first Americans in history had now actively fought and cooperated in battle with Chinese troops. They had marched and killed the enemy together. Americans had taken care of Chinese wounded as they did their own. They would now cooperate in the evacuation of the wounded as they had done after the Battle of Ritpong.

Tingkrukawng Dead and Wounded

	Americans	Chinese
Killed in action	4	5 or more
Died of wounds	2	1
Wounded	14	25
Total losses	20	31

Marauder Dead

Raymond Harris 36312550, T5g., Co. K, Orange
William F. Toomey, Jr. 13013923, Pfc., Co. K, Orange
William C. Noe, S.Sgt., Co. L, Orange
H. T. Pausch, Pfc., Co. K, Orange
John J. Osborne, Jr. 341093950, Pvt., Co. I, Khaki
Johnny Smith 34396554, Pfc., Co. I, Khaki

CHAPTER XX

Marauder Wounded

Carroll R. Molder 36107054, Pfc., Co.K , Orange
Robert E. Beach 20519495, T5g., med. detachment
Emanuel G. Valderama 6592386, Pfc., Co. L, Khaki
Layman Foundress 15045064, S.Sgt., med. detachment
Rubin M. Bey, T.Sgt., Hq. Co., Khaki
William R. Hubbard, Pvt., Co. I, Khaki
William J. Panetta Jr. 1308352, Pvt., Co. I, Khaki
Lee Miller 36740779, Pvt., Co. I, Khaki
Richard J. Hecht 12023794, Pvt., Co. I, Khaki
Paul R. Bickwell 35117641, T5g., Co. I, Khaki
George H. Hill, Sgt., Co. I, Khaki
Thomas J. Cross 35365918, Co. I, Khaki
Earl J. Torson 350l09584, Pfc., Co. I, Khaki
Clayton A. Vantol, Pvt., Co. K, Orange
William T. Bell, Capt., V.C., Third Battalion veterinarian.

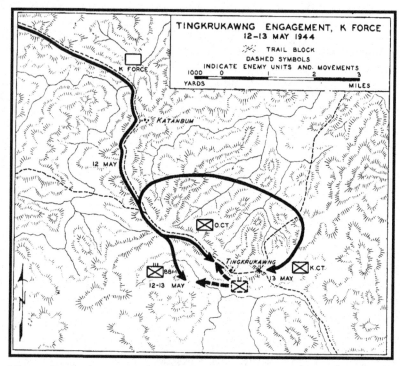

MAP 24. Tingkrukawng engagement: K Force, 12–13 May 1944.

CHAPTER XX

TINGKRUKAWNG TO MYITKYINA

Evacuation of the Sick and Wounded

The message went out that one battalion of Chinese would remain in the area for a brief period to keep the Japanese bottled up and harassed by mortar, machine-gun, and 77mm artillery fire. The rest of K Force was to be ready to depart on the fifty-mile march during the morning of 14 May 1944. One battalion of the Chinese 88th Regiment was to follow in the rear, protecting the walking wounded and carrying the stretcher cases. Every effort was to be made to reach Marawngkawng about ten miles to the southwest. The entire force would bivouac near here for the night of 14–15 May. After a successful airdrop of food and ammunition, sometime during 15 May the wounded would be taken by the Chinese to Arang, five miles to the northwest. When Colonel Hunter and his H Force had bypassed Ritpong on 10 May, they had gone directly to Arang. Here, as previously arranged, they had found a village guarded by Kachins, who as usual were cooperating with their American friends and the few Americans from Detachment 101 who from time to time were flown into safe areas.

Colonel Hunter's troops had improved the small, rough airstrip and had begun to supervise the evacuation of a hundred or more sick men from the Marauder First Battalion, as well as some ill Chinese from the 150th Regiment. Lieutenant Charlton Ogburn Jr., author of *The Marauders*, was in this group. Some of his comrades, who were also evacuated, were soon to die of scrub typhus.

When H Force pulled out, they left Major Dushkin and his surgical unit in charge of evacuation by small plane from the improvised airfield. They received and supervised the removal of more than a hundred sick and wounded from the Battle of Ritpong, who had arrived

471

on 11 May. Several small planes with their heroic sergeant pilots crashed. One crashed two times on the same day, and because of his injuries the pilot was flown out in a third plane. One plane later crashed into a tree, and a ladder had to be made of bamboo to get the pilot and passenger, both of whom had survived, out of the plane.

Shortly after the sick and wounded arrived from the Battle of Tingkrukawng, the Second Battalion of Marauders arrived at Arang. Operating as the M Force with a few Kachins, but with no Chinese, they had crossed the Kumon Mountain Range from the Hukawng Valley by an even more difficult route than the other two forces. They left a group of sick for evacuation, and in a few hours this group was followed by more of their sick, who had been left behind under command of Captain A. Lewis Kolodny. This group had a narrow escape: when they were about to run into a small bunch of Japanese, tragedy was averted when a patrol from the Third Marauder Battalion killed the enemy.

The sick and wounded, both Chinese and American, in spite of pain, fatigue, weakness, and their uncertain future, tolerated their problems with remarkable good humor and fortitude as the several-mile column of men and animals moved through the hot and humid jungle air along the rugged mountain trail. I knew Johnny Smith would soon die and decided to keep him with the Orange medical detachment until he did. We borrowed two Chinese litter bearers, who seemed to move easily along the trail with their burden. About noon Johnny died. We stopped by the trail just beyond a small mountain stream and dug a grave. I said a brief prayer, and this courageous young volunteer was laid to rest. He had served his country well at an age when some young men are still afraid of the dark.

Our cut-off point was reached about noon, and soon the ever-faithful C-47 pilots were over the jungle clearing known as Marawngkawng. As they banked their planes at three hundred feet elevation, our comrades the kickers pushed varicolored nylon parachutes through the side door. Much- needed K-rations, ammunition, and miscellaneous supplies floated over the designated area. Bags of oats came down, as a free drop, for the mules and horses. Resupplied, the Chinese with their sick and wounded charges were soon on their way, headed for Arang five miles to the northwest.

The proper supplies were distributed to the remainder of K Force and combat-loaded for an early departure in the morning of 15 May 1944. We all looked forward to a night of rest in spite of intermittent showers and a mattress of ground cover, no shelter but the open sky.

The March to Charpate

Numerous men were seeking medical advice from the platoon aid men and either Captain Jack Armstrong or myself. Many just felt bad, with such complaints as lack of appetite for the emergency field K-rations on which we had been living for more than ninety days. Recurrent chills, fever, joint, and muscle pain, weakness, weight loss, diarrhea, chest pain. shortness of breath, skin problems, chronic cough, backaches. and stomach problems were all frequent complaints. These complaints had all too often been heard in the past, and were not life-threatening. A new combination of complaints was now surfacing. Numerous men were complaining of severe headaches that persisted in spite of aspirin. The men also had skin rashes and swollen glands in their groins. We suspected that we were now seeing early cases of scrub typhus, the frequently fatal disease about which we had been warned when we were halfway across the mountain range.

The seriousness of the situation became increasingly apparent on 15 May, when we were well on our way toward Myitkyina about forty miles to the south. The march was a nightmare for most of the Americans. The Chinese, who were far behind, seemed to be free of significant medical problems. By the afternoon of 17 May we were at Hkumchet, having covered twenty-five miles—halfway to Charpate. Here, just short of Seingheing, an airdrop was attempted but had to be called off when a radio message ordered us to get to Myitkyina airfield as soon as possible. At Seingheing our officers were puzzled by a recent grave marked by a bamboo cross and the name of Joe Blow. The answer to the mystery was that Colonel Hunter's Force had buried some extra ammunition here.

A night march put the K Force into position to reach the Myitkyina area by the morning of 18 May, one day after H Force had overrun and captured the airfield. A message came through ordering K Force to capture and control Charpate, a small village five miles to the northwest of Myitkyina airfield. Now moving through open country, the

CHAPTER XX

Marauders forged ahead of the 88th Chinese Regiment and reached the outskirts of Charpate, which straddled the gravel road running from Kamaing in the west to Myitkyina in the east. Japanese reinforcements could be expected to be arriving along this road from Kamaing.

Occupation of Charpate

As the Marauder Third Battalion neared the village, our scouts picked up a Japanese machine gun dug in at the far end of the village. A fire fight broke out. After a brief period, the gun was knocked out and the village occupied. During this action Sgt. Frank H. Hunt from Khaki Combat Team was wounded by a bullet that entered the upper right pelvis and passed through his right buttock. A small plane was sent from the airfield, and Hunt was promptly evacuated to the field. He was soon on the way to the 20th General Hospital in Assam, India.

In spite of the obvious crisis from the serious breakdown of the health of the Third Battalion men, Colonel Beach continued to carry out all possible patrol, offensive, and defensive operations ordered by the Myitkyina task force headquarters, which was gradually arriving by small plane from their previous headquarters location on the Hukawng Valley side of the Kumon Mountains. The rumor, which later proved to be true, was that General Merrill had had a heart attack. We learned that he had not, as promised, come to the airfield immediately after its capture to take charge but had come in for a brief period on 18 May when he went out with a heart attack. This was to be his last official contact with the Marauders, but he was known to be active at Lord Louis Mountbatten's headquarters. It was at that location that he introduced General Stilwell to the resort society of Ceylon. This was during General Stilwell's working vacation, beginning several days before he was given a fourth star and while the Americans and Chinese were still fighting to capture the city of Myitkyina, which fell on 3 August 1944.

On 18 May, while a defensive perimeter was being set up about Charpate, Captain Jack Armstrong and I began to make arrangements to send the sickest men to the airfield for evacuation on C-47's. This required that they travel about three and one-half miles through no-man's territory accompanied by a combat patrol. This process would go on daily until fewer than a hundred men were left in the battalion by the last week in May.

Cpl. Bernard Martin, from Providence, Rhode Island, tells the story of his illness fifty years later:

> I had a headache. I talked to the medic about it. He said, "Let me bring the doctor up—a lot of men are getting headaches." So the doctor popped a thermometer in my mouth. He got some aspirin. He looked at the thermometer. He said, "Well, we have got some good news and some bad news." I said, "What's the bad news?" He said, "Well, if you were in the U.S.A., you would be in a hospital—but that's not your luck, and we don't know what it is." I said, "Give me one of those aspirins." I took a couple right away, and the headache started going away. When we were in the flat country we saw a sign that read Myitkyina. It didn't mean much to me, and it was so many kilometers up ahead. The only way I was able to walk was to hang on the ropes that were holding the rack equipment on a mule. I just could not put one foot in front of the other. Finally we got to where a battle was raging.
>
> It started all of a sudden, and Sergeant Ballard said, "There is a hole up ahead, and we will use that shell hole." As I was getting the radio off, the mule got shot, and I had a hell of a time rolling it over to get the equipment on the other side. We finally got a little equipment off, and one of the other mules got wounded—so we got him unloaded as soon as we could and got him off to a location away from the fighting. We had to crawl in and out of the hole to keep from getting shot. Sergeant Ballard said to me, "Send this out in clear text," and I remember it was 1430 hours or something like that. Just as I got through sending the message, the aerial got shot off. Sergeant Ballard was lying on the ground. He said, "Hang in there, I'll fix it myself." He crawled away and came back in about twenty minutes and gave me a piece of wire and said, "Tie it on the end of the antenna." So I tied it on, and he took the other end and crawled away. He had a tree branch in his hand, and he took this and tied the wire to it and stood it up against a piece of junk. I don't know what it was, but it looked like a truck or something that had been shot up years ago. It was a rusting hulk. I started collecting my traffic again, and that was the last I remember. When I woke up I was in a tent and a man was looking at me, and he said, "I am Doctor Seagrave." I said, "Where am I?"

CHAPTER XX

He said, "You are in a hospital, and you are on your way back to headquarters." I closed my eyes and said, "Thank God." I said, "What's wrong?" He said, "Well, you have a pretty high temperature. Your temperature is 105, and I think you have the Japanese typhus or Tsutsugmachi disease." I said, "That's all I need right now." They were feeding me atabrine or something else and it didn't do me any good. I could not move or get up. Either that day or the next day they put me on a C-47 with a bunch of others just like me on stretchers.

When we got back to the base I don't remember being unloaded off the airplane. When I came to it was in a hospital like a basha. It was clean and white, and the orderlies were wearing white. I said to the guy, "Where am I?" He said, "You are in a hospital" (Martin, videotape).

Martin made a gradual recovery. When he returned to the States he was sent to several hospitals so his blood could be studied in an attempt to learn more about the disease.

At that time no drug was available to arrest the condition. Martin was among the men evacuated on 18 May. On arrival, the situation was obviously critical. Hardly a man in our battalion was free of one or more significant illnesses. All were thought to have amoebic dysentery and chronic malaria. Many had broken through the prophylactic protection of atabrine and were showing signs of malaria in increasing numbers. We had no way of telling whether these patients with fever were suffering from malaria or the deadly scrub typhus. Early evacuation could mean the difference between life and death for the latter.

The Myitkyina task force headquarters had been told by numerous sources that the health of the men in the Second and Third Battalions had reached a critical point where men's chances for survival were at stake. We, as physicians, had been deceived and had from the onset of the third mission struggled with our consciences over being any part of an operation to be carried out by men in poor physical condition. Our opinion meant little. General Stilwell had the power to gamble with men's lives due to combat but also from any cause such as disease. He saw a chance to bring about a brilliant victory of questionable emergency value. It would obviously mean a fourth star for him if successful, and the Americans were paying the price. General Merrill had absolutely guaranteed that when the airfield was captured enough experienced Chinese would take over so the Marauders could be flown out on the same planes that had brought in the Chinese replacements. This promise was totally ignored. The Myitkyina task force headquarters seemed to radiate a sense that the airfield could be and would be overrun at any moment. The Marauders, even in their sad state of reduced numbers of sick and exhausted men, never for a moment shared this opinion (Hunter 1963, 137).

While attempting to carry out all combat duties, the three Marauder battalions—as well as the Chinese—suffered from a failure of the Myitkyina task force headquarters to have food and ammunition delivered as soon as the airfield was captured. The promised supplies did not come in until 21 May. This failure further contributed to the deterioration of the health of the Second and Third Marauder Battalions. Both battalions went several days without food. The forced starvation of the Chinese caused some units to refuse to carry out orders.

The officers and men soon learned, by observation and rumor, the situation in the Myitkyina area. The Third Marauder Battalion was immediately responsible for blocking all entrances from the northwest and north into the city. This covered an area running from the Irrawaddy River to Charpate, a distance of four miles.

The 89th Chinese Regiment had now joined the 88th Chinese Regiment, which was no longer a part of the Third Battalion since the K Force had been dissolved. Their sector ran from Charpate southwest to the Mogaung-Myitkyina Railroad.

The Second Marauder Battalion blocked any entrance or exit to the Myitkyina area between the railroad and the Namkwi Hka to the south.

The First Marauder Battalion—after capturing Pamati, Rampur, and the Zygun ferry, all to the south—was brought in to protect the airfield, where they would remain until the end of the campaign on 3 August 1944 (Hunter 1963, 137).

The three battalions of the 150th Chinese Regiment would be between the airfield and the western defenses of the city, three miles east of the airfield. The airfield was within easy artillery range of the Japanese heavy guns located on high ground behind the city defenses. The wide Irrawaddy River blocked entrance to the city from the east and south.

CHAPTER XX

The Morris Force, an ineffective, disease-ridden, and exhausted battalion from General Wingate's Chindits, was attempting to operate on the east side of the Irrawaddy River opposite the city of Myitkyina. Its forces would become rapidly depleted and would be quickly withdrawn.

Between 19 and 22 May the Third Battalion made a successful drive southeastward along the Kamaing-Myitkyina Road, stopping close to Radahpur about three miles north of the city. Two roads led from the north into the city. One passed through Radahpur into Myitkyina. The other ran along the western bank of the Irrawaddy River two miles to the east. Both were potential routes for Japanese supplies and replacements to get into the city.

The men of the Third Battalion were soon running into groups of Japanese arriving from the west, passing through Charpate, and threatening to surround our unit. The Charpate location was much better for defense, patrol, and offensive activity. We were ordered back to that location on 22 May after we had one man seriously wounded and another killed.

Pfc. Albert Mahmood from L Company, Orange Combat Team, while on patrol on 22 May, located a Japanese automatic weapon at about two hundred yards. Unfortunately he advanced well beyond the patrol and was crossing an open field. Some would say he used poor judgement in his attempt to reach and knock out the gun without help. He was hit while standing at a 150-yard range by a light machine-gun bullet. The bullet passed through his abdominal wall from front to back and passed out through the coccyx (tailbone) after perforating the large and small intestine. He walked back sixty yards and was then carried to the aid station. Evacuation was immediate, by hand-carried litter, five miles to Major Gorgon Seagrave's small military hospital at the airport. His life was saved by quick surgery. Long-term treatment was required to treat an ileostomy (drain in the small intestine) and a draining area over the tailbone.

Pfc. John W. Prate Jr. from headquarters company, Khaki Combat Team, was killed on 22 May. At 2300 hours, while in a defensive perimeter, he stood up in his foxhole. A night-time guard five yards in front of his location, mistaking him for a Japanese, turned suddenly and fired one shot from his M-1 weapon. He died instantly from a bullet through the chest.

On 23 May at 1000 hours another tragic death occurred. Sgt Willard G. Dills, L Company, Orange Combat Team, was a member of one of several five-man outposts at the Charpate perimeter defense. His outpost was near the road about four hundred yards out from the perimeter. The one Browning automatic rifleman and the four M-1 riflemen were well dug-in and located in jungle growth for good cover. They had been told that some Chinese would probably be coming in from the north. Dills saw a man at sixty yards' range and, thinking he was a Chinaman, went out to meet him. The man was a Japanese and shot him with a rifle bullet at fifty yards' range. He was immediately carried to the aid station, where plasma was given. His spine had been fractured. No litter plane was available, and he was carried to the 42nd Portable Surgical Unit, which was supporting the 88th Chinese Regiment. He died there fourteen hours later.

During the afternoon I walked approximately two miles to check on Dills's condition. The 42nd was set up just off the railroad track about three miles from the airport and four miles from the city. The doctors and medical personnel were living in foxholes lined with parachutes. The operating tables were litters set up on bamboo poles. Shelter was provided by parachutes. I was discouraged when I learned that Dills had a mortal wound and would soon die. It had been raining all day, and when I prepared to return to Charpate darkness was rapidly and unexpectedly descending. There was only one answer. I had to spend the night in the ditch beside the railroad track. During most of the night, tracer bullets were passing over from several directions. The next day it was made known that a battle had not been fought. Chinese units had been firing in an indiscriminate fashion at an imagined enemy. When I returned to Charpate in the morning, I soon learned that my own personal discomfort was nothing in comparison to what had happened to the Third Battalion during the night of 23–24 May.

The Battle of Charpate

During the late evening of 23 May, the rain continued at Charpate. Several officers were not happy with the defensive arrangements. The general opinion was that the perimeter was too large and the defensive plan not adequate. This region was quite flat, and most of the terrain was open. Early during the evening, twenty Chinese had passed one of the five-man outposts and on into the U.S. lines. At 2300 hours the night was very dark, the rain continued, and it was windy. A company of Japanese passed through one outpost before the Americans knew what had happened. For some reason they had no wire or radio communication with the perimeter. The only option was for the entire outpost to head through the brush for the perimeter. The Japanese beat them to the area. Other outposts mistook them for Chinese and were late in getting their guns into action. About thirty enemy got into the perimeter, while the rest deployed about the general area. During the fight that took place during the extreme darkness of this rainy, windy night, the Marauders had five killed and six wounded. The Japanese left fifteen dead inside the perimeter and had an estimated thirty-five wounded.

Grenades killed two Marauders and wounded three. One was wounded by a bayonet, one by bayonet and bullet, and the others by bullets.

S.Sgt. Thomas C. Schaffer, on his way back to the perimeter, stumbled into a group of enemy and was killed by a grenade and numerous bayonet wounds. S.Sgt Thomas C. Mattock was killed under circumstances similar to Schaffer's.

Sgt. M. M. Belger was wounded by grenade fragments while in a shallow foxhole. He had numerous flesh wounds.

S.Sgt. George O. Blazer had a serious penetrating wound of the right chest and lung, which resulted in long-term treatment.

Pfc. Stephen Komar (nicknamed "the Russian") was hit while firing his Thompson submachine gun. He had killed several enemy when a Japanese bullet struck him in the right arm. He was covered with the bloody intestines of one of the dead enemy when, according to many, he shouted, "Don't shoot!—it's the Russian." The bullet caused a severe compound fracture of the right lower arm.

Pfc. Charles A. Olden was with the outpost that was first alerted. He ran into a group of Japanese while on his way to L Company command post. He survived four bayonet wounds but required extensive hospital care.

Sgt. Melbourne M. Burton from the medical detachment was under a poncho without a foxhole. He attempted to crawl away and was shot by friendly fire with an M-1. Death was instant from a neck wound. His buddy stayed under the poncho and killed a Japanese with his pistol.

TINGKRUKAWNG TO MYITKYINA

1st Lt. John J. Hogan had crawled from his poncho-sheltered hole in order to man a radio. He was killed by a rifle bullet at close range while talking into the radio.

Lieutenant Warren A. Smith was in a kneeling position in a foxhole using a telephone when he was instantly killed by a bullet at a twenty yards' range. His heroic action south of Nhpum Ga, while managing his platoon in cooperation with 1st Lt. Logan Weston's courageous and heroic conduction of the running battle, saved the escape route of the Second and Third Battalions and should never be forgotten.

Pfc. Harold R. Stevenson had been in a jungle hammock acquired, in an undetermined fashion, from a trip to the airfield. He was out and crawling to assist Lieutenant Hogan when a Japanese bullet, fired at short range, caused a flesh wound over his lower abdomen.

During one of the actions at Charpate the Marauders were taking artillery fire. Tony Colombo has a few words about his association with Father Barrett:

> We were laying on the road at Charpate and were under artillery. We were lifted about two feet off the ground every time a shell would explode. The concussion was horrible. I don't think there is an infantryman alive who would not rather have a banzai attack than be shelled. It is a terrible thing because you can't shoot back. You just lay there and hope that one does not land on you. I guess it was Barrett's first encounter with artillery, and he looked at me. He was just trying to pacify me, as I was already dumbfounded and scared like hell. He looked up, and he said, "I only work for that guy up there. If he takes me here, I think it is a damn shame. Cancel out on your scotch and soda and use a little stronger language."

Father Barrett was evacuated the same day I was. He went out in the morning, and I got evacuated in the afternoon. He got evacuated because he was feverish. May 25 I believe the date was. In the afternoon I meandered, after Father Barrett was evacuated, out to Doctor Hopkins and asked him for some more codeine pills because I had a toothache. He had given me some codeine to relieve the pain previous to that, and I had run out. Well anyhow he said, "Look, Painless Parker is over at the airport," and he said, "If you will do me a favor and if you will evacuate four sick men, I'll give you some pills—but I have to warn you that the trail has been cut this morning by the Japanese." I said, "Sure, I will take them—but give me somebody that can shoot." He said, "No, these guys are just too sick." They were belly-down on horses, and I walked them through. Well, we didn't run into any Japanese, and when we got to the airport it was a mess, all you could see was piled debris, smoke, and cast-off equipment. It was a mess, but we got to the medical tents.

The nurse said, "What do we have here? Oh, you have four sick men to check—I'll check them out." I had just taken them in. She took them on in and she turned around and she said, "What are you here for?" I said, "I am here to see Painless Parker. I have a toothache." She said, "Well, let me see." She put her hand on my forehead, took a look at me, said, "You better take a check," shook a thermometer and stuck it in my face, and walked off. She came back, took the thermometer out, looked at it, shook it again, and stuck it back in my face. I said, "What the hell is she doing?" as she's hollering for some doctor. He comes out and she says, "Check that thermometer." He checks the thermometer, takes a little ticket out, and he writes FUO. I didn't realize it meant "fever of unknown origin."

Then he gave me the tag and said, "Get on that plane over there." I get on this C-47. It had bucket seats, and I sit down and there is a Chinaman sitting alongside me just grinning. All of a sudden he just flopped over and he was dead. They took him off the plane and put another one in. That was the last thing I remember until I awoke in the hospital.

When I awoke they had taken my .45 and they were scrubbing me down. They put me in a bed, and I was just out. Weeks out I got conscious. My musette bag was there, and I had two grenades in it. I started hollering and screaming that I wanted my .45 back, and it's Father Barrett's .45. Anyhow, what happened. . . . I went out again—I guess I was out for seven or eight days. I would wake up from time to time and find myself packed in ice. I remember a little nurse. Her name was Patricia Murphy. She would feed me ice cream, keep me cool, and talk to me. When I finally did come around I found out that I had a fever of one hundred and six. The whole thing lasted for about eighteen days, and it just went on until it got to a point where it began to subside and I started to come around. They were giving us beer for appetite. There was a case of beer under the cots. None of us could eat. We all wanted it but couldn't eat—our stomachs were shriveled up. I don't know how much I weighed then, but months later I weighed ninety-one pounds when I got off the plane in Florida.

From there I went on home and to Lovell General Hospital in Worcester, Massachusetts, and that went on for about thirteen months of hospitalization. Then they decided they were going to put me back in and use me during the Battle of the Bulge. They shipped me out to Fort Knox, Kentucky. I was supposed to be a demonstration sergeant. They were training officers at the time. I had one night of that, and I just said to hell with it. I am not going to do it tonight. The captain came to me the next morning and he said, "Look, you are going to have to do it." I said, "I just couldn't last night." He said, "Well, come along to the medics." So a little doctor came out. I was standing in the sick-call line and the doctor said to me, "You here again?" He didn't realize I was new and just mistook me for somebody else. I was just about to pop him in the pus and I said, "This is the first time I have ever seen you." The captain interjected and said, "This is the man I was talking to you about." The doctor said, "Oh! Get in that ambulance right there." The first thing you know they sent me to a hospital in Danville, Kentucky, and put me into some kind of rehabilitation thing and discharged me with a fifty-percent disability (Colombo, videotape).

The Last Days of the Third Battalion at Myitkyina

Because of the outlying exposed position of the decimated Third Battalion, Colonel Beach was ordered to move his men two miles to the south and set up on the northwest tip of the Chinese regiment's area. This move took place during the morning of 24 May. Several skirmishes took place during the move, but there were no American casualties. During the night a few Japanese artillery shells had fallen into the area, but we had no wounded.

On 24 May, one of the battalion's ten-man patrols, armed with four Browning automatic rifles, one Thompson sub-machine gun, and four M-1's, hit a group of forty-five Japanese armed with four light machine guns and a lone knee mortar. Twenty enemy were killed and a large number were wounded. No Marauders were injured.

On 26 May S.Sgt. Paul M. Mathis led a patrol out a hundred yards beyond his outpost. The area was thought to be free of any enemy. He advanced alone ahead of his patrol to the designated location. Here he unexpectedly encountered a Japanese who threw a grenade, resulting in numerous soft-tissue injuries. The sergeant made his way back for dressings and was evacuated.

CHAPTER XX

On 26 May, the American 209th Combat Engineer Battalion was taken from its work on the Ledo-Shingbwiyang Road and rushed to Myitkyina. They were sent out to join the Third Marauder Battalion. Colonel Beach and his men gave them emergency instruction in the use of the important infantry weapons. The bulldozer operators, truck drivers, and other engineer specialists were grateful for expert instruction in the care and use of grenades, M-1 rifles, Browning automatic rifles, Thompson submachine guns, flame throwers, mortars, and machine guns. The Marauders had a few nervous nights from indiscriminate firing of weapons by the engineers. Some of the Marauders volunteered to assist Colonel Beach in directing an attack by these replacements to take up a blocking area just south of Radahpur on the Radahpur-Myitkyina Road. This operation at the end of May was successful and was the beginning of the heroic offensive role the 209th Engineers played during the drawn-out battle for the capture of Myitkyina (Hunter 1963, 158; Romanus and Sunderland 1956, 237).

The roster of the Third Battalion now listed fewer than fifty sick and exhausted Marauders. Colonel Beach had been sent out sick. Colonel Kinnison had remained with the Chinese Regiment after K Force was dissolved. Unknown to the Marauder medical detachment, he had been ill for several days. When he came in around 30 May for a conference with General Boater, his condition was critical, with a high temperature. In spite of immediate hospital care, he soon died of scrub typhus.

About 30 May I took the three-mile trip to see Colonel Hunter at the airfield, and he advised me to use my own judgment about giving evacuation tags to all who required them. Since the few remaining men all had good medical reasons for evacuation, they were sent to the airport for final evaluation by Major Schudmak and any other medical officer who wished to express an opinion and act according to his judgement. None were turned down. I was glad to finally have the opportunity to seek treatment for a severe dysentery that had troubled me since the Battle of Nhpum Ga. The final diagnosis—made about four months later at Walter Reed Hospital—would be, as suspected, amoebic dysentery.

Between 26 May and 1 June, Stilwell's staff was rushing every American they could find, sick and otherwise, who had infantry experience and could hold a rifle, to the front (Romanus and Sunderland 1956).

The Second Battalion was in the process of being evacuated en mass because of chronic and acute illness and exhaustion. About two hundred men from the First Battalion, which had come through the campaign in slightly better condition than the others, would remain to protect the airfield. As explained later, numerous Marauders—later called Old Galahads—would volunteer to return in order to assist and train unorganized American replacements during the long, drawn-out battle for the capture of the city. Other sick and recuperating Marauders would be virtually shanghaied to return to the battle.

The epic battle against the Japanese was over for most of the Marauders. Every battle had ended in victory. Some of the Marauders would have to continue until 3 August under continuing adverse circumstances. The men continued to fight disease, thoughtlessness, administrative mistakes, inadequate food and ammunition, poor medical care, horrible living conditions, and a general lack of gratitude by General Stilwell and his Northern Combat Area Command.

Of the Third Battalion, 25 men had been killed, 17 died of wounds, and 109 others had been wounded. The battle casualties among the approximately 850 Third-Battalion men who had entered Burma totalled 151. The vast majority were among the six hundred or so riflemen who made up the infantry companies.

The care of the sick and wounded of the Third Battalion, while we were in the Myitkyina area, was a tremendous burden on the few remaining reasonably healthy men left in the battalion. With few exceptions we no longer had the service of the light planes. The men had to walk, ride horses or mules, or be carried the five miles through hostile, unsecured territory to the airfield. This primitive, slow, and physically difficult situation contributed to the death of some of the sick and wounded (Hunter 1963, 131).

Virtually the entire battalion had been partly or completely disabled by chronic or acute disease. General Merrill forbade any record keeping in Burma. The records of the rear echelon disappeared after the campaign. No complete roster of the unit has survived. Other members of the original volunteer group died in plane crashes, miscellaneous accidents, and additional combat at Myitkyina. The exact number of Third Battalion men who died of disease, if ever tabulated, has not been located. A conservative estimate would put this figure at thirty (Romanus and Sunderland 1956).

Third Battalion Dead at Charpate

John W. Pruitt, Jr. 16138944, Pfc., Hq. Co., Khaki
Thomas C. Schaffer 6978587, S.Sgt., Co. L, Orange
Milburn M. Burton, Sgt., medical detachment, Orange
Donald J. Hogan, 1st Lieutenant, Co. K, Orange
Warren A. Smith, 2nd Lieutenant, Co. K, Orange
Thomas C. Matlock 6978587, S.Sgt., Co. L, Orange
Willard G. Dills 3408879, Sgt., Co. L, Orange [died of wounds]

Third Battalion Wounded at Charpate

Frank H. Hunt 35117268, Sgt., Co. I, Khaki
Albert Mahmood 17107851, Pfc., Co. L, Orange
Mayo M. Belger 6927924, Sgt., Co. L, Orange
George O. Blazier 36610620, S.Sgt., Co. L, Orange
Stephen Komar 17047768, Pfc., Co. L, Orange
Charles A. Ogden 20106959, Pfc., Co. L, Orange
Harold R. Stevenson, Pvt., Co. K, Orange
Paul M. Mathis, S.Sgt., Co. K, Orange

Chapter XXI
Second Battalion Heads for Myitkyina

The battalion began the historic march, as scheduled, on 7 May. A lead platoon was well in advance and during the day reported a skirmish with the enemy. One man, a Kachin, had been wounded. The Japanese had then pulled out. The trail was proving to be almost impossible, and the battalion units were, by necessity, becoming wildly separated. The animals could not advance over the shorter primary trail and, on this the first day, had to be led over a longer but slightly easier trail. The pioneer and demolition platoon and a few Kachins were making a valiant effort to improve the trail. The steep up-and-down trails were very slippery because of continued rain.

Lieutenant Freer's I & R platoon had been sent out several days ahead of the battalion and by 5 May had reached the crest of the six-thousand-foot Hpunsimaru Bum. Lieutenant Witten's platoon and Captain Lyons's heavy weapons platoon had also been sent to join and back up the I & R. On 7 May, Freer reported by radio that three days of hard work would be necessary to make the trail passable for animals between Mgumaka on the west and Hpunsimaru Bum toward the east. Traveling to the east, two days' work would be necessary to make the trail passable for animals from Hpunsimaru Bum to the river that crossed the trail three miles to the east. The trail from Hkada Ga was very slippery and wet.

On 7 May, Freer's I & R was hit by a Japanese outpost, well concealed about eight hundred yards east of the river and one mile east of Hpunsimaru Bum. One of the Kachins traveling with the I & R was wounded. He was started on the way to evacuation from Naubum. A radio message was sent to Father Stewart at task force headquarters to inform him that the Kachin was being sent back for evacuation and treatment.

CHAPTER XXI

Freer had been ordered to avoid a major engagement. His platoon withdrew and set up a defensive area at the river. Offensive operations would await the arrival of Colonel McGee and the major portion of the Second Battalion.

The effort to envelop and destroy the Japanese position just west of Sharaw Kawng got under way on 10 May. A section of 81mm mortars, Witten's platoon, and a section of light machine guns under Captain Lyons moved up to the riverline below Sharaw Kawng, where the I & R was located. When all units were set, Sergeant Cobb took a section of the I & R platoon into the jungle on the right in an attempt to climb up the steep mountainside to get in back of the Japanese position.

After Cobb and his men were well on their way, Witten's platoon advanced up the trail to the position from which the enemy had first fired on the I & R on the 5th. They did not draw any fire. After advancing high enough to outflank all areas suitable for an ambush, the I & R group entered the trail and came down. They found no enemy but passed their last ambush site, which appeared to have recently been occupied by fifteen or twenty Japanese. The coals were still hot in a firebed. Now they had to keep this group of Japanese from setting up new ambushes on the trail leading to Muta Ga.

The delay at Sharaw Kawng had given the rest of the battalion time to catch up. From Hkada Ga the trail was up and down all the way and was by far the worst the battalion men had ever traveled on. In spite of all obstacles, the lead elements of the battalion arrived at Senjo Ga at 1480 hours on 7 May. They waited for the animals, which arrived at 1630. Animals and men were exhausted. Many animals had slipped and fallen down the trail or mountainside. Two animals had fallen to their death. The men would have to follow to rescue the surviving animals and the loads of the dead and living. It was obvious that no pack animal, camel, or elephant had ever passed over this trail. Rain continued, and the battalion bivouacked at Senjo Ga for the night.

Some monkeys were seen from time to time but no other animals. Jack Girsham, an officer in the Kachin Levies and a professional hunter, reported that one or two tigers were near the battalion's perimeter. The explanation was that he could smell them since they rolled in their urine. He had also heard a low-pitched call, which only an experienced hunter would hear. The following day Girsham was very ill with a severe attack of malaria and had to move back to Naubum with a Kachin escort.

On 11 May a group of about forty Kachins caught up to Lt. Edward Shearer's platoon, which was bringing up the rear of the Second Battalion. A Lieutenant Ward, of OSS, was with them but soon left to return to his base in the Tanai Hka area. This small unit would be the only group of Kachins to travel with the Second Battalion.

The men and animals struggled on but would not reach the summit of six-thousand-foot Hpunsimaru Bum until the afternoon of 11 May. They passed over the summit and went on to Sharaw Kawng, just beyond the area where the Japanese had fired on the I & R platoon. At this location they learned that Sergeant Perelli had gone over the side of a cliff with a mule. He survived, but the mule died. Here they picked up Pvt. Bert Fore, a sick Marauder who had to be carried many miles to Arang for evacuation.

A part of he battalion would not reach Hpunsimaru until 13 May. 1st Lt. Edward McLogan, of F Company, was in charge of this group. They were protecting and helping fifteen sick men who were under the care of the combat team's surgeon, Captain A. Lewis Kolodny. Most of the animals were also in this group and were able to reach Sharaw Kawng, on the side of the Hpunsi Bum, late in the day. They were well on their way toward Muta Ga on 14 May. The first day's march had been very difficult but less so than the six other days it had taken to reach this bivouac area east of Sharaw Kawng.

The I & R and other lead elements reached Muta Ga on 12 May. The village site was roughly circular and two hundred yards in diameter. A trail on the northeast led to Ritpong and one on the southeast to Arang. There were signs that the Japanese had stopped here but no indication which trail they had taken. Sergeants Collins, Kessler, and Lovejoy advanced up the trail toward Ritpong to set up a block. A short time later, gunfire was heard by the others. Collins soon came down the trail. His left shoulder was covered with blood. Major Rogoff, the battalion surgeon, had been traveling with the advance units of the battalion. He quickly evaluated and treated the sergeant's wound and made him comfortable before the trip to Arang. Sergeant Collins had run into two Japanese, one of which he had killed.

The airdrop of four days' rations was completed without problems.

CHAPTER XXI

The food was distributed to the men, and arrangements were made for the rest of the battalion to pick up their quota when they would arrive on 14 May. General Merrill flew over Muta Ga as a passenger in a liaison plane. He dropped a message of congratulations for passing over the mountains and requested that the battalion head for Myitkyina as soon as possible. All trails were blocked, and the men spent a peaceful night. The advance units departed Muta Ga at 0630 hour for Arang. General Merrill had promised to meet Colonel McGee at Arang on 14 May, but his plane did not show up. A radio message ordered the colonel to move to Myitkyina as soon as possible.

Lieutenant Shearer's platoon remained at Muta Ga to block the trails and guard the food until Major Healey arrived with the bulk of the battalion and animals during the afternoon of 14 May. Capt. Kolodny, with the sick and an equipment detail, had not yet arrived.

The battalion arrived at Arang at 1400 hours on 15 May. The men and animals were exhausted, and many men were sick with diarrhea, fever, weakness, muscle and back strains, and general malaise. No word had been heard from Captain Kolodny and his group of sick and injured. This group had reached Muta Ga on 15 May. They took the trail to Ritpong since they had not been told of a change in the destination. Just before they were about to run into a group of retreating Japanese infantry, a massacre of the Americans was prevented when a patrol from the Third Battalion—on a mopping-up operation from the battles of Ritpong and Tingkrukawng—caught and eliminated the enemy. Captain Kolodny and his charges were soon on their way to Arang for evacuation.

Captain Kolodny describes the incident:

> We were going up the trail toward Myitkyina. I had a point man, one in the rear, and two on the flanks. As I was walking—we had the sick and wounded walking or on horses or mules—the radio man reported that the Japanese were going to hit us on this trail. I pointed out to the guys what was going to happen. You never saw wounded or sick move so fast. We managed to evade the Japanese. The Third Battalion had cut them off on that trail. We got to the strip where we were going to evacuate the sick and wounded (Arang) just a few hours after the main body. They were very surprised to see us moving so fast, which points out the fact

that the adrenaline will really flow when your neck is in a sling (Kolodny, videotape).

On arrival at Arang, Colonel McGee found that the evacuation of the sick and wounded from the Battles of Ritpong and Tingkrukawng was almost completed. The Seagrave portable surgical unit, which had been left there on a temporary basis by H Force in order to help, was still directing the operation.

Doctor Kolodny and the bulk of the sick arrived on 15 May, and forty-nine Second Battalion men were added to those awaiting a flight out in the small liaison planes. When the battalion pulled out on 16 May, Captain "Doc" Stelling was left behind to look after the evacuation of the Second Battalion sick. He arrived at Myitkyina about a week later and was evacuated with hepatitis.

At the end of the campaign, "Doc" Stelling sent a very comprehensive medical report through channels. One paragraph gives interesting comments on the march over the Kumon Mountains:

> During the last half of the campaign following Nhpum Ga, the men were so thoroughly exhausted that when required to climb the five- to six-thousand-foot ranges of mountain they were forced to cross only by very slow, labored marching—with rest stops every five or ten minutes. The mules and horses were so exhausted and undernourished that they began falling down without being able to get up, even without packs and saddles. We were losing, toward the last day of these rugged mountain marches, as many as ten animals in a single day. Near the last, loads had to be left, and the few remaining animals had to be shuttled back and forth until the absolutely essential loads were brought through. Many animals and pack saddles and much ammunition and equipment had to be left behind with no hope of recovery. The battalion at times was scattered from ten to twenty-five miles along these mountain trails. If any sizable enemy force had been met or had ambushed or cut off segments of our columns, we would have been exterminated without a chance of holding our own (Stone 1969).

Later in the report he further describes the situation:

CHAPTER XXI

When the battalion finally reached Arang, some fifty men were incapable of marching because of exhaustion plus specific diseases, including advanced malaria, epidemic hepatitis, cholecystitis, chronic bloody diarrhea of weeks duration, and fevers of unknown origin. Several typhus cases developed out of this group. I made an insistent appeal to the battalion surgeon to put up a stand to evacuate the entire battalion at Arang, where an airstrip was available, as none of the men would be able to fight when they finished the march to Myitkyina. No man in the battalion was in condition for combat at Arang, and certainly the almost fifty miles that still lay ahead would not improve the condition of the men (Stone 1969).

It was also learned that the First Battalion had sent out a group of sick and injured. Among this group were several men critically ill with scrub typhus. Three and perhaps more of this group died of the disease. Fortunately, as of this date, no scrub typhus had shown up among the men of the Second Battalion. They would later learn that several of their men evacuated from Hsamshingyang had scrub typhus and that one had died.

Before leaving Arang a census of the Second Battalion listed 520 men and officers and 63 animals. During the seven-day crossing of the Kumon Mountains they had lost forty-six animals. Aside from the need for food for the men and animals, there was an urgent need for machine-gun and mortar ammunition. A request for an airdrop at Seingheing was made before departure from Arang on 16 May. The only orders were to get to Myitkyina as soon as possible. The I & R had departed for Seingheing on the 15th.

The Second Battalion moved out in the rain and kept bumping into the rear of the First Battalion of the Chinese 88th Regiment. This Chinese outfit had carried the casualties from Tingkrukawng to Arang. Unfortunately, their advance had left a muddy, slippery trail that the Americans had to follow. At noon the Second Battalion had about fifteen more miles before reaching Seingheing. They had now joined their I & R platoon and took a long noon break to attempt radio communication with the Myitkyina task force headquarters at Naubum and to let the Chinese get further ahead. The last drop of food had been consumed at Muta Ga on the 13th, and they now had little if any remaining. Headquarters could do no better than set an airdrop date for 18 May at Seingheing. This was most unsatisfactory. After a few more miles of marching, they bivouacked along a stream.

No rations were available on the 17th, and an increasing number of sick men were having trouble keeping up. The Chinese were still delaying the movement of the battalion. After marching nineteen miles in two days, the Second Battalion bivouacked about a mile north of Seingheing.

On the morning of the 18th they moved to the designated area to wait for an early airdrop. None had had food for twenty-four hours and some for forty-eight hours. Here they found the men who had been left by the First Battalion for evacuation. They assured Colonel McGee that arrangements had been made for evacuation. He took the opportunity to add twenty-one Second Battalion men, including Captain Stelling and Captain Beach. Captain Stelling had been running a fever for several days and now was showing signs of hepatitis, as were several of the other men.

The fate of this group of more than fifty men has been discussed with the history of the First Battalion's march to Myitkyina. In spite of the heroic effort of Captain Senff, who—while very ill—walked twenty miles through enemy territory to get help, they eventually had to walk the twenty miles back to Arang before those who were still living were evacuated.

Unanswered questions still remain about the sick left by the First and Second Battalions. The First Battalion left their sick on 15 May. K Force spent several hours there on 17 May, and there was no evidence of any of these men in the area. I remember seeing and puzzling over the Joe Blow grave, the buried ammunition site left by the First Battalion. Where were the sick? They were clearly at the area the Second Battalion identified as Seingheing when they passed through on 18 May. Did any of the sick actually die as a result of the failure of the Myitkyina task force to remember that these men had been abandoned?

Colonel McGee waited until 0900 hours for the airdrop of food. His only orders were to move as soon as possible. This seemed more important than food, and he therefore moved quickly over a route to the east of the slow-moving Chinese. Progress was satisfactory, and no enemy were encountered. They spent the night ten miles north of

Myitkyina. After a miserable night, they crossed the Mogaung-Myitkyina road and a little later the railroad. Try as he might, Colonel McGee was unable to make radio contact for information. As they neared the railroad, they sent the I & R platoon ahead to obtain information and orders. While waiting, they came under mortar fire from the east. The I & R eventually arrived at the recently captured airport, and it was determined that the fire was coming from the 88th Chinese Regiment. The mortar fire was stopped, and they were told that the Third Marauder Battalion was to the east on the road at the village of Charpate and two miles from their current location. This part of K Force was attempting to cover the three-mile northern boundary of the city of Myitkyina. The 88th Chinese Regiment was located two miles to the east on the railroad, from which location they were supposed to block the northwestern suburban boundary of the city.

The Second Battalion was ordered to occupy the town of Namkwi, located one mile south of the railroad on a convex curve of the Namkwi Hka on the eastern bank. This town was four miles from the airport. They were to cover the area from the railroad directly south for four miles and then tie in with Red Combat Team of the First Battalion located on the Irrawaddy River at the town of Pamati. As they were settling in for the night, they saw a lot of tracer fire to the east where the Chinese were rapidly using ammunition. They had reached the village of Namkwi free of enemy action and made bivouac at 0600 hours. Patrols brought back enough K-rations from the First Battalion for one meal. This was the first food they had eaten in seventy-two hours. They learned that no food had come in since the airport was captured on 17 May. General Merrill had promised Colonel Hunter that food and ammunition would arrive as soon as the airport was captured, and now the Second Battalion learned that this promise had not been kept.

Colonel McGee picked up some information from the commander of Red Combat Team, Captain John P. McElmurray. He explained that the airport had been taken without a fight and that so far there had been no reaction. He apparently did not know about the Third Battalion's skirmish at Charpate or White Combat Team's action south of Myitkyina. He must have had no knowledge of the numerous Chinese wounded.

SECOND BATTALION HEADS FOR MYITKYINA

Major Gordon S. Seagrave arrived by air with his nurses and surgical team on 18 May. His first two patients brought in on that day were dead. On 20 May he operated on 120 Chinese patients.

The morning of 20 May was rainy. The Second Battalion remained in bivouac and maintained contact with the Chinese 88th Regiment on the railroad. A pack train was sent to the airfield to pick up rations. Major Rogoff walked to the airport to deliver twenty-five sick for evacuation. On this hot, humid day the four-mile trip was very hard on the sick men. Major Schudmak, the Marauder regimental surgeon, was at Colonel Hunter's makeshift headquarters to process the sick and wounded. He was located at midfield on the west, and Major Seagrave's surgical unit was directly opposite on the east. Colonel McGee also traveled to the airport and met General Merrill's deputy, Colonel McCammon, who was in charge of the Myitkyina task force. He advised McGee to keep his battalion at its present location.

On 21 May the Second Battalion sent out another twenty-five sick men. Its strength was now only four hundred officers and men.

A patrol found that the Chinese had withdrawn without notifying Colonel McGee. Shortly after this information was learned, a message was dropped by liaison plane. The battalion was ordered to extend patrols four miles to Charpate and to the northwest. A note sent from headquarters informed McGee that six hundred Japanese were headed toward Myitkyina from a location eight miles west of Namkwi. Shortly after this information was obtained, a patrol ran into about thirty enemy near a railroad bridge about three miles west of Namkwi. They were not moving but had automatic weapons and knee mortars. Later they were joined by about 125 Japanese.

The several skirmishes with the enemy resulted in the death of one Second Battalion man and one wounded. During the day, seven sick were sent to the airfield for evacuation.

On 22 May, McGee got the only written order he had ever seen from Merrill. It was air-dropped as Field Order No. 10, "By Order of General Merrill," from task force headquarters. Colonel McGee had never heard of the other nine orders. It was an order for reconnaissance-in-force by a combat team of the First Battalion. On the 23rd they were to pass through the Second Battalion's sector and move on to contact the Third Battalion at Charpate. They would then return to the airfield. This order was later cancelled. The Third Battalion had been at Charpate since their arrival on 18 May, and this was the first that McGee knew of their arrival or location.

Colonel McGee was ordered to the airstrip on 23 May for an interview with Colonel McCammon. The four-mile walk was made in the rain. On arrival at the airfield he found that all flights had been cancelled because of the weather. This had been and would be a frequent problem. He soon learned that General Merrill had had a heart attack and had only been in for a short time on 19 May. Colonel McCammon had been informally promoted and advised to wear the stars of a brigadier general, since he was now in charge. An order on the 22nd had made him commander of the task force, which now included the three decimated Marauder battalions, the 88th and 89th Chinese Infantry Regiments from the 50th Division, and a combination of the 150th Regiment from the 30th Division and the 42nd from the 14th Chinese Division. The Chinese commanding generals had each arrived on the 23rd, well after their troops. The meeting was to notify Colonel McGee of the command situation. The Second Battalion was to remain at Namkwi.

The Japanese put a few mortar rounds on the Second Battalion's location on the 23rd. The I & R drove them off and captured a Japanese knee mortar.

On the 24th small groups of enemy were moving toward Charpate, and there were two skirmishes. The Marauders had two men wounded.

Radio communication with task force headquarters continued to be unreliable. Lieutenant Botts contacted Major Pilcher and asked for a telephone line to be put through.

Those of us who had been to the airfield were astonished to learn that the Myitkyina task force was very doubtful that the airfield could be held. The rumor had spread that Colonel McCammon was talking about a plan of evacuation in case the field was overrun. There was at no time any indication that Colonel Hunter or any of the battalion commanders or men even considered such a possibility. The Marauders knew that several thousand enemy were trapped in the town with little chance of replacements or additional supplies. There was never any evidence of fear or lack of confidence among the Marauders. General Stilwell had pushed us to the limit of human tolerance and endurance, but he had not destroyed our sense of duty to our country and our fellow Marauders. Those of us from the Pacific campaigns had found much to be disillusioned about. We had been in some poorly planned and poorly led campaigns with inadequate manpower or military power, but this campaign was the worst. American casualties had been unnecessarily excessive.

I, like many others, had volunteered for a brief and dangerous mission. We had been told that it was ordered by the President. The men expected to be assigned a well-planned mission with definite objectives and superb higher-echelon leadership. Our supplies and equipment had been well planned in the states. Our unit leaders did their best to make up what was left out. Now at Myitkyina our supplies and their delivery system had been removed from our control without consultation or previous notice and combined with the Chinese supply-and-delivery system. We had gone into action against an enemy who had very effective artillery, while we had none.

From the beginning, the health of the Third Battalion was way below standard, while a somewhat similar situation existed in the Second. The unit medical officers continued to struggle with medical problems but got little help from General Stilwell's CBI staff or the Northern Area Command. The 5307th Composite Unit was on the way into Burma before General Stilwell's chief medical officer knew that we were in the CBI.

Mortar and artillery fire hit McGee's battalion during the morning of the 26th. This was coming from Japanese located along the railroad to the west and would continue all day. Because of heavy rain the air force could not be called in, but the Japanese were hit with mortar. The Japanese were apparently trying to block the Second Battalion while they were moving troops into Myitkyina.

Colonel McGee had gone to the airfield, and in his absence Major Healy moved the battalion out of the area to prevent any further casualties. When the colonel returned he reported that the battalion had been ordered to move on 27 May to join the remnant of the Third Battalion at Charpate. He was also informed that a company of engineers would be joining the battalion.

Company C of the 209th Engineer Battalion joined the Second Marauder Battalion on 27 May. The move to Charpate was postponed, since the Japanese artillery was shelling the Third Battalion,

CHAPTER XXI

A few of the Second Battalion's recovered sick and wounded had been returning from hospitals in Assam. A current roster, which included the engineer company, showed 455 enlisted men, 24 officers, and 45 animals. Since the report of 27 April, the battalion had lost two hundred men and sixty-three animals.

A patrol was fired on in Namkwi village without any serious contact. The weather was good, and the air force gave the Japanese a good going over west of Namkwi.

The air corps had good days on both 29 and 30 May. The weather was clear, and Japanese replacements were on the move. The lull in fire fights and artillery and mortar attacks was used to give a brush-up course to the engineers on the use of infantry weapons and patrol activity. These men, fresh from road building, were eager students and quick learners. Two men were wounded during this period. On the 30th, word was received that General Stilwell had brought in General Boatner without telling him that he was coming in to replace Colonel McCammon. While at the airfield Stilwell told him that he was now the commanding officer of the Myitkyina task force.

Colonel McGee learned from Colonel Hunter on 31 May that his battalion would march immediately to the Third Battalion area at Charpate. The battalion moved out with the I & R in the lead and the engineers in the rear. They were starting two miles south of Namkwi and had to avoid the area on the six-mile march to Charpate. The detour took them through tall and thick elephant grass on a very hot day. As they approached the area on the railroad track where the Third Battalion had been, word came back that the area was booby trapped and had not been cleared. A horse was sent ahead in order to explode any uncleared explosives. The horse got through without injury, and the march continued.

At a point a mile further down the trail, a Japanese machine-gun opened up. A fight developed that continued during the entire afternoon. The battalion had one man killed and eleven wounded. Artillery fire was called in, and the battalion mortars were used. The unit spent the night in the battle area.

Colonel McGee tells of the plight of the Second Battalion at this time in his unpublished record, "The History of the Second Battalion, Merrill's Marauders" (1987).

In this history, he stresses the fatigue of the men and of himself. He recalls "numbness in the legs, difficulty of map reading, and a tendency to drop off."

During the night two Japanese—from the Third Battalion of the 114th Regiment—were killed by grenades. As would be expected from green troops, firing was heard from the engineer bivouac area.

On a rainy 1 June, the battalion remained in the area. Patrols were active. The night was quiet except from the engineer section, where there was intermittent grenade and rifle fire.

On 2 June, Colonel Hunter sent a platoon from the 236 Engineer Battalion from his position further east on the railroad back to the Second Battalion's position. A hand carried message ordered McGee to proceed with the attack on Charpate.

During the period of deploying the battalion to attack Charpate, Colonel McGee reached the wise decision to request that the battalion be relieved and moved to the airstrip. He also requested that C Company of the 209th Engineers be ordered to set up a perimeter defense and block the trail along the railroad track. Major Healy took both requests to Colonel Hunter, who granted them.

Both colonels had good reasons for their decisions. Any Japanese left at Charpate were not apt to offer trouble to the attacking troops. They were there to help strays and replacements to get into the city before they also tried to join their besieged comrades. Much better to let them starve there then throw exhausted and sick Americans into their machine guns, rifles, grenades, and mortars. The mission was not worth the sacrifice.

Colonel McGee had been with his men in Trinidad, through the long trip to India, over the strenuous training period, and during the five hundred or more miles and numerous battles in Burma. They had helped each other through death, wounds, acute and chronic illness, starvation, and thirst. Their minds had withstood emotional stress, and their bodies had survived extreme exertion, inadequate food, polluted water, and all the harmful results of acute and chronic tropical diseases. The commanding general had for months ignored their physical condition, and his martinets apparently had done nothing to change his mind. He had slowly pushed the Marauders to the brink of destruction. Colonel Hunter had also been with the Marauders from the beginning. He knew that there was hardly a man or officer who was not suffering from malnutrition, amoebic dysentery, chronic malaria, and exhaustion. These two West Point graduates had the courage to do the right thing by their men. All evidence points to the fact that they both were of the opinion that a crisis never existed once the airfield at Myitkyina had been captured. The Japanese only had an interest in holding the town until 1 August. They had been defeated on all fronts. Six fresh Chinese regiments and two battalions of American engineers were already in place. General Stilwell knew that twenty-six hundred American infantry replacements were already in India. He could have also called in the fresh British 36th Division.

The Second Battalion moved to the airfield, where they bivouacked for the night. Planes were available on 2 June and, after processing by Major Rogoff and Captain Kolodny, the Second Battalion completed its contribution to the Battle of Myitkyina.

Doctor Kolodny explains what happened:

> We had several battles there, and by this time people were flipping out very quickly. At one of the battles we had to leave because we ran out of ammunition just as the Japanese were coming into the village of Charpate. I had gone to sleep in a foxhole, and the group failed to mention to me that they were leaving Charpate. The last man going through happened to look in the foxhole and saw me. He yanked me out, and we started running with the Japanese on our tail. When we had the last battle, there were maybe a couple dozen of us left at the most. Colonel McGee was so exhausted he fell asleep in his foxhole. I have a picture of that. At the end of that battle we realized that we were no longer effective. Unfortunately, at that time they had orders that no one could be evacuated without the permission of the commanding general in that area. I felt he was stepping on my toes, which I resented very much. Bernie Rogoff (the other doctor with me) and I both decided we all had to be evacuated. We had no evacuation tickets—but we did have toilet paper, which I carried in my helmet. I pulled that out and wrote an evacuation ticket on each one. Each one was then taken to a plane. And as the last one got on the plane, including Colonel McGee, I wrote one for myself and got on the plane. And that was the last of our combat team (Kolodny, videotape).

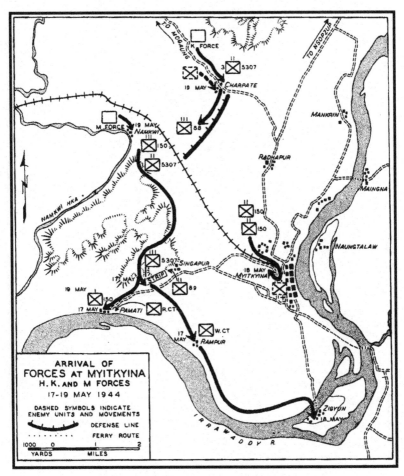

MAP 25. Arrival of forces at Myitkyina: H, K, and M Forces, 17–19 May 1944.

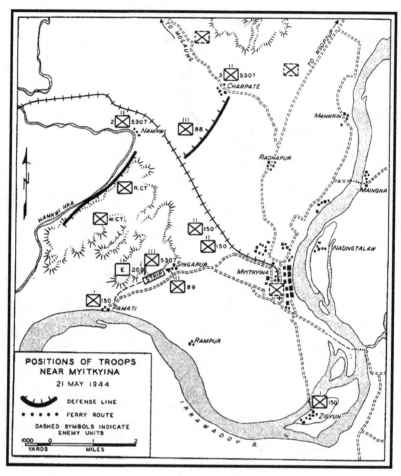

MAP 26. Positions of troops near Myitkyina, 21 May 1944.

Chapter XXII
Myitkyina
22 May–28 June 1944

5307th Under Colonel Hunter

22 May–4 June

A written order came through on 22 May that appointed Colonel John E. McCammon to the position of commanding officer of the Myitkyina area and all units therein. The order listed him as brigadier general.

K, H, and M Forces were now dissolved and the 5307th Composite Unit (Provisional) reestablished. Colonel Hunter was appointed commanding officer of all American forces in the Myitkyina area. The men of the unit now discovered that their official secret name was, and had always been, Galahad—a fact previously known to only a few.

The Second and Third Battalions were responsible for a five-mile, ill-defined area from Namkwi on the northwest to the Irrawaddy River on the northeast.

Colonel Hunter was ordered by General McCammon to send the Third Marauder Battalion against the Japanese defenses in an effort to secure the auxiliary airstrip, located just south of Radahpur and two miles north of the city, in an area heavily protected by entrenchments and infantry with machine guns and mortars. They were forced to dig in, early in the advance, at the Mankrin-Radahpur road junction. During the night the battalion was attacked from the rear, and on 22 May fell back to Charpate, which they had left at 1000 on 21 May. The Battle of Charpate, which took place on the night of the 23rd and the early morning of the 24th, has already been described.

The 22nd marked the day the Chinese units were complete, since the Chinese division commanders had arrived by this time with their headquarters staff. One of Colonel McCammon's first actions was to officially direct the Marauder First Battalion to provide security to the airfield, which meant that it would not be available for Colonel Hunter to use in combination with the other two Marauder battalions. With the continued poor communications it would be difficult for the colonel to actively supervise the work of the other two since they were on the periphery, three miles apart and four miles from the headquarters on the airfield. These battalions were isolated in enemy territory and far from their source of supply and medical assistance.

Without having been told by higher command, it was now known that the Marauders had lost their wonderful supply section. Everything in their warehouses, without previous notice, had been turned over to the headquarters of the Chinese Army in India. The battalions would have to send a daily supply train over four miles and back through no man's land to get food and ammunition, if available.

The two battalions, in spite of almost a hundred percent of their half-strength personnel suffering from tropical diseases, were expected to carry on with no help in sight. As discussed before, the Second Battalion was expected to hold Namkwi and patrol in all directions as well as keep a passageway open to the airfield. In spite of the tragedy of the night of 23–24 May, the Third Marauder Battalion was continuing to meet all of it patrolling obligations as well as advancing to retake the Mogaung-Myitkyina road junction two miles north of Myitkyina.

The Battle of Charpate ended during the morning of May 24th. Because of the isolation, the distance from the airport, and the difficulty in treating and evacuating the sick and wounded and obtaining supplies, Colonel Hunter ordered Colonel Beach to move the battalion to the railroad two and one-half miles to the south.

Shortly after Colonel Beach set up a defensive perimeter and base of operations in this area, Colonel Hunter temporarily moved his small headquarters to a location nearby. The new mission of the chronically and acutely ill men of the Second and Third Marauder Battalions was now not only to maintain security from the north but to attack the city from that direction. Considering the small force of available Americans and their poor condition, with very difficult supply, communication, and evacuation arrangements, this mission seemed irrational, impossible, and grossly unfair.

The Myitkyina task force headquarters was very disturbed by

Galahad's evacuation rate, now running between seventy-five and one hundred per day. At this time, fifteen to thirty men began to report daily, sick with symptoms of lethal mite or scrub typhus, and about eighty percent suffered from dysentery in various forms.

On the 24th Colonel McCammon tried to plan and initiate a major attack against the city. The 89th and 88th Chinese were to drive through the city to the riverbank on the 25th. There was total failure, since the Chinese failed to move out. Stilwell flew in to check on the situation.

During this visit, Colonel Hunter presented the general with a letter. Hunter states:

> By this time I was convinced that either General Stilwell was not acquainted with the condition of Galahad or he chose to ignore the dangerous situation developing before our eyes. I was also convinced that this chaotic direction of the military effort could only lead to disaster. I felt that Galahad needed some kind of encouragement if it were to remain longer and justify its presence in the area (Hunter 1963).

I might add, and Colonel Hunter would agree, that only a few of the men in the Second and Third Battalions were in condition to remain more than a few days.

Hunter continues:

> I had expected this letter to result in a series of questions that would afford an opportunity for a free and frank discussion. But I was never to have a free and frank discussion with this man who, to me, seemed unapproachable, though he was publicized as a soldier's soldier and cultured gentleman, masquerading under the acidulous demeanor. I never received a kind word of encouragement from the "Old Man," or a bit of advice, military or otherwise, although I was with him constantly for two days at one time. I never saw him talk man to man with an American soldier or make any attempt to familiarize himself with their problems, personal or otherwise. . . .
>
> I did not know at this time that Wingate's Special Force had been placed under Stilwell's command. Nor did I know of the seriousness of the situation on the West Burma front. . . .
>
> There was no attempt on the part of Stilwell or his staff, up to

now, to inform us of the situation as a whole in North Burma. "Ours not to reason why; ours but to do and die," is descriptive of the atmosphere (Hunter 1963).

Colonel Hunter had made the evacuation policy clear to the medical staff and had told General Stilwell, who agreed—but was later to deny that he knew so many men were sick.

During the last week in May, Colonel Hunter was on hand to watch about seventy-five Marauders, previously evacuated because of disease or injury, return to Burma. Their clothing was worn and filthy, and they were unshaven and ill-kept. Hunter states:

> Captain Benfield, who had arrived with this group, informed me that this group of men had been used as a spearhead for a Chinese regiment for some ten days or two weeks, and had been operating in the hills west of Kamaing. This group, plus the Chinese, had been called "Purple Force." They eventually became lost and returned to their base. Their commanding officer, an American colonel, had been relieved. After this futile exercise and under a new commander, they had started out once more—only to meet with the same sad fate again (Hunter 1963).

The group had just returned from this expedition, and they had not been given time to clean up or recuperate from the mission. The original group had included 200 men. There was no explanation as to what had happened to the other 125.

Benfield was able to explain why Marauders who had been evacuated earlier in the campaign with sickness or injury had not returned to the regiment. They had been assigned to the Northern Area Combat Command and were used to do guard duty about campsites, hospitals, the railroad, roads, and bridges in Assam. It seems that Generals Stilwell, Merrill, and Boatner could not find any help from the more than seventeen thousand service troops under the CBI Command and had to take these men, who were so badly needed by their comrades, the only American infantry soldiers fighting on the Asiatic continent. A little later, in May, another group of about two hundred Marauders were sent back to join the unit. They were mostly in poor condition, and ten were re-evacuated as patients. About half, according to

Colonel Hunter's statement in *Galahad,* were not fit for combat duty and were turned over to the Marauder First Battalion to sit in foxholes at the airport. The rest joined Benfield's men who had been sent to the Third Battalion, operating on the road and railroad near Radahpur.

Stilwell, after his trip to the airfield on 25 May, decided to take the 209th and 236 Engineer Battalions from their work on the Ledo Road and send them to the airfield as replacements. They arrived on the 27th and 28th. On arrival, it was obvious that they were not trained or equipped for this type of combat. Many had not seen a rifle since basic training.

Shortly after the 209th and 236th Engineer Combat Battalions started arriving at the airfield they were placed under Colonel Hunter's command, and he was given the title of commander of the American combat forces of the Myitkyina task force. Shortly after 1 June, Colonel Hunter moved his small headquarters from the airfield to the defensive base that Colonel Beach of the Third Battalion had set up on the railroad three miles north of the airport, two miles northeast of the Second Battalion on the Namkwi Hka, and two miles west of the road junction at Radahpur.

C Company from the 209th Engineers was sent to the Second Battalion, and the rest of the 209th—as well as the 236th—were sent to the Third Battalion. Many of the Marauders were quite optimistic about the security of the airfield, but there was evident a pervasive sense of doom among the officers of the task force headquarters. Men and officers were of the opinion that the Marauder First Battalion should have joined the two depleted battalions in covering the northeast and northwest boundaries of the siege line. This was not to be. The task force headquarters insisted, until the town fell on 3 August, that they continue to give airport security.

The Americans, by this date, had acquired four more pack howitzers, which brought their battery up to six guns. None of these guns had been authorized, and gun crews had to be found among the infantrymen. Ammunition would continue to be scarce.

All of the 81mm mortar ammunition was found to have defective fuses, and the fuses had to be removed from three thousand 60mm mortar shells and then screwed into the 81mm shells.

By the end of the first week in June, all but a few key and

reasonably healthful Marauders in the Second and Third Battalions had been evacuated because of battle wounds, accidental injuries, or sickness. These remaining Marauders were combined with the seventy-five men who had come in with Captain Benfield from the Purple Force and about half of the two hundred convalescent Marauders who came in a few days later. This American unit would now be known as the First Battalion or "Old Galahads." Colonel Hunter was able to place a few officers and men, who had not been considered sick enough to be evacuated to hospitals, in this small so-called battalion. There were others in the group who volunteered to return, as soon as they were discharged from hospitals, to limited duty.

Many uses in and out of combat were found for these, the remaining Marauders or Old Galahads. An I & R platoon was put together, and it operated very successfully until the town fell on 3 August. Men were shifted back and forth into the combat engineers to give them training in patrolling and the proper use of mortars and the other infantry weapons. Their presence helped the new and inexperienced men learn that the Japanese were not invincible and could always be defeated. These combat-experienced officers and men would also help organize and train the two battalions of poorly organized and trained, young, and inexperienced volunteer men and officers who would arrive in June.

The military activity of the Marauders at Myitkyina, up to this time, has already been discussed and will not be repeated. They had prevented many enemy reinforcements from reaching Myitkyina, had confined a group of enemy to Namkwi and another group to Charpate, and had assisted the Chinese in protecting the airfield.

As I have mentioned, S.Sgt. Ray Lyons had come in on 18 May to take over as sergeant major after Sergeant Major Doyer had been injured. Ray was bunking near the Myitkyina task force headquarters, and during May he did his best to work for the Myitkyina task force. This changed about the time that Colonel Hunter moved over to the location of the Third Battalion on the Mogaung-Myitkyina railroad tracks northwest of the city near the end of May.

Ray Lyons explains what happened to Colonel Hunter shortly after Colonel McCammon took over the command of the Myitkyina task force:

> Hunter was relieved of that command and went down and set
> up his headquarters in a wrecked C-47 that was left on the west

side of the field. One day an officer showed up, and he came over to me and introduced himself. He was an adjutant general from the back area sent to take over as adjutant of the task force. He was very pleased, obviously, to run into Sergeant Lyons, who had been sergeant major at the field all this time. I said, "Hey, I am glad to see you—here are all my notes," and I handed them over to him. The notes listed all the outfits around the field and what had transpired to the best of my knowledge. I said, "I am leaving; I am going back to Colonel Hunter. You can have all this." That's it. I walked away, and he was stunned. You can just picture him, coming into this combat situation from New Delhi, figuring that he was going to have the benefit of a sergeant who was on the ground and had been taking all the notes. I took off and never saw him again. I have no idea what his name was. I have often wondered what happened to those notes.

I went back down to Colonel Hunter. Partly why I did this was that to my mind, more than any other reason, Colonel Hunter was very much in command of what he was doing and what the Marauders were doing. All the rest of these characters who came to take command of this thing were not. They were up in the air about what was going on, and they didn't really have the ability. I can think of something else, for instance: Right after dark we got a radio message. It said that one of the forward groups, I am sure it was from the Marauders, saw a Japanese column just walk past, a column of like six hundred men, and they gave the coordinates of where they had seen them and the direction in which they were going. The idea was that we had no pack artillery, the Chinese had this, and there was a good chance to wipe out some of these Japanese who were marching into Myitkyina. The lieutenant who was in charge, he says, "Let's not shoot at them. If we shoot at them they will turn around and shoot at us. Let's all have a good night's rest and never mind shooting at them tonight." So we didn't shoot at them that night, and they went on into the town, and we were still trying to get them out months later. My reaction at the time was, "Hey, is this the way you fight a war? You think more about getting a good night's sleep than you do about wiping out the enemy." So I went down to Colonel Hunter at the plane and told him that I had given up on the guys at the headquarters and I wanted to be with him. He said, "Come on in and shack up in the plane" (Lyons, videotape).

CHAPTER XXII

Colonel Hunter's Headquarters at Radahpur

4 June–3 August

By 4 June the few men left in the Second and Third Battalions had been evacuated with Colonels Beach and McGee. The Marauder First Battalion, on 1 June, had a roster of 18 officers and 366 enlisted men. The battalion was and would remain at the airport until the Japanese were defeated on 3 August.

The failure of the air force to destroy the Namkwi railroad bridge continued to be a serious problem for the Marauders and the Myitkyina task force. After the Second Marauder Battalion had left the area to occupy Charpate to the northeast, the Japanese occupied the territory on either side of the bridge. Japanese replacements were using this bridge to cross the natural obstacle of the river. Lieutenant Scott had been garrisoning Pamati with about seventeen men. Colonel Hunter sent a jeep to bring him to the airfield. He agreed to ask the seventeen men at Pamati to volunteer to go with him in an attempt to destroy the bridge.

Theodore Zakonik describes the way things developed when Scott returned from the meeting with Colonel Hunter:

> Lieutenant Scott returned to Pamati. We had been there about two weeks. He said, "Fellows, I have volunteered." My 1st Sergeant Peters was there—he was also in charge of this group of us. He said, "I have volunteered the group of us. We are to blow up a bridge, a railroad bridge, and destroy telephone communications." There were three wires, as I recall, going into the town of Myitkyina. He said, "They are going to fly in TNT. There is a jeep there with a trailer. They are going to fill it full of TNT and bring it over here. We are going to show you what to do. Those who don't want to go don't have to, but I did volunteer to lead seventeen of us." They also threw in two bazooka teams. A team consisted of two men. I had never seen a bazooka. He took fifty-pound blocks of TNT, and he said, "Now I am going to take the packs and do each one on my own. I will wrap primacord around each one, and there will be primacord sticking out." Then he said, "Remember now, when you pull the cord it is going to detonate."
>
> We got to the Namkwi Hka and went across in a boat. On the other side there was a man with some Kachins. He was a major in the U.S. Army. He greeted us and said he and his Kachins would

guide us. He said, "Four of them will lead us up to the bridge. When they get to a certain point they will go no further after they show you the trail. You are then on your own." Lieutenant Scott, Sergeant Peters, and a patrol guy had field glasses, and they watched those birds [Japanese sentries]. Now this was patrolled by sentries, and they had to time this—and they did this all day and night. It took us several days to lay the charges on the bridge when the sentries were on the other side.

It was a stone bridge. There were seventeen of us, and we were going to lay our charges at the proper spot on the rails. We had two volunteers to shinny up the poles to actually chop the wires with bolo knives. Our charges were put in place first. When we pulled the primacords it just curled the rails up as it blew the bridge. It was successful.

When we did this we had to get out of there, and I mean now. We had to run down a steep bank, which was sheer gravel and had been hard to climb. Then we had to run across an open space about three hundred yards, and it was beginning to get daylight. When we got over there we were all spread out. We had been told that we would probably wind up on our own. Now everybody had a compass. We were told if we did spread up we would know how to get back. We just had to move through raw jungle. As it turned out, we split up and wound up in two groups. I was in the second group that got to Pamati.

We had no communication and no food. When Lieutenant Scott was arranging his packs, one of the fellows said, "What about food?" He said, "That's your problem—you take whatever you want." The fellow said, "Are they going to send us extra rations?" No such arrangements had been made. There was no room for anything but TNT (Zakonik, videotape).

The engineers, with the help of what was left of the Third Marauder Battalion, had captured Radahpur on 4 June, and Colonel Hunter moved his headquarters there from its previous location on the Mogaung-Myitkyina railroad. The small village of Radahpur is located at a road junction three miles north of the city. The northeast branch runs four miles to join a road that parallels the Irrawaddy River and passes through Mankrin to enter Myitkyina. The northwest branch goes two miles to Charpate and then on westward to Mogaung.

The 209th and the 236th Engineer Combat Battalions were put

under the command of Lt. William Combs, who came from his position as chief of American liaison to the 150th Chinese Infantry Regiment. The engineers would continue to be a very important part of the American force under Colonel Hunter.

The American force did not have access to any roads leading to the airport. Travel had to be overland, through or around swamps and flooded rice paddies. Many years before, during the monsoon season, the Irrawaddy River had swept around the city, leaving it as an island on high ground. The river no longer surrounded the city, but its previous seasonal course had left a crescent-shaped depression south of Manpin, Radahpur, east of the airport, and then south to the village of Pamati. The monsoon had produced many swamps and lakes, which blocked the advancing Chinese and Americans while offering protection to the Japanese, who were on the high ground.

Galahad's mission remained the same: Patrol and control the five-mile arc north of the city, be constantly on the offensive until the city has been entered and the Japanese destroyed. Colonel Hunter and his Americans knew that this mission was nearly impossible until the Japanese starved, died of disease, or ran out of ammunition. Any discussion of the problems involved met with the same response from General Boatner, which was "Get into Myitkyina."

It should be remembered that the First Battalion of the Marauders remained at the airfield during the rest of the campaign to give security to the Myitkyina task force headquarters. On several occasions Colonel Hunter attempted to have the Marauder First Battalion released for his use. The request was always refused, with the explanation that they would remain to protect the airfield. First Colonel McCammon and later General Boatner continued to be afraid that the airfield might be overrun at any time. This attitude was never shared by Colonel Hunter or the men of his command.

In spite of their location at the airport, the recently organized headquarters reconnaissance and security platoon, under the command of Lieutenant Phil Weld, frequently was able to make a round-trip visit to Colonel Hunter's headquarters. These Old Galahad veterans were a rugged bunch who always arrived bright and cheerful. They not only brought news but reassured those who had to travel back and forth that the route was free of Japanese.

Colonel Hunter was aware of the decision made by the War

Department in October 1943 that refilling Galahad (the Marauders) with individual replacements would be impracticable. He knew they had estimated that, after three months in the Burma jungle, the outfit would have suffered eighty-five percent casualties and would be used up. They had planned to form new units in the states and then ship them out intact. Any surviving Galahad veterans not eligible for return to the states would be assigned to key posts in the new units.

No one on Stilwell's staff had bothered to inform Colonel Hunter that in April 1944 the War Department had called for twenty-six hundred volunteers. After transport by ship, these men had arrived in Bombay Harbor on 25 May. They crossed India by train and air and arrived at Myitkyina airstrip during the first week in June. After a day or so spent in and about muddy foxholes, the first nine hundred were ordered to hike to Radahpur. Colonel Hunter, that morning, was notified that the advance element of an infantry battalion was marching the six miles out to his headquarters.

Doctor Sazama had arrived a day or so before to set up a battalion aid station. The headquarters had, by now, been able to set up the battery of pack-75mm artillery pieces. Colonel Hunter was on his way to check these installations when he spotted a column of troops resting beside the dirt trail. Some had broken ranks to get water out of numerous shell holes, old foxholes, and the flooded rice paddy. They ignored the fact that the water was contaminated. They failed to notice a concrete cistern filled with good water. None of the lieutenants with the unit would admit to being in charge.

The hot and exhausted men arrived and were turned over to Lt. Colonel Daniel Still, who had been operations commander under General Merrill and later second in command of the K Force. Colonel Hunter noticed a lack of discipline and soldierly appearance and was not able to find any officer who claimed to be in command.

The next day it was learned that this was not a regularly organized battalion. Previous information had been false. The men had been organized alphabetically into units designated solely for ease of shipment overseas. The senior officer in charge had been given no instructions to organize, instruct, classify, train, or indoctrinate the men.

Lieutenant Russell Shaver and 2nd Lt. Gordon W. Campbell explained the situation to Colonel Hunter in a letter dated 21 August 1944:

I certify that on May 28, 1944, the First Battalion train of GH 770A pulled into Ram Garth [Ramgarh]. I was met by Colonel Carroll, Post Commander at Ram Garth. A colonel of the First Battalion reported that his battalion was completely organized under T. O. strength, fully equipped, and thoroughly trained, ready for combat immediately. Such was not the case. Men and officers were practically strangers. Companies were organized hastily and without regard to qualifications of the men involved. Countless men were having their first initiation in the mechanical functioning of the M-1 rifle. Infantry tactics were, to a great number of men, something entirely alien from the training they had received in the States. Men were physically weak from the long ride on the troopship to this theater, and no time was given them to become acclimated. In fact, just forty days from the time we left the States, our men were in front-line combat. To the above-mentioned causes we attribute, to a great extent, the failure of our troops in their first phase of combat.

Colonel Hunter, as he turned the men over to Colonel Daniel Still for assignment, voiced his apprehension about sending this group of young and inexperienced Americans into combat. They had left the States six weeks before and had been confined to a boat, trains, and planes, Their physical condition had deteriorated from inactivity, and they were exhausted by the hike to Radahpur.

Steps were taken to bivouac them far enough away from headquarters to make sure that no one was wounded by their expected indiscriminate firing during the night. The next day Hunter was officially informed that the outfit was not a regularly formed battalion. He had been previously informed that it was. It was basically a group of men who had been obtained from replacement centers in the States. The battalion that later followed was of the same category. This second battalion would be put under an intensive combat training period, with its base at the airfield. It would be named Third Battalion (New Galahad). Numerous opportunities would arise to train the men against outlying groups of Japanese before it would take over the function of the other battalion in late July. Four hundred would be used as quartermaster troops.

The group of nine hundred men sent to Col. Hunter was given the name of Second Battalion (New Galahad). They would obtain their training under combat conditions with members of Old Galahad acting as their instructors.

Hunter immediately notified General Boatner of the condition and lack of training and organization into an infantry battalion. His protests were answered by sarcasm, and he was ordered to get into Myitkyina. Colonel Still and the Old Galahads frantically interviewed all the men and organized an infantry battalion. The next day they departed on their mission: to advance east three miles to Mankrin and then begin advancing toward the town, after which they were to coordinate an advance with the engineers with the object of capturing Myitkyina.

The American force available to Colonel Hunter was not large enough to give him the advantage of maneuver in the offensive operation that the Myitkyina task force headquarters had ordered. His engineer and infantry troops were inexperienced and not trained or organized for the type of offensive combat required for the aggressive siege operation that Generals Stilwell and Boatner were pushing. General Stilwell was not prepared to supply any more than token artillery or air support. It could be expected that the heat, monsoon rains, terrain, contaminated water, and tropical disease would give every advantage to the well-entrenched and fortified Japanese, whose veteran troops were well supplied with artillery, machine guns, and mortars. Colonel Hunter knew that no more replacements were available. There would be no way for him to give temporary periods of relief to his front-line men. When not burying their dead, treating or evacuating their wounded and sick, or advancing against machine guns, mortars, rifles, grenades, bayonets, and artillery, they would be trying to get rest in the mud of quickly dug foxholes.

The medical and surgical facilities near the front line were inadequate for the care of American front-line infantry troops. They were far below the standards of American military medicine that should have been available to the troops. The system of moving the sick and wounded from the front-line to the primitive above-mentioned medical facility was hit or miss. The men on the front line had to bring the sick and wounded back to the battalion and regimental aid stations the best way they could. The Myitkyina task force, General Stilwell's headquarters, and the Northern Area Combat Command were never able to supply stretcher bearers to the infantry. The

Chinese troops were much better supplied in that they had designated stretcher bearers.

The transport of the sick and wounded from Old and New Galahad's headquarters and rear base to the airfield was even more disgraceful. The monsoon season was now fully active. The numerous dirt paths that had been developed between the Marauder locations and the airfield before the heavy rains were now quagmires. These heavily rutted paths could no longer be traveled by the few available jeeps. The Northern Area Combat Command and the Myitkyina task force did not set up a system of evacuation by small planes. The only way to transport sick and wounded was to carry them by hand or by oxcart transport. Colonel Hunter was forced to hire primitive carts pulled by oxen. These carts were supplied by the native owners and drivers. Retired native military personnel from the area were used as escorts for the five-mile trip to the treatment and evacuation point at the airfield. This primitive evacuation system meant the death of some sick and wounded who might have survived by air transport.

Many highly qualified surgeons were available in the CBI for Generals Stilwell and Boatner to send to the aid of Galahad. Equal responsibility rests on the theater surgeon, Colonel Williams, and the Northern Area Combat Command surgeon, Colonel Peterson, for failure to supply a surgical portable hospital at all times to the Marauders.

With the headquarters at Radahpur, the only artillery available for the first two weeks was the two pack-75mm howitzers that had been parachuted to Beach's Third Battalion and used so effectively during the Battle of Nhpum Ga. Near the end of that battle, Captain Gordon Bonnyman had volunteered to command the artillery unit. He remained in command for Operation End Run (the Myitkyina operation). He and his volunteer gun crew struggled with the mules and guns as they brought them over the mountain range. They were used at Tingkrukawng. Colonel Hancock, back in Assam, was able to obtain four more howitzers, and the ever-helpful C-47 pilots gladly delivered them by parachute to Colonel Hunter. Captain Bonneyman and his men soon had a very efficient artillery battery. Ammunition for the guns was not plentiful, but here again the pilots and Colonel Hancock's men were most helpful. Daily barrages frequently silenced the heavier Japanese artillery and always gave our men encouragement. Used before each offensive operation of the two infantry and two engineer battalions, the artillery was never adequate—but always helpful. The guns were ready to fire at any time day or night, in spite of heat and monsoon downpours. They were responsible for saving many of our men. Enough artillery was stored in India to equip thirty Chinese divisions, and some of these guns could have easily been flown into Myitkyina.

During most of June and July the artillery battery had to fire at a range of two thousand yards or less. Howitzers are high-trajectory weapons. This frequently prevented their use when the Japanese fox-holes, dugouts, machine guns, and equipment were close to our front lines. Large trees in the area would be hit, and the tree burst of the exploding shell would be likely to kill or wound our men. Frequently the front-line troops would have to expose themselves while dynamiting these trees.

Galahad acquired, courtesy of Colonel Hancock, a 20-power scope. During periods of relative inactivity, Galahads would practice target shooting against any Japanese who dared to expose himself.

From the beginning, a squadron of P-51's was based at the airstrip. The Tenth Air Force apportioned fighter support on a daily pre-planned basis. Galahad could not designate targets the day before help was needed. Galahad requested and got a new plan. Captain Allred with his plane was assigned to Galahad for daily use. Even though he was eligible for rotation to the States, he agreed to stay with Galahad until the campaign was over. He would visit headquarters at Radahpur, and officers and men would direct him to the target by radio. This perfect fighter-bomber pilot was trusted to drop five-hundred-pound bombs and strafe within fifty yards of our lines.

I have previously mentioned that mortar ammunition was in short supply. The fuses in three thousand rounds of 81mm mortar shells were defective. Heavy weapons men had to spend time and energy, in spite of heat and rain, to remove fuses from 60mm mortar shells and screw them into the more powerful weapons. Near the end of June, Galahad acquired 4.1 mortars to replace the 81mm mortars, since the ammunition being supplied for the mortars was still defective. The engineers had a 37mm obsolete and ineffective anti-tank gun that had an inadequate sight. This gun soon proved to be useless.

Near the end of June the two engineer battalions were about

one-half strength, and replacements were essential. Stilwell and his staff rounded up 450 replacements and sent them out to Radahpur. Colonel Hunter states:

> The Galahad staff, at my direction, held them near Radahpur until their records were examined. I wanted an assessment of each individual's combat potential. I had been burned once, and I did not intend to be taken in a second time. My suspicions were confirmed. The records were examined to determine the answers to the following questions: What is his branch of service, what weapons had he fired and when, was he qualified in the weapons he had fired, how much basic training had he undergone, did his record show any advanced training, and so on. Of the 450, about half were rejected and returned to task force headquarters the next day. The new men were isolated under the command of a few trusted and experienced Old Galahads. In spite of instructions in promiscuous firing and self-inflicted wounds, both of these were at first a problem. So many wounded themselves that it became necessary to have line-of-duty proceedings forms mimeographed in order to save time. This group of men was a good example of what can happen when a unit is ordered to supply men for another area of operations. The company commander or first sergeant will, at times, volunteer certain undesirables out of their unit (Hunter 1963).

A cemetery had to be set up and decent burials arranged for all the dead whose bodies could be recovered. Father Barrett had died of scrub typhus, and no other chaplain would be available for the rest of the campaign. Each day a detail from the dead soldier's squad would bring their dead comrade or comrades to the cemetery, and Sergeant Lyons would see to proper burial after he said a simple prayer. Refugees from the town were hired to dig the graves and care for the area.

Sgt. Major Ray Lyons tells more about some of his thoughts and memories:

> Shortly after we left the field, Colonel Hunter was assigned to take all of the American troops, including the two engineer battalions—the replacements for the Second and Third Battalions— and move to a place called Radahpur. It took us a couple of hours to walk out there, which we did. Headquarters was alongside a road junction. On one side of the road was a portable surgical

hospital, the 44th Portable Surgical Hospital, commanded by a Major Sazama. Between us and the road there was a treeline. On the other side of the treeline there was a basha where the supplies were. There was a captain from the engineers whose name eludes me, but he came from Connecticut. It was an Irish name. I ran into a colonel from the 209th Engineers recently, and he mentioned the name. One day when they were airdropping grain or rice or whatever, it came tumbling down right through the roof of the basha and killed him instantly.

On the other side of that treeline we had a foxhole where the communications people were, and Colonel Hunter told me to set up my foxhole beside them, which I did. He was about fifteen or twenty yards away in a tent area that he had set up. We also set up a cemetery there, which turned out to be one of the biggest assignments I had. Anytime anybody died in that field hospital, that part of the surgical hospital, they would have natives dig a grave and they would call up Colonel Hunter. He would call me and say, "Sergeant, take over this burial detail and bury this guy." We had no chaplain. The only thing at the time was a prayer book. I looked through the prayer book and would find the prayer that seemed most appropriate when I was burying one of these guys. That's what I did. We had about four men and myself. When these guys died they were put on a stretcher, and we would carry the stretcher. When we got over to the grave we would wrap them in a blanket and lower them down into the grave. When I started I would get down into the grave in order to ease the transition. One day one character on this detail, I think I know who he is—though I said to him, "Weren't you that guy?" and he denied it—well anyway, he dropped his end of the blanket holding this guy whose stomach had been cut open and was full of blood—all of which came pouring out on me. I was just completely covered with blood all over. After that I decided to come up with a different system. I got some parachute cords and lowered the men down into the grave.This was a lot easier on me. I was still saying the prayers.

One day we got a visit from a detachment including Stilwell and a chaplain. I said to him, "Hey, we need a chaplain out here for these things that are going on," and he did not volunteer. I told him what I was doing. He said, "Good work, keep it up," and that was as far as he was concerned.

Hunter did not have a shirt anymore. His was in tatters so all he was wearing was pants. Stilwell took him and his escort, including the I & R platoon, out to Sitapur to hand out medals. I believe it was at that time that a lot of the guys got Silver Stars. We have a picture in our album of the awards except we don't have one of Hunter getting his Silver Star, which I am pretty sure he did. Once again, when I asked Colonel Hunter "Shall I go with you?" he said, "No, you stay here and mind the headquarters. When we look back on it now, it was a mistake. If I had gone out there we would have had somebody taking notes on a piece of paper as to who got what and who was promised what, as did happen subsequently.

Also one time we got a shipment of a case of whiskey that came into our headquarters, and he called me over and he said, "Distribute it." So I took the bottles and gave them to the runners to take to the different battalions, one to the I & R platoon, and one to our headquarters. I poured out his share. He didn't ask for his own bottle, but he held out his canteen and I poured his portion in and then poured my own. It was Scotch whiskey. All the men got their share.

He had me write a letter one time—everybody has heard of Sammy Wilson, who had been a lieutenant in the I & R—to recommend Sammy for assignment to West Point. He thought that Sammy was a good officer and he should get an appointment to West Point. He recommended that this happen while we were out there at Radahpur road junction. The troops were having a lot of trouble moving forward, and one day they got the air force to agree to bomb from B-25's on the Japanese, who were dug in deeply in front of our Third Battalion of New Galahad. So it came to pass. But when they did it was a tremendous sound—we were, I guess, about a mile away from it. Subsequently we discovered that instead of dropping them on the Japanese they dropped them on our troops, which caused a lot of casualties. This probably accounts for a lot of the thirty or so I buried on that day at that impromptu cemetery we had. It really was a terrible experience for those people, We could hear the noise but we didn't realize what it was happening to our own troops.

Colonel Hunter was soon able to convince the Myitkyina task force that food, ammunition, and supplies had to be supplied by air as they had been during February, March, April, and most of May. This was essential, since his command was five miles from the Myitkyina airfield. He now had a limited number of mules and muleskinners to cover the difficult and dangerous five-mile distance through and around flooded rice paddies and swamps. The dangerous round-trip would often not be completed before dark. The trip also required combat patrols. Food and ammunition were usually scarce when obtained in competition with the Chinese. The Americans fared much better with their own source of supply.

Several thousand refugees were being cared for and fed south of the town, but Colonel Hunter continued to be responsible for many in his area. Among this group he was able to hire thirty to forty Ghurkas, many of whom had some military experience. One Gurhka, their leader, formed a very well-disciplined and military-appearing group. They were frequently able to take over some of the duties of the Old Galahad headquarters reconnaissance and security platoon. The Ghurkas were soon assigned the duty of escorting the daily bullock train of wounded that was sent to the airport. Their job also included watching over Japanese prisoners and escorting them to the airport. Some coin money was available to pay these mercenaries, but most of their pay was in the form of food.

This history has explained that on 24 May Colonel Hunter presented General Stilwell with a letter in which he outlined some of the problems he had encountered during the campaign. Colonel Hunter had given copies of the letter to each battalion commander. The men, especially those Marauders (Old Galahads) who had been evacuated before the end of the first week in June, were especially grateful for Colonel Hunter's action. The points he made were well known to the men and were serious matters that had gradually accumulated since the formation of the Marauders. Rarely had any significant problem been corrected. Probably because of the letter to General Stilwell, Colonel Ernie Estabrook, one of his two sons-in-law on his staff, visited the so-called convalescent area in late June on an inspection tour. This visit became known to Colonel Hunter the day that General Boatner was replaced at Myitkyina, 25 June. Colonel Hunter was ordered to report to the Myitkyina airfield to be interviewed by the inspector general of the theater staff. Colonel Hunter informed the representative of the Myitkyina task force headquarters that it was customary for the inspector general to come to the officer under investigation at his command post.

The inspector general, Colonel Stanley Griswold, and his

stenographer made the hazardous five-mile trip out to Radahpur. Colonel Hunter was questioned on the letter, which is reproduced in full here:

> Subject: Galahad Project
> To: Commanding General, USAF-CBI, through the Commanding General, Rear Echelon. USAF-CBI, APO 885.

1. It is desired to bring to the attention of the commanding general certain facts which, in the opinion of the undersigned, either have not been brought to his attention before, or which are not being given sufficient weight in future planning.
   a. Morale: The morale of Galahad has been sustained only because of promises that:
      (1) Galahad would not be used as a spearhead for Chinese troops.
      (2) Immediately upon arrival at Myitkyina and the capture of the airfield, its personnel would be flown out for rest and reorganization.

2. Upon arrival in India, Galahad was treated by USAF-CBI Hq. as a visiting unit for which the theater felt no responsibility. It was, and still is the opinion that, so far as Combat Hq. is concerned, this attitude has not changed. The following facts bear out the following conclusions:
   a. No theater officer met Galahad on its arrival.
   b. Adequate preparations were not made for its reception.

3. Galahad was debarked at Bombay and moved to the transit camp at Deolali, where the accommodations and food furnished were a disgrace to the British Military authorities. The period of training at Deolali was entirely wasted, but health and food conditions were such that, in the opinion of the writer, they contributed to the later breakdown in health and morale experienced by the personnel from the South and Southwest Pacific Commands.

4. Since Colonel Brink was assigned to the G.S.C. and as such unable to assume command, but by your direction was charged with the responsibility for training, organization, and administration, many conflicts arose in jurisdiction between the undersigned and Colonel Brink as to the

amount of time to be devoted to organization, training, administration, sanitation, and basic subjects. Since the unit was to fight shortly, Colonel Brink insisted on—and the bulk of available time was spent on—combat training and organization, with a minimum of time being devoted to discipline and other essential subjects of a balanced training program for a newly organized unit, for example, such simple things as the issue, marking, care, and cleaning of equipment.

5. Galahad was organized as a composite unit which prevented its use of colors, insignia, or other morale-building paraphernalia normal to other units. This matter was taken up with Rear Esc. USAF-CBI several times with no apparent results.

6. Very few American officers visited this unit while in training as long as its status was indefinite, and it was difficult to get the normal support with reference to supply, morale, medical service, and other requirements normal to a unit assigned to the theater. Suddenly General Merrill was assigned to command the unit. Colonel Brink left, and the unit received treatment only comparable to that afforded the prodigal son. American soldiers being of a discerning nature and intelligent, naturally are sensitive to the treatment they receive from higher headquarters. Galahad personnel are all familiar with the conditions and facts outlined above and are gradually growing bitter. This is especially true of the officers, whose morale has been adversely affected by the following additional factors:

   a. General Merrill's statement that no officers would be promoted until the termination of the operation.
   b. Colonel Cannon's reported report that at Nhpum the undersigned was only worried about promotions for officers.
   c. The report freely circulated that General Boatner called Major Petito, Captain Bogardus, and Lieutenant Sievers "yellow."
   d. The unpleasant relationship existing between all Galahad officers and the officers of combat headquarters.
   e. The per diem situation now existent in the theater.

7. Repeated reports have made reference to the health of the command. Apparently these reports are not believed, since

no apparent effort has been made to verify this. It can be reiterated again that Galahad is practically ineffective as a combat unit at the present time, and its presence here as a unit is rapidly leading to a false sense of security, which is dangerous.

8. Although this unit had been in continuous contact with the Japanese and has performed capably in the field to date, no awards or decorations, no indication of appreciation, and no citations have been received by any personnel of this unit as far as can be determined by the writer, with the exception of the award of the purple heart, which is routine. This condition can only indicate a lack of interest by higher headquarters—or, worse, a "don't-care attitude," which creates hard feeling.

9. Conclusion: In view of the above, the following recommendations are submitted:
   a. That on the termination of the present operations, Galahad as an organization be disbanded and its personnel be reassigned to other units in the theater through the Army Classification Service.
   b. That in the future, American infantry combat units assigned to this theater be treated in such a manner as to instill in the unit a pride of organization, a desire to fight, and a feeling of being a part of a united effort, and further that every effort be made to overcome the feeling that such units are no better than Chinese troops and deserve no better treatment.
   c. That deserving promotions be awarded to officers of this command.
   d. That no other theater personnel be promoted as long as officers of this unit are not promoted.

Charles N. Hunter, Colonel, Infantry,
Commanding Officer, Galahad (Hunter 192–94)

Even though Colonel Griswold had interviewed Colonel Hunter on 25 June, there was no evidence that this meeting had anything to do with the improvement of the lot of the Marauders who had been discharged from hospitals. Some improvement did occur late in June and was probably due to action taken because of very critical dispatches by war correspondents. The report was never made available to Colonel Hunter or any members of the 5307th Composite Unit (Provisional).

Communications

During the first week after 17 May, the Myitkyina task force had an inadequate communication system—but a new radio officer, a wire officer, and switchboard and wire personnel soon improved the situation at the airport. A difficult problem existed at Colonel Hunter's command. A skeleton engineer regimental communications section, including radio, cipher, and wire personnel, was organized with men borrowed from the signal company, which had just arrived. After inspecting the service records of the newly arrived Galahads, trained but inexperienced men were found to cover the needs of the two battalions. A skeleton regimental section composed of men from the original liaison section was formed for Colonel Hunter's headquarters.

Major Milton A. Pilcher was the signal officer. The following statement is from his account in the *Burman News*:

> Wire was the primary means of communication during the final phase of the campaign. Personnel rapidly gained experience, and within two weeks communications organizations were functioning properly. Thirty-five miles of trunk line were installed, line outages were few, switchboard operation was courteous and efficient, and forward units made displacements as required with little loss of service. The battalions made good use of assault wire and sound-powered telephones in front-line companies, for heavy weapons support, and for rapid moves. Well-policed field wire followed the battalion and regimental CP's. It was found necessary to install two trunks over alternate routes to each lower headquarters to prevent outages due to enemy action or shell fragments. RL-24 mule-pack carriers were useful in this work, as manpower was scarce and jeeps could not traverse the trails.
>
> As much of the wire as possible was laid over brush or on poles, but sections of W-110-B laid across a gravel road and through swamp gave good service. W-130 did not hold up over long periods. A complete wire and radio installation for the force artillery battalion was also in operation during the final phase. Wire personnel should be included in all combat units in the future. Colonel Hunter's brigade headquarters switchboard now had

twenty-seven drops in use and was handling six hundred calls daily by the time Myitkyina fell on 3 August 1944 (Pilcher 1989).

Headquarters Under General Boatner

30 May–25 June

General Stilwell and Brigadier General Haydon L. Boatner flew in on 30 May 1944. Colonel Hunter states that he spoke to General Boatner about the circumstances of this visit. It seems that Stilwell asked him to accompany him to Myitkyina and said he might spend the night and had better have a toothbrush. When they arrived, Stilwell relieved McCammon and appointed Boatner commanding general. The Marauder officers had not been impressed by Colonel McCammon's knowledge of the operation or its units. It was also known that he was not well and had been treated for a medical condition before he joined General Merrill as his assistant at Naubum. As far as we knew, he had confined most of his activities to commanding the Chinese and had let Colonel Hunter supervise the activity of the Marauders. He had seemed to understand that the Marauders could not be effective without medical help. Certainly he was not responsible for the horrible staff mess that he inherited.

It seems likely that General Stilwell believed that Boatner would be the one member of his Chinese Army in India headquarters staff who could drive the Chinese. The record also shows that General Stilwell underestimated the number of Japanese defending the town. Colonel McCammon should not be held accountable for the three failed attempts of the Chinese to enter the town or for several other blunders the Chinese made that caused excessive casualties. We should not forget that, in the early stages of the siege of and battle for Myitkyina, the American and Chinese infantry had primitive and little artillery and mortar support. I have already mentioned that the 81mm mortar fuses were defective. Strafing and dive bombing was always limited. One late attempt at high-level heavy bombing was mishandled and buried a U.S. platoon. Food, ammunition, and medical care were totally inadequate during much of the campaign.

General Boatner failed to understand that the Second and Third Battalions of Merrill's Marauders were almost totally depleted by previous battle casualties as well as disease. Hardly any of the few remaining men in each battalion were free of chronic malaria, malnutrition, dysentery, or other disabling medical and surgical problems of a chronic nature. Many were being evacuated with scrub typhus, and about one-fourth of these were dying. He knew that the newly arrived two battalions of engineers were not trained for combat and had never been in combat. He now had four regiments of Chinese troops. The 88th had been in combat at Ritpong and Tingkrukawng, but the 89th and the 42nd Regiments had seen little action. The 150th Regiment had already suffered over seven hundred casualties at Myitkyina.

The Myitkyina task force was deficient in communications and all types of supplies—including food, ammunition, infantry weapons, and air support. Medical support, including procedures for the collection of casualties and their emergency treatment, was far below what should be expected by American troops.

In spite of the numerous problems I have mentioned, Boatner issued his first combat orders. The general attack was to begin on 30 May, the day after his arrival and appointment as commanding general. The Marauder Second Battalion, with one company of the engineers attached, was to take Charpate and then advance on Radahpur. The remains of the Third Battalion with the 209th Engineer Battalion was to block the Radahpur-Myitkyina Road south of Radahpur. The Chinese were to advance on the town of Myitkyina from the west and south.

I have already explained how the Second Marauder Battalion failed in its mission and how its men were evacuated to hospitals in Assam.

General Boatner made arrangements for a Chinese attack on 3 June. The 42nd and 50th Chinese Regiments, plus the First Battalion of the 89th Regiment, took part.

The Chinese 42nd Regiment reached the Waingmaw ferry south of the city. The road was twelve feet above the paddy fields and gave the Japanese a great advantage. The Chinese fell back but beat off a counterattack. The Chinese 150th reached the Irrawaddy riverbank and held.

The Chinese apparently decided that they did not want to sacrifice more men needlessly and began the old-fashioned siege operation of tunneling toward the Japanese. The 42nd, the 150th, and one battalion of the 89th Chinese Regiments took 320 casualties. Little advance was made. General Boatner reported to General Stilwell that if he had had air support about noon, he could have taken the town. Because of the Chinese casualties, the fall of his 75mm ammunition stock to six hundred rounds, and his .303 and belted .30-caliber ammunition limited to one day's supply, he reported that he would hold back until his supplies were built up. He reaffirmed his position a few days later, saying that the lack of an immediate Japanese threat and the need to cut Chinese casualties and to train U.S. troops inclined him to wait a few days more. He thought that the Japanese garrison was in bad condition.

The engineer action, with the support of Colonel Beach and some of the men from the Third Marauder Battalion, was very successful. This action is discussed in the next section.

The 209th and 236th Engineer Combat Battalions

25 May–7 June

The 209th and 236th Engineers were flown in between 25 and 29 May. Most remained near the airfield for several days. One group spent the night near a shell hole that contained the bodies of twenty-two dead Japanese. Their days and nights were spent in and about muddy foxholes. In this location they were used by the Marauder First Battalion to help protect the Myitkyina airfield. In spite of the rain and heat, the combat veterans used every safe period to instruct them in the use of M-1 rifles, carbines, machine guns, grenades, and mortars.

On 29 May some began moving through waist-deep swamps and over muddy trails to join the remnants of Colonel Beach's Third Battalion, which was slowly eliminating Japanese outposts as the men advanced toward the road leading from Radahpur into Myitkyina. This three-mile move proved to be very difficult; some of the men passed out, and others got rid of excess baggage.

The night of 29 May initiated the men to the danger of friendly fire. Sergeant Brinkman of B Company was shot and killed when he failed to halt or identify himself when ordered to stop.

Using a few key officers and men from the Third Battalion as instructors and aids, Colonel Beach moved the 209th Engineers rapidly forward and by 1730 hours on 1 June had them astride the road five hundred yards south of Radahpur. The force consisted of A, B, H, and S Companies. Foxholes, entrenchments, and lines of fire were rapidly completed. A few Japanese were eliminated.

At 2130 hours a convoy of three Japanese trucks drove toward the perimeter. In the darkness, machine guns, rifles, tommy guns, and BAR's opened up. Because of the pitch- black darkness, the results of the engagement could not be seen until daylight. Eighty-six dead Japanese were found. Pvt. Tommy Dolan was unfortunately killed by the engineers' own fire. The Americans had no other dead, but six had been wounded. There had been some hand-to-hand fighting and struggles in foxholes, with the enemy the constant losers. This first battle had shown that the untried engineers could be counted on in the future.

From 2 through 9 June the 209th Engineers traded mortar, machine-gun, and rifle fire with the enemy and had numerous dead and wounded. During this period the men had been subjected to daily rain and living in mud holes. The smell of dead Japanese was on every side, and the men—who had not been able to bathe, shave, or change their clothes—were filthy. Many had diarrhea, and many had ulcers on their legs.

A few were being killed or wounded daily as they held their position against the enemy or went on patrols. On 5 June, mail arrived for the first time. The men were sitting and squatting on the ground reading their letters when the Japanese suddenly attacked. They were soon repulsed, but Lieutenant Meyers was hit in the arm and several enlisted men were wounded.

While on a patrol led by Lieutenant Hillman on 7 June, Pvt. Clemons J. Meier was killed by machine-gun fire. On the same day a Japanese shell made a direct hit on a mortar crew. Private Simmons and Private Calvin Smith were seriously wounded, and Private Kurt Wolff and a T5g. had minor injuries.

On 1 June General Boatner sent the 236th Engineers four miles to the west of the airfield to attempt capture of the town of Namkwi. They were able to enter the town on this, their first combat action, but were soon driven out. They had fallen out for a rest period before setting up a defensive perimeter. The Japanese counterattacked and drove them out. This so-called training mission was a total disaster, sacrificing both men and the self-confidence of the troops.

CHAPTER XXII

Lt. John F. Eichelberger Jr. gives this interesting discussion about his experience as an officer in the 236th Engineers. His battalion of combat engineers had arrived in India just before the Marauders and had been building the Ledo Road from Assam, India, over the Patkai Mountains into Burma.

Without any warning or preliminary notice, we got an alert at 1500 that we were going into combat the next day, 27 May. We were told to be at the airstrip at 0600 at Ledo and that we would be fighting Japanese, which was our secondary mission.

On the flight in, I was in a C-47 with a jeep and a trailer load of ammunition plus the jeep driver, and that was all. The crew chief came back and got his head up in that little dome at the top of the plane and turned white. He then went back into the cabin and came back two or three times and said, "Hang on, I think we have a Zero on our tail." He said, "The pilot is going to take evasive action." He would go up to a hill and roll over the hill into the next valley and then over the next hill, all the way into Myitkyina. They finally found out it was a P-47—they look the same coming at you.

When we got to the all-weather airstrip, and I emphasize all-weather, it looked like no-man's land. There were more bomb craters on that place than Carter's got pills. The plane came down in a zig-zag fashion, and he still had to zig-zag after he got his wheels down. When we got off the plane there was another plane trying to steer right ahead of us. One of our lieutenants started lining his platoon up. He said, "Fall in." I hollowed, "No, don't do that." Now at this time one of the Marauders said, "You know you will get yourself killed." The Japanese opened up with artillery and they scattered.

The next day I went across the airstrip. I was told to go to a road and turn to the right. We were going to dig in over there. When I got across the airstrip I didn't see any road to the right and I just kept on the road and went by some Chinese. About a hundred yards down the road I looked at the jeep driver and said, "Do you see any wire over there?" He said, "No," and I said, "There ain't none over there either—turn this thing around." We went back to this Chinese position and the Chinese officer. He said, "See any Japanese?" I said, "No." He said, "How far did you go?" I said, "We turned around at five hundred yards." He said, "Ding how," and the Chinese moved up one hundred yards.

We finally found the road, which was little more than a cow path, and we went and got in with the rest of our battalion.

A couple of days later we went across the airstrip and went into the village of Pamati. That's where we got our baptism of fire. The men were scared to death, and that is putting it mildly. Some of them were really shaking. I could hear a lot of bird calls in the woods down by this stream. Some of the men wanted to go down and get some water. I said, "I wouldn't go down if I was you." They said, "It's okay, or those birds wouldn't be singing." I said, "I don't think they are birds." We found out later they were Japanese bird singers. We had one sergeant and about three others killed by one burst of machine-gun fire. We had one officer who got shook up when he heard a noise in the brush and shot one of his own men in the hip, and the man died of internal bleeding. Doctor Seagrave got all over our medics for not treating him for shock—then he opened him up and said, "Even I couldn't save him." I could say that Doctor Seagrave was a very human person. He put his hand on this boy's shoulder and apologized for the way he had talked to him.

From there we went over to a Y, and when we got to the Y the Galahad fellows were giving us instructions in BAR's, Bren guns, the 60mm mortars, and 90mm mortars. All the officers that went to OCS had taken an advanced officers course in mortars, but it seemed to me that I was the only one who knew how to set a mortar up. So I was made the mortar officer.

The Japanese were building a new airstrip in towards Myitkyina, and they asked me to set up our machine guns so we could hose down the strip to see if we could stop them. I had no kilometer so I used the arc on the trackfire and my compass to rig up the fire. They got a liaison plane up watching over the strip, and he said, "You ought to see those guys scampering off the strip." A couple days later we moved on down toward Charpate just below the Y there and got in there. The first day I saw a big Japanese mortar hit a tree. The big mortar shell hit in the top of a tree, slid down a branch, slid down the trunk, met a knot three quarters of the way down, jumped over the roots, and hit the grass. Walter Plummer, the company clerk, was there—he was speechless. I wasn't much better. No foxholes had been dug there.

We were told to set up a 37mm gun and fire into a rice paddy at a certain azimuth. It looked like jungle, but there were buildings in there. The shells blew all the camouflage away from them. The Japanese didn't like the gun and always threw a few rounds of mortar at you. They didn't like the bazooka either. I got the nickname "Bazooka Ike" because I always fired the bazooka when it looked like we needed it.

One day we got a little careless and the Japanese set up their main support weapon, with about a ten-inch barrel and a twelve-inch shell, across the rice paddy. Our men were having a big time settling themselves. All of a sudden this artillery came in. I called it a whiz bang. It went wham, whiz, burp. That's about the way it sounded. You heard the shell go off and then the wake of the shell and finally the gun.

My platoon sergeant got hit and was on a litter to be evacuated when they opened up again. I remember a boy by the name of Hoot Gibson. Anybody with the last name of Gibson, of course, was Hoot. He was pretty well shook up. I reached and got hold of his jacket on the left side and started pulling him in the hole with me and a shell hit his right hip and his right arm went down the hill. I looked down and Lindsey had been hit on the litter. It just opened him up. I hollered down the hill, I said, "Now Lindsey is dead, bring that litter up here and get Hoot out." He dumped Lindsey off, and when I counted three he grabbed that litter and ran up there and we put Hoot on. I put one arm around his neck and the other under his left arm. Two guys ran that litter up over the hill. As far as I know there was no artillery coming in. People who watched said machine-gun bullets chased them all the way up the hill. They missed. Then we started catching a lot of tree burst and I decided to do the only engineer job there was. I started cutting down trees to stop the tree bursts. I gathered up all kinds of dud shells and managed to get a couple cases of old water-logged TNT and some blasting caps and used the walkie-talkie to set the charges off. I would tie a block of TNT to a tree and add a 75mm shell and maybe a 4.5 bazooka shell, anything that had explosive in it. The biggest one I knocked down had a ten or twelve bowl, and that meant ten- or twelve-foot diameter. The 1st sergeant said, "If you disturb my tent, so help me, I'll kill you." All we got on the tent was some splinters, and the tree fell down in a place where our colonel had been trying to get me to send a patrol for three or four days and I kept saying there are too many booby traps in there. Well, it seemed that there were booby traps going off for about five minutes. The colonel got on horn and said, "What's all that shooting up there?" I said, "Sir, that's those booby traps you told me to send my men through." At the last tree I blew I was too close because I was using short telephone wire, and it blew my helmet off. I said, "Sir, that's the last tree I am blowing."

We were strafed by our own planes on 4 July. We were commenting how quiet it was for the 4th of July, and here comes our air force strafing. They killed one of our men and shot the heel off one of our officer's shoes and put his foot to sleep. He came out grinning from ear to ear—he wore size 13 and he said, "Well, I am going home now, they can't find shoes big enough for me." He kept on grinning, and here comes the supply sergeant with a pair of British brogans, those old hobnail jobs. The colonel said, "You got shoes." He said, "These are dog-gone horse shoes—I ain't going to wear them." So the colonel said, "You can either wear these or go barefooted, but you are not going out of here." So he put them on.

A couple days later we got a replacement captain in, and I was close enough to a five-hundred-pound bomb going off to throw dirt back overtop of me, and I moved on up there. The captain hollered his head off and said, "You darn fool, you will get yourself killed." About two or three days later he was hollering again because I was standing poking and waving my hands because people were strafing the wrong lines. We had told them to strafe a Y that had showed up on the map. What we didn't know was that there were two Y's, and he hit the wrong one. The bullets passed about ten feet on each side of me. I was outside the cone of fire (Eichelberger, videotape).

John F. Eichelberger Jr. continues his remembrance of the Battle of Myitkyina by discussing the oxcarts that served as ambulances:

We had a lieutenant who sent a patrol out, and it came back and said, "There is a Japanese pill box out there." He went striding out and said, "This I've got to see." He did—and he had his left leg sawed off at the knee. He was not evacuated right away. Sergeant White from A Company of the 236th Engineers went out when B Company refused to go out and rescue their officer. He was laying out in front of their line. White had a .45-caliber pistol strapped to his right hip—and, being a big football player, he threw his right hip into it when he saw a machine gun coming up. It tore the .45 to pieces and put another one in his leg so he couldn't use his leg for a while. He rode out in the oxcart. The guards I sent out with him, which we always had with an oxcart ambulance, said that he drank seven canteens of water. This would be seven pints or three and one-half quarts of water on the trip back to the airstrip. He kept begging the guards to give him a rifle or pistol so he could shoot himself. Said he was hurting so bad. Every step the oxen took jolted the cart from the ruts and that little old trailer. He had a five-mile trip of misery. He lived and remained in the army until he retired (Eichelberger, videotape).

This story has been told in order to stress one of the consequences of the failure of the command to arrange for evacuation from the Galahad headquarters back to the Myitkyina airstrip by the light planes, which had been used so successfully earlier in the campaign.

Near the end of the Battle of Myitkyina the engineer battalions were taken out of the offensive phase of the battle and sent back to the airstrip. They were now on airstrip security. Fortunately the Japanese did not know that they had only one belt of ammunition for each machine gun and one clip of ammunition for each carbine (Hunter 1963, 189).

Sgt. George Davey was in A Company of the 236th Engineers. Before combat he was a company bulldozer operator. He tells a story that could be representative of any infantry platoon in offensive jungle warfare against the Japanese:

> Lieutenant Eichelberger came up to the pit where we were working at Ledo and told us to get back to camp. We were told to be at the airstrip at six o'clock in the morning to be flown to Myitkyina to go into combat.
>
> We landed at the airstrip and almost immediately went into combat. We went to a small village, and no Japanese were there. In fact, the village was completely deserted. We were out of water at the time, and I had a half-dozen canteens to go down the river to get some water, and—not knowing there was a whole platoon behind me—I walked down this trail and there was a dead Japanese on a pile of brush. I stopped to look at him, and when I did the others crowded around and we were talking about it and one of the fellows came over and said, "I see a Jap." We thought he was talking about the one on the pile of brush. Just as he said that, a Japanese machine gun opened up, and we all took for cover. I got behind—I ran up a little glade and got behind a big tree. I was looking right down over where the Japanese were, and I looked out behind me. Well, first of all, the Japanese were firing the machine gun, and it was taking the bark off the tree. It was a huge tree. As I looked behind, all the other fellows were on the ground—including our lieutenant, his name was Lieutenant

Ebley. They wasn't doing anything, just laying there. The machine gun had wounded quite a few guys and they were all laying on the ground moaning and groaning directly in front of the machine gun. I fired my rifle a few times, but it didn't do any good. I couldn't pinpoint where the Japanese machine gun was. I ran back to the lieutenant and asked him if I could go get a bazooka. He told me to go ahead, so I ran up the trail to the village and saw Sergeant White coming up the trail. Someone had already told them what had taken place. So he came along with an armful of rockets and the bazooka. I grabbed the armful of rockets he was carrying, and down we went to where all the Japanese had all those fellows pinned down. We got up behind the big tree that I had been standing behind and knocked out the machine-gun nest. We picked up all the wounded and made makeshift stretchers. The Japanese had killed—I forget how many it was. It was certainly two or three dead and a lot of wounded. Anyway, we picked them all up and headed back to the airstrip. It poured cats and dogs.

The next morning we went back to our little bivouac area, which was up close to the railroad, and that day we took over the railroad block which the Chinese had before they moved on. We spent a day or two there. The Japanese at night would hit our perimeter, which we held. One of our lieutenants, who had been laying on the ground back at the village, shot this young fellow. It was his own fault, though. For some reason he stood up in his foxhole, and he shot him.

Dates don't mean a thing to me. I lost all track of time. We moved on to the Y and set up road blocks. Oh!—I got ahead of myself. Captain Elrod took us on, this is the whole company now, and got us lost. While we were thrashing around in the jungle the Japanese (or someone) shelled us. That was something wicked. We weren't dug in—we were just laying there—and to this day I don't know how no one got killed. We spent the night out in the jungle, and the next morning he sent for my squad leader, a fellow by the name of Diabla, and he had to go out on patrol. I happened to be in his squad. He took three of us. Myself and a fellow by the name of Wright went out on patrol. The object was to find a bridge, a railroad bridge. Well, we took off and we found the railroad. Diabla made us stay and cover him while he went out and crawled in the brush along the railroad to see if he could locate a bridge. I guess that was the object, and a few minutes later he came back and said, "There is no bridge in sight. Let's get back to the company." So he takes off. We were traveling with a compass, and right off the bat I knew he was going wrong. We were running now. I ran up to him and I stopped and I said, "Diabla, we are going wrong," and I insisted and we argued a little bit, and finally Wright spoke up and said I was right. So Diabla agreed to follow me and said he didn't think I was right. So we took off, and I was a pretty fast runner—especially with the Japanese behind us. Diabla and Wright were right behind me. We came to a long, narrow rice paddy, and as I saw it I knew we were on the right trail. We had crossed it on the way out. We ran across and right into our bivouac area. From then on, Diabla always picked George Davey to go on patrol with him.

An L-5 flew over and dropped a message for us to get out of there, we were in the wrong area. So we headed back toward the airstrip. In the meantime I think it was B Company that had a tangle with the Japanese at the railroad bridge. They lost a lieutenant who was captured by the Japanese. So they asked for volunteers to go out, and I volunteered. [Davey became so choked up at this point that the conversation had to be shifted to another subject.]

We spent sixty-four days on the front. We fought at least two weeks, maybe longer, before we got any air support. There was very little artillery support. We had a few mortars. It was just about all hand to hand. We spent sixty-four days in the same clothes we flew in with, except when I took off my shorts and threw them away and my stockings stood up by themselves and I threw them away. We were in complete tatters.

On the way out—I can't remember to this day whether it was on the road out or whether it was at the airstrip—General Sultan was standing, and he said, "Get these guys out of sight—they look just exhausted" (Davey, videotape).

First Mission of the Second Battalion of New Galahad

Colonel Still and a few Old Galahads quickly whipped the Second Battalion (New Galahads) into a organized battalion. Two days after arrival, they were on their way two miles northeast to Mankrin, which they occupied. The river road leading from the north into Mankrin and then Myitkyina was now blocked. Still informed Hunter that he was in position, but that if he moved out on the road to pass through a narrow area—with the river on the east and the flooded low ground on the right—he had reason to believe the troops would not follow.

Colonel Hunter ordered him to have his men set up a strong defensive line on either side of the road. From here they could prevent Japanese from leaving or entering the town. Patrol activity could be carried out, as well as a carefully planned and well-executed offensive. All the while they could hope for a Japanese banzai attack in order to annihilate as many as possible.

New Galahad advanced slowly day by day as they worked to knock out strong points. Each day, when the number of wounded sent to the aid stations and the surgical team reached twenty, the day's activity had to be discontinued.

General Boatner Orders a General Advance

General Boatner ordered a general advance of the entire Myitkyina force, against the well-entrenched defenders of the town of Myitkyina, to begin on 10 June. This advance by the poorly trained and ill-prepared American engineers and infantry across flat, swampy terrain was to be made with grossly inadequate artillery and air support. The Chinese, with their battalions greatly reduced in strength and their men not much better prepared and trained, faced similar obstacles. The allied forces had limited ammunition, short food supply, and totally inadequate medical backup for the job assigned.

The two engineer battalions, now under the command of Lieutenant Colonel William Combs, were entrenched a mile south of Radahpur across and on either side of the Radahpur-Myitkyina Road. Their blocking line ran about one and one-half miles to the west, where it met the northeast section of the Chinese line. From this point the Chinese blocked all western and southern entrances to the city. The Second Battalion of New Galahad defended a line running from the eastern edge of the engineer's sector northeastward through the town of Mankrin to the Irrawaddy River. The engineers were about two miles from the town, the Second Battalion of Galahad about three miles, and the Chinese about two thousand yards.

Colonel Osborne's original Marauder First Battalion, now numbering about one-third of its original strength, remained at the airport.

The 150th Chinese Regiment was to take positions in the railroad yard; the 42nd Regiment would go to the Irrawaddy; and the 89th Regiment, which had a zone twice that of the 42nd and 150th together, would attack directly toward the river. Chinese units lying west and south of Myitkyina were to move northeast into the town, then wheel east and drive to the river. The Second Battalion of New Galahad and the 209th Engineer Battalion would drive directly south toward the town.

Stilwell's Command Problems discusses the allied forces available for this general attack:

> Great though the endurance and devotion of the Chinese were, the steady drain of casualties was reducing their strength to dangerously low levels. This situation was called to General Boatner's attention on 7 June by the commanders of the 30th and 50th Divisions, who pointed out that the 150th and 89th Regiments mustered between them only one thousand men. The 88th and 42nd could each only find one battalion for an attack. The accuracy of these statements was confirmed by an American liaison officer.

No explanation was provided to explain why the Chinese regiments had so few infantrymen available during the early stage of the Battle of Myitkyina. A unverified rumor suggested that they were understrength before they departed for Myitkyina. I have earlier noted that one of the American liaison officers stated, before the mission began, that his Chinese regiment only had nine hundred rifles. On 7 June the Chinese had not had enough casualties to bring about such a reduction in their troops as they reported. The Myitkyina task force now had control of the Morris Force, a group of thirteen hundred British troops under the command of Brigadier G. R. Morris. They were now located on the east side of the river and were plagued by disease and loss of men to battle. They were covered by Japanese machine guns and surrounded by flooded rice paddies. Morris's men were sick and exhausted, and he was losing men daily. They were not in a position to give any significant assistance to the Chinese and Americans.

By mid-July the Morris Force, part of one of General Wingate's five brigades and located across the Irrawaddy River from Myitkyina, was down to twenty-five officers and men—down from the thirteen hundred they had on 31 May—and were withdrawn from combat.

Colonel Hunter was well aware that the Second Battalion (New Galahad) would suffer excessive casualties if they were pushed too hard in an offensive action. The 209th Engineers were already taking more casualties than was reasonable. He had to train and discipline the men as they advanced slowly against well-camouflaged trenches, covered dugouts, and interlacing automatic weapons, as well as mortars and artillery. One American liaison officer reported that the Chinese regiment to which he was attached was down to 481 officers and men. Boatner relayed this information to Stilwell, adding that the Chinese troops were taking casualties (121 on a comparatively quiet day) while he was trying to make the raw Americans battleworthy. Obviously, the two engineer battalions and the Galahad replacements represented the margin of numerical superiority over the Japanese garrison in Myitkyina—but because of the fixed belief that there were only five hundred Japanese in Myitkyina, the full import of this was not realized. Nonetheless, there was disquietude.

As will be reported later, the allied artillery, artillery ammunition, and air support was to be limited.

In front of the allied forces lay swamps and brush-covered terrain. The Japanese had the advantage of high ground, on which they had forced the Burmese to dig an extensive trench system. Numerous log-covered dugouts were present, and there were many islands of machine-gun and mortar emplacements. The Japanese now had four thousand troops defending the city. All during the Battle of Myitkyina, the number of enemy had been and would be underestimated by General Stilwell's son, Colonel Joseph Stilwell Jr., who was also his intelligence officer. Colonel Hunter was never fooled by the gross estimates that were continually presented. He had a good idea of how many reinforcements had arrived and how many had been killed. The Nisei members of the Marauders were able to obtain information from Japanese prisoners during the entire battle. Some of the Galahad staff suspected that the Myitkyina task force headquarters group purposely provided a low estimate of the Japanese defenders so that the Chinese would be more apt to take the offensive. On the morning of 10 June it was raining, but all of the allied units started as scheduled.

CHAPTER XXII

Action of the Second Battalion, New Galahad

10–17 June

The Second Battalion of New Galahad started the attack on their designated front as planned. Progress was careful, conservative, and slow, with a minimum of casualties as they were learning to destroy Japanese strong points. All went reasonably well with these poorly trained and unexperienced men until 13 June.

Galahad had only two pack-75 howitzers for support, with a minimum of ammunition. Most of the artillery was under the control of the Myitkyina task force headquarters, which was supporting the Chinese with two batteries and one platoon of 75mm howitzers, two 105mm, and two 155mm howitzers. They were to fire six hundred tons of ammunition, but rarely with massed fire.

A platoon of K Company was hit very hard by the Japanese on 13 June. Most of the company withdrew back to L Company's line. Under the leadership of two men with an automatic weapon and a machine gun, a few stayed in place and drove off the Japanese. This action took place near the river. To the west the Japanese were driven off with grenades and rifle fire. After the initial setback, the green troops had held against the veteran and aggressive enemy.

By 17 June, the Second Battalion of Galahad controlled the Maingna Ferry Road and a clear passage to the Irrawaddy River. They were one mile closer to the town than they had been on 13 June. The engineers and the rest of Galahad now also controlled the Myitkyina-Mogaung-Sumprabum road junction.

When his platoon leader was killed, Pvt. Howard T. Smith had taken charge of the platoon and single-handedly knocked out a Japanese pillbox. Pfc. Willard J. D. Lilly destroyed an enemy machine gun that was firing into his position. 1st. Lt. Melvin D. Blair rescued a wounded man and knocked out a machine gun while under fire. These three heroes were veteran Marauders. T.Sgt. Richard E. Roe of New Galahad was killed when he crawled forward to grenade a Japanese machine gun that was causing heavy casualties.

MYITKYINA

Action of the 209th Engineers

10–17 June

On this hot, humid day during a monsoon shower the 209th Engineer Combat Battalion went into their second major action. They were just two weeks off of their road- building job and a year or more away from basic training.

One of the engineer's mortars soon injured Perkins and Fraunberger. After the 209th Engineers advanced four hundred yards, the Japanese closed in back of A Company—which had led the advance. 1st Lt. Henrich was killed, Bucky Morris was listed as missing, and there were numerous other casualties.

During this same attack, B Company was under fire for an hour from mortars and machine guns. Slater and Rainwater were injured by enemy fire, and Cofill was hit when he set off one of the unit's booby traps. This was the first time A and B Companies had taken offensive action against Japanese who were so well entrenched. Fortunately the two companies were able to withdraw back to their original line.

It rained all night. The men rested until noon, 11 June, by which time men and equipment had dried out. The general attack, coordinated with the Second Battalion (New Galahad) on the left and Chinese on other fronts, began for the second day. During the advance the engineers hoped to capture a well that lay in their zone of advance. Now C Company was leading with B Company following. The men were encouraged by supporting mortar fire and several planes strafing and bombing ahead. Enemy fire was intense, and in spite of their courageous effort they were pinned down most of the afternoon. Their casualties and continued heavy opposition left no alternative but to withdraw for the night. The units on either side fared no better.

While eating their breakfast K-ration on the 13th, the 209th began to take very active artillery fire. T5g. Bodziak, T5g. Roonan, and Private Poobi were seriously wounded. In the afternoon 1st Lieutenant Stefi brought orders for B Company to move out in the morning. They were to infiltrate behind the enemy lines and establish a roadblock in back of the Japanese. The rest of the battalion was to follow.

CHAPTER XXII

In preparation for the move the men were to take their weapons, ammunition, and one meal of K-rations. All tracers were removed from machine-gun belts.

The company moved out at 0400 with Colonel Combs in command. Under cover of darkness they moved about one-half mile. Here they were hit by machine-gun fire, and T5g. John Nealaton was killed.

The position on the road was reached at dawn. Before the men could dig in, Pfc.'s Willie Jordan, Bullard, and Newfarmer were hit, and other casualties were increasing. Japanese small arms, machine-gun, and mortar fire was intense. Without adequate cover the men took up firing positions. Two machine guns were moved to give cover to the wounded, some of whom were trying to cross the road. Machine gunners Korzenowski, McGarey, and Tillema were hit almost immediately. The guns were immediately taken over by three other engineers.

Sgt. John McNiff, T5g. Kurowski, and Pfc. Marshall, located on the other side of the perimeter, saw a reed-and- bamboo basha filled with Japanese. These three men volunteered to knock them out with hand grenades. They each made several trips to get and throw grenades. The three men were wounded.

The battle continued for several hours, and it was decided that the platoon on the other side of the road had to be brought across to the perimeter where A and B Companies were continuing the battle. Staff Sergeant DeShane, Technician Birrer, and Private Avant crossed the road, which was still under heavy fire, to help bring back the wounded. The courageous action of these men was successful.

Near the end of the day, Japanese activity slackened, and the men were able to dig in. The two companies now reported a total of eight men killed and fifteen wounded. The two medics, Private Literio and Technician Maegho, continued to do a great job with their limited material. The former carried on in spite of his wounds. The misery of all, especially the wounded, was compounded by rain.

Word had reached the battalion C.P., before communications were cut off, and they made several nearly disastrous attempts to reach the two companies. They finally had to give up any rescue attempt.

16 June brought more rain and misery for all, but especially the sick and wounded. Staff Sergeant Kumcha was killed, and several were wounded. A Japanese officer called for their surrender and was always told to go to hell. Enemy fire continued, and the mortars were

especially accurate and deadly. Artillery was also hitting the perimeter. The situation was beginning to look quite hopeless, as the Japanese were mortaring the daylights out of the unit at point-blank range. Casualties were increasing, and many of the wounded were again hit by enemy fire. Hunger and rain added to the misery of the men.

Three Piper Cubs attempted to drop food and medicine. One parachute landed in the middle of the road, between Robbins's machine gun and the Japanese. Recovery was impossible. One Japanese tried, and he was killed. The Japanese then destroyed it with mortars. Artillery and mortar fire continued to cause casualties.

At dusk on the 16th, sixty hours after these men of the 209th Engineers had become trapped, enemy fire slackened and the two companies pulled out—carrying some wounded and helping others. Intense darkness and heavy rain were both a great help as they worked their way toward their battalion. Several wounded only made it back due to the heroic action of three men. Staff Sergeant Shockley and Privates First Class Osman and Miller swam back and forth across a swollen creek several times to bring them out. One man, Private First Class Bartley—who had a leg wound—drowned. Privates James, Pam, Pavone, and Sutherland were at the end of the perimeter and were not notified of the withdrawal. They soon realized that they were alone and made it back safely.

The hungry and exhausted men were greeted with considerable emotion as they came out of the misty and flooded paddy fields in the early morning. They would not recover quickly from this brush with death and the loss of the twenty men killed and twenty-five wounded in Company B, as well as the losses in Company A. One of the outstanding deeds was that of Private Rogers in staying with Technicians Birrer, Marshall, and Tillen while helping these wounded men return to safety. They expressed great admiration and respect for Lt. Colonel William H. Combs, who had been their leader until he was mortally wounded after he had killed three Japanese with his .45. He was posthumously awarded an Oak Leaf Cluster to the Distinguished Service Cross for this and other actions (Romanus and Sunderland 1956, 245).

The wounded were evacuated as quickly as possible. There being no jeep roads, they were hauled six miles on oxcarts to the airfield and then flown two hundred miles to the 20th General Hospital.

The change to hot meals was a welcome one. Nearly all of the men got a complete change of clothes and shaved for the first time in two weeks.

The 209th Engineers moved back to Radahpur for several days' rest and were replaced on the offensive line by the 236th Engineer Combat Battalion, which had also been pulled from their construction of the Ledo Road. Since their arrival by air several days after the 209th, they had been sent to Namkwi and other hot spots to gain combat experience against small groups of nonaggressive Japanese.

The Second Battalion of New Galahad was on their left flank. The 209th was put on the right flank of the 236th on 23 June. The Chinese were on their right flank.

Progress was slow along the Americans' front during the rest of June, but small gains were made during most days. Casualties continued to mount—both from battle and disease. Dysentery and skin ulcers were serious problems. By the end of the month, only forty men were left in B Company. Everyone agreed that the Japanese were beaten and their end was only a matter of time.

Lt. Colonel Harold Greenlee of New Galahad, Third Battalion, took over the combined engineers, and they fought effectively and bravely until they were taken out one week before the city fell on 3 August. At the end they were said to be as ill and as worn as the Marauders.

The 209th personnel had won a DSC, several Silver Stars, a half-dozen Bronze Stars, and 260 Purple Hearts. This brief summary of the brilliant combat record of the two engineer battalions does not do credit to these gallant and courageous Americans. Trained primarily as engineers, they were suddenly taken from noncombat and thrown into bitter offensive infantry battle. They fought in the tropical heat, rain, and mud with inadequate food, shelter, and contaminated water. Ammunition was in short supply, and artillery and air support were inadequate at all times. Transportation of the wounded from the front lines to the airfield was primitive, poorly planned, and inadequate. Early surgical care was inadequate and below standards that should have been expected.

During later action of the 236th Engineers, Sgt. Fres N. Coleman threw himself on a Japanese grenade and saved two comrades. He and S.Sgt. Alvin O. Miller of the 209th Engineers both received the Distinguished Service Cross for heroic action. While on patrol activity late in the campaign, Pfc. George C. Presterly of the engineers won the

Distinguished Service Cross when he moved out ahead of his patrol to assault a Japanese strongpoint. He was killed while firing his weapon during the lone attack.

Action of Chinese Regiments

10–17 June

On 14 June, two companies of the Chinese 42nd Regiment were able to get into Japanese territory. They held their position until night, when the Japanese counterattacked and wiped them out. The four Chinese regiments were otherwise unable to crack the Japanese defensive line in any sector.

General Boatner was forced to call a halt to the attempt to crack the Japanese defenses. On 18 June, headquarters of the Myitkyina task force ordered the Chinese to use tunneling in an attempt to close with the Japanese.

General Stilwell Visits the Front, General Boatner Removed from Command

28 June

General Boatner had informed General Stilwell that the "U.S. troops are shaky." General Stilwell promptly flew in to check for himself. Shortly after arrival, he traveled the five miles through rough and dangerous territory to Colonel Hunter's headquarters at Radahpur. Colonel Hunter in the next three paragraphs discusses his visit.

> General Stilwell's trip on 18 June was noteworthy for several reasons. He actually saw these unreliable troops, wounded and sick, being brought into aid stations. I believe for the first time he was seeing good, rich, American blood streaming from the agonizing but silent bodies of American soldiers. He may have witnessed such scenes in World War I; however, his record indicates such an experience to have been very unlikely. He saw no fear of death, no panic, no complaining. Sobered by what he saw, he passed a taciturn night in a foxhole at Radahpur during which there were no "alarms nor excursions." He saw the men up before daylight and, without extortion or shouting of instructions, go quietly about the

routine and sordid business of war. He saw our little cemetery with its crude bamboo crosses mutely marking the muddy mounds of earth; the eternal resting places of many Old and several New Galahad personnel. Disheartening as it all was, the atmosphere of routine indifference to fate must have somewhat restored his faith, and awakened in him, to some degree, a belief that all was not "kosher" with respect to the reports he had been getting.

While Stilwell was at Radahpur I explained to him the need for a maneuver element if we were to make any effective progress. I also stated that we did not fear a banzai attack; on the contrary, we would welcome them. He asked me if in my judgement a penetration of the Japanese defenses could be made from the north. I replied that given a four-hundred-man battalion I thought it could be done. He agreed and told me that on his return to the airstrip he would send out a good outfit of the agreed strength. He directed me to then attempt a penetration from the Mankrin area.

True to his word he issued the necessary instructions to send me a Chinese battalion of at least four hundred men. He explained that the purpose was to penetrate through the Japanese position to Sitapur roughly on a southeast azimuth, cutting off the north from Myitkyina proper. This order was issued to General Boatner, but before the general was able to act on it he came down with a recurrent malaria attack. General Stilwell used this as a good reason to send him to Assam for medical care. Among other things, Stilwell was disturbed that Boatner had not visited the American troops since he had been at Myitkyina. Boatner was evacuated on the 25th of June. After hospital care he returned to his old job as commanding general, Northern Combat Area Command (Hunter 1963, 154-57).

General Stilwell had conveniently brought Brig. Gen. Theodore Wessels along, and he was made the commander of all allied forces at Myitkyina on 26 June. The general had been on the staff of the Infantry School at Fort Benning, Georgia, when he was sent to the CBI as part of Stilwell's plans for training the Chinese army. When it became apparent that the Chinese army plans did not call for use of all 2,213 officers and men who had been sent to the CBI to train a second batch of thirty Chinese divisions, Wessels was sent to the Southeast Asia Headquarters.

Chapter XXIII
The Battle Continues
26 June–3 August 1944

While General Stilwell was debating what to do with General Boatner, General Wessels had several days to survey all aspects of the situation at Myitkyina. He took the trouble to visit every unit soon to be under his command. He made a point of talking to the junior officers, noncoms, and men who were on the front line. This did a lot for their morale. Those who had been in combat had a justified tendency to believe that they had been forgotten by headquarters personnel.

Stilwell's 22nd and 32nd Chinese Divisions and the Chindits defeated the Japanese at Mogaung on 26 June. This meant that a land route would soon be open to Myitkyina and the command would not have to worry about Japanese hitting from the rear. More supplies, men, and air support would be available.

The Massacre of F Company

Wessels promptly acted on General Stilwell's order to send a battalion of four hundred men to Galahad. The First Battalion of the 42nd Chinese Regiment was sent to carry out this mission, which had been planned by General Stilwell. They reported to Colonel Hunter on 28 June, and he promptly notified headquarters that instead of the promised 400 men, the battalion could only muster 250—and at least 50 were noncombat cooks and orderlies. He promptly protested to the Myitkyina task force headquarters and was told to do the best he could.

An I & R platoon from Galahad was attached, and the force set out on 29 June at 0530 hours. The small combat team passed through the Japanese lines without difficulty and reached their objective on the outskirts of Sitapur, about one mile from the northern edge of Myitkyina, at 0930 hours. They promptly dug in with a strong defensive perimeter. The Japanese immediately counterattacked with infantry, mortar, and artillery. They were supplied with adequate rifle and machine-gun ammunition to hold the Japanese off for an undetermined period but soon called for more. Numerous attempts were made to supply them with all that was required, but the perimeter was so small that only a few parachutes could get through on each flight. Most of the supplies landed in Japanese hands.

On 30 June, Colonel Hunter realized that their only chance for survival and a successful mission was to enlarge their perimeter. He ordered Colonel Osborne to send in a company of New Galahad in an effort to accomplish this by more manpower. Company F was to jump off early on the morning of 1 July from the Mankrin area. The weather was terrible, with heat, humidity, and rain. Preparations were slow, and darkness was approaching before they departed.

The company commander Captain McNight, S.Sgt. Tommy Roland, and others had been killed earlier in June. First Lieutenant Broadbrooks was now in command. They soon came to a large, flooded rice paddy, and as they started to cross came under heavy fire. They fell back and waited for daybreak. During the night a mortar squad and several automatic weapons were set up on the north bank of the flooded paddy field so as to give cover to the company as they crossed in the morning.

Just before daybreak the company, minus their supporting mortar squad, crossed the paddy, which was two feet under water and one hundred yards across. The company entered a bamboo grove and soon began to exit it. Lieutenant Broadbrooks, at the head of the emerging column, found himself in a large open area. He soon saw a parachute hanging in a tree at some distance off to the southwest. He knew that parachutes had been dropped to the surrounded Chinese battalion and assumed that he was looking at their perimeter. The truth was that the Chinese were well off to the southeast. He was looking at a parachute that had been dropped when an engineer company had been surrounded earlier in June.

Lieutenant Broadbrooks was not aware that he had lost his way when he noticed a group of Orientals ahead whom he decided were Chinese. The preliminary greeting of both groups was friendly, with "ding how" greetings all around. As the lieutenant and a scout called "Whitie" went to make further contact, the strangers suggested that they lay down their arms. Lieutenant Broadbanks is said to have immediately given the alarm to his men and was bayoneted to death as both sides opened fire.

The Japanese had their rifles and machine guns ready, and many of the Americans were slaughtered. A few surviving men withdrew, but at least twenty, still able to function, joined Corporal Anthony Firenze from Geneva, New York, in a valiant stand against overwhelming enemy. Firenze, with his courageous comrades, fought a delaying action of eight hours until the Japanese broke off when the Japanese commander was wounded and possibly killed. The corporal had been injured early in the ambush but had stayed with his machine gun until the attack was broken up and all but one of his gun crew were killed. Stragglers from the reliever company continued to drift in for three days. One incoherent survivor came in on the third day. His numerous wounds were covered with maggots and his body with leeches. He had been hiding during days and moving at night and had barely avoided capture and certain death. He surprised everyone by making a recovery.

Out of the company of 160 men, thirty-two survived. Cpl. Anthony F. Firenze received the Distinguished Service Cross.

Now we return to the Chinese battalion. Their part in this tragic episode is well described by Captain Paul L. Tobey in his book, *The Sitapur Incident*, published in 1987. The Chinese infantry battalion had marched, during the night of 27–28 June, about ten miles—from the southern perimeter of the battle area to Colonel Hunter's American sector. The 250 men included cooks, orderlies, radio personnel, and stretcher bearers. There was no motor transportation, mules, or horses. All equipment was carried by the men. Their two-mile advance toward Sitapur was all in enemy territory.

The company-sized battalion faced many obstacles:

1. Poor knowledge of what their mission was—other than to advance and dig in near the village of Sitapur deep in enemy territory.
2. Inadequate knowledge about the proper direction and terrain, much of which was under water.
3 No physical contact with the American units on the right or left flanks, which were supposed to advance but were unable to make any significant progress.

4. No safe overland route to the rear—and no route at all as soon as they were surrounded.
5. No doctors or medical technicians to care for the wounded.
6. No medical supplies other than insufficient battle dressings.
7. Inadequate food supplies
8. Poorly trained troops with Springfield rifles.
9. Unreliable radios and wire communication.
10. No artillery support.
11. Poor support from mortars in the American sector.
12. Limited ammunition.
13. Limited drinking water.
14. No means of evacuating the wounded.

On the positive side, the Chinese were accompanied by the New Galahad I & R platoon under the command of Lt. Jordan Adkins from Jumping Branch, Summers County, West Virginia. Captain Paul L. Tobey was their permanent liaison officer, and they could count on the American troop carrier command to deliver food and ammunition and all necessary supplies if at all possible.

Tobey had arrived at the Myitkyina airfield on 19 May 1944 as a U.S. Army infantry captain assigned as a liaison officer with the First Battalion, 42nd Regiment, 14th Division Chinese Army in India (CAI). The battalion consisted of 350 men. Once the battalion joined the rest of the regiment, Captain Tobey and the other battalion liaison officers were largely ignored by the Chinese senior battalion officers. During an attack on Myitkyina from 14 through 16 June the liaison officers had not been advised of the plans. The division had taken heavy losses, and two companies or the 42nd Regiment had been completely destroyed.

It is with this history that Capt. Paul Tobey was to serve with and watch the men of the Chinese battalion fight for their survival during 29 and 30 June and 1 and 2 July as they were surrounded in their small defensive perimeter deep in Japanese territory. They existed and fought under dreadful environmental and logistical circumstances while under constant machine-gun, mortar, and rifle attack. All the while they were surrounded by dead and wounded. There was little they could do for the latter. One courageous Chinese machine-gun platoon leader prevented a breakthrough after his crew had been killed. His only backup was the Galahad I & R platoon, stationed in the center of the perimeter to turn back a final assault.

General Wessels risked his future and the wrath of General Stilwell by ordering the abandonment of the defensive area and attempted a return to the American lines. This was carried out, with a surprisingly small loss of life, under the cover of well-placed mortar fire by Colonel Hunter's forces. Paul Tobey was cited for his part in leading many of the group to safety.

American Action at Myitkyina

3–11 July

General Wessels continued to evaluate the situation at Myitkyina and began a training program for New Galahad. The Third Battalion, which had up until this time been used mostly for patrol activity and training missions against small Japanese outposts, was started on an eight-hour-per-day training program. The Second Battalion of New Galahad, which was still on the front line, was allotted a four-hour training program. The rest of their time was devoted to knocking out Japanese strong points using their rifles, grenades, mortars, machine guns, and artillery with the cooperation of the assigned fighter plane. Colonel Hunter made every attempt to keep casualties at a minimum. The small unit aid station could barely handle more than thirty wounded per day. Evacuation of the wounded by oxcart over the six-mile route was still a major problem. The command was also beginning to recognize that the Japanese could not organize any major attack against the Americans or Chinese. They were no longer getting replacements or supplies and would soon be totally destroyed by artillery and air action as well as starvation and disease.

The fact that Colonel Peterson, the NAAC surgeon, had made no attempt to provide litter bearers, light planes, and other means of evacuating the wounded caused great hardship to the sick and wounded. The makeshift system of bullock cart transport with native drivers and guides was the only method available to the Americans. It certainly contributed to unnecessary misery, death, and delayed treatment of disease and battle casualties.

CHAPTER XXIII

General Wessels Attempts First Major Offensive

12 July

General Wessels had been planning a major attack for several days, and this process was still under way. Arrangements were far from complete. A radio message came from General Stilwell asking when the attack of the 12th was getting under way. Wessels took the hint, and the attack plans were hastily completed. On his own initiative, Major General Howard C. Davidson offered and arranged for a bombing by thirty B-24's. During the early part of the campaign, P-51 fighter support from the 88th Fighter Squadron had been of little help to Galahad since targets had to be designated a day ahead of time. Captain Allred and his P-51 fighter bomber was eventually assigned to Galahad and continued to serve the front-line troops daily. He became a much-admired hero of Galahad. He was also to help during the attack. As usual, his five-hundred-pound bombs and .50-caliber wing guns were to be counted on.

Before the attack, Colonel Hunter had requested that Galahad officers act as air controllers. His request was denied. The day of the attack, Galahad was not to use the combat air frequency on its radios. When General Stilwell had ordered the attack he had twenty-five American general officers at Myitkyina for a conference. Colonel Hunter was not asked to the conference, even though he had the title of commanding officer, American combat forces, Myitkyina task force.

Since General Wessels had arrived, Galahad had managed to advance two thousand yards, and the engineers had almost destroyed the Japanese defenses in front of their area. The two or three hundred recently arrived replacements, of questionable training and ability, had allowed the men to rotate from the front for a day or so to bathe, wash their clothes, and get a brief rest. Morale was good, and they were ready for the attack they hoped would end the battle.

In many places the Japanese were dug in fifty yards or less in front of Galahad and the engineers. In order to prevent friendly-fire casualties, the American front line was marked with white panels, and Galahad and the engineers pulled back two thousand yards just before the bombing attack was to begin. The B-24's could be seen coming in from the west long before they could be heard. They were supposed to come from the north. They drifted over the city and disappeared, only to appear a few minutes later at five thousand feet and coming in from the north. Their bomb bays could be clearly seen before they had reached the designated dropping site. Nothing could be done as the bombs came— and continued to come—on our front-line troops, two thousand yards off their mark.

Men were dazed and stunned along the line where forty percent of the bombs had fallen. One platoon was buried, and only six of its men survived. Needless to say, Galahad and the engineers did not attack. They were able, however, to get men back to their front before it was occupied by the Japanese. The disillusioned American infantrymen went back to their day-by-day advances, slowly driving the retreating Japanese. The Chinese were continuing their tunneling operations. The 88th and 89th Chinese Regiments had been involved in the attack and made little progress.

By mid-July the estimate was made that the Japanese garrison had suffered almost 800 dead and about 1,180 wounded.

The Final Weeks of Battle

13 July–3 August

In spite of the heat, rain, and horrible living conditions in and about their muddy foxholes, the dirty work of war went on. Pfc. Marvin H. Dean, a Marauder veteran, was lead scout of a patrol on 21 July. In this always-dangerous position he located a Japanese machine-gun position, which he destroyed. His self-reliance and courageous deed eventually won the Distinguished Service Cross (Romanus and Sunderland 1956, 251).

When Colonel Hunter had presented his letter of complaints and recommendations to General Stilwell on 25 May, item number eight concerned the matter of decorations: "Although this unit has been in continuous contact with the Japanese and has performed capably in the field to date, no awards or decorations, no indication of appreciation, and no citations have been received by any personnel of this unit as far as can be determined" (Hunter 1963, 192–95).

In the next several paragraphs, Colonel Hunter discusses the status of the decoration situation and General Stilwell's reluctant effort to partially correct his disgraceful, thoughtless, and unappreciative lack in carrying out this basic function:

Although many recommendations had been submitted for decorations, none had been received up to the end of May. A disconcerting thing that happened along this line, even after General Stilwell had had my letter for some time, was Major Schudmak's decoration. This decoration embarrassed all concerned, Schudmak most of all, when it was realized that the first man decorated was the surgeon who had originally evacuated General Merrill on the occasion of his first heart attack. This incident did not enhance the value or worth of those decorations subsequently awarded to members of the unit. Most recommendations were finally located, acted upon, and reported to the recipients sometime after they had left India and had reported to new assignments in the Zone of Interior. Merrill was the only officer to be decorated by the Chinese government, although in my opinion, Osborne and some of his men should have been given the recognition for their work in spearheading the Chinese into the Shaduzup area.

It appears that recommendations for decorations had been held without action, with Merrill's knowledge, somewhere in Assam. On learning of this some years later, I realized what probably was on Merrill's mind. I recalled that after Walawbum the battalion commanders were directed to submit written recommendations for awards. I was informed that an officer had told one of his men that he should write a recommendation on the officer and, in return, that officer would recommend that the soldier be decorated. When all the decorations were in, I advised Merrill that a couple of the recommendations were suspect and should be held up for verification by additional witnesses. It looks now as though Merrill may have sidetracked all recommendations thereafter. The only justification remotely possible for such action on his part was that—in accordance with his original promises—he hoped, after Myitkyina, to have the whole outfit assembled in a rest area where he personally would pin on all the medals. It may be that promotions were held up for the same reason. It may be that when Merrill suffered his second heart attack, the realization that he was in no position to fulfill his promises or realize his dreams was finally brought home to him by General Stilwell. Stilwell merely relates in his diary that Merrill on 19 May had had a heart attack and was given morphine by Peterson.

THE BATTLE CONTINUES

The rumor had gotten around that I had turned down a decoration offered by Stilwell. The facts behind this rumor show an interesting sidelight on General Stilwell's methods of conducting business. I was hurriedly called to the phone one day (Stilwell had come back on 23 July to check progress), and an excited staff officer told me that the general was on his way out to Radahpur to decorate some men; that he had with him two Distinguished Service Crosses and some six or seven Silver Stars; and further, that I was to write up some recommendations and have the men standing by when the general arrived. When I asked, "Why wasn't he using some of the many recommendations on hand?" I was given the old shrug-off and told to get busy. I pointed out that as much as I desired that the New Galahad men and the engineers be decorated, I thought it stunk not to act on the recommendations that they had been sitting on for some time. I did as directed, and after hastily getting the best information available, we started writing recommendations and assembling the men out of the lines. We managed to write as many recommendations and assemble as many men as Stilwell had medals. When he arrived, General Wessels and Captain Young, his aide de camp, were in the party. I lined up the men and waited for the general to proceed. He wasn't ready. He had neglected to bring a cameraman, and he wanted some pictures. I suppose he wanted to prove to Washington that he had issued some medals. By now all the photographers who had joined Galahad in India had fallen by the wayside. However, Doc Sazama had a small camera and some film. We sent for Doc and waited till he could arrive and record this historic event. The exposed film was taken by Captain Young and never seen again, until by some means Charlton Ogburn managed to dig up a couple of prints while researching material for *The Marauders*.

Some of the men to be decorated were at Radahpur, while the remainder were at Mankrin. When Stilwell had used up his allotted medals for the men stationed at Radahpur and I assumed he was through, he said, "Hunter, go get a shirt on so I can pin one of these on you." I modestly stated that I had done nothing unusual. He insisted, and after borrowing someone's shirt he pinned a Silver Star Medal on the flap of my left upper pocket, mumbling meanwhile something to the effect that "This is for doing a good job."

We then left for Mankrin by jeep. There were two routes by which one could go to Mankrin from Radahpur. One was by a good road leading north for almost five miles from where it turned east to the river and thence south to the village. This road took one within three miles of the Japanese general hospital. I considered this to be dangerous for use by the theater commander and General Wessels, although I "jeeped it all the time" when in a hurry. The other route, about three miles in length, skirted the rice paddy, and about midway between Mankrin and Radahpur a small stream—two to three feet in depth, depending on the amount of recent rains—had to be forded. The decorating party took this route. When we got to the ford, the leading jeep, in trying to get across the ford, got stuck. The water was too high. We were forced to dismount, wade across the stream, and continue on foot. In spite of General Stilwell's reputation he didn't like the idea of the hike he was forced to make. And of course he would have to walk back, too. I walked ahead rather nervous about the presence of the theater commander traversing this particular piece of terrain on foot, for it was the route usually crossed by Japanese stragglers in making their way into the city from the north. We arrived at Mankrin without incident and with only a few stray Japanese shots cracking a safe distance over our heads.

Stilwell had the requested number of men lined up and with the paperwork in hand. As the men lined up and were counted, Captain Young had to inform General Stilwell that there were not enough medals to go around. It was obvious what happened: his presentation of a medal to me had been done on impulse and without any prior preparation of a recommendation by the Myitkyina task force commander. To prevent embarrassment all around, I returned my decoration to Stilwell, and he pinned it on the soldier for whom it was originally intended. General Stilwell said he would have one sent to Dinjan for me. I wasn't too sure that I would ever receive it and forgot all about the matter until returning to the rear echelon in August, where I found a Silver Star awaiting me (Hunter 1963).

Since he had no official order, Colonel Hunter returned the Silver Star to the War Department in the spring of 1959. The official order reached him in February 1960. After the tragic bombing of Galahad by the American air force, General Wessels frequently visited the men on the front lines. They continued their methodical but successful daily gains against the Japanese defenses. Of the twenty-six hundred volunteer replacements who had arrived during the early part of June, the hastily organized Second Battalion of New Galahad was still on the front line with the two engineer battalions. About six hundred of the remainder had been assigned to numerous jobs such as muleskinners, truck drivers, medical personnel, and replacements for some of the sick, wounded, and dead. The remaining thousand men had been organized into the Third Battalion of New Galahad. They had been trained for about sixty days by sending them to various sections of the Myitkyina battle area to eliminate isolated clusters of Japanese, assist the First Battalion of Marauders (Old Galahad) in protecting the airfield, and perform numerous other functions assigned by the Myitkyina task force headquarters.

During the third week in July, General Stilwell suggested that a battalion of New Galahad be sent across the flooded rice paddy east of the engineer's position. The objective was to secure the partially completed airfield the Japanese had been constructing at the time we captured the airfield on 17 May. They had continued to control this important area. It was here that F Company of New Galahad had been destroyed on 2 July. It was apparent to General Stilwell, Colonel Hunter, and the men of Galahad that the Japanese defenders of Myitkyina were almost at the end of their ability to defend the city. As early as 19 July numerous small groups of Japanese were killed or captured as they attempted to escape on bamboo rafts floating down the Irrawaddy. Intelligence information obtained from a Japanese prisoner and passed to Stilwell on 26 July showed that only four hundred Japanese remained, many of whom were wounded and all of whom were starving. The command believed that the battle would soon be over. Of course it meant the death and wounding of more of Galahad's men, but General Stilwell was impatient and wanted the Battle of Myitkyina won without further delay, since he was due to leave in a few days to meet with Lord Louis Mountbatten in Ceylon, where he planned to spend one month.

The attack was set for 26 July. Colonel George W. Sliney, who had been with General Stilwell as artillery officer since the first Burma campaign, was now in charge of all artillery at Myitkyina. Rather than go to the airfield to work out arrangements with Colonel Sliney, as requested, Colonel Hunter, his junior in rank, asked him to come to Radahpur in order to get a better evaluation of what the artillery plans would be and how they were to be carried out. Sliney gracefully agreed to this change in his plans and made the trip to Radahpur. The plans made every effort to prevent friendly fire from the allied artillery barrages.

Lieutenant Colonel Gestring marched the now partially trained Third Battalion of New Galahad the five miles from the airstrip to Radahpur on 25 July. With the engineer battalions in place to the west and Second Battalion of New Galahad to the east, Colonel Gestring's force advanced on 26 July toward the designated area. Colonel Hunter states, "The attack was covered by a smoke barrage of 4.2 mortars and artillery, and the artillery was interspersed with high explosive. The battalion crossed the rice paddy and established themselves firmly in the north section of the city. I did not push them on. Now I told task force headquarters it was time for the Chinese to move" (Hunter 1963).

On 28 July, during the above action, Galahad veterans T5g. Russell G. Wellman and Pfc. Herman Manuel worked together to rescue a wounded companion while under heavy machine-gun and rifle fire. Even though they were wounded, they succeeded and won the Distinguished Service Cross (Romanus and Sunderland 1956, 252).

The successful advance of the Americans continued on the 29, 30, and 31 July. During this period Captains Shields A. Brubeck and John J. Dunn, and 1st Lt. Donald W. Delorey—all of New Galahad—fought with their units with valor and won the Distinguished Service Cross (Romanus and Sunderland 1956, 252).

Lieutenant Delorey was a machine-gun platoon leader in Company K. Machine-gun fire from the right flank had held up company advance, and the platoon leader on the right had been killed. Even though he was wounded, Lieutenant Delorey advanced and killed the Japanese machine-gun crew with a submachine gun. He left the field wounded but returned to fight the next day and was again wounded.

In his own words he tells some of the story:

> The engineers were sent to task force headquarters for rest and reorganization in preparation for their return to their engineering work. The 209th Engineers had taken forty-one percent battle casualties. Colonel Hunter was also now in a position where he could allow the Second Battalion of New Galahad to rotate men

out of combat for a chance to clean up and rest for a few days. They would then return to combat and join the Third Battalion in patrol and mopping up activities in Galahad's area of responsibility. American casualties continued, as did the foul weather—with daily rain, heat, and humidity (Romanus and Sunderland 1956, 292).

The Chinese 149th Regiment joined the 50th Division on 24 July. They were used to relieve portions of the Chinese 42nd and 150th Regiments. The First Battalion of the 90th Chinese Regiment took over a quiet sector on the 25th. The Chinese 50th Division was the one picked to carry out a new plan to enter the city of Myitkyina. General Pan Yul-kun offered his plan. A raiding party, formed into fifteen heavily armed sections, was to be organized and briefed on infiltrating the Japanese lines facing the 50th Division. Having made its way through the Japanese lines in darkness, it was to remain hidden until 0430 when the 50th would assault while the raiders spread confusion behind the Japanese lines.

The plan was carried out and, thanks to the efforts of the raiders and the preliminary stages of the Japanese evacuation, resistance was minimal—and the victory was complete by late afternoon. Of the 187 Japanese prisoners taken, most were sick or wounded. About six hundred Japanese and their commander, Colonel Maruyama, withdrew and thus escaped capture or death. Before agreeing to the withdrawal, Colonel Mizukami committed suicide on 1 August.

Hunter's Last Meeting with Stilwell

In *Galahad* (1963), Colonel Hunter tells of his final contact with General Stilwell:

> On the 29th of July I was directed to report to the airstrip and have lunch, at noon, with General Stilwell. I flew in, and while walking from the light airplane strip to the headquarters area, I fell in the mud while trying to negotiate the small embankment that skirted the edge of the field. Raising a foot to walk over an obstacle was beginning to require a conscious effort on my part. I suddenly realized that I was tired.
>
> I can't remember what I expected to happen at this luncheon except that I anticipated being fed a good meal, since Stilwell was

presumed to have a cook who could do wonders with the food available at the airstrip. As I approached the headquarters I was surprised to see Stilwell and Arms sitting under a small shelter—obviously the "Old Man's" private dining area. I approached and saluted. I was invited to sit down. The food came promptly, such as it was, and little was said while it was being consumed. When it was consumed Stilwell opened the conversation by stating, "Hunter, I am going to organize a brigade out of what is left of Old and New Galahad. We will organize the 475th Infantry Regiment. On the way and due in Bombay shortly is the 124th Cavalry. You can go back and get some teeth put in, take two months' leave in the States, and get back in time to move south with the 475th. How does that strike you? General Arms will be your brigade commander.

I was nonplussed. My first reaction was "Why Arms—why not Wessels as a brigade commander?" Of course I didn't voice this question. I got the picture. Wessels hadn't made the team either. I stalled for a minute by telling Stilwell that to get dental work done, I would have to go to Karachi on the other side of India, at least two thousand miles. He was quite surprised at this information. While he mulled this over I made up my mind and said, "General, I would prefer to go somewhere where I would command a conventional type organization, if I have a choice." Stilwell looked at Arms, ran his hand through his shock of hair, and took a deep breath.

The situation now became strained; however, I was asked who in my opinion, of the officers of Old Galahad, would make a good regimental commander for the 475th Infantry. I replied, "Osborne." With this the meeting broke up.

"You've made your bed, now lie in it," I said to myself as I got my pilot and started back to Radahpur. I called Osborne over to talk to him. I warned him that I had advised Stilwell that he would make a good regimental commander and that he should think it over. I explained to him why I had replied to Stilwell as I had:

1. My reputation and relationship with the NCAC had been such, and my confidence in that staff such, that I would be a detriment to the regiment rather than an asset.
2. I was not impressed by General Arms to a great degree. I felt very strongly that he was not physically capable of commanding the brigade. I was getting annoyed at my bosses getting fired or sick. Besides, I would most certainly not be

able to get along with Colonel Tack, who Arms proposed to appoint chief of staff of the brigade.

3. I was also opposed to commanding troops I had not trained. Therefore, if I accepted the job, I would take no leave and I would be without teeth as well.

4. Wessels had been apparently dumped, although he had done the best job of any of Stilwell's generals. Arms was an old friend of Stilwell's and had been picked over Wessels for that reason in my opinion.

5. Estabrook (General Stilwell's son-in-law) and young Joe Stilwell were around and might be shoved in on top of one of the regimental commanders.

6. And lastly, I told Osborne that the real war was over in the CBI.

I did not know it at time, but Stilwell left that afternoon for Kandy, Ceylon, after a short stop at Shaduzup, his normal forward headquarters. I was left for the dogs to chew on.

My attitude is better expressed by General Wedemeyer, who on leaving the service gives this as his reason: "When a situation develops wherein a member of the team feels he cannot in clear conscience subscribe to and support the leader, it is mandatory that he resign from the team." I was pretty sure that I had resigned from Stilwell's team. In his book, General Wedemeyer, in discussing his approaching duty in China with his aide, offered the following observation: "I told him that a year or so back I would have welcomed the opportunity to try to solve the problems of the China theater, but by now the difficulties seemed insurmountable. I had heard many times over that China was a graveyard for American officials, military and diplomatic; that you couldn't do anything with the Chinese, they just wouldn't cooperate, they led you into difficulties with your own government as well as with theirs, and so on. Many a good officer has had his career ruined in China." This statement could just as well have applied to the Burma portion of the theater as long as Chih Hui Pau was running the show under Stilwell.

A soldier is a human being. He has as great a capacity for love as any other human being. Officially, the military hierarchy attempts to instill in the soldier loyalty and respect for first his squad leader, then his platoon leader, then his company commander, and so on up through the chain of command. It is inherent in the system that those with the least experience, education,

CHAPTER XXIII

and training for leadership are first in the chain—i. e., the corporal as squad leader. It is just as self-evident that he is closest to the men he must command and lead into battle and possible death.

As the leader advances up the chain of command and grows in age as well as in experience, some also grow in understanding. Omar Bradley, for instance. Others grow in a different way. To these others, his officer subordinates and his troops are but stopping stones to success, invaluable to him during his journey upward but soon forgotten once the heights have been attained. Ambitious men look only forward, indifferent to the shambles left behind in their mad scramble to the top in pursuit of their personal aims.

The men of Galahad were soldiers who respected only their own officers and noncommissioned officers. They loved their mules and horses. Everyone else was an outsider. No one seemed to like them, so why should they bestow respect on people who were unsympathetic to their needs? It became a unit with a chip on its shoulder. Denied a set of colors, they carried with them into battle no symbol of the great country for which they were fighting. Denied a shoulder patch, the small can opener that came with the C- ration, affixed to the shirt lapel, became the unit's adopted symbol.

Had Galahad had an American flag to raise over Myitkyina as did the marines at Tarawa, its presence flying proudly there in rain and fog might have inspired greater sacrifice, and a less discouraging chapter in American military history might now be penned. What stupid ass made the decision that Galahad was not to carry the American flag into battle? As a reminder of the American heritage being enhanced here in Southeast Asia, on July 4th 1944 I ordered each man under my command to fire forty-eight rounds into the Japanese lines; every mortar, machine gun, and artillery piece also fired forty-eight rounds. We all felt pretty good that day. A soldier fights not for money, but for his country. He needs the symbols—the flag, a regimental set of colors, a shoulder patch, and a band playing the good old songs from time to time—to remind him that the homeland still exists, should he live to return to it, even at the moment he is separated from it by ten thousand miles of land and ocean. Galahad had no symbols other than a little tin can opener on the shirt, a dirty set of jungle greens, a heavy beard, some leeches sucking on his legs, and a fever gnawing on his innards.

It is a sad commentary on life that one may deny to others that which he covets most. General Stilwell's policy on decorations was not understandable. In January 1944, Merrill told me that General Stilwell was very sensitive to the fact that he (Stilwell) had not received adequate recognition (i.e., decoration for valor) for his service to date. He failed to realize that others might also become sensitive to similar neglect on the part of his staff. It often appeared that he did not check on the little things that most great combat leaders are interested in when talking with the men they command (Hunter 1963, 208–12).

Myitkyina Falls

3 August

At 0300 hours on 3 August, the Chinese 50th Division sent several raiding parties into the town of Myitkyina. They attracted little enemy attention and were soon followed by Chinese regiments all along the line of attack. By 1545 hours on 3 August the town of Myitkyina was in the hands of the Allies.

Sgt. Major Ray Lyons has this to say about the end of the Battle of Myitkyina:

> They hauled a whole bunch of us to the 20th General Hospital. Hunter went. I went. In the hospital, I kept to myself on the ward where I was. There was actually nothing wrong with me, but they were trying to find out if there was something wrong. I didn't realize this until long after the war when I read this book that the medical department put out, in which they indicated that the 20th General Hospital, in particular, had gotten into trouble over sending boys who were not in good physical condition back to Myitkyina. Then it dawned on me that, after the battle was over, they were not going to let anybody out of that hospital until they were sure they were in good shape (Lyons, videotape).

General Stilwell was not available in or near Myitkyina. He had left the area on 29 July with his son Colonel Joseph Stilwell to travel for a four-week vacation in the resort area of Kandy, Ceylon. The official purpose of the trip to Ceylon was to act as Lord Mountbatten's deputy while he spent the month of August in England. Stilwell, by his own admission, turned the work over to Lieutenant General Pownall and spent his stay sightseeing and resting. General Merrill was in Kandy and introduced him to society at a cocktail party on 2 August. He remained at Kandy until 30 August.

The Marauders, the 209th and 236th Engineers, the poorly trained volunteers of New Galahad, numerous other American and British units, and the Chinese had served him well. The capture of Myitkyina airfield and the town, as well as the defeat of of the Japanese in North Burma, climaxed his career. Just before the fall of Myitkyina he was made a four-star general, a rank only achieved by Generals Marshall, MacArthur, Eisenhower, and Arnold.

The word that Stilwell was now a four-star general was not met with enthusiasm when it gradually became known among the men who had sacrificed so much for their country under his command. Other important information slowly became known to the men. The 5307th Composite Unit (Provisional) was cited in War Department General Orders No. 54 dated at Washington 5 July 1944. The citation by the theater commander, United States Army forces in China-Burma-India, was confirmed in the name of the president of the United States as public evidence of deserved honor and distinction. The citation read as follows:

> The 5307th Composite Unit (Prov.) was the first United States ground combat force to meet the enemy in World War II on the continent of Asia. After a series of successful engagements in the Hukawng and Mogaung Valleys of North Burma during March and April 1944, the unit was called on to lead a march over jungle trails through extremely mountainous terrain against stubborn resistance in an attack on Myitkyina. The unit proved equal to its task, overcame all the obstacles put in its way by the enemy and the weather, and, after a brilliant operation 17 May 1944 seized the airfield at Myitkyina, an objective of great tactical importance in the campaign, and assisted in the capture of Myitkyina on 3 August 1944. The successful accomplishment of this mission marks the 5307th Composite Unit (Prov.) as an outstanding combat force and reflects great credit on Allied Arms.

The next-to-last sentence had originally only cited the unit for capturing the airfield. This was changed on 8 November 1944. I know of no effort made by General Stilwell to express his congratulations and thanks to the American and Chinese troops. He never visited the troops during their training period. He was seen by some of the men when he stood beside a jungle trail for a brief period when one battalion crossed into enemy territory. He visited Colonel Hunter on two occasions while he was at Radahpur. Late in the campaign, in what seemed to be an afterthought, he hurriedly presented some decorations to Galahad. It seems unlikely that he ever had a word of praise or encouragement for the men in the field. At no time was there any gathering of the men (Old or New Galahad) to show appreciation for the courageous way they had performed and the sacrifices they had made for their country. It seems that he was incapable of expressing admiration and thanks either in private or public. In his diary, when victory was presented to him, he never mentioned Galahad.

Colonel Hunter Is Relieved of Command

On the morning of 3 August 1944, Colonel Willis Tack gave Colonel Hunter a note relieving him of command of Old and New Galahad. It was generally known that Galahad was to be disbanded on 10 August. As previously recounted, Stilwell on 29 July had told Colonel Hunter that he was going to organize a brigade with what was left of Old and New Galahad combined with the 124th Cavalry, which was on its way to Bombay. From these units he would form the 475th Infantry Regiment. He had offered Colonel Hunter the position of commander of this new regiment, and Colonel Hunter had turned him down.

Needless to say, Colonel Hunter was shocked to learn of his dismissal. He had expected to remain in command until 10 August and then to be reassigned. He was further dismayed when he learned that General Arms had been ordered, on 29 July, to assume command of Provisional Unit No. 5307 (Galahad) pending orders from theater headquarters. Neither General Stilwell nor Arms had the nerve to tell Colonel Hunter what they had planned for his immediate future. In spite of the "arbitrary and ignominious manner" in which he was relieved, Colonel Hunter was given a "superior" rating. He was directed to return to the Marauder rear base at Dinjan, Assam, India, where he was to await further orders. He was soon directed to return by ship to the United States "in the best interest of the service." After arriving in San Diego in early

October, he was directed to report to the War Department in Washington on about 24 November for a new assignment.

Before Colonel Hunter left Dinjan for the States he verified that all radio messages to and from the front were present at Dinjan safely in the headquarters file. Sometime later the files disappeared and have never been found.

When Colonel Hunter departed, he took with him the affection and gratitude of New and Old Galahad. He had been the first and last senior officer in Galahad. He was always there when we needed him, and his devotion to the men and his duty and country was an inspiration to the men of Galahad. The men knew he could be counted on as a great leader, infantry officer, and advocate. From the very beginning he had recognized the frequent mishandling of problems forced upon the men of Galahad, and as they continued to occur fought valiantly to make higher command recognize and correct them.

Casualty Records, Second North Burma Campaign: October 1943–August 1944

An accurate record of the Marauder dead, sick, and wounded has never been recorded. Records of many aspects of the campaign seem to be permanently lost. All radio transmissions between the combat troops and the rear echelon were carefully recorded, preserved, and available after the campaign—but soon disappeared, never to be located. By 4 June Old Galahad (the Marauders) had had 1,908 men withdrawn because of sickness, 93 dead as a result of combat, 30 dead from disease, 8 missing, and 293 sent out with wounds. No accurate records were kept of the wounded who remained in combat. On the above date, of the approximately 2,600 Marauders who had entered combat, 2,394 had been lost. The Marauders had suffered approximately eighty-five percent casualties up to this time. Some were killed or died of disease after this date. Many had fought with such problems as chronic malaria, amoebic dysentery, various forms of chronic skin diseases, and various lung, gastrointestinal, genito-urinary, neurological, bone and joint, and other conditions. Many were not diagnosed and treated until they served in the states or were diagnosed and treated after discharge.

The adjutant general lists the Marauder casualties as of 4 June as follows:

Casualty	Number
Battle deaths	93
Nonbattle deaths	30
Wounded	293
Missing	8
Amoebic dysentery	503
Scrub typhus	140
Malaria	203
Psychoneurosis	72
Miscellaneous	930
Total	2,394

As an example of how inaccurate the above record is, it should be noted that the Marauder regimental headquarters stated that 314 were wounded at Nhpum Ga.

It seems reasonable to assume that after Walawbum virtually every man in the Marauders was inoculated with the malaria parasite and infected with amoeba. Malnutrition was a significant problem. It has been estimated that the average loss of weight was thirty pounds.

The official report of Chinese and American casualties at Myitkyina offers the following statistics:

	Killed	Wounded
Chinese	972	3,184
American	272	955
Total	1,244	4,139

It has not been possible to locate the figures for the number of sick Americans and Chinese during the Burma campaign.

Chinese casualties in North Burma from the fall of 1943 through 13 April 1944 total 1,450 dead and 3,450 wounded.

The Chinese Army of India pushed on after 13 April and, with the aid of the Marauders and the Third Indian Division, had cleared the

Japanese from the Hukawng and Mogaung valleys by 27 June. Unfortunately, *Stilwell's Command Problems* does not list the number of Chinese dead and wounded for this part of the campaign.

Not counting the unlisted Chinese casualties, they had 2,633 dead and 7,589 wounded in the North Burma campaign, which ran from the fall of 1943 until 3 August 1944. Before Myitkyina, the Marauders operated in front of the 22nd and 38th Chinese Divisions. On the march to Myitkyina they led a regiment from the 30th Chinese Division and one from the 50th Chinese Division. The Marauders (Old Galahad) plus New Galahad and the 209th and 236th Engineer Battalions lost, during the North Burma campaign, 395 dead and 1,249 wounded seriously enough to be evacuated.

Other Americans who died or were wounded are not part of this record. They would be located among air corps, medical, quartermaster liaison, and personnel not a part of the ground-combat troops.

General Wingate's Third Indian Division was made up of six brigades totalling twenty thousand men. Five of these brigades—seventeen thousand men—had come under the control of General Stilwell to be a part of the North Burma campaign. One of these long-range penetration units had walked five hundred miles from Ledo, India, to set up a strong point far south of the Hukawng and Mogaung area of operations. The other four units were flown in by plane to set up strong points on or near the railroad about a hundred miles south of Mogaung. Their function was to harass the Japanese from strong points, block their flow of supplies, and kill as many as possible. Admiral Mountbatten's fiscal report lists their casualties as follows: 1,005 killed in action, 2,531 wounded, 473 missing, and 7,317 evacuated to hospital care because of illness. At the end of their respective periods in combat, which varied from early March to 3 August, they had few men suitable for combat without hospital care, rest, and rehabilitation. From their problems with exhaustion and disease their record was as bad if not worse than that of the Marauders.

Stilwell's Command Problems has this to say about Japanese casualties: "The Japanese paid heavily to hold North Burma and prolong the blockade of China. The 18th Division lost fifty percent of the strength with which it began the action" (Romanus and Sunderland 1956).

Lieutenant General Tanaka was interviewed by the G-2 of the U.S. Army Far East Command in April 1949. He had been the commander of the Japanese 18th Division in North Burma during the campaign. He stated that the peak strength at Myitkyina was forty-six hundred, and he believed that no more than six hundred escaped (Chan 1986, 125).

None of the casualty records should be considered one hundred percent accurate. One hundred and eighty-seven Japanese prisoners had been taken. Most of them had been wounded or were sick or incapacitated by near death from starvation and disease.

The Comfort Girls

Kim, a young Korean girl, was brought in on 3 August. She was a "comfort girl" and looked the part, as a short dress was all she was wearing. Captain Won-Loy Chan, an intelligence officer in the theater from January 1943, was with the Myitkyina headquarters during much of the battle for the town. He questioned twenty other "comfort girls" brought in by the Marauders on 8 August. He was able to question them in a well-guarded tent before they were turned over to the British at Ledo, who were responsible for all prisoners.

The comfort girls had been taken by the Japanese—for the most part forcefully—from their family farms and homes in Korea. They were only for the pleasure of the Imperial Japanese troops. They were dressed in ill-fitting soiled dresses and baggy pants and blouses. An older Japanese mama-san was their supervisor as they squatted or sat on mats in the tent. They were young, 18 to 25, and in spite of no grooming were attractive women. Some were tearful, some embarrassed, and some defiant. They knew little Japanese.

From an intelligence standpoint, in spite of kindness and diplomacy, no important military information was obtained. One produced a picture of Colonel Maruyma, the commander of the 114th Regiment. She obviously knew him well.

The mama-san asked if the girls could know their fate. They were told their confinement was only temporary. They would be sent to India and eventually to Korea. She slowly began to unwind a sash from around her abdomen. When the girls fled Myitkyina she had collected

CHAPTER XXIII

their pay and tips, which was in the form of Japanese occupation money. The money, of course, was worthless.

The night before they were to leave, three Japanese-Americans in the G-2 section visited them for the last time. They held a sing-along. One G.I. had a guitar. They sang Japanese, Hawaiian, and American songs, while the girls in turn sang "Airiang," the Korean love song, to the G.I.'s.

Chapter XXIV
THE END OF MERRILL'S MARAUDERS

The number of Marauders available for combat at any given time cannot be given with total accuracy. All records were kept at the rear base located at Dinjan, Assam, India. As previously explained, these records disappeared—presumably in late 1944. At the beginning, the roster listed 2,997 men. During the trip to India, the training period, and the train and riverboat passage to Ledo, Assam, India, approximately 250 men were lost because of acute or chronic disease or accidents. Approximately two hundred men, most of whom were declared unfit for combat because of chronic medical problems, were used to organize and operate a quartermaster supply section. In January, three weeks before our twelve-hundred-mile trip to Assam, it was learned that we would be under the command of General Stilwell instead of the British commander General Wingate. Inexperienced men were sent with our supplies to Dinjan, Assam, India, where they were quickly trained to pack our supplies, attach them to parachutes, and push them out of planes to our infantry in Burma.

A small group of communication men, about eighty muleskinners, and a few other specialists joined us in January 1944. Approximately twenty-six hundred men were available to march into enemy territory on 9 February 1944. By the time the third mission—the march to Myitkyina—began, the Marauders had lost over eight hundred of the twenty-six hundred men. Seventy-six were dead, 231 had wounds serious enough to require loss to combat, and over 500 had been sent out because of sickness or accidental injury. About sixteen hundred men started on "End Run," General Stilwell's name for the mission to Myitkyina.

About thirteen hundred Marauders reached the Myitkyina airfield or its periphery. The First Battalion, with the 150th Chinese Regiment, had arrived and captured the airfield on 17 May. The Third Battalion and the attached 89th Chinese Regiment had been delayed because of the three-day Battle of Ritpong and the two-day Battle of Tingkrukawng. The Second Battalion, which had started last and had crossed the mountains by a very difficult route, came in on the 19th.

The Marauder combat surgeons had done all they could to inform the Marauder regimental staff that the survivors of three months' combat behind Japanese lines were on the verge of total medical collapse. Their advice was ignored. General Merrill, on one of his brief stays at Naubum, made it clear that he was speaking for General Stilwell. His words were spoken to Colonel Hunter and a few senior officers. General Stilwell was calling on the men for more effort than could be fairly expected, but he considered it his only option. Because of the exhaustion of the unit he authorized General Merrill to begin evacuating Galahad, as soon as the airfield had been captured—without further orders, if everything worked out.

Colonel Charles Hunter gives a very clear account of his conversations with General Merrill:

> Merrill had a meeting of the Galahad staff and the battalion commanders to brief them on the future. At this meeting it was explained that, should we succeed in capturing the airstrip, Galahad personnel would be relieved and flown to an already-selected site, where a rest and recreational area would be constructed. Merrill at some time even stated the amount of money budgeted or set aside for this purpose. There was some restriction put on this information.
>
> When I held the initial briefing for the officers and senior noncommissioned officers of Task Force H of the Myitkyina task force, I warned them that the war would not be over for them should Myitkyina be captured, since most of them had been overseas less than a year. Coupled with Merrill's promise was the thought that those men approaching sufficient overseas time to warrant their being rotated to the ZI would be sent home. [This would apply to two-thirds of the survivors] This promise by Merrill was to become a key factor affecting Galahad's future actions. It was also the initial indication that there were no plans at that time, late in April, to retain Galahad personnel at Myitkyina (if captured) beyond the time to effect an early relief by Chinese units, i.e., the remainder of the 50th and 30th Chinese Divisions.

THE END OF MERRILL'S MARAUDERS

> I had several conversations with Merrill concerning the relief by the Chinese—covering such matters as the disposal of individual arms, unit equipment, and animals. He even went so far as to question the battalion commanders, asking them if the men so closely attached to the animals might not want to march back to Assam, thereby ensuring that the animals would not be turned over to the Chinese (Hunter 1963, 123).

The men and junior officers of the Marauders were not happy over the sudden decision to move toward Myitkyina. During the previous month, unverified information had reached the men that Stilwell's North Burma campaign would soon be called to a halt. The general impression was that the Marauders would be sent out for rest, medical evaluation, and treatment. Some would return to the States. The Americans had led the Chinese out of the Hukawng Valley into the Mogaung Valley. They would wait out the monsoon and be ready to advance toward Kamaing and Mogaung in the fall.

In spite of the sudden decision of Stilwell to send them over a series of mountain ranges and then more than one hundred miles to capture an enemy airfield, there was little significant opposition expressed by the men. The general attitude was "what the Hell—let's get it over with." No doubt General Merrill's promise of immediate evacuation for rest and medical treatment as soon as the airfield was captured helped to give them a positive attitude about this new and unexpected mission.

The continued efforts of the combat surgeons to impress upon the regimental command that hardly a man was free of some medical problem that, under normal circumstances, would require hospital or extensive outpatient care did not seem to matter. It should be remembered that General Merrill and his regimental staff had marched far behind and had never been involved in any significant enemy action. They always traveled under the best of circumstances with adequate animal transportation and could make comfortable arrangements for sleep, preparation of food, and boiling of water. None of them had been or would ever be in combat. There was no proof that General Stilwell had ever been in combat. General Merrill had left his regimental headquarters with chest pain one month previously, just before the major eleven-day Battle of Nhpum Ga began.

A third of the Marauders had been through intensive and prolonged infantry fighting in the Pacific. We had seen many of our comrades killed or wounded. There we had learned of the horrors of war. Here in Burma we had been conducting a vicious three-month offensive against Japanese veterans. Our men had fought five major battles and numerous skirmishes. Every day we lived with the physical misery present in a hostile environment. Rain, humidity, tropical heat, mountainous terrain, and lack of rest and sleep left the men constantly fatigued. Malaria, dysentery, gastrointestinal problems, weight loss, malnutrition, arthritis, bursitis, backaches, skin problems, foot ailments, etc. were always present. The young soldiers lived with death, wounds, and disease on a daily basis. Most especially we had learned that an infantry soldier is not apt to get out of combat unless he is killed or wounded or the enemy is defeated. Frequently he has never seen the general who is moving pins on a map, issuing orders, and thinking of his next promotion. During my combat experience in the South Pacific and Burma I never saw a general at the front where machine guns, rifles, artillery, mortars, grenades, air strafing, and bombing were frequently being used.

The general attitude of the Marauders was that this new mission was foolish and should not be undertaken. We had driven the enemy deep into their own defensive system and found them no match for our aggressive and courageous offensive activity. They had been defeated in every engagement. It seemed sensible to regroup during the monsoon season and then destroy them in the fall. All information suggested they could be quickly driven from Burma by a well-organized offensive of British, Chinese, and Americans when the weather would allow use of land vehicles, maximum air activity, maximum artillery, and the proper treatment of the sick and wounded. No matter what our officers and men thought, there was only Stilwell's way. We would never have the opportunity of having him or General Merrill explain any of their plans, since they never visited the troops. As loyal American soldiers, we could only follow their orders.

The passage to Myitkyina turned out to be just about the worst that anyone could imagine. Several days after we had been struggling toward the first mountain pass at sixty-five hundred feet, word reached us that some of our men who had recently been sent out with fever and multiple complaints had a disease we had not heard of. Thirty-five men were critically ill with scrub typhus, and three were already dead. They could tell us little about the disease. Many years later I learned that the disease had first appeared among the Chinese and some American personnel in the fall of 1943. No one on General Stilwell's staff had thought it necessary to warn the Marauders of this deadly disease. The men had now paid a great price, and this tragedy would significantly contribute to the eventual medical destruction of the Marauders.

On arrival in the vicinity of Myitkyina there was hardly an officer or man among the Marauders who was not sick or suffering from some problem or problems that, under ordinary circumstances, would have been disabling until studied and and treated. The airfield was firmly in the hands of the First Battalion and four regiments of Chinese infantry by 22 May. On or about this time the Second and Third Battalions of Marauders were put under the command of Colonel Hunter. Colonel McCammon, who was now in charge of the Myitkyina task force, ordered the First Marauder Battalion to remain at the airfield to prevent its recapture.

General Merrill had failed to keep his promise that he would be the first man on the airfield when it was captured on 17 May. He did not put in an appearance until 19 May, and then only for a brief period. The food and ammunition that was to have arrived on the day of capture did not come in until 21 May. This failure of a central command and lack of supplies was most likely the main reason the Chinese were unable to make any progress in capturing the city. Some of the Marauder staff were shocked at the defeatist attitude of the Myitkyina task force command group. They freely circulated the fearful opinion that the airfield might be overrun at any time. From the very beginning, the Second and Third Marauder Battalions, who were fighting on the northwest periphery, and the First Battalion were confident that the Japanese would soon be defeated if proper pressure were applied.

The men and officers of the Marauder unit knew that total success depended on promised supplies and the rest of the 30th and 50th Divisions arriving quickly by air. None of these promises were kept. No plan was presented for the capture of the town before Japanese replacements arrived in large numbers. Stilwell had condemned Galahad to extinction by not honoring Merrill's promises of food, ammunition, and relief by adequate and qualified Chinese troops (Hunter 1963, 116, 126).

The Marauders could not understand why General Stilwell's four American-trained and equipped Chinese infantry regiments could not be depended on to hold the airfield and capture the city. The Chinese had been well cared for and had seen little of the hardship and combat the Marauders had been enduring for four months.

During the first week in the vicinity of Myitkyina, the Marauder Third Battalion had fought one major battle, and sections of the unit had been in numerous skirmishes. Over one hundred of its men had been evacuated with scrub typhus, and several had died from the disease. Each day my battalion's medical section had been sending men seriously ill from other causes to the airfield for evaluation by Major Schudmak, the regimental surgeon. Colonel Hunter had found it necessary to put strict limits on the sick before they could leave their posts at the front.

General Stilwell ordered the 209th and 236th American Combat Engineer Battalions from their noncombat work on the Ledo Road into combat at Myitkyina. They arrived by air on 28 and 29 May. On the day that General Boatner took over command of the Myitkyina task force, 30 May, he ordered the Second and Third Marauder Battalions to eliminate Japanese troops at Charpate and Radahpur.

The Second Battalion, plus a company of engineers, was unable to drive the Japanese out of Charpate. The sick and exhausted Marauders were unable to muster enough men to do the job. The engineers could not attack without help. Colonel McGee was forced to request that his half-strength battalion be evacuated for evaluation, hospital treatment as necessary, and then rehabilitation and rest. Because he now had the two engineer battalions, Colonel Hunter granted his request.

At this time, 30 May, the Third Battalion mustered less than a company of men. The few who were able to march several miles into combat joined the 209th Engineers and, with Colonel Beach's help, set up a very effective roadblock south of Radahpur.

Shortly after the Radahpur action, Colonel Beach was sent out sick. I could see no reason to keep the few sick and exhausted men of the Third Battalion in Burma. With this in mind I took the dangerous and fatiguing five-mile trip to the airfield, where I located Colonel

Hunter. He agreed with me and suggested that I send the men to the airfield with medical emergency tags for final evaluation before evacuation. He stated, as he had before, that he did not anticipate any significant aggressive action by the enemy. He implied that banzai attacks would be welcome as a way to kill more Japanese. The engineers, although ill-prepared for combat, would be able to control the situation on the northwest perimeter. He would also soon have two battalions of replacements from the States. The sick and exhausted survivors of the Third Marauder Battalion went out over a period of two or three days. I was among the last to leave, with the hope of diagnosis and treatment of a severe chronic dysentery.

The First Battalion kept between one and two hundred men at the airfield until the town fell on 3 August 1944. Colonel Hunter had attempted to get the Myitkyina task force headquarters to release them to his command, but his request had been denied. There continued to remain the fear that, in spite of the presence of four regiments of Chinese infantry, the Japanese might attempt to overrun the airport and the task force headquarters.

The medical evacuation of the decimated Second and Third Battalions was not the end of the 5307th Composite (Provisional) Unit at Myitkyina. As has been reported, the new First Battalion—and the two battalions of engineers who fought at Myitkyina during June, July, and August under Colonel Hunter's command—was made up using Marauders who at various times had been released from hospitals as fit for duty. This new First Battalion was called Old Marauders or Old Galahads. The controversial aspects of the return of the men to form this rather small battalion have been previously discussed.

In spite of General Merrill's failure to keep his promise to send the Marauders out as soon as the airfield was taken, the Marauders never failed to carry out any mission assigned. They would be the first to admit that their job had been made much more difficult by the failure of General Stilwell's staff to deliver food and ammunition for three days after the airfield was captured. Needless to say, their respect for General Stilwell and the Northern Area Combat Command had reached a very low point by the first of May, and would never change—especially after their subsequent treatment in Assam, India.

CHAPTER XXV
THE POSTCOMBAT PERIOD

Evacuation to Ledo

The flight out of Myitkyina in the C-47 freight plane seemed like luxurious travel after four months under combat in Burma. As the plane skirted the southern portion of the Kumon Mountains the single Kamaing-Myitkyina Road could be clearly seen. We then crossed over the mountaintop where we had fought for two weeks, up the five-mile trail, to defeat the enemy-reinforced battalion that had surrounded the Second Battalion at Nhpum Ga. The area was then turned over to the 112th Regiment of Chinese, putting them twenty miles north of the Japanese stronghold of Kamaing. The Chinese would capture Kamaing on 22 June.

If we had flown twenty miles south of Kamaing we would have passed over Mogaung, which would be captured by the Chinese, together with the last of Wingate's exhausted and diseased Chindits, on 27 June.

When we were over Nhpum Ga, the sites of the Battles of Ritpong and Tingkrukawng lay over the Kumon Mountain ridges about forty miles to the northeast. Myitkyina is about eighty miles south of those locations.

Next we passed near Inkangahtawng on the Ledo-Kamaing Road, where the Second Battalion had slaughtered many Japanese. Ten miles to the north we flew over Shaduzup, where the First Battalion had fought and defeated the Japanese before turning their roadblock over to the Chinese regiment that had followed them over tortuous trails through the eastern foothills of the Kumon Mountains.

The plane next flew over the pass at Jambu Bum, the mountain pass that separates the Hukawng Valley to the north from the Mogaung Valley to the south. The Chinese had advanced down the

Ledo-Kamaing Road to capture this location. This advance of the Chinese had been coordinated with the Marauder action at Shaduzup and Inkangahtawng.

Soon we recognized the jungle area surrounding Walawbum, where the Third Battalion had fought without food for three days and destroyed more than four hundred Japanese. Nearby was the jungle clearing of Lagang Ga, where so many of our men had been hit by Japanese artillery, and nearby the area where the Second Battalion had set up a roadblock. These successful actions forced the Japanese 18th Division to withdraw from Maingkwan ten miles to the north and retreat to Jambu Bum pass, thirty miles south of that city. After overrunning Maingkwan, the 64th, 65th and 66th Chinese Regiments were soon in a position to take Jambu Bum.

Last below us we quickly passed over the numerous mountains making up the Patkai Mountain Range, which separates North Burma from Assam, India. We had marched about one hundred and fifty miles over a narrow dirt track that American engineers had carved with bulldozers through these mountains. Now, at times, we could get a glimpse of the snakelike Ledo Road through the gigantic trees that covered the numerous mountains and valleys. On the twelve-day march into Burma, the highest area we had crossed was fifty-two hundred feet in elevation. We had seen a snow-covered peak about one hundred miles to the left of this area, where it marked the border between China, India, and Burma. On this flight we could see this mountain peak at over nineteen thousand feet, as well as another to our left and one to our right—both over nine thousand feet in elevation.

As the plane flew on toward the airstrip at Ledo, India, I looked at my comrades in the plane resting on the floor and miscellaneous baggage. They were all underweight, haggard, and bearded. Many had ulcers on their legs; many had skin rashes. Their clothes were torn and dirty, and their shoes showed extensive wear. Some were flushed with fever, and others had chills or were vomiting. None were complaining, and all had a look of peace and bewilderment on their faces. I, just as they, could hardly believe that the nightmare of four months in Burma was at an end.

I thought of our comrades who had died of enemy action, injury, or disease and was grateful for my own survival. The sick and wounded were being given an opportunity to get on with their lives. I could not help but be very proud of having been part of this magnificent unit of volunteer foot soldiers. All had struggled for five hundred miles, and some for two or three hundred more. There had been seven major battles and many violent contacts with the enemy. Our men had never been defeated as they fought the veteran 18th Japanese Division, the conquerors of Nanking, Singapore, Malaya, and Burma. We had spearheaded four Chinese divisions and helped destroy the 18th Japanese Division. We knew that Myitkyina would soon fall and some of our unit would be there until the end. We did not, at this time, understand the epic nature of our contribution.

Hospital Care in Assam, India

The C-47 came to a bumpy landing on the airfield nestled between the giant teakwood and ironwood trees. I said a silent prayer of thanks for my deliverance. We had not expected a band or a committee to greet us and indeed found none. An army truck was there instead. We wearily but eagerly climbed aboard and were soon bumping along the main street of Ledo. The small village of tin-roofed shacks was quickly left behind. Instead of going north a few miles to the 20th General Hospital, where our sick and wounded had been cared for up to this time, we headed south. The driver explained that our destination was the 14th Evacuation Hospital at mile nineteen on the road into Burma. We, at that time, did not think about the significance of this change in the care of our sick and wounded from a well-established general military hospital to a recently assembled evacuation hospital

The trucks eventually pulled off the dusty road, and we learned that we had arrived at our destination, the 14th Evacuation Hospital. Those of us who could walk climbed out of the truck onto the dusty driveway. Others were taken out on stretchers. The hospital was housed in native bashas made of reeds and bamboo. Other sections were housed under tents. I, like most of the sick men, was soon resting on an army cot that was one of many set up on a dirt floor in a rather large native basha. Windows were open spaces that could be closed by lowering a bamboo reed-covered trap door. There was no need to worry about the storage of personal effects, since we had only our worn-out shoes and dirty, frayed fatigue jackets and pants. Most of us had no underwear or socks.

The hospital seemed to be understaffed by doctors, nurses, order-lies, and technicians, but they were very kind and helpful. We were soon supplied with standard army pajamas and well-prepared standard army canned food. For the first few days most of the diagnostic studies and medical treatment seemed to be concentrated on the acutely ill men—especially the scrub typhus patients, one or more of whom were dying each day.

We soon learned that critically ill men who had been evacuated during the last ten days in May had not been sent to the 20th General Hospital but to either the 14th Evacuation Hospital or the 111th Station Hospital. We had known that during March, February, April, and the first three weeks in May these Marauders had been sent to the 20th General Hospital for care. This change in plans seemed quite odd, and at this time I did not understand its reason—or the effect it was to have on the care of the sick men.

For the first week I spent most of my time resting, eating, and wondering when I would learn the cause of my chronic weakness, fatigue, abdominal cramps, and loose stools. My weight had gone from 200 pounds when the campaign started to 170. I knew that the weight would soon return to normal with adequate food. When I was discharged after twelve days of rest with the diarrhea, cramps, and weakness still present and no diagnosis or adequate plan of treatment, I was disappointed and apprehensive. I was more disturbed when I learned that many others did not consider themselves adequately treated or diagnosed, either.

Shortly after my admission I heard my name being called, in a garbled and plaintive manner, from the wet and muddy area between the bamboo shack I was in and the adjacent one. I went to the open space, which served as a window, and saw Lieutenant Pat Perrone wandering about. He was soon brought back to his cot and found to have the potentially fatal disease cerebral malaria. Fortunately, after treatment he made a recovery—but would continue, to this day, to be afflicted with serious permanent complications of cerebral malaria.

The understaffed and ill-supplied hospital personnel were doing all they could to take care of the sick Marauders, but it was not enough. Later, statistics would show that during May and July 1944 the 14th Evacuation Hospital reported the following figures for disease in the men of the 5307th when they were evacuated from Myitkyina. Some of those who arrived in June came from New Galahad, but of the group of 1,905 at least 1,500 probably came from Old Galahad.

Gastrointestinal disease	616
Malaria	516
Upper respiratory infections	301
Exhaustion syndrome	35
Scrub typhus	93
Undiagnosed fevers	109
Neuropsychiatric conditions	42
Dermatological infections and diseases as the primary cause of admission	31
Miscellaneous	65
Total	1,905

It seems only logical to assume that many of the men had more than one condition. It should be noted that the diagnosis of amoebic dysentery was not made. Personal experience and knowledge of the campaign suggests that a majority of the Marauders at the end of the campaign had active amoebic dysentery or chronic amoebic dysentery. I was told that the hospital laboratory did not have facilities for culture of bacteria but that they were able to do microscopic examinations for amoeba. Since they did not break down the number of gastrointestinal diseases into definitive lists, it must be assumed that they were unable to diagnose, with confidence, the numerous diseases that fall under this group.

Activity at the Staging Area

I was discharged from the 14th Evacuation Hospital on 16 June 1944 with the diagnosis of dysentery, unclassified, chronic.

Major Thomas J. Morrison, the chief of the medical section, recommended me for convalescence at the Shillong Rest Camp, several hundred miles distant. I did not accept this recommendation, since I wished to return to help Marauders who were being sent from the various medical facilities to the so-called convalescent center. This proved to be a clearing in the jungle, located near Ledo and Margherita, which was called a staging area. Here were found numerous dilapidated, deteriorating bamboo-and-reed buildings with dirt floors and open spaces for doors and windows. None had plumbing or screens. Unscreened open pits nearby served as latrines. Walks consisted of muddy paths. A few locations provided running water from a single faucet. No shower facilities were available.

Since no convalescent area had been set up as promised by General Merrill, this run-down area had been quickly designated as a convalescent area for the Marauders. Up until early April, when sick and wounded Marauders began to arrive in large numbers, the 20th General had been able to accommodate these men and keep them in the hospital until they were well on the way to cure and rehabilitation. Many of the six or seven hundred early patients had been discharged before the march on Myitkyina. Few had been returned to Burma to rejoin their comrades. Instead of this logical and very necessary action, many of these men had been placed in noncombat jobs in the Assam area. No documentation of this action has been found, but it was rumored that they were used to do guard duty, drive trucks, and take unfilled positions in the numerous service organizations in the area. Approximately 250 of this group made up the Purple Force, which, as I have previously mentioned, were sent on an illogical, poorly organized mission with a regiment of Chinese troops.

I had not known about this use of convalescent Marauders until I arrived in the staging area. Early in April, these men—who had been released from area hospitals, many prematurely on limited-duty status—were quickly rounded up and sent on a mission with the 149th Chinese Regiment of the 50th Division. This was a flanking mission to the west as part of the operation against the Japanese stronghold at Kamaing. The mission was futile, as was a second one. The surviving Marauders were then sent, in spite of their deplorable physical condition, to join the depleted Marauder force at Myitkyina.

After my brief inspection of the staging area I located some of the Third Battalion men bunking in a run-down, mildewed basha with a leaking roof. Army cots had already been set up in neat rows on the dirt floor. Each was furnished with a blanket. No tables or chairs were available, and no storage facilities were provided. Since none of the late arrivals had belongings, this luxury had to be worked out later from odds and ends.

Bashas that had not collapsed were occupied by convalescent Marauders who had been cleared out of the 20th General Hospital in late April and May to make room for the large a number of Chinese, as well as Old and New Marauders, who were arriving daily from the Myitkyina combat area.

The convalescents from each Marauder battalion were gathered in battalion areas. No senior officers were present. Colonel Beach and Colonel McGee had departed or would depart for the states as soon as they left the 20th General Hospital. Colonels Hunter and Osborne were still retained at Myitkyina. The Northern Combat Area Command had not provided any staff to run this old staging area, now designated as a hospital convalescent area. The management of the area was taken over by several senior lieutenants and sergeants who set up supply, kitchen, transportation, communication, and clerical arrangements. On my arrival I joined Captain A. Lewis Kolodny in staffing a medical detachment. We set up a sick-call arrangement that ran twenty-four hours daily.

Unbeknownst to any of the Marauders, but apparently known to the hospitals and the Northern Combat Area Command, the convalescents were all carried on a limited-duty status. This was supposed to acknowledge that they were still patients and presumably not available for military duty until their status had changed.

I soon learned that a daily effort was being made to round up as many convalescent men as possible and ship them back to Myitkyina. This effort had been going on since the last week in May. Evidence was not difficult to obtain. Orders had been issued through the Northern Area Command that hospitalized members of the 5307th who were able to walk were to be shipped back to Myitkyina. The so-called convalescent section in the old staging area was also raided. About two hundred men were literally shanghaied for the so-called emergency at Myitkyina. Colonel Hunter has already spoken of the arrival of these men and his disgust with the methods used and the condition of the men. Some had to be immediately returned because of their obvious poor condition. Most served gallantly until the battle was over.

This battle without weapons between Stilwell and his staff on the one hand and the hospital and Marauder physicians on the other lasted until the end of June. Some Marauders voluntarily returned to combat before they were declared fit for duty. Second Lieutenant Charlton Ogburn was in this group. He had not recovered from a severe injury of his heel and chronic malaria, as well as general debility and weakness. He was promptly sent back to the convalescent camp by Colonel Osborne. Colonel Hunter had also interviewed him shortly after he arrived at the Myitkyina airfield and appointed him as adjutant of the convalescent area.

Captain A. Lewis Kolodny, who had been evacuated because of illness with his medical detachment and the rest of the Second Battalion, had played a major part in working individually and with the area hospital staff to prevent sick men from returning to combat. One day he and I, both convalescent medical officers, learned that several hundred sick and convalescent Marauders were traveling by truck to the Dinjan airfield for transport to Myitkyina. Under his leadership the convoy was intercepted and forced to return the men to the convalescent area. The doctors had won a decisive victory over the poor judgment and ignorance of the Northern Area Combat Command.

Battalion kitchens were set up in tents, each near an outside cold-water faucet. The Northern Combat Area Command offered little help. Supplies were obtained with difficulty, and most information was simply rumor.

Before we had departed from this area in early February for the march into Burma, all personal belongings had been placed in a native warehouse, made of bamboo and reeds, for safekeeping. Shortly after acquiring my sleeping area I was told that little remained of our stored property. A personal inspection verified this when I looked over the contents of the storage facility. Everything had been thoroughly ransacked, all valuables were missing, and the rest had been destroyed by rain and mildew. After considerable controversy we were issued the basic articles of clothing.

Each day, men were breaking through atabrine prophylactic prevention measures and were presenting themselves with clinical malaria. Many were seen with chronic recurrent bacillary and amoebic dysentery. Flareups of joint pain, bursitis, and muscle problems were frequent. Many men had chronic coughs and chest complaints, which suggested the need for diagnostic studies and long-term treatment. Some had continued weight loss, weakness, fatigue, or esophageal and stomach complaints. Numerous minor psychological complaints, as well as some major psychiatric conditions, were evaluated. It was obvious that quite a few men should still be under hospital care.

For many of the problems picked up at sick call, our only recourse was to tag the men with an emergency medical tag and send them off for further evaluation and care. This action was not received kindly by the commanding officer of the 14th Evacuation Hospital or the chief surgeon of the Northern Area Combat Command. Many of our suggestions for further care and diagnostic studies were not acted on, and we were informed that we were out of line. With considerable difficulty because of transportation problems, I obtained interviews with the commanding officers of the 111th Station Hospital, the 14th Evacuation Hospital, and the 20th General Hospital. The C.O.'s of the 111th Station Hospital and the 20th General were very sympathetic. They indicated that everything possible would be done to offer complete diagnosis and treatment. Improvement took place. Colonel Isidore Ravdin was able to talk General Stilwell's New Delhi headquarters into sending some air conditioners to be used in the scrub typhus ward. The action probably saved the lives of some of the Marauders, as well as other victims.

During June and July, little improvement took place at the convalescent area. The majority of the men did their best to put up with the horrible living conditions. They understood that a camp such as this would not be tolerated at home or in any other allied theater of war. They had been through hell and back, and were thankful they had survived. Now the hope of a future and the fact that they had been able to do their duty seemed more important than obtaining gratitude for their service and decent living conditions.

The men from the Pacific had not had running water or facilities for washing their clothes or taking showers for many months before they volunteered for the dangerous and hazardous mission. Slit trenches had been taken for granted. Conditions did not improve during their two-month training period in India. While in combat in Burma they had lived like animals and seen death almost daily. A few more months would not make that much difference.

CHAPTER XXV

At the end of July, Lieutenant Ogburn submitted a report to Colonel Hunter. The colonel speaks of this and the lack of any action after the inspector general was sent to Myitkyina in response to the report that he (Colonel Hunter) had given Stilwell in late May:

> That—in spite of the inspector general having made a report on the state of morale—nothing was being done was made clear to me in a report submitted August 1st by Lt. Charlton Ogburn Jr., the adjutant of the staging area. This report detailed incredible conditions existing in the staging area and went on to describe the violations of discipline taking place. Things had apparently gone to hell in a big way (Hunter 1963).

The men continued to be disturbed over the failure of General Merrill to keep his promise about flying the unit out of Burma as soon as the Myitkyina airfield was captured. They also had good reason to doubt General Merrill's sincerity when they failed to find a well-ordered convalescent camp. They had been promised the best that money could buy until they returned to the states or entered another period of combat.

Above all, the Marauders were disgusted by the failure of Generals Merrill and Stilwell to meet them in small groups or as a unit to express some gratitude to them and their dead and seriously wounded or sick comrades. The Stilwell way was to forget that the Marauders had ever existed as a unit. This great volunteer outfit, with its gallant men and officers and its fantastic esprit de corps, was to disappear without written history, colors, insignia, or future. No effort was made to act on the numerous recommendations made for battle decorations. These were not to be acted on until the individual men had returned to the states for discharge or service in other units. Some were not to get recommendations for months or years.

When the men got their first pay, some turned to undisciplined and irresponsible activities. A local alcoholic mixture spiked with marijuana led to fights, thievery, and numerous episodes of AWOL. All of the above could probably have been avoided by thoughtful help and encouragement from higher authority. From beginning to end the men were treated as if they had never existed except as pawns to be used to spearhead the Chinese during the Burma offensive. They were forced to assume that the rear-echelon officers of the Northern

Combat Area Command cared little whether they lived or died.

Official leave authorizations among the convalescent area residents were scarce. As mentioned, the 14th Evacuation Hospital had recommended that I have convalescent leave for twenty-one days. The authorization for this came through on 21 June. At this time I was so disturbed by the situation at the convalescent camp that I decided to write a report that would give an outline of the history of the 5307th Composite Unit (Provisional) from the time of its origin through its entire existence.

By 22 June I had produced a preliminary document and forwarded a copy to Colonel Hunter, at Myitkyina, to go through channels to the surgeon general of the United States. I suggested that Doctors Henry G. Stelling and A. Lewis Kolodny of the Second Battalion also write reports. These reports can be found in the book *Crisis Fleeting*, compiled and edited by James H. Stone, formerly a military historian for the CBI and later with the Department of Humanities, San Francisco State College. Several supplements to my report followed in June and July. These reports, together with the Voorhees Report and extensive narrative discussions by James Stone, make up chapter five, titled "The Marauders and the Microbes."

Instead of departing for twenty-one days of authorized leave at the Shillong rest camp, I decided to take my report to the theater surgeon, Colonel Robert P. Williams, M.C., at Stilwell's headquarters in New Delhi. On the 26th I departed for New Delhi by military plane. After several stops I was in flight from Agra to New Delhi when I was taken sick with malaise, chills, and fever. I had continued to take the one tablet of atabrine each day and had now obviously broken through this preventive measure.

On arrival at New Delhi I was admitted to the 100th Station Hospital. My malaria was promptly evaluated, and treatment was started. The next day I called the theater surgeon's office and was informed that he was in Washington and that Colonel George E. Armstrong was in charge of the office. The colonel came on the line and agreed to visit me at the hospital.

On the first visit I presented a copy of my report to the colonel and explained that the original had gone through channels for eventual delivery to the Office of the Surgeon General in Washington. I was given the opportunity to explain the situation at the so-called convalescent camp. He was made aware of the inadequate diagnosis and treatment of the Marauders. His help was requested in obtaining a complete medical evaluation of the Marauders. This had to be done before those eligible for return to the states were scattered and before the rest would be sent into further combat in Burma.

Colonel Armstrong visited me a second time. He told me that General Stilwell had been authorized to return all men to the states who, in the opinion of the treating hospital, would not be ready for duty for sixty days. He promised to look into the medical situation as soon as possible.

I ignored the authorized leave to Shillong and departed on 5 July for the convalescent camp and my bunk in Assam. At the first stop in Agar I was approached by Colonel Tracy S. Voorhees, of the judge advocate general's office. He had been sent to the theater to investigate the medical supply system. The colonel asked me about the Marauders. This seemed like a good opportunity to get further help, and I provided him with a copy of my report.

Shortly after my arrival in Assam I received a message from the colonel explaining that he had destroyed the report. He had spoken to Colonel Armstrong and became aware that the colonel did not want the report to leave the theater. A message soon came from Colonel Armstrong requesting that I burn the report. This request was not complied with since I had no guarantee that the report would ever reach the surgeon general.

A few days after my return, General Stilwell's son-in-law, Colonel Ernest F. Estabrook of the Northern Combat Area Command, arrived to conduct an inspection of the convalescent camp. He was conducted about by 2nd Lieutenant Charlton Ogburn Jr. The colonel left after a brief visit. No report was returned about the result of the inspection, and that was the last we heard of any interest in the welfare of the men. The conditions as described did not change.

About a week after my return from New Delhi I was notified that orders had been issued by the Northern Area Combat Command. I was to be immediately transferred out of the 5307th Composite Unit (Provisional) to China as an unattached medical replacement. My good friend and comrade Captain A. Lewis Kolodny of the Second

Battalion, who had served with exceptional heroism and attention to the welfare of the men, came to my rescue. With his tongue in his cheek and his fingers crossed he informed the responsible staff officers that I was a troublemaker and that, if the order was not cancelled, the consequences would be impossible to explain or eliminate. When Colonel Hunter heard of the order he reminded the responsible officers that he was the commanding officer of the Marauders and he wanted the order cancelled. He advised me to forget that it had ever been issued, and that was the end of the matter.

The Marauder medical staff continued to fight for the welfare of the men. Living conditions did not improve, but the health of the survivors did. As the sick officers were treated and cured of exhaustion, dengue fever, chronic malaria, bacillary, amoebic, and unclassified diarrhea, gastrointestinal problems, bronchitis, scrub typhus, and skin diseases, as well as chronic bone, joint, and muscle problems, they began to assume their proper functions in the convalescent area.

Two events took place that in their own way did a lot for the esprit de corps and morale of the men. Second Lieutenant Charlton Ogburn, after release from the 20th General Hospital, was one of several who designed the unofficial Marauder insignia. The design has never changed. At the top of a shield are the words *Merrill's Marauders*. The border has a thin band of red, inside of which is a blue background. The central background is green. A red streak of lightning passes diagonally through the center. The Kuomentaing Sun of China is located to the right of the lighting bolt and the Star of Burma to the left. Ogburn painted a reproduction on sheet metal, and it was available for all to see for a brief period before it disappeared.

The second event was the appearance in the *CBI Roundup* (newspaper) of a ten-stanza poem written by Ogburn. It extolled the Marauder campaign.

During the four months we had been fighting in Burma, our warehouses were maintained fifty miles west of Ledo in an area called Dinjan. Nearby was a tent camp used to house the men of the rear echelon. Near the end of July this camp was enlarged and improved. Many surviving Marauders who were not still under active hospital treatment, had not been sent home disabled, or were still fighting at Myitkyina were gradually moved by truck to this area.

CHAPTER XXV

At Dinjan we found screened kitchens and a dining area. Latrines and shower areas were satisfactory. The camp was located near a military airfield. All military installations were surrounded by large tea plantations. We were now out of the damp jungle, but not out of the tropical heat and rain showers. The well-run 111th Station Hospital was nearby to provide diagnostic and treatment facilities. Here we were no longer at the end of the supply line. The men now had access to toilet articles, one or two beers per week, newspapers, magazines, and an occasional candy bar.

The battalion medical detachments at Dinjan were combined into one unit and continued to offer all possible diagnostic and treatment facilities. The hospitals had more available beds and made every effort to offer complete diagnostic and treatment facilities. Food was adequate, and there was time for rest. The better condition of the men and treatment of all chronic malaria and other multiple problems made the men much more resistant to the various tropical diseases. Everyone took the prophylactic dose of atabrine, and the tendency to break through with attacks of malaria was much less than while in combat.

What little spare time I had was used to complete my study dealing with all aspects of the cause of combat deaths and wounds among the men of the First and Third Battalions. This study had begun while I was in combat with the First Battalion of the 37th Division on the island of New Georgia in the Solomon Island chain. My purpose was to determine the value of a better helmet and a trunk protector for infantry troops.

The convalescent and recovered Marauders were continually informed that they were on a standby status until the Battle of Myitkyina ended. The War Department authorization to send all men home who would not be eligible for combat within sixty days was not honored.

There was much conversation and joy, but not much celebration, when word came that Myitkyina had fallen on 3 August 1944. I don't recall any information reaching the camp about the citation of the 5307th by the War Department.

As pointed out earlier, in General Order No. 54, dated 5 July 1944, the unit was cited by the theater commander, United States Army forces in China-Burma-India, and confirmed in the name of the president of the United States as public evidence of deserved honor and distinction.

Few of the Marauders knew, at this time, of the great honor that had been bestowed on their unit. I first learned it when, some months later, I obtained a copy of *The Marauders*, which had been recently published by the War Department for the information of the men who had been members of the unit.

At the end of July a rumor reached Dinjan. General Stilwell, on his last brief visit to Myitkyina, had informed Colonel Hunter that the men in the 5307th who were not eligible to return to the United States would, with New Galahad, form the 475th Infantry Regiment. They would join the 124th Cavalry, which was soon to arrive in Burma. The combined outfit would be under command of General Arms and would be part of a planned fall advance into south Burma. Since the above was only a rumor, we had not learned of the details. We did learn that Colonel Hunter had been offered the job of commanding officer of the 475th Infantry Regiment but had refused the offer. The details of the meeting and his reason for declining the offer have been recorded earlier in this history.

A day or so later, several rumors about General Stilwell reached our ears. He had been promoted to a four-star general, thus joining Eisenhower, Arnold, MacArthur, and Bradley. He had departed to look after Lord Louis Mountbatten's headquarters in Ceylon. Both of these events were said to have taken place several days before the fall of Myitkyina. The rumored knowledge of these two events in the life of General Stilwell did not elicit any enthusiasm among the Marauders. The general impression was that it was good to get him out of the area. One man was heard to say that one day he had the S.O.B. in his gunsight at Myitkyina. Only his Christian upbringing had kept him from pulling the trigger.

A day or so after the fall of Myitkyina, on 3 August 1944, Colonel Hunter arrived at our Dinjan camp. We soon learned of his summary dismissal, on 3 August 1944, as commander of the American forces at Myitkyina. He managed to keep his mouth mostly shut, but every Marauder experienced feelings of disgust about Stilwell's treatment of this West Pointer who had the respect of every man and officer. He was later to write:

That I was relieved of command of Galahad in an arbitrary and ignominious manner came as no particular surprise to me after having spent almost a year observing the manner in which business was conducted in the theater. I had known on 3 August that Galahad was to be disbanded on 10 August. Military tradition, if followed in this instance, would have dictated that I be placed on leave until that date and then be temporarily assigned to some sinecure of a job.

Arbitrary relief of command, in my case as in that of General MacArthur's, was and is the prerogative of the commander. The exercise of this prerogative in war is not unusual but generally is followed by the officer being court-martialed or being placed before a reclassification board. In my case I was given a "superior" rating, ordered to Dinjan to await further orders, given no leave, and returned by ship to the United States "in the best interest of the service." It was 23 August before I was allowed to leave Assam on the long journey home. I arrived in San Diego early in October and was ordered to duty in Washington with a reporting-for-duty date on or about the 24th of November 1944 (Hunter 1963).

The men and officers were shocked and disgusted with General Stilwell when we learned the details of Colonel Hunter's departure for home. Instead of traveling by plane, he was to travel by boat. It was well known that the common and proper way for most officers to travel to the States was by air. It had never occurred to us that an officer of his rank and importance would travel home by any other means. There could be only one reason for this disgraceful delay in Colonel Hunter's departure and his means of travel. The men and officers freely expressed the obvious fact that General Stilwell wanted Colonel Hunter kept out of the States until the discussion of the disgraceful handling of the Myitkyina campaign by General Stilwell and his staff had died down and all investigations had been completed.

At my suggestion, the officers contributed money to be eventually used to purchase a gift as our expression of admiration and gratitude for the great job he had done. Later, when I was in the States, I sent him a sterling-silver water pitcher.

The record clearly shows that Colonel Hunter's leadership contributed as much as—if not more than—any officer to the success of the Marauders. Without Colonel Hunter and the sacrifice, patriotism, courage, and brilliant tactics of the officers and men under the part-time leadership of General Merrill, the second Burma campaign would have been a failure.

On 10 August 1944 the 5307th Composite (Provisional) Unit ceased to exist. It was now the 475th Infantry Regiment. All men of Old and New Galahad who were fit and had less than the required overseas duty were now active members of this regiment. Colonel William Lloyd Osborne, formerly commander of the First Battalion, became the regimental commander. He would organize, train, and equip the unit. A new military camp would soon begin to grow a few miles north of Myitkyina. It would be named Camp Landis in honor of Private Robert W. Landis, who had been the first Marauder killed in Burma at the beginning of the campaign.

The 475th Infantry Regiment would soon be joined by the 124th Cavalry Regiment, dismounted (and new in the CBI theater). These two regiments, with other supporting service units, made up the Mars Force, which was to open up the third Burma campaign during October 1944, in cooperation with four Chinese divisions and the British-Indian 36th Division, a force of about a hundred thousand.

Chapter XXVI
The End of the Burma Experience

Shortly after deactivation of the 5307th, a recent regulation became known to us. The War Department authorized return home of all who had served more than two years of foreign duty. This forced the Northern Area Combat Command to authorize and begin shipping arrangements for most of the men in the Second and Third Battalions. On the evening of 17 August 1944, fourteen officers, myself included, and fifty noncommissioned officers were ordered to prepare for departure to the United States of America. Early in the morning we traveled by truck to Tinsukia Station of the Bengal-Assam Railroad. The majority were equipped with little more than the clothes they were wearing. I had rescued a mildewed canvas bedding roll from the ransacked bamboo-and-reed warehouse where our belongings had been stored before combat. My most important souvenir was still intact and well-hidden in the bedroll. This rare and prized short Japanese carbine rifle and bayonet would travel with me. A few other souvenirs were placed in an army footlocker that had followed me around the world. Believe it or not, it would eventually arrive at my home in Maryland—but, unfortunately, with most of its contents removed.

The fact that this group, the first large one returning to the states, was made up of officers and noncommissioned officers disturbed me and others. Certainly many of lower rank had served just as much—or more—time overseas as some of the chosen group. The only explanation I could think of was that the individuals in our group were needed for training and placement in new infantry divisions. The need for experienced officers offered further proof that Colonel Hunter's departure was being held up for political reasons.

Our departure for the station involved mixed emotions. We were all happy and grateful that we were returning home in one piece to our families and friends. On the other hand we were sad to leave friends who in many cases meant more to us than any others we had known. When you are living and serving in combat with men, you get to know them better than you might at any other period in your life. Some of us were saying goodbye to comrades who had saved our lives. Others were leaving the buddy who had shared the misery of field life, the rigors of training, and the life-or-death situations of battle. You get to know people very well when you are blunting a banzai attack or crawling forward to knock out an enemy machine gun or laying on the ground when artillery or mortar shells are exploding all about you.

We soon learned that our destination was Karachi, India, a distance of twenty-five hundred miles. The rest of our trip halfway around the world would be by air. Enough K-rations were supplied to feed us until we arrived at Karachi. We were well aware of sleeping and other accommodations in the boxcar-like, rickety coaches. You slept on bench-like seats, on the floor, or on a baggage rack. Toilet facilities consisted of a hole in the floor. Large metal cans were available to be filled with water for drinking at some of the numerous stops. As on our two other long trips by train in India, the men were welcomed at each stop by vendors selling fruits, various cooked dishes, and hot tea. No one went hungry, but the desire for fresh beef prompted a group of our men to purchase a steer. Some had training as butchers and made use of this knowledge to provide all of us with fresh meat. Small gasoline stoves miraculously had appeared for the first time, and these were used for hot drinks and numerous delicious dishes made from the K-rations, the fresh meat, and spices and vegetables purchased from the vendors.

First we crossed the mighty Brahmaputra River on barges. After the crossing, we transferred to rickety cars traveling on wider-gauge tracks. When we reached the Ganges, at a location just north of Calcutta, the train was broken into sections that were ferried across and then reattached to the engine for the rest of our journey. Because of an increasing number of sick, I asked for a more modern coach as a hospital car. This was procured and greatly appreciated by my small staff and our patients. Unlike the other cars, this one had more comfortable benches on which the men could sleep. Before we left Dinjan our supply section had provided us with a few newly introduced aerosol insect spray containers. One was used in the coach, and the biggest cockroaches I have ever seen crawled out of many hiding places.

THE END OF THE BURMA EXPERIENCE

As we crossed India there was a never-ending change of scenery, including jungle, farming country, deserts, mountains, and plains. The innumerable towns, villages, and railroad stations all seemed the same. Evidence of poverty was seen in all areas. Coaches packed with representatives of every caste and religion were frequently attached to our train. At times more individuals were riding on top of the coaches than inside.

We arrived at our destination and the end of the line, Carica, India—now Carica, Pakistan—on 28 August, the eleventh day of our journey. As I now think of that trip with the primitive accommodations, it should have been a nightmare—but, strangely enough, I remember it as an interesting and happy period, and the anticipation of arriving home transcended every hardship and inconvenience we encountered.

The rumor that the rest of our journey would be by plane now became reality. Special restricted orders from headquarters, CBI Air Forces Training Command, authorized our passage to the United States. Among other orders we were not to disclose information concerning the War Department, the army, or our activities within the theater through newspapers, magazines, radio, lectures, books, or by any other means without first securing a clearance from the War Department Bureau of Public Relations or from appropriate public relations officers of the various army installations. We were advised that seven dollars per day would be allowed for food and lodging, where not furnished by the government.

After a five-day layover at a hot, dusty, and primitive Indian military camp, I boarded a C-47 plane with some of our detachment. Nine hours and several stops later we were in Cairo, Egypt. As I remember, we arrived on a Sunday and were forced to produce all of our baggage for inspection by U.S. Army officers at the airport. I had my Japanese rifle and extensive records on dead and wounded. The first batch dealt with the First Battalion of the 37th Division during the Battle of New Georgia Island of the Solomon group. The second listed the casualties of the Marauder First and Third Battalions.

In back of the censor's counter I saw a pile of souvenir weapons, presumably from the African campaigns. My chance of keeping the Japanese carbine and bayonet looked hopeless. As a last resort I obtained the name of the general in charge. A telephone call took him away from his Sunday dinner. Permission was immediately denied.

CHAPTER XXVI

When he heard that I was a Marauder, his attitude changed. He must have heard of our reputation or perhaps had encountered the determination of other Marauders who on their way to the States had refused to take no for an answer.

My next job was to get my records safely by the censor. He was a young lieutenant who seemed somewhat awed by the fact that I was a Marauder. I assumed and continued with a very positive attitude. He eventually accepted my suggestion that my records be sent to me in care of the surgeon general of the United States. This arrangement relieved me of trouble and responsibility and guaranteed that the surgeon general's officer would know who I was when I went to pick up the records.

While resting in the airport, Anne Sheridan, the first movie actress I had ever seen in person, passed through. Our men were very excited over this chance encounter. They decided that the pin-up pictures were definitely on the accurate side.

An attractive young Englishwoman introduced herself to me with the explanation that she was on her way to Philadelphia to join her American husband. She had gone through the worst of the London blitz when she met her future husband, an American doctor in the U.S. Army. I was surprised to learn that a modern-day woman would need someone to look after her while traveling on a military plane but gladly assumed the mission of watching over her as we prepared for and then departed on our 4 September flight in a C-47 to Casablanca. After several stops and ten hours we reached Casablanca.

Two days gave everyone time to spend money and see all the traps that would later be there for tourists. Our plane was now a four-motored job with comfortable seats instead of the bucket seats on the others. After a flight of twenty-three hours with a stop in the Azores and Newfoundland, we arrived in New York City at 1200 hours on 7 September 1944. Our biggest thrill was a view of the Statue of Liberty, the first time most of us had seen it. We exited the plane like routine passengers, with no welcoming committee or band.

A bus was waiting to take us to a secure room in the city. Here we were greeted like criminals by an officer from the adjutant general's office. We were told that we must not discuss or give interviews on any political or tactical situation concerning the Burma campaign. The officer presented his instructions in such a way that most of us were inclined to believe that the mishandling of our 5307th Composite (Prov.) Unit during the Burma campaign had stirred up a real hornet's nest in the United States.

Routine orders allowed each of us twenty-one days' leave after we had reported to replacement depots near our homes. Lieutenant Logan Weston and I were directed to report to the public relations officer at the Pentagon before we took our leave. Logan Weston and I immediately purchased new uniforms before boarding a train for Washington.

Our initial stay in Washington was brief but productive. At the Pentagon, Weston and I were both given the opportunity to offer suggestions to members of the War Department Historical Branch and Military Intelligence Division who were writing the pamphlet *Merrill's Marauders*. This was part of the "American Forces in Action" series published for the information of wounded men.

Lieutenant Weston was then given an opportunity, by the Infantry Training Division officers, to explain infantry tactics that had been helpful in combat. He was soon ordered to Fort Benning to teach officer candidates the tactics he had developed.

After World War II, Weston returned to his religious studies but had to interrupt this course of action because of his physical condition. He, in the post-discharge period, had had many recurrent attacks of malaria, and his health had seriously deteriorated. The best plan seemed to return to active duty. He was soon in Japan and shortly thereafter in Korea as a company commander. After a long period of intense combat he was critically wounded, but he survived to return to combat.

He eventually retired as a colonel after service in Germany, Vietnam, and numerous posts in the United States. He was recently inducted into the Ranger Hall of Fame. Colonel Weston is possibly the most decorated soldier in American history. The Marauders will never forget his courageous stand south of Nhpum Ga, where his platoon held up a reinforced battalion of Japanese for four days until the Second and Third Battalions were able to slip out of a trap. The Marauders, as well as General Stilwell's second Burma campaign, were saved by this action. This godlike man is a great patriot whose life has touched the hearts and souls of many in combat and civilian life.

CHAPTER XXVI

After leaving the Pentagon I visited the Office of the Surgeon General, also in Washington. At the information desk I was told that Surgeon General Kirk had left instructions that I see him on my arrival. My wound ballistic records and a copy of my report on the medical aspects of the Burma campaign had arrived before I did. General Kirk and General Love, of the Historical Section, now had a first-hand account of the history and medical situation. I was immediately asked to talk to the staff of the surgeon general's office and was offered clerical and statistical services to record my thoughts on medical service overseas and in combat. General Love encouraged me to begin immediately on the task of writing a wound ballistic report based on my records. This would be the first record ever put together that discussed all aspects of the total battle casualties in individual battalions. General Love understood that my primary purpose was to show the need for a better battle helmet and for a ballistic trunk protector (armored vest).

I immediately reported to the Fort Meade Replacement Depot, where my orders were changed from a twenty-one-day leave to duty in the Office of the Surgeon General. Here I produced the New Georgia-Burma Wound Ballistic Report, which pointed out several important facts. The old theory that no more than two percent of battle casualties were caused by friendly fire was shown to be inaccurate. This study suggested that over fifteen percent of our dead and a comparable number of wounded were due to friendly fire. Our helmet was shown to save lives and prevent wounds but was demonstrated to be totally inadequate. The fact that about forty-five percent of all fatal casualties were due to hits in the head and neck and forty-five percent over the trunk proved that a better helmet and a trunk protector for men in combat was essential.

After taking a course at Carlisle Barracks in preparation for an overseas job as a division surgeon, I was made a staff surgeon at Walter Reed Hospital. While in this position I worked with the New Development Division and the Ordnance Division of the army to produce an armored vest. I lobbied for this vest with an infantry committee at Fort Benning. Material was set aside to produce a vest for use in the invasion of Japan. Pressure continued by myself and others, and today we have a better helmet and a standard armored vest. Both have saved lives in Korea, Viet Nam, Granada, Panama, Haiti, and the Persian Gulf. Let us hope that the military services never forget the need for continued research to improve our helmets and trunk protectors. They should also have available and use face and neck protectors.

Within two or three months all Marauders with enough points returned home. Some came by air, but most by boat. Many interesting stories could be told. S.Sgt. Clarence Branscomb, who was Lieutenant Sam Wilson's right-hand man in the First Battalion's White Combat Team I & R, recently sent a description of his trip home to be published in the *Burman News*, the Marauders Association newspaper. His letter to the editor is quoted here in a shortened form to give another history of the trip home:

In your letter, you seemed surprised that I've finally surfaced. Well, time is quite a healer, and after forty-five years the bitterness has gone. I was pretty disgusted with the whole military establishment, including Merrill's Marauders—and to top it off, after we had gotten out of Burma and were camped by the river, the monsoons were well on their way. The point system had been enacted, and I had lots of points, so they decided to ship me stateside. I had no clothes to leave with, but it didn't seem to be anyone's concern but mine, so I finally went over to a huge pile of mildewed clothing that had been dumped out of barracks bags, picked out a shirt and pair of pants, and hitchhiked to Chu. There I boarded an ATC plane headed west. All this without a thanks or goodbye or anything.

I left India very much alone. When I got to Karachi, they put me in a general hospital. I had doubled up with cramps in the old stomach again. The hospital staff had a very bad attitude about anyone going home while they had to stay there. They started to prepare me for surgery. Well, I wasn't about to have my appendix out. So, as soon as I found my clothes, I went out a window and caught the next plane going west. I did stop in Accra, on the Gold Coast, for almost a week going swimming in the Atlantic and washing my clothes to get India out of my system.

After having arrived in the U.S., I reported to the armory in Monterey, California, where I had been drafted four years before. Some shavetail collected a bunch of us and said, "We're going to give you the best time of your lives for the next few days at the Miramar Hotel in Santa Barbara." When we showed up there some other officer, with a touch more rank, said, "You're not going to bring that lot in here. They're probably full of all kinds of exotic disease."

So they shipped us back up to Camp Beale in northern California, where we were supposed to be discharged from the army. Some medical officer said, "You can't turn these men loose until they have had a medical examination." Which made some sense. So they gave us a one week furlough home. When I reported back, I was put in Hoff General Hospital in Santa Barbara for nine months, during which time I learned to go out the window after lights out and head downtown.

It was on one of these outings that I spotted Colonel Hunter on the corner of the street—with his wife, I presume. Well, we both ran out in the middle of the street and threw our arms around each other. No saluting or anything, and his wife still on the sidewalk. He said he was going back to Washington to the Army War College, and was there anything he could do for me. I told him I couldn't stand the natives around this part of the world and wanted to go back, but on my terms. He agreed and said he would contact G-2 and have them make me an officer with orders to go to China and be dropped someplace in Northern China by parachute to organize some sort of attack on Japan.

The day I was to receive my discharge, the sealed orders arrived, but I wouldn't have a chance to read them until I was out of the U.S. So I took the discharge and decided to try to adapt (Branscomb 1989, letter).

Many interesting stories have yet to be told about how various men and groups of men returned to the United States. Little mattered, however, except getting home.

Unfortunately, I can find no evidence that any organized attempt was made by the War Department to arrange for a careful medical evaluation of the returnees. After a period of authorized leave and evaluation by replacement depots, they were assigned duty wherever men were needed. Many ended up in hospitals because of chronic problems such as recurrent malaria, amoebic dysentery, and numerous ill-defined medical and surgical problems. I have mentioned that S.Sgt. Clarence Branscomb spent nine months in a military hospital. I was troubled for about a year with a chronic intestinal problem before the presence of amoebic dysentery was proven and treated. Captain A.

THE END OF THE BURMA EXPERIENCE

Lewis Kolodny, while on the staff of a military hospital, became comatose from cerebral malaria. Lieutenant Tom Chamales, after writing the book *Never so Few*, committed suicide. Lieutenant Colonel Charles E. Beach, commander of the Third Battalion, killed himself. Captain Winston Steinfield, a member of the Second Battalion medical detachment, was lost at sea while sailing with his wife. General Merrill died of a heart attack in 1955. General Stilwell died in 1946, presumably from a malignant condition that was troubling him while still in the CBI.

No study has ever been made of the postwar military and civilian careers of the survivors of Merrill's Marauders. The list would be very impressive. Many officers, noncommissioned officers, and privates came up from the ranks and served during the rest of World War II and/or Korea and Vietnam. Our volunteer veterans can also be found in many professions and businesses.

Epilogue

The legacy of the Marauders was put on hold when the 475th Infantry was deactivated in China on 1 July 1945. The 475th was reactivated on 21 June 1954 and allotted to the Regular Army on 26 October 1954. On 20 November 1954 it was activated in Okinawa and again deactivated on 21 March 1956. In 1969, Philip B. Piazza, Merrill's Marauders Association president, presented the Marauder colors at a ceremony activating the 75th Ranger Regiment. Major General Kenneth D. Wilkins, adjutant general, ordered the 75th Regiment, which traced its origin to the 5307th Composite Unit (Provisional)—Merrill's Marauders—to accept the unit as its parent organization. Authorization was given for the cloth insignia of the Marauders to be incorporated into the design of the organizational flag of the 75th Rangers. The men wear the metal insignia as their distinctive emblem.

From time to time I have had opportunities to contemplate and discuss the many unusual—and at times positive—aspects of the Marauders' remarkable campaign in Burma. The many unique characteristics of the organization and campaign created an unusually close bond among the men and officers—one that has never been broken over the years. That bond has been kept alive by a quarterly newsletter, the Merrill's Marauders Organization, and a yearly meeting. Like parents who see the example of their lives carried forth by a growing family, the Marauders take pride in the fact that the young volunteers who make up their military descendent, the 75th Infantry Ranger Regiment, continue our traditions, and that our patch and colors will continue to represent one of the world's outstanding ranger regiments into the distant future.

The origin of the outfit was unique. Its international flavor and the important people involved in its formation add to its historic interest.

EPILOGUE

It was probably the first and only time in World War II that the political head of one government, Prime Minister Winston Churchill, asked the dominant figure in another government, President Franklin Roosevelt, such a unique favor. The request was that three thousand volunteer infantrymen, trained in jungle warfare and in superb physical condition, be supplied to fight—halfway around the world—in a remote part of the British Commonwealth. These men were to train in India as three small units, each with two combat teams of about four hundred men. Their training would be under the supervision of a controversial British military figure, General Orde Wingate. He had fought in Ethiopia and had organized and trained the Israeli army. In 1943 he had sent three thousand men into Burma to harass the Japanese. On this so-called long-range penetration campaign, he had lost more than a third of his men. All supplies had been delivered, when possible, by parachute, and he had had no way to evacuate the sick and wounded.

The American volunteers requested by Wingate were to join his new long-range penetration force of eighteen thousand men. General Marshall and President Roosevelt agreed to send not only the men but also a private air force to be used in the operation. All combat supplies needed by the Americans were to be shipped by boat and delivered in time for combat.

The Joint Chiefs of Staff expected the unit to take eighty-five percent casualties and to be no longer fit for combat after three months, when the unit would be dissolved. There would be no plan for replacements. This was to be a one-shot deal in the attempt to help drive the Japanese out of Burma and reopen a land route to China.

The Marauders knew little about the origin or political implications of their outfit until long after the campaign was over. We only knew that President Roosevelt was requesting volunteers for a dangerous and hazardous mission. We also knew nothing of the allied infighting and political maneuvering that resulted in the transfer of our unit, just before combat, from General Wingate's command to that of General Stilwell. This was to change our mission from one of long-range penetration and enemy harassment to one of spearheading the Chinese advance into Burma.

Many of the special type of individuals who had the courage and love of country to volunteer with little or no hesitation welcomed the opportunity to get out of an unfavorable or dead-end situation. This sudden opportunity to have some say in our future appealed to most of us. The unexpected opportunity of the volunteers from the Caribbean and the States—to spend a month at sea while cruising through the Pacific—was a bonus to the men. Those from the south and southwest Pacific were thrilled and grateful for the rest, medical attention, and good food. The danger of enemy surface ships and submarines was not as disturbing as combat on the ground. The chance to take a boat ride halfway around the world was an inviting prospect— one that promised a memorable experience for all of us.

In spite of the problems associated with illness, training, poor food and living conditions, isolation, and lack of attention by the British-dominated Southeast Asia Command and the CBI theater headquarters, the total experiences were interesting and never to be forgotten. Travel in India—by foot, dilapidated train, and paddlewheel boat— never failed to be interesting. The opportunity (seized by about half of the Third Battalion men) to ignore military discipline and take well-deserved leave, without permission, from a few days to a several weeks, provided many unforgettable stories, which would be told many times both in and out of combat.

The relationship between the men and officers was one of total respect. This attitude—present from the beginning— was never to wane. As the years have gone by and the number of survivors slowly decreases, the men and officers still behave like brothers. Every state was represented on our roster, and many of the men were second- or first-generation Americans originally from Europe, Asia, South and Latin America, China, and Japan. We could count few college graduates, but among the many young men of limited education a high number would go on after discharge to take advantage of the G.I. Bill of Rights and gain high-school or higher education.

We could be proud of the fact that few if any American combat units of comparable size had ever entered and operated for long periods deep in enemy territory. The feat accomplished by various sections of the Marauders of marching and fighting between 500 and 750 miles through jungle and over mountains seems to break a record for combat troops. This was accomplished in spite of the superior forces of

EPILOGUE

Japanese veterans and the absence of any allied forces to prevent possible annihilation of the Americans.[*]

At a Merrill's Marauders reunion in 1971, one of our members said:

> There was no historical precedent for the Marauders' activity. It had always been considered far too hazardous for any small unit to operate behind enemy lines and run the risk of encirclement, such as happened to Custer in 1876.
>
> There has been no march in all world military history that can quite compare with that of the Marauders. Washington marched three times through the impenetrable forest to take Fort Duquesne, but he never got behind it; and though his ragged and ill-supplied army marched more than two hundred miles from the Hudson River to reach Baltimore, where they boarded ships to complete their journey to nearby Yorktown, they had the advantage of a mild climate, roads, cultivated land, and no enemy in sight during the march. MacArthur went behind the enemy by sea at the Inchon landing in Korea, but that was no jungle, and visibility was perfect. Hannibal came closest by crossing the Alps and taking Rome from behind, but again visibility was perfect. Jeb Stuart did it in the Civil War, but he had visibility, and he wasn't walking.

One must remember that, for six months, Merrill's Marauders was the only American infantry unit fighting on the Asiatic mainland. We upheld the honor and demonstrated the will of America to support the Chinese against a common enemy. They were given assurance that, with our help, the enemy would be driven from China and a land route would be opened to their country.

Our unit pioneered long-range military activities in jungle and mountainous areas. These included patrol, major ambush operations, and offensive and defensive battle tactics. At the end of the campaign we were there to train and help stabilize untrained and poorly

---

[*] The Chinese were always in the rear until the last mission. At that time, the Chinese who were sent to help the Marauders were allies who had never been in combat and were neither fully trained, staffed, nor supplied with adequate automatic weapons. The men of several of the Chinese regiments were in poor physical condition. British troops did not enter Burma until the Marauders had dealt a vital blow to the enemy, thirty miles in front of the Chinese, at Walawbum.

organized engineer and casual replacement Americans who had been rushed into battle.

Our Burma experience showed how isolated infantry troops can operate successfully for months in hostile territory when supplied by courageous and innovative pilots. These professionals could and did accomplish miracles when backed up by well-stocked warehouses and dedicated servicemen to fulfill all orders, no matter how urgent. Our rear-echelon men came from the original volunteers and for the most part had been declared unfit for ground combat. Their courage and dedication was continually demonstrated as they rode with the planes and pushed life-saving supplies out to our men on the ground. No matter what the time or weather, the pilots and their Marauder crews never failed us.

Some say that the Marauders accomplished more with less than any comparable-size unit in the history of the U.S. Army in World War II. This group of men overcame many ill-founded decisions, administrative obstacles, and mistakes to complete one of the most productive campaigns in the history of America. Their ability to ignore disease, constant fatigue, poor food, obvious lack of appreciation, death, and wounds—while forging ahead again and again into hostile territory and more battles—will continue to deserve the honor of future generations.

Appendix I
Decorations

This list of decorations received by the 5307th Composite Unit (Prov.), with minor modifications, is copied from *Merrill's Marauders (February–May 1944)*, Armed Forces in Action Series, Military Intelligence Division, U.S. War Department, 1945. It is recognized that the list is not complete.

The Bronze Star medal was later authorized for every member of the organization. The courageous engineers and infantry replacements are not included in this list.

Purple Hearts are not included. Posthumous awards are indicated by an asterisk.

Distinguished Service Cross

1st Lt. Melvin R. Blair
Pfc. Marvin H. Dean
Pfc. Willard I. D. Lilly
Pfc. Herman Manuel
Pfc. Howard T. Smith
T5g. Russel G. Wellmam

Legion of Merit

S.Sgt. John A. Acker
Capt. Charles E. Darlington
S.Sgt. Roy H. Matsumoto
Major Melvin A. Schudmak (British Army}
T.Sgt. Francis Wonsowicz

Silver Star

T.Sgt. Edward C. Ammon
Pfc. Marvin H. Anderson
1st Lt. Paul E. Armstrong M.C.

APPENDIX I—DECORATIONS

M.Sgt. James C. Ballard
Pfc. Earnest C. Banks
Lt. Col. Charles E. Beach
Pfc. Paul R. Bicknell
Capt. George G. Bonnyman
1st Sgt. Clarence E. Branscomb
Maj. Edwin J. Briggs
Pfc. Damiel F. Carrigan
S.Sgt. Ellsworth Dalmus
T4g. Lewis Day Jr.
Pfc. Harold E. Dibble
M.Sgt. Ralph E. Duston
Capt. John R. Fair
T5g. Joseph N. Gomez
Pfc. Everett E. Hudson
Col. Charles N. Hunter
T5g. Emory Jones
Col. Henry L. Kinnison, Jr.
1st Lt. William Lepore
S.Sgt. Earl Little
S.Sgt. James I. Marsh
Lt. Col. George A. McGee, Jr.
Pvt. Paui V. Michael
T4g. William H. Miles*
1st Lt. Robert C. Newman
Pfc. Lambert L. Olson*
Pfc. Leonard G. Porath
S.Sgt. Salvidore F. Rapisarda
1st Sgt. Worth E. Rector
S.Sgt. Ernest W. Reid
T5g. Luther E. Satterfield*
Sgt. Harold Shoemaker
2nd Lt. Winslow B. Stevens
2nd Lt. John W. Travis
Pvt. Clayton A. Vantol
1st Lt. Victor J. Weingartner

2nd Lt. Philip S. Weld
1st Lt. Samuel V. Wilson

Soldier's Medal

Capt. John M. Jones

Bronze Star

Capt. John H. Ahrens
Sgt. Clifford Allen
T5g. Geoge J. Anderson
T5g. Eugene F. Arnold
T5g. Louis F. Barberi
Capt. Thomas E. Bogardus
Capt. George G. Bonnyman
S.Sgt. Charles H. Branton
Maj. Edwin J. Briggs
T4g. Robert L. Carr
1st Sgt. Linwood C. Clements
CWO Thomas J. Dalton
Pfc. Claude F. Davis
Maj. Raymond L. Derraux
S.Sgt. John F. Doran
T.Sgt. Woodrow H. Gelander
1st Lt. William C. Grissom
T5g. Koore W. Hanson
Maj. Richard W. Healy
2nd Lt. George S. Hearn
Maj. George H. Hestad
Capt. James E. T. Hopkins M.C.
1st Lt. Theodore Hughes, Jr.
Maj. Caifson Johnson
Sgt. Edward C. Kohler
S.Sgt. Robert B. Kroy
Capt. Kenneth S. Lancy
1st Lt. Lawrence V. Lindgren
S.Sgt. Francis K. Luke
S.Sgt. Roy H. Matsumoto

APPENDIX I—DECORATIONS

Sgt. Jack V. Mayer
1st Lt. Maurice F. Metcalf
1st Lt. Edward F. McLogan
Lt. Col. William L. Osborne
S.Sgt Allen H. Overby
Pfc. Wayne M. Price
Pvt. Paul L. Rogers
Maj. Bernard Rogoff M.C.
T.Sgt. Frank Russel
2nd Lt. Warren R. Smith
S.Sgt. Charles R. Stewart
Pfc. Milton Susnjdr
Pfc. Joseph F. Sweeney
Sgt. Perlee W. Tintary
Pfc. Darrel M Tomlinson
T5g. Harland Vadnas
Sgt. Arthur A. Werner, Jr
1st Lt. Logan E. Weston
1st Lt. Samuel V. Wilson
2nd Lt. William E. Woomer
Pfc. Leonard F. Wray
Pfc. Edward F. Yardley
Sgt. Osiride O. Zanardelli
S.Sgt Jack F. Zosel

Oak Leaf Cluster to Siver Star

Lt. Col. Charles E. Beach
S.Sgt Ellsworth Dalmus
1st Lt. Samuel Wilson

Appendix II
Records Available

We have been unable to locate any of the following:

1. The roster of the three battalions of volunteers who arrived in Bombay Harbor on 29 October 1943.
2. A list of those who were lost before 24 February 1944 due to death in combat or death from illness or injury.
3. A record of those who joined the unit during the training period in India.
4. A list of those who remained in Assam with the rear echelon headquarters to support the troops in Burma.
5. A list of those who entered combat on 24 February 1943.
6. A complete list of dead and wounded Marauders.
7. A complete list of those who died of disease during the campaign.
8. A complete list of nonfatal battle and accidental injuries.
9. A complete list of dead, wounded, and sick among the replacement combat engineers and infantrymen who fought at Myitkyina.
10. A list of those who remained in Burma until the town of Myitkyina was taken on 3 August 1944.
11. A list of the survivors of the 5307th Composite Unit (Provisional) who went on the Mars Force campaign in late 1944 and early 1955.
12. A roster of the 31st, 33rd, and 35th Quartermaster Pack troops.
13. A record of the men who joined the Third Battalion from the 25th, 43rd, 37th, and Americal Divisions in the Pacific.
14. A list of the men who left San Francisco with the First Battalion.
15. A list of the men who fought at Myitkyina as members of the 209th and 236th Combat Engineers.
16. A list of infantry replacements who arrived at Myitkyina during the last week of May and June.
17. A list of combat engineers and infantry replacements lost to death, injury, or illness.

18. A list of men in all units who died of scrub typhus and other medical conditions.

Some of the following records are available:

1. A complete roster of the Second Battalion as it existed on 5 January 1944. This roster can be found in the unpublished "History of the Second Battalion, Merrill's Marauders," compiled by the commanding officer Colonel George A. McGee in 1967.
2. The names of the officers and enlisted personnel of the Second and Third Battalion medical detachments are recorded in Chapter IV. The officers of the First Battalion medical detachment are listed, but a list of enlisted men could not be found.
3. The record most nearly resembling a roster of all survivors of the original 5307th plus the infantry replacements. This record, "Headquarters, 475th Infantry, General Order Number 3," dated 24 August 1944, has been published in the *Burman News*. It lists 3,899 men, including some dead, such as 2nd Lt. Warren R. Smith and 1st Lt. Donald J. Hogan from Orange Combat Team, who were killed at Charpate on 23 May 1944.

DEAD AND WOUNDED

Marauders Killed in Action or Died of Wounds

First Battalion

Crawley L. Myers 34132652, Pfc., Co. B
William E. Clary 38273868, Pfc., Co. C
Edward E. Foronof 35035009, Pvt., Co. C
William A. Stitt, T5g., Co. C
James R. Welch 33392021, Pvt., Hq. Co.
Lambert L. Olson 20604521, Pfc., Co. B
Richard S. Murphy 6147306, T5g., Co. C
Dervie J. Allen 37240530, Pfc., Hq. Co.
Robert Allen Johnson 0-422409, 1st Lt.
Deck V. Grant 34087208, Pvt., Co. B
Herman Johnson 35106065, Pvt., Hq. Co.
Russell J. Plunkett 35027412, Pfc., Co. C
Raymond K. Chambers 7025667, Sgt., Hq. Co.
Melvin Krul 36217430, Pfc.
William E. Clark 38273866, Pfc., Co. C
Aubrey H. Clark 0-1298194, 1st Lt., Co. B

Second Battalion

Robert Landis 15071424, Pfc., Hq. Co.
William E. Thornton, Pfc., Co. G
Darrell F. Avery, Pfc., Co. G
Hugh H. McPherson 37160239, T5g., Co. F
George C. Jerry 20127616, Pvt., Co. E
Louis Black, Cpl., Co. G
John Lockner, Pvt., Co. G
Charles Varela, Pfc., Co. G
Willard C. Arnett 15061160, Sgt., Co. E

APPENDIX III—DEAD AND WOUNDED

Brendon Lynch 01301657, 1st Lt., Hq. Co.

John C. Carter 36368347, Pvt., Co. F

Perry L. Coltrane 34430074, Pfc., Co. F

Wayne Robinson, Pvt. Co. G

Norman H. Lusaidi 36456337, Pvt., Hq. Co.

Robert F. Noonan 13022665, Cpl., Co. F

Curtis Fountain 14064074, Pvt., Co. F

Robert C. Noel 34155721, Pfc., Co. F

Max C. Cercelius 3572002, Pvt., Hq. Co.

Joseph N. Cotton, Pfc., Co. G

Raymond Bressler 13116687, Pvt., Hq. Co.

John H. McDevitt 31227929, Sgt., Co. E

Albert G. Wankel, Pfc., Co. G

Ellis C. Yoder, Pfc., Co. G

Robert K. Thompson 13041380, Pfc., Co. F

George Bryant, Pvt., Co. G

Julina D. Belk, T5g., Co. G

Leo G. Godkin, Pfc., Co. G

Robert W. Henneburg 12066903, T5g., Co. F

Albert S. Evans 0-489062, 1st Lt., Hq. Co.

Harold E. Asher 37513522, Pvt., Hq. Co.

John F. Magiowysh, Sgt., Co. F

Clarence E. Pyle, T5g., Co. G

James D. Praire 31223692, Pfc., Co. F

William M. Brophy 7041243, Pfc., Hq. Co.

Third Battalion

Pete Leightner 34200282, Pfc., Orange I & R

Lionel J. Paquette 20637964, Cpl., Orange I & R

Clarence J. Bruno 6904202, Co. K, Orange,

William F. Hoffman 39450269, Sgt., Hq. Co., Khaki

Carter F. Pietsch, Pfc., Co. L, Orange

John Zokoski, S.Sgt., Co. K, Orange

Raymond F. Bratten, Pfc., Khaki I & R

Leroy E. Brown 31019775, Pfc., Co. L, Orange

Edgar Robertson 3543040, Cpl., Co. L, Orange

John L. Ploederl 3620824, S.Sgt., Co. L, Orange

APPENDIX III—DEAD AND WOUNDED

Ryland A. Howard, T5g., Co. K, Orange
Daniel V. Carrigan 36605795, Pfc., Co. K, Orange I & R
William W. Scott 20609921, Pfc., Co. L, Orange
Robert H. Sanders 230649662, 1st Sgt., Co. I, Khaki
Thomas F. Nichols 35686178, Pfc., Co. K, Orange
Edward Nichols 20509310, Pvt., Co. I, Khaki
Luther E. Satterfield 38022721, T5g., Co. I, Khaki
Heinz H. Sander, Pvt., Co. I, Khaki
Raymond J. Bokelman 32306750, Pfc., Co. I, Khaki
Leone R. Wralstead 6837940, Pfc., Co. I, Khaki
Charles A. Bias 35208149, Pfc., Co. I, Khaki
Keith B. Carnes 1900638, S.Sgt., Co. I, Khaki
Paul W. LaPanne 20150281, Pvt., Hq. Co., Khaki
Bernard J. Marshall 3112506, Pfc., Hq. Co., Khaki
Robert W. Norling 20504451, Cpl., Hq. Co., Khaki
Alfred L. Fine 36306304, T5g., Co. I, Khaki
Charles B. Page 34304426, Pvt., Co. I, Khaki
Raymond Harris 36312550, T5g., Co. K, Orange I & R
William F. Toomey, Jr. 13013923, Pfc., Co. K, Orange
William C. Noe, S.Sgt., Co. L, Orange
John J. Osborne 341093850, Pvt., Co. I, Khaki
Johnnie Smith 34398554, Pfc., Co. I, Khaki
H. T. Pausch, Pfc., Co. K, Orange
John W. Pruitt, Jr. 14138944, Pfc., Hq. Co., Khaki
Willard G. Dills 3408879, Sgt., Co. L, Orange
Thomas C. Shaffer 6978587, S.Sgt., Co. L, Orange
Thomas C. Mattlock, S.Sgt., Co. L, Orange
Milburne M. Burton, Sgt., Orange med. det.
Donald J. Hogan, 1st Lt., Co. K, Orange
Warren A. Smith, 2nd Lt., Co. K, Orange

Headquarters

Barlow G. Coon, Pvt.
William Laffin, Capt.

Additional Dead

The following list of dead (provided by Robert E. Passanisi, Merrill's Marauder historian) may include the thirty nonbattle deaths, those missing in action, and some members of the several hundred Marauders who remained or returned to fight at Myitkyina:

Donald R. Adams 31284990, Pfc.
Sandolid C. Alvarez 34543583, Pvt.
Arthur Ams, Jr. 32735589, Pvt.
Bill E. Anderson 15382513, Pvt.
Floyd R. Austin 32838650, Pfc.
William R. Bader 33573161, Sgt.
Luther E. Bagley 34440458, Pfc.
Charles H. Bame 35422015, Pfc.
Thomas E. Barrett, Rev. (typhus)
Pasquale S. Barttromd 32805097, Pfc.
Julian T. Belk 14009065, T5g.
Harold J. Berrett 11018122, Pvt.
Stanley J. Bethke 6134215, S.Sgt.
Dale R. Bostwick 35002538, Sgt.
Lewis F. Broadbooks 1299677, 1st Lt.
George Brooks 39410916, Pfc.
John N. Brown 0-1302770, 2nd Lt.
Arthur Burrell 35790336, Pvt.
Angelo J. Caruso 32838645, Pfc.
John W. Chapman 321766433, Pvt.
Oscar Chappell 35790498, Pfc.
Roman Cherubini 20226610, Pvt.
Thomas R. Clinard 34723201, Pvt.
Joseph D. Coburn, Jr. 34543548, Sgt.
Robert L. Crane 39402027, Pvt.
Richard M. Dawson 13016729, Pfc.
Philip W. Daye 31319369, Pvt.
Fred G. Eagan 34260944, Pvt.
Fritz Euhrich (typhus)
Robert Evans 33353519
William H. Freeman, Jr. 35629104, Sgt.

APPENDIX III—DEAD AND WOUNDED

Joseph A. Gaia 31357982, Pvt.
Philip J. Geary 36882938, Pvt.
Guido G. Giaquinta 35607478, Pfc.
Ernest W. Gibson 36054286, Sgt.
Calvin E. Goff 31375603, Pvt.
John O. Goodknight 38149437, Pfc.
Milton J. Goralski 33558651, Pvt.
James F. Graham
Joseph C. Hagerman
Johnny Harris
Richard S. Hewy 31317051, Pvt.
Leslie A. Holtzapfel 32751123, Pvt.
Rufus L. Ingram 34428879, Pfc.
Robert C. Kadgihn, Capt.
Keith Karnes
Mack Kidd 35774963, Pvt.
Henry L. Kinnison, Col. (typhus)
Joseph Krug
Joseph Lapsiak
Floyd R. Leighliter 33684515, Pvt.
William S. LePore 0-1289101, 1st Lt. (typhus)
Harold P. Lichtenau 32806593, Pvt.
Vita Luceno, Jr. 32766593, Pfc.
Daniel B. Manasco 35725874, Pvt.
Bernard J. Marshall 3112506, Pfc. (typhus)
Kenneth E. Matson 15065014, Pvt.
Mike R. McDowell 35790891, Pvt.
Paul V. Michel 15010345, Pfc.
Horace H. Middleton 33501351, Pvt.
George O. Moran 39704212, Pvt.
Fred D. Newman 34543665, Pfc.
Henry S. Nowocinski 31316118, Pfc.
Robert J. O'Donell 6142416, T4g.
Primo J. Pescatore 31325725, Pvt.
Wilfred W. Poulin, Jr. 11016679, Pvt.
Vincent Rapoaci
David Richter 32172514, Pfc.

APPENDIX III—DEAD AND WOUNDED

Paul Rossochacy
James C. Roten 34605605, Pvt.
Richard P. Schmidt 33788642, Pvt.
Eugene A. Siedler 32833143, Pvt.
Wilbur Smawley (typhus)
Walter L. Sokolowski 33463716, Pfc.
Jerome E. Stone 32846675, Pfc.
Herman J. Sunstad 1299324, 1st Lt.
Charlie H. Thomson 35130856, Pfc.
Dillard L. Triplett 34606335, Pfc.
Charles R. Ullery 35629565, Pvt.
Ernest L. Valentine 35547545, Pfc.
Robert L. Vincent 35725281, Pfc.
Henman Vohnson 35106065, Pvt.
James W. White 35628445, Pfc.
Thomas E. White 38556502, Pvt.
Earl Wolf 31513980
William Yardley
Joseph S. Zikas 32810706, Pfc.
Robert L. Zimmer 35048239, Pvt.

We believe the majority of the deaths listed here were due to Tsutsugmachi fever (typhus). We know of one death from suicide, one from leukemia, one accident, and two from drownings. No complete list of these men has been located.

The official list includes 503 with amoebic dysentery, 140 with typhus, 296 with malaria, 72 with psychoneurosis, and 950 miscellaneous.

No adequate analysis of the disease casualties has ever been made. Personal obseration showed that virtually all the Marauders were suffering from amoebic dysentery, chronic malaria, and malnutrition. Many had chronic bronchitis, varying degrees of dermatitis, arthritis, and a form of chronic fatigue syndrome. Near the end of the campaign the highly fatal scrub typhus struck the 1,300 or so remaining men. Between 150 and 200 required immediate hospitalization, and at least 30 died.

APPENDIX III—DEAD AND WOUNDED

Lost in Flight

The following dead were among the Marauders assigned to pack and deliver freight from the C-47 planes of the Second Troop Carrier Squadron, 443rd Troop Carrier Group, 10th Air Force, based at Dinjan, India:

Benjamin J. Jones, Pfc., Travelers Rest, S.C.
Howard K. Moss, Pf., Maryville, Tenn.
Walter B. Owensby, Pfc., Ashville, N.C.
Vidas D. Parker, S.Sgt., Fond de Lac, Mich.

All four of the above men were lost on a flight to Myitkyina in May 1944. Their remains were found about forty years later. Also lost were the pilot, 2nd. Lt. Ernest R. Wilson of Monticello, Miss.; the radio operator, Sgt. Allen W. Beeler of Roselawn, Ind.; and the flight officer, Andrew Maligo.

Unofficial records show that more than one hundred aircraft were missing in flight in northern Burma.

Additional Wounded

Among the original Marauders who either returned to combat or remained in combat at Myitkyina until the Japanese were defeated on 3 August 1944, the following men were wounded in battle:

(NFN) Bigham 38000703, Cpl., Hq and Hq. Det., 30 June, Clifton, Ariz.
George G. Bonnyman 0-413059, Capt., Hq. and Hq. Det., 25 June, Nashville, Tenn.
Thomas W. Brymer 39030664, Pfc., Co. C, 29 July, San Francisco, Calif.
Evert L. Cranke 6578495, S.Sgt., Co. A, 28 July, Lompoe, Calif.
Hunt D. Crawford 15334309, T.Sgt., Hq and Hq. Co., 12 June, Louisville, Ky.
Ralph E. Duston 6883461, M.Sgt., Hq and Hq. Det., 12 July, Sharon, Pa.
William G. Emerick 0-284760, Capt., Co. K, 29 June, Akron, Ohio
Arnold T. Geissler 36216067, T5g., 28 July, Chippewa Falls, Wisc.
Sidney German 33297096, Pfc., Hq. and Hq. Det., 30 June, Brooklyn, N.Y.
Daniel J. Grady 32535893, Sgt., Co. B, 28 July, Yonkers, N.Y.

Frank M. Guth 32766387, Sgt., 28 July

John J. Hewitt 6899288, Pfc., Co. C, 22 July, Fontrose, Va.

Talmadge A. Hinson 7085154, Pfc., Co. E, 22 July, Winnsboro, S.C.

Johnnie B. Holmes 6342203, S.Sgt., Hq. Co., 29 July,
Washington, D.C.

Elwin H. Laetech 31031543, Sgt., Co. C, 28 July, Reading, Mass.

Carlyle A. Lilly 35429239, Pfc., Co. F, 14 July, Crab Apple Orchard,
W.Va.

Joseph R. Linthwaite, 11008786, Pvt., Co. A, 28 July,
Longmeadow, Mass.

Manuel B. Maclas 38100318, Pfc., Co. K, 27 July, Waco, Tex.

Herman Manuel 20845086, Pfc., Co. B, 28 July, Scottsdale, Ariz.

Harry M. Paris 16040658, T4g., Co. C, 28 July, Staunton, Ill.

Henry Parsons, Jr. 15065904, T5g., Co. C, 27 July, Covington, Ky.

Robert E. Passanisi 12064098, S.Sgt., 1 July

Arthur J. Richards, Jr. 33353539, Cpl., Co. E, 27 July

Charles F. Slusser 15042717, Sgt., Co. E, 28 July, Lima, Ohio

Richard B. Thomas 12024710, T4g., Co. G, 28 July, Marcy, N.Y.

(NFN) Williamson 39404023, S.Sgt., Hq. Co., 28 July, Doye, Calif.

Total Battle Casualties

The following statistics do not include engineers and infantry replacements.

Battle deaths (our records)	97
Battle deaths (official records)	93
Battle wounds (our records)	383
Battle wounds (official records)	293
Missing in action (official records)	8
Nonbattle deaths (official records)	30

NOTES ON JUNGLE WARFARE

These notes have been compiled by John M. Jones based on his World War II experience in Burma as a captain with Merrill's Marauder Rangers.

1. Train plenty of messengers—not just any man, but a soldier with guts who will take a message over dangerous country at night and get it through. All messengers should be taught to ride a horse (if available, basic cavalry).

2. SCR 536 is good on the drop field, on marches, and in bivouac areas, but very little use in combat due to range limitation. SCR 300 is tops for combat—each platoon could use one. Their range of three miles in the jungle covers most tactical situations. SCR 264 is splendid for units more than three miles apart but not more than fifteen.

3. In the jungle the tommy gun is tops—junior officers should carry them—you need something with stopping power and a fast rate of fire. Your ranges usually are less than forty yards—sometimes ten.

4. An extra canteen cover for carrying two or three grenades is good. Some heavy-weapons men should carry incendiary grenades to destroy mortars if you have to abandon them quickly; flame-thrower teams should carry incendiary grenades in case their flame thrower doesn't ignite—throw the incendiary grenade and shoot the oil on it.

5. For perimeter defense, plenty of grenades are essential—especially at night.

6. Every man should have some guide or pamphlet to get information from natives. An interpreter for each platoon should be provided if the natives actually go with a combat team on an independent operation.

7. Some simple map should be provided for every soldier, not only for possible use in case he becomes lost but to orient himself on the situation.

8. In the jungle a kukri or machete is about fifty percent as useful as the dah.

9. No one takes vitamin tablets in the jungle—why not use that space in the jungle first-aid kit for a small can of foot powder?

10. K-ration should be supplemented with C-ration or the meat component as often as once a week. One pound of rice per man per week would also help—however, they tire of it if they get it too often.

11. A drop of one can of fruit juice and one pound coffee per man per week would help—he would drink the fruit juice on the spot and carry the coffee.

12. 10-in-1 rations whenever the unit is stopped for more than a day helps morale.

13. The short wrap-type leggings are very good for jungle wear. They keep out leeches and are easy to put on and take off. Most men cut G.I. leggings off three-quarters of the way up. The regular legging is too high on the leg for most men.

14. A spoon and the bottom of your mess gear is enough when you have to carry your own pack and rations for long periods.

15. A drop of toilet paper in each ration would be a good thing. Irritation almost always develops from using leaves.

16. Men should be trained to keep their heads up when they hit the ground—what they see sometimes would make them move before they get shot and would also enable them to see the enemy first—sometimes.

17. Be sure your code clerks and radio operators are well trained. It is better to have a good operator who can't shoot than a good shot who is only a fair operator.

18. Some of the most valuable men in our outfit were the Nisei Japanese interpreters—not with the battalion and regimental headquarters but with a platoon in contact on the perimeter. The Japanese talked loudly sometimes before they attacked, and on several occasions the Japanese interpreters told us exactly what the enemy was shouting and enabled us to get set for an attack from a certain direction. Once an interpreter caused the Japanese to attack into a trap by shouting orders to them.

APPENDIX IV—NOTES ON JUNGLE WARFARE

19. Always have somebody else read your messages to check the meaning before sending them out. Sometimes important things are left out, even though you are thinking about them.

20. It is easy to teach a man to look for different type shoeprints on a trail. On two occasions a suspicious looking shoeprint caused us to surprise the Japanese, whereas if we hadn't noticed it they probably would have surprised us.

21. Marching at night in the jungle is very difficult for men over good trails. Over fair or poor trails it is almost useless and is practically impossible for animals.

22. When ordered to get animals off a trail quickly, take them off in pairs—they go better and don't bray as much.

23. If a man is busy under fire he doesn't get so scared or nervous. What is bad, however, is to sit without anything to do but listen to them whistle over.

24. 81mm mortars are very accurate and can be fired safely fifty to one hundred yards in front of our front lines. H.H. heavy is good for close-in work.

25. The Japanese is no suicide soldier—he will run and retreat if surrounded, and once you get him on the run he is not nearly so effective.

26. The best defense against snipers is to move fast. When you hit the ground, crawl a little farther and keep your head up to see what's going on.

27. If your arches are O.K. you will like jungle boots, as they are much lighter than G.I. shoes.

28. Always carry an extra piece of silk rope (obtainable from parachutes after an airdrop). You always have to tie something on to your pack—and silk rope will untie easily.

29. A G.I. shovel is worth its weight in gold when you start digging. Two colonels dug with helmets and knives while I dug with my shovel once when the shells were coming over. That is something I guarded with my life. Also if a man has no shovel, chances are he won't bury his body waste.

30. Many men throw away helmets before they have been under shell fire—after that, they never throw them away. Although they won't stop a bullet, they frequently change its course—and they will stop

shell fragments. No one ever uses the chin strap under his chin—hook it on the back of the helmet out of your way, but don't cut it off—you'll need it when you want to carry water in your helmet.

31. Insist that men don't dig foxholes near trees—either dig away from them or cut them down. Tree bursts are responsible for many unnecessary casualties.

32. Watch your men carefully to see that they halazone their water. If they fail to do it one time and get away with it, then first thing you know they never halazone water and brag about it till somebody comes down with dysentery. Educate them to the value of atabrine and halazone—man's good friends in the jungle.

33. The K-ration tastes good as long as you are doing hard physical work—after that it is nauseating.

34. Flexible cellophane bags to carry your maps are invaluable. The top of your helmet is a good spot for mosquito head net (seldom used) and the map you are using.

35. Practically everybody uses a horseshoe type pack—rations in the pack, and blanket and poncho in the horseshoe.

36. It pays big dividends to have men and officers know as much about the situation as possible—an officers meeting in the field should be arranged so that they can get the news to their officers and men that day—before it becomes history.

37. The few officers who took enough interest in their men to write a short letter to a man's family found that it produced amazing results in morale. A letter from his platoon leader when a man is promoted or does a good job has a good effect on the whole platoon—the word gets around.

38. See that someone in every platoon carries an oil stone when you go into the field. They are worth their weight in gold to a man who has a dull knife.

39. We drove a mule in front of us over a trail we thought might be booby trapped. It was, and the mule was killed.

40. Expect knee-mortar fire within three minutes from the time you hit the enemy. It is amazing how quick and how accurate knee mortar can be.

41. An S.O.P. for various situations is a good thing even though you might not use it. Somehow it gives both men and officers confidence.

42. If you do march at night, compass tied on the back of a man's pack helps keep the column together—especially on a dark night. The phosphorescent lines stand out clearly.

43. If you are in or near enemy territory, don't walk around at night—even to relieve yourself. There is always a trigger-happy guy who shoots first even though you are miles from the enemy.

44. The Japanese taught us a good trailblock. It is in the shape of an "S," with the trail running down the middle and automatic weapons on the humps and ends, if available. Riflemen are scattered in between.

45. Field glasses were almost never used by us in the jungle—and then only to look for snipers in the trees.

46. One of our patrols took the same route that a previous patrol had used and was ambushed. The Japanese are cagey—they will follow a patrol sometimes for long distances, then set an ambush in case it comes back.

47. Close-order drill and a full field inspection one day after coming off the front lines snapped one of our battalions back into shape quick. They had lost noncoms and officers and had been fighting steadily for two weeks. Their discipline and morale was low, and they were tired and very sluggish. They were mainly veterans of Guadalcanal and New Guinea, and considered themselves above this sort of thing (close-order drill). However—although they objected strenuously—they did it with snap, and the outfit benefitted greatly. It gave the new platoon leaders, platoon sergeants, and squad leaders a chance to see what their men looked like and to give them a few orders. I believe practically every man in the organization recognized the excellent results obtained.

48. The new plastic oil-filled wrist compass is excellent—preferable to the new oil-filled lensatic compass because it appears to be more waterproof and is easier to read.

49. The intelligence and reconnaissance platoon should have one more animal to carry a 60mm mortar and ammunition. At the present time it has no machine guns or mortars.

50. G.I. wristwatches don't stand up in the jungle. We need a good waterproof wristwatch with an easy-to-read face.

List of Works Cited

Chan, Won-Loy. 1986. *Burma, The Untold Story.* Presidio.

Dorn, Frank. 1971. *Walkout, with Stilwell in Burma.* Thomas Y. Crowell Co.

Freeman, Paul D. Interviews. USAMH.

George, John B. 1981. *Shots Fired in Anger.* National Rifle Association.

Hill, Russell F. 1944. "S-3 Journal, Third Battalion, 5307th Composite Unit (Provisional)." Hoover Institution on War, Revolution, and Peace.

Hunter, Charles N. 1963. *Galahad.* The Naylor Co.

Jones, John M. 1944. "War Diary of the 5307th Composite Unit (Provisional)." Orginal copy, censored copy appendix 16 of *History of Northern Area Combat Command.* War Department Special Staff.

McGee, George E., Jr. 1987. *The History of the Second Battalion, Merrill's Marauders.* Privately printed.

Ogburn, Charlton, Jr. 1956. *The Marauders.* Harper and Brothers.

Romanus, Charles F. and Sunderland, Riley. 1956. *Stilwell's Command Problems.* U.S. Army, Office of the Chief of Military History.

Seagrave, Gordon S., M.D. 1964. *Burma Surgeon Returns.* W.W. Norton and Co.

Stilwell, Joseph W. 1948. *The Stilwell Papers.* Edited by Theodore H. White. William Sloane Associates.

Stone, James H. 1949. "Evacuation of the Sick and Wounded in the Second Burma Campaign, 1943–45." *Military Review* 29, no. 2.

———. 1949. "The Marauders and the Microbes." *Infantry Journal* 64, no. 3.

LIST OF WORKS CITED

———. 1959. "Surgeon in Battle: The Mobile Surgical Hospital in Burma, 1943–45." *Military Surgeon* 311–20.

———. 1969. *Crisis Fleeting: Original Reports on Military Medicine in India and Burma in the Second World War.* U.S. Army, Office of the Surgeon General.

Stuart, Father. 1984. "Chronicle of the Marauders." *Burman News,* Merrill's Marauders Association, Inc.

U.S. War Department, History Section. 1945. *Merrill's Marauder's.* American Forces in Action Series.

Van Der Vat, Dan. 1944. *The Pacific Campaign.* Simon and Schuster.

Weston, Logan E. 1992. *The Fightin' Preacher.* Vision Press.

Glossary

ALBACORE—Code name for Stilwell's three-phase, Ledo-to-Myitkyina plan to retake North Burma.

B-25—USAF four-engine bomber.

Banzai charge—Wild charge of a Japanese infantry unit.

Basha—Name applied to native living quarters in India and Burma. Usually made of bamboo and reeds.

Bum—Burmese term for hill or mountain.

Bushido code—Ancient Japanese warrior code. His ultimate duty was to die in defense of his country. It was modified into the soldier's code, which glorified suicidal tactics. Death was necessary instead of capture. Failure to comply caused their name to be removed from official records and disgraced their family.

C-46 and C-47—USAF two engine freight planes. Used in CBI for troop transport and all types of freight.

CBI—China-Burma-India theater of operations.

Chiang Kai-shek (1887–1975)—President of China from 1941. This amounted to a dictatorship. From 1925 as a Chinese nationalist general he ruled China. Allied supreme commander of the China theater of operations after Pearl Harbor.

Chih Hui Pu—Name of Chinese Army headquarters in India.

China Incident—Term applied by the Japanese to their armed operation in China between 1931 and 1941.

Chindits—Brig. Gen. Orde Wingate's name for his long-range penetration forces. Name derived from Burmese Canthi, the mythological bird that guarded temples.

Chop—Seal usually made of ivory, which the Japanese and Chinese used to sign documents.

Combat team—Each Marauder battalion was divided into two equal units by order of Brig. Gen. Orde Wingate.

GLOSSARY

Comfort girls—Japanese sex slaves. See description of group captured at Myitkyina.

CP—Command post of a squad, platoon, company, or any size infantry unit.

Div.—Division.

End Run—Stilwell's code name for his plan to capture Myitkyina.

G-1—Personnel. The letter "G" is used for divisions or higher. If less than a division, the letter is "S."

G-2—Intelligence.

G-3—Operations.

G-4—Logistics.

Galahad—Code name for shipments 1688 A, B, and C, later to become 5307th Composite Regiment (Provisional). When General Merrill was named commanding officer, it was still the code name for what was now a unit instead of a regiment. At Myitkyina, when about two hundred of the original men were left, this group plus two battalions of engineers and two thousand untrained and unorganized infantry replacements were generally called Galahad. Up until the Battle of Myitkyina, the Marauders had not been aware of the name.

Hka—River.

Hump—The air route over the Himalayas between Assam, India, and Kunming, China. It was also called the Aluminum Trail because of the crashes that marked the route from the Brahmaputra valley in India to Kunming in China. Supply missions began in 1942 and continued until 1945, when the Burma Road was opened.

L-4/5—USAF light, single-engine aircraft used for liaison, casualty evacuation, and intelligence gathering.

LRP—American long-range penetration units, such as Merrill's Marauders.

LRPG—Wingate's Chindits. First formed as 77th Indian Brigade spring of 1942 from British, Ghurka, and Burmese units. Raided north central Burma for three months in 1942. In 1943 entered Burma as 3rd Indian Division with five brigades.

Mars Task Force—The few remaining Marauders and the survivors of the twenty-six hundred casual replacement troops who fought at Myitkyina were first formed into the 75th Infantry Regiment and shortly afterwards into the 475th Infantry Regiment. In late September they were joined by the 124th Cavalry Regiment, dismounted from Texas to form the 5332nd Brigade.

Mitch—Slang word for Myitkyina.

MP—U.S. Military Police.

MT—Myitkyina Task Force.

NCAC—U.S. Northern Combat Area Command.

NCO—U.S. Noncommissioned officer.

Nisei—Second-generation Japanese Americans.

OSS—U.S. Office of Strategic Services.

P-40/51—USAF fighter aircraft.

Ping—Chinese soldier.

POW—Prisoner of War.

Rect—Regiment.

SEAC—Southeast Asia Command. Allied command for Burma-Malaya-Thailand Singapore theater with headquarters in India. Set up November 1943 with Admiral Mountbatten as the supreme commander and General Joseph Stilwell as deputy supreme commander.

Shin—GOSLING for Shingbwiyang.

SOS—U.S. Services of Supply.

USAF—United States Army Air Force.

Bibliography

Anders, Leslie. *The Ledo Road.* University of Oklahoma Press, 1965.

The Army Lineage Book. "Mars Force, 475th and 75th Infantry Regiments."

Boatner, Hayden L. "Account of Services in Southeast Asia." Unpublished papers, USAMHI Archives.

Chan, Won-Loy. *Burma, The Untold Story.* Presidio, 1986.

Dorn, Frank. *Walkout, with Stilwell in Burma.* Thomas Y. Crowell Co., 1971.

Eldridge, Fred. *Wrath Over Burma.* Doubleday and Company, Inc., 1948.

Fischer, Edward. *The Chancey War.* Orion, 1991.

Frank, Richard B. *Guadalcanal.* Random House, 1990 Freeman, Paul D. Interviews. USAMH.

George, John B. *Shots Fired in Anger.* National Rifle Association, 1981.

Hill, Russell F. "S-3 Journal, Third Battalion, 5307th Composite Unit (Provisional)." Hoover Institution on War, Revolution, and Peace, 1944.

Hoyt, Edwin. *Merrill's Marauder's.* Pinnacle, 1980.

Hunter, Charles N. *Galahad.* The Naylor Co., 1963.

Infantry, vol. 2 of *The Army Lineage Book.* Office of the Chief of Military History, 1953.

Jones, John M. "War Diary of the 5307th Composite Unit (Provisional)." Orginal copy, censored copy appendix 16 of *History of Northern Area Combat Command.* War Department Special Staff.

Masters, John. *The Road Past Mandalay.* Harper and Brothers, 1961.

McGee, George E., Jr. *The History of the Second Battalion, Merrill's Marauders.* Privately printed, 1987.

BIBLIOGRAPHY

Merrill's Marauders Association. *Merrill's Marauders War in Burma.* Volume 1.

Ogburn, Charlton, Jr. *The Marauders.* Harper and Brothers, 1956.

Romanus, Charles F. and Sunderland, Riley. *Stilwell's Command Problems.* U.S. Army, Office of the Chief of Military History, 1956.

Seagrave, Gordon S., M.D. *Burma Surgeon.* W.W. Norton and Co., 1943.

————. *Burma Surgeon Returns.* W.W. Norton and Co., 1964.

Southeast Asia Command. *Report to the Combined Chiefs of Staff by the Supreme Allied Commander* (Admiral Lord Louis Mountbatten, Southeast Asia). London: H.M. Stationary Office, 1951.

Stanton, Shelby L. *Ranger's War: LRRP's in Vietnam.* Ivy Books, 1992.

Stilwell, Joseph W. *The Stilwell Papers.* Edited by Theodore H. White. William Sloane Associates, 1948.

Stone, James H. "Evacuation of the Sick and Wounded in the Second Burma Campaign, 1943–45." *Military Review* 29, no. 2 (1949).

————. "The Marauders and the Microbes." *Infantry Journal* 64, no. 3 (1949).

————. "Surgeon in Battle: The Mobile Surgical Hospital in Burma, 1943–45." *Military Surgeon* 311–20 (1959).

————. *Crisis Fleeting: Original Reports on Military Medicine in India and Burma in the Second World War.* U.S. Army, Office of the Surgeon General, 1969.

————. "United States Army Medical Service in Combat, India and Burma." Declassified, unpublished history. Library of AMSS, BAMC, Ft. Sam Houston, Texas, 1945.

Stuart, James. "Chronicle of the Marauders." *Burman News,* Merrill's Marauders Association, Inc. (1984).

Tobey, Paul. "The Sitapur Incident." Unpublished document.

U.S. War Department, History Section. *Merrill's Marauder's.* American Forces in Action Series. 1945.

Van Der Vat, Dan. *The Pacific Campaign.* Simon and Schuster, 1944.

Weston, Logan E. *The Fightin' Preacher.* Vision Press, 1992.

About the Authors

James E. T. Hopkins, a physician, graduated from the Johns Hopkins University Medical School in 1941 and was in first-year surgical training when the Japanese struck at Pearl Harbor. He soon volunteered for duty and entered the army as a first lieutenant. He was in the Pacific with the 18th General Hospital during the Battle of Midway. A year later he volunteered to go to Guadalcanal as a battalion surgeon with the 37th Division (Ohio National Guard). The division was soon in the Northern Solomon Islands, fighting in the Battle of New Georgia. It was there, after the campaign, that he volunteered for the "dangerous and hazardous mission" that would take him to Burma. He served during the entire Burma campaign as Orange Combat Team surgeon with the Third Battalion, sometimes called C Battalion.

✿ ✿ ✿

The collaborating author, Captain (later Lieutenant Colonel) **John M. Jones,** of Greenville, Tennessee, volunteered for the unit while serving in the office of the assistant commandant of the U.S. Army Infantry School, Fort Benning, Georgia, in the fall of 1943. He was a graduate of what was then the Tennessee Military Institute, in Sweetwater, Tennessee, a military high school from which he received, in the mid 1930's, an ROTC commission as a second lieutenant in the army. He later graduated form Washington and Lee University, Lexington, Virginia.

His first assignment, after being called to active duty in early January 1942, was as a platoon commander with troops at Fort McClellan, Alabama. There he saw in graphic detail the extreme lack of preparedness of the country. It was not possible to train troops without modern rifles and mortars.

His unit was preparing to go overseas in the spring of 1943. The unit was eventually sent to the South Pacific as replacements, and Captain Jones would have gone with them had he not been a patient in the hospital recovering from a serious case of pneumonia.

Following his release from the hospital, he was sent to Fort Benning for a thirteen-week infantry officer training course. After completing that, he was named an instructor in the machine-gun section of the Infantry School. He later served on the staff of the assistant commandant of the school, where he was responsible for handling intelligence matters.

Captain Jones and another officer from the Infantry School learned of the call for soldiers for "a hazardous mission somewhere in the world," volunteered for it, and were flown to New Delhi, India, in advance of the other members of Merrill's Marauders.

At the time Captain Jones and the other officer from Fort Benning flew into new Delhi, the new unit was not assigned to the China-Burma-India theater (CBI) but to the Southeast Asia Command (SEAC). Because of that fact, Colonel James Wagner Bellah, of SEAC, ordered the two officers to visit British assault units and train with them where possible. This training was designed to prepare for the possibility that the new unit would be entering Burma with British General Orde Wingate's Chindits, which sometimes moved by air or made landings from the sea. The regiment was at a training camp in Central India. When he reported there, Captain Jones was assigned to work with Captain William Laffin, the unit's intelligence officer.

Shortly after the Marauders entered Burma, Captain Jones suggested to General Frank Merrill, the commanding officer, that he (Jones) maintain a diary on the unit's operations and send out the handwritten material when wounded members were being evacuated. He was never officially a unit historian, although his notes became an informal history of the Merrill's Marauder campaign.

Captain Laffin assigned him to work with Father James Stuart, an Irish Roman Catholic missionary in Burma. On a strictly personal basis, Father Stuart served as a liaison with the Kachins, a native people in northern Burma who were a major source of intelligence for the Marauders.

Jones worked largely with the Kachins but also took out intelligence patrols and made a number of flights in small airplanes for intelligence-gathering purposes. He continued to work with General Merrill's command group, and later Colonel Charles N. Hunter's command group, until he (Jones) was evacuated with amoebic dysentery. Like most others in the unit, he had experienced significant weight loss by that time. He had weighed 189 pounds before entering Burma in early February; he weighed 126 pounds when he was flown out to the hospital in Ledo, Assam, in mid-May.

He spent a number of weeks in hospitals in Assam and later in Colombo, Ceylon (now Sri Lanka). While in the hospital at Colombo, he was brought to Kandy, Ceylon, to receive a decoration. On that occasion, he became acquainted with Admiral Lord Louis Mountbatten, the supreme commander of the Southeast Asia Command. Admiral Mountbatten questioned him at length about the Marauder operations.

Subsequently, while continuing his recuperation, Captain Jones was provided with secretarial help to transcribe and amplify his notes from the Marauder operations. These were the notes he had sent out by plane with the wounded Marauders being evacuated. The notes were among the material later used by Charlton Ogburn and others in writing about the unit.

Jones was later appointed an aide to Lt. General Raymond A. Wheeler, India-Burma theater commander, and American aide-de-camp to Admiral Mountbatten. He returned to the United States in October 1945 with General Wheeler, who had been appointed U.S. Army Chief of Engineers.

Jones was released from army service in December 1945. Later that month he entered the newspaper business, joining his family in newspaper publishing and, later, in magazine publishing and broadcasting.

PLATE 1. View of a small section of a column of Marauders hiking the twisting, turning, up-and-down 110-mile dirt tract over the Patkai Mountain Range from Ledo, India, to the Chinese/American forward military base of Shingbwiyang, North Burma. The road would eventually be twenty-eight feet wide and covered with gravel.

PLATE 2. The Marauders' training camp on the Betwa River, near the small village of Deogarh in central India. This isolated and desolate area had been picked by the British Gen. Orde C. Wingate, under whose command we were supposed to fight in Burma. It was our home and training area for nine weeks until we departed for Burma at the end of January 1944.

PLATE 3. General Joseph W. Stilwell: commanding general, United States Army forces, China, Burma, and India theater of operations; acting deputy supreme Allied commander, Southeast Asia; commanding general, Chinese Army in India; and commanding general, Northern Combat Area Command. The Marauders were shifted to his command during early January 1944 in order to spearhead two Chinese divisions in their drive against the Japanese. After completing two successful missions, we led two Chinese regiments to capture the all-weather airfield at Myitkyina and later assisted the Chinese in capturing the town. Few Marauders had the opportunity to see the general. He avoided the Marauders before, during, and after the great victories, even though our efforts had won him a fourth star.

PLATE 4. Brig. Gen. Frank D. Merrill (with pipe) joined the
Marauders just before combat but was not with them in the field
during April and May because of chronic heart trouble. Shortly after
assuming command, his sensible approach and positive personality
gained the confidence and respect of the men. Lt. Col. Charles
Beach came to his position as commander of the Third Battalion as a
National Guard veteran of the Solomon Island campaign. He was a
courageous leader who guided and led his men and officers with
great ability during the entire campaign.

PLATE 5. Colonel Charles N. Hunter (right) observes an infantry drill
with Colonel Beach. While at Fort Benning, Hunter became the first
member of the volunteer unit. He served as commanding officer longer
than anyone else. His West Point background and knowledge of men
was very important in and out of combat. This brilliant and effective
leader and tactician was not one of Stilwell's men and got what
amounted to a raw deal at the hands of Stilwell.

PLATE 6. The headquarters tent at Deogarh, where they combined infantry training with paperwork. Much of the paperwork was eliminated when most of the staff marched into Burma as infantrymen.

PLATE 7. Marauders prepare a raft for practice crossing of the Betwa River. Unfortunately, this part of the training had to be delayed until just before we left for Burma. We had been waiting for the arrival of our mules and horses to assist in the crossing. The operation was very dangerous because few of the men could swim, and two men drowned during an exercise.

PLATE 8. The ground cover in the wilderness at Deogarh was not like
the rain forest of Burma. Here we trained in furnacelike heat during
the day and bone-chilling temperatures at night. The ground cover in
many areas consisted of thorn-covered bushes. The training was realis-
tic, with long marches and practice in the use of all infantry weapons.

PLATE 9. Admiral Lord Louis Mountbatten, the supreme Allied commander, Southeast Asia Command, talks to members of the Third Battalion shortly before we leave for Burma. His visit was well received by the Marauders. Neither General Stilwell nor any of his staff had bothered to meet the men.

PLATE 10. A battalion exits its troop train on the ten-day, twelve-hundred-mile trip (by train, paddleboat, and foot) to the combat area, awaiting arrangements to board another troop train on a different gauge track.

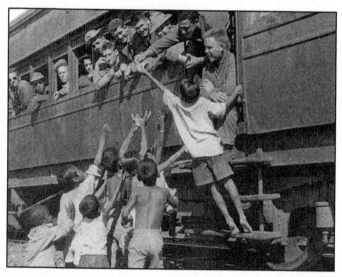

PLATE 11. Members of the Third Battalion medical detachment ride in style in a Pullman car on the trip toward Burma. Other members of the battalion rode in wooden coaches with wooden benches and a hole in the floor for bathroom facilities.

PLATE 12. During a brief rest on the Ledo Road near the India-Burma border, the men look south toward the mountains they must climb and further on to the rainforests of Burma.

PLATE 13. The India-Burma border at Borderville, Pansau Pass, elevation five thousand or more feet. From here we thought it would all be downhill, but that was not to be. There were many more long steep grades up and down. (I still remember the pull on my kneecaps on the down grades.) The march from Ledo to D day on the banks of the Tanai totaled about 140 miles.

PLATE 14. Manna from heaven. There had been no practice airdrops, and we had anxiously awaited the real thing. All knew that the viability of this method of supplying food and ammunition to a large number of men and animals had not been proven. Everything depended on the rear-echelon suppliers, packers, freight kickers, and pilots; fortunately, all went well. In the future they rarely failed us in spite of many periods of dense clouds, rain, and enemy action.

651

PLATE 15. D day, 24 February. Starting at 0600 the Marauders began crossing the Tarung Hka, with the First Battalion in the lead. We were now in enemy territory, and all who crossed were eligible for the Combat Infantryman's Badge. All ranks were notified that if anyone became sick or wounded they might have to be left on the trail.

PLATE 16. On 25 February 1944, Corporal Werner Katz of Orange Combat Team I & R was wounded and killed the first enemy soldier. This picture, taken a short time later by Yank correspondent Dave Richardson, shows the crease of a machine-gun bullet on his left cheek but not the laceration on the left side of his nose. This veteran of Guadalcanal was with his platoon during the entire campaign in Burma.

PLATE 17. These Marauders are looking for Japanese outposts to the right of the trail on 24 February 1944. With the exception of small clearings at villages, the mountainous and hill country of north Burma was covered with dense jungle vegetation. Much of the Hukawng and Mogaung Valleys were covered by elephant grass six to ten feet tall.

PLATE 18. Three heroes of the Second Battalion. From left to right: Red Maoris, while serving as first scout near Walawbum, was the first in his battalion to kill a Japanese soldier. Sid Savitt lost an eye when hit on the front line at Nhpum Ga. Robert Landis, a veteran of the 37th Division in the Solomon Islands and the first Marauder to be killed in action, died at Lanem Ga on 25 February 1944 while serving as first scout in the battalion's I & R platoon.

PLATE 19. A patrol of the Second Battalion passes dead enemy soldiers just killed by their lead scouts near Walawbum. Note the ever-present elephant grass, the leaves of which could cut like a knife. This grass, because it provided good cover and forced the men to stick to the trails, made it possible for the Japanese to set up frequent ambushes with machine guns and mortars.

PLATE 20. Lieutenant Philip Piazza searches dead enemy soldiers to gather intelligence. They frequently carried maps and other valuable information.

PLATE 21. An L-4 cub liaison plane has been converted into an ambulance at Lagang Ga. Generals Merrill and Stilwell had presented no plans for evacuation of the sick and wounded. From this time on, Marauder sick and wounded were sent from combat to hospital by the small liaison planes. The L-1 and L-4 could take one patient, while the L-5—available late in the campaign—was able to accommodate one stretcher case and three sitting wounded. At times the casualties had to walk or be carried fifteen or twenty miles to a sandbar or village rice paddy large enough to accommodate the planes. The heroic sergeant pilots never failed the Marauders. They paid a heavy price in men and planes for their great work.

PLATE 22. 3 March 1944: Lt. Pat Perrone (with the bayonet) and some headquarters men inspect the end results of an ambush that Perrone set up at Lagang Ga. The Japanese attempted to hit the central part of the Third Battalion column as it passed through Lagang Ga on the way to Walawbum.

PLATE 23. Lieutenant Logan Weston (left) and his interpreter, Sgt. Henry Gosho, of Orange Combat Team's I & R platoon. This photograph was taken early in the campaign just after the Battle of Walawbum, before they had lost weight and become debilitated. Weston's brilliant leadership during his platoon's battle across the river on 4 April contributed a great deal to the success of the Battle of Walawbum and saved many men. His action qualified him for the Congressional Medal of Honor—for which, unfortunately, he was not recommended. Gosho's nickname was "Horizontal Hank" from the many times he crawled toward enemy lines to gather information.

PLATE 24. When the Marauders had the Japanese in retreat near the end of the Battle of Walawbum, the Chinese—whom they were spearheading—began to arrive. A Chinese company mistook a section of the First Battalion for Japanese and fired on them. Not knowing that the action was that of Chinese allies, the Marauders fired in return. The wounded Chinese were given immediate medical attention. Fortunately, none were killed.

PLATE 25. On 18 March the Second and Third Battalions crossed
this bamboo bridge on the Tanai Hka. For several days we had
been following the river, which runs south to north in a narrow
gorge between two ranges of the Kumon Mountains. Directly
across the bridge we climbed two thousand feet in elevation to
Janpan. The climb was so steep that our hands frequently touched
the ground.

PLATE 26. On the way to the second mission of the Second and Third Battalions, General Merrill set up headquarters at Janpan on 18 March. The village, located on a mountaintop at thirty-two hundred feet elevation, was thirty miles northeast of the expected battle of Inkangahtawng. General Merrill is making friends with the Kachins by passing out costume jewelry and useful articles such as sewing kits.

PLATE 27. A battalion medic treats a Kachin child. Many of the native children had skin disease as well as enlarged spleens due to chronic malaria. Much malnutrition was also evident.

PLATE 28. During the first week in April, a Third Battalion 81mm mortar crew waits for a firing order. They are supporting the riflemen of Orange Combat Team on the trail from Hsamshingyang as they advance toward the Second Battalion on "Maggot Hill" at Nhpum Ga.

PLATE 29. A Third Battalion heavy machine-gun crew supports the
Third Battalion riflemen as they knock out Japanese machine guns,
riflemen, and mortars along the four-mile, razorback mountaintop
trail leading to the Second Battalion, which was surrounded at
Nhpum Ga.

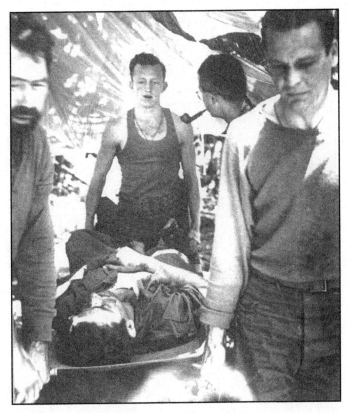

PLATE 30. At Nhpum Ga, battalion surgeon Captain L. Lewis Kolodny (with pipe) prepares to treat a wounded man. Fellow rifle-men have brought him in from the battalion perimeter.

PLATE 31. On 9 April 1944, the defeated Japanese are driven from Nhpum Ga Hill. The sick and wounded are now walking or being carried the four miles to the airstrip at Hsamshingyang. The action has cost the Marauders 52 dead and 302 wounded. Many of the wounded were able to remain in combat and were later able to take part in the Myitkyina mission. Three hundred and forty-nine sick and wounded were evacuated in small planes from Hsamshingyang.

PLATE 32. "Mass of deliverance," 9 April 1944. Father Barrett, a young Catholic priest, had been flown in to join the Third Battalion on their second mission. His devotion to duty and courage was an inspiration to all. He was equally helpful to men of all faiths.

PLATE 33. Pfc. Sid Savitt (with the patch over his destroyed eye) and others—whose appearance is consistent with their ordeal at Nhpum Ga—take the walk to Hsamshingyang, 9 April 1944.

PLATE 34. More wounded are carried four miles to the evacuation point on 9 April 1944. Note the improvised stretcher and what appears to be a poncho or blanket.

PLATE 35. An infantryman who has just come through the ordeal at Nhpum Ga checks for the grave site of a friend in the emergency cemetery there.

PLATE 36. On 9 April 1944, Easter Sunday, Father Barrett hears the confession of a GI who has just come off the line after the relief of the Second Battalion.

PLATE 37. Father Barrett prepares for Mass on Easter Sunday.

PLATE 38. S.Sgt. Roy Matsumoto, "The Hero of Nhpum Ga." He was awarded The Legion of Merit for tapping the Japanese telephone lines at Walawbum. His information alerted General Merrill to the pending withdrawal of the 18th Division. It also led to the destruction of a large ammunition dump by American P-51 planes. At Nhpum Ga, Matsumoto volunteered many times to crawl out to the Japanese lines to learn their attack plans. His information on several occasions enabled the battalion to repulse suicide attacks.

PLATE 39. After the Battle of Nhpum Ga, advance elements of the Chinese regiment arrive at Hsamshingyang to occupy the territory the Marauders have captured. Corporal Bernard Martin, Orange radioman, takes the opportunity to meet a Chinese soldier and compare weapons.

PLATE 40. This little plane at Hsamshingyang—and flying ambulances like it—always did a good job of getting our men out, and were the best morale builders we had. All sick and wounded knew they would never be left behind and would soon get the best medical care available to the Northern Combat Area Command troops.

PLATE 41. After the Battle of Nhpum Ga, Colonel Hunter decided that close-order drill would be good for morale. At any rate it seemed not to lower it. The men have been supplied with fresh clothing and have been able to bathe and get some rest. Note the strip of dirt in this rice paddy at Hsamshingyang. Such dirt had been removed from other areas to construct the small airstrip.

PLATE 42. Major Briggs, commanding officer of Khaki Combat Team, Third Battalion, holds an equipment inspection before the unit departs for the Myitkyina mission.

PLATE 43. A conference with General Merrill at Naubum before the march to Myitkyina. From left to right: General Sun Li-jen, commanding general of the Chinese division the Marauders had been spearheading into Burma; Colonel Henry Kinnison, brought in from Stilwell's staff to command the newly formed K Force; and General Merrill, who has returned to set up his headquarters at Naubum and organize and command the Myitkyina task force. Only one month earlier, he had been evacuated with a heart attack. We would not see him again, as he had another heart attack when he flew to Myitkyina airfield the day after it was captured. Kinnison died of scrub typhus a few days after we captured the airfield.

675

PLATE 44. Lieutenant Logan Weston waits for D day on the march
to capture the airfield at Myitkyina. He has survived a trail-blocking
operation against a reinforced battalion of Japanese infantry with a
battery of four artillery guns. He and his I & R platoon, later reinforced by Lieutenant Smith and his infantry platoon, delayed the
Japanese for four days. This heroic and brilliant blocking action
allowed the Second and Third Battalions to carry out their roadblock and get back into Nhpum Ga, where they could prevent the
Japanese from outflanking Chinese troops. The action of Weston
and his men saved the Marauders from almost total destruction.
The Marauders would likely have been trapped, and the Chinese
would have lost their spearhead and failed to advance further in
1944. Weston and Smith's platoons next played a major part during
the Battle of Nhpum Ga. His action and that of Lieutenant Smith,
if under different command, could have justified recommendation
for the Medal of Honor.

PLATE 45. The officers talk over the proposed mission to Myitkyina. From left to right: Major Hodges and Colonel Combs were liaison officers with the 150th Regiment, the Chinese component of H Force of the Myitkyina task force. Colonel Hunter, who commanded H Force, had taken over command of the Marauders when General Merrill left with a heart attack on 28 March. A few days after the airfield was captured, he was appointed commander of all American troops in the Myitkyina area. For no apparent reason, Stilwell relieved him of his command on 29 July, four days before the Battle of Myitkyina was over.

PLATE 46. D day for the Third Battalion, 28 April 1944. Three days of K-rations are passed out as the men leave for the climb to the Naura Hkyat Pass over the Kumon Mountain Range at sixty-one hundred feet. Many were suffering from chronic malaria and/or amoebic dysentery, severe weight loss, bronchitis, arthritis, skin problems, exhaustion syndrome, and other problems. Approximately fifty percent of the Marauders had been lost to combat and disease, and no replacements were available.

PLATE 47. The L-5 Stinson was used as a flying ambulance at Arang to fly approximately 250 sick and wounded Marauders and Chinese to medical facilities on the Ledo-Kamaing Road.

PLATE 48. This airdrop (4 May 1944) at Salawng Hkayang, located about five miles east of Naura Hkyat Pass, was our first since late in the day on 28 April. The men and animals had gone two days without rations.

PLATE 49. The Myitkyina airfield is under Japanese artillery attack a day or so before the nearby city would be captured. This had been a daily occurrence since the strip was captured by the Chinese and Americans on 17 May.

PLATE 50. This fourteen-year-old Kachin guerilla proved to be a first-class soldier when he joined a Marauder on the front line at Myitkyina.

PLATE 51. A machine-gun crew takes action at Myitkyina on the northwestern sector of the Marauder position. The bamboo-and-reed basha was typical in the villages of North Burma.

PLATE 52. Suicide by hanging was frequent among the few Japanese who were left as a rear guard when the few remaining members of the 18th Japanese Division fled rather than be captured.

PLATE 53. The U.S. military cemetery at Myitkyina. Here were buried most of the 272 Americans who died during the seventy-eight-day Battle of Myitkyina.

Index

INDEX

INDEX

INDEX

INDEX

INDEX

INDEX

INDEX

INDEX

INDEX

CPSIA information can be obtained
at www.ICGtesting.com
Printed in the USA
BVOW03s1504191217
503017BV00004B/128/P